BUILDING AN OBJECT-ORIENTED DATABASE SYSTEM

THE STORY OF O_2

THE MORGAN KAUFMANN SERIES IN
DATA MANAGEMENT SYSTEMS

Series Editor, Jim Gray

BUILDING AN OBJECT-ORIENTED DATABASE SYSTEM: THE STORY OF O_2
Edited by François Bancilhon (O_2 Technology),
Claude Delobel (O_2 Technology), and
Paris Kanellakis (Brown University)

TRANSACTION PROCESSING
Jim Gray (Digital Equipment Corporation) and
Andreas Reuter (Stuttgart University)

DATABASE TRANSACTION MODELS FOR ADVANCED APPLICATIONS
Edited by Ahmed K. Elmagarmid (Purdue University)

A GUIDE TO DEVELOPING CLIENT/SERVER SQL APPLICATIONS
Setrag Khoshafian (Portfolio Technologies, Inc.),
Arvola Chan (Versant Object Technology),
Anna Wong (CLaM Associates), and
Harry K. T. Wong (Nomadic Systems)

THE BENCHMARK HANDBOOK FOR DATABASE AND TRANSACTION PROCESSING SYSTEMS
Edited by Jim Gray (Digital Equipment Corporation)

CAMELOT AND AVALON: A DISTRIBUTED TRANSACTION FACILITY
Edited by Jeffrey L. Eppinger (Transarc Corporation),
Lily B. Mummert (Carnegie Mellon University),
and Alfred Z. Spector (Transarc Corporation)

DATABASE MODELING AND DESIGN: THE ENTITY-RELATIONSHIP APPROACH
Toby J. Teorey (University of Michigan)

READINGS IN OBJECT-ORIENTED DATABASE SYSTEMS
Edited by Stanley B. Zdonik (Brown University) and
David Maier (Oregon Graduate Center)

READINGS IN DATABASE SYSTEMS
Edited by Michael Stonebraker (University of California at Berkeley)

DEDUCTIVE DATABASES AND LOGIC PROGRAMMING
Jack Minker (University of Maryland)

Contents

Preface **xxi**

Acknowledgements **xxv**

Part I Introduction to Object-Oriented Database Systems 1

1 The Object-Oriented Database System Manifesto **3**
Atkinson, Bancilhon, DeWitt, Dittrich, Maier, and Zdonik

1 Introduction 3
2 Mandatory Features: The Golden Rules 5
2.1 Complex Objects 5
2.2 Object Identity 6
2.3 Encapsulation 7
2.4 Types and Classes 8
2.5 Class or Type Hierarchies 10
2.6 Overriding, Overloading, and Late Binding 11
2.7 Computational Completeness 12
2.8 Extensibility 12
2.9 Persistence 13
2.10 Secondary Storage Management 13
2.11 Concurrency 13
2.12 Recovery 14
2.13 Ad Hoc Query Facility 14
2.14 Summary 14
3 Optional Features: The Goodies 15
3.1 Multiple Inheritance 15
3.2 Type Checking and Type Inferencing 15
3.3 Distribution 15
3.4 Design Transactions 16
3.5 Versions 16
4 Open Choices 16
4.1 Programming Paradigm 16

4.2 Representation System 16
4.3 Type System 17
4.4 Uniformity 17
5 Conclusion 17
6 Acknowledgements 18
References 18

2 The Story of O_2 **21**
Deux et al.
1 Introduction 21
1.1 A System Overview 21
2 A Programmer's View of the System 22
2.1 The Data Model and the Data Definition Language 23
2.2 The O_2 Languages 29
2.3 Development and Execution Modes 33
2.4 Distribution 33
3 Looks, the User Interface Generator 34
3.1 Major Features of Looks 34
3.2 A Simple Programming Example 36
4 OOPE, the Programming Environment 37
4.1 The OOPE Design Principles 38
4.2 The Programming Functionalities 38
4.3 The Programming Tools 39
5 The Implementation 41
5.1 System Decomposition and Process Layout 43
5.2 The Schema Manager 44
5.3 The Object Manager 44
6 Performance of the O_2 Prototype 52
6.1 Simple Tests 52
6.2 Wisconsin Benchmark Selection Times 54
7 Conclusion 55
8 Acknowledgements 56
References 56

Part II The O_2 Data Model 59

3 Introduction to the Data Model **61**
Kanellakis, Lécluse, and Richard
1 Historical View of the O_2 Approach 62
2 Objects Versus Values in OODBs 63
3 The O_2 Data Model 65

3.1 Values and Objects 65
3.2 The Syntax of Types and Classes 67
3.3 Class Hierarchy and Subtyping 67
3.4 The Semantics of Types and Classes 69
3.5 Methods 70
3.6 Database Schema 72
3.7 Instances of a Database Schema 73
4 Acknowledgements 74
5 A Roadmap for Part 2 74
References 75

4 O_2, an Object-Oriented Data Model 77
Lécluse, Richard, and Vélez
1 Introduction 77
2 Overview 79
3 Objects 80
4 Types 83
4.1 Type Structures 85
4.2 Methods 89
4.3 Type Systems 92
5 Databases 93
6 Conclusion 95
7 Acknowledgements 96
References 96

5 Object Identity as a Query-Language Primitive 98
Abiteboul and Kanellakis
1 Introduction 98
1.1 The Structural Part 100
1.2 The Operational Part 101
1.3 Expressive Power 103
1.4 Type Inheritance 104
1.5 Value-Based versus Object-Based 104
1.6 Relation to O_2 104
2 An Object-based Data Model 105
3 The Identity Query Language 107
3.1 Syntax 108
3.2 Semantics 109
3.3 Shorthands and Examples 111
4 IQL Expressibility 114
5 The Sublanguages of IQL 118
6 Type Inheritance 119

7 A Value-based Data Model 122
8 Acknowledgements 124
References 124

6 Method Schemas 128
Abiteboul, Kanellakis, and Waller
1 Introduction 128
2 Method Schemas 131
2.1 Syntax 131
2.2 Semantics 133
2.3 Consistency 135
2.4 Variations 135
3 Recursion-Free Schemas 136
4 Schemas with Recursion 138
5 Covariance 139
6 Practical Issues 140
6.1 Avoiding Recursion 140
6.2 Updates 142
7 Acknowledgements 143
References 143

7 A Framework for Schema Updates in an Object-Oriented Database System 146
Zicari
1 Introduction 146
1.1 Preliminary O_2 Concepts 146
1.2 Updates: What Do We Want to Achieve? 148
1.3 Organization of the Paper 149
2 Ensuring Structural and Behavioral Consistency 149
2.1 Structural Consistency 149
2.2 Behavioral Consistency 151
2.3 The Interactive Consistency Checker 151
3 Schema Updates 152
3.1 Changes to the Type Structure of a Class 152
3.2 Changes to the Methods of a Class 152
3.3 Changes to the Class-Structure Graph 153
3.4 Basic Schema Updates 153
4 Method Updates 154
4.1 Adding a Method in a Class 154
4.2 Dropping a Method from a Class 156
5 Type Updates 159
5.1 Structural Consistency 159

5.2 Behavioral Consistency 160
6 Class Updates 162
6.1 Addition of an Edge 163
6.2 Removal of an Edge 163
6.3 Addition of a Node 168
6.4 Deletion of a Node 169
7 Implementation Issues 171
8 Related Work 172
9 Conclusion and Future Work 174
9.1 Data Structure 174
9.2 Update-Execution Model 174
9.3 Object Updates 175
9.4 High-Level Restructuring 175
9.5 Tools 176
9.6 Incomplete Types 176
10 Acknowledgements 176
References 177
Appendix: Cost Analysis 179
A.1 Architecture 179
A.2 Parameters 179
A.3 Assumptions 180
A.4 Notations 180
A.5 Costs 181

Part III The Languages 183

8 Introduction to Languages **185**
Bancilhon and Maier
1 A Brief Survey 187
2 Historical View of the O_2 Approach 188
2.1 The O_2 Database Programming Language 188
2.2 The O_2 Query Language 190
3 Language Integration in OODBs 190
4 A Roadmap for Part 3 192
References 193

9 The O_2 Database Programming Language **195**
Lécluse and Richard
1 Introduction 195
2 Objects and Values in O_2 196
3 Types and Classes 197

3.1 The Schema Definition Language 198
3.2 Object Creation 199
3.3 Naming and Persistence 199
4 Manipulation of Objects and Values 200
4.1 Method Definition 200
4.2 Manipulating Values 201
4.3 Iterator 202
5 Subtyping and Inheritance 203
5.1 Subtyping 203
5.2 Inheritance 204
5.3 Late Binding 205
6 Interesting Features 206
6.1 Exceptional Attributes 206
6.2 Exceptional Methods 206
7 Type Checking 207
8 Related Work 207
8.1 Other OODBs 207
8.2 Other Systems 210
9 Conclusion 211
10 Acknowledgements 212
References 212

10 Lisp O_2: A Persistent Object-Oriented Lisp 215
Barbedette
1 Introduction 215
2 Object-Oriented Features 216
2.1 Objects and Classes, Values and Types 217
2.2 Inheritance 219
2.3 Operation Implementations: Methods 222
2.4 Object Creation: Constructor 223
2.5 Coping with Faults: Exceptions 225
2.6 Type-Checking Methods 225
3 Integrating Persistence Facilities in the Language 227
4 System Design 228
4.1 The Persistent Layer 228
4.2 The Object Layer 229
5 Related Work 230
6 Future Work 231
7 Acknowledgements 231
References 232

11 A Query Language for O_2 **234**
Bancilhon, Cluet, and Delobel

1 Introduction 234
2 Object-Oriented Database System 235
3 Uses of the Query Language 236
3.1 For Ad Hoc Queries 237
3.2 For Access to the Database 237
3.3 For Simple Programs 238
3.4 For Shortcuts in the Programming Language 238
4 The Design of a Query Language 238
4.1 Relationship with Encapsulation 238
4.2 Data versus Methods 239
4.3 The Answer to a Query 239
4.4 Integration in the Programming Language 240
4.5 Relationship with the Type or Class System 241
5 The O_2 Data Model 241
6 Design Choices 244
7 The Query Language 244
7.1 Simple Queries 245
7.2 Access to All Levels of a Structure 246
7.3 Lists and Sets inside a Query? 247
7.4 Flat and Nested Values 248
8 Semantics of the O_2 Query Language 250
9 Other Query Languages 252
9.1 The Query Language for Orion 252
9.2 OSQL, the Iris Query Language 252
9.3 The Query Language for Exodus 253
9.4 Two Query Languages for O_2 253
References 254

12 Reloop, an Algebra-Based Query Language for O_2 **256**
Cluet, Delobel, Lécluse, and Richard

1 Introduction 256
2 An Example 257
2.1 The Designer's View 257
2.2 The User's View 259
3 Design Issues 259
3.1 Classes and Encapsulation 260
3.2 Values 261
4 The Reloop Language 262
5 Reloop Semantics through an Algebra 266
5.1 The Algebra Operators 266

5.2 Reloop Semantics 267
6 Translation from Reloop to CO_2 271
6.1 The CO_2 Language 271
6.2 The Macro-Algebra 272
7 Conclusion 274
8 Acknowledgements 274
References 275
Appendix: Construction of the Algebraic Macro-Operators 276
A.1 The ⊙ Operator 276
A.2 The ⊎ Operator 277

13 Using Database Applications to Compare Programming Languages 278
Gamerman, Lanquette, and Vélez
1 Introduction 278
2 The Applications 280
2.1 The Bill of Materials Application 280
2.2 The Unix Mail Application 280
3 C+SQL 281
3.1 Developing the Bill of Materials Application in C+SQL 281
3.2 Developing the Unix Mail Application in C+SQL 282
3.3 Conclusions 283
4 Basic-Pick 283
4.1 Developing the Bill of Materials Application in Basic 284
4.2 Developing the Unix Mail Application in Basic 284
4.3 Conclusions 285
5 Prolog 285
5.1 Developing the Bill of Materials Application in Prolog 286
5.2 Developing the Unix Mail Application in Prolog 286
5.3 Conclusions 287
6 Smalltalk-80 287
6.1 Developing the Bill of Materials Application in Smalltalk-80 287
6.2 Developing the Unix Mail Application in Smalltalk-80 288
6.3 Conclusions 289
7 The O_2 System 290
7.1 Developing the Bill of Materials Application in O_2 290
7.2 Developing the Unix Mail Application in O_2 291
7.3 Conclusions 292
8 Conclusions 292
8.1 Development Time 292
8.2 Code Size 293
8.3 Number of Variables 294
8.4 Conformity to Specifications 294

6.2 Starting O_2 from a Workstation 379
6.3 Handling Abnormal Process Terminations 380
7 Related Work 380
References 382

17 Clustering Strategies in O_2: An Overview **385**
Benzaken, Delobel, and Harrus
1 Introduction 385
2 The O_2 Clustering Strategies 387
2.1 Placement Trees 390
2.2 A Clustering Algorithm 395
3 Self-adaptative Clustering Strategies 397
3.1 Definition of Good Placement Trees 398
3.2 Simplifying Assumptions 399
3.3 Cost Function 399
3.4 Automatic Derivation of Placement Trees 402
4 Performance Measurements 404
4.1 Early Measurements 404
4.2 From Hypermodel to CluB-0 405
5 Conclusion 408
6 Acknowledgements 408
References 408

18 Three Alternative Workstation-Server Architectures **411**
DeWitt, Futtersack, Maier, and Vélez
1 Introduction 411
2 The Three Workstation-Server Architectures 412
2.1 The Object-Server Architecture 413
2.2 Page-Server Architecture 415
2.3 The File-Server Architecture 417
3 Prototyping the Workstation-Server Architectures 418
3.1 File Server 420
3.2 Page Server 420
3.3 Object Server 422
3.4 Concurrency Control and Recovery 423
4 The Altaïr Complex-Object Benchmark 423
4.1 Database Design 424
4.2 Queries 427
4.3 Benchmark Organization 429
5 Performance Evaluation 429
5.1 Test Environment 430
5.2 Database Build Time 431
5.3 Clustering and Smearing Tests 431

5.4 Impact of Workstation Buffer Space 438
6 Related Work 441
7 Conclusions 442
8 Acknowledgements 444
References 444

19 Consistency of Versions in Object-Oriented Databases 447
Cellary and Jomier
1 Introduction 447
2 The Database-Version Approach 449
3 Object-Version Identification 451
4 Operating on Objects 453
4.1 Reading 453
4.2 Updating 453
4.3 Deletion 456
4.4 Creation 456
5 Concurrency Control 456
6 Version Management of Composite Objects 456
7 Conclusions 458
8 Acknowledgements 460
References 460

20 Integrating Concurrency Control 463
Cart and Ferrié
1 Introduction 463
2 User Transactions and O_2 Objects 464
2.1 Representation of O_2 Objects 465
2.2 Hierarchy of Abstraction Levels 467
3 Constraints upon Concurrency 468
3.1 Classification of Methods on Classes and Instances 468
3.2 Compatibility of Methods 469
3.3 Access Control of Classes and Instances 471
3.4 Creation and Deletion of Instances 472
3.5 Creation and Deletion of Classes 474
4 Object and Operation Properties Exploited by CC 474
4.1 Primitive and Constructed Objects 474
4.2 Compatibility and Commutativity between Operations 475
4.3 Independence of Objects at the Same Abstraction Level 475
5 Impact of a One-level Transaction Model 476
5.1 Physical Locking 477
5.2 Physical and Logical Locking 477
6 Impact of a Multilevel Transaction Model 478

6.1 Necessity of Object Independence 480
6.2 Multilevel Two-phase Locking 481
6.3 Exploiting Method Commutativity 482
7 Conclusion 483
8 Acknowledgements 483
References 483

Part V The Programming Environment 487

21 Introduction to the Programming Environment **489**
Delobel, Kanellakis, and Plateau
1 The Technical Challenges 490
1.1 Interaction between User and Database 490
1.2 The Software Engineering Problems 491
2 Historical View of the O_2 Approach 491
3 A Roadmap for Part 5 492
References 494

22 Building User Interfaces with Looks **496**
Plateau, Borras, Lévêque, Mamou, and Tallot
1 Introduction 496
1.1 Existing User-Interface Tools 497
1.2 Looks 498
2 The Looks Data Model 498
3 Main Features of Looks 499
3.1 Generic Presentations 499
3.2 Editing Presentations 500
3.3 Masks 501
3.4 Placements 502
3.5 Modes 503
3.6 Links 503
3.7 Interactive Method Activation 504
3.8 Specific Presentations 504
4 A Programming Example 505
5 Conclusion 505
References 506

23 The O_2 Programming Environment 508
Borras, Doucet, Pfeffer, and Tallot

1 Introduction 508
2 Design Principles 509
3 Programming with OOPE 510
3.1 Programming Tools 511
3.2 A Tour with OOPE 513
4 Related Work 519
5 Implementation Choices and Future Improvements 520
6 Conclusion 521
7 Acknowledgements 521
References 521

24 Using a Database System to Implement a Debugger 523
Doucet and Pfeffer

1 Introduction 523
2 The Compiling Process 524
3 The O_2 Debugger 524
3.1 Information Managed by Debuggers 524
3.2 The O_2 Debugger Architecture 526
3.3 The O_2 Debugger Paradigm 526
4 The Symbol Database 527
4.1 Fine Granularity 527
4.2 Creation of a Symbol Database 527
4.3 Structure of a Symbol Database 527
5 Database Management during the Debugger Process 531
5.1 Dynamic Binding 532
5.2 Management of the Execution Stack 533
6 Evaluation of Gains 534
6.1 Performance Gain 534
6.2 Space Gain 534
6.3 Functionality Gain 535
7 Related Work 536
7.1 A Similar Symbol Table Organization 536
7.2 Debuggers That Use a Database 537
8 Conclusion and Future Work 538
9 Acknowledgements 539
References 539

25 Incremental Compilation in O_2 **541**
Larchevêque
1 Introduction 541
2 A Survey of Language-based Editors 542
3 Main Functionalities 543
3.1 Programs and Applications 543
3.2 User Interaction 543
4 The Semantic Component 544
4.1 Code Generation 544
4.2 Parse-time Semantic Actions 546
5 The Syntactic Component 546
5.1 Conventions 546
5.2 Requirements and Assumptions for the Incremental Parser 547
5.3 Extended Example 548
5.4 Augmenting the Parser for Optimal Context Reuse 550
5.5 Adding Flexibility to the Parser 552
6 Further Research 552
References 553

26 Self-explained Toolboxes **555**
Arango
1 Introduction 555
2 The Toolbox Approach 556
2.1 What Is a Toolbox? 556
2.2 Class Identification 557
2.3 Classification of Operations 559
3 The Business-Application Toolbox 561
3.1 The Learning Mechanism 561
3.2 Using the Toolbox 562
3.3 Extending the Toolbox 565
4 Conclusions 565
5 Acknowledgements 566
References 566

Part VI Examples of O_2 Applications 569

27 A Guided Tour of an O_2 Application **571**
Grosselin and James
1 The Altaïr Travel Agency 571
2 Displays and Data Capture 574
3 The O_2 Query Language 577

4 Multimedia Objects 579
5 The O_2 Programming Environment 581

28 Geographic Applications: An Experience with O_2 585
Scholl and Voisard
1 Introduction 585
2 Map Model and Query Language 587
2.1 The Map Model 588
2.2 Examples of Queries on Maps 591
3 Architecture of the Prototype 592
3.1 Available Functionalities 592
3.2 Architecture 593
4 Implementation of the Map Level 594
4.1 Expressive Power of the O_2 Query Language 594
4.2 Integration of the O_2 Query Language 595
4.3 Implementing Generic Relational-Algebra Operations 595
4.4 Design of a Query Language 596
4.5 Current Implementation 596
5 Implementation of Geometric Functions 598
5.1 Queries 598
5.2 Structure 599
5.3 Methods 602
6 The User Interface 605
6.1 Functionalities of the Interface 605
6.2 Current Implementation 607
7 Conclusion 608
8 Acknowledgements 609
References 610
Appendix I: An O_2 Schema for the Geometry of a Map 613
Appendix II: Extension of CO_2 for Implementing Relational Operations 616

Index 619

Preface

Object-oriented database systems are new software systems integrating techniques from databases, object-oriented languages, programming environments, and user interfaces. We believe (and hope to convince the reader) that this particular synthesis of computer science ideas and software tools is larger than its parts. In fact, it is creating a new generation of database technology.

This book provides an in-depth perspective of the new technology through the description of a complete example prototype: the object-oriented database system O_2. The exposition ranges from the data model through the system implementation to applications. The format of the book is a commented and edited collection of papers that cover all aspects of the prototype software system O_2 (focusing on its V1 version). The authors are designers, implementors, and users of this system.

The articles collected here contain a wealth of essential details on all aspects of building an object-oriented database system. This is knowledge that can help researchers, database designers, and users to assess the nature and potential of the new technology.

Although they have long been successful in business, database systems have not been fully utilized for advanced applications such as office information systems (OIS) and computer-aided design (CAD). These applications have new requirements in design environments, transaction mechanisms, and complex or multimedia data types. O_2 has been built with such advanced applications in mind. It is not just an extension of a network or relational database system tailored to specialized applications, but represents an integrated approach to software engineering that combines object-oriented programming and database technology.

During the last decade, object-oriented programming concepts (such as classes of objects with methods and inheritance) and languages (such as Smalltalk or C++) have received a great deal of attention. One reason for the popularity of object-oriented paradigms is that data abstraction, modularity, and code reusability are key elements in building large software systems. Languages and programming environments that emphasize these three principles are bound to impact experimental computer science. However, one should bear in mind that the software engineering problems (which object-oriented languages were designed to address) are very different from the problems that originally led to the development of database management systems.

Database systems evolved, quite independently from programming languages, because of the practical need for efficient manipulation of large amounts of structured information. The insight that data is an integrated resource which is independent of application programs has led to more than twenty-five years of database technology. Four particular themes have been central in database research and development: (1) data persistence beyond the scope of application programs, (2) very high level but reasonably fast query languages that are independent of the physical organization of the data, (3) efficient secondary storage management for large amounts of structured information, and (4) transaction management guaranteeing access by concurrent users, data integrity, security, and recovery from faults.

This overall emphasis of database technology on performance has made its integration with object-oriented programming a challenging task. For example, specific concrete types, such as records and lists, were given prominent roles in various data description languages (DDLs). This made good implementations possible, but resulted in reduced flexibility of data abstraction. Reasonably efficient but ad hoc data manipulation languages (DMLs) were developed. Unfortunately most were largely incompatible with the widely used programming languages. The resulting "impedance mismatch" between the database query language and the general-purpose or host language motivated the research on language integration in database systems.

There are some obvious ways of approaching the integration of host and query language. One approach is to add database features, such as persistence, to a widely used general-purpose language. Pascal/R and PS-Algol represent pioneering efforts in this direction. Another approach is to extend a successful query language toward the closest programming language. For example, the research on databases and logic programming was largely motivated by the potential uses of Prolog+database; after all, logic programming is the computing paradigm closest to relational query languages. From this emerged a number of interesting prototypes (e.g., LDL or NAIL!).

Here we should point out that adding database capabilities to the *appropriate* general-purpose language can bring significant benefits, beyond any improvement of the query/host language interface. If the programming language was designed a priori to support a rich set of data abstractions, modularity, and code reusability, then its persistent version is an excellent candidate for nonstandard database applications, such as OIS and CAD. For example, the potential of rich type systems with semantic features, such as inheritance, was illustrated in various prototype languages (e.g., ADABTBL, Galileo, Taxis, Trellis/Owl).

Beyond persistence, a database version of a language offers schema-management facilities. In this case, the schema is the persistent set of type declarations and comes with mechanisms for concurrency control, recovery, versioning, library management, and more generally for schema evolution. Object-oriented languages were designed precisely for building and evolving large software systems; they facilitate the development of programming environments and user interfaces. In this light, adding persistence and other database functionalities to Smalltalk in the Gemstone system was a natural, but very important, step in demonstrating the feasibility of a new technology:

object-oriented database systems (OODBs).

At present there is a lot of experimental work under way which has resulted in prototype and even commercial systems claiming the OODB label (or claiming to incorporate major object-oriented programming concepts). There are also many proposed designs and some theoretical analysis. For example, proceeding alphabetically, and fully aware of the everchanging nature of this list, we can mention some of the better-known implemented systems: Cactis, Damokles, Encore/ObServer, Exodus, G-Base, GemStone, Iris, O_2, Ode, Ontos/VBase, Orion, Probe, Postgres, and Vision.

We will not attempt a detailed survey or classification of these systems. A new software technology is typically a creative synthesis of older ideas, tools, and concepts. Its multiple origins make reaching agreement on its precise specification impractical and even damaging to the diversity of the field. Therefore, the goal of this book is not to give a definition of "The OODB" but to clarify (by example) what seem to be the principal OODB components and the design choices made in building them.

The first chapter in this book, entitled "The Object-Oriented Database System Manifesto," was an attempt to outline a commonly accepted part of the OODB specifications. Historically it followed most of the other papers in this book, and it is in large part based on the lessons of building a number of OODBs. Since O_2 is one of these systems, the rest of the book makes concrete the manifesto's many and rather forcefully described golden rules.

The book presents a complete and consistent view of the Altaïr project—a five-year research and development effort to build O_2 that started in September 1986. All aspects of the project are described. For consistency, we focus on the V1 version of the prototype, which was operational in September 1989 and has been distributed to more than 30 sites. The V1 version followed an initial experimental V0 version and preceded the various commercial product versions. As this book goes to press, a commercial release of the industrial version of O_2 is available (since June 1991). Many of the functionalities are similar to the ones described here, although there are some differences.

The most interesting papers related to the O_2 project are presented in what we feel is the most sensible expository sequence. The material in the chapters consists (primarily but not exclusively) of papers which have appeared in the proceedings of internationally recognized computer science conferences. The papers were edited and reformated to make the presentation as uniform as possible.

The book is divided into six parts. Part 1 consists of two papers: the "Manifesto" and "The Story of O_2." It is intended to provide a good overall summary, and we hope it will entice the reader to venture further in the text.

The papers in parts 2 to 5 are related to each other and to the whole through short introductions. The introduction to part 2 contains a complete definition of the O_2 data model; the introduction to part 3 contains a detailed discussion of query/host language integration; and the introductions to parts 4 and 5 contain summaries of the key technical issues related to the system and the programming environment, respectively. The introductions also contain comments on the history of the O_2 contributions, and they close with a roadmap to each part's contents. Part 6 concludes the exposition with descriptions of two applications.

As editors we were faced with the hard task of choosing which parts to emphasize (through the selection of specific papers) from a large project with many contributors. For the data model we focused on the clean synthesis of object-oriented concepts and database complex structures that O_2 offers, on a novel analysis of the power of object identity, and on new ways of controlling schema updates. For the language part we emphasize the multilanguage aspect of O_2—a characteristic that distinguishes it from other efforts in the field. The papers in this part describe the integration with programming languages such as C, Basic, and Lisp, as well as the development of specific query languages. For the system part we have tried to present as many details as possible: on object manager, object clustering, distribution, alternative architectures, version management, and concurrency. The programming environment part is devoted to software engineering tools and the user interface; this reflects the revolutionary impact that high-resolution bitmap workstations have had on computing and the importance for any new database technology of a high-quality interface with the overall programming environment.

In the next chapter we use the golden rules of the object-oriented database manifesto as a way to introduce the material in this collection. If one reverts to the original historical sequence, these rules also provide an accurate set of conclusions. However, let the reader beware. Manifestos invariably reflect the experiences of their authors but also their biases.

We hope that the computer science experiment described in these pages will provide readers with the expertise to follow the final rule of the opening manifesto—"Thou shalt question the golden rules"—and to decide for themselves what object-oriented databases are or should be.

François Bancilhon
Altaïr

Claude Delobel
Université de Paris-Sud

Paris Kanellakis
Brown University

Acknowledgements

The O_2 system is the result of a group effort and this book is the collective work of all those who contributed to the Altaïr[1] project. The editors wish to thank the following people.

The technical staff and the researchers who participated in the design and/or implementation of the system: Gustavo Arango, Gilles Barbedette, Véronique Benzaken, Guy Bernard, Pascale Biriotti, Patrick Borras, Patrice Boursier, Philippe Bridon, René Cazalens, Sophie Cluet, Vineeta Darnis, Christine Delcourt, Anne Doucet, Denis Excoffier, Philippe Futtersack, Sophie Gamerman, Olivier Grémont, Constance Grosselin, Gilbert Harrus, Laurence Haux, John Ioannidis, Mark James, Geneviève Jomier, Jean Marie Larchevêque, Christophe Lécluse, Carol Lepenant, Didier Lévêque, Joëlle Madec, Jacques Madelaine, Jean-Claude Mamou, Jean-Baptiste N'dala, Patrick Pfeffer, Didier Plateau, Bruno Poyet, Michel Raoux, Philippe Richard, Michel Scholl, Dominique Stève, Didier Tallot, Fernando Vélez, and Roberto Zicari.

The students who participated in the project: Laurent Alonzo, Thomas Baudel, Yves Branwschweig, Yveline Cessou, Xavier Crinon, Fabrice Laurence, Sabine Letellier, Vincent Marfaing, Eli Nakdimon, Marc Poinot, and Yves-Henri Saliou.

The consultants who helped at many stages of the design: Michel Adiba, Malcolm Atkinson, Haran Boral, Peter Buneman, George Copeland, Joëlle Coutaz, David DeWitt, Gilles Kahn, Sacha Krakowiak, David Maier, and Marc Shapiro.

The colleagues who agreed to have their papers included in this book: Serge Abiteboul, Michéle Cart, Wojciech Cellary, Klaus Dittrich, Jean Ferrié, Stan Zdonik.

The administrative staff, thanks to whom the group was able to operate efficiently: Eve-Lyne Daneels, Florence Deshors, Hélène Gans, Karine Maillard, Pauline Turcaud, and Carole Viard.

[1]Altaïr is a consortium funded by IN2 (a Siemens subsidiary), INRIA (Institut National de Recherche en Informatique et Automatique), and LRI (Laboratoire de Recherche en Informatique, University of Paris-Sud and CNRS). It is a five-year research and development project started in September 1986. Bull joined the consortium in 1989. Its goal is to design and implement a next-generation database management system. The project is supported by the members of the consortium, by a Eureka convention, BD 11, and by two Esprit projects, FIDE and ITHACA.

The editors would also like to thank the Defense Advanced Research Projects Agency, the National Science Foundation, and the European Community Esprit projects for their support of the task of editing and commenting on (via introductions) the material in this volume.

Finally, detailed credits for the various research activities described in this book are listed under "Acknowledgements" at the end of each chapter.

Part I

Introduction to Object-Oriented Database Systems

CHAPTER 1

The Object-Oriented Database System Manifesto

MALCOLM ATKINSON FRANÇOIS BANCILHON
DAVID DEWITT KLAUS DITTRICH
DAVID MAIER STANLEY ZDONIK

1 Introduction

Object-oriented database systems (OODBSs) are currently receiving a lot of attention from both the experimental and the theoretical standpoint, and there has been considerable debate about the definition of such systems. The field at this stage is characterized by (1) the lack of a common data model, (2) a lack of formal foundations, and (3) strong experimental activity.

Whereas Codd's original paper (Codd 1970) gave a clear specification of a relational database system (data model and query language), no such specification exists for object-oriented database systems (Maier 1989). We are not claiming here that no complete object-oriented data model exists; indeed, many proposals can be found in the literature (e.g., Albano et al. 1985; Carey, DeWitt, and Vandenberg 1988; Lécluse and Richard 1989; see chapter 9 of this book), but rather that there is no consensus on a single one. Opinion is slowly converging on the gross characteristics of a family of object-oriented systems, but at present there is no clear consensus on what an object-oriented system is, let alone an object-oriented database system.

The field lacks a strong theoretical framework. To compare object-oriented programming to logic programming, there is no equivalent of Van Emdem and Kowalski 1976. The need for a solid underlying theory is obvious: the semantics of concepts such as types or programs are often ill-defined, and consensus on the data model is almost impossible to achieve.

Finally, a lot of experimental work is under way: people are actually building systems. Some of these systems are just prototypes (Bancilhon et al. 1988; Nixon et al. 1987; Banerjee et al. 1987; Skarra, Zdonik, and Reiss 1986; Fishman et al. 1986; Carey et al. 1986), but some are commercial products (Atwood 1985; Maier et al. 1986; Caruso and Sciore 1987; G-Base 1988). The interest in object-oriented databases seems to be driven by the needs of design-support systems such as computer-aided design (CAD), computer-aided software engineering (CASE), or office information systems (OIS). These applications require databases that can handle very complex data, that can evolve gracefully, and that can provide the high performance dictated by interactive systems.

The implementation situation has similarities (and differences) with that of relational database systems in the midseventies (though there are more start-ups in the object-oriented case). For relational systems, even though there were some disagreements on a few specific points such as the form of the query language or whether relations should be sets or bags, these distinctions were in most cases superficial, and there was a common underlying model. People were mainly developing implementation technology. Today, we are simultaneously choosing the specification of the system and producing the technology to support its implementation.

Thus, with respect to the specification of the system, we are taking a Darwinian approach: we hope that, out of the set of experimental prototypes being built, a fit model will emerge. We also hope that viable implementation technology for that model will simultaneously evolve. Unfortunately, with the flurry of experimentation, we risk a system emerging as *the* system, not because it is the fittest, but because it is the first one to provide enough of the functionality demanded by the market. It is a classical, and unfortunate, pattern of the computer field that an early product becomes the de facto standard and never disappears. This pattern is true at least for languages, such as Fortran, Lisp, Cobol, and SQL, and for operating systems. Our goal here is not to standardize languages, however, but to refine terminology.

It is important to agree on a definition of an object-oriented database system. As a first step, this paper suggests the characteristics that such a system should possess. We expect that the paper will be used as a straw man, and that others will either invalidate or confirm the points mentioned here. This paper is not a survey of the state of the art of OODBS technology, and it does not pretend to assess the current status of the technology; it merely proposes a set of definitions.

We have separated the characteristics of object-oriented database systems into three categories: *mandatory,* the ones that the system must satisfy to deserve the label; *optional,* the ones that can be added to make the system better but which are not mandatory; and *open,* the ones where the designer can select from a number of equally acceptable solutions. There is also some leeway as to how each characteristic, mandatory as well as optional, should be formulated.

The rest of this chapter is organized as follows. Section 2 describes the mandatory features of an OODBS, section 3 describes its optional features, and section 4 presents the degrees of freedom left to the system designers.

2 Mandatory Features: The Golden Rules

An object-oriented database system must satisfy two criteria: it should be a database management system (DBMS), and it should be an object-oriented system—that is, it should be consistent with the current crop of object-oriented programming languages as far as possible. The first criterion translates into five features: persistence, secondary storage management, concurrency, recovery, and an ad hoc query facility. The second criterion translates into eight features: complex objects, object identity, encapsulation, types or classes, inheritance, overriding combined with late binding, extensibility, and computational completeness.

2.1 Complex Objects

Thou shalt support complex objects.

Complex objects are built from simpler ones by applying constructors to them. The simplest objects are integers, characters, byte strings of any length, Booleans, and floats (one might add other atomic types). There are various complex object constructors: tuples, sets, bags, lists, and arrays are examples. The minimal set of constructors that the system should have are set, tuple, and list. *Sets* are critical because they are a natural way of representing collections from the real world. *Tuples* are critical because they are a natural way of representing properties of an entity. Of course, both sets and tuples are important because they gained wide acceptance as object constructors through the relational model and its extensions. *Lists* or *arrays* are important because they capture order, which occurs in the real world. They arise in many scientific applications, where people need matrices or time-series data.

The object constructors must be orthogonal to the objects; that is, any constructor should apply to any object. The constructors of the relational model do not meet this requirement, because the set constructor can only be applied to tuples and the tuple constructor can only be applied to atomic values. Furthermore, in non-first-normal-form relational models the top-level construct must always be a relation.

Appropriate operators must be provided for dealing with complex objects, whatever their composition. That is, operations on a complex object must propagate transitively to all its components. Examples include the retrieval or deletion of an entire complex object, or the production of a "deep" copy (in contrast to a "shallow" copy, where components are not replicated but are instead referenced by the copy of the object root only). Additional operations on complex objects may be defined, of course, by users of the system (see the extensibility rule below). However, this capability requires some system-provided provisions, such as two distinguishable types of references ("is-part-of" and "general").

2.2 Object Identity

Thou shalt support object identity.

Object identity has long existed in programming languages. The concept is more recent in databases (see Hall, Owlett, and Todd 1976; Maier and Price 1984; Khoshafian and Copeland 1986). The idea is that in a model with object identity, an object has an existence which is independent of its value. Two objects can be identical (they are the same object) or they can be equal (they have the same value). Identical objects can be distinguished from equal objects in two ways: object sharing and object updates.

Object sharing. In an identity-based model, two objects can share a component. Thus, the pictorial representation of a complex object is a graph, whereas in a system without object identity it is limited to be a tree. Consider the following example: the object Person has a name, an age, and a set of children. Assume Peter and Susan both have a 15-year-old child named John. In real life, two situations may arise: Susan and Peter may be parents of the same child, or there may be two children involved. In a system without identity, Peter is represented by

```
(peter, 40, {(john, 15, {})})
```

Susan is represented by

```
(susan, 41, {(john, 15, {})})
```

Thus there is no way of expressing whether Peter and Susan are the parents of the same child. In an identity-based model, however, these two structures can either share the common part (john, 15, {}) or not, thus distinguishing between the two possible situations.

Object updates. Assume that Peter and Susan are indeed the parents of a child named John. In this case, all updates referring to Susan's son will be applied to the object John, and consequently also to Peter's son. In a value-based system, by contrast, the two subobjects must be updated separately.

Object identity is also a powerful data-manipulation primitive that can be the basis of set, tuple, and recursive complex-object manipulation (Abiteboul and Kanellakis 1989).

Supporting object identity implies offering operations such as object assignment, object copy (both deep and shallow copy), and tests for object identity and object equality (both deep and shallow equality). One can simulate object identity in a value-based system by introducing explicit object identifiers. However, this approach places the burden on the user to insure the uniqueness of object identifiers and to maintain referential integrity (and this burden can be significant for operations such as garbage collection).

Identity-based models are the norm in imperative programming languages: each object manipulated in a program has an identity and can be updated. This identity either comes from the name of a variable or from a physical location in memory. But the concept is quite new in pure relational systems, where relations are value based.

2.3 Encapsulation

Thou shalt encapsulate thine objects.

The idea of encapsulation comes from (1) the need for a clear distinction between the specification and the implementation of an operation, and (2) the need for modularity. Modularity is necessary to structure complex applications designed and implemented by a team of programmers. It is also necessary as a tool for protection and authorization.

There are two views of encapsulation: the programming language view, which is the original view since the concept originated there; and the database adaptation of that view.

The idea of encapsulation in programming languages comes from abstract data types. In this view, an object has an interface part and an implementation part. The interface part is the specification of the set of operations that can be performed on the object. It is the only visible part of the object. The implementation part has a data part and a procedural part. The data part is the representation or state of the object, and the procedural part describes, in some programming language, the implementation of each operation.

The database translation of the principle is that an object encapsulates both program and data. In the database world it is not clear whether the structural part of the type is part of the interface (this depends on the system), whereas in the programming language world the data structure is clearly part of the implementation and not of the interface.

Consider, for instance, an Employee object. In a relational system, each employee is represented by some tuple. It is queried using a relational language, and later an application programmer writes programs to update this record—for example, to reflect a raise in the Employee's salary, or termination of the Employee. These updates are generally written either in an imperative programming language with embedded DML (data manipulation language) statements, or in a fourth-generation language. They are stored in a traditional file system and not in the database. Thus in this approach there is a sharp distinction between program and data, and between the query language (for ad hoc queries) and the programming language (for application programs).

In an object-oriented system, we define Employee as an object that has a data part, probably very similar to the record that was defined for the relational system, and an operation part, which consists of the *raise salary* and *fire* operations and other operations to access the Employee data. When storing a set of Employees, both the data and the operations are stored in the database. Thus there is a single model for data and operations, and information can be hidden. No operations other than those specified in the interface can be performed. This restriction holds for both update and retrieval operations.

Encapsulation provides a form of "logical data independence": we can change the implementation of a type without changing any of the programs using that type. Thus the application programs are protected from implementation changes in the lower layers of the system. We believe that proper encapsulation is obtained when only the operations are visible and the data and the implementation of the operations are hidden in the objects.

There are cases where encapsulation is not needed, however, and the use of the system can be significantly simplified if the system allows encapsulation to be be violated under certain conditions. For example, with ad hoc queries the need for encapsulation is reduced, since issues such as maintainability are not important. Thus, an encapsulation mechanism must be provided by an OODBS, but there appear to be cases where its enforcement is not appropriate.

2.4 Types and Classes

Thou shalt support types or classes.

There are two main categories of object-oriented systems, those supporting the notion of class and those supporting the notion of type. In the first category are systems such as Smalltalk (Goldberg and Robson 1983), Gemstone (Maier et al. 1986), Vision (Caruso and Sciore 1987), and more generally all the systems of the Smalltalk family; and Orion (Banerjee et al. 1987), Flavors (Bobrow and Steifik 1981), G-Base (G-Base 1988), Laure (Caseau 1989), and more generally all the systems derived from Lisp. In the second category we find systems such as C++ (Stroustrup 1986), Simula (Simula 1967), Trellis/Owl (Schaffert et al. 1986), Vbase (Atwood 1985), and O_2 (Bancilhon et al. 1988).

A *type*, in an object-oriented system, summarizes the common features of a set of objects. It corresponds to the notion of an abstract data type. It has two parts, the interface and the implementation (or implementations). Only the interface part is visible to the users of the type; the implementation of the object is seen only by the type designer. The interface consists of a list of operations together with their signatures (i.e., the type of the input parameters and the type of the result).

The type implementation consists of a data part and an operation part. In the data part, one describes the internal structure of the object's data. Depending on the power of the system, the structure of this data part can be more or less complex. The operation part consists of procedures which implement the operations of the interface part.

In programming languages, types are tools to increase programmer productivity, by insuring program correctness. By forcing the user to declare the types of the variables and expressions he or she manipulates, the system reasons about the correctness of programs based on this typing information. If the type system is designed carefully, the system can do the type checking at compile time; otherwise some of it might have to be deferred to run time. Thus types are mainly used *at compile time* to check the correctness of the programs. In general, in type-based systems, a type is not a first-class citizen; it has a special status and cannot be modified at run time.

The notion of *class* is different from that of type. Its specification is the same as that of a type, but it is more of a run time notion. It contains two aspects: an object factory and an object warehouse. The object factory can be used to create new objects, by performing the operation *new* on the class or by cloning some prototype object representative of the class. The object warehouse allows the class to be attached to its extension, that is, the set of objects that are instances of the class. The user can manipulate the warehouse by applying operations on all elements of the class.

Classes are not used for checking the correctness of a program but rather for creating and manipulating objects. In most systems that employ the class mechanism, classes are first-class citizens; they can be manipulated at run time, that is, updated or passed as parameters. In most cases, while providing the system with increased flexibility and uniformity, this renders compile time type-checking impossible.

Of course, there are strong similarities between classes and types. The names have been used with both meanings, and the differences can be subtle in some systems.

We do not feel that we should choose one of these two approaches. We consider the choice between the two should be left to the designer of the system (see section 4.3). We require, however, that the system should offer some form of data-structuring mechanism, be it classes or types. Thus the classical notion of a database schema will be replaced by that of a set of classes or a set of types.

We do not, however, feel that is necessary for the system to maintain automatically the extent of a type (i.e., the set of objects of a given type in the database) or, if the extent of a type is maintained, for the system to make it accessible to the user. Consider, for example, the rectangle type, which can be used in many databases by multiple users. It does not make sense to talk about the set of all rectangles maintained by the system or to perform operations on them. We think it is more realistic to ask each user to maintain and manipulate his or her own set of rectangles. On the other hand, in the case of a type such as *Employee,* it might be nice for the system to automatically maintain the *Employee* extent.

2.5 Class or Type Hierarchies

Thy classes or types shall inherit from their ancestors.

Inheritance has two advantages: it is a powerful modeling tool, because it gives a concise and precise description of the world; and it helps in factoring out shared specifications and implementations in applications. An example will help illustrate the interest in having the system provide an inheritance mechanism. Assume that we have two kinds of objects, Employees and Students. Each Employee has a name, an age above 18, and a salary; and he or she can die, get married, and be paid (how dull is the life of the Employee!). Each Student has an age, a name, and a set of grades. He or she can die, get married, and have his or her grade-point average (GPA) computed.

In a relational system, the database designer defines a relation for Employee and a relation for Student; he or she writes the code for the *die, marry,* and *pay* operations on the Employee relation and writes the code for the *die, marry,* and *GPA computation* for the Student relation. Thus the application programmer writes six programs.

In an object-oriented system, using the inheritance property, we recognize that Employees and Students are Persons; they have something in common (the fact of being a Person), and they also have something specific. We introduce a type, Person, which has attributes **name** and **age**, and we write the operations *die* and *marry* for this type. Then we declare that an Employee object is a Person. It inherits the attributes and operations of Person, and it also has a special attribute, **salary**, and a special operation, *pay*. Similarly, we declare that a Student object is a Person with a specific **set of grades** attribute and a special operation, *GPA computation*. In this case, we have a better-structured and more concise description of the schema because we factored out specification, and we have only written four programs because we factored out implementation. Inheritance helps code reusability, because every program is at the level at which the largest number of objects can share it.

There are at least four kinds of inheritance: *substitution* inheritance, *inclusion* inheritance, *constraint* inheritance, and *specialization* inheritance.

In *substitution inheritance,* we say that a type t inherits from a type t' if we can perform more operations on objects of type t than on objects of type t'. Thus any place where we can have an object of type t', we can substitute for it an object of type t. This kind of inheritance is based on behavior and not on values.

Inclusion inheritance corresponds to the notion of classification. It states that a type t is a subtype of a type t' if every object of type t is also an object of type t'. This kind of inheritance is based on structure and not on operations. An example is a Square type with methods *get* and *set(size),* and a *Filled-square* subtype with methods *get, set(size),* and *fill(color).*

Constraint inheritance is a subcase of inclusion inheritance. A type t is a subtype of a type t' if every object of type t is not only an object of type t'

but also satisfies a given constraint. For example, Teenager is a subtype of Person: the type Teenager doesn't have any more fields or operations than the type Person, but it obeys a more specific constraint—a teenager's age must be between 13 and 19.

With ***specialization inheritance,*** a type *t* is a subtype of a type *t′* if objects of type *t* are objects of type *t′* but with more specific information. For example, an Employee object is a Person with some extra fields such as **salary**.

Various degrees of these four types of inheritance are provided by existing systems and prototypes, and we do not prescribe a specific style of inheritance.

2.6 Overriding, Overloading, and Late Binding

Thou shalt not bind prematurely.

There are cases where one wants to have the same name used for different operations. Consider, for example, the *display* operation, which takes an object as input and displays it on the screen. Depending on the type of object, we might want to use different display mechanisms. If the object is a picture, we want it to appear on the screen. If the object is data about a person, we want some form of a tuple printed. If the object is a graph, we want its graphical representation. Consider the problem of displaying a set whose members are of types that are not known at compile time.

In an application using a conventional system, we have three operations: *display tuple, display bitmap,* and *display graph.* The programmer will ascertain the type of each object in the set and use the corresponding display operation. This forces the programmer to be aware of all the possible types of objects in the set, to be aware of the corresponding display operations, and to use them accordingly.

```
for x in X do
  begin
    case of type(x)
      tuple: display(x);
      bitmap: display-bitmap(x);
      graph: display-graph(x);
    end
  end
```

In an object-oriented system, we define the display operation at the object-type level (the most general type in the system). Thus *display* has a single name and can be used indifferently on graphs, tuples, and pictures. However, we redefine the implementation of the operation for each of the types according to the type; this redefinition is called *overriding.* This redefinition results in a single name, *display*, denoting three different programs; this is called *overloading.* To display the set of elements, we simply apply the *display* operation to each one of them, and let the system pick the appropriate implementation at run time.

```
for x in X do  display(x)
```

Here we gain a different advantage: the type implementors still write the same number of programs, but the application programmer does not have to worry about three different programs. In addition, the code is simpler because there is no case statement on types. Finally, the code is more maintainable; when a new type is introduced and new instances of the type are added, the display program will continue to work without modification (provided that we override the display method for that new type).

In order to provide this new functionality, the system cannot bind operation names to programs at compile time. Therefore, operation names must be resolved (i.e., translated into program addresses) at run time. This delayed translation is called is called *late binding*. Late binding makes type checking more difficult (and in some cases impossible), but it does not preclude it completely.

2.7 Computational Completeness

Thou shalt be computationally complete.

From a programming-language point of view, computational completeness is obvious. It simply means that one can express any computable function using the DML of the database system. From a database point of view this is a novelty; SQL, for instance, is not complete. We are not advocating here that designers of object-oriented database systems design new programming languages; computational completeness can be introduced through a reasonable connection to existing programming languages. Most systems indeed use an existing programming language (Banerjee et al. 1987; Fishman et al. 1986; Atwood 1985; Bancilhon et al. 1988); see Bancilhon and Maier 1988 for a discussion of this problem.

Computational completeness is different from being "resource complete," that is, being able to access all resources of the system (e.g., screen and remote communication) from within the language. The system, even though computationally complete, might not be able to express a complete application. It is, however, more powerful than a database system which only stores and retrieves data and performs simple computations on atomic values.

2.8 Extensibility

Thou shalt be extensible.

The database system comes with a set of predefined types. These types can be used at will by programmers to write their applications. This set of types must be extensible; that is, there must be a means to define new types and there must be *no distinction in usage between system-defined and user-defined types*. Of course, there might be a strong difference in the way system-defined and

The authors have not reached consensus on whether the following features should be mandatory or optional.

- View definition and derived data
- Database administration utilities
- Integrity constraints
- Schema evolution facility

3 Optional Features: The Goodies

In this section we discuss things which clearly improve the system, but which are not mandatory to make it an object-oriented database system. Some of these features are of an object-oriented nature (e.g., multiple inheritance). They are included in the category of optional features because, even though they make the system *more* object oriented, they are not core requirements.

Other features are simply database features (e.g., design-transaction management). These characteristics usually improve the functionality of a database system, but they are not core requirements and they are unrelated to the object-oriented aspect. In fact most of them are targeted at serving new applications (CAD/CAM, CASE, office automation, etc.) and are more application oriented than technology oriented. Because many object-oriented database systems are currently aiming at these new applications, there has been some confusion between these features and the object-oriented nature of the system.

3.1 Multiple Inheritance

Since the object-oriented community has not yet agreed on multiple inheritance, we consider that providing it is optional. Note that once one decides to support multiple inheritance, there are many possible solutions for dealing with the problem of conflict resolution.

3.2 Type Checking and Type Inferencing

The degree of type checking that the system will perform at compile time is left open, but the more the better. The optimal situation is where a program that was accepted by the compiler cannot produce any run time type errors. The amount of type inferencing is also left to the system designer; but the more there is, the better. The ideal situation is where only the base types have to be declared, and the system infers the temporary types.

3.3 Distribution

Distribution is orthogonal to the object-oriented nature of the system; that is, the database system can be distributed or not.

3.4 Design Transactions

In most new applications, the transaction model of classical business-oriented database systems is not satisfactory. Transactions tend to be very long, and the usual serializability criterion is not adequate. Thus many OODBSs support design transactions (long transactions or nested transactions).

3.5 Versions

Most of the new applications, such as CAD/CAM and CASE, involve a design activity and require some form of versioning. Thus many OODBSs support versions; but providing a versioning mechanism is not a core requirement.

4 Open Choices

Every system which satisfies the 13 rules deserves the OODBS label. In designing such a system, there are still choices to be made about the degrees of freedom for the OODBS implementors. The characteristics described in this section differ from the mandatory ones in that the scientific community has not yet reached a consensus about them. They also differ from the optional features in that we do not know which of the alternatives are more or less object oriented.

4.1 Programming Paradigm

We see no reason why we should impose one programming paradigm rather than another. The logic programming style (Bancilhon 1986; Zaniolo 1985), the functional programming style (Albano et al. 1985; Banerjee et al. 1987), or the imperative programming style (Stroustrup 1986; Eiffel 1987; Atwood 1985) could all be chosen. Another solution is that the system be independent of the programming style and that it support multiple programming paradigms (Skarra, Zdonik, and Reiss 1986; Bancilhon et al. 1988).

Of course, the choice of the syntax is also free, and people will argue forever whether one should write "john hire" or "john.hire" or "hire john" or "hire(john)".

4.2 Representation System

The representation system is defined by the set of atomic types and the set of constructors. Even though we gave a minimal set of atomic types and constructors (elementary types from programming languages and set, tuple, and list constructors) that are available for describing the representation of objects, they can be extended in many different ways.

4.3 Type System

There is also freedom with respect to the type formers beyond type constructors. The only type formation facility we require is encapsulation. There can be other type formers, such as generic types or a type generator (for example, set(T), where T can be an arbitrary type), restriction, union, and arrow (functions). Another option is whether the type system is second order. Finally, the type system for variables might be richer than the type system for objects.

4.4 Uniformity

There is a heated debate on the degree of uniformity one should expect of OODB systems: Is a type an object? Is a method an object? Or should these three notions be treated differently? We can view this problem at three different levels: the implementation level, the programming-language level, and the interface level.

At the implementation level, one must decide whether type information should be stored as objects, or whether an ad hoc system must be implemented. This is the same issue faced by designers of relational database systems when they have to decide whether to store the schema as a table or in some ad hoc fashion. The decision should be based on performance and ease of implementation. Whatever decision is made, however, is independent from the one taken at the next level up.

At the programming-language level, the question is: Are types first-class entities in the semantics of the language? Most of the debate is concentrated on this question. There are probably different styles of uniformity (syntactical or semantical). Full uniformity at this level is also inconsistent with static type-checking.

Finally, at the interface level, another independent decision must be made. One might want to present the user with a uniform view of types, objects, and methods, even if in the semantics of the programming language these are distinct notions. Conversely, one could present them as different entities, even though the programming language views them as the same. That decision must be made based on human-factor criteria.

5 Conclusion

Several authors, including Kim 1988 and Dittrich 1986, argue that an OODBS is a DBMS with an underlying object-oriented data model. If one takes the notion of a data model in a broad sense, especially if it includes the additional aspects going beyond record orientation, then this view is in accordance with our approach. Dittrich 1986, 1988 introduces a classification of object-oriented data models (and consequently of OODBSs): if it supports complex objects, a model is called structurally object oriented; if extensibility is provided, it is called behaviorally object oriented; a fully object-oriented model has to offer both features. This definition also requires persistence, disk management, concurrency, and recovery; and it at least implicitly assumes most of the other features (where applicable, according to the various classes). In total, it is thus slightly more liberal than our approach. However, as most current systems and prototypes do not fulfill all the requirements mandated by our definition anyway, Dittrich's classification provides a useful framework for comparing both completed and ongoing work.

We have proposed a collection of defining characteristics for an object-oriented database system. To the best of our knowledge, the golden rules presented in this paper are currently the most detailed definition of an object-oriented database system. The choice of the characteristics and our interpretation of them devolves from our experience in specifying and implementing the current round of systems. Further experience with the design, implementation, and formalization of object-oriented databases will undoubtedly modify and refine our stance. (In other words, don't be surprised if you hear one of the authors lambasting the current definition in the future.) Our goal is only to put forth a concrete proposal to be debated, critiqued, and analyzed by the scientific community. Our last rule is:

Thou shalt question the golden rules.

6 Acknowledgements

We wish to thank Philippe Bridon, Gilbert Harrus, Paris Kanellakis, Philippe Richard, and Fernando Vélez for suggestions and comments on earlier drafts of the paper. David Maier's work was partially supported by NSF award IST 83-51730, co-sponsored by Tektronix Foundation, Intel, Digital Equipment, Servio Logic, Mentor Graphics, and Xerox.

References

Abiteboul, S., and P. Kanellakis. 1989. Object identity as a query language primitive. In *Proceedings of the 1989 ACM SIGMOD conference.*

Albano, A., G. Gheli, G. Occhiuto, and R. Orsini. 1985. Galileo: A strongly typed interactive conceptual language. *ACM Transactions on Database Systems* 10(2): 230–61.

Atkinson, M., F. Bancilhon, D. DeWitt, K. Dittrich, D. Maier, and S. Zdonik. 1990. The object-oriented database system manifesto. In *Proceedings of the first international DOOD conference.*

Atkinson, M., P. J. Bayley, K. Chilsom, W. Cockshott, and R. Morrison. 1983. An approach to persistent programming. *Computer Journal* 26(4): 360–65.

Atwood, T. 1985. *An object-oriented DBMS for design support applications.* Ontologic, Inc., Report.

Bancilhon, F. 1986. A logic programming object-oriented cocktail. *ACM SIGMOD Record* 15(3): 11–21.

Bancilhon, F., and D. Maier. 1988. Multilanguage object-oriented systems: A new answer to old database problems. In *Future generation computer II*, ed. K. Fuchi and L. Kott. North-Holland.

Bancilhon, F., G. Barbedette, V. Benzaken, C. Delobel, S. Gamerman, C. Lécluse, P. Pfeffer, P. Richard, and F. Vélez. 1988. The design and implementation of O_2, an object-oriented database system. In *Proceedings of the second international workshop on object-oriented database systems,* ed. K. Dittrich.

Banerjee, J., H-T. Chou, J. Garza, W. Kim, D. Woelk, N. Ballou, and H. J. Kim. 1987. Data model issues for object-oriented applications. *ACM TOIS* 5(1): 3–26.

Bobrow, D., and M. Steifik. 1981. *The loops manual.* Technical report no. LB-VLSI-81-13, Xerox Palo Alto (Calif.) Research Center, Knowledge Systems Area.

Carey, M., D. DeWitt, J. E. Richardson, and E. J. Shekita. 1986. Object and file management in the Exodus extensible database system. In *Proceedings of the 12th VLDB conference.* Morgan Kaufmann.

Carey, M., D. DeWitt, and S. Vandenberg. 1988. A data model and query language for Exodus. In *Proceedings of the 1988 ACM SIGMOD conference.*

Caruso, M., and E. Sciore. 1987. The VISION object-oriented database management system. In *Proceedings of the workshop on database programming languages.* ACM Press.

Caseau, Y. 1989. A model for a reflective object-oriented language. *Sigplan Notices*, Special issue on concurrent object-oriented programming (March).

Codd, E. F. 1970. A relational model for large shared data banks. *Communications of the ACM* 13(6): 377–87.

Dittrich, K. R. 1986. Object-oriented database system: The notions and the issues. In *Proceedings of the 1986 international workshop on object-oriented database systems*, ed. K. R. Dittrich and U. Dayal, IEEE, Computer Science Press.

———. 1988. Preface. In *Advances in object-oriented database systems*, ed. K. R. Dittrich. Lecture Notes in Computer Science, vol. 334. Springer-Verlag.

Eiffel. 1987. *Eiffel user's manual.* Publication no. TR-EI-5/UM. Interactive Software Engineering.

Fishman, D., D. Beech, H. P. Cate, E. C. Chow, T. Conners, J. W. Davis, N. Denett, C. G. Hoch, W. Kent, P. Lyngbaek, B. Mahbod, M. A. Neimat, T. A. Ryan, and M. C. Shan. 1986. Iris: An object-oriented database management system. *ACM TOIS* 5(1): 48–69.

G-Base. 1988. *G-Base version 3: Introductory guide.* Graphael.

Goldberg, A., and D. Robson. 1983. *Smalltalk 80: The language and its implementation.* Addison-Wesley.

Hall, P., J. Owlett, and S. Todd. 1976. Relations and entities. In *Modeling in data base management systems*, ed. G. M. Nijssen. North-Holland.

Khoshafian, S., and G. Copeland. 1986. Object identity. In *Proceedings of the first ACM OOPSLA conference.*

Kim, W. 1988. *A foundation for object-oriented databases.* MCC Technical Report.

Lécluse, C., and P. Richard. 1989. The O_2 database programming languages. In *Proceedings of the 15th VLDB Conference.*

Maier, D. 1989. Why isn't there an object-oriented data model? In *Proceedings of the IFIP 11th world computer conference.*

Maier, D., and D. Price. 1984. Data model requirements for engineering applications. In *Proceedings of the first international workshop on expert database systems.*

Maier, D., J. Stein, A. Otis, and A. Purdy. 1986. *Development of an object-oriented DBMS.* Report no. CS/E-86-005, Oregon Graduate Center.

Nixon, B., L. Chung, D. Lauzon, A. Borgida, J. Mylopoulos, and M. Stanley. 1987. *Design of a compiler for a semantic data model.* Technical note no. CSRI-44, University of Toronto.

Schaffert, C., T. Cooper, B. Bullis, M. Kilian, and C. Wilpolt. 1986. An introduction to Trellis/Owl. In *Proceedings of the first OOPSLA conference.*

Simula. 1967. *Simula 67 reference manual.*

Skarra, A., S. Zdonik, and S. Reiss. 1986. An object server for an object oriented database system. In *Proceedings of the 1986 international workshop on object oriented database systems.* IEEE Computer Science Press.

Stroustrup, B. 1986. *The C++ programming language.* Addison-Wesley.

Van Emdem, M., and R. Kowalski. 1976. The semantics of predicate logic as a programming language. *JACM* 23(4): 733–42.

Zaniolo, C. 1985. Object-oriented programming in Prolog. In *Proceedings of the first workshop on expert database systems.*

CHAPTER 2

The Story of O_2

O. DEUX ET AL.

1 Introduction

Altaïr is a five-year project which began in September 1986. Its goal is to design and implement a next-generation database system. The five-year period was divided into two phases: a three-year prototyping phase and a two-year development phase. The three-year prototyping period has now ended and version V1 of the prototype is operational as scheduled.

The actual design of the system started in February 1987. We first built a throwaway prototype, which was demonstrated in December 1987 and is described in Bancilhon et al. 1988. We started a new design in January 1988 and had a new working prototype in March 1989. From March to September 1989 we improved the prototype, both by adding new features and by making the code more robust. A subset of the code is now being distributed to a set of selected partners for a first evaluation. The current system is operational on Sun workstations.

1.1 A System Overview

Our main technical choices can be summarized as follows. We implemented an *Object-Oriented Database System*, O_2. This OODBS supports a set of *Database Programming Languages*, CO_2 and BasicO_2 ; a set of *User-Interface Generation Tools* (Looks); and a *Programming Environment* (OOPE).

Thus, O_2 consists of eight functional modules: OOPE, the Alphanumeric Interface, Looks, the Language Processor, the Query Interpreter, the Schema Manager, the Object Manager, and the Disk Manager.

The Disk Manager takes care of input/output (I/O), data placement, indexing, and buffering. The Object Manager maps the abstract object data model onto the disk representation. The Schema Manager deals with schema information such as types and programs. The Language Processor manages the commands of the Data Definition Language and manages the compilation of programs. It also populates the schema by sending orders to the Schema Manager. The Query Interpreter is responsible for interpreting queries, using the Object Manager and the Schema Manager. Looks manages the screen, displays objects and values, and handles their interaction with the Object Manager. OOPE is the programming environment; it uses Looks to display and manage data on the screen. The Alphanumeric Interface provides direct access to the various languages of the system, without using graphical facilities.

The rest of this paper is organized as follows. Section 2 gives a programmer's view of the system. It presents the O_2 data model, the data definition language, the query language, and the programming language, and how all these languages interrelate (this corresponds to the Language Processor and Query Interpreter modules). Section 3 describes the user-interface generation tools—the Looks module. These tools are used by the O_2 application programmer. We also used them to implement the programming environment (the OOPE module), which is described in section 4. Section 5 describes the implementation of the system—the Schema Manager, Object Manager, and Disk Manager modules. Section 6 is devoted to a performance evaluation of the system.

2 A Programmer's View of the System

The standard interface to the O_2 system is OOPE, the O_2 Programming Environment. This environment provides graphical tools to update and consult the database schema and to browse through and edit the database. This interface is described in section 4. We also provide a more classical alphanumeric interface. This interface supports the Data Definition Language (DDL), the Query Language, and the Database Programming Languages (DBPLs).

Programming a database application using O_2 involves the following two steps:

Schema definition: The application programmer generates a *schema,* using the O_2 data definition language (O_2 1989). The schema consists of *classes* which describe the internal structure (*type*) of objects and their behavior (*methods*). Classes are related by an *inheritance* relationship. The underlying data model and the Data Definition Language are described in section 2.1.

Method implementation: The next step is the implementation of the *methods* attached to the classes. Methods are implemented using one of the two O_2 database programming languages. These languages are C and Basic, enhanced with an object-oriented layer which is in charge of object and complex value manipulations (O_2 1989).

Furthermore, the user can also interact with the database in an ad hoc fashion, using the O_2 Query Language (O_2 1989). This language can be used interactively and is interpreted by the system. It is described in section 2.2.2.

2.1 The Data Model and the Data Definition Language

O_2 is object oriented: information is organized as *objects,* which have an identity and encapsulate data and behavior. Manipulation of objects is done through *methods,* which are procedures attached to the objects. Object identity is useful for supporting object sharing, and provides simple update semantics.

2.1.1 Objects and Values in O_2

In O_2 we provide the user with the possibility of defining not only objects but also complex *values.* The following are typical O_2 objects:

```
i0: tuple(name: "Eiffel Tower",
          address: i5,
          description: "a famous Paris monument",
          closing_days: list("Christmas", "Easter", "August 15th"),
          admission_fee: 25)
i1: tuple(name: "Paris",
          map: i2,
          hotels: set(i3, i4))
i5: tuple(city: i1,
          street: "Champs de Mars",
          number: 1)
```

Objects are (identifier,value) pairs. For example, the first object has identifier i_0 and a tuple-structured value. The value is built using atomic values (e.g., "Eiffel Tower"), structured values (e.g., the **closing_days** value), or objects through their identifiers (i_1, i_2, etc.—we have not detailed here the objects i_2, i_3, and i_4, which represent respectively a bitmap and two hotels). Objects are encapsulated; that is, their value is not directly accessible and they are manipulated by methods, as explained in section 2.2. On the other hand, values are manipulated by primitives.

2.1.2 Types and Classes

In O_2, the user may choose between two kinds of organization: *classes,* whose instances are objects and which encapsulate data and behavior; and *types,* whose instances are values. Values are not encapsulated; that is, their structure is known by users and they are manipulated by operators. To every class is associated a type, describing the structure of its instances. Classes are created explicitly using commands and are part of the inheritance hierarchy. Types appear as components of classes. The underlying model is presented and analyzed in Part 2 of this book (Lécluse and Richard 1989; Abiteboul and Kanellakis 1989).

Types are constructed recursively using the O_2 atomic types (integer, float, double, string, char, Boolean, and bits) and classes from the schema, and applying to them the set, list, and tuple constructors. The following expression is an O_2 type:

```
tuple (name: string,
       map: Bitmap,
       hotels: set(Hotel))
```

This type describes cities. The **hotels** attribute has a set-structured value. Hotel is a class name.

In O_2, the schema is a set of classes related by inheritance links and/or composition links. A class describes the structure *and* the behavior of a set of objects. The structural part of a class is a type as defined above, and the behavioral part is a set of methods (see section 2.2). Classes are created using schema-definition commands as follows:

```
add class City
        type tuple(name: string,
                   map: Bitmap,
                   hotels: set(Hotel))
add class Monument
        type tuple(name: string,
                   address: Address,
                   description: string,
                   closing_days: list(string),
                   admission_fee: integer)
add class Address
        type tuple(street: string,
                   city: City)
add class Hotel
        type tuple(name: string,
                   address: Address,
                   facilities: list(string),
                   stars: integer,
                   rate: float)

add class Restaurant
        type tuple (name: string,
                    address: Address,
                    menus: set(tuple(name: string,
                                     rate: float)))
```

2.1.3 Naming and Persistence

In O_2, objects and values can be named. The following are examples of name definitions of objects:

add name Eiffel_Tower: Monument
add name Paris: City

The name Eiffel_Tower will stand for an object of class Monument. In the same way, one can name a value as follows:

add name Paris_monuments: **set**(Monument)

Paris_monuments is a name for a value of type set of Monument. Such a name can be seen as a global variable dynamically attached to a given object or value. The attached object can be changed by assignment. For instance, we can write:

Eiffel_Tower = **new**(Monument)

This instruction attaches a newly created object to the name Eiffel_Tower. The initial value of the object is the tuple default value corresponding to the type. This object will always be accessible through the name Eiffel_Tower until the user makes another assignment.

In O_2, persistence is attached to names. The persistence rules are:

- Every named object or value is persistent.
- Every object or value which is a part of another persistent object or value is persistent.

For example, if we consider that the name Eiffel_Tower has been attached to the object i_0 defined at the beginning of section 2.1, then the object i_1 will become persistent, since it is a component of i_0 together with the strings "Eiffel Tower" and "a famous Paris monument", which are the values of the `name` and `description` attributes. The same holds for the values of the `closing_days` and `admission_fee` attributes.

The *extension* of a class is the set of all objects created using the **new** command (see section 2.2.1) applied to that class. The system provides the user with an automatic management of class extensions if required by the programmer. This is done using a set value which collects all the objects of a class. For instance, we could have defined the class City as follows:

```
add class City with extension
        type tuple(name: string,
                   map: Bitmap,
                   hotels: set(Hotel))
```

The optional **with extension** clause in the class definition tells the O_2 system to create a named value of type set(City) with name City. Every city created by the **new**(City) command will be automatically inserted in this set and will thus persist as a component of a persistent set. Note that, according to our persistence rules, objects of a class without extension will not persist unless they are explicitly named or become components of some other persistent object or value. Classes without extension are a natural way of dealing with transient objects.

In O_2, objects are not explicitly deleted; they disappear by becoming unreachable from the persistence roots (the named objects and values). Thus one does not delete objects, one deletes links between objects. This is commonly called *garbage-collection semantics.* Of course, special treatment must be given to the extensions of classes. These are persistent and objects in them are persistent by definition and would never be deleted otherwise. Thus we have a **remove** primitive which deletes the object from the class extension in case no other object points to it.

2.1.4 Methods

Objects are manipulated using *methods.* A method is a piece of code which is attached to a specific class and which can be applied to objects of this class. In O_2, method definition is done in two steps. First, the programmer declares the method by giving its *signature*—that is, its name, the class to which it is attached, the type or class of the arguments, and the type or class of the result, if there is one. Then he or she gives the implementation of the method. The following is a method declaration:

add method check_rates(): Boolean **in class** Hotel

This method checks whether the rates of the hotel are correct with respect to its category (the **stars** attribute). It is attached to the Hotel class, it has no parameter, and it returns a value of type Boolean. Methods can be *private* or *public.* Private methods are visible only within their class, that is, in the methods attached to that class. Public methods are visible by every class and can be used freely. When declaring a method, the programmer can add the keywords **is private** in order to make it private. The default is public. The following declares a private method for the Monument class:

add method increase_fee(amount: integer) **in class** Monument **is private**

The description of method implementation is given in section 2.1.1.

2.1.5 Subtyping and Inheritance

Inheritance allows the programmer to define classes in an incremental way by refining already existing ones. O_2 provides the user with an inheritance mechanism based on subtyping.

A type is a subtype of another if and only if every instance of this type is also an instance of its supertype. This allows statements like "A person is a mammal" or "An employee is a person." A tuple type is a subtype of another if it is more defined, that is, if it contains every attribute of its supertype plus some new ones and/or it refines the type of some attributes of its supertype. The following example illustrates this.

```
tuple(name: string,
      address: Address,
      description: Text,
      closing_days: list(string),
      admission_fee: integer,
      facilities: list(string),
      stars: integer,
      rate: float)
```

is a subtype of

```
tuple(name: string,
      address: Address,
      description: Text,
      closing_days: list(string),
      admission_fee: integer)
```

Another characteristic of this subtyping relationship is that a set-structured type set(T) is a subtype of set(T′) if and only if T is a subtype of T′. For instance,

```
set(tuple(name: string,
          address: Address))
```

is a subtype of

```
set(tuple(name: string))
```

The same relationship holds for lists. The subtyping relationship is inferred by O_2. Based on this subtyping relationship, O_2 offers an *inheritance* mechanism. We can define the Historical_hotel class as follows:

add class Historical_hotel **inherits** Monument, Hotel

The effect of this declaration is the definition of a Historical_hotel class whose associated type is a subtype of the Monument type and of the Hotel type.

The programmer only has to give the extra attributes (the others are taken from the definition of the inherited classes) and the redefined attributes. The O_2 command interpreter checks whether the inheritance definition is legal (i.e., there is no subtyping violation) and creates the subclass according to the subtyping rules. An object of class Historical_hotel will automatically be considered as an object of class Monument and as an object of class Hotel. This results in the possibility of applying any method of classes Monument or Hotel to Historical_hotel objects. Note that we do not infer the subclass relationship, which is user defined. The system just checks whether it is legal with respect to the subtyping rules.

As shown by this example, O_2 supports *multiple inheritance.* As opposed to simple inheritance, possible ambiguities may arise when an attribute or a method name is defined in two or more superclasses. The user either has to explicitly redefine the attribute or method name where needed or explicitly give the inheritance path using the **from** keyword.

We assume that historical hotels can have higher rates than other hotels of the same category. This can be done by overriding the *check_rates* method of the class Hotel as follows:

add method check_rates(): Boolean **in class** Historical_hotel

This *check_rates* method for historical hotels will then be used instead of the one for hotels generally whenever a historical hotel is concerned.

2.1.6 The Object Class

The system offers a predefined class named Object. This class is the root of the class hierarchy, and every class implicitly inherits from it. It implements methods that are common to all objects in the system. These methods are thus inherited by every class. Among these predefined methods are those which implement the classical identity or equality tests for complex objects (e.g., the methods *is_same, is_value_equal,* and *is_deep_equal*) and the corresponding copy methods.

2.1.7 Exceptional Attributes and Methods

Due to the semantics of types, a tuple value can have extra attributes. Consider the Monument class: the Eiffel_Tower object can have a value which also contains an attribute **height**. This extra attribute will not be dealt with by the methods associated to the Monument class; however, the standard operators available on tuple values will handle it. For instance, the following is a correct value for an object of class Monument:

tuple(**name**: "Eiffel_Tower",
    address: i_5,
    description: "a famous Paris monument",
    closing_days: **list**("Christmas", "Easter", "August 15th"),
    admission_fee: 25,
    height: 315)

The **height** attribute is exceptional, since it does not appear in the type associated to class Monument. Exceptional attributes are allowed for any tuple object or value, named or not.

One can also associate specific methods to named objects. These methods are used to characterize the exceptional behavior of an object. One can also override an existing method in the class of the object with an exceptional method. An example of this mechanism is:

add method increase_fee(amount: integer) **in object** Eiffel_Tower
add method increase_height(amount: float) **in object** Eiffel_Tower

This second method will be used to increase the `height` attribute of the Eiffel_Tower object. The method is associated with the name and not with a particular object, and the actual object associated to the name Eiffel_Tower can change at run time. The late-binding process will associate the exceptional method to the object currently bound to the name.

2.2 The O_2 Languages

Besides the Data Definition Language, O_2 offers two types of languages: DBPLs to write the code of methods and a query language for ad hoc querying of the database. This subsection describes these languages.

2.2.1 The Database Programming Languages

We chose to be language independent in the DBPL design. We defined an O_2 layer which handles (1) object and values declaration, (2) object manipulation (i.e., message passing), and (3) value manipulation (i.e., primitives). This layer is language independent and depends only on the O_2 data model. We can add this layer to existing languages, turning a language L into the language LO_2. In the process, we adapt the syntax of the O_2 layer to that of the host programming language so that the merge is smooth and natural.

At this stage, we have implemented two languages, CO_2 and BasicO_2. The CO_2 (or BasicO_2) programming language is a superset of the C (or Basic) language. CO_2 and BasicO_2 respect as much as possible the style and philosophy of the host language. Furthermore, there is an implicit correspondence between O_2 atomic types and C or Basic types. Thus, every atomic value manipulation is done using the C or Basic language without the need of conversions, while the object-oriented layer is in charge of complex-value and object manipulations. The syntax of the object-oriented layer closely follows that of the host language. For example, in CO_2, set union resembles C integer addition, and tuple projection is similar to the extraction of a field of a C record. This helps the programmer to learn the LO_2 language quickly, provided he or she knows L. In this paper, we report only on CO_2, for space reasons. For more details see chapter 9.

We give below, as an example, the code of a method *increase_fee* for the Monument class.

```
body increase_fee(amount: integer) in class Monument
    co2 { *self.admission_fee += amount; }
```

The curly brackets delimit the CO_2 block of code, as in pure C. The value of an object is obtained using the "dereferencing" operator, "*"; thus "self" is the object and "*self" is the associated value. This illustrates the association between objects and values. As in standard programming languages, objects can be seen as pointers to values. In this example, the value "*self" is a tuple, and access to an attribute is obtained using the dot operator. The assignment is done as in C; it increments the integer value representing the admission fee. Notice that we stick to the C syntax for manipulating O_2 values such as dereferencing or extracting a tuple field.

A method is applied to an object by *message passing,* whose syntax is:

[receiver selector(arguments)]

where "receiver" denotes an object to which the method with name "selector" is applied. This may return either a value or an object, depending on the method signature. For example, the method *increase_fee* is applied to the Eiffel_Tower object using the following message passing:

[Eiffel_Tower increase_fee(3)]

The keyword "self" in the code of *increase_fee* will refer to the object attached to the name Eiffel_Tower.

Object creation. Objects are created through a command called **new**. This command takes a class name as input. For example, the following creates a new Monument object:

Eiffel_Tower = **new**(Monument);

Value manipulation. The CO_2 language allows the construction of O_2 values using the set, list, and tuple constructors. We can, for instance, write a set value containing four integers as follows:

set(1, 4, 34, -21)

The following associates a value to a newly created object:

```
*Eiffel_Tower = tuple(name: "Eiffel Tower",
                      address: Eiffel_address,
                      description: "famous Paris monument",
                      closing_days: list("Christmas", "Easter",
                                         "August 15th"),
                      admission_fee: 25);
```

The "*" operator can only be used in a method of the class of the receiver (in this case, the Monument class), except if it was declared public. Eiffel_address is a variable which denotes an object of class Address. We have seen that we can extract a field of a tuple value using the "." operator. All the CO_2 value manipulations are done in this way, using the classical C syntax. For instance, to append elements to the `closing_days` list of the Eiffel_Tower object, one can proceed as follows:

*Eiffel_Tower.**closing_days** += **list**("June 6th");

O_2 provides the programmer with the usual set and list operators (union, intersection, difference, cardinality, concatenation, etc.) whose syntax follows the C syntax.

Iterator. CO_2 provides the programmer with an iterator that enables easy set or list manipulations. This iterator can be applied on set-structured or list-structured *values*, but not on objects. Of course, the set value can contain either values or objects. Indeed, objects are encapsulated, and one should not know the structure of the encapsulated value.

for (x **in** S [**when** condition]) <statement>

This is an extension of the classical C iterator. It applies the given statement with the variable *x* bound to every element of the set (or list) value S that satisfies the optional condition. The **when** clause adds no power to the **for** iterator, but allows some optimization when the condition is directly evaluable by the object manager. For instance, we can write:

o2 Monument x;
for (x **in** Paris_monuments **when** (*x.**admission_fee** <= 20))
    [x increase_fee(3)];

The above code increases the value of **admission_fee** for all the monuments located in Paris whose admission fee is less than or equal to Fr 20. The expression "**o2** Monument x" declares an O_2 variable which is used to denote objects of class Monument. Paris_monuments is a named value of type set (Monument), which is supposed to contain all Paris monuments. The **for** iterator is more flexible and powerful than the classical selection operation.

2.2.2 The Query Language

In an object-oriented environment, doing a simple retrieval of information can be a complex task if the only means of interaction with the system is a database programming language that respects encapsulation. Thus we want to provide the user with a simple means of ad hoc interaction with the system. This can be done in two ways: through a graphical interface (see the OOPE description in section 4) and through a query language (chapter 11), which we discuss in this subsection. The query language has the following characteristics.

- It is a two-mode language. It can be used within programs to write applications (thus as a data manipulation language), and it can be used interactively for ad hoc queries. In the first mode (the programming mode), it cannot violate encapsulation; that is, it cannot access the value of an object otherwise than through its public methods. In the second mode (the ad hoc mode), the query language may violate encapsulation; it may directly access the values of the objects.

- A query returns an object or a value. Returned objects are those already existing in the database. A query can generate new values, however.
- The query language is functional and first order. It is defined by a set of basic functions and a way of building new functions from these, through composition and iterators.
- The query language is a subset of the programming language. This avoids the impedance mismatch in the embedded mode and avoids the need to learn a new language.

We now present examples of O_2 queries. The query language offers basic queries for objects, tuples, and sets of lists.

Objects. Let us suppose we are given the *is_open_on* method on the Monument class that, given a day, checks whether the monument is open on that day. For example, *Is the Eiffel Tower open on the 14th of July, Bastille day?* A valid query is:

```
Eiffel_Tower is_open_on("Bastille day")
```

Tuples. For example, *On which days does the Eiffel Tower close?*

```
Eiffel_Tower.closing_days
```

Sets and lists. We have chosen a standard SQL-like syntax for filtering lists or sets. For example, *What are the names of the hotels in Paris that have air conditioning?*

```
select h.name
from  h in Paris.hotels
where "air_conditioning" in h.facilities
```

Constructing values is possible through the standard constructors—tuple, set, and list. Lists and sets are also built through filters. In our last example, a new set has been created, one that contains the names of the Paris hotels which have air conditioning.

The language being functional in nature, all consistent combinations are possible. This property gives the language completeness, while keeping it understandable by all since only a few basic concepts have to be assimilated. Here is an example of a more elaborate query: *What are the restaurants in Paris where one can eat for less than Fr 50? What are their menus?*

```
select tuple(restaurant: r.name,menu: m.name)
from  r in Restaurant,
        m in r.menus
where m.rate < 50 and r.address.city.name = "Paris"
```

The filter operator features three clauses. The variables of the **from** clause are defined from set- (or list-) resulting queries. They could be filters, unions of filters, set-resulting methods, and so on. The **select** clause accepts any sound query as an argument: filters, field extractions, method call, and the like. The **where** clause only accepts queries that return Booleans, such as Boolean method call or membership test.

2.3 Development and Execution Modes

O_2 provides two modes for running an application. The first, called *development* mode, corresponds to what has been previously described. In development mode, the programmer interactively modifies the schema by creating or deleting classes, methods, and named objects or values. He or she also defines applications with their programs, and can run and test programs and methods at any time. In this mode, O_2 is highly interactive and makes full use of features such as late binding. The price of this flexibility is reduced performance for method execution and the possibility of run-time errors due to possible inconsistencies in the schema. For example, a method may call another one which has been deleted. This is reasonable, however, since the applications are in a development phase and since their designers need dynamicity more than security and performance.

When an application is completed and debugged, it will be used by end users. In this context, performance and safety are crucial. Furthermore, there is no need for schema evolution. This is why O_2 provides end users with an *execution* mode, in which the schema is frozen. This allows the system to optimize late binding by replacing dynamic name solving with function calls whenever possible. However, some schema operations, such as class or method deletions, are no longer permitted on the frozen schema. The execution mode for an application is generated by the command:

compile Tour_operator

The effect of this command is to compile the whole application and to produce an optimized executable code. The consistency between this completed application and the development process (command interpreter) is ensured by forbidding updates on the part of the schema concerning the compiled application.

2.4 Distribution

The distributed architecture is visible to the application programmer. The programmer is aware of the existence of two machines (the server and the workstation) and may explicitly specify on which of the machines a message-passing expression is to be executed. Any method call can have a site specification as follows:

[**on server** Eiffel_Tower increase_fee(3)] or

[**on workstation** Eiffel_Tower increase_fee(3)] or

[**on other** Eiffel_Tower increase_fee(3)]

As shown in the example, the site definition can be absolute ("server" or "workstation") or relative ("other"). Note that we associate location with message invocation and not with the methods themselves: the same method can run both on the server and on the workstation, if the programmer decides so. For messages without site specification, execution is local.

3 Looks, the User Interface Generator

The O_2 user-interface generator, Looks, is a toolkit extension designed to meet the O_2 programmer's requirements in terms of end-user interaction. Looks addresses three problems:

- It allows the programmer to create simple user interfaces quickly by means of predefined generic dialogue components. Thus programmer productivity can be significantly improved.
- It permits the programmer to customize these predefined dialogue components in order to match the requirements of specific applications.
- It is in charge of the dialogue with the end user.

Looks supports the graphic and interactive manipulation of complex O_2 objects and values.

3.1 Major Features of Looks

Looks is a user-interface server which provides functions to create, remove, edit, and save. It maintains the consistency of the *presentations* of any O_2 value or object. A complete description of the Looks external behavior and the programming interface can be found in O_2 1989. Looks is implemented in Le_Lisp on top of the Aïda toolkit (Devin and Duquesnoy 1988). The communication between server and client is supported by a general Remote Procedure Call (RPC) mechanism. RPC is implemented on top of Unix sockets.

The major features of Looks are outlined in this subsection.

3.1.1 A Two-dimensional Space of Generic Display Algorithms

Each O_2 object or value can be arbitrarily complex; it can be viewed as the root of a hyperobject graph. Looks provides two parameters to control the display of any value: expansion and placement. O_2 values constitute graphs connecting atoms (integer, string, etc.) and constructors (tuple, set, and list) through "part-of" relationships. Because these value graphs can be arbitrarily large and cyclic, a display operation must define how much of the graph should be shown. We call this operation graph expansion. Figure 2.1 shows a single hotel object displayed with each of the three predefined expansions supported by Looks: "icon" (upper left), "level_one" (lower left), and "all_you_can_show" (right).

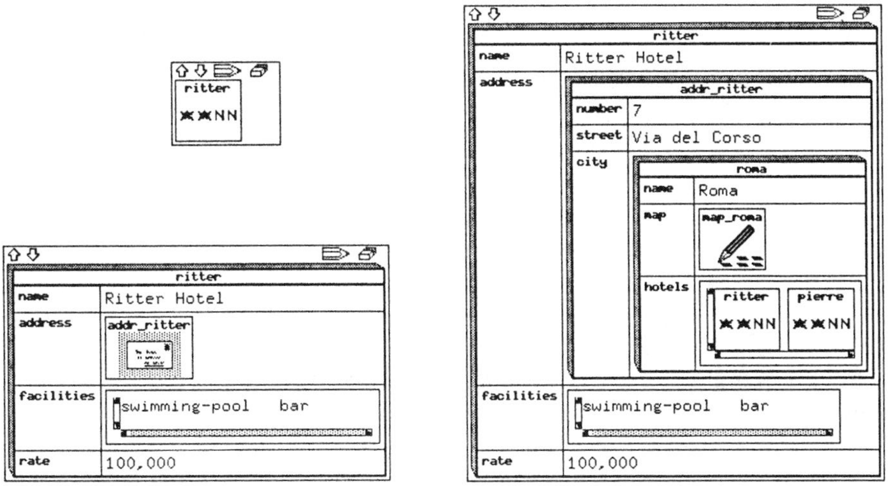

Figure 2.1. Three presentations of the same object

Once a presentation is built, we must decide where to display it on screen. Looks provides several placement algorithms to the programmer: tiling, stacking, interactive, mouse, and coordinate.

3.1.2 Specific Presentations

Because generic presentations cannot satisfy the needs of every application, specific presentations can be defined. Looks supports specific presentations of the O_2 bitmap, text, and pie-chart classes. Each of these classes has an O_2 structure which does not appear explicitly on the presentation. For instance, text is stored in O_2 as a list of strings. In the current version, building a customized presentation in Looks requires writing Lisp code.

3.1.3 Structured Edition

Once a value is displayed, its presentation can be edited. Editing is based on cut, copy, paste, and create operations. These operations are performed either with the keyboard or by direct manipulation with the mouse. Because values are typed, some editing operations are not valid. For instance, one cannot paste a list of monuments in a set of hotels or type characters in an integer field. Looks interactively controls the editing operations to guarantee type consistency.

3.1.4 Interactive Method Activation

Looks provides the possibility of interactively activating a method from the presentation of an object. Assume, for instance, that a *book_a_room* method is associated with City objects and consists of choosing a hotel from the `hotels` list for a particular city. The method has one hotel argument. Once a City object is displayed, the end user can decide at any time to activate the *book_a_room* method. Looks automatically produces a presentation into which the user can paste the chosen hotel. Method activation is performed by selecting the name of the method from a menu. At run time, a method can be inhibited by the application and later reactivated.

3.1.5 Browsing and Querying the Database

Database browsing is supported by two mechanisms. The first one relies on the ability to display the subobjects of any object already displayed on screen. For instance, to consult a Person subobject within a list, the end user can scroll the list and then display the appropriate Person. Subobject display operations are implemented as O_2 methods so that they can be redefined by programmers.

The scrolling and displaying subobject functions are not appropriate for browsing large lists. To speed up browsing, the second mechanism implements a search facility.

3.2 A Simple Programming Example

To describe all the 14 primitives supported by Looks would be beyond the scope of this paper (see O_2 1989 for a complete description). Instead, let us look at a short example which illustrates the main features of Looks. Here is the code for entering data about a new hotel:

```
hotel_object = new(Hotel);
hotel_presentation = present(hotel_object, ALL_YOU_CAN_SHOW);
map(hotel_presentation, MANUAL);
user_answer = lock(hotel_presentation);
if user_answer == ERASER then < cancel hotel creation >;
else {
        consult(hotel_presentation, &hotel_object);
        < check consistency and process the hotel creation >;
        }
unmap(hotel_presentation);
remove(hotel_presentation);
```

The first line of the program creates an O_2 Hotel instance.

present is a Looks primitive which creates a presentation object for a "Hotel" object. The image is created using the "all_you_can_show" expansion. This means that the presentation will show as much information as fits in a given window size, following a breadth-first expansion strategy.

map displays the presentation on screen; "manual" tells that the presentation is to be placed by the end user at run time. Figure 2.2 shows the result of the sequence.

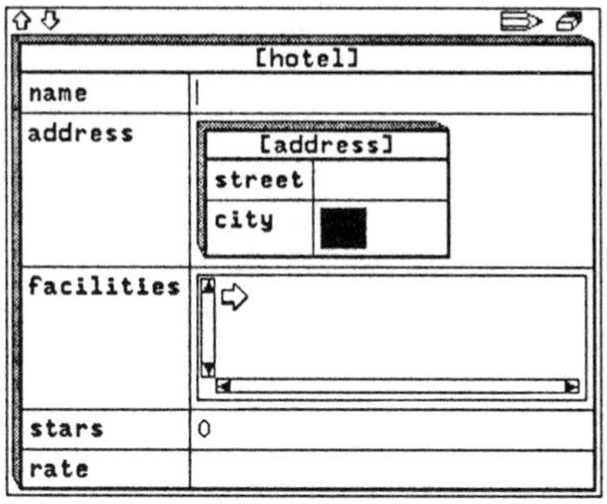

Figure 2.2. Interactive creation of a new Hotel object

lock suspends the execution until the user has filled the presentation. To do so, the user edits the presentation and clicks the "pencil" button. To cancel the operation, the user can click the "eraser" button (see figure 2.2). Notice that while this piece of code is in the suspended state, the application process is available to process any user query (to run a method, for instance). **lock** is a very important primitive: it offers a mechanism to transfer dialogue control from the application to the end user and back.

If the user_answer is "eraser," it means that the user wants to cancel the operation. Otherwise, **consult** returns the value entered by the user at the "hotel_object" address. The application checks whether this value is consistent and processes the creation.

unmap is used to erase the hotel presentation from screen, and **remove** is used to remove it.

4 OOPE, the Programming Environment

OOPE is a graphical programming environment supporting the development of O_2 applications. It allows the programmer to browse, edit, and query the data and the schema, and to edit, test, and debug methods and programs. In addition to this basic functionality, it provides tools to simplify the programmer's work. Finally, it provides a tool box (Arango 1989) containing predefined classes, objects, and values which the programmer can use as software components in his or her programs. It can also be used by the casual user who wants to interact with the database. This "naive" user will be able to browse through, query, and edit both the database and the schema.

OOPE is fully described in O_2 1989. It is implemented in CO_2, and its interface is built using Looks. It is therefore an O_2 application.

4.1 The OOPE Design Principles

OOPE is fully object oriented. It makes full use of graphics, and has an all-object design philosophy—that is, every piece of information is represented by an object, every action is performed by sending a message to an object, and all objects are displayed in a generic fashion.

When OOPE is invoked, a set of objects, named "Tools," is displayed on the screen. It contains all the tools used to build an application. We distinguish between two kinds of tools: those that deal with programs themselves, and those that help improve programmer productivity.

4.2 The Programming Functionalities

Application programming in O_2 consists of defining a schema and writing, editing, compiling, and testing the bodies of the methods. We describe in this subsection how these operations are performed with OOPE.

4.2.1 Classes

A class in OOPE is represented by an object of type tuple, as shown in figure 2.3. This tuple specifies the name of the class, its type, its position in the hierarchy (its superclasses and subclasses), and its methods (private and public). It also indicates whether the structure of the class is public or private, and whether it has an extension. Additional information (such as documentation) is grouped in an Infos field.

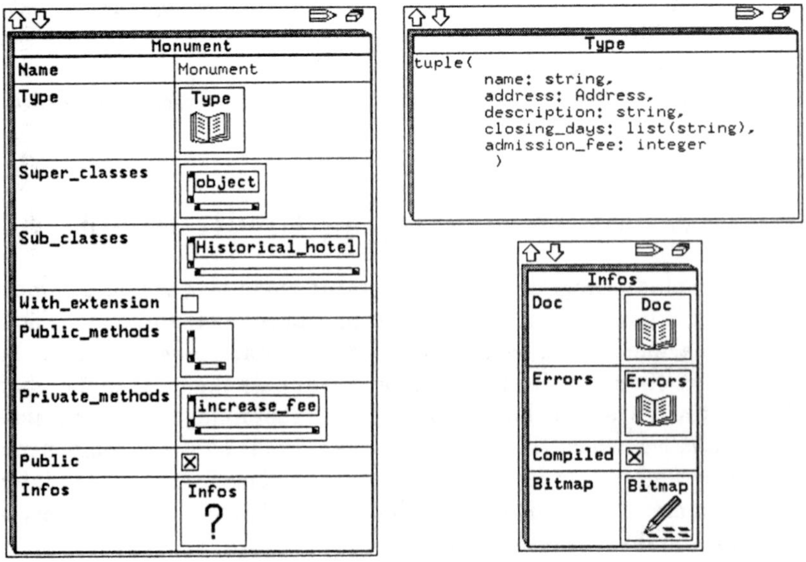

Figure 2.3. The class Monument

Methods defined on this object allow the addition of a subclass, the addition of public and private methods, the display of the class hierarchy, the compilation of the class, and the deletion of the class. It is also possible to create named instances for a class. The programmer fills a frame displayed on the screen with a name and a value.

4.2.2 Methods

A method in OOPE is represented by an object of a tuple type, which contains the signature of the method (its name, its parameters, its result, and the class to which its receiver is attached), the language in which the method is written, the body of the method, and some other information. An example of a method display is given in figure 2.4.

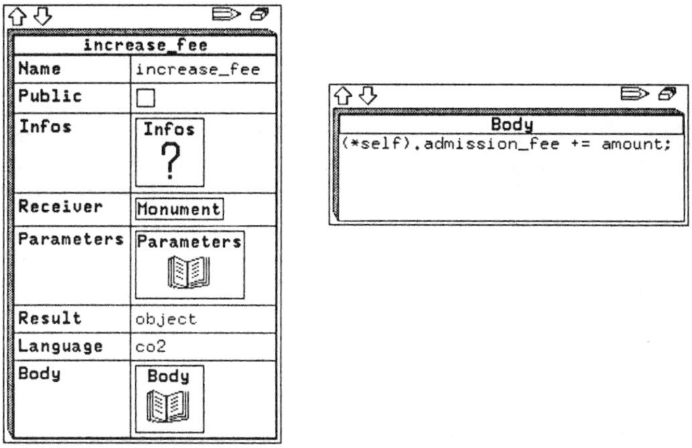

Figure 2.4. The method *increase_fee* of the class Monument

As it is very convenient and time-saving to test a method just after its compilation, OOPE offers the possibility of running a method just after compiling it: a new and empty instance of the receiver class is created and displayed. After editing this instance, the user can apply the method to it.

4.3 The Programming Tools

OOPE also provides tools to help the programmer.

4.3.1 The Browser

The browser provides access to the objects of the database, thus allowing the user to navigate through the database. Once an object is displayed, it is possible to navigate through the objects it references, using the browsing facility provided by Looks. The browser also allows the display of the class hierarchy, with the class Object as a root.

The browser is the starting point of any programming session. Since classes, named objects, and values are represented as objects, the programmer accesses them through the browser. The names of these objects are displayed upon user demand. Selecting one of them causes the corresponding object to be displayed.

4.3.2 The O_2_Shell

OOPE provides a standard class Text, whose objects are displayed as text editors. It offers all the traditional facilities of a full-screen text editor. The O_2_Shell, an object of class Text, is used to edit and execute O_2 code in alphanumeric mode. The programmer can use it to save pieces of code which can be used later as a test set. The O_2_Shell also provides access to the Unix file system, by allowing reading and writing of Unix files.

4.3.3 The Workspace

Building applications requires access to classes and objects. As explained above, object retrieval is usually done by the browser. To avoid a sometimes tedious navigation through the database, it can be very convenient to keep the objects the programmer is working on, from one session to another. A workspace is an object whose type is a set of objects; anything in the database can be stored in it. During a session, the programmer stores in a workspace the objects he or she wants to retrieve in the next session.

Workspaces are named objects and are therefore persistent, as is the data they contain. A programmer can create as many workspaces as he or she wants, and can keep different workspaces corresponding to different activities. The named workspaces are displayed in Tools and are immediately accessible at the beginning of a session. All the programmer needs to do is open a workspace in order to retrieve his or her working data.

Objects are stored in a workspace as icons. The methods defined for these objects can be activated. The workspaces can be seen as entry points to the browsing and programming activities.

4.3.4 The Debugger

The debugger (Doucet and Pfeffer 1989) follows the OOPE design principles: debugging is done by browsing through and editing database objects. These objects represent the current state of a program running under the control of the debugger.

The O_2 debugger is *symbolic, multilanguage, interactive,* and *graphic.* It is fully integrated within OOPE. Its use is very simple: a program under debugger control updates a set of objects that reflect its state. The programmer controls the behavior of his or her program by editing the Execution Manager, which is a named object.

The O_2 debugger provides the functionality usually offered by traditional debuggers, such as the display of variable values, the execution of functions and instructions of the program, and the dynamic modification of a variable. The O_2 debugger offers additional functionality directly associated with the object-oriented features of O_2. It is, for instance, possible to interactively control message passing: these can be skipped or replaced by other messages or values. This allows the execution of partially written programs and can avoid the need for recompilations.

The O_2 debugger is written in CO_2, and consists of four objects: the Execution Manager, the Symbol Tables, the Execution Stack, and the Editor.

The *Execution Manager* is displayed as a control panel. It allows the programmer to control the execution of the program. This control includes interactively setting and clearing breakpoints on line numbers and methods, displaying the lists of breakpoints, running the execution, choosing an execution mode (step or next), and controlling message passing.

The *Symbol Tables* contain static information about methods. Instead of having one common Symbol Table, we use one Symbol Table per method. It is created at compile time, and stored with the information concerning the method.

The *Execution Stack* is a stack of Symbol Tables. It is created and managed during the execution of the program. It allows the programmer to visualize the sequence of message invocations (i.e., the execution) and to display information about the method. Each time a message is sent, the corresponding Symbol Table is pushed onto the stack. When the execution is finished, it is popped from the stack. This stack helps the programmer to understand the execution of the program by visualizing the method calls.

The *Editor* is an object of type Text, used to display the source of the debugged method.

An example of the debugger is shown in figure 2.5. The O_2 code being executed is shown in the Shell. It contains a call to the method *increase_fee*, whose body is displayed in the Body window. The Execution Stack shows the order of the message passing: *increase_fee*, called by *execute_body*, is on top of the stack. The Execution Manager indicates the lists of breakpoints (lines 4 and 6) for the method *increase_fee*, and it allows the execution mode (step or next) to be modified, and message passing to be controlled. The variables of the current method are displayed in the Declaration Table window. They can be consulted and edited.

5 The Implementation

The O_2 system consists of eight functional modules: OOPE, the Alphanumeric Interface, Looks, the Language Processor, the Query Interpreter, the Schema Manager (SM), the Object Manager (OM), and the Disk Manager (DM).

In *development mode*, all these modules are present, and the application programmer directly interacts with OOPE. In *execution mode*, the application

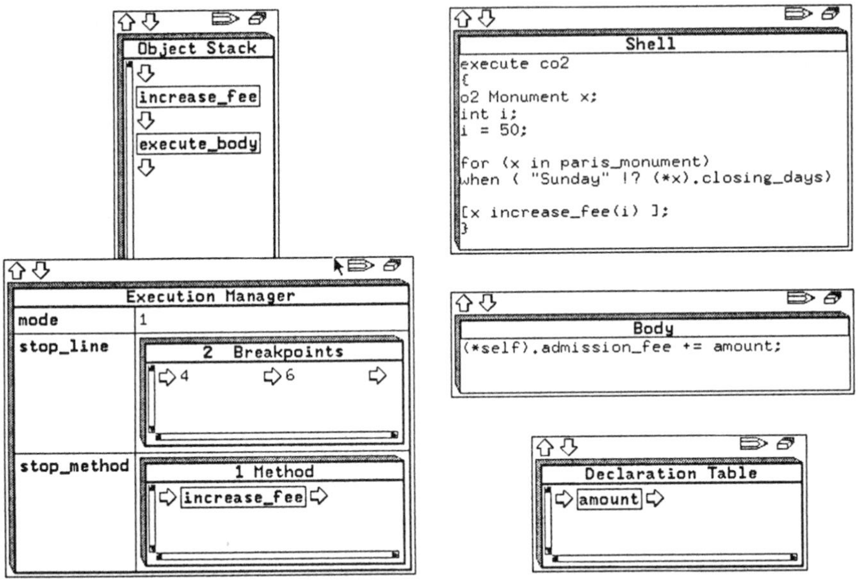

Figure 2.5. The O_2 debugger

runs on top of the Object Manager, the Schema Manager, and Looks. Of course, OOPE is discarded, and so are the Query Interpreter and the Language Processor: the application is compiled into object code with calls to the Object Manager, the Schema Manager, and Looks.

The system has a *workstation version* and a *server version*. The two versions have almost the same interface. The main distinction is in the actual implementation: the workstation version is single-user and memory based, while the server version is multiuser and disk based.

In development mode, the Alphanumeric Interface, Looks, the Language Processor, and the Query Interpreter are on the workstation. There are different versions of the Schema Manager and the Object Manager on the workstation and the server. The disk is only managed by O_2 on the server.

In execution mode, the application code is distributed (with possible replication) between the workstation and the server. It runs on the workstation on top of Looks, a reduced Schema Manager, and the workstation version of the Object Manager. It runs on the server on top of the same reduced version of the Schema Manager and the server version of the Object Manager, which in turn uses the Disk Manager.

In what follows, we concentrate on the system aspects of O_2—the Schema Manager, the Object Manager, and the Disk Manager.

5.1 System Decomposition and Process Layout

The system is composed of three main layers. The upper layer is the Schema Manager. It is responsible for monitoring the creation, retrieval, update, and deletion of classes, methods, and global names. It is also responsible for enforcing the semantics of inheritance and for checking the consistency of a schema.

The Object Manager is the middle layer. It handles complex objects with identity and complex values regardless of whether they are persistent or not. It also handles message passing and the distributed server/workstation configuration. It implements persistence, garbage-collects unreferenced objects, and implements indexes and clustering strategies based on complex objects and inheritance. Finally, it offers transaction modes which adapt the system to execution mode or development mode.

The innermost layer is WiSS, the Wisconsin Storage System (Chou et al. 1985), which is our Disk Manager. It provides persistence, disk management, and concurrency control for "flat" records. WiSS provides the following persistent structures: record-structured sequential files, unstructured files, and long data items. All these structures are mapped into pages, the basic unit of persistence. WiSS provides indexes for disk management as well as full control of the physical location of pages on disk. It bypasses the OS file system and does its own buffering. We ported it to Unix (SunOS 4.0).

The main advantage resulting from implementing the SM on top of the OM is an improved speed of development because of the uniformity of the system: access to the schema information is handled as with regular objects. Furthermore, mechanisms such as crash recovery are directly available for classes and methods.

The SM is entirely dependent on the O_2 data model. The OM is much less dependent: the part of the OM depending on classes and methods is essentially the message-passing mechanism and has been clearly isolated from the rest of the system. The OM was built with an architectural requirement of canonicity in mind. It implements state-of-the-art complex objects. The main difference with nested relational kernels is that the latter are geared toward optimizing selections and joins, and support neither traversing the composition graph nor important (object-oriented) functionalities such as identity, persistence, or garbage collection.

The following process layout has been adopted: on the workstation, an application (i.e., an execution mode application or the development module consisting of the programming environment, the query interpreter, and the compilers) and the workstation versions of the SM and the OM form one single process. There are as many processes as running applications.

For each process running on a workstation, there is a *mirror* process running on the server, composed of the server versions of the SM, the OM, and WiSS. In addition, there may be some *terminal* application processes running on the server which do not have any corresponding "partner" on a workstation. On the server, the OM is compiled as reentrant library modules to be shared among all applications. The lock table and the buffer managed by WiSS are shared by all processes. The Object Memory of the OM is also a global buffer in shared memory, as detailed below.

5.2 The Schema Manager

The SM interacts with the Schema Command Interpreter, the CO_2 compiler, the BasicO_2 compiler, and OOPE. The interaction with the Command Interpreter takes into account the creation and removal of classes, types, named objects and/or values, and methods. It also supports creation and removal of applications and programs. The interaction with the compilers and the OOPE consists mainly of retrieval of information from classes, types, and methods.

As the SM is implemented on top of the Object Manager, there is a Class class and a Method class in the system (but they are not visible to programmers: see section 2). Instances of these classes are class-defining objects and method-defining objects. Similarly, there is an Application class and a Program class.

Classes in O_2 are included in an inheritance hierarchy and a composition graph. We do not force people to follow any particular order when creating classes. Therefore, classes can be momentarily incompletely specified. For instance, a class C can be defined with an attribute of class C' that is not defined. In this case, C is said to be a shadow class, and consistency will be checked as much as possible using available information. When class C' is created, it is seen as a leaf of the inheritance hierarchy and consistency is checked. This triggers "lighting up" C and checking its consistency. Furthermore, a shadow class can appear in a method signature (or in the definition of a named value); but no implementation of a method can be compiled in this case.

Class deletion is done in a more orderly manner. Deletion of a class which is not a leaf in the inheritance hierarchy, or which is used in another class or in a method signature, is forbidden. More precisely, a class is deleted only if (1) it has no instances, and (2) no other classes depend on it through composition, specialization, or method signatures. To avoid the problem of mutually referencing classes, it is possible to remove a list of classes. Deletions of methods can entail two types of inconsistency: on the one hand, conflicting inheritance paths for the method in the class and some of its subclasses, and on the other hand, invalid message passing, involving instances of the definition class or its subclasses. Checks for the first type of inconsistency are done synchronously; the second type of inconsistency is detected at run time.

5.3 The Object Manager

The OM has an external layer composed of a Complex Object Manager, a Message-Passing Manager, a Transaction Manager, a Clustering Manager, and an Index Manager. It has an intermediate layer, which manages the object buffer, and a communication layer. On the server, the Communication Manager listens to requests coming from the workstation and dispatches them to the corresponding module.

5.3.1 The Complex Object Manager

The Complex Object Manager performs the following tasks: (1) creation and deletion of objects (recall that objects are deleted only if they are not referenced by any other object), (2) retrieval of objects by name, (3) support for the predefined methods for objects (the predefined methods in class **Object** are **value_equal**, **deep_equal**, **value_copy**, **deep_copy**, **display**, and **edit**), and (4) support for set-, list-, and tuple-structured objects. In this subsection, we elaborate on two important issues: how to implement identity and how to represent complex objects both on disk and in main memory.

Object identifiers. Objects are uniquely identified and accessed by object identifiers (oids). The object identifiers could have been "logical," giving no information about their location in secondary memory, as in GemStone (Maier and Stein 1987), Orion (Kim et al. 1988), and ObServer (Hornick and Zdonik 1987). In this case, a correspondence table between oids and physical addresses would be needed. This table could be very large, as it would contain one entry for each object in the database. Probably one disk access would be required to retrieve the object-table entry of the object, and a second to retrieve the object. This is why we decided to implement persistent identifiers. Roughly speaking, an object will be stored in a WiSS record and the object identifier will be the record identifier, an RID. To move objects on disk, we don't change their identifiers; otherwise, we would need to keep backward reference links to attain all objects referencing the object we want to move, and we consider these too heavy to maintain. Rather, we use the well-known forward-marking technique (as in relational data managers such as System R). WiSS already implements this mechanism as a side-effect of a record update that makes the record too big for the page it resides on.

Objects are generally created on the workstation, and physical identifiers representing RIDs are only delivered on insertion of the corresponding WiSS record. Persistent identifiers are assigned at transaction-commit time (according to the clustering mechanism described below) in order to avoid extensive message exchange between the two machines. Temporary oids are generated for new objects, and they are changed before commit. This also implies changing any references to these objects from old (and new) objects.

Object representation. The O_2 model distinguishes objects from values. In the OM, structured values are given an identifier and are stored and retrieved as objects, mainly for reasons of homogeneity. The extra cost comes from generating levels of indirection; but this is alleviated by our clustering mechanism, which tries to put values in the same page as the object to which they belong.

The system supports both the primitives for manipulating values and the message-passing mechanism for objects. There are primitives which distinguish oids denoting objects from oids denoting values. For example, the primitive to add an oid to a set uses a different membership test depending on whether the oid denotes an object or a value: in the former case, the membership test is object identity, whereas in the latter it is value equality; in addition, as values are not shared, when inserting a value into a set the value is copied first and then the copy is inserted.

Tuples: On disk, a *tuple* is represented as a record stored on a page. When a tuple outgrows a disk page, we switch to a different representation suitable for storing long records, the long data item (LDI) format provided by WiSS. An LDI consists essentially of a directory record pointing to records containing the LDI data, each on a different page. The oid of the tuple is unchanged: it is the RID of the original record. In main memory, the representation is as a contiguous chunk containing the actual values, with the exception that strings are stored separately from the main chunk, which contains pointers to the proper locations. This way, the strings may grow or shrink without having to change the location of the entire object.

Lists: *Lists,* which are more accurately termed *insertable arrays*, are represented as ordered trees (with slight modifications to allow fast scans). An ordered tree is a kind of B-tree in which each internal node contains a count of the nodes under it. The insertion and deletion procedures have to update node counts (this is the essential difference from standard B-tree management). This structure is very efficient for storing small and large lists. In Exodus (Carey et al. 1986), this structure has been used to implement long data items.

Sets: A *set* of objects is itself an object containing the object identifiers of its members (the objects themselves are stored according to clustering strategies described below). The representation for large sets of objects needs to be such that (1) membership tests are efficient, and (2) scanning the elements of the set is also efficient. WiSS provides indexes, which are convenient data structures to assist in these two functions. Two types of indexes are provided: hash indexes and B-trees. For a membership test in a large set, hashing is better. But for scanning a set, B-trees are far more efficient because, as the oids of the elements are sorted, the physical order of elements on disk coincides with the order in which they are retrieved, thereby minimizing disk-arm moves. We therefore use B-tree indexes to represent large sets. However, using an index for a small set would be too costly. Therefore, there is a limit under which a set is represented as a WiSS record; a convenient value for this limit is the maximum record size in WiSS. Small sets are kept ordered. This decision was motivated by the fact that large sets are kept ordered, and binary operations on sets take advantage of this uniformity: unions, intersections, and differences are programmed using merge algorithms.

Multimedia objects: From the system point of view, texts are atomic values of type string and bitmaps are atomic values of type bits, an unstructured byte string preceded by its length. When the size of these values exceeds the size of a WiSS page, they are stored as LDIs on disk.

5.3.2 The Message-Passing Manager

The Message-Passing Manager exists both on the workstation and on the server. In development mode, it supports late binding and also handles the application of the selected binary code to the receiver object. Binding is done in constant time because there is no run-time lookup of the ancestors of a class. In fact, information about inherited method is duplicated down the inheritance hierarchy. Methods are dynamically loaded into the system process. To this end, a high-performance dynamic loader has been developed.

In execution mode, message passing is implemented by function calls whenever possible (i.e., when the message is not overridden in a subclass). Otherwise, an ad hoc function call for each of the possible implementations of a message will be generated in the code. Methods are statically loaded when an execution-mode application is started. Another optimization of execution-mode applications is that access to tuple attributes by name is replaced by physical offsets. (This is not always possible due to multiple inheritance. In these cases, the compiler generates a late-binding call for attribute names.)

These optimizations are made possible by restricting changes to the classes used by an application. Changes dealing with the structure of a class are disallowed. However, the operational parts of classes and the extensibility of the system are preserved: methods can be added, dropped, or redefined, and classes may be refined into subclasses. These changes are not reflected in existing execution-mode applications unless they are recompiled.

5.3.3 The Transaction Manager

The system is used either by a full-fledged execution-mode application or by a programmer in development mode. Transactions are dealt with at the OM level. In a development-mode session, the SM always calls the OM primitives within a transaction. Our notion of transaction differs from the classical database notion of transaction (namely, an atomic and serializable sequence of database commands) in the following respects.

First, we distinguish concurrency on the schema from concurrency on objects, and allow objects to be activated or deactivated independently. For example, in execution mode, one can choose to run with concurrency on objects but no concurrency on schema. The converse makes sense when running in development mode under the Schema Manager.

Second, recovery may be switched on or off. When running prototype applications, one may be willing to sacrifice safety for the sake of performance. If recovery is enforced, the programmer may set savepoints in order to avoid losing arbitrary amounts of work if transactions are large (for example, when designing applications in development mode).

Finally, a transaction may choose to run in *object fault* mode or in *resident* mode. The former is the normal operation mode of most data managers: objects are loaded on demand. The latter is used for in-memory applications: the system loads all persistent data in main memory at the beginning of the transaction to enhance execution speed. Note that the choice of object-fault mode or resident mode is orthogonal to the choice of execution mode or development mode; it is possible to have a mixture of resident and execution mode, as well as of resident and development mode. This is specified at run time, not at compile time; the same transaction may run in a different mode from one session to another. A good candidate to run in resident mode is the Schema Manager; in this case, before beginning a session all the schema information is loaded in memory. This is a significant improvement from the first version of the system (Bancilhon et al. 1988), in which the choice was hard-wired in the code. In the current version, the Schema Manager can run in object-fault mode if it wishes to.

An O_2 transaction maps directly to a WiSS transaction. The Transaction Manager supports the functionality just described, and it handles concurrency according to the following strategy. Concurrency on objects is handled by WiSS on the server by a two-phase locking algorithm on pages and files. However, transactions update objects on the workstation where there is no concurrency-control code, as workstations are considered to be single-user. Our solution to ensure consistency was the following. Before reaching the workstation, objects are read-locked. When a transaction updates an object in the workstation, first we ask explicitly for a write lock on the object's page (this is transparent to the programmer), and then the update proceeds in the workstation asynchronously without waiting for an answer. If the response to a write-lock request is "abort" because of a deadlock, the process running the transaction in the workstation is informed and the transaction is aborted. This "optimistic" approach reduces the network traffic and the work to be done by the server. At transaction commit, the workstation process asks the server process if all requested write locks have been granted, and only if this is the case are the objects transferred to the server.

We handle concurrency on the schema differently from concurrency on objects. This is a consequence of our application requirements, but it is also due to the observation that in development mode the schema is the hot spot of the system. The page granule is too large; also we would like, for example, two programmers to be able to add different methods to the same class concurrently. Therefore, a custom concurrency control for the schema takes into account semantic information about schema updates to allow for increased parallelism. This module runs on the server and is monitored by the SM from the workstations.

5.3.4 The Communication Manager

Our design choices in the implementation were made according to the criteria of simplicity, transparency, performance, and reliability.

Simplicity (and thus portability) is achieved by choosing standard and well-proven tools. The local area network which links the workstations and the server is Ethernet; the transport protocols are TCP/IP. *Transparency* results from the fact that the end user is never concerned with either the client/server task distribution or the heterogeneity of the machines. *Performance* is obtained by execution migration and by designing a communication protocol optimized for object moves, which are the main potential bottlenecks of any client/server architecture. Lastly, *reliability* is obtained by a failure-detection mechanism that prevents indefinite resource holding, which might result from an abnormal process termination.

When an application is started on a workstation, a mirror application process must be started on the server in order to interact with the lower layers of the system. A daemon process, which is always running, accepts connection requests from a workstation (or from the server, as we support terminals attached to the server also), creates the mirror application process on the server, and loops back, waiting for the next connection request. This daemon process also supports the failure-detection mechanism of both the workstation and the mirror processes.

Objects are transferred from one site to the other independently. However, when several objects are to be transferred (for example, dirty objects at commit time), we group them in a single message to minimize the number of network accesses. The main reason for doing this is to handle heterogeneity between machines. Before sending an object, we encode it using the XDR, presentation protocol, and it is decoded on reception at the other site.

To handle execution migration, the system keeps track of the set of dirty objects (this includes newly created objects) on the server and the set on the workstation. When control is transferred from one site to another, these two sets, as well as the objects referenced to by these sets, are also transferred. In this way, transactions preserve their execution context. Furthermore, embedded execution transfers may appear, and they have to be handled. For instance, if a method that selects tuples of a large set displays one tuple per 100 tuples selected, the programmer may specify that the selection is to be run in the server, and that the display is to be done on the workstation. This way, the two sites may act alternatively as client or server. Our execution-migration protocol is thus more than a classical, unidirectional Remote Procedure Call mechanism.

5.3.5 Persistence

In the O_2 model, persistence is defined as reachability from persistent root objects, which are named objects or values. Persistence is implemented by associating with each object a reference count. An object persists as long as this count is greater than zero. When an object is made persistent, all its components are made persistent too; conversely, when the reference count of an object drops to zero, the reference count of all its components is decremented. Circular garbage (for example, two objects pointing to each other and not being accessible from any other object), if any, would be recovered at suitable intervals by a mark-and-sweep algorithm beginning from the persistence roots. Space for objects in memory and disk is recovered at transaction-commit time.

5.3.6 The O_2 Buffer Manager

The intermediate layer takes care of translating object identifiers into memory addresses. This includes handling object faults for objects requested by the application and not currently in memory. The Buffer Manager is also responsible for managing the space occupied by objects in main memory. As in Orion (Kim et al. 1988) and GemStone (Maier and Stein 1987), a dual buffer-management scheme is implemented: a page buffer implemented by WiSS and an object-buffer pool, the O_2 buffer. Objects in the page buffer are in their disk format. In the object memory, they are in their memory format.

On the server, an object fault implies reading a WiSS record and transferring it from the page buffer to the server O_2 buffer. Even though an object corresponds (roughly) to one WiSS record, on every object fault all the valid records on the same page as the object in question are transferred into the object memory. This strategy is based on the fact that objects which have a strong correlation between them are clustered on the same page or on nearby pages, and reading an entire page will accelerate further processing. As some degree of sharing is expected among applications, the server O_2 buffer is implemented as a data segment shared by all the concurrent processes.

On the workstation, the O_2 buffer is private to each application. The memory allocation and deallocation tasks are left to the Unix virtual-memory mechanism. If the process runs out of swap space, space for objects is freed until we attain a given threshold (we start first by freeing clean objects; dirty objects have to be written back to disk). An object fault is addressed to the Communication Manager, which in turn asks the server mirror process to send the object across the network.

On both the server and the workstations, the memory address at which an object is stored (after reading from disk or on creation) never changes until the object migrates to another machine or is written out to disk. While an object is in memory, in order to access it given its identifier, we use an object table. This table is hashed on identifier values and contains entries for resident objects only. On the workstation, each application has its own object table, whereas on the server the object table is shared among all applications.

5.3.7 The Clustering Manager

Placement of objects on disk depends on control information given by the database administrator (DBA) describing the placement of objects—the placement trees (for a complete description, see Benzaken and Delobel 1989). A placement tree expresses the way in which a complex object and its components will be clustered together. Roughly speaking, a placement tree for a class C is a subtree of the composition class hierarchy rooted at C. For example, the DBA may write the following command to create a placement tree for the class Monument defined in subsection 2.1.2:

> **add cluster tree for class** Monument
>   **desc tuple** (address: **tuple**(city: City [**tuple**(hotels: **set**(Hotel))]))

This placement tree says that the set of the hotels of the city of the address of a monument have to be stored as close as possible to one another on disk. If no indication is given by the DBA, the system will generate a default placement tree in which all complex values of Monument will appear as branches.

The clustering algorithm operates at commit time on a set of objects and values that are newly created by the transaction (which have a temporary identifier) and on objects and values which have been accessed by the transaction (which have a persistent identifier). The purpose is to place a newly created object according to the placement tree defined for classes that are related by composition to the class they belong to. The physical unit of clustering is the WiSS page. When inserting a record, one has the option of specifying the identifier of another record, R, and WiSS tries to store the new record on the same page as R or on a nearby page.

The placement trees can be modified over time, and they are completely separated from any schema information. (This is the main difference from other approaches, such as the concept of a composite object in Orion [Kim et al. 1988.]) The placement-tree strategy that has been implemented aims at determining a good initial placement of an object, but it does not take into account dynamic evolution.

5.3.8 The Index Manager

The Index Manager implements indexes that take into account the specificities of the O_2 data model—in particular, the inheritance hierarchy and the composition hierarchy. The relationship of indexes with each kind of hierarchy has been explored separately in Kim et al. 1988 and in Maier and Stein 1987. It is constructed directly above the WiSS layer supporting indexes. We currently support indexes on extensions of classes (not on arbitrary sets or lists). The selection criteria associated to an index can involve a path expression applied to members of a class, as in Maier and Stein 1987. For example, the following command creates an index on the Restaurant class which can be used to retrieve instances of restaurants given the name of the city in which they are located.

add index Rest_city_name **on class** Restaurant **path** address.city.name

In our implementation, we decompose indexes defined on paths along the composition hierarchy in a sequence of basic index components, one for each link in the path. Scans on composite indexes are compound operations on these basic indexes. Decomposing a composite index into basic ones is necessary in order to take into account updates in the intermediate links of the paths. Known advantages of this approach are that (1) if the paths of two or more indexes share a common prefix, the indexes will share the index components on the common prefix, and (2) any prefix of a path is also indexed.

Indexes also "understand" the inheritance hierarchy: the index defined above for the Restaurant class will contain entries for all Restaurant objects and objects of other subclasses of the class Restaurant. Furthermore, if the city of the address of a Restaurant object is an object of a subclass of City—say, Beautiful_city—the index should still map the name of the Beautiful_city object to the restaurant. This is called *class-hierarchy indexing.* An alternative solution would be to have one index for each subclass; this is called *single-class indexing.* As inheritance in O_2 has an inclusion semantics, queries addressed to a class extension C will implicitly refer to subclasses of C as well. Kim et al. 1988 have shown that in this case, class-hierarchy indexing is better in general than single-class indexing. Fast retrieval from this index can still be performed for a query on a subclass of the indexed class. In our implementation, we structure the leaves of the index in such a way that we retrieve all objects of a subclass in a single block, without having to scan the whole leaf. This is an improvement with respect to the implementation proposed in Kim et al. 1988.

6 Performance of the O_2 Prototype

Since the prototype of the O_2 system has recently been completed, we have just begun to study its performance. In the following sections we describe some of the tests we have done, along with what we have learned from these tests. We are currently implementing the Sun and Tektronix benchmarks, which will be used to further evaluate the prototype. The results of these tests will be presented in a future report. The tests presented here were performed on the July 1989 version of the O_2 prototype running in development mode on a Sun 3/280.

6.1 Simple Tests

This set of tests includes three simple but frequently executed operations in the O_2 system: object creation, access to the field of a tuple object, and method invocation. In order to filter out the cost of disk accesses (which are addressed in the next subsection) these tests were conducted using a "warm" system. That is, the persistent objects referenced were first faulted into the O_2 object cache, and then the tests were conducted. The results presented below represent the average central processing unit (CPU) time for each operation.

6.1.1 Object Creation

In the first test we created three different types of objects in the object cache, using the CO_2 instruction:

```
obj = new(Class);
```

where Class has either a tuple, set, or list structure. The results of these tests are contained in table 2.1.

Table 2.1. Object-Creation Time

	Creation Time (ms)
Tuple	1.8
Set	1.6
List	1.6

6.1.2 Access to the Field of a Tuple Object

For the second test, we measured the time required to read or write a field of a tuple object (the *write* operation does not involve either locking or logging code). Two types of objects were considered: temporary objects created during the measurement session, and named persistent objects that had been faulted into the object cache. For each type of object, two alternative cases were considered. In the first case, the class of which the object was an instance was created as the first step of the test. In the second case, the object was an instance of a previously defined persistent class. The results from these tests, presented in table 2.2, illustrate several points about O_2. First, temporary objects are less expensive to access because they are accessed directly using a virtual-memory address pointer into the object cache. On the other hand, named objects, even if they reside in the object cache, are accessed by translating the name into a virtual-memory address via the hashing function. A similar name-translation step is also needed when an object of a persistent class is accessed. The cost of this translation accounts for the differences between the values in the two columns.

Table 2.2. Time to Read or Write an Attribute of a Tuple Object

	New Class (ms)	Persistent Class (ms)
Temporary Object	0.29	0.44
Named object	0.58	0.97

6.1.3 Method Invocation

In the third test we measured the time needed to apply a null method to an instance of a class containing twenty methods. As with the previous test, we considered both the case when the object was an instance of a newly created class and the case when it was an instance of a previously created persistent class. In order to test the significance of the position of the method in the class definition, the test was repeated for methods 1, 10, and 20. The results of these tests are given in table 2.3. Several comments are in order. First, the time to invoke a method is only slightly sensitive to the position of the method in its class definition. However, compared to the cost of invoking a null function (measured to be 0.002 ms) the cost of invoking a method is fairly high. The reason is that since this test was conducted with the system in development mode, late binding was used to bind a message to the appropriate method. When the system is run in execution mode (see section 5.3.2), most method invocations can be replaced with a direct function call. To support late binding in development mode, the Schema Manager maintains the mapping from messages to methods on a class basis, and it uses O_2 list and tuple values to do so. Thus accesses to tuple fields and a list lookup must be performed for each message-passing operation.

Table 2.3. Time to Apply a Null Method to an Object

	New Class (ms)	Persistent Class (ms)
Method #1	0.60	0.90
Method #10	0.65	0.93
Method #20	0.70	0.98

6.2 Wisconsin Benchmark Selection Times

In order to determine the maximum rate at which objects can be processed, we implemented the nonindexed selection operation from the Wisconsin benchmark. In table 2.4, we present the time required to scan a set of 10,000 tuples (each 208 bytes long) for three different selectivity factors. The qualifying tuples were placed into another set. These tests were run on a cold system. We measured the elapsed time for the operation. Needless to say, the results of these tests indicate a number of problems that will have to be corrected in the production version of the system.

The first serious problem is apparent if we consider the 0% selection query. The execution time for a comparable implementation of this operation written in C directly on WiSS (using a file for the objects and a clustered, unique index on the oids of the objects as the set mechanism) executes in 12.8 seconds. Several factors contribute to this performance degradation. The first factor is that the class definition for each object must be interpreted, to determine the

Table 2.4. Time to Scan a Set of 10,000 Tuple Objects

Selectivity Factor	Elapsed Response Time (s)
0%	28.7
10%	35.3
100%	99.1

type and offset of the attribute against which the predicate is to be applied. This is because our tests were carried out in development mode. As shown in table 2.2, this step takes approximately 0.44 ms per object (or 4.4 seconds for 10,000 objects). The second factor is that, as explained in section 5.3.6, objects are not manipulated directly in the WiSS buffer pool but are instead copied into an object cache. Furthermore, as objects are moved into the cache, variable-length components are stored as separate objects. Thus each tuple requires four mallocs: one for the fixed-length portion of the tuple and one for each of the three string fields. Four calls to malloc plus the corresponding copy operations cost another 0.71 ms per object (or 7.1 seconds for 10,000 objects). The solutions are obvious. First, the overhead of schema interpretation can be eliminated in the execution mode of the system. Second, objects should be manipulated directly in the buffer pool of the system and should not be copied into a separate object cache.

The second serious problem indicated by the results in table 2.4 is O_2's use of "true" sets. As indicated in section 5.3.1, large sets are implemented in O_2 via a B-tree on oid. As tuples are inserted into the result set, their oids are inserted into a B-tree to check for duplicates. This operation is very expensive, especially when the size of the B-tree is larger than the buffer pool. To avoid this problem, future versions of O_2 will provide both bags and sets, and users will be warned that they should not use sets unless they are willing to accept their associated cost.

7 Conclusion

We have described the status of the current O_2 prototype. O_2 is an object-oriented database system which includes a programming environment and user-interface generation tools. It operates on a single-server/multiple-workstation configuration. It is multilanguage, distributed, and bimode. All the features described in this paper have been implemented and are operational.

We now plan to derive a product from the prototype. This calls for a complete evaluation of the prototype, its interface, its architecture, its specific algorithms, and the quality of its code. This evaluation will be done on the functional side by writing a number of applications using the system, and on the performance side by measuring and benchmarking it. Then we will rewrite whatever percentage of the code is necessary to build a robust and efficient prototype.

8 Acknowledgements

O_2 is the result of a group effort; this is why we have chosen to attribute the paper to a pen name. The following persons participated in the design or implementation of the system: Gustavo Arango, François Bancilhon, Gilles Barbedette, Véronique Benzaken, Guy Bernard, Pascale Birrioti, Patrick Borras, Philippe Bridon, René Cazalens, Sophie Cluet, Christine Delcourt, Claude Delobel, David DeWitt, Vineeta Darnis, Anne Doucet, Denis Excoffier, Philippe Futtersack, Sophie Gamerman, Olivier Grémont, Constance Grosselin, Gilbert Harrus, Laurence Haux, Yannis Ioannidis, Mark James, Geneviève Jomier, Pâris Kanellakis, Jean Marie Larchevêque, Christophe Lécluse, Didier Lévêque, Joëlle Madec, Jean-Claude Mamou, Patrick Pfeffer, Didier Plateau, Bruno Poyet, Michel Raoux, Philippe Richard, Dominique Steve, Didier Tallot, and Fernando Vélez.

References

Abiteboul, S., and P. Kanellakis. 1989. Object identity as a query language primitive. In *Proceedings of the 1989 ACM SIGMOD conference.*

Arango, G. 1989. *O_2 predefined classes: Functional specification.* Altaïr Technical Report.

Atkinson, M. et al. 1989. The object-oriented database manifesto. In *Proceedings of the international conference on deductive and object-oriented databases.*

Bancilhon, F., G. Barbedette, V. Benzaken, C. Delobel, S. Gamerman, C. Lécluse, P. Pfeffer, P. Richard, and F. Vélez. 1988. The design and implementation of O_2, an object-oriented database system. In *Proceedings of the second international workshop on object-oriented database systems,* ed. K. Dittrich.

Bancilhon, F., S. Cluet, and C. Delobel. 1989. A query language for the O_2 object-oriented database. In *Proceedings of the second workshop on database programming languages.*

Benzaken, V., and C. Delobel. 1989. *Dynamic clustering strategies in the O_2 object-oriented database system.* Altaïr Technical Report.

Carey, M., D. DeWitt, J. E. Richardson, and E. J. Shekita. 1986. Object and file management in the Exodus extensible database system. In *Proceedings of the 12th VLDB conference.*

Cazalens, R. Building user interface with the LOOKS hyper-object system. *To be published.*

Chou, H-T. et al. 1985. Design and implementation of the Wisconsin storage system. *Software Practice and Experience* 15(10).

Deux, O. et al. 1989. *The complete story of O_2.* Altaïr Technical Report.

______. 1990. The story of O_2. In *Transactions on knowledge and data engineering* 2(1): 91–108.

Devin, M., and P. Duquesnoy. 1988. *Aida version 1.2, manuel de référence.* ILOG, Gentilly.

Doucet, A., and P. Pfeffer. 1989. A debugger for O_2, an object-oriented language. In *Proceedings of the first international conference on technology of object-oriented languages and systems.*

Hornick, M., and S. B. Zdonik. 1987. A shared, segmented memory for an object-oriented database. *ACM TOIS* 5(1).

Kim, W., N. Ballou, H-T. Chou, J. F. Garza, D. Woelk, and J. Banerjee. 1988. Integrating an object-oriented programming system with a database system. In *Proceedings of the 1988 OOPSLA conference.*

Lécluse, C., and P. Richard. 1989. The O_2 database programming languages. In *Proceedings of the 15th VLDB Conference.*

Lécluse, C., P. Richard, and F. Vélez. 1988. O_2, an object-oriented data model. In *Proceedings of the 1988 ACM SIGMOD conference.*

Maier, D., and J. Stein. 1987. Development and implementation of an object-oriented DBMS. In *Research directions in object-oriented programming,* ed. B. Shriver and P. Wegner. MIT Press.

O_2. 1989. *O_2 manual.* Altaïr.

Vélez, F., G. Bernard, and V. Darnis. 1989. The O_2 object manager: An overview. In *Proceedings of the 1989 VLDB conference.*

Part II

The O_2 Data Model

Chapter 3

Introduction to the Data Model

Paris Kanellakis
Christophe Lécluse
Philippe Richard

The goal of this introduction is to give a clear, concise, and complete definition of the O_2 data model. The presentation summarizes a number of publications and adapts their contents. It is a faithful description of what is implemented in the V1 version of the system. Since the data model synthesizes a fair number of ideas that have been proven useful in practice, the resulting exposition requires some technical detail. We hope that any effort spent on mastering these definitions will greatly facilitate the reading of the papers in this collection.

The O_2 data model mixes, in a harmonious way, the object-oriented and value-oriented worlds. Its design is a synthesis of database and object-oriented programming concepts and is the basis for the data definition language (DDL) in the O_2 system. It is also used in the database programming language compilers of the system, in particular for static type-checking in the presence of inheritance and overloading. From this introduction the reader can verify that the O_2 data model is a synthesis realizing a large part of the object-oriented database manifesto requirements (Atkinson et al. 1989; see chapter 1).

Of course, another crucial part of data models is the data manipulation languages (DMLs). A large part of this collection deals with the question: What are the right DMLs for the O_2 DDL presented in this introduction? This emphasis reflects the importance of the question and the effort devoted to it in the O_2 project. We encourage the reader to proceed to the DMLs once he or she has gained some familiarity with the DDL. For an analysis of the expressive power of DMLs using the "structural" part of O_2 (without methods), see chapter 5.

For an analysis of O_2's "behavioral" part (with methods), see chapters 6 and 7. For concrete and implemented designs of DMLs, see chapters 9, 10, 11, and 12.

The study of data models has been a major topic of database theory and practice. Since at least the mid-1970s, extensions of the relational model and semantic data models have been a very active area of research. Much of this work has been of use in the recent development of OODBs. Given the focus of this book on one system and the extent of recent efforts, it is impossible to survey the area accurately. In the following discussion we provide some references to work that has directly influenced the design of the O_2 data model. For a more accurate historical account of the database concepts used in O_2 we refer the reader to two relatively recent in-depth surveys, Hull 1987 and Hull and King 1987, as well as to the shorter technical exposition in Abiteboul and Kanellakis 1990.

This introduction is divided into four sections. We start with a brief history of the design. We then expand on the slightly controversial issue of objects versus values—a technical issue in the semantic data model literature that was highlighted (and to some extent resolved) by the O_2 effort. This brings us to the principal section, which deals with the data model itself. Finally, we provide a roadmap to the contents of part 2.

1 Historical View of the O_2 Approach

A first version of the O_2 data model (Lécluse, Richard, and Vélez 1988; see chapter 4) was produced for the V0 prototype of the system. Complex values without identity were not part of this version. It combined structures, very similar to those of the logical data model (LDM) of Kuper and Vardi 1984 and Kuper 1985, with inheritance as in Cardelli 1988, and with methods. We have included Lécluse, Richard, and Vélez 1988 (see chapter 4) in this collection for two reasons: because of its general impact on the development of OODBs and in order to illustrate the evolution of the O_2 design.

A second version of the data model was designed for the V1 prototype. This is the version described in detail in section 3 of this chapter and implemented in V1. Features of this version have been described in a number of publications (Lécluse and Richard 1988, 1989a, 1989b; Abiteboul and Kanellakis 1989; see also chapter 5). The data model was designed to generalize structures of both LDM and complex-value models without identity as in Abiteboul and Beeri 1987 and Bancilhon and Khoshafian 1986. Its type system augments that of Abiteboul and Beeri 1987 with recursive types. Note that Bancilhon and Khoshafian 1986 proposes an essentially untyped language. Inheritance and methods were also generalized from the first version.

The principal feature of the V1 version—that is, the combination of objects with identity and values without identity—was first described in Lécluse and Richard 1989b. The semantics of recursive types is given in Abiteboul and Kanellakis 1989 (see chapter 5). Naming mechanisms for persistence and other features are described in Lécluse and Richard 1989a. The data model definitions used in the prototype (described in Abiteboul and Kanellakis 1989 and Lécluse and Richard 1989a, 1989b) are summarized in section 3. In fact, we included Abiteboul and Kanellakis 1989 (see chapter 5) in our collection because of its additional theoretical analysis of data manipulation.

Finally, note that Lécluse and Richard 1988 proposes techniques (not yet implemented) for extensions involving parametric polymorphism. The integration of parametric or "ML-like" polymorphism in the prototype would represent an important advance. It would augment the code-reusability capabilities that are already provided by method inheritance.

2 Objects Versus Values in OODBs

A goal of every object-oriented database system is to provide programmers with powerful applications development support that uses encapsulation and inheritance. This important step forward should not be canceled by an increased complexity in structure manipulations and by loss of data independence due to navigation through object identifiers.

What the optimum balance is between object-oriented programming concepts and value oriented database concepts has been the subject of many lengthy technical (and often nontechnical) discussions under the heading of objects versus values.

In the O_2 data model we allow both the concept of object and that of value. Data can be either objects with identity and encapsulation (manipulated through methods) or complex values (manipulated through algebraic operations). Note that the term *complex object* is often used in the database literature instead of *complex value*; here we follow the object-oriented programming terminology.

The coexistence of both concepts is a departure from the "pure" object-oriented tradition, where every piece of information must be an object. We believe that this is one of the principal tradeoffs that must be made in databases. It means that, in the definition of an object, the component values of this object do not necessarily contain only objects, but can also contain other values.

In O_2 the user may choose between two kinds of organizations: classes, whose instances are objects and which encapsulate data and behavior; and types, whose instances are values. We emphasize that values are not encapsulated; that is, their structure is known by users, and they are manipulated by algebraic operations. To every class is associated a type, describing the structure of its instances. Classes are created explicitly using commands and are parts of the inheritance hierarchy. Types are not created explicitly, since they appear only as components of classes and do not appear in the inheritance hierarchy.

Our design choices were based on our experience that pure object-oriented database systems have severe drawbacks. The user has to define a new class every time he or she needs a complex value. This results in an undesirable growth of the class hierarchy. We believe that the class hierarchy should contain only classes which correspond to data shared by distinct software modules. It should not be polluted by classes which are only used to describe nonshared values.

We also believe that our design has significant advantages over other OODBs from the point of view of data manipulation. It facilitates expressing simple queries in a simple fashion, because *both* objects and values are very useful. Without objects, the semantics of queries are often obscured by the syntax. Without values, the data manipulation language has difficulty maintaining temporary results and eliminating duplicates, and it uses too many redundant identifiers. This experience is illustrated in the language IQL (see chapter 5) and in the language CO_2 (see chapter 9).

Let us now clarify these points with some discussion of the original OODB designs. In classical object-oriented languages such as Smalltalk (Goldberg and Robson 1983), the value encapsulated in an object is always an atom or a tuple of other objects. In many object-oriented (Maier, Otis, and Purdy 1985 and Banerjee et al. 1987) and semantic (Kuper 1985) data models, this value is a tuple or a set of objects, since databases must provide flexible management of large sets of data. However, this value is always a flat value, as it can only contain identifiers of other objects, and not directly other complex values. This limitation is exactly the same as the limitation of relational systems which has motivated the introduction of nested relations and (more generally) complex values. Of course, complex values can always be modeled through the use of identifiers, but we think that this solution is awkward, as is the modeling of nested relations with surrogates in relational systems.

Many of the original OODB designs were modified, interestingly, along lines similar to the design choices of O_2. Early on, some authors already felt the need for dealing with both objects and values. In Banerjee et al. 1987, there is a notion of exclusive relationship between an object and some of its components; when an object is exclusively owned, it cannot be shared. The same notion is introduced in Carey, DeWitt, and Vandenberg 1988, where the programmer can specify whether he or she deals with a reference to a complex value or with the complex value itself, and also whether an object can be shared by several objects or is exclusively owned by an object. This notion introduces the desired distinction, but values are still implemented and manipulated as objects. Thus our concept of values can be used in a similar way to the concept of *composite object* of Orion (Kim et al. 1987) or the *own attribute* of Exodus (Carey, DeWitt, and Vandenberg 1988). In the new version of FAD (Danforth, Khoshafian, and Valduriez 1987), one can manipulate objects and values. A value in FAD is either atomic or structured. A structured value contains values. An object in FAD has an identifier and a state. A state is either an atomic value or a structure containing objects and values. Objects may be updated, values may not. FAD objects allow sharing.

In summary, the dichotomy of values and objects is used to generalize data description languages with and without identity. In O_2 the objects versus values issue is dealt with in a clear and precise fashion. Most important, the proposed solution is used to simplify the data manipulation languages. Similar ideas are presently used in many object-oriented database systems.

3 The O_2 Data Model

Our exposition proceeds through a number of simple steps. It follows Lécluse and Richard 1989b and Abiteboul and Kanellakis 1989 (see chapter 5). We first define *values* (definition 1) and *objects* (definition 2) and describe their structure through *types* (definition 3) and the *class hierarchy* (definition 4). The class hierarchy must be well formed; that is, it must satisfy a structural compatibility condition enforced using *subtyping* (definition 5). We provide semantics to our notions of classes (definition 6) and types (definition 7), which capture *type inheritance.*

These structural aspects of the data model are complemented with behavioural aspects (or abstract data types as opposed to concrete ones): *methods* are attached to classes (definition 8). This leads naturally to *method inheritance*; here we also assume some well-formedness conditions. The methods *encapsulate* code, and their only visible part is their *signatures* (also definition 8). In the tradition of object-oriented programming, the evaluation of methods is performed using *name overloading* and *late binding.*

Based on this dual framework, which represents both traditional or complex-structure databases and object-oriented programming concepts, we define *database schemas* (definition 9) and *instances* (definition 10).

3.1 Values and Objects

To start, we need a small amount of preliminary notation; the special atomic type names **integer, string, float, Boolean,** and their natural pairwise disjoint corresponding domains; the special name **nil,** representing the "undefined value"; and four pairwise disjoint sets:

- The set **D** of atomic values is the union of the four atomic type domains.
- The set **A** of symbols called *attributes*, such as `age` or `name`. We use a typewriter font for the names of attributes.
- The set **I** of *object identifiers*, such as #32 or #765. We use # followed by numerals.
- The set **C** of *class names*. We begin class names with a capital letter.

We can now define values via atomic values, object identifiers, the undefined value, tuples, sets, and lists. The only subtle point is making a set I of object identifiers into values.

Definition 1. Let I be a subset of $\mathbf{I}$. A *value over* I (or just a value, if I is understood) is defined as follows.

1. Every element of $\mathbf{D}$ or I is a value.
2. The special name **nil** is a value.
3. If $v_1, \ldots, v_n$ are values, then $[\mathbf{a}_1 \colon v_1, \ldots, \mathbf{a}_n \colon v_n]$ is a (tuple) value. [ ] is the empty tuple value. (We assume the attributes $\mathbf{a}_i$ are distinct; the attribute order is meaningless.)
4. If $v_1, \ldots, v_n$ are distinct values, then $\{v_1, \ldots, v_n\}$ is a (set) value. {} is the empty set value. (These are finite sets; the order of elements is meaningless.)
5. If $v_1, \ldots, v_n$ are values, then $< v_1, \ldots, v_n >$ is a (list) value. $< >$ is the empty list value. (These are finite lists; the order of elements is meaningful.)

We denote $\mathbf{V}(I)$ the set of all values over I, and $\mathbf{V} = \mathbf{V}(\mathbf{I})$. We can now define objects by the pairing of object identifiers and values.

Definition 2. An *object* is a pair (i, v), where i is an identifier of $\mathbf{I}$ and v is a value of $\mathbf{V}$.

Here are some examples of values.

```
[name: "Eiffel_Tower",
 address: [city: #432,
           street: "Champ de Mars"],
 description: "a famous Paris monument",
 admission_fee: 25]
```

```
{#23, #54}
```

The following are examples of objects.

```
(#23, [name: "Eiffel_Tower",
       address: [city: #432,
                 street: "Champ de Mars"],
       description: "a famous Paris monument",
       admission_fee: 25])
```

```
(#432, [name: "Paris",
        country: "France",
        population: 2.6,
        monuments: {#23, #54}])
```

3.2 The Syntax of Types and Classes

We now present the language used to describe common structure in values. The only subtle point is the use of a set of class names C in this language. This is analogous to the use of object identifiers in values.

Definition 3. Let C be a subset of $\mathbf{C}$. We call *types over* C (or just types, if C is understood) the expressions constructed as follows.

1. The atomic types **integer**, **float**, **Boolean**, and **string** are types.
2. The class names of C are types.
3. If $t_1, \ldots, t_n$ are types, then $[\mathtt{a}_1\colon t_1, \ldots, \mathtt{a}_n\colon t_n]$ is a type. (As with tuple values, the attributes are disjoint and their order is meaningless.)
4. If t is a type, then $\{t\}$ is a type.
5. If t is a type, then $<t>$ is a type.

We note $\mathbf{T}(C)$ the set of all types together with the special name **any**. We use $\mathbf{T}$ for $\mathbf{T}(\mathbf{C})$. (Note that **any** is a "default" used as a type, but not as a subexpression of another type.)

The following are examples of types referencing the classes Monument and City.

```
[name: string,
 address: [city: City,
           street: string],
 description: string,
 admission_fee: integer]
```

```
[name: string,
 country: string,
 population: float,
 monuments: {Monument}]
```

A class is defined as the association of a class name c and a type $\sigma(c)$. The contents of a class will be objects, and this association describes the structure of the vs for the objects (i, v) in the class. This association must be well formed. Section 3.3 makes this precise.

3.3 Class Hierarchy and Subtyping

Inheritance is a central concept in object-oriented (database) systems. It allows the user to derive new classes from existing classes by refining their properties. For example, the Monument class can be specialized into a Historical_monument class. We say that the Historical_monument class inherits from the Monument class. The interaction between inheritance and typing has been studied and formalized by many authors; one can find detailed surveys in Cardelli and Wegner 1985 and in Danforth and Tomlinson 1988.

A class hierarchy is made of two components: a finite set of class names with types associated to them, and a subclass relationship. The type associated with a class describes the structure of the objects which are instances of the class. The subclass relationship describes the *user-defined* inheritance properties between classes.

Definition 4. A *class hierarchy* is a triple $(C, \sigma, \prec)$, where C is a finite set of class names, σ is a mapping from C to $\mathbf{T}(C)$, and $\prec$ is a partial order on C (i.e., $\prec$ is reflexive, antisymmetric, and transitive).

The idea is that the type $\sigma(c)$ of the class named c denotes the internal structure of the objects in c. Here we impose a well-formedness condition. We do not allow two related classes ($c \prec c'$) to have arbitrary associated types. For example, an object of a class (say Employee) being also an object of its superclass (say Person), we want Employee to be "structurally compatible" with Person. More precisely, we require the following condition. If c and c' are two related classes ($c \prec c'$), then we require that $\sigma(c) \leq \sigma(c')$. This compatibility is based on the *subtyping* relationship $\leq$, which is induced from the subclass relationship $\prec$ as follows.

Definition 5. Let $(C, \sigma, \prec)$ be a class hierarchy. Then the *subtyping* relationship $\leq$ on $\mathbf{T}(C)$ is the smallest partial order which is closed under the following rules.

1. $\vdash c \leq c'$, for all c and c' in C such that $c \prec c'$.

2. $\vdash [\mathsf{a}_1\colon t_1, \ldots, \mathsf{a}_n\colon t_n, \ldots, \mathsf{a}_{n+p}\colon t_{n+p}] \leq [\mathsf{a}_1\colon s_1, \ldots, \mathsf{a}_n\colon s_n]$, for all types t_i and s_i, $i = 1, \ldots, n$, such that $t_i \leq s_i$.

3. $\vdash \{t\} \leq \{s\}$, for all types t and s such that $t \leq s$.

4. $\vdash <t> \leq <s>$, for all types t and s such that $t \leq s$.

Finally, $t \leq$ **any**, for all types t (i.e., the default **any** is the top of the type hierarchy).

The first rule in definition 5 just says that subclasses are subtypes. We then have one rule per type structure. Notice that we can refine tuples by refining some fields or by adding new ones. Also, note that given $\prec$ it is easy to check for $\leq$.

We say that the class hierarchy $(C, \sigma, \prec)$ is *well formed* if for all classes c and c': if $c \prec c'$ then $\sigma(c) \leq \sigma(c')$. Hence we deal only with well-formed class hierarchies.

The following is an example of a well-formed class hierarchy.

```
σ(Monument) = [name: string,
               address: [city: City,
                         street: string],
               description: string,
               admission_fee: integer]

σ(Historical_hotel) = [name: string,
                       address: [city: City,
                                 street: string],
                       description: string,
                       admission_fee: integer,
                       facilities: <string>,
                       rate: integer,
                       stars: integer]

σ(City) = [name: string,
           country: string,
           population: float,
           monuments: {Monument}]

Historical_hotel  ≺  Monument
```

This class hierarchy is consistent because the type associated to class Historical_hotel is a subtype of the type associated to class Monument. Note, however, that Monument and City have mutually recursive types.

3.4 The Semantics of Types and Classes

The semantics of types and of classes are essentially defined together. This is to handle mutually recursive types. For this we use the *oid assignments* from chapter 5, which describe the contents of classes. The mathematical formalization is related to "non-well-founded sets."

Definition 6. Let $(C, \sigma, \prec)$ be a subclass hierarchy. A *disjoint oid assignment* is a function π_d mapping each class name to a disjoint set of object identifiers. The *oid assignment* π (inherited from π_d) is a function mapping each class name c of C to a set of object identifiers as follows:

$$\pi(c) = \pi_d(c) \cup \{\pi_d(sc) \mid sc \in C, sc \prec c\}.$$

When we use the term *oid assignment* we will mean the oid assignment π, inherited from a disjoint oid assignment π_d. It is clear that for pairs of classes (c, c') in C such that $c \prec c'$, we have $\pi(c) \subseteq \pi(c')$. Thus the constraint satisfied by an oid assignment maps the inheritance links from the classes to the instances. It means that an employee is a person and that a hotel is a monument.

This definition is slightly more constrained than assigning oids to classes and treating $\prec$ as set inclusion. It reflects the practical fact that an object is created in a *single* class (which gives us π_d). When this happens the created object is considered as an instance of this class, but also as an instance of all the superclasses of this class. This definition also simplifies type checking.

Definition 7. Given an oid assignment, the *interpretation* dom(t) of a type t in $\mathbf{T}(C)$ is defined as follows.

1. If $I = \cup\{\pi(c) \mid c \in C\}$, then dom(**any**) $= \mathbf{V}(I)$.
2. For every atomic type, take its corresponding natural domain.
3. $\text{dom}(c) = \{\textbf{nil}\} \cup \pi(c)$ for all $c \in$ C.
4. $\text{dom}([\mathsf{a}_1\colon t_1, \ldots, \mathsf{a}_n\colon t_n]) = \{[\mathsf{a}_1\colon v_1, \ldots, \mathsf{a}_n\colon v_n, \mathsf{a}_{n+1}\colon v_{n+1}, \ldots, \mathsf{a}_{n+m}\colon v_{n+m}] \mid v_i \in \text{dom}(t_i),\ i = 0, 1, \ldots, n\}$.
5. $\text{dom}(\{t\}) = \{\{v_1, \ldots, v_n\} \mid v_i \in \text{dom}(t),\ i = 0, 1, \ldots, n\}$.
6. $\text{dom}(<\!t\!>) = \{<\!v_1, \ldots, v_n\!> \mid v_i \in \text{dom}(t),\ i = 0, 1, \ldots, n\}$.

The domain function is built in the usual way. Condition 1 expresses that the only valid object identifiers are those of the existing instances. We follow the Cardelli 1988 approach for the domain of tuple types, and we allow tuple values with extra attributes. This definition leads to a domain-inclusion semantics for subtyping:

for all types t and t' in $\mathbf{T}(C)$ such that $t \le t'$, we have $\text{dom}(t) \subseteq \text{dom}(t')$.

Until now we have presented the structural part of the data model. Methods are associated to classes and define the behavior of objects of the corresponding class.

3.5 Methods

A method contains the code (e.g., CO_2 code) that defines functions on objects. Typically, a method is stored "intensionally"; that is, the code of the method is part of the database. For a particular database instance, the meaning of this code is a finite input-output relation—that is, the "extension" of the method. The only visible part of a method, for the purposes of data description, is its signature. So for the moment let us ignore the data-manipulation code.

Definition 8. Let (C, σ, $\prec$) be a well-formed class hierarchy. To every class in C we attach a set of *methods*. Each method has a *signature*—that is, an expression $m\colon c \times t_1 \times \ldots \times t_n \rightarrow t$, where m is the name of the method and c, $t_1, \ldots, t_n, t$ are types over C. The first type c of a method signature is the class to which the method is attached; it is called the *receiver class* of the method.

One important feature of the object-oriented paradigm is *encapsulation.* The objects of a class can only be manipulated using the methods associated with this class. A method can be seen as a function from a source domain to a range domain. For example, the method

get_name: Monument $\rightarrow$ string

can be applied to objects belonging to class Monument, and the result will be a value of type string.

Another important feature of object-oriented systems is the notion of *overloading* and *late binding.* A method m can be defined with *the same name* in several classes. Given an object and a method name, the method code to be executed is determined at run time (late binding) by searching for a method of that name in the class hierarchy. (Of course, the redefinitions of a method in subclasses of a class must follow some typing rules in order to avoid inconsistencies.) This is expressed more formally as follows.

If m is a method name and c a class of C, we say that *m is defined in c* if there is a method with signature m: $c \times t_1 \times \ldots \times t_n \rightarrow t$. We say that *$m$ is reachable from c* if there is (at least) one superclass of c in which m is defined. This notion of reachability defines method inheritance. The inheritance rule is: *A class inherits a method from the least ancestor where this method is defined.*

Method inheritance must follow some typing rules in order to avoid (1) structural incompatibilites, and (2) inheritance conflicts.

Structural compatibility simplifies type checking and is similar to the one for class hierarchies. For inheritance conflicts, if two noncomparable classes (say c and c') with method m, have a common subclass (say c''), then the method m can be inherited from any of these superclasses. The semantics of method inheritance must ensure that the application of a method to an object is uniquely defined.

Let $(C, \sigma, \prec)$ be a well-formed class hierarchy with a set of method signatures. We say that the signatures are *well formed* if two conditions are met:

1. If m is defined at both c, c', and $c \prec c'$, then m: $c \times t_2 \times \ldots \times t_n \rightarrow t$, and m: $c' \times t'_2 \times \ldots \times t'_n \rightarrow t'$, and $t_i \leq t'_i$, and $t \leq t'$. (This is known as the covariant condition.)

2. If there are classes c and c' having a common subclass c'', with a method of name m defined on both c and c' but not defined at c'', then there is a subclass c''' of c and c' of which c'' is a subclass in which m is also defined. (Thus, c'' inherits m from c''' and there is no ambiguity.)

The first property ensures that the method overloading is done with compatible signatures, and the second eliminates the multiple inheritance conflicts (see figure 3.1). In section 3.6, we consider only well-formed class hierarchies associated with a well-formed set of signatures.

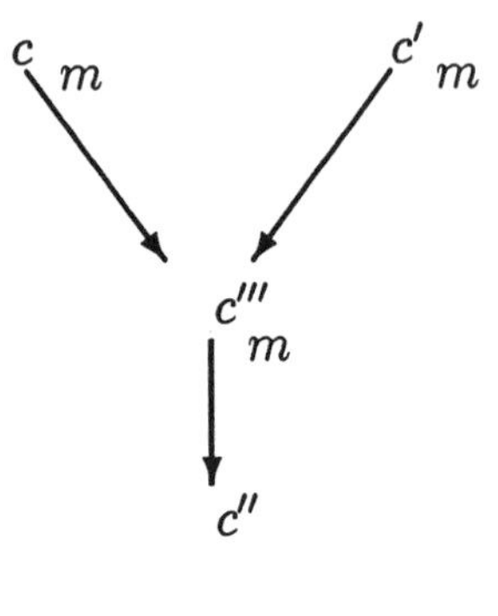

Figure 3.1. Resolving multiple inheritance conflicts

3.6 Database Schema

A database schema models both the structural and the behavioral parts of the database. Its main component is the class hierarchy and the method signatures that describe the programming interface of the objects in the classes.

Definition 9. A *database schema* S is a 5-tuple $(C, \sigma, \prec, M, G)$, such that

- $(C, \sigma, \prec)$ is a well-formed class hierarchy
- M is a well-formed set of method signatures
- G is a set of names with a type associated to each name

The names of G are the entry points in the database. They serve as handles for some objects (or values) which are of a particular importance. In many object-oriented systems, the database entry points are the "extensions" of the classes. We want to be more general and define entry points which are arbitrary values or objects.

As database entry points, the names of G (global names) are also used to define the persistence semantics with the following rules:

1. Every object or value with a global name is persistent.
2. Every object or value that is part of a persistent object or value is also persistent.

The global names are the roots of the persistence mechanism. We shall see in section 3.7 that classes can be attached extensions which are defined as special cases of global names. As a consequence, every instance of a class with an extension can be persistent.

3.7 Instances of a Database Schema

Definition 10. An *instance* of a database schema S consists of a 4-tuple (π, ν, μ, γ), where

- π is an oid assignment for the schema and $I = \cup\{\pi(c) \mid c \in C\}$.
- ν is a mapping from object identifiers to values; that is, ν is a function from I to $\mathbf{V}(I)$. This function defines the value associated to all the database object identifiers. Of course, these values must be consistent with the type of the corresponding classes, and we impose that $\forall j \in \pi(c)$ we must have that $\nu(j) \in \mathrm{dom}(\sigma(c))$.
- μ is a mapping from method signatures in M to finite input-output relations. We have that $\mu(m\colon w \rightarrow t) \in dom(w)^{dom(t)}$ is the input-output relation defined by the method code given the instance. If the method m is overloaded with two different signatures $w \rightarrow t$ and $w' \rightarrow t'$, such that $w \leq w'$ and $t \leq t'$, then functions $\mu(m\colon w \rightarrow t)$ and $\mu(m\colon w' \rightarrow t')$ agree on $\mathrm{dom}(w)$.
- γ is a function associating each name of G, of type t, to a value of $\mathrm{dom}(t)$. This value is the value currently assigned to the global name. This can be used to define persistence of class contents or "extents," sets of values, individual objects or values, and so on.

Finally, in every instance we have some defaults. We only assume one predefined class, named **Object**. This class is intended to be the top of any class hierarchy. The associated type is **any**. It implements the methods that are common to all objects in the system. The following are examples of such methods, indicating the variety of notions of equality in our data model.

is_same: **Object** × **Object** → **Boolean**

This method returns true if the argument and the receiver are the same object (they have the same identifier), and false otherwise.

is_value_equal: **Object** × **Object** → **Boolean**

This method returns true if the argument and the receiver have the same value (not necessarily the same identifier), and false otherwise.

is_deep_equal: **Object** × **Object** → **Boolean**

This method returns true if the argument and the receiver are isomorphic copies (are the same up to a one-to-one mapping of their involved identifiers), and false otherwise.

This completes our presentation of the data description language (DDL) of the O_2 data model. There are a number of additional details and specialized features that are best explained in the appropriate context. In particular, for other predefined methods (for objects) and algebraic primitives (for values) we refer to part 3. For schema modifications we refer to chapters 6 and 7. For the treatment of database versions we refer to part 4.

4 Acknowledgements

The work on the data model and the database programming language(s) benefited from help and feedback from many of the Altaïr members. We are particularly indebted to our colleagues in the language team, the system team, and the evaluation team. We also especially acknowledge F. Vélez who participated in the design of a first version of the model, S. Abiteboul who participated in the formalization and analysis of the second version of the model, and C. Delobel who defined an object-oriented data model from which we took inspiration. Finally, we wish to thank the anonymous reviewers for their helpful comments on this exposition.

5 A Roadmap for Part 2

Let us now outline the chapters in part 2. Chapters 4, 5, and 6 are edited versions of conference proceedings papers (respectively, Lécluse, Richard, and Vélez 1988; Abiteboul and Kanellakis 1989; Abiteboul, Kanellakis, and Waller 1990), and chapter 7 was written for this collection (see also Zicari 1991).

Chapter 4, "O_2, an Object-Oriented Data Model," gives the original design of the data model. A comparison with the description in this introduction shows how the basic concepts matured during the development of the system. A reader familiar with the model may in fact proceed directly to chapter 5 without loss of continuity.

Chapter 5, "Object Identity as a Query-Language Primitive," is a theoretical analysis of the structural part of the new data model. Its principal goals are to clarify the role of object identity in OODBs (beyond structure sharing and updates), and to determine what the computable database queries are for databases with identity, complex structures and inheritance. It characterizes these queries using the rule-based language IQL.

Chapter 6, "Method Schemas," is a theoretical analysis of a simplified behavioral part of the new model. The concept of method schemas is proposed as a simplified model for object-oriented programming with features such as classes with methods and inheritance, method name overloading, and late binding. The static consistency problem for method schemas is analyzed in general and for various restrictions on the methods, e.g., nonrecursive, monadic, covariant, etc. The motivation for this is as follows. The *schema update* problem (Zicari 1991) can be formalized and heuristically solved using the incremental consistency of method schemas. The static analysis in this paper is the natural first step in understanding schema updates.

Chapter 7 is an analysis of the schema update problem in the full O_2 data model. "*A Framework for Schema Updates in an Object-Oriented Database System*" provides the first cost analysis of different alternative implementations of schema update policies in the O_2 system. In this sense it strongly complements the analysis of the simplified model in the previous paper.

References

Abiteboul, S., and C. Beeri. 1987. On the power of languages for manipulating complex objects. In *International workshop on theory and applications of nested relations and complex objects.* (Also INRIA technical report no. 846, 1988.)

Abiteboul, S., and P. Kanellakis. 1989. Object identity as a query language primitive. In *Proceedings of the 1989 ACM SIGMOD conference.* (Also INRIA technical report no. 1022, 1989.)

———. 1990. Database theory column: Query languages for complex object databases. *Sigact News* 21(3): 9–19.

Abiteboul, S., P. Kanellakis, and E. Waller. 1990. Method schemas. In *Proceedings of the ninth ACM PODS conference.*

Atkinson, M., F. Bancilhon, D. DeWitt, K. Dittrich, D. Maier, S. Zdonik. 1989. The object-oriented database system manifesto. In *Proceedings of the first international conference on deductive and object-oriented databases.*

Banerjee, J. et al. 1987. Data model issues for object-oriented applications. *ACM TOIS* 5(1): 3–26.

Bancilhon, F., and S. Khoshafian. 1986. A calculus for complex objects. In *Proceedings of the ACM PODS conference.*

Cardelli, L. 1988. A semantics of multiple inheritance. *Information and Computation* 76(2): 138–64.

Cardelli, L., and P. Wegner. 1985. On understanding types, data abstraction, and polymorphism. *ACM Computing Surveys* 17(4): 471–522.

Carey, M., D. DeWitt, and S. Vandenberg. 1988. A data model and query language for Exodus. In *Proceedings of the 1988 ACM SIGMOD conference.*

Danforth, S., S. Khoshafian, and P. Valduriez. 1987. *FAD: A database programming language.* MCC Technical Report.

Danforth, S., and C. Tomlinson. 1988. Type theories and object-oriented programming. *ACM Computing Surveys* 20(1).

Goldberg, A., and D. Robson. 1983. *Smalltalk 80: The language and its implementation.* Addison-Wesley.

Hull, R. 1987. A survey of theoretic research on typed complex database objects. In *Databases*, ed. J. Paredaens. Academic Press.

Hull, R., and R. King. 1987. Semantic Database modeling: Survey, applications, and research issues. *ACM Computing Surveys* 19: 201–60.

Kuper, G. M. 1985. *The logical data model: A new approach to database logic.* PhD thesis, Stanford University.

Kuper, G. M., and M. Y. Vardi. 1984. A new approach to database logic. In *Proceedings of the third ACM PODS conference.*

Kim, W., J. Banerjee, H-T. Chou, J. F. Garza, and D. Woelk. 1987. Composite object support in an object-oriented database system. In *Proceedings of the OOPSLA conference.*

Lécluse, C., and P. Richard. 1988. Modeling inheritance and genericity in object-oriented databases. In *Proceedings of the second ICDT conference.*

______. 1989a. Manipulation of structured values in object oriented databases. In *Proceedings of the DBPL2 workshop.*

______. 1989b. Modeling complex structures in object-oriented databases. In *Proceedings of the ninth ACM PODS conference.*

Lécluse, C., P. Richard, and F. Vélez. 1988. O_2, an object-oriented data model. In *Proceedings of the ACM SIGMOD conference.*

Maier, D., A. Otis, and A. Purdy. 1985. Development of an object-oriented DBMS. *Quarterly Bulletin of IEEE Computer Science Technical Committee on Database Engineering* 8(4).

Skarra, A., and S. Zdonik. 1987. Type evolution in an object-oriented database. In *Research directions in object-oriented programming*, ed. B. Shriver and P. Wegner. MIT Press.

Zicari, R. 1991. A framework for schema updates in an object-oriented database system. In *Proceedings of the IEEE Data Engineering Conference.*

CHAPTER 4

O_2, an Object-Oriented Data Model

C. LÉCLUSE
P. RICHARD
F. VÉLEZ

1 Introduction

One of the objectives of the Altaïr Group is to develop a new-generation database system. The target applications are traditional business applications, transactional applications (excluding very high performance applications), office automation, and multimedia applications. The system we are designing is object oriented. We briefly recall the main features of the object-oriented paradigm:

1. Object identity. Objects have an existence which is independent of their value. Thus two objects can be either identical (that is, they are the same object) or equal (that is, they have the same value).

2. The notion of *type*. A type describes a set of objects that have the same characteristics. It describes the structure of data carried by objects as well as the operations (*methods* in the object-oriented terminology) applied to these objects. Users of a type only see the interface of the type—that is, a list of methods together with their signatures (the type of the input parameters and the type of the result). This is called *encapsulation*. (The term *class* is frequently used; however, in addition to the intensional notion of type, it contains an extensional aspect, as it denotes the set of all objects of the system which conforms to the type at a given time.)

3. The notion of *inheritance*. Inheritence allows objects of different structures to share methods related to their common part. Types are organized in

an inheritance (or *subtype*) hierarchy, which factorizes common structures and methods at the level at which the largest number of objects can share them. (Another mechanism allowing objects to share operations is called *delegation*. It is the basis of the so-called Actor languages. We will not consider it in this paper.)

4. *Overriding* and *late binding*. The body of a method in a given type may be redefined at any moment in any of its subtypes, while keeping the same name. This frees the programmer from remembering the name of an overridden method in a given type; therefore the code is simpler, and it is reusable because it is independent of the types that existed at the time the program was written. To offer this functionality, the system has to bind method names to binary code at run time.

There is a clear interest in the database community about the object-oriented technology. First of all, types and inheritance are a powerful tool to model the real world. They also make systems extensible: by adding new types in a system, one can extend its capabilities. Object identity allows modeling object sharing and provides a natural semantics for object updates (Copeland and Khoshafian 1986). Second, this technology provides a framework to represent and manage both data and programs. It is a promising paradigm for solving the *impedance mismatch*—the awkward communication between a query language and a programming language that results when applications are developed with a database system. Third, it provides good software-engineering tools that make the programming task much easier.

Object-oriented database systems are currently being built. Most of them are prototypes (Banerjee et al. 1987; Zdonik 1984; Nixon et al. 1987; Bancilhon et al. 1987), and few of them are commercial products (Copeland and Maier 1984; Andrews and Harris 1987). The overall objective of these systems is to integrate database technology (such as data sharing, data security, persistency, disk management, and database query languages) with the object-oriented approach in a single system. However, a strong theoretical framework is lacking for object-oriented systems. This paper is a step toward such a framework. It sets out the data model foundations for an object-oriented database system. The originality of this model, called O_2, lies in its type system, which is defined within the framework of a set-and-tuple data model. Our approach is different from other object-oriented approaches because we use set and tuple constructors to deal with arbitrary complex objects. The type system enforces strong typing, yet overriding is allowed.

Models already exist that deal with inheritance, such as those of Bruce and Wegner 1986 and Cardelli 1984. In Bruce and Wegner 1986, types are modeled as many-sorted algebras. A type is a subtype of another if there exist suitable (not necessarily injective) "coercion" operators which behave as homomorphisms between the algebras. Cardelli 1984 proposes a safe, strongly typed system in which the semantics of subtyping for tuple-structured types corresponds to set inclusion between the corresponding type interpretations; this semantics is different from that of Bruce and Wegner. Functions are typed, and rules for subtyping among functional types are given.

We have borrowed Cardelli's interpretation for tuple types, as it leads to an intuitive notion of the subtyping of tuple structures. Our model is different from Cardelli's in that (1) we propose a different rule for the inheritance of methods (for functional subtyping, in Cardelli's terms); (2) we introduce set-structured objects, and objects may form a directed graph in which cycles are allowed; and (3) methods can be directly attached to objects. Our tuple-and-set construction of objects is similar to that of Bancilhon and Khoshafian 1986 and especially to that of Kuper and Vardi 1984, who also introduce identifiers, called addresses.

This paper is organized as follows. Section 2 gives an informal overview of our approach and illustrates it through examples. Section 3 defines the notion of objects. Section 4 gives the semantics of types and of the inheritance relationship. Section 5 introduces the notion of a database. Section 6 contains some concluding remarks and notes some problems that remain open.

2 Overview

Let us introduce some of the notions of the O_2 model with examples. Objects represent things or people in the world. They are made up of an object identifier (a name for the object) and a value. Values can be atomic (strings, integers, reals, and so on), tuple-structured, or set-structured. For example:

$(o_1,$ [**name**: "Smith", **age**: 32]$)$

$(o_2,$ [**name**: "Doe", **age**: 29, **salary**: 9700]$)$

$(o_3, \{o_1, o_2\})$

The first two objects are examples of tuple objects; the third is a set object. In these examples, the ages and names are atomic objects; they also have identifiers (see below). Objects can reference other objects, and this allows the definition of complex objects. We can have mutually referencing objects, as in the following example:

$(o_4,$ [**name**: "John", **spouse**: o_5]$)$

$(o_5,$ [**name**: "Mary", **spouse**: o_4]$)$

This possibility makes our objects more general than the simple, nested, tuple-and-set objects. A type has a name, and it contains a structure and a set of methods applying to these objects. The structure will be either a basic structure (such as string, integer, or real), a tuple structure, or a set structure. The following examples of type structures will be used throughout this paper:

Person = [**name**: string, **age**: integer, **sex**: string]

Employee = [**name**: string, **age**: integer, **sex**: string, **salary**: integer]

Male = [**name**: string, **age**: integer, **sex**: "male"]

Persons = {Person}

Employees = {Employee}

Married_person = [**name**: string, **spouse**: Married_person, **children**: Persons]

The type structure Person represents the set of all tuple objects having a name field which is a string, and an age field which is an integer. The type structure Male is the same as Person, except that the sex field is restricted to contain the string "male". The type structure Persons represents all objects which are sets of persons. Given a set of objects Θ, we call the interpretation of a type structure (say Person) the set of all objects of this set having the corresponding structure. If Θ is the set of all objects o_1 to o_5, then the interpretation of Persons will be the object o_3, whereas the interpretation of Person will be the two objects o_1 and o_2. Indeed, these two objects have name and age fields with the corresponding structures (string and integer). Notice that we allow the objects to have additional fields (for example, the object o_2 also has a salary field). In the same manner, the interpretation of the Employee structure is the set containing only the o_2 object. So the interpretation of Employee is included in the interpretation of the type structure Person. This is an intuitive result, because we want to say that every employee is a person. This "is_a" relationship between type structures is called *inheritance* in the object-oriented terminology.

The notion of inheritance involves the concept of methods. As employees are persons, a method defined for every Person object can be applied to an Employee object. Moreover, if a method (say *name*) is defined for both Person and Employee objects, then we shall put some constraint on these two methods, in order to make them compatible. Such compatibility is necessary for type checking.

3 Objects

In this section, we define the notion of objects. We suppose given:

- A finite set of *domains* $D_1, \ldots, D_n$, $n \geq 1$ (for example, the set $\mathbf{Z}$ of all integers is one such domain). We note $\mathbf{D}$ the union of all domains $D_1, \ldots, D_n$. We suppose that the domains are pairwise disjoint.

- A countably infinite set $\mathbf{A}$ of symbols called *attributes*. Intuitively, the elements of $\mathbf{A}$ are names for structure fields as we shall see later.

- A countably infinite set **ID** of symbols called *identifiers*. The elements of **ID** will be used as identifiers for objects.

Let us now define the notion of *value*.

Definition 1.

1. The special symbol *nil* is a value, called a *basic value.*
2. Every element v of **D** is a value, called a *basic value.*
3. Every finite subset of **ID** is a value, called a *set-value.* Set-values are denoted in the usual way using brackets.
4. Every finite partial function from **A** into **ID** is a value, called a *tuple-value.* We denote by $[a_1\colon i_1, \ldots, a_p\colon i_p]$ the partial function t defined on $\{a_1, \ldots, a_p\}$ such that $t(a_k) = i_k$ for all k.

We denote by **V** the set of all values.

We can now define the notion of object.

Definition 2.

1. An *object* is a pair $o = (i, v)$, where i is an element of **ID** (an identifier) and v is a value.
2. We define, in an obvious way, the notion of *basic* objects, *set-structured* objects, and *tuple-structured* objects.
3. **O** is the set of all objects; that is, $\mathbf{O} = \mathbf{ID} \times \mathbf{V}$.

This "tuple-and-set" construction of objects is similar to that of Bancilhon and Khoshafian 1986 and especially to that of Kuper and Vardi 1984 where identifiers (called addresses) were also introduced.

We add some further technical notations:

- If an object $o = (i, v)$, then ident(o) denotes the identifier i, and value(o) denotes the value v.
- We will denote by *ref* the function from **O** in $2^{\mathbf{ID}}$ which associates to an object the set of all the identifiers appearing in its value, i.e., those referenced by the object.

We can use a graphical representation for objects as follows.

Definition 3. If Θ is a set of objects, then the graph graph(Θ) is defined as follows.

1. If o is a basic object of Θ, then the graph contains a vertex with no outgoing edge. The vertex is labeled with the value of o.
2. If o is a tuple-structured object $(i, [a_1\colon i_1, \ldots, a_p\colon i_p])$, the graph of o contains a vertex, say v, represented by a dot ($\bullet$) and labeled with i, and p outgoing edges from v labeled with $a_1, \ldots, a_p$ that lead respectively to the vertices corresponding to objects $o_1, \ldots, o_p$, where o_k is an object identified by i_k (if such objects exist).

3. If o is a set-structured object $(i, \{i_1, \ldots, i_p\})$, the graph of o contains a vertex, say v, represented by a star (*) and labeled with i, and p unlabeled outgoing arcs from v that lead respectively to the vertices corresponding to objects $o_1, \ldots, o_p$, where o_k is an object identified by i_k (if such objects exist).

We illustrate this definition with an example. Let Θ be the set consisting of the following objects:

$$o_0 = (i_0, [\texttt{spouse}: i_1, \texttt{name}: i_3, \texttt{children}: i_2])$$
$$o_1 = (i_1, [\texttt{spouse}: i_0, \texttt{name}: i_4, \texttt{children}: i_2])$$
$$o_2 = (i_2, \{i_5, i_6\}),\ o_3 = (i_3, \text{“Fred”}),\ o_4 = (i_4, \text{“Mary”})$$
$$o_5 = (i_5, \text{“John”}),\ o_6 = (i_6, \text{“Paul”})$$

Θ is represented by the graph shown in figure 4.1.

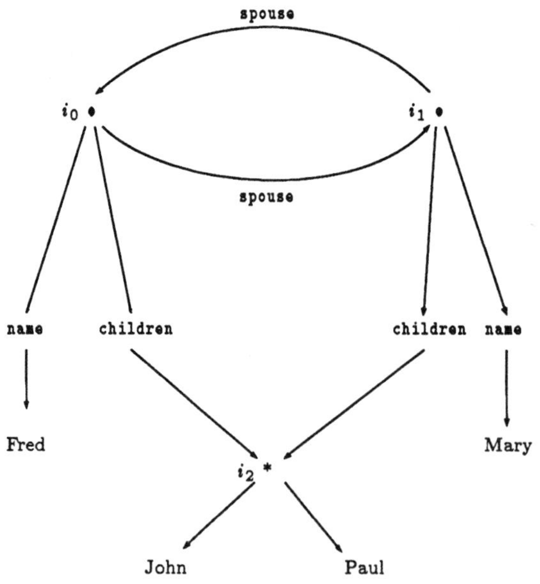

Figure 4.1. Graph of a set of objects

We cannot build the graph representation of every set of objects. For example, if an identifier i appears in a value, there must be an object identified by it. Intuitively speaking, identifiers are pointers on objects, and there must be no dangling pointers in our set of objects. This leads us to the notion of consistency for a set of objects.

Definition 4. A set Θ of objects is consistent iff:

1. Θ is finite.
2. The *ident* function is injective on Θ (i.e., there is no pair of objects with the same identifier).
3. For all $o \in \Theta$, ref(o) $\subseteq$ ident(Θ) (i.e., every referenced identifier corresponds to an object of Θ).

We denote by Θ(i) the value v such that the object (i, v) is in Θ.

In value-based systems (i.e., systems where no object identity exists, such as relational systems) there is no need to distinguish between identical objects and equal objects, since the two notions are the same. Object-oriented systems need to distinguish them, however, as there is a sharp distinction between values and objects.

Definition 5.

1. Two objects o and o' are 0-equal (or *identical*) iff $o = o'$ (in the sense of mathematical pair equality).
2. Two objects o and o' are 1-equal (or simply *equal*) iff value(o) = value(o').
3. Two objects o and o' are ω-equal (or *value-equal*) iff span-tree(o) = span-tree(o'), where span-tree(o) is the tree obtained from o by recursively replacing an identifier i (in a value) by the value of the object identified by i.

Equality implies value equality; but the converse is not true, since many distinct objects may have the same span tree. These definitions of equality correspond to those of identity, shallow equality, and deep equality for Smalltalk 80 (Goldberg and Robson 1983). The span-tree built from an object may be infinite, in the case of cyclic objects; so this construction cannot be used (directly) as a decision procedure for testing value equality.

4 Types

A type is an abstraction that allows the user to encapsulate in the same structure both data and operations. In our model, the static component of a type is called a type structure. Our notion of type bears some similarity to abstract data types. Users of a type only see its abstract part—that is, the interface of its methods—whereas the programmer of the type is concerned with the implementation. However, a type has only one implementation.

In what follows, we decompose the process of defining the syntax, semantics, and subtype relationship among types into two steps. In section 4.1 we define the syntax of type structures as well as the notion of a schema. Then we give the semantics of a schema with respect to a consistent set of objects. We define a partial order among type structures, using this semantics. In section 4.2 a similar treatment is given to methods. We bring the pieces together in section 4.3, with the notion of type systems.

We begin by defining the set of type names.

Definition 6. *Bnames* is the set of names for basic types that contains the following:

1. The special symbols *any* and *nil*.

2. A symbol d_i for each domain D_i. We note $D_i = \text{dom}(d_i)$.

3. A symbol $'x$ for every value x of $\mathbf{D}$, the union of all domains $D_1, \ldots, D_n$.

Cnames is the set of names for constructed types that is countably infinite and disjoint with *Bnames*.

Tnames is the union of *Bnames* and *Cnames*. It is the set of all names for types.

In order to define types, we assume that there is a finite set $\mathbf{M}$ whose elements are called methods and play the role of operations on our data structures. For the moment, we can think of the elements of $\mathbf{M}$ as uninterpreted symbols. We define them in section 4.2.

Definition 7. A *type* is either a basic or a constructed type.

A basic type, or Btype, is a pair (n, M) where n is an element of *Bnames* and M is a subset of $\mathbf{M}$. (The link between basic types and domains D_i is given in definition 10.)

A constructed type, or Ctype, is one of the following:

- A triple (s, t, M) where s is an element of *Cnames*, t is an element of *Tnames*, and M is a subset of $\mathbf{M}$. We denote such a type by $s = (t, M)$.

- A triple (s, t, M) where s is an element of *Cnames*, t is a finite partial function from $\mathbf{A}$ to *Tnames*, and M is a subset of $\mathbf{M}$. We denote such a type by $s = ([a_1\colon s_1, \ldots, a_n\colon s_n], M)$, where $t(a_k) = s_k$. We call it a *tuple-structured type*.

- A triple (s, s', M) where s is an element of *Cnames*, s' an element of *Tnames*, and M is a finite subset of $\mathbf{M}$. We denote such a type by $s = (\{s'\}, M)$. We call it a *set-structured type*.

The set of all types is denoted by $\mathbf{T}$.

4.1 Type Structures

In this subsection we are interested in the static part of a type, its structure.

Definition 8. Let $t = (n, M)$ be a basic type. We call n the ***basic type structure*** associated to t.

Let $t = (s = x, M)$ be a constructed type. We call "$s = x$" the ***constructed type structure*** associated to t.

Given a type t, its structure part will be denoted by struct(t) and its methods part by methods(t). Intuitively, a type structure is a type in which the methods part is hidden; that is, it is the data part of the type. Note that recursion (or transitive recursion) is allowed in type definitions; that is, one of the s_i may be s. The type structure Married_person is an example of a recursively defined type. Type structures are analogous to Galileo's concrete types (Albano et al. 1985), except that type structures only exist within types.

We need a notion of consistency for a set of expressions defining type structures. In order to define it formally, we need some technical notations.

- If t is a type, then name(t) is the name of the type, that is, the first component in its definition.
- If st is a type structure associated to the type t, the name of the type structure st is the name of t. We note name(st) = $name(t)$.
- If st is a type structure associated to a type t, the set of all type names appearing in the structure st is called the set of type references for st. We denote this set by ref(st).

Definition 9. A set Δ of constructed type structures is a *schema* iff:

1. Δ is a finite set.
2. *name* is injective on Δ (only one type structure for a given name).
3. For all $st \in \Delta$, ref(st) $\cap$ $Cnames \subseteq$ name(Δ); that is, there are no dangling identifiers.

Note that in a schema we can identify a type name, name(Δ), with the corresponding type structure in Δ. We use this convention in the remainder of this chapter.

We illustrate the notion of a schema with two examples. Let Δ be the set consisting of the following type structures:

Age = integer,

Person = [**name**: string, **age**: age]

Δ is a schema. If we remove the type structure Age from Δ, it is no longer a schema. On the other hand, the following set of type structures is also a schema:

$$\text{Person} = \text{Human}$$
$$\text{Human} = \text{Person}$$

This set of type structures may not be useful, but it is well defined and has an interpretation (see the next subsection).

4.1.1 Interpretations

This subsection deals with the semantics of the type-structure system. An *interpretation* is a particular function which associates subsets of a consistent set of objects to type-structure names.

Definition 10. Let Δ be a schema, and let Θ be a consistent subset of the universe of objects **O**. An *interpretation* I of Δ in Θ is a function from *Tnames* in $2^{\text{ident}(\Theta)}$ that satisfies the following properties.

For basic type names:

1. $\text{I}(\text{nil}) \subseteq \{i \in \text{ident}(\Theta)/(i, \text{nil}) \in \Theta\}$
   (Ident(Θ) denotes the set of the identifiers of all objects of Θ; $\Theta(i)$ denotes the only value v for which (i, v) is in Θ.)
2. $\text{I}(d_i) \subseteq \{i \in \text{ident}(\Theta)/\Theta(i) \in D_i\} \cup \text{I}(\text{nil})$
3. $\text{I}('x) \subseteq \{i \in \text{ident}(\Theta)/\Theta(i) = x\} \cup \text{I}(\text{nil})$

For constructed type names:

1. If $s = [a_1\colon s_1, \ldots, a_n\colon s_n]$ is in Δ, then

$$\text{I}(s) \subseteq \{i \in \text{ident}(\Theta)/\Theta(i) \text{ is a tuple structured value defined (at least) on } a_1, \ldots, a_n, \text{ and } \Theta(i)(a_k) \in \text{I}(s_k) \text{ for all } k\} \cup \text{I}(\text{nil})$$

2. If $s = \{s'\}$ is in Δ, then

$$\text{I}(s) \subseteq \{i \in \text{ident}(\Theta)/\Theta(i) \subseteq \text{I}(s')\} \cup \text{I}(\text{nil})$$

3. If $s = t$ is in Δ, then

$$\text{I}(s) \subseteq \text{I}(t)$$

For undefined type names:

If s is neither the name of a basic type nor a name of the schema Δ, then

$$\text{I}(s) \subseteq \text{I}(\text{nil})$$

Definition 11.

1. An interpretation I is *smaller* than an interpretation I′ iff for all $s \in$ *Tnames*, $I(s) \subseteq I'(s)$

2. Let Δ be a schema and let Θ be a consistent set of objects. The *model* M of Δ in Θ is the greatest interpretation of Δ in Θ.

Intuitively, the model M(s) of a constructed type structure of name s is the set consisting of all objects (or identifiers of objects) having this structure. For example, if Θ is the set

$$\{(i_0, \text{nil}), (i_1, i_2, i_3), (i_2, 1), (i_3, 4), (i_4, [a\colon i_2]), (i_5, [a\colon i_2, b\colon i_3])\}$$

and Δ is the schema

$$\{s_1 = [a\colon \text{integer}], s_2 = [a\colon \text{integer}, b\colon \text{integer}], s_3 = \{\text{integer}\}\}$$

then:

$$\begin{aligned} M(s_1) &= \{i_0, i_4, i_5\} \\ M(s_2) &= \{i_0, i_5\} \\ M(\text{integer}) &= \{i_0, i_2, i_3\} \\ M(s_3) &= \{i_0, i_1\} \end{aligned}$$

The value of an interpretation of a basic type name does not depend on Δ; this is an intuitive result. Moreover, if (the identifier of) an object belongs to the model M(s) of a tuple structure, then it also belongs to the models of tuple type structures which are substructures of s. In the example just given, i_5 is in M(s_2) but also in M(s_1). This property will allow us to give a simple set-inclusion semantics for the subtyping relation among type structures, which is defined in definition 12. This interpretation is derived from one originally proposed in Cardelli 1984. Note that any attribute could be added to a tuple-structured object and the latter would still have a well-defined type. We refer to such added attributes as "exceptional"; their manipulation is considered in subsection 4.3.1.

We now have to prove that our definition of the model of a schema is well founded. Given a schema Δ and a consistent set of objects Θ, there is a finite number of interpretations of Δ defined on Θ. Therefore, in order to prove that the greatest interpretation exists, we just have to prove that the union of two interpretations is an interpretation.

Let I_1 and I_2 be two interpretations, and let I be the function defined by $I(s) = I_1(s) \cup I_2(s)$, for every type name s. This function I clearly verifies properties 1, 2, and 3 of definition 10 for basic type names. If $s = [a_1\colon s_1, \ldots, a_n\colon s_n]$ and i is an element of I(s) (for example, an element of $I_1(s)$), then $\Theta(i)(a_k)$ is in $I_1(s_k)$ for all k, because I_1 is an interpretation. So $\Theta(i)(a_k)$ is in $I(s_k)$ for all k, and I verifies property 1 of definition 10 for constructed type names. We can show in the same manner that I also verifies properties 2 and 3 of definition 10 for constructed type names.

In conclusion, there is a greatest interpretation M, and we have:

$$\mathrm{M}(s) = \bigcup_{\mathrm{I} \in \mathrm{INT}(\Delta)} \mathrm{I}(s)$$

for every type name s, where INT(Δ) denotes the set of all interpretations of Δ (in Θ).

4.1.2 Partial Order among Type Structures

Definition 12. Let s and s' be two type structures of a schema Δ. We say that s is a substructure of s' (denoted by $s \leq_{st} s'$) iff $M(s) \subseteq M(s')$ for all consistent sets Θ.

For example, if Δ consists of the following type structures:

$$\begin{aligned} s_1 &= [a\text{: integer}] \\ s_2 &= [a\text{: integer}, b\text{: integer}] \\ s_3 &= [c\text{: } s_1] \\ s_4 &= [c\text{: } s_2] \\ s_5 &= s_1 \\ s_6 &= s_2 \\ s_7 &= [a\text{: } '1] \end{aligned}$$

then the following relationships hold among these structures:

$$s_2 \leq_{st} s_1, \quad s_4 \leq_{st} s_3$$
$$s_7 \leq_{st} s_1, \quad s_6 \leq_{st} s_5$$

The first relationship, $s_2 \leq_{st} s_1$ comes from the interpretation of tuple type structures. Let us establish the second one, $s_4 \leq_{st} s_3$. Let i be the (identifier of an) object belonging to I(s_4). We know from the definition that $\Theta(i)(c)$ belongs to I(s_2), and so to I(s_1) because we have $s_2 \leq_{st} s_1$. We conclude that i belongs to I(s_3), and so I(s_4) $\subseteq$ I(s_3). The inequality $s_6 \leq_{st} s_5$ can be established in the same manner; and the relation $s_7 \leq_{st} s_1$ is obviously true.

Definition 12 is a semantic definition of the subtyping relationship $\leq_{st}$. The following theorem gives a syntactic characterization of it.

Theorem 1. Let s and s' be two type structures of a schema Δ. s is a substructure of s' ($s \leq_{st} s'$) iff one of the following conditions is met:

1. s and s' are tuple structures $s = t$ and $s' = t'$, such that t is more defined than t'; and for every attribute a such that t' is defined, we have $t(a) \leq_{st} t'(a)$.

2. s and s' are set structures $s = s_1$ and $s' = s'_1$, and we have $s_1 \leq_{st} s'_1$.

3. $s = 'x$, s' is a basic type structure, and x is in dom(s').

Proof. The validity of this characterization can be easily established by induction. The completeness can be established with a case study inspecting successively tuple-structured types, set-structured types, and basic types.

This theorem gives a syntactical means for checking type-structure subtyping.

4.2 Methods

In section 4.1, we presented the syntax and semantics of type structures. In this subsection we define, in the same way, the syntax and semantics of operations, which in this context we call methods. These operations will consist of (first-order) functions.

We assume that we have a countable set *Mnames* of symbols that will be used as names for methods.

Definition 13. Let Δ be a schema. A *signature* over Δ is an expression of the form

$$s_1 \times s_2 \times \ldots \times s_n \longrightarrow s$$

where $s_1, s_2, \ldots, s_n$, and s are type names corresponding to type structures in Δ, or basic type names.

A method m is a pair (n, σ) where n is a method name (an element of *Mnames*) and σ is a signature. We denote by name(m) the name of the method m, and by sig(m) the signature of the method m.

In the object-oriented formalism, methods are related to types (or type structures) using the first argument of their signature, so we have the following definition.

Definition 14. Let $m = (n, s_1 \times \ldots \times s_n \rightarrow s)$ be a method. We say that *m is defined on* s_1.

4.2.1 Interpretation

In this subsection, we define the model of a signature σ.

Definition 15. Let Δ be a schema and σ a signature over $\Delta(\sigma = s_1 \times \ldots \times s_n \rightarrow s)$. If Θ is a consistent set of objects, then the *model of* σ *in* Θ is the set of all partial functions from $\text{M}(s_1) \times \ldots \times \text{M}(s_n)$ into $\text{M}(s)$ where $\text{M}(s_k)$ is the model in Θ of the structure of Δ identified by s_k.

Let us illustrate these definitions by an example. Let Δ be the schema introduced in section 2, which is restricted to the type structures Person, Persons, Employee, Employees, and Male. We now consider the following signatures:

$$\sigma_1 = \text{Persons} \times \text{Person} \rightarrow \text{Boolean}$$
$$\sigma_2 = \text{Employees} \times \text{Employee} \rightarrow \text{Boolean}$$
$$\sigma_3 = \text{Person} \rightarrow \text{Person}$$
$$\sigma_4 = \text{Male} \rightarrow \text{Employee}$$
$$\sigma_5 = \text{Employee} \rightarrow \text{integer}$$

We take the following set of objects Θ as an interpretation domain:

$$(i_0, \text{nil}), (i_1, [\texttt{name}\colon\ i_{16}, \texttt{age}\colon\ i_7\texttt{sex}\colon\ i_8])$$
$$(i_2, [\texttt{name}\colon\ i_{17}, \texttt{age}\colon\ i_9, \texttt{sex}\colon\ i_{10}])$$
$$(i_3, [\texttt{name}\colon\ i_{18}, \texttt{age}\colon\ i_9, \texttt{sex}\colon\ i_8, \texttt{salary}\colon\ 9i_{11}])$$
$$(i_4, [\texttt{name}\colon\ i_{19}, \texttt{age}\colon\ i_{13}, \texttt{sex}\colon\ i_{12}, \texttt{salary}\colon\ i_{11}])$$
$$(i_5, i_1, i_2), (i_6, i_3, i_4), (i_7, 20), (i_9, 25), (i_{11}, 130000)$$
$$(i_{13}, 35), (i_8, \text{"male"}), (i_{10}, \text{"varying"})$$
$$(i_{12}, \text{"female"})$$
$$(i_{14}, \text{false}), (i_{15}, \text{true}), (i_{16}, \text{"Smith"})$$
$$(i_{17}, \text{"Blake"}), (i_{18}, \text{"Jones"}), (i_{19}, \text{"Nash"})$$

Using definition 9, we can build the models of the type structures defined in Δ:

$$\text{M(Person)} = i_0,\ i_1,\ i_2,\ i_3,\ i_4$$
$$\text{M(Persons)} = i_0,\ i_5,\ i_6$$
$$\text{M(Employee)} = i_0,\ i_3,\ i_4$$
$$\text{M(Employees)} = i_0,\ i_6$$
$$\text{M(Male)} = i_0,\ i_1,\ i_3$$
$$\text{M("male")} = i_0,\ i_8$$
$$\text{M(string)} = i_0,\ i_8,\ i_{10},\ i_{12},\ i_{16},\ i_{17},\ i_{18},\ i_{19}$$
$$\text{M(integer)} = i_0,\ i_7,\ i_9,\ i_{11},\ i_{13}$$
$$\text{M(Boolean)} = i_0,\ i_{14},\ i_{15}$$

The model of the signature σ_1 is the set of all partial functions from $\{i_0, i_5, i_6\} \times \{i_0, i_1, i_2, i_3, i_4\}$ into $\{i_0, i_{14}, i_{15}\}$. Intuitively, the model of the signature σ_1 is the set of functions assigning a Boolean object to some pairs (i, j) where i is (the identifier of) a set of Person objects and j is (the identifier of) a Person object.

4.2.2

We use the interpretation of signatures, defined in the previous subsection, to introduce an ordering among signatures.

Definition 16. Let Δ be a schema and f and g two signatures over Δ. We say that f is smaller than g (or that f *refines* g) iff $M(f) \subseteq M(g)$ for all consistent sets Δ. This ordering will be denoted by $\leq_m$.

Looking at the schema of the previous example, we can see that the following inequalities hold: $\sigma_2 \leq_m \sigma_1$, and $\sigma_4 \leq_m \sigma_3$. In fact, let Θ be any consistent set of objects and f be a partial function in $M(\sigma_2)$. f is a (partial) function from M(Employees)×M(Employee) in M(Boolean). We have seen in section 4.1.2 that Employees $\leq_{st}$ Persons and Employee $\leq_{st}$ Person, and hence M(Employees) $\subseteq$ M(Persons) and M(Employee) $\subseteq$ M(Person). So f is also a partial function from M(Persons) × M(Person) in M(Boolean); so f is in $M(\sigma_1)$. A similar proof can be constructed for the inequality $\sigma_4 \leq_m \sigma_3$.

Intuitively, $\sigma \leq_m \sigma'$ means that we can use a method of signature σ' in place of a method of signature σ. In the example above, we can apply a method of signature σ_1 to a set of Employees and to an Employee because employees are persons. This partial order models the inheritance of methods, just as the ordering $\leq_{st}$ models inheritance of data structures. In section 4.3 we put data structures and methods together to define type systems, and we use the ordering $\leq_{st}$ and $\leq_m$ to define inheritance of types. The following theorem gives an easy syntactical equivalent to the definition of the partial order $\leq_m$ among signatures.

Theorem 2. Let f and g be two signatures over a schema Δ. Then $f \leq_m g$ iff all of the following conditions are met.

1. $f = s_1 \times \ldots \times s_n \rightarrow s$
2. $g = s'_1 \times \ldots \times s'_n \rightarrow s'$
3. $s_k \leq_{st} s'_k$ for $k = 1, 2, \ldots, n$
4. $s \leq_{st} s'$

Proof. In order to clarify the proof, we assume, without loss of generality, that the method signatures are of the forms $\sigma = s_1 \rightarrow s$ and $\sigma' = s'_1 \rightarrow s'$. Suppose that $\sigma \leq_m \sigma'$. Every partial function from $M(s_1)$ to $M(s)$ is then a partial function from $M(s'_1)$ to $M(s')$. So, we necessarily have $M(s_1) \subseteq M(s'_1)$ and $M(s) \subseteq M(s')$.

Conversely, if these two inclusions hold, then every partial function from $M(s_1)$ to $M(s)$ is clearly also a partial function from $M(s'_1)$ to $M(s')$.

As far as methods are concerned, our definition differs from the classical definitions of data-type theory (Bruce and Wegner 1986; Cardelli 1984; Albano et al. 1985). In these settings, functional types may be constructed: the type $r \rightarrow s$ has as instances functions having r as domain and s as codomain. The general rule of subtyping among functional types can be expressed as follows:

$$\text{If } r' \leq r \text{ and } s \leq s', \text{ then } r \rightarrow s \leq r' \rightarrow s'$$

This means that a function with domain r and codomain s can always be considered as a function from some smaller domain r' to some larger codomain s'. This is a necessary condition for the type system to be *safe*, that is, to guarantee that a run-time error will never be caused by a syntactically well-typed expression. If we had adopted this rule in our framework, the subtype relation would be inverted between the right-hand sides of the signatures in theorem 2; that is, $s' \leq s$ instead of $s \geq s'$.

Our choice leads to a less restrictive type system, but we give up safety. There are three main reasons for such a choice. First, we want to be able to inherit an *add* method defined on sets. Suppose there are two types s and t such that $s \leq_{st} t$; then we have $s \leq_{st} t$. Let add_s be a method of signature $s \times s \rightarrow s$, and let add_t be a method of signature $t \times t \rightarrow t$. Then we want $add_s \leq_m add_t$, which is a necessary condition to have $s \leq t$ (see definition 18). Second, this model is intended to be a foundation for an object-oriented layer on top of C, which itself is not type safe. Third, we shall implement run-time checking for the cases where static type-checking is not sufficient.

4.3 Type Systems

Definition 17. A set of types Π is a *type system* iff:

1. The set of structures associated to Π is a schema.
2. For all types $t \in \Pi$, and for all methods $m \in$ methods(t), m is defined on struct(t). (Methods(t) denotes the set of methods of the type t.)

Now, given a type system Π, we must be able to compare two types t and t', with respect to their structures and to the methods they contain.

Definition 18. Let Π be a type system, and let t and t' be two types of Π. We say that t *is a subtype of* t' and we note $t \leq t'$ iff:

1. struct(t) $\leq_{st}$ struct(t').
2. For all $m \in$ methods(t), there exist $m' \in$ methods(t') such that name(m) = name(m') and sig(m) $\leq_m$ sig(m').

We illustrate this by the following example. Let Π be the type system given as an example in section 4.2.1, in which

Methods(Person) = (husband, σ_3)
Methods(Persons) = (parent, σ_1)
Methods(Employee) = (husband, σ_3), (salary, σ_5)
Methods(Employees) = (parent, σ_1), (manager,σ_2)
Methods(Male) = (hire, σ_4), (husband, σ_3)

In this type system, the following subtype relationships hold: Employee $\leq$ Person, Male $\leq$ Person, and Employees $\leq$ Persons.

4.3.1 Objects Revisited

We now extend the definition of an object in order to encapsulate in the same structure both data and operations.

Definition 19. An object o is a triple (i, v, M), where i is an identifier of $\mathbf{I}$, v is a values of $\mathbf{V}$, and M is a set of methods. The first component of the signature of every method of M is a type structure whose interpretation contains o.

The set of methods of an object can be empty, and in this case it will be manipulated through the methods of the type it possesses. This notion is useful in the following cases.

1. When handling exceptions. For example, let us assume that we define in type Employee a method *increase salary* to compute the salary of an employee. Suppose that one of these employees is the chief executive officer (CEO), and that his salary has to be computed differently than for regular employees. One could create a specific subtype of Employee in order to override the *increase salary* method of Employee. This would be heavy, and it is more natural to define a specific method for the CEO object.

2. In the handling of "exceptional" attributes (see subsection 4.1.1). As full encapsulation is preserved, the only way to access and/or modify an exceptional attribute of an object is via a method attached to the object.

3. When representing the data model in terms of itself. This kind of self-representation is very frequent in object-oriented frameworks (the predefined classes "class" and "metaclass" of Smalltalk 80 are a good example). Types could be represented as objects belonging to a predefined type Type, and type methods could easily be defined to attach them to these objects. An example of a type method for a type t is a customized method for instantiating instances of t.

5 Databases

Informally, a database is a type system together with a consistent set of objects that represent the instances of the types at a given moment.

Definition 20. A database is a tuple $(\Pi, \Theta, <_{db}, \text{ext}, \text{impl})$, where

- Π is a type system, and Δ is the associated schema.
- Θ is a consistent set of objects.
- $<_{db}$ is a strict partial order among Π.
- *ext* is an interpretation of Δ in Θ.
- *impl* is a function assigning a function to every method m of a type t.

Moreover, we impose that the following properties hold:

1. $t <_{db} t'$ implies $t \leq t'$.

2. If $t <_{db} t'$ and $t <_{db} t''$, then t' and t'' are comparable.

3. $\Theta = \bigcup_{t \in \Pi} \text{ext}(t)$

4. $\text{ext}(t) \cap \text{ext}(t') = \emptyset$ if t and t' are not comparable.

5. If t is a type of Π and m is a method of t having signature $t \times \ldots \times s_n \rightarrow s$, then $\text{impl}(m)$ is a function defined at least from $\text{ext}(t) \times \ldots \times \text{ext}(s_n)$ in $\text{ext}(s)$.

This definition deserves some comments. The extension of a type is an interpretation, but it may not be a model. Indeed, a model contains all the possible objects which satisfy a given structure. For example, there may be two types of structure *integer* (say Age and Weight) in a data base. These types have the same model, but a given extension as defined by a user will not contain the same objects. The $\leq$ ordering of definition 18 models the notion of subtyping. That is, two types t and t' are comparable using $\leq$ if one *can be* a subtype of the other. The ordering $<_{db}$ is the actual hierarchy of inheritance types, as *defined* by the user. This ordering must satisfy property 1; that is, the user can declare that t is a subtype of t' ($t <_{db} t'$) only if it is allowed by the model ($t \leq t'$). For example, the type system may contain the types

$$\text{Age} = (\text{integer}, +, -) \text{ and}$$
$$\text{Weight} = (\text{integer}, +, -)$$

with corresponding signatures for the methods $+$ and $-$. We have the inequalities (Age $\leq$ Weight) and (Weight $\leq$ Age), but the user does not intend to consider an age as a weight nor a weight as an age, and Age and Weight will be incomparable for $<_{db}$. Property 2 says that we do not allow multiple inheritance. This is a constraint we introduced for the O_2 system because it is still an open problem to decide whether multiple inheritance is a useful modelization tool. In any case, our semantics would still be valid in the context of multiple inheritance. Property 3 says that Θ is the union of all type extensions. There are no database objects not belonging to any type extension. Property 4 says that an object o cannot belong to the extension of two types t and t' if they are incomparable for $<_{db}$. Consider the types Age and Weight. The object $(i_1, 1)$ belongs to the model of Age and to the model of Weight, but if we allow this object to belong to both ext(Age) and ext(Weight), we violate the user's intention, which was to isolate these two types.

6 Conclusion

The main contribution of this paper is to propose a data model for an object-oriented database system. The model includes the following features.

1. Objects may have a tuple or set structure (or be atomic). They form a directed graph in which cycles may appear. Consistent sets of objects are used as interpretation domains for type structures and method signatures.

2. Types consist of a type structure and a set of methods. Their structure may be recursively defined. The interpretation of tuple-structured types is unusual in the database world and follows the original proposal of Cardelli 1984. It allows one to give a simple set-inclusion semantics to the partial order among type structures ($\leq_{st}$). Methods are defined as a name together with a signature, and a method is interpreted as a function. The interpretation of method signatures allows a simple set-inclusion semantics for the partial order among signatures ($\leq_m$). The subtyping relationship is defined using the ordering $\leq_{st}$ and $\leq_m$. Although our database definition restricts inheritance to simple inheritance, our model deals with multiple inheritance.

3. The $\leq_m$ relation differs from other proposals (Cardelli 1984; Bruce and Wegner 1986) in that it is less restrictive; but the type system is no longer safe (that is, run-time errors may be caused by a syntactically well-typed expression). This decision was mainly motivated by the desire to increase flexibility and by the fact that we are not building a new language but rather an object layer on top of existing programming languages with unsafe type systems, such as C and Lisp.

4. A database is a type system, together with a consistent set of objects (database instances) and a subtyping relationship satisfying some constraints.

We are currently working on some extensions of the model. The first one concerns object naming. Up to now, the only handle that a programmer has had on a object has been through the name of one of its types. So, to retrieve an object of the database, the programmer has to send a message to the extension of the type with some key as argument. Such a problem is introduced by persistency: in standard programming languages, we name objects using temporary variable names. Object names seem to be needed in the model.

A second extension concerns the introduction of variables in the construction of types in order to model genericity (also called parametric polymorphism) of types and methods. Genericity can be simulated with inheritance (Meyer 1986), but in a heavy and nonintuitive way.

A third extension is to increase the modeling power of the model: a list constructor should be included in order to model ordered collections of data (it could be implemented as a recursive tuple type, but we would lose expressiveness).

Finally, in this model, we made the simplifying assumption that the methods are not objects of the model. So methods have to be modeled as first-order functions. It should be interesting to extend the model to treat methods as objects and to allow higher-order methods.

7 Acknowledgements

Most of the ideas presented here were generated with F. Bancilhon. This paper also benefits from the careful reading of S. Abiteboul and our colleagues from Altaïr, in particular D. Excoffier. Thanks also go to P. Buneman, A. Borgida and D. DeWitt for the fruitful discussions we had on this model.

References

Albano, A., L. Cardelli, and R. Orsini. 1985. Galileo: A strongly typed, interactive conceptual language. *ACM TODS* 10(2): 230–61.

Andrews, T., and C. Harris. 1987. Combining language and database advances in an object-oriented development environment. In *Proceedings of the OOPSLA conference.*

Bancilhon, F., and S. Khoshafian. 1986. A calculus for complex objects. In *Proceedings of the ACM PODS conference.*

Bancilhon, F., V. Benzaken, C. Delobel, and F. Vélez. 1987. *The O_2 object manager architecture.* Altaïr technical report no. 14/87.

Banerjee, J., H-T. Chou, J. Garza, W. Kim, D. Woelk, N. Ballou, and H. J. Kim. 1987. Data model issues for object-oriented applications. *ACM TOIS* 5(1): 3–26.

Bruce, K. B., and P. Wegner. 1986. An algebraic model of subtypes in object-oriented languages. SIGPLAN *Notices* 21(40).

Cardelli, L. 1984. A semantics of multiple inheritance. In *Lecture notes in computer science*, Vol. 173. Springer-Verlag.

Copeland, G., and S. Khoshafian. 1986. Object identity. In *Proceedings of the first ACM OOPSLA conference.*

Copeland G., and D. Maier. 1984. Making smalltalk a database system. In *Proceedings of the ACM SIGMOD conference.*

Goldberg, A., and D. Robson. 1983. *Smalltalk 80: The language and its implementation.* Addison-Wesley.

Kuper, G. M., and M. Y. Vardi. 1984. A new approach to database logic. In *Proceedings of the ACM PODS conference.*

Lécluse, C., P. Richard, and F. Vélez. 1988. O_2, an object-oriented data model. In *Proceedings of the ACM SIGMOD conference.*

Meyer, B. 1986. Genericity versus inheritance. In *Proceedings of the OOPSLA conference.*

Nixon, B. et al. 1987. Implementation of a compiler for a semantic data model: Experience with Taxis. In *Proceedings of the ACM SIGMOD conference* .

Zdonik, S. 1984. Object management system concepts. In *Proceedings of the ACM SIGOA conference on office systems.*

CHAPTER 5

Object Identity as a Query-Language Primitive

SERGE ABITEBOUL
PARIS C. KANELLAKIS

Is object relations theory simply a new name for what classical theorists have been doing all along, or is it a fundamentally new system, or an excursion into new realms wholly compatible with classical theory?

From the cover of *Object Relations in Psychoanalytic Theory* (1983), by J. R. Greenberg and S. A. Mitchell

1 Introduction

Object-oriented database systems will, most probably, be the next generation of commercial database systems (see Bancilhon 1988). They are currently the focus of a great deal of experimentation and research (e.g., Maier, Otis, and Purdy 1985; Zdonik 1985; Banerjee et al. 1987; Fishman et al. 1987; Carey, DeWitt, and Vandenberg 1988; Bancilhon et al. 1988). These recent developments in databases are largely based on concepts and software tools from object-oriented programming (e.g., Goldberg and Robson 1983; Bancilhon 1988; Kim 1988). More generally, the integration of programming languages and database systems is an important research activity. For a detailed exposition of the state of the art, see Atkinson and Buneman 1987.

Unfortunately, much of the terminology currently used in object-oriented database systems is overloaded, and experts disagree on the precise meaning of concepts such as object identity, types, inheritance, methods, and encapsulation. Consequently, there has been very little progress on understanding the principles of object-oriented databases. This is in marked contrast with the previous generation of database systems, where the relational model of Codd 1970 provided the basis for many successful implementation efforts and, at the same time, for the development of an elegant and relevant theory (Ullman 1988; Kanellakis 1988).

An attempt is made in this paper to clarify some of the foundations of object-oriented databases, by showing that they are "an excursion into new realms wholly compatible with classical theory." In particular, we demonstrate that the concept of *object identity* (oid) is a powerful programming primitive for database query languages by *having oids as the centerpiece of a data model with a rich type system, inheritance, and a powerful query language*, called Identity Query Language (IQL).

Oids have been part of many data models; for example, they are called *surrogates* in Codd 1979, *l-values* in Kuper and Vardi 1984, and *object identifiers* in Abiteboul and Hull 1987. They have recently been highlighted as an essential part of object-oriented database systems (Khoshafian and Copeland 1986). A variety of reasons have been given for their use; for example, structure sharing, updates (Abiteboul and Hull 1987), or the encoding of cyclicity (Kuper and Vardi 1984). We use oids for the traditional encoding of directed (perhaps cyclic) graphs, but also for the manipulation of sets and for making our query language fully expressive. At an intuitive level, oids are "typed pointers," and IQL is based on a controlled use of "indirection."

The structural part of the object-based model described here is a synthesis of elements that existed in the literature. It generalizes the relational data model (Codd 1970), most complex-object data models, (e.g., Abiteboul and Beeri 1987; Fischer and Thomas 1983; Jaeschke and Schek 1982; Korth, Roth, and Silberschatz 1985; Schek and Scholl 1986; Verso 1986.), and the logical data model (LDM) (Kuper and Vardi 1984; Kuper 1985). It can be viewed as the common upper bound of the models used in Kuper and Vardi 1984 and in Abiteboul and Beeri 1987. The pleasant surprise is that little mathematical simplicity had to be traded off in order to achieve this synthesis. The actual definitions are not much longer than those for the relational model.

The operational part of the data model, the language IQL, is also surprisingly simple in both syntax and semantics. It has three basic properties: (1) it is rule based; (2) it can be statically type checked; and (3) it is complete, in the sense that it expresses exactly all database transformations with certain desirable properties. Let us comment on these three points. The first highlights the declarative nature and mathematical clarity of the programming paradigm used; the second illustrates what is controlled about the use of pointers; and the third involves generalizing the basic theorem of Chandra and Harel 1980 from the relational model to a data model with first-order and recursive types.

As in the relational model, there is a clear separation of the notions of instance and schema. As a consequence, the typing of IQL is similar to that of the query languages in Kuper and Vardi 1984, Abiteboul and Beeri 1987, and Abiteboul and Grumbach 1988; and it corresponds to the strong typing in programming languages. A number of recent language proposals in this area do not have these properties. For example, in Bancilhon and Khoshafian 1986, Maier 1986, and Kifer and Wu 1989 there is no instance-schema separation, and the query languages can be viewed as untyped extensions of Prolog.

We now turn to brief overviews (by example) of the structural and operational parts of our data model. The detailed definitions are in sections 2 and 3, respectively.

1.1 The Structural Part

An *instance* consists of data in the form of (1) a finite set of *o-values*, that is, values containing oids, and (2) a *partial function*, ν, of oids to o-values; this mapping is the essence of the data model. Oids and constants are o-values, but so are finite trees built out of constants and oids via finite tuple or set constructors. We allow ν to be partial in order to model incomplete information; this will be very useful in the operational part of the model. Repeated applications of ν on oids give us *pure values*, which are regular infinite trees.

A *schema* contains the information on the structure of the data allowed in an instance. In current terminology, it contains the names and types of persistent data. We have chosen to include two forms of information: (1) *relation names*, R, for naming relations, that is, finite sets of o-values of the same type $\mathbf{T}(R)$; and (2) *class names*, P, for naming classes, that is, finite sets of oids, where these oids are mapped through ν to o-values of the same type $\mathbf{T}(P)$. An important assumption is that the classes of any legal instance are pairwise disjoint sets of oids.

The type language and interpretation is presented in a somewhat nonstandard fashion for the recursive case (i.e., without a μ constructor). The subtle point is that the recursion is captured by having the types $\mathbf{T}(R)$ and $\mathbf{T}(P)$ refer to base domains or class names.

The dichotomy between relations and classes is the only design decision that slightly complicates the structural part. Its justification is that it greatly simplifies the operational part. Since relations are sets of o-values, duplicates are eliminated from them at a logical level. Thus it is possible to program directly in popular rule-based formalisms, such as Datalog. Relations can name subsets of classes and can function as useful temporaries. Also, this distinction allows a direct generalization of both Kuper and Vardi 1984 and Abiteboul and Beeri 1987.

Example 1. (taken from *Genesis* 4 and 5.) Schema S has class names 1st-gen (for first generation) and 2nd-gen, and relation names Founded-lineage and Ancestor-of-celebrity. Their types are defined as follows:

$\mathbf{T}$(1st-gen) = [`name`: string, `spouse`: 1st-gen, `children`: {2nd-gen}]

$\mathbf{T}$(2nd-gen) = [`name`: string, `occupations`: {string}]

$\mathbf{T}$(Founded-lineage) = 2nd-gen

$\mathbf{T}$(Ancestor-of-celebrity) = [`anc`: 2nd-gen, `desc`: (string $\vee$ [`spouse`: string])]

Note that the types can refer to the base domain *string* and to class names, but not to relation names. Also, note the cyclicity in the type associated with 1st-gen, and the presence of union types.

Now let us come to an instance I of S. To each relation name R, the instance associates a finite set $\rho(R)$ of o-values of the right type. So, strictly speaking, the type of $\rho(R)$ is $\{\mathbf{T}(R)\}$. To each class name P, the instance associates a finite set $\pi(P)$ of oids. Classes are assigned disjoint sets of oids. Partial function ν assigns o-values to the oids of the instance. Each one of these oids has a value of the right type or is undefined. So, again strictly speaking, the type of $\pi(P)$ is $\{P\}$ and the type of $\nu(\pi(P))$ is $\{\mathbf{T}(P)\}$.

In instance I, we denote the oids as *adam, eve, cain, abel, seth,* and *other.* Note that the oid *adam* is distinct from the string "Adam". I is cyclic; one can see this by following the ν mapping of the oids.

π(1st-gen) = {*adam, eve*},
π(2nd-gen) = {*cain, abel, seth, other*},
ρ(Founded-lineage) = {*cain, seth, other*},
ρ(Ancestor-of-celebrity) = {[`anc`: *seth*, `desc`: "Noah"], [`anc`: *cain*,
`desc`: [`spouse`: "Ada"]]},
ν(*adam*) = [`name`: "Adam", `spouse`: *eve*, `children`: {*cain, abel, seth, other*}],
ν(*eve*) = [`name`: "Eve", `spouse`: *adam*, `children`: {*cain, abel, seth, other*}],
ν(*cain*) = [`name`: "Cain", `occupations`: {"farmer", "nomad", "artisan"}],
ν(*abel*) = [`name`: "Abel", `occupations`: {"shepherd"}],
ν(*seth*) = [`name`: "Seth", `occupations`: { }]
ν(*other*) is undefined (*Genesis* is rather vague on this point).

1.2 The Operational Part

The design of IQL was greatly influenced by both the COL language of Abiteboul and Grumbach 1988, for the manipulation of sets, and by the detDL language of Abiteboul and Vianu 1988, for the invention of new oids. The focus was on adding the minimum to Datalog rules in order to obtain an object-based language that can express all computable queries.

In summary, IQL is inflationary Datalog with negation (Kolaitis and Papadimitriou 1987; Abiteboul and Vianu 1988), combined with set/tuple types, invention of new oids, and a weak form of assignment. Inflationary semantics were chosen because of their simplicity and their generality as a mechanism for the flow of control. We feel that to get the same expressive power, similar kinds of extensions would have to be considered, if an algebraic language or a language based on any other paradigm were chosen instead of rules.

The flexibility of a type system, such as the one used here, allows multiple representations of the same information and translation from one representation to another, as illustrated in the next example.

Example 2. Let the input schema be just a relation R with $\mathbf{T}(R) = [A_1\colon D, A_2\colon D]$, and let the output schema be P with $\mathbf{T}(P) = [A_1\colon D, A_2\colon \{P\}]$. The input instance I represents a directed graph G with nodes in D. The desired query is to transform the input instance I into an output instance J representing the same graph. In this new representation every node is associated with an oid, whose value is the pair with the node name for first component and the set of successors for second component. The individual oids used in the output do not matter, only their interrelationships do. Let us examine the computation in IQL in four stages.

During the first stage, we produce (in standard Datalog fashion) the set of node names. We use a relation R_0 with $\mathbf{T}(R_0) = [A_1\colon D]$. As a shorthand, we do not list the attributes A_1, A_2, $A_3, \ldots$ in the rules, but think of them as first argument of relation, second argument of relation, and so on. The following rules are used:

$$R_0(x) \longleftarrow R(x, y)$$
$$R_0(x) \longleftarrow R(y, x)$$

In the second stage, we produce two oids per node, using a semantics in the style of detDL (Abiteboul and Vianu 1988). We use a relation R' with $\mathbf{T}(R') = [A_1\colon D, A_2\colon P, A_3\colon P']$, whose tuples contain oids from class P and from class P'. Class P' is a class with $\mathbf{T}(P') = \{P\}$; that is, its oids have values that are sets of oids from P. The following rule invents two oids for each node, one of which will go into class P and the other into class P':

$$R'(x, p, p') \longleftarrow R_o(x)$$

Note how the variables p and p' in the head are not in the body. When the new oids are invented, they are placed in the proper classes, and they are automatically assigned default values: p is undefined and p' is the empty set (because of the set-valued type of P').

In the third stage, we nest the oids representing nodes in P into sets of successors of a node. This nesting of elements q is done by using the oids p' of P' as temporary names. Each p' is set valued, and its value, noted $\widehat{p'}$, is a set in which the corresponding qs are collected. This dereferencing and assignment to objects in P' simulates the effect of a COL data-function (Abiteboul and Grumbach 1988) or a grouping in LDL (Beeri et al. 1987).

$$\widehat{p'}(q) \longleftarrow R'(x, p, p'), R'(y, q, q'), R(x, y)$$

In the final stage, the nodes of P have been grouped into P', and the connection in R' between x, p, and p' is used to produce the desired result. Note that the value of some node p is a tuple with the name of the node as first component and a set of P-oids as second component. This weak form of assignment is performed only when $\hat{p}$ was undefined (see Abiteboul and Hull 1988). No further changes are made to $\hat{p}$.

$$\hat{p} = [x, \widehat{p'}] \longleftarrow R'(x, p, p')$$

We have presented the program in four separate stages; but one need not separate the stages. It is possible through standard techniques (using negation) to slightly modify the rules given above and to think of them as operating in parallel with inflationary semantics. A useful construct, definable in IQL, is that of sequential composition (;). In fact, only the last rule needs to be modified by separating it with a ";" from the rest of the rules.

1.3 Expressive Power

An important primitive in the language is the invention of oids. This serves a triple goal: (1) objects may be part of the result, and oids must be assigned to them; (2) invented oids are used for set manipulation; and (3) they are also used to obtain completeness in the sense of Chandra and Harel 1980. The reason we use 1 is to code the sharing of structures and cyclic structures. Regarding 2, the rule-based language does not need to have any mechanism such as grouping in LDL (Beeri et al. 1987), data-functions in COL (Abiteboul and Grumbach 1988), or universal quantification (Kuper 1987). Thus one of our contributions is to show that *the manipulation and creation of sets can be realized using only invented oids.*

We examine 3 in detail in section 4. Chandra and Harel's (1980) notion of completeness is adapted to our context. Intuitively, the language must capture all transformations that are recursively enumerable and that preserve some isomorphism properties (Chandra and Harel 1980; Hull 1986). A basic contribution is a completeness result for IQL. *For disjoint input-output schemas, we show that all database transformations are expressible in IQL, up to copy elimination.* In many cases we can express copy elimination in IQL, but it is an open question whether this technical restriction is necessary. Disjoint input-output schemas are sufficient for the study of queries and updates, such as insertions. To obtain completeness for nondisjoint schemas, we need to add noninflationary features to IQL. These are based on the study of deletions in Abiteboul and Vianu 1988. (For other completeness results, see Abiteboul and Vianu 1987, 1988; Hull and Su 1989; Dahlaus and Makowski 1986.)

In section 5 we specialize IQL, using a number of syntactic restrictions. This specialization allows us to discover as IQL *sublanguages most of the popular rule-based formalisms.* We also show that these restrictions can be used to guarantee efficient query evaluation (i.e., with PTIME data-complexity); see also Abiteboul et al. 1989.

In summary, IQL is both a mathematical model of computation with types and (particularly in its range-restricted form IQL^{rr}) a useful high-level query language. Like Prolog, it can be used to manipulate unbounded structured terms; but unlike Prolog it is typed, it has negation, it is a good candidate for conventional database optimizations, and its semantics are not complicated by depth-first search strategies.

The last subsequent sections of our paper deal with two issues that we believe are orthogonal to the structural and the operational parts of our object-based model. These are type inheritance (section 6) and the relationship of object-based to value-based systems (section 7).

1.4 Type Inheritance

In all the development of IQL we make crucial use of a technical condition, the pairwise disjointness of the various classes of an instance. This condition guarantees the soundness and the static typability of IQL programs. However, the removal of this condition is necessary if one is to study *type inheritance* as proposed in Cardelli 1988. With inheritance, the disjointness condition on the classes is replaced by a less restricted condition that, we argue, is natural. We show that, under this limited addition, type inheritance has simple semantics. The union types of our object-based data model are critical in this development. We observe that union types are a more general mechanism for sharing structure than type inheritance. As a result, IQL can be used (at no cost of expressive power) to deal with schemas with inheritance.

1.5 Value-Based versus Object-Based

Oids can be viewed as a syntactic trick to avoid manipulating recursive objects. The same is true for the use of class names in the type syntax. Even with these devices, recursive structures stay in the background in a fundamental way. Object-based systems often allow features such as *equality by value*, which is a precise way of addressing the underlying infinite objects. We illustrate a natural connection with a value-based model founded on regular infinite trees (Courcelle 1983). Our analysis allows us to show that IQL can serve as a language for this model as well. Object identities, in this context, lose all semantic denotation to become purely primitives of the language. This is a nontrivial link between the value-based and object-based approaches (Ullman 1987). A value-based point of view can be used to understand *pure values* (no oids), *pure types* (no classes in the type syntax), and equality by value (as a coercion mechanism).

1.6 Relation to O_2

A major motivation for our work was the study of the formal aspects of the O_2 system (Bancilhon et al. 1988). O_2 is a multilanguage, object-oriented database system (around, for instance, C and Basic). Its structural data model (Lécluse et al. 1988; Lécluse and Richard 1989; see chapter 4) is a subset of the structural data model with inheritance described here. The prototype implementation presented in Bancilhon et al. 1988 does not have union types, but it does have type inheritance. Inheritance in O_2 is constrained by (pure) type compatibility;

this facilitates coercions and the use of inheritance in queries (Lécluse et al. 1988; see chapter 4). Some stand-alone query languages, besides CO_2, are investigated in Bancilhon et al. 1989 (see chapter 11).

Because of space limitations we have omitted proofs and many important details from this chapter; for these see Abiteboul and Kanellakis 1989.

2 An Object-based Data Model

We assume the existence of the following countably infinite and pairwise disjoint sets of atomic elements: (1) *relation names* $\{R_1, R_2, \ldots\}$, (2) *class names* $\{P_1, P_2, \ldots\}$, (3) *attributes* $\{A_1, A_2, \ldots\}$, (4) *constants* $D = \{d_1, d_2, \ldots\}$, and (5) *object identities* or oids $O = \{o_1, o_2, \ldots\}$. Throughout our exposition, we use the generic notation $[A_1\colon \cdots, \ldots, A_k\colon \cdots]$ (where k is a nonnegative integer) for a *tuple* formed using any k distinct attributes $A_1, \ldots, A_k$ (when $k > 0$) and for the *empty tuple* $[\,]$ (when $k = 0$). The empty set is denoted $\emptyset$ or $\{\}$.

Definition 1. The set of *o-values* is the smallest set containing $D \cup O$ and such that if $v_1, \ldots, v_k$ ($k \geq 0$) are o-values then so are $[A_1\colon v_1, \ldots, A_k\colon v_k]$ and $\{v_1, \ldots, v_k\}$.

Definition 2. Let $\mathbf{R}$ be a finite set of relation names and let $\mathbf{P}$ be a finite set of class names.

1. An *o-value assignment* for $\mathbf{R}$ is a function ρ mapping each name in $\mathbf{R}$ to a finite set of o-values.

2. An *oid assignment* for $\mathbf{P}$ is a function π mapping each name in $\mathbf{P}$ to a *finite* set of oids. We call π *disjoint* if $P \neq P'$ implies $\pi(P) \cap \pi(P') = \emptyset$ (where $P, P' \in \mathbf{P}$).

By finiteness, each relation $\rho(R)$ ($R \in \mathbf{R}$) and each class $\pi(P)$ ($P \in \mathbf{P}$) is itself an o-value. Since o-values are defined using finite tupling and finite subsetting, it is possible to represent them using *finite trees* with base, set, and tuple nodes.

The syntax and semantics of types are now defined using a given finite set of class names $\mathbf{P}$ and an oid assignment π for $\mathbf{P}$. The set of *type expressions*, called types($\mathbf{P}$), is given by the following abstract syntax, where τ is a type expression, P an element of $\mathbf{P}$, and $k \geq 0$:

$$\tau = \emptyset \mid D \mid P \mid [A_1\colon \tau, \ldots, A_k\colon \tau] \mid \{\tau\} \mid (\tau \vee \tau) \mid (\tau \wedge \tau)$$

For an oid assignment π, each type expression τ is given a set of o-values as its *interpretation* $[\![\tau]\!]_\pi$, in the following natural fashion:

- $[\![\emptyset]\!]_\pi = \emptyset$
  $[\![D]\!]_\pi = D$
  $[\![P]\!]_\pi = \pi(P)$ (for each $P \in \mathbf{P}$)
- $[\![(\tau_1 \vee \tau_2)]\!]_\pi = [\![\tau_1]\!]_\pi \cup [\![\tau_2]\!]_\pi$
  $[\![(\tau_1 \wedge \tau_2)]\!]_\pi = [\![\tau_1]\!]_\pi \cap [\![\tau_2]\!]_\pi$
- $[\![\{\tau\}]\!]_\pi = \{\{v_1, \ldots, v_j\} \mid j \geq 0,\ v_i \in [\![\tau]\!]_\pi,\ i = 1, \ldots, j\}$
- $[\![[A_1\colon \tau_1, \ldots, A_k\colon \tau_k]]\!]_\pi = \{[A_1\colon v_1, \ldots, A_k\colon v_k] \mid v_i \in [\![\tau_i]\!]_\pi,\ i = 1, \ldots, k\}$

We sometimes represent a type expression τ by its *parse tree*, which has internal nodes labeled by tupling ($\times$), finite set construction ($\star$), union ($\vee$), and intersection ($\wedge$). We say that

- τ is *intersection reduced* if in τ's parse tree no $\wedge$ node is an ancestor of a $\times$, $\star$, or $\vee$ node
- τ is *intersection free* if τ's parse tree has no $\wedge$ node

Two type expressions, τ_1 and τ_2, are *equivalent* (*over disjoint oid assignments*) if for each (disjoint) oid assignment π they have the same interpretations. By easy algebraic manipulation, we have the following proposition.

Proposition 1. For each type expression, there is (1) an intersection-reduced, equivalent type expression, and (2) an intersection-free, equivalent-over-disjoint-oid-assignments type expression.

Most of our analysis uses disjoint oid assignments; therefore, by this proposition, intersection can be eliminated. After these preliminaries, we present schemas and instances and comment on their definitions.

Definition 3. A schema S is a triple $(\mathbf{R}, \mathbf{P}, \mathbf{T})$, where $\mathbf{R}$ is a finite set of relation names, $\mathbf{P}$ is a finite set of class names, and $\mathbf{T}$ is a function from $\mathbf{R} \cup \mathbf{P}$ to types($\mathbf{P}$).

Definition 4. An instance I of schema $(\mathbf{R}, \mathbf{P}, \mathbf{T})$ is a triple (ρ, π, ν), where ρ is an o-value assignment for $\mathbf{R}$, π is a disjoint oid assignment for $\mathbf{P}$, and ν is a partial function from the set of oids $\cup\{\pi(P) \mid P \in \mathbf{P}\}$ to o-values, such that

1. $\rho(R) \subseteq [\![\mathbf{T}(R)]\!]_\pi$, for each $R \in \mathbf{R}$
2. $\nu(\pi(P)) \subseteq [\![\mathbf{T}(P)]\!]_\pi$, for each $P \in \mathbf{P}$
3. ν is total on $\pi(P)$, for each $P \in \mathbf{P}$ with $\mathbf{T}(P) = \{\tau\}$

It is important to note that each oid occurring in I (i.e., in the ranges of ρ, π, and ν) must belong to some $\pi(P)$ (where $P \in \mathbf{P}$). This easily follows from conditions 1 and 2 of the instance definition and from the semantics of types.

Let $I = (\rho, \pi, \nu)$ be an instance of a schema $S = (\mathbf{R}, \mathbf{P}, \mathbf{T})$. A *set-valued* oid in I is an oid belonging to a class P, where $\mathbf{T}(P) = \{\tau\}$ for some τ. Since an oid can only belong to one class, this is a well-defined notion. The information contained in I can be represented in a "logic programming" notation as follows:

$$\begin{aligned}\text{ground-facts}(I) = {} & \{R(v) \mid v \in \rho(R), R \in \mathbf{R}\} \\ & \cup \{P(o) \mid o \in \pi(P), P \in \mathbf{P}\} \\ & \cup \{\hat{o}(v) \mid v \in \nu(o), o \text{ set-valued}\} \\ & \cup \{\hat{o} = v \mid v = \nu(o), o \text{ non-set-valued}\}.\end{aligned}$$

It is easy to see that ground-facts(I) is an alternative representation of I. Recall condition 3 in Definition 4, that ν must be total for set-valued oids. Based on this, we follow the convention that if for some set-valued oid o there is no ground fact $\hat{o}(v)$, then $\nu(o) = \{\}$; and if for some non-set-valued oid o there is no ground fact $\hat{o} = v$, then ν is undefined at o.

We use the following terminology: instances(S) for the set of all instances of schema S; objects(I) for the set of all oids occurring in I; constants(I) for the set of all constants occurring in I.

Remark The structural part of the model generalizes that of many previously introduced data models, for example, the relational model and most complex-object data models, as well as LDM. Incomplete information can be modeled using oids with undefined value. Besides this, there is an important technical reason for having oids with undefined values. The language IQL builds objects in stages, and oids with undefined values are used in the intermediate stages. For o-values of set type $\{\tau\}$, we use $\{\}$ in order to achieve the same effect without any ambiguity.

3 The Identity Query Language

We first need to define projections of schemas and instances, in order to describe the inputs and outputs of programs. A schema $S' = (\mathbf{R}', \mathbf{P}', \mathbf{T}')$ is the *projection* of schema $S = (\mathbf{R}, \mathbf{P}, \mathbf{T})$ if we have $\mathbf{R}' \subseteq \mathbf{R}$, $\mathbf{P}' \subseteq \mathbf{P}$, and $\mathbf{T}'$ is the mapping $\mathbf{T}$ on $\mathbf{R}' \cup \mathbf{P}'$. Given an instance I of S, its projection on S', denoted $I[S']$, is defined in the obvious way and is an instance of S'.

An Identity Query Language (IQL) program $\Gamma(S, S_{\text{in}}, S_{\text{out}})$ consists of rules over schema S and expresses a binary relation on instances. This relation is between instances over the *input schema* S_{in} and instances over the *output schema* S_{out}, where S_{in} and S_{out} are two projections of S. Intuitively, the input to a program is an instance I over S_{in}, the computation of the program defines an instance J over S, and the output is $J[S_{\text{out}}]$.

3.1 Syntax

The syntax for a program $\Gamma(S, S_{\text{in}}, S_{\text{out}})$ is a finite set of rules over $S = (\mathbf{R}, \mathbf{P}, \mathbf{T})$, where terms, literals, and rules are defined as follows.

3.1.1 Terms

Assume that there are pairwise disjoint, countably infinite sets of variables for each τ in types($\mathbf{P}$), and that $k \geq 0$. The *terms* and their types are as follows.

- Each variable x of type τ is a term of type τ.
- Each R in $\mathbf{R}$ is a term of type $\{\mathbf{T}(R)\}$ and each P in $\mathbf{P}$ is a term of type $\{P\}$.
- For each P in $\mathbf{P}$ and variable x of type P, $\widehat{x}$ is a term of type $\mathbf{T}(P)$.
- For $t_1, \ldots, t_k$ terms of type τ, $\{t_1, \ldots, t_k\}$ is a term of type $\{\tau\}$.
- For $t_1, \ldots, t_k$ terms of types $\tau_1, \ldots, \tau_k$, $[A_1\colon t_1, \ldots, A_k\colon t_k]$ is a term of type $[A_1\colon \tau_1, \ldots, A_k\colon \tau_k]$.

3.1.2 Literals

Let t_1 and t_2 be terms; then $t_1 = t_2$ and $t_1(t_2)$ are *positive literals*, and $t_1 \neq t_2$, and $\neg\, t_1(t_2)$ are *negative literals*. A literal (positive or negative) is *typed* when:

- for literals $t_1(t_2)$ or $\neg\, t_1(t_2)$, the term t_1 is of type $\{\tau\}$ and the term t_2 is of type τ
- for literals $t_1 = t_2$ or $t_1 \neq t_2$, the terms t_1 and t_2 are both of type τ

A *fact* is any typed positive literal of the following forms:

- $R(t)$ for R in $\mathbf{R}$, $P(t)$ for P in $\mathbf{P}$
- $\widehat{x}(t)$, where $\widehat{x}$ is of set type, or $\widehat{x} = t$, where $\widehat{x}$ is not of set type

3.1.3 Rules

A *rule* r is an expression of the form $L \longleftarrow L_1, \ldots, L_k$ $(k \geq 0)$, where L is a literal called head(r) and $L_1, \ldots, L_k$ is a set of literals called body(r), and:

1. head(r) is a fact and thus is typed.
2. All literals in body(r) are typed, except for $t_1 = t_2$ with t_1 of type τ and t_2 of type $\tau \vee \tau'$.
3. Each variable occurring in head(r) and not in body(r) has type P for some P in $\mathbf{P}$.

Remark Terms, literals, and rules as defined here are pretty much standard, with some important additions: (1) the typing for R, P, and $\hat{x}$ in terms, (2) the relationship of the syntax of heads or facts with the ground facts of an instance, (3) the more liberal typing of equality in the bodies that will be used to deal with the union of types, and (4) the type restriction for variables in the heads and not in the bodies. We have not included among the terms any constants for the elements of D. This is in order to study a "pure" language as in Chandra and Harel 1980, Abiteboul and Vianu 1988. Constants can be added easily without changing the framework.

3.2 Semantics

The semantics of program $\Gamma(S, S_{\text{in}}, S_{\text{out}})$ is a binary relation $\gamma = \gamma(\Gamma)$ on instances. The pair (I, I') is in γ if I is in instances(S_{in}), I' is in instances(S_{out}), and $I' = J[S_{\text{out}}]$ for some J in instances(S) where (I, J) is in the program's *inflationary fixpoint operator* γ_∞.

We now formally define the inflationary fixpoint operator of a program, using valuations, satisfaction, and the one-step inflationary operator. These notions are straightforward extensions of those used for the semantics of detDL in Abiteboul and Vianu 1988. They are slightly complicated by two aspects of the language: (1) the particular mechanism used for oid invention, and (2) the weak assignment of o-values to non-set-valued oids based on condition (*) below.

3.2.1 Valuations

Given an instance $I = (\rho, \pi, \nu)$, a valuation θ is a partial function from variables to o-values such that if θx is defined and x is of type τ, then (1) θx is in τ's interpretation given π, and (2) the constants occurring in θx are from constants(I). A valuation (given I) can be extended to terms t as θt, defined below. Note that θ is a partial mapping on variables, so θt may be undefined for some variables and some terms.

- $\theta R = \{v \mid R(v)$ in ground-facts$(I)\}$ and $\theta P = \{o \mid P(o)$ in ground-facts$(I)\}$.
- $\theta\hat{x} = \{v \mid$ ground fact $\widehat{\theta x}(v)$ is in ground-facts$(I)\}$, where $\hat{x}$ is of set type.
- $\theta\hat{x} = v$ if ground fact $\widehat{\theta x} = v$ is in ground-facts(I), where $\hat{x}$ is not of set type.
- $\theta\{t_1, \ldots, t_k\} = \{\theta t_1, \ldots, \theta t_k\}, \theta[A_1\colon t_1, \ldots, A_k\colon t_k] = [A_1\colon \theta t_1, \ldots, A_k\colon \theta t_k]$ $(k \geq 0)$.

3.2.2 Satisfaction and Valuation Domain

Let I be an instance and θ a valuation (given I) that must be defined on terms t_1 and t_2.

1. $I \models \theta[t_1(t_2)]$ if $\theta t_2 \in \theta t_1$
2. $I \models \theta[t_1 = t_2]$ if $\theta t_1 = \theta t_2$
3. $I \models \neg\theta[t_1(t_2)]$ if $\theta t_2 \notin \theta t_1$
4. $I \models \theta[t_1 \neq t_2]$ if $\theta t_1 \neq \theta t_2$.

In addition, let r be a rule. We say that $I \models$ body(r) if I *satisfies* ($\models$) all the literals in body(r).

Given a program Γ and an instance I, the *valuation domain*, denoted val-dom (Γ, I), is defined as follows.

$$\text{val-dom}(\Gamma, I) = \{(r, \theta) \mid r \in \Gamma, I \models \theta\text{body}(r)$$

where θ is a valuation exactly on variables in body(r), and there is no extension $\bar{\theta}$ of θ such that $I \models \bar{\theta}$head(r)}. By the extension $\bar{\theta}$ of θ, we mean a valuation (given I) that agrees with θ on the variables occurring in body(r) and that is also defined on the variables occurring in head(r) but not in body(r).

The significance of the valuation domain is that if one thinks of I as the "current state," then each (r, θ) contributes to augmenting I. Thus the valuation domain is the set of valuations that participate in the derivation of new ground facts. New ground facts can be added to I either using old oids and constants, or inventing new oids. Here are the laws governing the invention of oids.

3.2.3 Invention and Valuation Map

A *valuation map* η, for program Γ and instance I, is a function defined on val-dom(Γ, I) with the following properties. For each (r, θ) we have that $\eta(r, \theta)$ is a valuation of the variables in r such that

- if x in body(r), then $\eta(r, \theta)x = \theta x$; that is, $\eta(r, \theta)$ is an extension of θ
- if x in head(r) and not in body(r), then $\eta(r, \theta)x$ is in (O − objects(I)); that is, $\eta(r, \theta)x$ is new (recall that x has type P for some P in $\mathbf{P}$)
- if x in head(r) and not in body(r), and x' in head(r') and not in body(r'), then $r \neq r'$ or $\theta \neq \theta'$ or $x \neq x'$ implies $\eta(r, \theta)x \neq \eta(r', \theta')x'$; that is, all inventions happen in parallel, producing distinct oids for each parallel branch.

3.2.4 Inflationary Operators

Given program Γ, the *inflationary one-step operator* γ_1 is a binary relation on instances. The pair of instances (I, J) is in γ_1 if there exists a valuation map η for Γ and I and:

ground-facts(J) = ground-facts(I) ∪
  {$\eta(r, \theta)$head(r) | for some r and θ subject to condition (∗) below} ∪
  {$P(o)$ | for some r, θ and x of type P, $o = \eta(r, \theta)x$ and o is invented}

(∗) Let o be non-set-valued. If $\widehat{o}$ is undefined in I and a single new ground fact $\widehat{o} = v$ is derived, then it is added to ground-facts(J). If $\widehat{o}$ is defined in I or if two distinct new facts $\widehat{o} = v$ and $\widehat{o} = v'$ are derived, then the new derived ground facts about $\widehat{o}$ are ignored.

Given program Γ, its inflationary fixpoint operator γ_∞ is a binary relation on instances. The pair of instances (I, J) is in γ_∞ if there exists a finite sequence $I_0 = I, \ldots, I_i, \ldots, I_n = J$ with (1) for all $i > 0$ we have $(I_{i-1}, I_i) \in \gamma_1$, and (2) for all J' if $(J, J') \in \gamma_1$ then $J = J'$.

3.2.5 A Determinate Naive Inflationary Evaluator

It is possible to have nonterminating computations in IQL; see condition 2 just above. Also, because of the quantification over valuation maps η in the definition of γ_1, the binary relation γ_1 contains (I, J) pairs for all possible legal choices of invented oids. It follows that there could be many J associated to a single instance I, as pairs (I, J) in γ. However, as we shall see in theorem 1, all these J are isomorphic to each other. It is easy to define an algorithm for evaluating IQL programs, based on the semantics above. This *naive inflationary evaluator* proceeds in iterations: in each iteration it determines the valuation domain and picks a valuation map; it stops if no ground fact is added. The output is independent of the choice of valuation map made by this evaluator, up to the renaming of invented oids.

In IQL, one goal of type checking is to guarantee the soundness of programs. In other words, type checking is used to guarantee that the result is a correct instance. Another goal is to increase the *efficiency of evaluation*, for example, to decrease the size of the valuation domain and the cost of computing it. This latter use is a major justification for the separate notions of schema and instance in data models. The schema contains the type information that is used to make retrieval efficient. It is easy to see that IQL programs can be statically type checked. There is one exception: the treatment of ground facts $\widehat{o} = v$ involves some checking during the evaluation; see condition (∗) in the definition of the one-step inflationary operator. However, this exception does not invalidate our claim. The dynamic check performed here is of very small cost and does not entail checking the whole type. We check only if an oid has a value or is undefined. The cost is less even than that of recording the derived facts. Unfortunately, statically deciding if this inexpensive check will be used in some evaluations is not recursive; see Abiteboul and Hull 1988.

3.3 Shorthands and Examples

We accept $R(t_1, \ldots, t_k)$ as an alternative notation for $R([A_1\colon t_1, \ldots, A_k\colon t_k])$, when some implicit ordering on the attributes is understood. It is now clear that each *Datalog* program can be viewed as a valid IQL program on a relational schema, and that its Datalog and IQL semantics are identical. The same applies to *Datalog with negation and inflationary semantics.*

Continuing with relational schemas, other relational languages can be viewed as IQL sublanguages, for example, detDL (Abiteboul and Vianu 1988). The differences between detDL and IQL restricted to relations are (1) slightly different semantics for valuation domains, and (2) invented constants in detDL versus invented oids in IQL. However, it is very simple to simulate detDL in IQL.

It is shown in Abiteboul and Vianu 1988 that control mechanisms such as *composition*, *if-then-else*, and *while-statements* can be simulated in detDL (using negation and inflationary semantics). These mechanisms can now be used as shorthands. In particular, we use ";" to denote composition. The transformation expressed by an IQL program $\Gamma_1;\Gamma_2$ is the composition of the transformations expressed by Γ_1 and Γ_2. Using composition, it is easy to see that *relational calculus* queries and *Datalog with stratified negation* are expressible in IQL almost verbatim.

Now consider complex objects. The best-known operations on complex objects are *nest* and *unnest*. Nest/unnest in IQL resembles the expression of these operations in the language COL (Abiteboul and Grumbach 1988; Abiteboul et al. 1989). The next example shows the IQL realization. For greater clarity we use capital letters, such as X or Y for set variables.

Example 3. Let $(\mathbf{R},\mathbf{P},\mathbf{T})$ be a schema, $R_1, R_2, R_3 \in \mathbf{R}$, $\mathbf{T}(R_1) = \mathbf{T}(R_3) = [A_1\colon D, A_2\colon \{D\}]$, and $\mathbf{T}(R_2) = [A_1\colon D, A_2\colon D]$. We want to unnest R_1 into R_2, and then nest R_2 into R_3. For unnesting, use the single rule

$$R_2(x,y) \longleftarrow R_1(x,Y), Y(y)$$

For nesting, use an auxiliary class P associated with $\mathbf{T}(P) = \{D\}$, and auxiliary relations R_4 and R_5 associated with $\mathbf{T}(R_4) = D$, $\mathbf{T}(R_5) = [A_1\colon D, A_2\colon P]$. Nesting is realized with $\Gamma_1;\Gamma_2$, where Γ_1 is

$$R_4(x) \longleftarrow R_2(x,y)$$
$$R_5(x,z) \longleftarrow R_4(x)$$
$$\hat{z}(y) \longleftarrow R_2(x,y), R_5(x,z)$$

and Γ_2 is

$$R_3(x,\hat{z}) \longleftarrow R_5(x,z)$$

Γ_1 creates one oid z per x in the A_1-column of R_2. The value of the oid z is the set of values paired to its x in the A_2-column of R_2. The program Γ_2 starts after Γ_1 completes and constructs the result. Note how attributes were omitted from the rules, without any ambiguity.

No invention is required in COL to perform the nesting: it is realized using *data functions.* A data function can be viewed as a *parametrized relation* and is therefore based on a more elaborate concept than the relations in IQL. However, data functions can be simulated in IQL using invented oids. We chose here to have oid invention, since such a feature serves many other purposes as well in our context.

One can show that each COL query can be computed using an IQL program. The proof is easy, given the above programs for nest/unnest. As a consequence, all *algebraic operations on complex objects* of Fischer and Thomas 1983, Jaeschke and Schek 1982, Schek and Scholl 1986, and Abiteboul and Beeri 1987, and the calculus queries of Abiteboul and Beeri 1987, and Korth, Roth, and Silberschatz 1985 are expressible in IQL. Also, it is easy to show that all calculus and algebra queries in LDM can be simulated in IQL.

One important operation found in the algebra for LDM and the algebra for complex-objects of Abiteboul and Beeri 1987 is *powerset.* This operation is expensive: it is exponential in the input size. Indeed, we will emphasize sublanguages of IQL that cannot express the powerset but can express important classes of queries evaluable in the time polynomial in the input instance size. The powerset operation is considered in the next example, which provides all the necessary guidelines for the restrictions imposed on IQL to obtain efficiently evaluable sublanguages.

Example 4. First suppose that the input consists of a single relation R of type D, and the output of a single relation R_1 of type $\{D\}$. The powerset of R is computed in R_1 by

$$R_1(X) \longleftarrow X = X$$

where X is a variable of type $\{D\}$. Indeed, since R is the single input relation, by the definition of valuation (given I) the variable X will range only over the subsets of R, and R_1 will contain the powerset of R.

The obvious problem is that the variable X is not *range restricted* in the program (see section 5 for a formalization of range restriction). However, the powerset can also be computed in a range-restricted manner using oids. Let R and R_1 be the input and output as above. We also use a class P with type $\{D\}$, and an auxiliary relation R_2 with type $[A_1\colon \{D\}, A_2\colon \{D\}, A_3\colon P]$.

The powerset program has the following rules:

$$\begin{aligned}
&R_1(\{\}) \longleftarrow \\
&R_1(\{x\}) \longleftarrow R(x) \\
&R_2(X, Y, z) \longleftarrow R_1(X), R_1(Y) \\
&\widehat{z}(x) \longleftarrow R_2(X, Y, z), X(x) \\
&\widehat{z}(y) \longleftarrow R_2(X, Y, z), Y(y) \\
&R_1(\widehat{z}) \longleftarrow P(z)
\end{aligned}$$

One can check that this computes the powerset in a constructive way. Suppose that relation R is $\{d_1, d_2, d_3\}$. Then $\{\}$, $\{d_1\}$, $\{d_2\}$, and $\{d_3\}$ are first obtained, then $\{d_1, d_2\}$, $\{d_2, d_3\}$, and so on. In this computation some subsets are obviously derived more than once.

Note that in this second way of computing the powerset, invention of oids occurs in a "loop." Such recursion with invention of oids may be the cause of nonterminating computations. For instance, let R_3 be a relation with $\mathbf{T}(R_3) = [A_1\colon P, A_2\colon P]$. Then the rule

$$R_3(y,z) \longleftarrow R_3(x,y)$$

may cause the nontermination of the computation.

As illustrated by the graph example of section 1.2, IQL also allows the creation of objects and the sharing of objects. We refer to that example for many features of IQL, such as Datalog rules, set manipulation, invention of oids bounded by a polynomial in the size of the input, composition, and weak assignment to nonset oids.

The union of types is treated in IQL in a special fashion, based on allowing the use of a less constrained typing condition in the rule bodies. This condition (2 in the syntax of rules) can be viewed as equality modulo *coercion*. The following is an example involving union types.

Example 5. Consider the two schemas S and S':

- S has only one class P, with $\mathbf{T}(P) = P \vee [A_1\colon P, A_2\colon P]$.
- S' has only one class P', with $\mathbf{T}'(P') = [A_1\colon \{P'\}, A_2\colon \{[A_1\colon P', A_2\colon P']\}]$.

We use one temporary relation R, with $\mathbf{T}(R) = [A_1\colon P, A_2\colon P']$; and we omit the attributes when there is no ambiguity.

Instances over S can be "losslessly" transformed to S' instances using these rules:

$$R(x,x') \longleftarrow P(x)$$
$$\widehat{x'} = [\{y'\},\emptyset] \longleftarrow R(x,x'), R(y,y'), y = \hat{x}$$
$$\widehat{x'} = [\emptyset,\{[y',z']\}] \longleftarrow R(x,x'), R(y,y'), R(z,z'), [y,z] = \hat{x}$$

An "inverse" mapping from S' to S can be realized using these rules:

$$R(x,x') \longleftarrow P'(x')$$
$$\hat{x} = w \longleftarrow R(x,x'), R(y,y'), y = w, \widehat{x'} = [\{y'\},\emptyset]$$
$$\hat{x} = w \longleftarrow R(x,x'), R(y,y'), R(z,z'), [y,z] = w, \widehat{x'} = [\emptyset,\{[y',z']\}]$$

Note the use of coercions in the bodies. For instance, in the the first program, $\hat{x}$ is of type $P \vee [A_1\colon P, A_2\colon P]$, whereas y and z are of type P. In the second program, w has type $P \vee [A_1\colon P, A_2\colon P]$, different from the types of y and $[y,z]$. We use w in order to have typed heads.

4 IQL Expressibility

We call an isomorphism h on $D \cup O$, which maps D to D and O to O, a DO-isomorphism. Clearly, each such isomorphism can be extended to o-values and instances. An *O-isomorphism* is an isomorphism on O. Each O-isomorphism can be viewed as a DO-isomorphism by extending it with $hd = d$ for each d in D. Thus an O-isomorphism can be viewed as an isomorphism over o-values and instances.

The following definition states the four conditions that a binary relation on instances should satisfy in order to qualify as a db-transformation. The first three conditions are standard and capture *well-typedness*, *effective computability*, and *genericity*. The justification for genericity is that a query language should not "interpret" atomic elements such as constants and oids (see Chandra and Harel 1980 and Hull 1986). The fourth condition is new and expresses a form of *functionality*.

Definition 5. A binary relation γ on instances is a *db-transformation* if

1. $\exists\ S, S'$ such that $\gamma \subseteq$ instances(S) $\times$ instances(S').
2. γ is recursively enumerable.
3. h is a DO-isomorphism and $(I, J) \in \gamma$ imply that $(hI, hJ) \in \gamma$.
4. $(I, J_1), (I, J_2) \in \gamma$ imply that there exists an O-isomorphism h' such that $h'J_1 = J_2$.

It follows from conditions 3 and 4 that no new constants can appear in the output. More precisely:

If (I, J) is in a db-transformation γ, then constants(J) $\subseteq$ constants(I).

In contrast, the kind of functionality enforced by condition 4 allows the presence of oids in the output that were not in the input. This is a significant addition to the frameworks of Abiteboul and Vianu 1988, and Chandra and Harel 1980. It is important to be able to create new oids in the output if one wishes to manipulate in a general fashion the types available in the data model.

Another intuition formalized by condition 4 is that the oids as atomic elements are irrelevant; only their interrelationships matter. Consider the IQL example of section 1.2. The oids of the nodes of the output instance do not matter: if two instances are O-isomorphic, they contain the same information.

We now prove a soundness theorem: that IQL programs define only db-transformations. It follows that IQL programs are determinate in the sense of condition 4. Note that the disjointness of oid assignments is important to guarantee soundness (see Abiteboul and Kanellakis 1989).

Theorem 1. The semantics of an IQL program is a db-transformation.

This soundness theorem raises a natural completeness question: are all db-transformations expressible in IQL? Consider a relation name R common in both input and output schemas. A problem is that the inflationary semantics of IQL do not allow deleting ground facts $R(v)$ from the input, even if the db-transformation we are trying to compute specifies that they are not in the output.

Following Abiteboul and Vianu 1987, 1988, we first consider only disjoint input-output schemas. These suffice for a general study of database *queries* and *insertions*. The disjoint input-output db-transformations (*dio-transformations*) are all db-transformations

$$\gamma \subseteq \text{instances}(S_{\text{in}}) \times \text{instances}(S_{\text{out}})$$

where for some schema S with disjoint projections S_{in} and S_{out} and for every $(I, J) \in \gamma$ we have that I and J are projections of *one* instance of S on S_{in} and S_{out}.

For *relational* schemas, the dio-transformations (by definition) are the same as the graphs of computable queries as defined in Chandra and Harel 1980. For *acceptors* (programs that answer *yes*, *no*, or *loop for ever*) we use the set of *yes/no db-transformations*: these are all db-transformations with an output schema consisting of a single relation of type the empty tuple.

Proposition 2. Each dio-transformation for relational schemas is the semantics of some IQL program.

Proposition 3. Each yes/no db-transformation is the semantics of some IQL program.

For dio-transformations, we generalize proposition 3 to obtain completeness of IQL up to copy elimination. We show that given a dio-transformation γ, there is an IQL program which on input I_0 constructs finitely many copies of images of I_0 through γ. These copies are guaranteed to be identical up to renaming of the oids and are distinguishable from each other (but we don't know whether one of these copies can be selected by an IQL program).

One may attempt a direct analogy between Turing Machines (TMs) and IQL programs. A function is TM computable iff its graph is TM acceptable. To show this, one uses the fact that a TM can easily enumerate the integers. The enumeration of instances in IQL is not as simple. So, unfortunately, from the fact that yes/no db-transformations are expressible one cannot directly derive the fact that arbitrary db-transformations can be computed by IQL programs (as one can for TMs). This is the reason for the technical restriction of "up to copy elimination," which we formalize below. Note how the different copies are separated by using distinct sets of oids, given explicitely in a new relation.

Definition 6. Let S be a schema with classes $\{P_1, \ldots P_n\}$, and let I be an instance of S. We define $\bar{S}$, the *schema for copies* of S by augmenting S with a single new relation name $\bar{R}$ with associated type $\{P_1 \vee \ldots \vee P_n\}$. An instance $\bar{I}$ of $\bar{S}$ is an instance with copies of I if there are O-isomorphic copies $I_1, \ldots, I_n$ of I such that:

1. ground-facts$(\bar{I}[S])$ = ground-facts$(I_1) \cup \ldots \cup$ ground-facts(I_n).

2. $\bar{I}(\bar{R}) = \{objects(I_1), \ldots, objects(I_n)\}$, where objects($I_i$) ($i = 1, \ldots, n$) are pairwise disjoint.

We say that binary relation γ is binary relation $\bar{\gamma}$ *up to copy* when we have:

- If $(I_0, I) \in \gamma$, then for some $\bar{I}$, $(I_0, \bar{I}) \in \bar{\gamma}$, and $\bar{I}$ is an instance with copies of I.
- If $(I_0, \bar{I}) \in \bar{\gamma}$, then for some I, $(I_0, I) \in \gamma$, and $\bar{I}$ is an instance with copies of I.

We now come to the principal result of this section.

Theorem 2. Each dio-transformation is the semantics of some IQL program up to copy elimination.

Is copy elimination expressible in IQL? A positive answer would imply the conjecture that each dio-transformation is the semantics of some IQL program. In many important cases, this conjecture is true. Natural programs, such as the graph example of section 1.2 or the examples from section 3, do not use copy elimination. More specifically, we can show the following propositions.

Proposition 4. If γ is a dio-transformation, such that the output schema contains no class, then γ is the semantics of some IQL program. In particular, each query in the calculus/algebra of the complex-objects model of Abiteboul and Beeri 1987 is expressible in IQL.

Proposition 5. If γ is a dio-transformation, such that D does not occur in the output schema, then γ is the semantics of some IQL program.

Proposition 6. Each query in the calculus/algebra of the Logical Data Model of Kuper and Vardi 1984 is the semantics of some IQL program.

As in Abiteboul and Vianu 1988, one can introduce *nondeterministic* dio-transformations and a nondeterministic variant of IQL that expresses all of them. (With nondeterminism, selection of one out of a set of copies is easy.) Also, one can in the style of Abiteboul and Vianu 1988 consider "ordered databases" and prove completeness of IQL in this setting.

IQL has inflationary semantics and is a simple and elegant model for queries and insertions. However, because of monotonicity it cannot express deletions of ground facts from the input. Let IQL* be the language obtained by allowing negative facts in heads of rules and interpreting them as *deletions* in the style of the "*" languages of Abiteboul and Vianu 1988. IQL* allows manipulation of arbitrary input-output schemas. All the propositions, remarks, and open questions above can be extended analogously, from disjoint to nondisjoint input-output schemas.

5 The Sublanguages of IQL

A major strength of IQL is that it contains, as syntactically defined sublanguages, many popular, declarative database query formalisms. For example, with small modifications of the syntax: on relations, we can identify Datalog, relational calculus, and Datalog with negation (stratified or inflationary); on complex objects, we can identify the restricted calculus of Abiteboul and Beeri 1987 and COL with range restriction (Abiteboul et al. 1989). All these sublanguages have PTIME *data complexity*: *each fixed program can be evaluated in time that is polynomial in the input instance size.* (The size of an instance is assumed to be the size of some standard encoding of the instance.)

In this section, we use syntactic conditions to obtain the sublanguages IQL^{rr} and IQL^{pr}, where $\text{IQL}^{\text{rr}} \subset \text{IQL}^{\text{pr}} \subset \text{IQL}$. These sublanguages have PTIME data complexity. Also, all the above popular query formalisms are contained in IQL^{pr}. The containment is proper, because many queries on cyclic schemas (such as the graph example from section 1.2) are IQL^{rr} expressible. We first consider the PTIME-restricted language.

Definition 7. A program is *PTIME restricted* if all its rules are PTIME restricted. A rule is PTIME restricted if all variables occurring in its body are PTIME restricted. Let r be a rule.

1. Each variable of a type without the set constructor is PTIME restricted in r.

2. If all variables in t_1 are PTIME restricted and $t_1(t_2)$, $t_1 = t_2$, $t_2 = t_1$ is a positive literal in the body of r, then all variables in t_2 are also PTIME restricted.

Our further choices are determined by the features of the second example in section 3.3: (a) variables must be restricted, and (b) invention must be controlled. First, a program is *invention-free* if no variable occurs in the head and not in the body of a rule.

Let Γ be an IQL program, such that the leftmost symbol of each rule is a relation name. Γ is *recursion-free* if the directed graph $G(\Gamma)$ is acyclic. The nodes of $G(\Gamma)$ are the relation and class names of the program; there is an arc in $G(\Gamma)$ from a node n to a node n' if in some rule r: (1) n is a relation name R or a class name P occurring in body(r); or n is a class name P and a variable of type P occurs in body(r); and (2) n' is the leftmost symbol R' in the rule, or n' is some class name P' occurring in $\mathbf{T}(R')$, where R' is the leftmost symbol of the rule.

The following definition is based on invention freedom, recursion freedom, and composition (;).

Definition 8. An IQL^{pr} program Γ is an IQL program if it is of the form $\Gamma_1; \ldots; \Gamma_k$, where for each i in $1 \ldots k$, Γ_i is PTIME restricted and is either recursion-free or invention-free.

We could have chosen more involved criteria. The rationale for our definition is that it is simple, it subsumes most popular query languages, and it suffices to show the principal result of this section.

Theorem 3. Each query expressed by an $\mathrm{IQL}^{\mathrm{pr}}$ program can be answered in time polynomial in the size of the input instance.

In $\mathrm{IQL}^{\mathrm{pr}}$ we have guaranteed program termination and polynomial data-complexity. From a practical standpoint this is not enough. It is also critical to limit the possible valuations of variables to o-values that already exist in the database—because searching over type interpretations built from the constants in the database is in theory polynomial, but in practice it is too expensive. This additional requirement leads naturally to the definition of range restriction and to $\mathrm{IQL}^{\mathrm{rr}}$, where statement 1 of definition 7 is replaced by "Each variable of type P for some class P is range-restricted."

6 Type Inheritance

In this section, we add type inheritance to our object-based data model. Let us extend the definition of schema as follows.

Definition 9. A schema S is a quadruple $(\mathbf{R}, \mathbf{P}, \mathbf{T}, \leq)$, where $\mathbf{R}$ is a finite set of relation names, $\mathbf{P}$ is a finite set of class names, $\mathbf{T}$ is a function from $\mathbf{R} \cup \mathbf{P}$ to types($\mathbf{P}$), and $\leq$ is a partial order on $\mathbf{P}$ called an *isa hierarchy*.

A common use of type inheritance is to specify, by the addition of an isa hierarchy to the schema, that certain classes share certain structural properties. It is possible to express this intended meaning of isa statements, by schemas and instances without isa. The main reason is the inclusion of union types in our type system. So, given union types, one can think of isa as a convenient shorthand.

We proceed in two steps. First, we reexamine one of our basic assumptions, namely, *the disjointness of oid assignments.*

Inherited oid assignments. To preserve static type-checking, it seems necessary to know a priori what type of result we get at evaluation time, when we valuate terms such as $\hat{x}$. This means static knowledge of which classes oids can belong to. We formalize this static knowledge using a common engineering intuition: oids are created in a single class and automatically belong to the ancestors of this class in the isa hierarchy.

Definition 10. Let $\mathbf{P}$ be a set of class names and $\leq$ a partial order on $\mathbf{P}$. An *inherited oid assignment* $\bar{\pi}$ for $\mathbf{P}$ is an oid assignment for which there exists a disjoint oid assignment π such that for each P in $\mathbf{P}$:

$$\bar{\pi}(P) = \cup\{\pi(P') \mid P' \in \mathbf{P}, P' \leq P\}$$

At this point, we must deal with the meaning of $\mathbf{T}$ (the types in the schema), given inherited oid assignments. Let us first examine a frequently quoted example.

Example 6. Let our schema contain four classes:

$P_1 \equiv$ Person, with $\mathbf{T}(P_1) = [\texttt{name}\colon D]$

$P_2 \equiv$ Student, with $\mathbf{T}(P_2) = [\texttt{name}\colon D, \texttt{course-taken}\colon D]$

$P_3 \equiv$ Instructor, with $\mathbf{T}(P_3) = [\texttt{name}\colon D, \texttt{course-taught}\colon D]$

$P_4 \equiv$ TA, with $\mathbf{T}(P_4) = [\texttt{name}\colon D, \texttt{course-taught}\colon D, \texttt{course-taken}\colon D]$

With a disjoint oid assignment, we can capture the meaning of TAs, that is, teaching assistants (these are π(TA)), of instructors who are not TAs (these are π(Instructor)), and so on. But we would also like to say that every TA isa Student and Instructor, every Student isa Person, and every Instructor isa Person. This is expressed by the partial order $P_4 \leq P_3$, $P_4 \leq P_2$, $P_3 \leq P_1$, $P_2 \leq P_1$, and it can be realized by using the inherited oid assignment $\bar{\pi}$.

Now the type information in $\mathbf{T}$ must apply to $\bar{\pi}$ and not to π. For instance, if R is a relation of type $[A_1\colon \text{Student}, A_2\colon \text{Instructor}]$, we expect to find in R tuples $[o, o']$, where o is in π(Student) and o' in π(Instructor), but also such tuples with o in π(TA) and o' in π(Instructor), and so on.

In this example, there is no restriction on the types of classes related via the "isa" relationship; isa and types are declared separately and independently. Given $\bar{\pi}$, the type interpretations (as defined in section 2) determine what are the possible o-values. Thus instances can be defined by a single modification of definition 4: in conditions 1 and 2 use:

$$[\![\mathbf{T}(\cdot)]\!]_{\bar{\pi}} \quad \text{instead of} \quad [\![\mathbf{T}(\cdot)]\!]_{\pi}$$

where $\bar{\pi}$ is the oid assignment inherited from π.

Wherever $\bar{\pi}(P)$ appears in the modified definition it can be replaced by $\cup\{\pi(P') \mid P' \leq P\}$. This corresponds to replacing, in the types, a class P by the disjunction of its "smaller-or-equal" classes; for example, replacing Student by Student $\vee$ TA.

$*$-Interpretations. The purpose of type inheritance is to specify structure sharing. So we cannot reasonably assume that isa and types are declared separately and independently. Interestingly, their interaction does not significantly complicate things, and it can be captured using a $*$-interpretation in the style of Cardelli 1988: in all cases, replace $[\![\ldots]\!]_{\pi}$ by $[\![\ldots]\!]_{\pi*}$ except for tuples where

$$\begin{aligned}
&[\![[A_1\colon \tau_1, \ldots, A_k\colon \tau_k]]\!]_{\pi*} \\
&\quad = \{[A_1\colon v_1, \ldots, A_k\colon v_k, A_{k+1}\colon v_{k+1}, \ldots, A_l\colon v_l] \mid \\
&\qquad\quad \text{for some } A_{k+1}, \ldots, A_l,\ (l \geq k) \text{ distinct from } A_1, \ldots, A_k \\
&\qquad\quad \text{and } v_i \in [\![\tau_i]\!]_{\pi*},\ i = 1, \ldots, k\}.
\end{aligned}$$

Observe that, in this definition, $v_{k+1}, \ldots, v_l$ are o-values of totally unconstrained types. One can show an analogue to proposition 1:

Proposition 7. For each type expression, there is (1) an intersection-reduced, $*$-equivalent type expression, and (2) an intersection-free, $*$-equivalent-over-disjoint-oid-assignments type expression.

Let us come back to the canonical example.

Example 7. A more succinct specification of the schema of example 6 is:

Person has-type $\tau_1 = [\texttt{name}: D]$

Student has-type $\tau_2 = [\texttt{course-taken}: D]$ and Student isa Person

Instructor has-type $\tau_3 = [\texttt{course-taught}: D]$ and Instructor isa Person

TA isa Student and TA isa Instructor.

The intention here is to have the isa hierarchy force a certain structural similarity. For this, interpret the types using $*$-interpretations of types given $\bar{\pi}$, where $\bar{\pi}$ is the inherited oid assignment. The type of Person is τ_1, the type of Student is $\tau_1 \wedge \tau_2$, the type of Instructor is $\tau_1 \wedge \tau_3$, and the type of TA is $\tau_1 \wedge \tau_2 \wedge \tau_3$. Using proposition 7, we can eliminate the intersection and get the type expressions explicitly given in the previous example.

Clearly, the $*$-interpretation forces some compatibility of the types of classes connected via isa. Otherwise, their conjunction may end up being the empty type or some trivial type.

Following through with this kind of approach, one can find a serious drawback with exclusive use of $*$-interpretations. It leads to legal instances with attributes that do not appear in the schema. Thus there is insufficient information in the schema to describe the instance and, consequently, little hope of finding a complete query language according to our requirements.

This suggests a blend of the two possibilities. One would like to use the starred interpretation to force inheritance of structure. But one would also like to use the unstarred interpretation on the disjoint oid assignment π that generates $\bar{\pi}$. For instance, the value of an object in $\pi(\text{TA})$ in example 6 should have exactly type $[\texttt{name}: D, \texttt{course-taught}: D, \texttt{course-taken}: D]$, and no other attributes.

In this spirit, let P be in $\mathbf{P}$. We construct τ_P such that

$$[\![\tau_P]\!]_{\bar{\pi}*} = \cap \{[\![\mathbf{T}(P')]\!]_{\bar{\pi}*} \mid P \leq P'\}.$$

Such a type expression τ_P exists by proposition 7. Now we can put everything together in a new definition of instance, which gives meaning to isas.

Definition 11. An instance I of schema $(\mathbf{R}, \mathbf{P}, \mathbf{T}, \leq)$ is a triple (ρ, π, ν), where ρ is an o-value assignment for $\mathbf{R}$, π is a disjoint oid assignment for $\mathbf{P}$, and ν is a partial function from the set $\cup\{\pi(P) \mid P \in \mathbf{P}\}$ to o-values, such that

1. $\rho(R) \subseteq [\![\mathbf{T}(R)]\!]_{\bar{\pi}}$ (for each $R \in \mathbf{R}$)
2. $\nu(\pi(P)) \subseteq [\![\tau_P]\!]_{\bar{\pi}}$ (for each P in $\mathbf{P}$)
3. if $\mathbf{T}(P) = \{\tau\}$, then ν is total on $\pi(P)$ (for each $P \in \mathbf{P}$)

where $\bar{\pi}$ is the oid assignment inherited from π.

The language IQL can now be used with no modification.

7 A Value-based Data Model

In this section we introduce a value-based data model and relate it to the object-based model of the previous sections. We use a simplified framework: only class names $\mathbf{P}$ and v-types($\mathbf{P}$). The set v-types($\mathbf{P}$) consists of all type expressions in types($\mathbf{P}$) constructed without $\vee$, $\wedge$, and $\emptyset$; that is, we assume only base, finite set, and finite tuple construction.

The value-based schemas have the form $(\mathbf{P}, \mathbf{T})$ and should be compared to object-based schemas of the form $(\emptyset, \mathbf{P}, \mathbf{T})$. For simplicity both are denoted $(\mathbf{P}, \mathbf{T})$. We also limit consideration to IQL programs from input schema S to output schema S', where S and S' are disjoint value-based schemas. We use IQL^v for this subset of IQL.

The *pure values* that are considered here can be defined as trees, in the style of o-value representations. They have the same kinds of nodes (base, finite set, finite tuple) but there are two differences: (1) no oids occur in them; and (2) they can have infinite depth. These *infinite trees* are variants of the infinite trees in Courcelle 1983. For example, the set nodes do not have a fixed arity and the order of their children is not significant, whereas all functions in Courcelle 1983 do have a fixed arity. However, using the fact that the sets that are considered are finite, it is an easy but tedious exercise to show that the properties of the infinite trees in Courcelle 1983 also hold for pure-value infinite trees.

The assignments and type interpretations of section 2 have analogues in the value-based case. Given a set of class names $\mathbf{P}$, a *finite assignment* I for $\mathbf{P}$ is a function from $\mathbf{P}$ to finite sets of pure values. Each finite assignment I defines a function from v-types($\mathbf{P}$) to sets of pure values, called the type *interpretation* given I.

This function $[\![\cdot]\!]_I$ is analogous to $[\![\cdot]\!]_\pi$ of section 2 (i.e., $[\![P]\!]_I = I(P)$, for each P, and $[\![\cdot]\!]_I$ extends to v-types($\mathbf{P}$) by structural induction).

Definition 12. A *v-schema* S is a pair $(\mathbf{P}, \mathbf{T})$, where $\mathbf{P}$ is a finite set of class names and $\mathbf{T}$ is a function from $\mathbf{P}$ to v-types($\mathbf{P}$) such that $(*)$ for each $P \in \mathbf{P}$, $\mathbf{T}(P)$ is not a class name. A v-instance I over $(\mathbf{P}, \mathbf{T})$ is a finite assignment for $\mathbf{P}$ such that $I(P) \subseteq [\![\mathbf{T}(P)]\!]_I$ for each $P \in \mathbf{P}$.

Note the simplicity of these definitions, which generalize complex-object data models by adding cyclicity to both schemas and instances. The technical condition $(*)$ on the $\mathbf{T}$ of a v-schema is imposed to avoid pathological cases, such as $\mathbf{T}(P_1) = P_2$, which does not specify any structure for P_1.

A regular tree is a tree with a finite number of subtrees (Courcelle 1983). An important consequence of the finiteness of assignments is that each value occurring in a v-instance is a regular tree.

Proposition 8. Each pure value occurring in a v-instance is a regular tree.

Now let us compare object-based and value-based instances over schema $(\mathbf{P}, \mathbf{T})$. It is simple to define translations of pure values into objects and vice versa: φ can be thought of as producing o-values by adding oids, and ψ as producing pure values by losing oids. In the absence of union types, we can show that these translations preserve information in the following sense.

Proposition 9. For each v-instance I, $\psi\varphi I = I$.

Propositions 8 and 9 have some interesting consequences for computable queries in the value-based model. Regularity guarantees the existence of a simple encoding of v-instances on Turing-machine tapes, so it is possible to compute. Genericity is defined in the usual way. A *vdio-transformation* is a transformation from v-instances over a v-schema S to v-instances over a disjoint v-schema S', which is recursively enumerable and generic. A language is *vdio-complete* if it expresses exactly the vdio-transformations.

Let Γ be an IQL^{v} program from v-schema S to disjoint v-schema S'. Γ transforms $\varphi(I)$ into some instance J. We also say that Γ transforms I into $\psi(J)$. So by using Γ for the value-based model, we mean that it is preceded by the fixed transformation φ and followed by the fixed transformation ψ. First, note that this defines a mapping. It is easy to check that this mapping is recursively enumerable and generic. Recall that IQL can express all dio-transformations (up to copy). Using this completeness theorem, and noticing that automatic copy elimination is performed in ψ, we have the following theorem.

Theorem 4. IQL^{v} is vdio-complete.

Cyclicity in schemas and instances has been treated using one basic idea: class names are part of the type syntax. Is it possible to separate class names and class types? This removal of the Ps from type expressions would give us a notion of the pure structure of a class (which might be useful for determining coercion strategies).

A natural semantic definition for the *pure type* of a class P in a schema S would be $\{v \mid \exists \text{ instance } I \text{ over } S \text{ such that } v \in I(P)\}$, that is, the set of all values that may be members of P. In Abiteboul and Kanellakis 1989 we exhibit a constructive definition of a pure type and show that the two definitions are equivalent. Let us present the basic intuition via an example.

Example 8. Consider the following:

$$\mathbf{T}(P_1) = [A_1\colon D, A_2\colon D]$$
$$\mathbf{T}(P_2) = [A_3\colon D, A_2\colon P_1]$$
$$\mathbf{T}(P_3) = [A_1\colon D, A_2\colon P_3]$$

Intuitively, the pure type of P_1 is given by $[A_1: D, A_2: D]$, and of P_2 by $[A_3: D, A_2: [A_1: D, A_2: D]]$. On the other hand, the pure type of P_3 should be some recursive type with certain regularities. If one were to use recursive syntax here, a fixpoint type constructor, such as $\mu x.\tau$, would have to be added and its fixpoint semantics specified. An important point is that the straightforward least fixpoint constructions do not work. In this example, such constructions would give empty sets for P_3. The problem is that such approaches specify finite trees, and we want v-instances with infinite trees. Perhaps greatest fixpoints would be more appropriate.

Instead of introducing recursive syntax it is simpler to define the pure type of P_3 using a sequence of finite types which are better and better approximations of P_3 Courcelle 1983:

$$[A_1: D, A_2: \Omega], [A_1: D, A_2: [A_1: D, A_2: \Omega]],$$
$$[A_1: D, A_2: [A_1: D, A_2: [A_1: D, A_2: \Omega]]], \ldots$$

The basic intuition is to consider these types as sets of partially defined finite trees (they have leaves labeled $\perp$). Now the constructive definition of pure type of P_3 is: the set of regular trees that are limits of sequences of partially defined trees.

8 Acknowledgements

The work of the second author was supported by NSF grant IRI-8617344, ONR grant N00014-83-K-0146 ARPA order no. 4786 and an Alfred P. Sloan Fellowship. We want to thank the people in the Altaïr and Verso groups for fruitful discussions and arguments, and in particular, François Bancilhon, Claude Delobel, Sophie Gamerman, Stéphane Grumbach, Christophe Lécluse, Philippe Richard and Fernando Vélez. We also thank Maria-Teresa Otoya for pointing out that object relations have been studied for a century in psychology.

References

Abiteboul, S., and C. Beeri. 1987. *On the manipulation of complex objects.* INRIA Technical Report.

Abiteboul, S., and S. Grumbach. 1988. COL: A logic-based language for complex objects. In *Proceedings of the first conference on extending database technology.*

Abiteboul, S., S. Grumbach, A. Voisard, and E. Waller. 1989. An extensible rule-based language with complex objects and data-functions. In *Proceedings of the DBPL-II workshop.*

Abiteboul, S., and R. Hull. 1987. IFO: A formal semantic database model. *ACM TODS* 12: 525–65.

———. 1988. Data-functions, datalog and negation. In *Proceedings of the ACM SIGMOD conference.*

Abiteboul, S., and P. Kanellakis. 1989. *Object identity as a query language primitive.* INRIA Technical Report. Also In *Proceedings of the ACM SIGMOD conference 1989.*

Abiteboul, S., and V. Vianu. 1987. A transaction language complete for database update and specification. In *Proceedings of the ACM PODS conference.*

———. 1988. Procedural and declarative database update language. In *Proceedings of the ACM PODS conference.*

Atkinson, M., and P. Buneman. 1987. Types and persistence in database programming languages. *ACM Computing Surveys* (June).

Bancilhon, F. 1988. Object-oriented database systems. In *Proceedings of the 1988 ACM PODS conference.*

Bancilhon, F., G. Barbedette, V. Benzaken, C. Delobel, S. Gamerman, C. Lécluse, P. Pfeffer, P. Richard, and F. Vélez. 1988. The design and implementation of O_2, an object-oriented database system. In *Proceedings of the second international workshop on object-oriented database systems,* ed. K. Dittrich.

Bancilhon, F., S. Cluet, and C. Delobel. 1989. Query languages for object-oriented database systems. In *Proceedings of the DBPL-II workshop.*

Bancilhon, F., and S. Khoshafian. 1986. A calculus for complex objects. In *Proceedings of the ACM PODS conference.*

Banerjee, J., H-T. Chou, J. Garza, W. Kim, D. Woelk, N. Ballou, and H. J. Kim. 1987. Data model issues for object-oriented applications. *ACM TOIS* 5(1): 3–26.

Beeri, C. et al. 1987. Sets and negation in a logic database language (LDL1). In *Proceedings of the ACM PODS conference.*

Cardelli, L. 1988. A semantics of multiple inheritance. *Information and Computation* 76: 138–64.

Carey, M. J., D. J. DeWitt, and S. L. Vandenberg. 1988. A data model and query language for Exodus. In *Proceedings of the 1988 ACM SIGMOD conference.*

Chandra, A., and D. Harel. 1980. Computable queries for relational data bases. *JCSS* 21(2): 156–78.

Codd, E. F. 1970. A relational model of data for large shared data banks. *Communications of the ACM* 13(6): 377–87.

Codd, T. 1979. Extending the database relational model to capture more meaning. *ACM TODS* 4(4): 397–434.

Courcelle, B. 1983. Fundamental properties of infinite trees. *TCS* 25: 95–169.

Dahlaus, E., and J. Makowski. 1986. Computable directory queries. In *Proceedings of the CAAP*. Springer-Verlag.

Fishman, D., D. Beech, H. P. Cate, E. C. Chow, T. Conners, J. W. Davis, N. Denett, C. G. Hoch, W. Kent, P. Lyngbaek, B. Mahbod, M. A. Neimat, T. A. Ryan, and M. C. Shan. 1987. Iris: An object-oriented database management system. *ACM TOIS* 5(1): 46–69.

Fischer, P., and S. Thomas. 1983. Operators for non-first-normal-form relations. In *Proceedings of the COMPSAC conference.*

Goldberg, A., and D. Robson. 1983. *Smalltalk 80: The language and its implementation.* Addison-Wesley.

Hull, R. 1986. Relative information capacity of simple relational schemata. *Siam J. of Computing* 15(3).

Hull, R., and J. Su. 1989. Untyped sets, invention and computable queries. In *Proceedings of the ACM PODS conference.*

Jaeschke, B., and H.J. Schek. 1982. Remarks on the algebra of non-first-normal-form relations. In *Proceedings of the ACM PODS conference.*

Kanellakis, P. 1988. Elements of relational database theory. Brown University Technical Report. (To appear as a chapter in the *Handbook of theoretical computer science.*)

Khoshafian, S., and G. Copeland. 1986. Object identity. In *Proceedings of the first ACM OOPSLA conference.*

Kifer, M., and J. Wu. 1989. A logic for object-oriented logic programming (Maier's o-logic: revisited). In *Proceedings of the ACM PODS conference.*

Kim, W. 1988. *A foundation for object-oriented databases.* MCC Technical Report.

Kolaitis, P. G., and C. H. Papadimitriou. 1987. Why not negation by fixpoint? In *Proceedings of the ACM PODS conference.*

Korth, H. F., M. A. Roth, and A. Silberschatz. 1985. *Extended algebra and calculus for not 1NF relational databases.* University of Texas, Austin, Technical Report.

Kuper, G. M. 1985. *The logical data model: A new approach to database logic.* PhD thesis, Stanford University.

———. 1987. Logic programming with sets. In *Proceedings of the ACM PODS conference.*

Kuper, G. M., and M. Y. Vardi. 1984. A new approach to database logic. In *Proceedings of the ACM PODS conference.*

Lécluse, C., and P. Richard. 1989. Modeling complex structures in object-oriented databases. In *Proceedings of the ACM PODS conference.*

Lécluse, C., P. Richard, and F. Vélez. 1988. O_2, an object-oriented data model. In *Proceedings of the ACM SIGMOD conference.*

Maier, D. 1986. A logic for objects. In *Proceedings of the workshop on foundations of deductive databases and logic programming.*

Maier, D., A. Otis, and A. Purdy. 1985. Development of an object-oriented DBMS. *Quarterly Bulletin of IEEE on Database Engineering* 8(4).

Schek, H., and M. Scholl. 1986. The relational model with relation-valued attributes. *Information Systems.*

Ullman, J. D. 1987. Database theory—past and future. In *Proceedings of the ACM PODS conference.*

———. 1988. *Principles of database and knowledge-base systems,* Vol. 1. Computer Science Press.

Verso, J. 1986. Verso: A database machine based on non-1NF relations. In *Nested Relations and Complex Objects.* Springer-Verlag.

Zdonik, S. 1985. Object management systems for design environments. *Quarterly Bulletin of IEEE on Database Engineering* 8.

CHAPTER 6

Method Schemas

SERGE ABITEBOUL
PARIS C. KANELLAKIS
EMMANUEL WALLER

1 Introduction

Object-oriented database systems are the focus of a great deal of current experimentation and research (for motivation and terminology see Bancilhon 1988). Although most of the work to date has concentrated on system development (e.g., Maier, Otis, and Purdy 1985; Zdonik 1985; Banerjee et al. 1987; Fishman et al. 1987; Bancilhon et al. 1988), some of the principles of these new systems have also been investigated. For example, Abiteboul and Kanellakis 1989 (see chapter 5) and Hull and Su 1989 address the expressibility of languages in this new context, and they use many of the tools of typed complex structure and semantic modeling research. Here, we do not examine such "structural" aspects, but focus instead on some of the "behavioral" aspects of the object-oriented paradigm (for some other recent work in this direction see Borgida 1989; Hull, Tanaka, and Yoshikawa 1989).

We propose *method schemas* as a simple model of the object-oriented programs that are being used in most of the existing database prototypes. The critical features are *classes with methods and inheritance*, a syntax involving *method-name overloading*, and a semantics involving *late binding*. A key computational problem is *consistency maintenance of method schemas*. Its solution has many applications. For example, it can be used to facilitate the support of schema evolution (e.g., Banerjee et al. 1987; Skarra and Zdonik 1987). Let us briefly outline our formalization.

Syntax We have an *isa* hierarchy of classes, where each class is a set of objects. Each object has an associated set of methods and no other "visible structure."

All objects in a class have the same methods, and methods can be inherited along the class hierarchy. Method names can be reused in different parts of the hierarchy; that is, there is overloading. We consider two kinds of methods: the *base* methods, which can be viewed as defined extensionally, that is, as materialized functions with particular signatures; and the *coded* methods, which consist of pieces of code (i.e., programs) built using base and coded methods. We consider very simple programs, which are directed acyclic graphs labeled by method names.

Semantics We propose an operational semantics. For a given finite interpretation of the base methods, the coded methods are defined using rewriting. Because of overloading, a given method call is rewritten based on its context, that is, on the classes of its arguments. This models late binding. An inconsistency is raised when a method is called with arguments for which this method is undefined. Rewriting is important in order to handle recursive calls. Without recursion, the semantics is function composition.

Consistency We study the consistency problem. More precisely, we want to check whether a given method schema can possibly produce an inconsistency for some finite interpretation of the base methods. Our analysis of consistency also provides signatures to the coded methods—in this sense we study type inference in an object-oriented database context. Our contributions are (1) *a formalization of method schemas*, and (2) *a static analysis of method-schema consistency*. This static analysis is the first important step if one is to understand incremental algorithms for problems such as schema evolution. Based on our analysis, we outline (3) *a sound heuristic for method-schema consistency maintenance in an object-oriented database system.*

The syntax and the semantics we use for method schemas are reasonably language independent. Our syntax and semantics provide an abstract view of flow of control based on method composition and possibly recursive method calls. We are consistent with any programming paradigm based on inheritance, overloading, and late binding. In this sense, the present work is similar to research on recursive applicative program schemas (Greibach 1975; Luckham, Park, and Paterson 1970). However, there are some important differences from traditional program schemas: (1) the class hierarchy with its inheritance mechanism replaces the interpreted **if-then-else** construct for coded methods; (2) the overloading of base method names is also outside the traditional framework; and (3) the signature information for base methods is particular to the new setting and is important for database applications.

The operational semantics that we use can be viewed as an abstraction of a Smalltalk interpreter, and it is relatively straightforward. On the other hand, it is much harder to analyze methods statically (at compile time). This difficulty is substantiated by the undecidability of consistency checking, even in our simple model. We prove undecidability by reduction of problems involving program schemas. It turns out that the main feature in program schemas (conditional binary transfer) can be simulated using method overloading. Richard Hull proved undecidability of "reachability" for a different model of method schemas[1] by reduction of the Post correspondence problem. Almost the same proof can be used for showing undecidability of consistency in our model. However, we believe that our (approximate) simulation of program schemas provides some additional insights into the relationship with the theory of program schemas.

Undecidability comes from the simultaneous presence of recursion and the use of multiple-argument methods to represent contexts. Practical programs are often less complex. Thus we analyze in detail the consistency problem for *monadic* and/or *recursion-free* method schemas, which happens to be decidable. We also quantify the effect of *covariance*, which is a widely used constraint on the signature of methods.

1. **In the case of schemas that are both monadic and recursion-free,** consistency checking can be done using finite-state automata. The use of pattern-matching techniques leads to PTIME solutions. Inheritance and overloading introduce some nondeterminism in the consistency checking, but the covariance constraint removes it. Checking a single coded method for consistency is logspace-complete in NLOGSPACE, whereas it is in DLOGSPACE and in linear time if covariance is assumed. The linear time bound is an interesting application of two-way deterministic pushdown automata (Cook 1971).

2. **In the monadic case,** the set of possible computations can be described using a context-free language. An inconsistency may be reached if this language has a nonempty intersection with a particular regular language. The decision procedure is in EXPSPACE. To handle overloading, our proof uses a modification of a technique of Ashcroft, Manna, and Pnueli 1973.

3. **In the recursion-free case,** the consistency problem is coNP-complete, even for a single coded method. Some special cases can be shown to be in PTIME, using tree automata techniques (Doner 1971; Vardi 1989). Although covariance does not help in the multiargument recursive case, we show that there is a PTIME test for a single coded method in the recursion-free covariant case. This is interesting in practice, because it motivates a heuristic for the general case.

In an object-oriented context, it is not reasonable to recompile all methods each time the schema is updated. The problem is to obtain an *incremental* consistency checking algorithm that would avoid redoing the same verifications/computations. A solution that is adopted practically (e.g., Bancilhon et al. 1988) is to maintain a dependency graph of the methods and to recompile only methods that may have been affected by the update. Understanding what

[1] Private communication to the authors, June 1989.

can be affected is the key; this is where our analysis contributes. We briefly discuss this aspect and refer to Waller 1989 for more details.

The paper is organized as follows. In section 2, we present the model. Recursion-free schemas are considered in section 3, and schemas with recursion in section 4. Section 5 deals with covariance. Some practical aspects are considered in section 6.

2 Method Schemas

2.1 Syntax

We assume the existence of the following disjoint countable sets: of *class names* $(c_1, c_2, \ldots)$, and of *method names* $(m_1, m_2, \ldots)$. For each method name m, the *arity* of m is an integer greater than or equal to zero ($\text{arity}(m) \geq 0$). A *signature* is an expression $c_1, \ldots, c_{n-1} \rightarrow c_n$, where each c_i is a class name.

An n-*term* for some $n \geq 0$ is a finite, rooted, ordered direct acyclic graph (DAG) such that (1) vertices are labeled either by method names or by integers in $\{1, \ldots, n\}$; (2) each vertex labeled by a method name of arity k has k children; (3) all vertices of out-degree zero are called *inputs*, and each vertex labeled with an integer is an input; (4) the children of each vertex are ordered, and thus the DAG comes with a uniquely defined depth-first search order. For example, the terms t and t' in figure 6.1 are 1-terms. They are, by definition, also 2-terms, 3-terms, and so on.

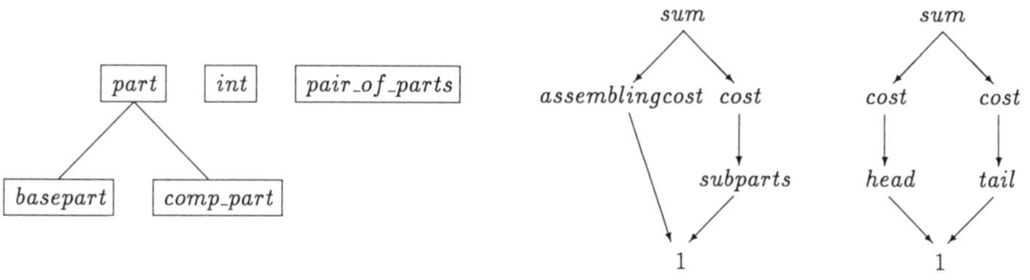

isa hierarchy term t term t'

Figure 6.1. Hierarchy and terms

A *base definition* of m at $c_1, \ldots, c_{n-1}$ is a pair $(m, (c_1, \ldots, c_{n-1} \rightarrow c_n))$, where m is a method name of arity $n-1$, and the remaining part is a signature. A *coded definition* of m at $c_1, \ldots, c_n$ is a triple $(m, (c_1, \ldots, c_n), t)$, where m is a method name of arity n, each c_i is a class name, and t is an n-term.

For example, consider the definitions

$$(\mathit{price}, (\text{Basepart} \rightarrow \text{Int}))$$
$$(\mathit{cost}, (\text{Basepart}), s)$$
$$(\mathit{cost}, (\text{Part}), t)$$

where t is as in figure 6.1, and s is a single arc with tail *price* and head 1. They are represented syntactically using intuitive lambda or graphical notation. (Note that a colon (:) is used for base, and an equals sign (=) is used for coded methods.)

$$methodprice \text{ @Basepart: Int}$$
$$methodcost \text{ @Basepart} = \lambda x_1.price(x_1)$$
$$methodcost \text{ @Part} = \lambda x_1.sum(assemblingcost(x_1), cost(subparts(x_1)))$$

Definition 1. A *method schema* is an expression $(C, \leq, \Sigma_0, \Sigma_1)$, where:

1. C is a finite set of classes, and $\leq$ is a forest on C.
2. Σ_0 is a set of base definitions with class names from C and $M_0 = \{m \mid (m, \ldots) \in \Sigma_0\}$.
3. Σ_1 a set of coded definitions with class names from C and $M_1 = \{m \mid (m, \ldots) \in \Sigma_1\}$. The n-term method-name labels of Σ_1 are from $M_0 \cup M_1$. We require that $M_0 \cap M_1 = \emptyset$.
4. Each method of arity k has at most one definition at $c_1, \ldots, c_k$ for each $c_1, \ldots, c_k$.

Example 1. Consider the class hierarchy of figure 6.1 and the terms t and t' in that figure. Using either a lambda or a graphical notation, the method definitions are as follows:

method	*sum*	@Int, Int	:	Int
method	*head*	@Pair_of_parts	:	Part
method	*tail*	@Pair_of_parts	:	Part
method	*price*	@Basepart	:	Int
method	*subparts*	@Part	:	Pair_of_parts
method	*assemblingcost*	@Part	:	Int
method	*cost*	@Part	=	t
method	*cost*	@Basepart	=	$\lambda x_1.price(x_1)$
method	*cost*	@Pair_of_parts	=	t'
method	*sum2*	@Int, Int, Int	=	$\lambda x_1 x_2 x_3.sum(sum(x_1, x_2), x_3)$

2.1.1 Method Inheritance

A method schema $(C, \leq, \Sigma_0, \Sigma_1)$ contains *explicit* definitions of methods (i.e., Σ_0, Σ_1), but it is also used to define methods *implicitly*, for the convenience of code reuse. So, in addition to the explicit definitions for a method name, method definitions are implicitly inherited along the class hierarchy. If a method m is explicitly defined on classes $c_1, \ldots, c_k$, then its definition implicitly applies to $c'_1, \ldots, c'_k$, where $c'_i \leq c_i$ for $i = 1, \ldots, k$.

2.1.2 Overloading

Method inheritance implies that we can have several definitions for the same base or coded method name at the same class names (although by condition 4 of the definition of method schema, there can be only one explicit definition). This creates overloading of names. To illustrate overloading, consider the method *cost* in the example. That method is explicitly defined on Part, implicitly inherited by Basepart, and explicitly redefined on Basepart.

The resolution of method name overloading consists of finding a unique definition for a given method name and given classes. The resolution of a method m at some $c'_1, \ldots, c'_k$ is the explicit definition of m for the "componentwise smallest" $[c_1, \ldots, c_k]$, for which m has an explicit definition and $c'_i \leq c_i$, for all i such that $1 \leq i \leq k$ (if such a unique componentwise minimum exists). If m has a resolution at $c'_1, \ldots, c'_k$, we say that m is *well defined* at $c'_1, \ldots, c'_k$. Otherwise, we say that m is *undefined* at $c'_1, \ldots, c'_k$.

Note that nondefinition can come either because there is no definition of m above $c'_1, \ldots, c'_k$ or because there is ambiguity of the definitions above $c'_1, \ldots, c'_k$. Note also that for methods of arity 1, ambiguity cannot arise because of the forest hierarchy.

Example 2. Let c_1, and c_2 be methods with $c_1 \leq c_2$, and consider the schema with explicit base definitions of m at c_1, c_2 and c_2, c_1. Then m is undefined at c_2, c_2 (no definition) and m is undefined at c_1, c_1 (ambiguity of definitions).

2.2 Semantics

We assume the existence of a countably infinite set of *objects* $(o_1, o_2, \ldots)$ disjoint from class and method names. We use object assignments (Abiteboul and Kanellakis 1989; see chapter 5) to provide semantics for classes with inheritance. The semantics of base methods is defined using mappings that satisfy certain signature constraints. The semantics of coded methods is defined using the semantics of base methods and a rewriting technique. Without recursion, this rewriting is equivalent to function composition. The operational style of the rewriting models the intuitive notion of *late binding.*

Definition 2. A *disjoint object assignment* ν for a set of class names C is a mapping from C to finite sets of objects such that distinct class names are mapped to disjoint sets of objects. For each c, we denote with $c*$ the union of all classes below c. Therefore $\nu(c*) = \bigcup_{c' \leq c} \nu(c')$.

Definition 3. An *interpretation* of a schema $S = (C, \leq, \Sigma_0, \Sigma_1)$ is a pair $I = (\nu, \mu)$ where ν is a disjoint object assignment for C and μ a mapping from the names of the base methods in S to partial functions such that:

1. If m has arity k, $\mu(m)$ is a partial function from O^k to O, where O is the set of objects in ν.
2. For each $c_1, \ldots, c_k$, if the resolution of m at $c_1, \ldots, c_k$ is $(m, (c_1, \ldots, c_k \rightarrow c))$, then we have that $\mu(m)\mid_{\nu c_1 \times \ldots \times \nu c_k}$ is a total mapping into $\nu(c*)$, else $\mu(m)$ is undefined everywhere in $\nu c_1 \times \ldots \times \nu c_k$.

Let us first give some intuition for the rewriting of coded methods. Consider a depth-one n-term, whose one internal node is labeled m and whose inputs have been replaced by objects, as a "procedure call" to m. Based on the classes of the arguments, we can replace m either by some object/code, if it is defined, or by an error message if it is undefined. In general, given a term to obtain a new term we "reduce" the first (in the depth-first ordering) method name with instantiated leaves as children. We can continue this process, and we will either obtain a result (i.e., an object), reach an inconsistency, or not terminate. A (partial) sequence of rewritings for example 1 is shown in figure 6.2, where o is in the class Pair_of_parts, and o' and o'' are in the class Basepart.

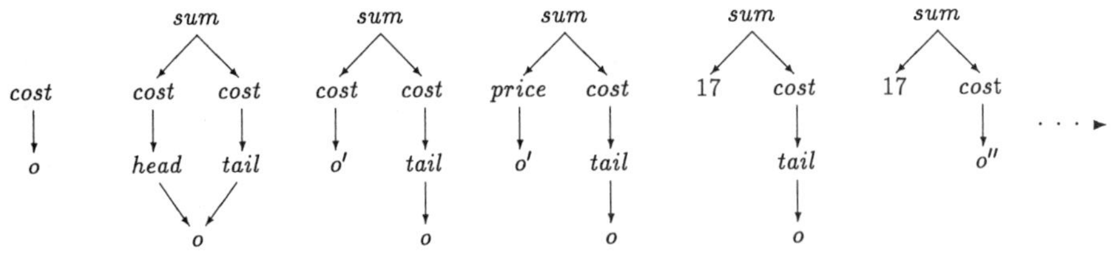

Figure 6.2. A (partial) sequence of rewritings

An *instantiated term* in interpretation I is an n-term whose integer labels have been replaced by objects. Let $c_1, \ldots, c_k$ be classes, let m be a method of arity k, and for each i let o_i be in c_i. Then an instantiated term consisting of a single vertex labeled m and having k inputs, labeled respectively $o_1, \ldots, o_k$, is said to be a *redex*. Let *first-redex* be the first vertex in the depth-first ordering of an instantiated term, whose induced subterm is a *redex*. This first-redex is uniquely determined.

Definition 4. Let I be an interpretation of method schema S, t an instantiated term, v the first-redex of t, and m the label of v. Let $o_1, \ldots, o_k$ be the labels of the children of v belonging respectively to classes $c_1, \ldots, c_k$. The *reduction* $I(t)$ of t in I is obtained as follows.

1. $I(t)$ is a special symbol $\perp$ if m is undefined at $c_1, \ldots, c_k$.
2. If m is a base method, then $I(t)$ is the instantiated term obtained by removing from v the outgoing edges and changing its label to $\mu(m)(o_1, \ldots, o_k)$.

3. If m is a coded method, then $I(t)$ is the instantiated term obtained by substituting (with the natural renaming of inputs) the vertex v by the DAG s, where (m, σ, s) is the resolution of m at $c_1, \ldots, c_k$.

2.3 Consistency

We are interested in the rewriting sequences of a particular set of instantiated terms; that is, these are the initial "procedure calls" that make sense according to a method schema. More formally, we have the following. Let S be a method schema with interpretation I, let $c_1, \ldots, c_k$ be classes, let m be a method of arity k well defined at these classes, and for each i let o_i be in c_i. Then an instantiated term consisting of a single vertex labeled m and having k inputs, labeled respectively $o_1, \ldots, o_k$, is said to be a *start-redex*.

Definition 5. A method schema S is consistent if for each interpretation I of S it is impossible to rewrite any start-redex into $\perp$ in a finite number of steps.

A variety of questions are important in this setting; for example: (1) Is a schema consistent? (2) Are there possible/certain diverging computations? (3) Is method m (at c) possibly/certainly reachable from m' (at c')? We concentrate here on 1, although most of the techniques that we develop can be used for studying other problems such as 2 or 3.

Two properties simplify consistency: monadic arity and absence of recursion. *Monadic schemas* are schemas where all methods have arity exactly 1. A schema is *recursion-free* if there is no cycle in the *method-dependence graph* (the vertices of the method-dependence graph are the method names, and there is an edge from m to n iff m occurs in the code of n). A schema is *simple* if only base methods occur as labels in its coded definitions. Simple schemas are important subcases of recursion-free schemas. Indeed, the study of recursion-free schemas can be reduced to that of simple schemas.

2.4 Variations

To conclude section 2, we consider some important variations of the above definitions.

1. Constraints can be imposed on method signatures, for example, "covariance."

2. "Virtual" classes can be considered.

3. The isa order on classes may be more complicated. In particular, one may allow a class to have more than one direct superclass, that is, to have "multiple inheritance."

4. In some proposals, it is required that the first argument, called the receiver, of a method must determine the resolution. Each instance of a method is then viewed as "attached" to the class of the first argument.

In section 5 we consider covariance and mention briefly some unexpected aspects of virtual classes. We do not address multiple inheritance and attachment to first argument. We believe that for these cases, once the resolution mechanism is determined, our techniques are also applicable.

3 Recursion-Free Schemas

In this section, we study recursion-free schemas. We consider the monadic, then turn to the general case. We first present an example that illustrates the consistency-checking technique for simple monadic schemas.

Example 3. Consider the schema:

$$\begin{array}{llll} \text{class} & c & & \\ \text{class} & c' & \text{isa} & c \end{array}$$

$$\begin{array}{lllll} \text{method} & m_1 & @c & : & c' \\ \text{method} & m_2 & @c & : & c \\ \text{method} & m_2 & @c' & : & c' \\ \text{method} & m_3 & @c' & : & c \end{array}$$

Consider the definitions:

$$\begin{array}{lllll} \text{method} & m & @c & = & \lambda x_1.m_1(m_2(m_1(x_1))) \\ \text{method} & m' & @c & = & \lambda x_1.m_3(m_3(m_1(x_1))) \end{array}$$

The algorithm first transforms the method schema into a nondeterministic FSA. The start states represent start-redexes (this is the reason for having states *start*, *sc*, *sc'*). The other states (ic, ic') correspond to the classes. The nonempty transitions to all but the *final* state represent all possible well-defined base methods at classes. The nonempty transitions to the *final* state represent where base methods are undefined. The reason for the empty transitions (ϵ) is as follows. Consistency checking is essentially nondeterministic because of the semantics of signatures. A definition ($m_3, c' \rightarrow c$) indicates that given an object in c', m_3 returns an object in c or in a subclass of c (here, c').

Of the coded definitions, the first is consistent and the second is not. To verify that, it suffices to check that the words $cm_1m_2m_1$ and $c'm_1m_2m_1$ are rejected by the FSA of figure 6.3 and that the word $cm_1m_3m_3$ is accepted.

The same automaton of the above example can be used to detect that an "inferred signature" of m is $c \rightarrow c'$. But the nondeterminism in consistency checking also implies that disjunction is needed to describe inferred signatures of coded methods, as shown by the following example.

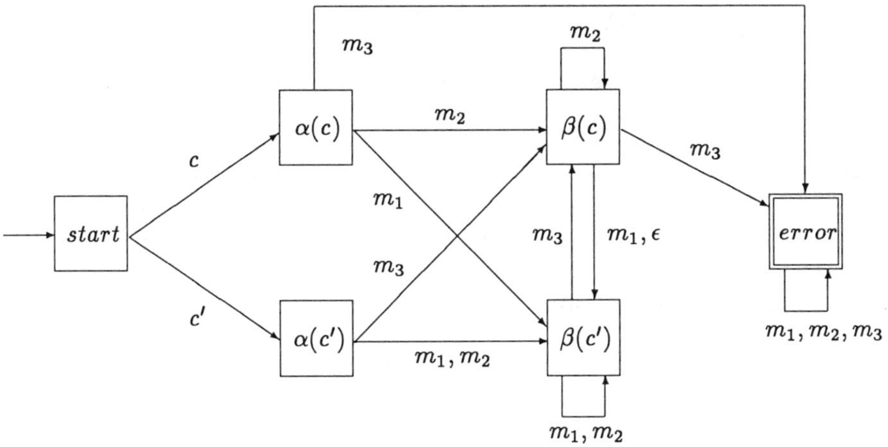

Figure 6.3. The finite state automaton (FSA) for testing consistency

Example 4. Consider the schema:

$$\begin{array}{lll} \text{class} & c_0 & \\ \text{class} & c & \\ \text{class} & c' & \text{isa} \quad c \end{array}$$

$$\begin{array}{llcll} \text{method} & m_4 & @c & : & c \\ \text{method} & m_4 & @c' & : & c_0 \\ \text{method} & m'' & @c & = & \lambda x_1.m_4(m_4(x_1)) \end{array}$$

Then an inferred signature of m'' is $c \rightarrow c \vee c_0$.

Finite state automata techniques provide necessary and sufficient conditions for consistency of simple monadic schemas. Moreover, testing a single method is linear in the size of the method to be checked, but quadratic in the size of the class hierarchy. Using this, one can show that:

Theorem 1. Consistency of recursion-free monadic schemas can be tested in PTIME.

The situation is more complicated if methods with multiple arguments are considered. An exhaustive algorithm and a reduction from 3DNF tautology suffice to show that:

Theorem 2. Consistency of recursion-free schemas is in EXPTIME. Deciding whether a simple schema with a single coded method definition is consistent is coNP-complete, even if all arities are bounded by 2.

If the code of the methods to be checked is required to be a tree, consistency checking is in PTIME. This bound is obtained by generalizing the automaton technique to tree automata (Doner 1971; Vardi 1989).

4 Schemas with Recursion

In this section we allow recursion in method definitions. We first consider the monadic, then turn to the general case.

In the monadic case, one can use context-free language techniques to show that the problem is decidable. Intuitively, the possible prefixes of computations are described using a context-free language. The computations leading to inconsistencies are described using a regular language. The problem is therefore reduced to testing emptiness of the intersection of a context-free language and a regular one, that is, to testing emptiness of a context-free language.

Theorem 3. Consistency of monadic schemas is in PTIME.

We now consider the most general case. In particular, we show that the consistency problem for arbitrary schemas is undecidable. (This was first shown by Richard Hull for a different method formalism.[2]) To prove this result, we show that method schemas and program schemas have "approximately" the same power. We "approximately" simulate program schemas by method schemas and, conversely, method schemas by program schemas. The undecidability results then come from the undecidability results for program schemas of Luckham, Park, and Paterson 1970 (see also Greibach 1975 for linear recursion).

Theorem 4. Consistency of method schemas is undecidable, even if all arities are bounded by 2 and only linear recursion is used.

Due to space limitations, we do not provide here the simulation of program schemas by method schemas. We only illustrate how to simulate a fundamental feature of program schemas, namely, the **if-then-else** statement. Consider a statement:

$$\textbf{if } P(x) \textbf{ then } F(y) \textbf{ else } G(y)$$

We assume that we have a class D which has two subclasses D_P and $D_{\overline{P}}$. We use a method m of arity 2 defined as follows:

$$\begin{array}{llll} \text{method} & m(x,y) & @D & = m(x,y) \\ \text{method} & m(x,y) & @D_P & = F(y) \\ \text{method} & m(x,y) & @D_{\overline{P}} & = G(y) \end{array}$$

The intuition is that the elements in the domain of the program schema are represented by objects. The elements for which P holds are in D_P; those for which P doesn't hold are in $D_{\overline{P}}$. Elements strictly in D prevent us from obtaining a "perfect" simulation. They have to be treated in an ad hoc manner depending on the problem that is addressed. In the above example, the method loops on such objects.

[2]Private communication to the authors, June 1989.

Our simulation is of independent interest; using results in Luckham, Park, and Paterson 1970, one can show the undecidability of a variety of problems, such as consistency, reachability, divergence on *all/some* valid calls, and termination on *all/some* valid calls. Indeed, this strongly suggests that most non-trivial properties of method schemas are undecidable.

We consider in this paper finite interpretations of method schemas. Undecidability results hold for all (finite and infinite) interpretations, by the same reduction and Luckham, Park, and Paterson 1970.

5 Covariance

In this section we consider covariance and show that it simplifies the consistency problem. We first consider simple schemas.

For simple schemas, covariance is the following constraint on the signatures of base methods. A simple schema is *covariant* if for each m and for each pair of definitions of a base method m:

$$(m,(c_1,\ldots,c_k \rightarrow c)), \quad (m,(c'_1,\ldots,c'_k \rightarrow c'))$$

we have that $(\forall i \; c_i \leq c'_i) \Rightarrow c \leq c'$.

First consider the schema of example 3, which is covariant. Suppose that we tested the prefix of a coded method and reached $\boxed{ic}$. We can either read a new method name or follow the ε edge to move to $\boxed{ic'}$. Suppose that a word ω moves the automaton from $\boxed{ic'}$ to $\boxed{\text{error}}$. Because of the covariance, one can show that the same word moves from $\boxed{ic}$ to $\boxed{\text{error}}$. Thus there is no need to follow the ε transition to detect the error. Therefore, in the covariant case, it is possible to remove the ε transitions of the automaton and still have the property that a definition is consistent iff the associated word is rejected by the automaton.

From the example, intuitively, the covariance condition on the base methods simplifies consistency checking. Indeed, the following result contrasts the consistency checking of simple monadic schemas with and without covariance.

Theorem 5.

1. Consistency for simple monadic schemas is logspace-complete in NLOGSPACE.

2. Under the covariance restriction, the consistency of monadic schemas is in DLOGSPACE.

It turns out that under covariance, the consistency of simple monadic schemas can be checked in linear time. This bound is obtained by showing that it can be checked using a deterministic two-way pushdown automaton. Note that naive use of the isa can be quadratic.

Theorem 6. Under the covariance restriction, the consistency of simple monadic schemas can be tested in linear time.

Let us now consider simple polyadic schemas. We assume that arities are polyadic, but bounded by a constant (unbounded arities are unreasonable from a practical standpoint). In that case, a problem may arise if (1) a method is called with arguments for which it is undefined, or (2) an ambiguity is encountered. These two kinds of problems can be easily detected. Indeed, we have a result that should be contrasted with theorem 2.

Theorem 7. Under the covariance restriction and with arities bounded by a constant, the consistency of simple schemas can be tested in PTIME.

To test for the consistency of a simple schema, one has to check that (1) no ambiguity can arise, and (2) no illegal call can arise. Checking for ambiguity can be easily done in PTIME. Checking that a call to a particular method m in a class $c_1, \ldots, c_k$ cannot lead to illegal calls, one can proceed as follows. The leaves of the code of m at $c_1, \ldots, c_k$ are marked by $c_1, \ldots, c_k$. The code is traversed bottom-up while marking the internal leaves with class names. The marking is given by the definitions of base methods.

A virtual class c is a class that is required always to have an empty interpretation; that is, $\nu(c) = \emptyset$. Virtual classes are useful for expressing the exact union of two classes. If virtual classes are considered, the consistency of simple, monadic schemas is still in PTIME. However, with virtual classes, the consistency of simple, covariant schemas is coNP-hard. This indicates a subtlety of virtual classes.

To conclude this section, we consider schemas that are not simple. Here, the definition of covariance is obvious only for the base methods. Covariance does not help in the general (recursive) case, because the method schemas constructed to simulate program schemas are covariant with respect to the base methods. Another difficulty in this context is that, although covariance of the base methods can be tested easily, testing the covariance of the inferred signatures of coded methods is in general undecidable. This is because the inferred signatures of the coded methods must be computed first.

6 Practical Issues

In this section, we briefly consider practical issues. First we consider a heuristic solution to the consistency problem in the general case, then we consider the problem of checking incrementally for consistency.

6.1 Avoiding Recursion

While doing the consistency checking, we implicitly (if not explicitly) produce inferred signatures for the coded methods. Let us assume now that extra signature information on coded methods is provided. This can be viewed as transforming the type-inference problem that we have considered so far into a type-checking problem; and it leads to the notion of constrained schema.

A constrained method schema is a pair (S, τ), where $S = (C, \leq, \Sigma_0, \Sigma_1)$ is a schema and τ a mapping from Σ_1 to classes. Intuitively, for each coded method definition, τ indicates the class of the return value. *Consistency* of constrained method schemas also requires the satisfaction of the constraints τ.

We next provide a sound but incomplete consistency heuristic for constrained schemas. Let (S, τ) be a constrained schema. We construct a simple schema S_τ from S. The schema S_τ is on the same classes as S, with the same hierarchy. Furthermore, each base method in S is also a base method in S_τ, with the same base definitions. For each coded method m in S that occurs in the code of another method, let m_τ be a new base method in S_τ, and let its signatures be as follows. For each $\alpha = (m, (c_1, \ldots, c_k), t)$ in Σ_1, $(m_\tau, (c_1, \ldots, c_k \rightarrow \tau(\alpha)))$ is a base definition of m_τ. For each coded definition (m, σ, t) in S, S_τ contains a definition (m, σ, t') where t' is obtained from t by replacing each method name n by n_τ. Clearly, S_τ is a simple schema. Now we have:

Proposition 1. For each S and τ, if (S_τ, τ) is consistent, (S, τ) is consistent.

This leads to a heuristic for testing consistency of S, assuming certain constraints τ. First, construct the associated simple constrained schema and test it for consistency. To check whether (S_τ, τ) is consistent, one would have also to consider the inferred signatures of coded methods and verify that they do not violate τ. This can be done with the techniques outlined in the previous sections. Accept (S, τ) if (S_τ, τ) is accepted.

The algorithm is sound; and it is obviously not complete. Furthermore, even in simple cases it depends heavily on the "tightness" of the constraints specified by τ, as illustrated by the following example.

Example 5. Let c be a class, and let c' be a subclass of c. Consider the schemas S and S_τ defined on $\{c, c'\}$ as follows:

S:

method	m'	$@c$	:	c		
method	m'	$@c'$	:	c'		
method	m_0	$@c'$	:	c'		
method	m	$@c'$	=	m'	:	c'
method	m	$@c$	=	$\lambda x_1.m(m'(x_1))$	:	c
method	m_1	$@c$	=	$\lambda x_1.m_0(m(x_1))$	:	c'

S_τ:

$$\begin{array}{llllll} \text{method} & m' & @c & : & c & \\ \text{method} & m' & @c' & : & c' & \\ \text{method} & m_0 & @c' & : & c' & \\ \text{method} & m_\tau & @c' & : & c' & \\ \text{method} & m_\tau & @c & : & c & \\ \text{method} & m & @c' & = & m' & : c' \\ \text{method} & m & @c & = & \lambda x_1.m_\tau(m'(x_1)) & : c \\ \text{method} & m_1 & @c & = & \lambda x_1.m_0(m_\tau(x_1)) & : c' \end{array}$$

The above algorithm will detect an inconsistency in the definition of m_1 in S_τ. (An object in $\nu(c)$ may be mapped by m_τ to an object in $\nu(c)$, and m_0 is undefined on $\nu(c)$.) However, a more careful analysis of S shows that the output of m has to be an object in $\nu(c')$. Therefore, no inconsistency can be reached with models of S. Indeed, the above algorithm would succeed if the second definition of m is replaced by:

$$\text{method } m@c = \lambda x_1.m(m'(x_1)) \text{: } c'.$$

Unconstrained method schemas: Suppose now that the schema is not constrained, or that only partial constraint information is available. Some preanalysis of S can suggest the choice of candidate constraints for the various methods. Furthermore, if the algorithm fails, one may attempt to refine the constraints on the basis of the information gathered by this first phase. In this context, covariance may be useful to reduce the search space of candidate constraints.

So the proposed *heuristic for consistency* consists of a signature preanalysis phase and one or more constrained method-schema-testing phases. (This approach forces coded methods to have signatures of the form $c_1, \ldots, c_k \rightarrow c$. Clearly, this can be extended to allow disjunction in signatures of coded methods.)

6.2 Updates

It is unreasonable, when the schema is updated, to recompile all the methods of the schema. Therefore there is a need for incremental algorithms. We first consider the insertion of a method. We present an example of an update that may yield problems, discuss it, and mention some other open problems.

Example 6. Let c, c' be two classes, with $c' \leq c$. Let the definitions be

$$m'@c\text{: } c'$$
$$m''@c'\text{: } c'$$
$$m@c = \lambda x_1.m''(m'(x_1))$$

The schema is consistent. Let us now insert a new base definition $m'@c'$: c. The schema is no longer consistent because of m, although we have apparently not modified m; we have not even touched the execution of m on objects strictly in c. However, by inheritance, m should also apply to c'-objects, and this may now lead to an inconsistency.

The problem is caused here by the compacted form of the information in a method schema (inheritance). It is possible to make explicit such information, which would facilitate the detection of update effects; but such a technique defeats space efficiency and code reusability.

One may think that the above problem would disappear if covariance is assumed. Indeed, under covariance, if a coded method definition is inserted, it is not necessary to recompile the schema. The code of the new method only has to be checked. However, we can identify the following problems.

The inferred signatures of the previously inserted methods may be refined by this insertion. As a consequence, covariance may have been lost. So covariance would only be good for one insertion, and the consistency-checking algorithm may have to recompile at least part of the schema if completeness is to be achieved in future insertions. (For detailed examples and some techniques for special cases, see Waller 1989.)

Finally, covariance does not help with deletions. To see this, consider the following example.

Example 7. Let c, c', c'', Int be four classes with $c' \leq e$, and $c'' \leq c$. Let the definitions be

$$m@c\colon c$$
$$m@c'\colon c''$$
$$m''@c''\colon \text{Int}$$
$$m'@c' = \lambda x_1.m''(m(x_1))$$

The schema is consistent and covariance holds. Let us now delete the base definition $m@c'\colon c''$. The schema is no longer consistent, even if m is still well defined in c and its subclasses.

7 Acknowledgements

The work of the second author was supported by NSF grant 1RI-8617344, ONR grant N00014-83-K-0146 ARPA order no. 4786 and an Alfred P. Sloan Fellowship. We thank Richard Hull for discussions on the topic.

References

Abiteboul, S., and P. Kanellakis. 1989. Object identity as a query language primitive. In *Proceedings of the ACM SIGMOD conference.*

Abiteboul, S., P. Kanellakis, and E. Waller. 1990. Method schemas. In *Proceedings of the 9th ACM SIGACT-SIGART conference on principles of database systems.*

Ashcroft, E., Z. Manna, and A. Pnueli. 1973. Decidable properties of monadic functional schemas. *JACM* 20(3): 489–99.

Bancilhon, F. 1988. Object-oriented database systems. In *Proceedings of the ACM PODS conference.*

Bancilhon, F., G. Barbedette, V. Benzaken, C. Delobel, S. Gamerman, C. Lécluse, P. Pfeffer, P. Richard, and F. Vélez. 1988. The design and implementation of O_2, an object-oriented database system. In *Proceedings of the second international workshop on object-oriented database systems,* ed. K. Dittrich.

Banerjee, J., H-T. Chou, J. Garza, W. Kim, D. Woeld, N. Ballou, and H. J. Kim. 1987. Data model issues for object-oriented applications. *ACM TOIS* 5(1): 3–26.

Banerjee, J., W. Kim, H. J. Kim, and H. F. Korth. 1987. Semantics and implementation of schema evolution in object-oriented databases. In *Proceedings of the ACM SIGMOD conference.*

Borgida, A. 1989. Type systems for querying class hierarchies with non-strict inheritance. In *Proceedings of the ACM PODS conference.*

Cook, S. A. 1971. Linear-time simulation of deterministic two-way pushdown automata. In *Proceedings of the IFIP congress.*

Doner, J. E. 1971. Tree acceptors and some of their applications. *JCSS* 4: 406–51.

Fishman, D., D. Beech, H. P. Cate, E. C. Chow, T. Conners, J. W. Davis, N. Denett, C. G. Hoch, W. Kent, P. Lyngbaek, B. Mahbod, M. A. Neimat, T. A. Ryan, and M. C. Shan. 1987. Iris: An object-oriented database management system. *ACM TOIS* 5(1):46–69.

Greibach, S. A. 1975. Theory of program structures: Schemes, semantics, verification. In *LNCS* Vol. 36.

Hull, R., and J. Su. 1989. On accessing object-oriented databases: Expressive power, complexity, and restrictions. In *Proceedings of the ACM SIGMOD conference.*

Hull, R., K. Tanaka, and M. Yoshikawa. 1989. Behavior analysis of object-oriented databases: Method structure, execution trees and reachability. In *Proceedings of the third international conference on foundations of data organization and algorithms.*

Luckham, D. C., D. M. R. Park, and M. S. Paterson. 1970. On formalized computer programs. *JCSS* 4: 220–49.

Maier, D., A. Otis, and A. Purdy. 1985. Development of an object-oriented DBMS. *Quarterly Bulletin of IEEE on Database Engineering* 8(4).

Skarra, A., and S. Zdonik. 1987. Type evolution in an object-oriented database. In *Research directions in object-oriented programming*, ed. B. Shriver and P. Wegner. MIT Press.

Vardi, M. Y. 1989. Automata theory for database theoreticians. In *Proceedings of the ACM PODS conference.*

Waller, E. 1989. *Vérification de type en présence d'héritage et de surcharge.* DEA PhD thesis, Orsay.

Zdonik, S. 1985. Object management systems for design environments. *Quarterly Bulletin of IEEE on Database Engineering* 8.

CHAPTER 7

A Framework for Schema Updates in an Object-Oriented Database System

ROBERTO ZICARI

1 Introduction

Schema evolution is a concern in object-oriented systems because the dynamic nature of typical OODB applications calls for frequent changes in the schema (Panel 1989). However, updates should not result in inconsistencies either in the schema or in the database. While most of the work done on schema updates has concentrated on the structural consistency of objects when the type definition changes, an important and difficult area of investigation is behavioral consistency. We present a framework for schema updates for the O_2 object-oriented database system (Bancilhon 1988; Lécluse, Richard, and Vélez 1988; see chapter 4) that takes into account the issues of both structural and behavioral consistency; and we evaluate the cost of an implementation.

1.1 Preliminary O_2 Concepts

In this section we briefly recall the fundamental concepts of O_2 which are relevant for our discussion. The reader is referred to Lécluse and Richard 1988, 1989a, and 1989b (see chapter 9) for a formal definition of the O_2 data model and to Vélez et al. 1989 (see chapter 15) for a description of the system architecture.

In the O_2 data model, both objects and values are allowed; in the definition of an object, its component values can contain not only objects but also values. We have two distinct notions: classes, whose instances are objects and which encapsulate data and behavior; and types, whose instances are values. To every class is associated a type, describing the structure of its instances. Classes are created using schema-definition commands. Types are constructed recursively using *atomic types* (such as integer, string, etc.), *class names*, and the *set*, *list*, and *tuple* constructors; types can be complex.

Objects have a unique internal identifier and a value which is an instance of the type associated with the class. Objects are encapsulated, their values are not directly accessible, and they are manipulated by methods. Method definition is done in two steps: first, the user declares the method by giving its *signature*, that is, its name, the type of its arguments, and the type of the result (if any). Then the code of the method is given. In O_2, the schema is a set of classes related by inheritance links and/or composition links. The inheritance mechanism of O_2 is based on the subtyping relationship, which is defined by a set-inclusion semantics. Multiple inheritance is supported. O_2 offers a compile-time type-checker in an attempt to statically detect as many illegal manipulations as possible of objects and values. Objects are created using the **new** command.

If a class is created with extension, then a named set value is created which will contain every object of the class and will persist. Deletion of objects or values is obtained by removing the links which attach them to the persistence roots (names). Classes with extension are also provided with a *delete* method, which allows objects to be removed from the class extension when no other objects or values refer to it. O_2 allows objects values to be manipulated by methods other than those associated with the corresponding class. This feature is obtained by making "public" the type associated with the class.

Methods in O_2 can call other methods of the same class, or public methods defined in other classes. They may access directly a type associated to a class (besides the class to which they are associated) if this type has been defined as public. The inheritance scope of a method can be changed by application of the @ feature, which allows a reference to a method from outside the scope of the method.

Example. Given two classes, C and C_2 in the class structure shown in figure 7.1.

$C\ m$: $(C \rightarrow C')$
|
$C_2 m$: $(C_2 \rightarrow C'')$
m_2: $(C_2 \rightarrow C'')$
body.m_2: $[\ldots m@C \ldots]$

Figure 7.1. Structure of classes C and C_2

It is possible, in the body of method m_2, to refer to a method m defined in C instead of the method m redefined in class C_2, as the scope rule would normally imply.

When a class inherits methods or types from more than one class (multiple inheritance), conflicts with names of methods and type attributes have to be explicitly solved by the designer. For example, two methods with the same name defined in different superclasses will not be inherited by the common subclass. The designer has two possible choices to solve the conflict: either (1) redefine the method in the subclass, or (2) specify which method he or she wants to inherit using a **from class** clause which specifies the inheritance path. We have retained this philosophy of O_2 in the schema update mechanism, and the system does not try to solve automatically ambiguities arising in performing an update. The system guides the designer in order to avoid inconsistencies in the schema and the database if the advisor solution is chosen (see section 9).

1.2 Updates: What Do We Want to Achieve?

Updates can be performed both at the schema level and at the object level. An update is a dynamic modification. Changing the schema may logically imply changing all the objects related to the portion of the schema which has been updated. Changing a specific (named) object does not imply a schema update; the update is limited to the object(s) specified and possibly to some other object(s) related to the object which has been modified. The main goal of this paper is to define a reasonable minimal set of primitives for updating an O_2 schema, and to show the problems which need to be solved in order to obtain a usable schema-update mechanism.

Informally, the problem with updates can be stated as follows: We want to change the structural and behavioral part of a set of classes (schema updates) and/or of a set of named objects (object updates) without this resulting in run-time errors, "anomalous" behavior, or any other uncontrollable situation. In particular, we want to ensure that the semantics of updates are such that when a schema (or a named object) is modified, it is still a consistent schema (object). Consistency can be classified as follows:

1. *Structural consistency* refers to the static part of the database. Informally, a schema is structurally consistent if the class structure is a direct acyclic graph (DAG), and if attribute- and method-name definitions, attribute- and method-scope rules, and attribute types and method signatures are all compatible. An object is structurally consistent if its value is consistent with the type of the class it belongs to.

2. *Behavioral consistency* refers to the dynamic part of the database. Informally, an object-oriented database is behaviorally consistent if each method respects its signature and if its code does not result in run-time errors or unexpected results (see section 2).

A more precise definition of consistency is given in section 2.

We will consider acceptable only those updates that do not introduce structural inconsistency. We will allow behavioral inconsistencies that do not result in run-time errors. Any kind of behavioral inconsistency that has been caused by an update will be reported to the user (designer).

1.3 Organization of the Paper

In the rest of this paper, we concentrate on the problem of schema updates. The problem of object updates will be addressed in a forthcoming paper.

The paper is organized as follows. Section 2 describes in some detail the distinction between structural and behavioral consistency for the O_2 object-oriented database system. The semantics of schema-update primitives is that of transforming the schema from one state which is structurally and behaviorally consistent, to another state which is structurally and possibly behaviorally consistent. Behavioral consistency is much harder to obtain than structural consistency. Therefore, we will accept some kinds of behavioral inconsistencies, that is, those inconsistencies that do not produce run-time errors; and we will signal to the user (designer) all behavioral anomalies that may be induced by an update. Section 2 also briefly describes how updates could be performed by invoking an interactive tool. Section 3 defines the set of primitives for updating the schema. We present a fill list of update primitives, and then show how this list can be reduced to a minimal set of basic updates, sufficient to implement all other updates. We classify updates in three categories; these are explained in detail in sections 4, 5, and 6. Section 4 describes schema updates that modify only methods. Section 5 describes schema updates that modify only the type associated to a class. Section 6 describes schema updates that modify a class as a whole entity. Problems arising from all such updates are illustrated in the respective sections. Section 7 describes some implementation issues. Section 8 compares our approach with related work. In section 9 we present the conclusions and state some open problems. Finally, in section 10 we sketch a first cost analysis for different strategies of update implementations.

2 Ensuring Structural and Behavioral Consistency

In this section, we discuss the two basic types of consistency relevant to the O_2 system (and to every object-oriented database system): *structural* and *behavioral* consistency.

2.1 Structural Consistency

The formal definition of the O_2 data model is given in chapter 3. We recall here only the following notation and definitions of the O_2 database schema.

We denote $\mathbf{T}(C)$ the set of all types defined over a class C. $\mathbf{T}(C)$ includes atomic types, class names, and tuple, set, and list types. Inheritance between classes defines a class hierarchy: A class hierarchy is composed of class names with types associated to them, and a subclass relationship. The subclass relationship describes the inheritance properties between classes. A class hierarchy is a triple $(C, \sigma, \prec)$, where C is a finite set of class names, σ is a mapping from C to $\mathbf{T}(C)$ (i.e., $\sigma(C)$ is the structure of the class of name C), and $\prec$ is a strict partial ordering among C.

The semantics of inheritance is based on the notion of subtyping. The subtyping relationship $\leq$ is derived from the subclass relationship as defined in chapter 6, section 2.3, definition 5 of this book.

As inheritance is user given, some class hierarchies can be meaningless.

In a class hierarchy an instance of a class is also an instance of its superclasses (if any). Therefore, if class c' is a superclass of class c, then we must have that the type of c is a subtype of the type of c'. More formally:

A class hierarchy $(C, \sigma, \prec)$ is consistent iff for all classes c and c', if $c \prec c'$ then $\sigma(c) \leq \sigma(c')$.

A schema is also constituted of methods attached to classes. Methods have signatures.

A method signature in class C is an expression m: $c \times t_1 \times \ldots \times t_n \rightarrow t$, where m is the name of the method and $c, t_1, \ldots, t_n$ are types. The first type c must be a class name; it is called the receiver class of the method.

An O_2 *database schema* is a quintuple $S = (C, \sigma, \prec, M, N)$, where $(C, \sigma, \prec)$ is a consistent class hierachy, M is a set of method signatures in C, and N is a set of names with a type associated to each name. A schema is therefore composed of classes related by inheritance which follow the type compatibility rules of subtyping and a set of methods. Attributes and methods are identified by name. When we do not want to distinguish between a type attribute and a method name, we simply use the term *property*.

Now we are ready to define what we mean by structural consistency for a database schema.

Definition 1. A database schema S is *structurally consistent* iff it satisfies the following properties:

1. If $c \prec c'$, and the method m is defined in c with signature m: $c \times t_2 \times \ldots \times t_n \rightarrow t$, and method m' is defined in c', with signature m': $c' \times t'_2 \times \ldots \times t'_2 \rightarrow t'$, and m and m' have the same name, then $t_i \leq t'_i$ and $t \leq t'$ (covariant condition).

2. The class hierarchy is a DAG.

3. If there are classes c_1 and c_2 having a common subclass c_4, with a property name p defined in both c_1 and c_2 but not in c_4, then there is another subclass c_3 of c_1 and c_2 in which the property p is also defined, and c_4 is a subclass of c_3.

The first property assures that method overloading is done with compatible signatures; the second property constrains the structure of the class hierarchy; and the third property eliminates multiple inheritance conflicts (also called *name conflicts*). Definition 1 is important because we consider only schemas that are structurally consistent. An update to a schema is a mapping which transforms a schema S into a (possibly) different schema S'. Schemas S and S' have to be structurally consistent. The semantics of the schema-update primitives will have to ensure *at least* that structurally consistent schemas are produced as a result of an update. In this approach, name or type conflicts occurring as a consequence of an update will not be solved automatically by the system.

2.2 Behavioral Consistency

Behavioral consistency ensures that methods do indeed perform the desired task. As we have seen, the signature of a method is used to type-check the compatibility of the method in the class structure. This kind of check is therefore part of the process to ensure structural compatibility. However, checking the signature of a method is not sufficient to ensure behavioral consistency of the method. Updating a schema could result in anomalous behavior of some methods due to *method dependency* (i.e., methods in their body may refer to other methods or public types), and in some subtle cases, due to the change of method signatures resulting from a change of the class hierarchy.

Behavioral inconsistencies do not always result in run-time errors. There may be methods that do not fail as a consequence of an update but behave in a modified way after an update. The two notions of *method failure* (i.e., run-time errors) and *method's change of behavior* (i.e., the expected result of the method is different) are to be distinguished. In the rest of this paper, however, we do not make this distinction; we use only the general term *behavioral inconsistency.* We take the approach of allowing transformations of schemas that may lead to behavioral inconsistencies which do not result in run-time errors (updates that cause run-time errors are refused), signaling to the designer all methods which may potentially be affected by an update, and leaving to the user the responsibility for acting on these warnings.

This paper concentrates mainly on behavioral consistency. A detailed analysis of structural consistency is reported in Delcourt and Zicari 1989.

2.3 The Interactive Consistency Checker

The way the designer updates the schema is a dialogue with an interactive tool called the Interactive Consistency Checker (ICC). The ICC is a basic update tool which, given a schema and a proposed update, detects whether inconsistencies may occur. It then refuses those updates that produce structural inconsistencies or behavioral inconsistencies which may imply a failure of some methods (i.e., run-time errors). The consistency check is performed in two steps: first the structural check, and then the behavioral check. If structural inconsistencies arise, the behavioral check is not performed and the update is refused. The reason for the refusal of the update is always given to the user. A description of the system architecture is given in section 7, and in section 9 there is a brief description of a more advanced schema tool.

3 Schema Updates

We present in this section a complete list of the basic updates one may want to perform on an O_2 schema. Updates are classified in three categories: updates to the type structure of a class, to methods of a class, and to the class as a whole. This classification is fairly similar to that of Banerjee et al. 1987a and 1987b. However, the semantics of some updates is different. The main differences between the schema-update characteristics of O_2 and of other relevant systems is discussed in section 9.

3.1 Changes to the Type Structure of a Class

Because in O_2 types can be arbitrarily complex, we have different ways to modify a class type. We can think of an update u, which modifies the type structure T of a class C, as a mapping between types, u: $T \rightarrow T'$. Updates of this kind can be broadly classified in two categories: those for which $T' \leq T$ (we call them type-preserving), and those for which $T' \not\leq T$ (we call them non-type-preserving). Of all possible type updates we list here only the most elementary ones:

1.1 Add an attribute to a class type.

1.2 Drop an existing attribute from a class type.

1.3 Change the name of an attribute of a class type.

1.4 Change the type of an attribute of a class type.

Updates 1.1 and 1.3 are type-preserving; updates 1.2 and 1.4 are non-type-preserving.

3.2 Changes to the Methods of a Class

The method updates are:

2.1 Add a new method.

2.2 Drop an existing method.

2.3 Change the name of a method.

2.4 Change the signature of a method (this update may be also implied by a change to the class-structure graph as defined below).

2.5 Change the code of a method.

3.3 Changes to the Class-Structure Graph

The class updates are:

3.1 Add a new class.

3.2 Drop an existing class.

3.3 Change the name of a class.

3.4 Make a class S a superclass (or subclass) of a class C.

3.5 Remove a class S from the superclass (or subclass) list of C.

A set of more involved changes to a schema (defined as a tree) can be found in Abiteboul and Hull 1988.

3.4 Basic Schema Updates

The list can be reduced to a basic set of updates which can be used to execute all other updates:

1.1 Add an attribute to a class type.

1.2 Drop an attribute from a class type.

2.1 Add a method.

2.2 Drop a method.

3.1 Add a class.

3.2 Drop a class.

3.3 Change the name of a class.

3.4 Make a class a superclass (or subclass) of C.

3.5 Remove a class from the superclass (or subclass) list of C.

The other updates can be executed using sequences of basic updates:

$1.3 = < 1.2,\ 1.1 >$ (This equivalence does not hold at instance level.)
$1.4 = < 1.2,\ 1.1 >$ (This equivalence does not hold at instance level.)
$2.3 = < 2.2,\ 2.1 >$
$2.4 = < 2.2,\ 2.1 >$
$2.5 = < 2.2,\ 2.1 >$
$3.3 = < 3.2,\ 3.1 >$ (This equivalence does not hold at instance level.)

The sequence of basic updates corresponding to a nonelementary update has to be atomic, to avoid inconsistency.

The*completeness* of a set of basic updates at *schema level* (Banerjee et al. 1987b)—that is, whether the set of basic updates subsumes every possible type of schema change—is not necessarily the same as its completeness at the *database instance level.*[1]

4 Method Updates

In this section we consider only the two basic method updates as defined in section 3.4: add a method m in class C, and drop a method m in class C. The other updates to methods can be executed by using the two basic ones.

4.1 Adding a Method in a Class

We have a schema, and we want to add a method to a class of this schema. The syntax of the update is:

```
add_method <m> in <C> [<signature>, <body>] || [from <C'>]
```

Square brackets indicate an optional parameter; the notation $(p_1) \,||\, (p_2)$ is used to denote two alternative parameters, p_1 or p_2; and:

- $< m >$ is the name of the method to be added.
- $< C >$ is the class where the method is added.
- The parameter $<$ *signature* $>$, $<$ *body* $>$ (if specified) defines the method signature and the body of method m.
- The parameter **from** $< C' >$ (if specified) indicates that the signature and body of the new method are those of a method with the same name m defined in a class C', with $C' \neq C$.

Structural consistency of the schema implies that, when adding a method, we must ensure that no problems arise in (1) the class structure, (2) the resolution of the method names, or (3) the compatibility of the method signatures. The addition of a new method m in class C modifies the scope of all methods with the same name defined in the superclasses of C. The system must automatically ensure such modifications. The scope of the new added method is the standard one (see section 2). The introduction of a new method may result in a name conflict in the same class C (i.e., a method with the same name was already defined in C) or in a subclass C' of C in case of multiple inheritance with other classes. In either case, the update is refused.

The insertion of a new method implies a static check of its signature. The signature of the new method should be type compatible with the signatures of existing methods with the same name and related to it by class inheritance.

[1]D. Maier, private communication to the author, October 1989.

An incompatible signature will imply the refusal of the update. The detailed specifications of the algorithms for preserving structural schema consistency are given in Delcourt 1989. Adding a method to a class does not require one to logically update the class extension.

The addition of a method to a class may lead to behavioral inconsistencies. These must be checked for by looking at the method code. In particular, we may have inconsistencies if:

1. The code of the new method m contains references to methods or classes that do not exist in the schema. In this case the update is refused, and the designer first has to define those methods and classes which are not already created.

2. Other methods have in their code a method with the same name but a different signature.

Because of the method-calling dependency, other methods may be affected as well by the update. For this purpose a *method-dependency graph* can be extracted by looking at the code of each method. The vertices of the method-dependency graph are the method names, and there is an edge from m to n iff m occurs in the code of n. In order to ease the task of building the method-dependency graph, and also to reduce the search for dependent methods (see also section 5), the system associates (1) to each class, an import list which tells whether the class is using methods of other classes, and also some information which tells what other classes (their public types, to be precise) are accessed without using encapsulation by methods of the class; and (2) to each method, the list of methods which are called outside the class where the method is defined, and which types the methods access without encapsulation. We call this information *dependency information.*

Before inserting a method, besides checking its signature, one has to analyze and type-check its body in order to avoid run-time errors. The body of a method can be rather complex; it is therefore important to be able to extract the relevant information when type-checking the method code. When an update is performed, this information can be used to decide whether the method still works properly or needs to be recompiled, or whether in any case the method will not work any more (see section 4.2).

We can think of a method as mainly based on one syntactical construct: concatenation $m_1; m_2$ (which means that method m_2 is executed immediately after method m_1). For the type checking, conditional combinations, such as **if** p **then** m_1 **else** m_2 (which corresponds to the conditional execution of m_1 or m_2 depending on a state predicate p on the database state S) and looping, such as **while** p **do** m, can be expressed by concatenation.

The idea behind this reasoning is the following. Consider a method M with signature $C \rightarrow C_1$. The assumption here is that if the body of M does not contain any call to other methods, then the type of the object which M manipulates is completely specified by its signature (M gets an object of type C and returns an object of type C_1). Things change when in the body of a method there is a call to another method.

Consider the method $M(C \rightarrow Y)$.

```
Body of M:
{sequence of statements
 method call M'
 sequence of statements
 method call M''
 sequence of statements}
```

The method signatures are

$$M'(C \rightarrow X), \quad M''(X \rightarrow Y)$$

M gets an object of type C, which gets to M', M' returns an object of type X in accordance with its signature. This object gets to M'', which then results in an object of type Y. This can be expressed by the concatenation of the two method calls: $M = M'; M''$. A first formalization of the problem of the behavior of methods is presented in Abiteboul, Kanellakis, and Waller 1989 (see chapter 6), for the subclass of monadic and/or recursion-free methods; and in Hull, Tanaka, and Yoshikawa 1989, where the emphasis is on nontermination and the reachability of method executions.

4.2 Dropping a Method from a Class

The syntax of the update to delete a method in a class is:

```
delete_method <m> in <C>
```

where $< m >$ is the name of the method to be deleted, and $< C >$ is the class where m is defined.

It is not possible to delete a method which is inherited from another class. Method m must be locally defined in C. Deletion of a method m also implies the deletion of all references to m using the m **from** C' clause. When removing a method from a class (as for all updates) we should assure the structural consistency of the schema and detect possible behavioral inconsistencies. The reader is referred to Delcourt and Zicari 1989 and Delcourt 1989 for a detailed analysis of the issue of structural consistency.

Deleting a method m from a class C can cause name conflicts and signature incompatibility if C inherits from more than one class. This is due to the change of method scopes after the update. Detection of structural inconsistencies results in the refusal of the update. We are currently designing a tool to help the designer find method dependency, in this case method references using the **from** clause. If we consider an intelligent advisor to aid schema updates, we could have a different solution (see section 9). Deleting a method does not imply a logical update to the class's objects.

Behavioral problems can be detected by checking the signature of a method, by looking at the method dependency graph, and, most importantly, by looking at the code of the method. Some kinds of behavioral problems are obvious, such as a reference to a method which has been deleted (and not replaced through the inheritance mechanism by another method); these are solved by analyzing the method-dependency graph. There are, however, other cases of inconsistencies that are not so immediate. We present the problem by means of two examples.

Example. Consider a class Window with two subclasses Icon and Point. The class Window has a method *print* associated to it which is inherited by Point. The class Icon redefines the method *print*, and it has a local method called *print_context*. The classes and the methods, with their signatures, are illustrated in figure 7.2.

```
            Window
         /          \print(Window)
       /              \
     Icon            Point
   print(Icon)
print_context(Icon)
body.print_context = [print]
```

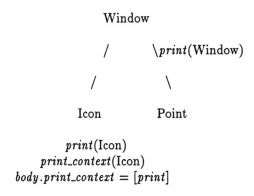

Figure 7.2. Structure of classes Window, Icon, and Point

In the body of *print_context* there is a call to method *print*. By the scope rule, *print* is the method redefined in class Icon. Therefore, the type inference of the body of the method *print_context* is as follows: *print*, as defined in Icon, gets an object of class Icon as input. This is represented by the following notation:

o(Icon) →*print*@Icon

where *o*(Icon) indicates an object of class Icon, and the symbol @ is used to denote the class (here, Icon) in which a method (here, *print*) is defined.

Suppose we perform the update **Delete method** ***print*** **from** Icon. This update results in the new schema of figure 7.3.

Because of the inheritance hierarchy, after the update the body of method *print_context* refers to *print* as defined in class Window. In this case the type inference is:

o(Icon) → *print*@Window

Window

/ \ *print*(Window)

/ \

Icon Point

print_context(Icon)
body.print_context = [*print*]

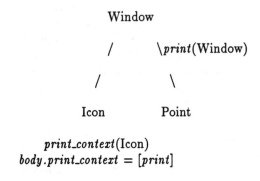

Figure 7.3. Updated schema

That is, method *print* now expects as input an object of class Window, but instead it gets an object of class Icon. Type compatibility is satisfied, since Icon is a subclass of Window, but there is no guarantee that the method *print_context* will work as before.

Example. Consider three classes: C, and two subclasses C_1 and C_2. Class C has a method m which is inherited by C_2. C_1 redefines m, and has a local method m'. C_2 also has a local method m''. The classes and the methods, with their signatures, are defined in figure 7.4.

C

m: $(C \rightarrow C)$ \

/ \

C_1 C_2

m: $(C_1 \rightarrow C_2)$ m'': $(C_2 \rightarrow \text{int})$

m': $(C_1 \rightarrow \text{int})$

$body.m' = [m; m'']$

Figure 7.4. Classes C, C_1, and C_2

The body of m' is defined as a concatenation of methods m and m'', that is, it contains first a call to m and then a call to m''. Type-checking method m' works fine, as can easily be seen from the method signatures.

Now suppose we perform the update **Delete method m from C_1**. This update will result in a failure of m'.

Before performing the update we had the following situation. Method m' got an object of class C_1 (because of its signature); this object went as input to method m (because of the definition of the body of m'), which returned an object of class C_2 (because of the signature of m). This resulting object was given as input to method m'', which returned an object of type *integer*. The equivalent notation is

$o(C_1) \rightarrow m \rightarrow o(C_2) \rightarrow m'' \rightarrow o(\text{int})$

After the update, we have for the same method m':

$o(C_1) \rightarrow m \rightarrow o(C) \rightarrow m''$

Method m' gets as before an object of class C_1, and this is given to m, but now m results in an object of class C. This creates the problem; method m'' gets an object of class C instead of C_2, with C a *superclass* of C_2, and therefore will fail.

These two examples show that deletion of a method may imply either a different behavior or even a run-time error of other methods defined in the schema, which is not predictable by looking only at the method signatures and at the method-dependency graph. In particular, the last example indicates that there is a need to "remember" how the type-checking has been performed in order to guarantee the consistency of a method after an update to the schema.

5 Type Updates

This section describes the basic updates which modify the type associated to a class: delete an attribute from the type associated to a class, and add an attribute to the type associated to a class. The results we present for these two updates also characterize the other possible O_2 class-type updates. We discuss the effects of type updates on structural and behavioral consistency separately.

5.1 Structural Consistency

The type changes proposed do not affect the class DAG. A structural check must be performed to detect whether the new class-type definition does not result in:

1. Name conflicts; for example, the same attribute name is defined in two or more superclasses. This problem is similar to that of updating a method (see section 4).
2. Type incompatibility in the inheritance hierarchy.

(See Delcourt and Zicari 1989.) For such cases the update is refused.

When performing an addition or deletion of an attribute (and in general for any change in the class type) it is also necessary to logically update the class extensions. The object belonging to the class extension need to conform to the new class-type definition. Default values can be assigned to the new attributes; the values which correspond to the attributes removed from the schema must be deleted. A logical update to a class extension does not necessarily correspond to a physical update in the database (see section 7).

5.2 Behavioral Consistency

In presenting the issue of behavioral consistency when updating a class type, we restrict the discussion to a simplified case where class types are tuples and no inheritance is defined. The approach can be extended to the more general case of complex types and multiple inheritance, as reported in Zicari 1989 (the present paper is a shortened version of that report).

Example. Consider the class Person, defined as follows (We use the "M→T (*attributes*)" notation to denote which portion of the type T the method M is using in its body):

```
Class Person
Type tuple Tp(id:  integer, age:  integer)
Add Method M1(), with M1→Tp(id, age)
Add Method M2(), with M2→Tp(age)
```

In this example, M_1 uses all type T_p, while M_2 only uses the **age** attribute of the tuple T_p.

Suppose we perform the update **Drop id from T_p in class** Person. This update maps the type T_p to a type $\hat{T_p}$ as follows:

$$T_p = (\texttt{id, age}) \rightarrow \hat{T_p} = (\texttt{age})$$

Behavioral inconsistencies can be detected for this simple case in two ways: with a naive approach, or with a less naive approach.

5.2.1 The Naive Approach

With the naive approach, the information available to the O_2 system does not specify which portion of a type a method is using. Therefore for the given example we know only that $M_1 \rightarrow T_p$, and $M_2 \rightarrow T_p$, by the definition of the class Person and the encapsulation property. ($M \rightarrow T$ is a short notation to denote that M uses the entire type T). Therefore:

1. We must mark M_1 and M_2 as potentially invalid (we shall call them "unsafe" from now on), because the update has modified the type T_p. The user gets an appropriate warning.

2. We must find all methods M_i defined in other classes which refer to either M_1 or M_2 (if M_1 and M_2 are defined as public) or directly to the type T_p associated to Person (if T_p has been defined as public). This requires looking at the code for all methods of all classes. All methods which refer to either M_1 or M_2 are marked unsafe, and signaled to the user. We call methods which refer to other methods "dependent" methods. Note that with these assumptions it is irrelevant whether methods M_1 and M_2 refer to each other.

We have the following disadvantages:

- Methods are signaled as unsafe even if they are not (such as M_2 in the example).
- The cost of looking at the code of all methods is high.

To improve the situation, we define another approach.

5.2.2 A Less Naive Approach

We need to express some metainformation about the behavior of methods with respect to the type of the class. In particular we should be able to get information that answers these questions: (1) What are the classes (methods) using the public methods of Person and/or using directly the public type T_p? and (2) For each method of Person, what portion of the type T_p is really used? The O_2 system has been extended in order to express this information. In particular, question 1 is answered by keeping the method-dependency graph, as defined in section 4. Question 2 is answered by attaching some extra information to each method, which tells what portion of the class type the method actually uses in its body. Having this extra information corresponds to knowing the following dependencies:

$T_p = (\texttt{id, age})$
$M_1 \rightarrow T_p(\texttt{id, age})$
$M_2 \rightarrow T_p(\texttt{age})$
$M_i, \ldots, M_j \rightarrow M_1, M_2$ (This notation denotes method dependencies, that is, methods $M_i, \ldots, M_j$ refer to M_1 or M_2 in their body.)

The above information is kept by the system. The given update transforms the type $T_p = (\texttt{id, age})$ into the type $T_p\hat{} = (\texttt{age})$. With the dependency information we have, we can say that:

1. Method M_1 is affected by the update.
2. If method M_2 is not dependent on method M_1 (this can be checked by looking at the method-dependency graph), then it is easy to prove that method M_2 is not affected by the update.

The advantages over the naive approach are:

- We signal to the user only those methods which may be really affected by the update.
- We eliminate the cost of searching methods unnecessarily.

The disadvantage is that we have to keep extra information in the system, which has to be updated as well.

The situation can be expressed more formally with the help of figure 7.5, where the class structure and the type lattice are defined. To each class C there corresponds one type T. To each method m_i of C there corresponds a type T', with T' either the same as T or a supertype of T by the definition of type-compatibility. Dropping an attribute in C corresponds to changing the type T to $T^{\wedge}$, the new type associated to C.

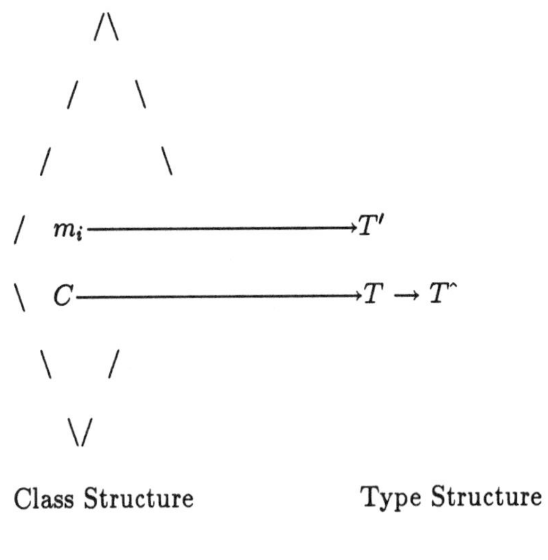

Figure 7.5. Class structure and type structure

In Zicari 1989, more complicated examples with single and multiple inheritance are presented. The naive and less naive approaches are still applicable. In particular, when updating types and multiple inheritance is considered, it is also useful to know what portion of the type of a subclass comes from the various superclasses (if any).

6 Class Updates

Updates to a class as a whole entity are equivalent to the operations of manipulation of a graph (i.e., the class DAG):

- Adding a node is equivalent to adding a class.
- Deleting a node is equivalent to dropping a class.
- Adding an edge is equivalent to making a class a superclass (or a subclass) of another class.
- Removing an edge is equivalent to removing a class from the list of superclasses (or subclasses) of another class.

There are different ways to give the semantics to these updates. We provide a set of *parameterized* primitives to perform class updates which the designer will use to define his or her own update semantics. In particular, the updates which may have different semantic interpretations are deletion of an edge, addition of a node, and deletion of a class. For such updates, the problems are (1) Where to connect a class if it becomes disconnected from the DAG after the update? (2) Do the types and methods of the subclasses change after deletion of a superclass or removal of a class from their superclass list? and (3) Where to place a newly created class in the DAG?

6.1 Addition of an Edge

Adding an edge in the class structure corresponds to making a class C a superclass (or a subclass) of another class S. A structural check has to be done in order to ensure that no name conflicts or type incompatibility arise. Adding an edge modifies the scope of attribute and method names in the inheritance hierarchy. The update must not introduce cycles in the DAG. The update has a logical impact on the class extensions, because the attributes of C have to be added to all instances of subclasses of C (if any).

The syntax of the update is:

```
add_edge <S-C>
```

where S and C are classes already existing in the DAG. Class C is made a direct subclass of class S. The addition of an edge may create behavioral problems in the same way as when adding a method or an attribute to a class.

6.2 Removal of an Edge

Removing an edge may be obtained in different ways. Suppose we have an inheritance hierarchy composed of three classes, Person, PhD, and Employee, with associated types T_a, T_c, and T_b, as shown in figure 7.6.

We want to perform the update **Remove class** PhD **from the superclass list of** Employee. This update is equivalent to saying **Remove edge** < PhD–Employee >. For this particular schema, the effect of this update is to disconnect the class Employee from the DAG; in fact, PhD is the only superclass of Employee. To preserve class consistency, the class Employee has to be connected to some other class(es) in the DAG. There are two possibilities:

1. Class Employee is made a direct subclass of all direct superclasses of PhD—class Person in the example—or

2. Class Employee is made a direct subclass of the system class OBJECT.

Both approaches are reasonable, depending on what the user wants to do with the class Employee.

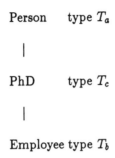

Person type T_a

|

PhD type T_c

|

Employee type T_b

Figure 7.6. Classes Person, PhD, and Employee

Moreover, when deleting the edge PhD–Employee we also must define what happens to the attributes of the type T_b (associated to Employee) which are inherited from the class PhD and not redefined in Employee. There are two possibilities:

1. Class Employee loses all attributes inherited from PhD; or

2. Class Employee does not lose attributes inherited from PhD; attributes which were inherited become locally defined in Employee.

Again, the two approaches are both reasonable. The same considerations hold for methods as well. The use of a parameterized update operator allows the definition of different update strategies. The syntax of the **delete edge** primitive is

```
drop_edge <S-C> [[connect <C> to <class_list>],
                 [type and methods_of <C> are not preserved]
```

where S is a superclass of class C. Brackets indicate an optional parameter.

The semantics of the update is as follows:

- $< S\text{–}C >$ is the edge to be removed. It is removed from the class DAG.

- The parameter **connect** $< C >$ **to** $<$ *class_list* $>$ (if specified) indicates that in case class C becomes disconnected from the class DAG after deletion of the edge (i.e., S is the only superclass of C), then class C is made a direct subclass of the classes listed in $<$ *class_list* $>$. Note that classes in the < *class_list* > do not necessarily have to be superclasses of S. The update is refused if name conflicts or type incompatibility arise when trying to connect class C. If the parameter is not specified, then class C is made a direct subclass of the system class OBJECT. In this case, neither type incompatibility nor name conflicts occur.

- The parameter *type* **and** *methods_of* < C > **are not preserved** (if specified) indicates that both the attributes of the type of class C and the methods inherited from class S and not redefined in C are deleted; this also implies the deletion in the subclass of C (if any) of all methods and type attributes that were inherited from the disconnected superclass and not locally redefined in the subclass. If the parameter is not specified, then the type of C is unchanged (i.e., attributes which were inherited now become locally defined in C), and the methods of C are also unchanged. Deletion of attributes in C may lead to name conflicts and type incompatibility; in this case the update is refused.

Let us consider a simple example to show how this parameterized update models several useful situations.

Example. Consider the schema S composed of the inheritance hierarchy of classes Person, PhD, and Employee, as shown in figure 7.7.

OBJECT

|

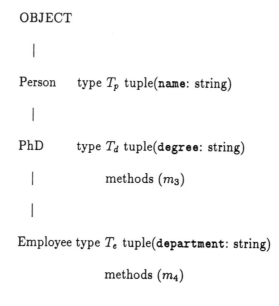

Person type T_p tuple(**name**: string)

|

PhD type T_d tuple(**degree**: string)

| methods (m_3)

|

Employee type T_e tuple(**department**: string)

methods (m_4)

Figure 7.7. Schema S

The class Person is of type T_p and has methods m_1 and m_2. Class PhD inherits in its type T_d the attribute **name** from T_p and has the attribute **degree** locally defined. PhD has a local method m_3. Class Employee inherits the attributes **name** and **degree** respectively from Person and PhD, and has a local method m_4.

Consider the following update:

```
drop_edge <PhD-Employee> connect <Employee> to <Person> (S)
```

This update results in the schema shown in figure 7.8.

OBJECT

|

Person T_p = (**name**), m_1, m_2

/ |

Employee PhD T_d = (**degree**), m_3

T_e = (**name**, **degree**,

department)

m_1, m_2, m_3, m_4

Figure 7.8. Updated schema S

Employee is now a subclass of Person. Its type and methods have not been changed. Methods m_1, m_2, and m_3 are now locally defined in Employee. Method m_4, which was locally defined in Employee before the update, is also unchanged. Note that after the update, all attributes of the type T_e are *locally defined.*

It is also possible to specify that the **name** attribute of T_e be the one inherited from Person. This can be done with either of the following two updates:

```
<(delete_attribute name in Employee), (add_attribute name
  in Employee from Person)>
```

or

```
delete_attribute name in Employee
```

In this example it is not necessary to add the attribute, because class Employee does not inherit from multiple superclasses and therefore no name conflicts occur in Employee.

Consider this other update on the previous schema S:

```
drop_edge <PhD-Employee> connect <Employee> to <Person>
type and methods_of <Employee> are not preserved (S)
```

This update results in the same schema as the previous update, but with the difference that the type T_e does not have the **degree** attribute any more; that is, T_e = (**department**) and **name** is inherited from Person. Employee has method m_4 locally defined, does not have method m_3 any more, and inherits m_1 and m_2 from Person.

Consider another update:

```
drop_edge <PhD-Employee> (S)
```

It results in the schema shown in figure 7.9.

```
                    OBJECT
                     /  |
                   /    |
        Employee     Person
$T_e$= (name, degree,      $T_p$ = (name), $m_1$, $m_2$
        department)          |
   $m_1$, $m_2$, $m_3$, $m_4$     PhD
                     $T_d$ = (degree), $m_3$
```

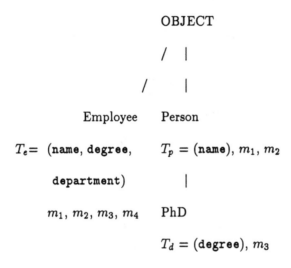

Figure 7.9. Schema S after update

Employee is a direct subclass of OBJECT. Its type and methods are unchanged.

If we consider the update

```
drop_edge <PhD-Employee>
type and methods_of <Employee> are not preserved (S)
```

we have as a result same schema as the previous update, with the difference that Employee does not inherit the attributes **name** and **degree** any more (that is, T_e = (**department**)), and it has lost methods m_1, m_2, and m_3.

As these examples show, the use of a parameterized operator allows the expression of several useful and consistent updates. The update has a logical impact on the class extensions if the class type C has to be changed; that is, if attributes are deleted in the class type of C.

6.3 Addition of a Node

Adding a node corresponds to adding a new class in the class DAG. We allow addition of a class *in any position* in the class DAG. To preserve DAG consistency, when no position in the DAG is specified the new class is by default made a direct subclass of the class OBJECT. Adding a class in a different position in the class hierarchy implies adding an edge to a superclass S and/or an edge to a subclass C. The semantics of the update is the following:

1. The new class must not have a name which is already used for another class in the schema.
2. The new class becomes by default a direct subclass of the class OBJECT unless a different position is specified.
3. When adding a class C in an inheritance hierarchy, no automatic attribute propagation is performed. The type C must be completely redefined in order to be type-compatible with the types of the superclasses and subclasses of class C. If redefinition of attributes is not desired, the update has an option which allows it to refer to attributes defined in superclasses of C.

The syntax of the update is:

```
add_class <C> [connect to <superclass Su> [before <subclass Sb>]]
type is <attribute definition> [from <class name>]
```

Brackets indicate an optional parameter, and:

- $< C >$ is the new class.
- **connect to** $<$ *superclass* $>$ [**before** $<$ *subclass* $>$] indicates the position in the hierarchy where the new class has to be placed. *Sb* is a direct subclass of *Su*. If the subclass *Sb* is not indicated, then the new class is a leaf of the DAG. Note that only one superclass and one subclass can be specified in the update. If class C has to be connected to more than one superclass or subclass, the explicit *add-edge* update has to be used. If the **connect** parameter is not specified, then class C is connected directly to the class OBJECT.
- **type is** $<$ *definition* $>$ (**from** $<$ *class* $>$) defines the type associated to the class. If the **from** parameter is used to define an attribute of the type, then it refers to an existing attribute defined in the class S or in a superclass of S (if any).

Example. Consider the schema shown in figure 7.10.

OBJECT

|

Person T_1 = (`name`)

|

Employee T_3 = (`name`, `degree`, `department`)

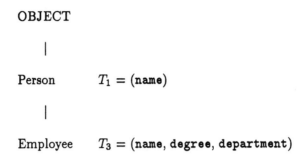

Figure 7.10. Schema before update

The following update

```
add_class <PhD> connect to <Person> before <Employee>
    type is tuple(name: string, degree: string)
```

results in the schema shown in figure 7.11.

OBJECT

|

Person T_1 = (`name`)

|

PhD T_2 = (`name`, `degree`)

|

Employee T_3 = (`name`, `degree`, `department`)

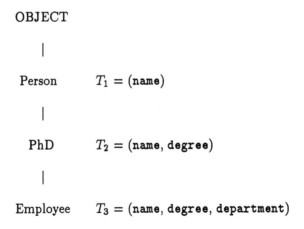

Figure 7.11. Schema after update

Note that T_2 redefines the `name` attribute.

6.4 Deletion of a Node

Deleting a node corresponds to dropping a class in the class DAG. We allow the deletion of a class in any position in the class DAG. Deleting a class with this assumption is an involved operation. The semantics of the update is the following.

Deletion of a class C corresponds to the deletion of all edges to the subclasses of C (if any), the deletion of all edges to the superclasses of C and the deletion of the class C from DAG. Because of the possible different semantics of the delete-edge update, we have different alternatives when deleting a class. The alternative semantics of deleting a class are obtained by composition of the different semantics resulting from deleting edges. The update will have parameters to specify such alternatives. We do not indicate then here, but instead define some constraints when deleting a class:

1. Deleting a class can only take place if its class extension is empty.

2. No system-defined classes can be deleted.

3. Deletion of a class can only take place if the class is not referred to in method signatures or in types of other classes.

4. A class cannot be deleted when its only superclass is the system class OBJECT and the class is not a leaf in the DAG.

Condition 1 restricts the deletion of a class C to the case where there are no objects associated to the class. It also implies no automatic coercion to other class types in the schema (e.g., to a superclass of C) of objects belonging to the extension of C. We assume the existence of explicit updates to delete objects or to change the object class types (see section 9). Condition 2 is obvious. Condition 3 avoids type inconsistency for method signatures and attribute types. Condition 4 preserves the DAG consistency.

Deletion of a class C may create behavioral inconsistency. In particular, all other methods in the schema which depend on class C—either by calling methods of C or by using directly the type T of C (if T is defined as public)—must be marked unsafe. The dependency information introduced in section 4.1 helps in detecting unsafe methods.

Example. Consider the schema shown in figure 7.12. Deletion of the class PhD can be expressed in different ways, depending on the resulting schema we want to obtain (we consider the extension of the class PhD empty). Here is one example:

```
delete_class <PhD> = T1: <(drop_edge <PhD-Employee>),
  (drop_edge <Person-PhD), (remove <PhD>)>
/* the class Employee is made a subclass of OBJECT,
   its type is unchanged */
```

The deletion of the class PhD can also be specified so that the type of Employee is changed (i.e., it loses the attributes defined in PhD).

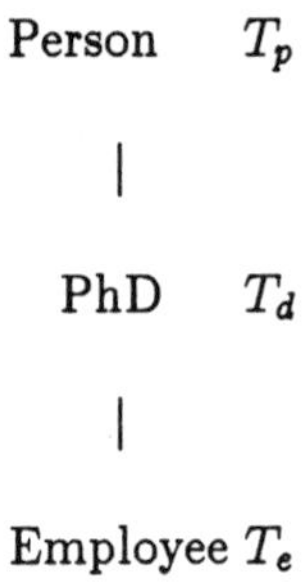

Figure 7.12. Schema prior to update

7 Implementation Issues

This section describes a few issues related to the implementation of the schema-update operators we have seen so far. Updating the schema implies structural changes to the schema itself. Object instances have to be modified in accordance with the schema change.

There are two basic approaches to performing schema updates with respect to the database (i.e., the set of persistent objects):

1. *Screening.* This approach defers (possibly indefinitely) the modification to the database; values are either filtered or corrected before they are used. Encore (Skarra and Zdonik 1986, 1987) uses filters placed between instances of an older version of a class and methods that expect instances of a newer version of the class. Orion (Banerjee et al. 1987a, 1987b) uses persistent screening on all objects presented to an application. The representations of objects are corrected as they are used; this is a late binding on the representation of objects.

2. *Conversion.* This approach changes all instances of the class to the new class definition, ensuring that auxiliary definitions (such as the class's methods) agree with the new definition. GemStone (Penney and Stein 1987) employs a conversion approach. When a class is modified, GemStone attempts to coerce the underlying database to conform to the new class definition. GemStone provides the option of keeping metainformation on instances of a class to ease the effort in modifying the class. However, we do not have further information regarding what kind of metainformation GemStone is actually using.

Both approaches have serious drawbacks. In the screening approach, execution speed may be compromised by screening; in the conversion approach, time can be consumed at the time a class is modified.

The current state of our implementation is as follows. The ICC tool is operational (Delcourt 1989), and we are currently implementing updates to the database with an immediate conversion approach; that is, all objects are immediately updated after a schema change. We are also considering the alternative of updating objects *on demand*, that is, only when they are really used. We intend to compare the two approaches with cost-analysis and simulation techniques to help us make a final decision on how to implement schema updates in O_2. A first cost analysis has been done (Harrus, Vélez, and Zicari 1990); it is briefly reported in section 10. To conclude this section, we give our solutions to the three fundamental issues identified in Panel 1989 for supporting schema evolution:

- *Architecture.* Consistency checking is a separate layer in the system and is performed by the ICC tool. The ICC interacts with the O_2 Schema Manager (called the Type and Method Manager), which is responsible for actually updating the schema, and with the Object Manager, which implements object changes (Vélez et al. 1989; see chapter 15).

- *Compile-time versus run-time approach.* O_2 provides two modes of operation: *development mode* and *execution mode* (Vélez et al. 1989; see chapter 15). These two modes correspond respectively to a run-time (development mode) and a compile-time (execution mode) way to generate code for methods and supporting schema evolution. In our current implementation we use nonnaive behavioral validation (see section 5) only in development mode. This is because in execution mode the system optimizes late binding by replacing dynamic name resolution with function calls whenever possible. The ICC tool is only used in development mode; in execution mode validation checks are performed by the compiler.

- *Primitives*: We have observed that the set of primitives for schema change does not necessarily correspond to the set of primitives for object updates. Completeness at schema level does not imply completeness at database instance level (see section 3). This explains why our set of basic schema-update primitives contains some redundancy.

8 Related Work

Structural consistency is assured by all systems supporting a mechanism for changing the schema. To compare the different solutions is not always easy, because there is no underlying common model for such systems. The pioneering work in the field of schema manipulation in the context of object-oriented database system is that proposed for the Orion database system. In Banerjee et al. 1987a and 1987b, a complete taxonomy of schema-update operations is presented, and for each update the semantics is given with a set of rules to preserve some "invariants" of the schema. Our definition of structural consistency implies the invariants of Orion: (1) class lattice invariant, (2) distinct name invariant, (3) distinct identity (origin) invariant, (4) full inheritance invariant, and (5) domain compatibility invariant.

The O_2 and Orion data models differ in a number of characteristics; we briefly list them here. The existence in O_2 of types as well as classes is not present in Orion. The O_2 typing system can be viewed in the schema-update context as a set of additional constraints which modify the Orion invariants 4 and 5. In O_2, methods and attributes in an inheritance hierarchy have to be type compatible; this is taken into account in the definition of a consistent schema. Both systems allow multiple inheritance. O_2 has a set-inclusion semantics for subtyping; Orion has no set-inclusion semantics. In O_2, multiple inheritance conflicts are solved by the designer; when there is an ambiguity in the inheritance of a method or attribute, the designer must specify which one he or she wants to inherit, or must redefine it. By contrast, Orion automatically solves ambiguities. The system maintains an ordering among the superclasses which overrides ambiguities in the inheritance of methods. This difference modifies the Orion invariant 3.

The O_2 distinction between objects and values is also present in Orion. In Orion, however, the notion of a complex value is implemented as a dependent object (composite object); that is, nonshared values are still objects with a constraint enforcing their privacy. Because of these differences in the two data models, the update semantics are also different. In particular, class updates in O_2 provide parameters to allow the designer to specify the semantics he or she wants to have. Orion adopts a default-approach semantics for update operations; for example, when removing an edge $< S\text{–}C >$ in the DAG, if the class C becomes disconnected then it is automatically reconnected to all superclasses of S. The attributes of the type of class C which are inherited from S and not locally redefined in C are lost. No other possibilities are allowed.

GemStone (Penney and Stein 1987) follows an approach similar to Orion to ensure structural consistency when the schema is updated; it also uses invariants. The major differences from the O_2 system are that GemStone does not support types, that it has only objects and no values, and that it supports simple inheritance. Therefore structural problems are simpler than for systems which allow types, such as O_2 and Vbase (Andrews and Harris 1987), and multiple inheritance, such as Orion and O_2. Vbase has types, but it supports only single inheritance.

The issue of behavioral consistency is not considered in many object-oriented database systems. To our knowledge, Orion (Banerjee et al. 1987a, 1987b; Kim et al. 1988), GemStone (Penney and Stein 1987), and Vbase do not support any mechanism for dealing with behavioral inconsistency in the database. In Orion it is the user's responsibility to avoid (or cope with) the possible occurrence of dangling references when he or she is updating composite objects. In fact, in Orion it is possible to delete a class when the class extension is not empty. All objects of the deleted class are logically deleted. If the deleted object is part of another object (composite objects), then all dependent objects are recursively deleted.

The Encore data model (Skarra and Zdonik 1986, 1987; Zdonik 1987) is similar to that of O_2; it provides types and multiple inheritance. Encore ensures structural consistency and provides an interesting mechanism for behavioral consistency based on versions of types and exception handlers. A change to a type creates a new version of the type. Exception handlers are associated to versions of types in order to allow different instances of different types to be used uniformly. Errors resulting from methods using a method or an attribute which are undefined or unknown are processed by the appropriate handlers. Versions of schemas are proposed in Orion (Kim and Chou 1988). This solution has the advantage of allowing different programs to use different versions of the schema. In our current solution for updating an O_2 schema, we did not consider creating versions either at schema level or at object level.

Other OODB systems, such as Iris, Zeitgeist, and Trellis/Owl (although it is not a true OODBS), do support schema changes (Panel 1989), but we are not aware of the types of updates they provide and the ways they implement them. A different approach is taken in the LOGRES project (Cacace et al. 1990), an integration of the object-oriented data-modeling paradigm with the rule-based approach, where updates are expressed in modules by appropriate logical rules.

9 Conclusion and Future Work

We have outlined in this paper the primitives for schema manipulation currently available in the O_2 object-oriented database system. We have defined a set of basic schema updates, and two kinds of consistency (structural and behavioral) which are desirable when performing a schema update. More work is needed to improve our current approach. This section outlines the work we plan to do.

9.1 Data Structure

We plan to define a suitable data structure and more efficient algorithms to perform behavioral checks. In general, feedback from users will give us more insight into this issue and will allow us to optimize our schema-evolution implementation.

9.2 Update-Execution Model

We plan to develop an update-execution model and perform some simulations in order to compare the cost of immediate versus on-demand object updates. This study will help us to choose the appropriate alternative for the final implementation of schema updates in O_2.

9.3 Object Updates

We plan to investigate the problem of object updates. Possible updates on objects are:

1. Create a (named) object.
2. Destroy a (named) object.
3. Change the value of a (named) object.
4. Change the class for a set of (named) objects.

The first three types of updates have been formally studied in the context of semantic database models (Abiteboul and Hull 1987), and they seem to be adaptable, with some modifications, to the O_2 data model. Updates of type 4 are an open research area. The following is an example of our idea of how to perform a subset of updates of this kind. The approach is based on the possibility for objects in O_2 to have *exceptional attributes* (with reference to the class structure) and *exceptional methods* (with reference to the set of methods associated to the class). We could define an update

```
move (select <C:T> where <P(T(C)>) to <C1: T1>
```

which selects a subset of the objects of a class C, with type T, based on a predicate P on the object structure $\mathbf{T}(C)$, and moves them to the extension of a different class C_1, with type T_1, iff T is a subtype of T_1, that is, $T \leq T_1$. For those objects that have been moved, the attributes which do not correspond to the new type T_1 will become exceptional, and so will those methods which do not correspond to the methods of the new class C_1. This update would be very useful to allow a split of one class into other classes. The update would eliminate those structural and behavioral problems, described in Zdonik 1987, that occur when the types of objects are changed. The update does not modify the structure of the objects and does not modify object identifiers.

A very interesting solution to the problem of object updates in the presence of integrity constraints is offered by the Cactis object-oriented database system (Hudson and King 1989). In Cactis, integrity constraints are expressed by attribute-evaluation rules attached to attributes. An efficient incremental update algorithm is used to perform object updates. When an update is performed, the system identifies and performs indirect updates to bring the system up to date with respect to all attribute-evaluation rules.

9.4 High-Level Restructuring

We plan to define a set of high-level restructuring operations on the schema. We can view the schema tool manager as providing the basic mechanisms that can be used to build on top of it a more sophisticated object-oriented design tool, such as a tool which will enable compositions of classes, the creation of superclasses given a set of classes, and so on. This design tool would only be used to modify the schema, with no actual database (i.e., a pure design phase). Interesting restructuring operations based on rewriting rules for schemas defined as a tree have been proposed in Abiteboul and Hull 1988. The same techniques could perhaps be applied to schemas defined as a graph.

9.5 Tools

We plan to design an intelligent advisor tool for schema manipulation, and a set of tools for helping the designer perform schema updates. The advisor would participate in schema-update manipulations, including testing and validation, and also would suggest to the user a set of possible update alternatives (which may imply an interactive reply from the user) whenever some inconsistency might arise. At update time, if a test shows that an update is illegal, then the advisor augments the update with secondary updates to obtain a transaction that is illegal. This process is recursive, because the secondary updates might require tertiary updates and so on.

The consistency-advisor tool transforms an illegal update into an and/or tree of updates from which the user can construct a legal *transaction* (Zicari 1989) that includes the original illegal update. The advisor produces a set of hints, which the user does not necessarily have to follow. However, the advisor does not produce an exhaustive list of update alternatives. The criterion for generating alternative update strategies is that, in transforming an illegal update into a new one, undesired inconsistencies are not produced. The notion of transaction update has also been introduced in Gottlob, Paolini, and Zicari 1988, in the context of the view-update problem.

9.6 Incomplete Types

We plan to allow type transformation with incomplete types and object values (Zicari 1989; Gottlob and Zicari 1988).

10 Acknowledgements

Several discussions with Serge Abiteboul and Paris Kanellakis helped in improving our understanding of the problems. In particular, problem 2 in section 5.2.2 is from Serge Abiteboul and problem 1 in section 5.2.2 is from Paris Kanellakis. David Maier advised me to distinguish between the notion of completeness at schema level and the one at database level. The members of the Altaïr group, in particular François Bancilhon, Christine Delcourt, Claude Delobel, Gilbert Harrus, Sophie Gamerman, Christophe Lécluse, David Maier, Mark James, Claudia Medeiros, Philippe Richard, and Fernando Vélez provided useful comments on an earlier version of this chapter. In particular, Christine Delcourt designed and implemented the ICC tool, and Gilbert Harrus designed and ran the cost analysis.

References

Abiteboul, S., and R. Hull. 1987. IFO: A formal semantic database model. *ACM TODS* 12: 525–65.

______. 1988. Restructuring hierarchical database objects. *Theoretical Computer Science* 62.

Abiteboul, S., and P. Kanellakis. 1989. Object identity as a query language primitive. In *Proceedings of the ACM SIGMOD conference.*

Abiteboul, S., P. Kanellakis, and E. Waller. 1989. Method schemas. *Submitted for publication.*

Andrews, T., and C. Harris. 1987. Combining language and database advances in an object-oriented development environment. In *Proceedings of the OOPSLA conference.*

Banerjee, J., H-T. Chou, J. Garza, W. Kim, D. Woelk, N. Ballou, and H. J. Kim. 1987a. Data model issues for object-oriented applications. *ACM TOIS* 5(1): 3–26.

Banerjee, J., W. Kim, H. J. Kim, and H. F. Korth. 1987b. Semantics and implementation of schema evolution in object-oriented databases. In *Proceedings of the ACM SIGMOD conference.*

Bancilhon, F. 1988. Object-oriented database systems. In *Proceedings of the ACM PODS conference.*

Cacace, F., S. Ceri, S. Crespi-Reghizzi, L. Tanca, and R. Zicari. 1990. Integrating object-oriented data modeling with a rule-based programming paradigm. In *Proceedings of the ACM SIGMOD conference on management of data.*

Delcourt, C. 1989. *The integrity consistency checker (ICC): Detailed specifications.* GIP Altaïr Report.

Delcourt, C., and R. Zicari. 1989. *Preserving structural consistency in an object-oriented database.* GIP Altaïr Report.

Delobel, C. 1989. *A formal framework for the O_2 data model.* GIP Altaïr Report.

Gottlob, G., P. Paolini, and R. Zicari. 1988. Properties and update semantics of consistent views. *ACM TODS* 13(4).

Gottlob, G., and R. Zicari. 1988. Closed-world databases opened through null values. In *Proceedings of the 14th VLDB conference.*

Harrus, G., F. Vélez, and R. Zicari. 1990. Implementing schema updates in an object-oriented database system: A cost analysis. Altaïr Report.

Hudson, S., and R. King. 1989. Cactis: A self-adaptative, concurrent implementation of an object-oriented database management system. *ACM TODS* 14(3).

Hull, R., K. Tanaka, and M. Yoshikawa. 1989. Behavior analysis of object-oriented databases: Method structure, execution trees, and reachability. In *Proceedings of the 1989 FODO conference.*

Kim, W., N. Ballou, H-T. Chou, J. F. Garza, D. Woelk, and J. Banerjee. 1988. Integrating an object-oriented programming system with a database system. In *Proceedings of the OOPSLA conference.*

Kim W., and H-T. Chou. 1988. Versions of schema for object-oriented databases. In *Proceedings of the 14th VLDB conference.*

Lécluse, C., and P. Richard. 1988. Modeling inheritance and genericity in object-oriented databases. In *Proceedings of the ICDT-88 conference.*

______. 1989a. Modeling complex structures in object-oriented databases. In *Proceedings of the ACM PODS conference.*

______. 1989b. The O_2 database programming language. In *Proceedings of the 15th VLDB conference.*

Lécluse, C., P. Richard, and F. Vélez. 1988. O_2, an object-oriented data model. In *Proceedings of the ACM SIGMOD conference.*

Panel on Schema Evolution and Version Management. 1989. Report on the object-oriented database workshop. *SIGMOD Record* 18(3).

Penney, D. J., and J. Stein. 1987. Class modification in the GemStone object-oriented DBMS. In *Proceedings of the ACM OOPSLA conference.*

Skarra, A., and S. Zdonik. 1986. The management of changing types in an object-oriented database. In *Proceedings of the ACM OOPSLA conference.*

______. 1987. Type evolution in an object-oriented database. In *Research directions in object-oriented systems,* ed. B. Shriver and P. Wegner. MIT Press.

Vélez, F., G. Bernard, and V. Darnis. 1989. The O_2 object manager: An overview. In *Proceedings of the 15th VLDB conference.*

Zdonik, S. B. 1987. Can objects change types? In *Workshop on object-oriented databases.*

Zicari, R. 1989. A framework for O_2 schema updates. GIP Altaïr report no. 38–89. Also in Proceedings of the 7th IEEE international conference on data engineering. 1991.

Appendix: Cost Analysis

This section gives a sketch of the first cost analysis of Harrus, Vélez, and Zicari 1990. First, we briefly describe some system-implementation details, and then we present the results of the analysis.

A.1 Architecture

The O_2 system is composed of two main layers, if we ignore the language environment and the user interfaces (Vélez et al. 1989; see chapter 15). The upper layer of the system is the Schema Manager (called the Type and Method Manager). It manages the schema and is responsible for enforcing the semantics of inheritance and for checking the consistency of the schema. It is built on top of the Object Manager, which is the lower layer of the system. The Object Manager handles complex objects with identity and complex values. Objects are uniquely identified and accessed by their object identifiers (oids). The object internal representation contains (in the header) the identification of the class to which the object belongs and the identifier of the type to which its value belongs. The Object Manager also handles message passing and the distributed server/workstation configuration. It implements persistence, garbage-collects unreferenced objects, and implements indexes and clustering strategies based on complex objects and inheritance. Finally, it offers transaction modes which adapt the system to *execution* mode or *development* mode.

A.2 Parameters

We considered three parameters in our study: (1) types of updates, (2) modes of updates, and (3) implementation of class extensions.

A.2.1 Types of Updates

We considered only updates to the schema, u, which imply updating the database as well. Updates u can be grouped in three categories with respect to their implementation:

a. Updates which change the type field in the object header: updates 1.1 and 1.2.

b. Updates which insert or delete oids in class extensions: updates 3.1 and 3.4.

c. Updates which insert or delete oids and change the type field of the object header: update 3.5.

A.2.2 Modes of Updates

We considered two alternative approaches to updating the database (see section 7):

- *Immediate mode*: objects are updated immediately after the schema modification.
- *Deferred mode*: objects are updated only when used.

The deferred mode implies a way to "remember" the update history for each object in the database (see the discussion of costs in section 10.5). This ensures that objects are up to date with respect to the schema modifications.

A.2.3 Class-Extension Implementation

Logically each class C in a schema has associated an extension ext(C), that is, the set of objects (oids) of that class. The inheritance relationships implies that the extension of C also contains the oids of all subclasses of C (if any). We considered three alternative ways to implement class extensions:

- *Global extension*: ext(C) contains the oids of all objects of class C and all subclasses of C.
- *Local extension*: ext(C) contains only the oids of objects of class C.
- *No extension*: the system does not keep the class extension.

A.3 Assumptions

We restricted our attention to a system with the following simplified assumptions:

- Tuple-structured objects have only atomic attributes.
- The system is in development mode.
- The test database is already in main memory.

We plan to extend our results to take into consideration disk-access time.

A.4 Notations

The mean cost of a schema update u (i.e., the time needed for the central processing unit (CPU) to update all objects affected by the update) is denoted $C(tsm)$, where

t is the type of update (a, b, or c).

s is the class-extension implementation (global, local, or no extension).

m is the update mode (immediate or deferred).

$C(tsm)$ depends on the following parameters:

N, the number of objects in the database.

p, the problem of objects concerned with the update. pN is the total number of objects which has to be updated.

C_{ro}, the CPU time to access an object (given its oid).

C_{ins}, the CPU time to insert an object in its class extension.

C_{tu}, the mean cost of a tuple update.

C_{ac}, the mean cost of accessing the information to decide whether a class has been updated in the current session.

C_{sr}, the mean cost of keeping the object-update history; that is, the time to decide if an object is up to date with respect to the updates of its class.

R, the access rate to objects.

q, the proportion of objects in the database that belong to an updated class.

Table 7.1 shows some measured values for the above parameters.

Table 7.1. Values of Parameters

N	1000–10000
p	0.0–1.0
C_{ro}	0.05 ms
C_{ins}	0.40 ms
C_{tu}	0.15 ms
C_{ac}	0.08 ms
C_{sr}	0.40 ms
R	200–2000
q	0.0–1.0

A.5 Costs

Table 7.2 displays the mean CPU time required by each type of update. Local class extensions give minimal CPU costs. For deferred updates, there is an additional cost: the system overhead for storing and accessing each object's update history, given by

$$qRC_{sr} + (1 - q)RC_{ac}$$

Table 7.2. Costs for Schema Updates

	Type of Update		
	a	b	c
Global extensions			
Immediate	$pN(C_{ro} + C_{tu})$	$pN(C_{ro} + C_{ins})$	$2pN(C_{ro} + C_{ins} + C_{tu})$
Deferred	$pN\,C_{tu}$	$pN\,C_{ins}$	$2pN(C_{ins} + C_{tu})$
Local extensions			
Immediate	$pN(C_{ro} + C_{tu})$	0	$2pN(C_{ro} + C_{tu})$
Deferred	$pN\,C_{tu}$	0	$2pN\,C_{tu}$
No extension			
Immediate	$N(C_{ro} + pC_{tu})$	0	$2N(C_{ro} + pC_{tu})$
Deferred	$pN\,C_{tu}$	0	$2pN\,C_{tu}$

A.5.1 Overheads

To compute the system overhead for an update in deferred mode, we considered two hypothetical situations:

- Configuration A (business application): few classes (less than 10); large q (more than 50%); only updates of type a are made; high object-access rate R (from 1000 to 2000); low-computation methods.
- Configuration B (CAD application): many classes (more than 50); frequent updates of types b and c; large q (more than 50%); small R (200 to 400); each method requires high computation.

Table 7.3 shows some values for the overhead required by deferred updates for the two configurations. The dominating factor is R.

Table 7.3. Examples of Overhead in Deferred Mode

	Configuration A			Configuration B		
	$R = 1000$	$R = 1500$	$R = 2000$	$R = 200$	$R = 300$	$R = 400$
$q = 0.50$	24	36	48	4.8	7.2	9.6
$q = 0.75$	32	48	64	6.4	9.6	12.8
$q = 1.00$	40	60	80	8.0	12.6	16.0

Part III

The Languages

CHAPTER 8

Introduction to Languages

FRANÇOIS BANCILHON
DAVID MAIER

Database systems include a number of language components. The data definition language (DDL) of the O_2 data model was discussed in part 2 of this book. In part 3 we focus on data manipulation languages (DMLs) to access and modify the database. In particular, we examine

- programming languages to write database application programs in
- query languages to access data in an ad hoc fashion or from a programming language

Relational systems have privileged the ad hoc query language components (where a user interactively extracts data from the database) over the programming ones (where a programmer writes an application, generally more complex and longer lasting, for an end user). Thus relational systems offer a DML whose main component is a query language (most probably SQL) which is simple and powerful but not complete. Because of this incompleteness, the application programmer has to use an external programming language in which to embed DML commands.

Unfortunately, relational data manipulation languages and classical programming languages do not fit together well. This *impedance mismatch* is largely due to three causes:

1. *Type mismatch.* The type system of the programming language and the database system DDL are not the same. Relational databases deal with sets of flat tuples, while programming languages often deal with single hierarchical records. Therefore the programmer must take care of the conversion when storing in the database or retrieving from it.

2. *Set versus element programming.* Relational database systems operate on sets of tuples as a whole through macro-operations such as join, select, and project; whereas programming languages deal with one record at a time.

3. *Declarative versus imperative programming.* One of the more attractive features of relational query languages is their declarativeness. They specify *what* the user wants and not *how* it should be computed. Unfortunately, this is accompanied by a tradeoff in expressive power and implementation complexity. In contrast, the most widely used programming languages are imperative. This reflects the reality of practice in the early 1990s; although imperative programming is not as user friendly as declarative programming, it uses well-understood implementation technology.

The impedance mismatch has a number of undesirable consequences. Faced with both a query language and a programming language, the programmer has to decide where to put the boundary between the extraction of data from the database and the processing of this data. More code has to be written because the programmer has to handle data conversion and the binding of variables. This additional code is hard to write and to read because it is awkward and unrelated to the problem the programmer is treating. It also introduces a lot of unnecessary communication between the programming language and the database system, thus creating a performance loss. Finally, more errors result from the minimal type checking performed across the boundary between the programming language and the database.

In the last decade, there have been numerous attempts to solve this mismatch. Examples of such attempts are *persistent programming languages,* which result from the introduction of database functionality in existing or new programming languages; *database programming languages,* which result from the extension of data manipulation languages to make them complete; and *deductive databases,* which result from the extension of relational languages to give them the power of logic programming languages.

In object-oriented databases, the same need is taken into account by providing complete database programming languages. However, the common practice is that these languages complement but do not replace traditional query languages. Thus some OODBs (O_2 included) simultaneously support a query language for ad hoc interaction and a programming language for coding of methods. However, in OODBs (unlike in relational systems) the main language component is the programming language component.

The position exemplified by O_2 is the "realist" one, which involves a number of language components, as opposed to the "idealist" all-in-one language approach. In particular, we believe that query languages are still needed because they provide:

- simplicity of expression
- associative and declarative access to bulk data
- the ability to query the database in an ad hoc fashion (without having to actually use a programming language)

Having argued for the presence of query languages, we should point out that there are technical difficulties. The design of query languages for object-oriented databases raises a number of issues not taken into account in relational query languages. This is because such query languages involve:

- complex objects instead of flat relations
- objects which encapsulate data and operations
- a connection to the database programming language, minimizing the impedance mismatch

The rest of this introduction is divided into four parts. We start with a brief survey of the language components of other OODBs. We then present a historical view of the O_2 approach. This brings us to a more detailed discussion of language integration in OODBs. Finally, we provide a roadmap for part 3 of this book.

1 A Brief Survey

We present here a survey of some of the major object-oriented database systems in terms of their database programming languages and their query languages.

GemStone's (Maier, Otis, and Purdy 1985) data model is based on the programming language Smalltalk. The system uses an extension of Smalltalk as its database programming language and its data definition language. This extension also includes a query language facility, which provides associative access to data (via predicates based on structural selection applied to a single set).

Orion (Banerjee et al. 1987) has its own data model, which incorporates the most common object-oriented features. It uses an extension of Lisp for its method language. This extension embeds a query language (Banerjee, Kim, and Kim 1987) which does not violate encapsulation. Queries are based on methods only. Access to the database is gained through the extensions of the database classes. The output of a query is always a subset of the instances of a class. Unless classes are related through a "composition" link, the query language only allows access to a single class at a time.

Vbase (Atwood 1985; Ontologic 1986; Andrews and Harris 1987) originally had its own data model and provided two different languages: TDL, a data definition language, and COP (for C Object Processor) to define methods. COP was an extension of C. A query language of the SQL type was added later on.

Iris (Fishman et al. 1987) was originally based on a functional data model, which later evolved into an object-oriented one. It supports the OSQL query language (Beech 1988), which has an SQL-like syntax. OSQL is not only a query language but also the comprehensive language vehicle for the model. In that respect Iris has been largely influenced by the relational paradigm and its standard SQL. As with SQL, OSQL serves as a data description, data manipulation, and query language. However, it cannot address some complex problems, which have to be solved by a call to external functions. Those functions have to be written in a foreign programming language, C in the Iris prototype. Thus Iris does not have a complete database programming language per se.

Exodus (Carey, DeWitt, and Vandenberg 1988) is based on the Extra data model. The Excess query language has a QUEL syntax and allows modification of a database as well as querying. It also provides facilities to define new functions. Objects are queried through appropriate functions; values are queried according to their structure and appropriate functions. The output of a query is always a set value.

2 Historical View of the O_2 Approach

2.1 The O_2 Database Programming Language

The design of the O_2 database programming language went through various stages, not all of them successful! The experience gained in this effort was valuable, and led to CO_2 as the preferred database programming language of prototype V1. It also made it easy to integrate other (similar) programming languages in subsequent versions of O_2, the important example being the language C++.

The original goal was to define an *independent* language layer, O_2, which could be added to any programming language. Thus C plus O_2 would become CO_2, Basic plus O_2 would become BasicO_2, and Lisp plus O_2 would become LispO_2. These three languages were the original target list. C was chosen because it was a good implementation language and, in 1986, C++ had not yet gained the wide acceptance it now has. Basic was chosen because it was the application language used by our main industrial sponsor. Lisp was chosen because it was so widely different from the other two, and it would make the point that the list of languages could be extended easily.

2.1.1 The V0 Prototype

In the original V0 prototype the layer was defined independently of the programming language and then incorporated into C. The first CO_2 compiler was operational in September 1987, and a number of toy applications were written using it. The process of integrating the O_2 layer into Basic and Lisp was investigated.

The lesson learned from this effort was that unless the layer was specifically designed (at least syntactically) for the language to which it was added, the end result was cumbersome and not very natural to use.

2.1.2 The V1 Prototype

For the V1 prototype it was decided to proceed differently. The team defined the semantics of the layer independently, then the syntax was adapted to each of the languages. Here is what happened for C and Basic.

The experiment was carried through, in the sense that CO_2 and $BasicO_2$ were defined in 1988 and the compilers for both of them were implemented in 1989. The CO_2 language of the V1 prototype is described in Lécluse and Richard 1989 (see chapter 9). The V1 prototype did actually support objects having methods written in both CO_2 and $BasicO_2$. The conclusion was mixed:

- The group was indeed able to build a multilanguage system that managed objects and classes having methods in both CO_2 and $BasicO_2$ (even in the same class). The communication problem between CO_2 and $BasicO_2$ was solved, and a common layer was defined for both languages, even though that layer had a different syntax in C and in Basic. The use of language-specific syntax allowed a nice embedding of the common layer in each host language.

- The development of a specific technology which would allow us to define the implementation of the layer in an easy and incremental way on an existing compiler was less successful. The CO_2 implementation was done by a CO_2 preprocessor which generated C; that preprocessor happened to do quite a lot of work (it performed a complete type checking of the programs). The $BasicO_2$ implementation was done through a $BasicO_2$-to-C compiler, which turned out to be a major job. Thus, developing a new language LO_2 from a language L using this approach meant in fact rewriting a complete compiler for the LO_2 language (making limited use of the existing L compiler).

We are not saying there is no other way to do it. We are merely saying we solved one of the problems and did not investigate the second one for enough to develop a suitable new technology.

2.1.3 The $LispO_2$ Stand-alone Prototype

When trying to make Lisp one of our method languages, we were confronted with some major problems, indicating some of the naiveté of the original goals.

1. Integrating a language like Lisp within a strongly typed framework such as O_2 was not a good idea, because most of the benefits of Lisp were lost in the process.

2. Lisp users would not want to write Lisp code within an O_2 framework but only to access the O_2 facilities from a Lisp environment. They would be interested in accessing O_2 from Lisp, but not Lisp from O_2.

3. It was possible to write O_2 methods in Lisp, but not to benefit from the Lisp run-time environment in O_2.

We therefore changed our strategy and, instead of trying to integrate Lisp into our O_2 environment in the same way as C and Basic, we decided to start an independent experiment with Lisp, making LispO_2 a stand-alone prototype separate from the V1 prototype. This experiment is recounted in Barbedette 1990 (see chapter 10).

2.2 The O_2 Query Language

We did a number of experiments before actually choosing the O_2 query language. One of these experiments is reported in Cluet et al. 1989 (see chapter 12), which presents the Reloop query language together with its formal semantics. Delobel et al. 1988 presents a different aspect of this language. A purely functional language, Lifoo (Boucelma and Lemaître 1988), was designed and implemented by a group in Marseille. These two articles were not included in this book; the original Reloop paper was edited to remove redundancy with respect to chapter 11 (Bancilhon, Cluet, and Delobel 1990).

We drew many lessons from these experiments and defined a new language, described in Bancilhon, Cluet, and Delobel 1990 (again, see chapter 11). This language is the one supported as the O_2 query language of the V1 prototype.

3 Language Integration in OODBs

The design of a database programming language for an object-oriented database system raises a major issue: given a data model and a programming language, how do we connect them? We can list four approaches to this problem that impact the choice of language in an OODB.

1. *The new language approach:* We define a new language, specifically suited for the design task at hand. It has to be a full-blown programming language with complete language features, such as I/O. As far as we know, no *complete* OODB has taken this solution. Galileo (Albano, Cardelli, and Orsini 1985), is close to an example of this approach.

2. *The existing language approach:* We choose an existing programming language (Smalltalk, C, Pascal, or Modula); we can base our choice on various factors, such as popularity or ease of description of the applications envisioned. Then we extend that language by its connection to the data model. This approach was taken in GemStone (Maier, Otis, and Purdy 1985) by

extending Smalltalk, in Orion (Banerjee et al. 1987) by extending Lisp, and in Vbase (Ontologic 1986) by extending C.

3. *The multilanguage approach:* We allow the user to write methods in a set of existing programming languages. Thus we have to define a connection mode which will work for all of them. This was the original O_2 approach, which was carried through to the extent described in the previous section.

4. *The program object approach:* We view programs as objects. For example, a program is stored as a database object. It is structured by **while** loops or **if-then-else** constructors. It can be executed and has its own semantics. Given such program objects (as the internal machine representations) they can be made to resemble (in their display to the user) various programming languages. This is an ambitious area, but as far as we know it is still unexplored.

All these approaches have pros and cons, which we now list.

The new language approach. On the minus side, designing a language is a long task, which can take years and require specialists. Getting the compiler to produce fast code takes time and talent. The new language will meet user resistance; nobody likes to switch to a new programming language—it will require teaching and selling. A complete library will have to be developed for this language.

On the plus side, because the language is specifically designed for that purpose, the connection between the language and the database will be smooth and natural.

The existing language approach. On the minus side, the system will be easily accepted only by those who already use the programming language. With all other programmers, we will meet user resistance. There is also a risk that, in connecting the language to the data model, one may introduce unnatural features to take into account the idiosyncrasies of the language. In the long run, such features may prove counterproductive.

On the plus side, it will be easy to sell to people familiar with the chosen programming language. The system will be able to make use of the existing library for this language, thus avoiding the need to develop a new one. Because we develop a connection between the programming language and the data model, and because in practice we have full control over the data model, we can fit the two reasonably well. We will have no language to define and no code generation to perform; a simple precompiler should be sufficient to process the extended language.

The multilanguage approach. On the minus side, we will need to write n precompilers, where n is the number of supported languages. If we want the system to support multilanguage applications, we will have to write n^2 data-conversion procedures to accomodate the built-in data types of those languages (such as strings). The connection has to be made between the data model and a set of languages that is not known a priori (we might want to add new languages later without destroying the edifice); so the connection will be based on general principles and might not fit very well with each particular language. In summary, because we have to satisfy different families of customers with the same product, the product will not be as customized.

On the plus side, we have a large potential market of users: all the users of the programming languages are potential customers, who could switch to the new system without too much training. Users will have the ability to write multilanguage applications; complex applications with several specialized parts could be written in this fashion, each part written in the best adapted language. After all, n^2 is not prohibitive if n is small. Because the connection has to be made between the data model and a set of languages, the layer added to each programming language will be clean and language independent; this might prove to be a major advantage in the long run. Of course, we will not have to write entire compilers, and we will have the availability of large libraries.

The program object approach. On the minus side, we will have to do complete code generation and compilation. The approach relies on fairly new technology. Program objects will not be totally compatible with existing programming languages.

On the plus side, we are back to the solution of the new-language approach, and we have all of its advantages of smooth connection to the data model. Because we can make the program objects look like C or Pascal code, they could easily be accepted by users familiar with those programming languages. Finally, programs will be stored and manipulated as objects.

4 A Roadmap for Part 3

The rest of part 3 consists of five chapters, which are edited versions of papers previously published in conference proceedings. Chapters 9, 10, 11, and 12 (Lécluse and Richard 1989; Barbedette 1990; Bancilhon, Cluet, and Delobel 1990; Cluet et al. 1989) describe languages which were developed as part of the O_2 project; chapter 13 (Gamerman and Vélez 1989) addresses the problem of evaluating languages through the encoding of benchmark applications.

Chapter 9, "The O_2 Database Programming Language," gives a complete description of the O_2 database programming language as it is implemented in the V1 prototype.

Chapter 10, "LispO_2, a Persistent Object-Oriented Lisp," reports on the experiment of integrating the O_2 data model in a Lisp environment.

Chapter 11, "A Query Language for an Object-Oriented Database System," provides a general discussion on object-oriented database query languages and presents informally the final query language of the V1 prototype.

Chapter 12, "Reloop, an Algebra Based Query Language for an O_2," reports on one of the query languages defined for O_2 and on its formal semantics.

Chapter 13, "Using Database Applications to Compare Programming Languages," is an attempt to provide an empirical metric for the comparison of database programming languages. It uses a benchmark approach, defining a simple set of applications, writing them in various languages, and commenting on programmer productivity.

References

Albano, A., L. Cardelli, and R. Orsini. 1985. Galileo: A strongly typed, interactive conceptual language. *ACM TODS* 10(2): 230–61.

Andrews, T., and C. Harris. 1987. Combining language and database advances in an object-oriented development environment. In *Proceedings of the OOPSLA conference.*

Atwood, T. 1985. *An object-oriented DBMS for design support applications.* Ontologic, Inc., Report.

Bancilhon, F., S. Cluet, and C. Delobel. 1990. A query language for an object-oriented database system. In *Proceedings of the second database programming language workshop.* Also in *The O_2 queries syntax and semantics.* Altaïr Technical Report no. 45–90.

Banerjee, J., H-T. Chou, J. Garza, W. Kim, D. Woelk, N. Ballou, and H. J. Kim. 1987. Data model issues for object-oriented applications. *ACM TOIS* 5(1): 3–26.

Banerjee, J., W. Kim, K. C. Kim. 1987. *Queries in object-oriented databases.* MCC Technical Report, no. DB 188–87.

Barbedette, G. 1990. LispO_2, a persistent object-oriented Lisp. In *Proceedings of the second conference on extending database technology.*

Beech, D. 1988. A foundation for evolution from relational to object databases. In *Proceedings of the first conference on extending database technology.*

Boucelma, O., and J. Lemaître. 1988. Lifoo, un language d'interrogation fonctionnel pour une base de donnée orienté-objet. Université de Marseille, Technical Report.

Carey, M., D. DeWitt, and S. Vandenberg. 1988. A data model and query language for Exodus. In *Proceedings of the 1988 ACM SIGMOD conference.*

Cluet, S., C. Delobel, C. Lécluse, and P. Richard. 1989. RELOOP, an algebra based query language for an object-oriented database system. In *Proceedings of the first conference on deductive and object-oriented databases.*

Delobel, C., C. Lécluse, and P. Richard. 1988. LOOQ: A query language for object-oriented databases. In *Proceedings of the AFCET conference on knowledge and object-oriented database systems.*

Fishman, D., D. Beech, H. P. Cate, E. C. Chow, T. Conners, J. W. Davis, N. Denett, C. G. Hoch, W. Kent, P. Lyngbaek, B. Mahbod, M. A. Neimat, T. A. Ryan and M. C. Shan. 1987. Iris: an object-oriented database management system. *ACM TOIS* 5(1): 46–69.

Gamerman, S., and F. Vélez. Using a set of database applications to compare programming languages. In *Proceedings of the fourth PRC BD3.*

Lécluse, C., and P. Richard. 1989. The O_2 database programming language. In *Proceedings of the fifteenth conference on very large databases.*

Maier, D., A. Otis, and A. Purdy. 1985. Development of an object-oriented DBMS. *Quarterly Bulletin of IEEE on Database Engineering* 8(4). Also in *Proceedings of the 1986 OOPSLA conference.*

Ontologic. 1986. *VBase functional specification.* Ontologic, Inc., Billerica, Mass.

CHAPTER 9

The O_2 Database Programming Language

C. LÉCLUSE
P. RICHARD

1 Introduction

The major objective of Altaïr is to prototype a complete development environment for data-intensive applications. The functionalities of such a system should include those of a DBMS, those of a programming language, and those of a programming environment. We decided to build an object-oriented database system, named O_2, and its programming environment. Our motivations for this choice are the following:

- We believe that one of the main limitations to the productivity of the application programmer is the impedance mismatch between the programming language and the database. This impedance mismatch cannot be solved by redefining the database box (i.e., by changing the frontier between the programming language and the database system). It is necessary to mix database technology and programming-language technology to build a complete system with the functionalities of both a DBMS and a programming language.

- We believe that, among the available technologies produced by programming-language people and among the possible approaches, the object-oriented approach is the best one to mix with database technology. This is due both to the intrinsic characteristics of the approach and to the appeal this paradigm has for programmers.

The next choice concerned the programming language of the system. Among the possible solutions—extending an existing language, designing a new language, or being language independent—we chose the last one, mainly for marketing reasons (from a purely technical point of view the second was probably the best). The system is viewed by the user as consisting of a data definition language (DDL) by which the user can manipulate a hierarchy of classes. He or she can attach methods to classes or to objects by writing these methods in various languages. Our first target set of languages consists of C and Basic. Rather than speaking of the O_2 database programming language, one can think of the O_2 database programming languages. Programming in O_2 is done in two distinct steps. First the programmer defines classes using O_2 commands. Then he or she programs the code of his or her methods, using one of the O_2 programming dialects. For the time being, two programming languages are specified: the CO_2 language, which relies on C; and the BasicO_2 language, which relies on Basic. In this paper, we specifically report on the merging of programming-language technology and database technology (Atkinson and Buneman 1987). We describe only CO_2, as it is the first language we have implemented. The approach followed for BasicO_2 is similar to that for CO_2 . A full description of the O_2 object manager can be found in Vélez, Bernard, and Darnis 1989 (see chapter 15).

This paper is organized as follows. Section 2 contains an informal presentation of objects and values in O_2. Section 3 describes the data organization in O_2 through examples. Section 4 shows how programming is done, and illustrates it using CO_2. Section 5 explains how inheritance works in O_2, and justifies its foundations through subtyping. Section 6 illustrates the features of O_2 which deal with sets and exceptions. Section 7 briefly describes how methods are type checked in O_2 and how method safety is ensured. Section 8 compares the O_2 system with several other object-oriented database systems. Finally, we present some conclusions in section 9.

2 Objects and Values in O_2

O_2 is object-oriented. This means that information is organized as *objects*, which have an identity and encapsulate data and behaviour. Manipulation of objects is done through *methods*, which are procedures attached to the objects. Object identity is useful for supporting object sharing and update management. The theoretical foundations for object identity as a programming language primitive can be found in Abiteboul and Kanellakis 1989 (see chapter 5).

In O_2 we provide the user with the possibility of defining not only objects but also *values*, as in standard programming languages or in the so-called complex-object languages (Abiteboul and Beeri 1987; Kuper 1985; Bancilhon and Khoshafian 1986). ("Complex objects" are not objects in the object-oriented terminology but rather complex values.)

Consider the following three objects (the object identifiers are written in italics):

```
eiffel_tower:
tuple(name: "Eiffel Tower",
      address: eiffel_address,
      description: "a famous Paris monument",
      admission_fee: 25)

eiffel_address:
tuple(city: paris,
      street: "Champ de Mars")

paris:
tuple(name: "Paris",
      country: "France",
      population: 2.6)
```

While both *paris* and *eiffel_address* were modeled as objects in this example, we believe that they should be treated differently: *eiffel_address* is nothing more than a pair of strings, and it appears only in the value of *eiffel_tower*. On the other hand, cities evolve (for example, the population may change), and they might contain other monuments; therefore we wish to model *paris* as an object. In our system, the object *eiffel_tower* should be modeled as follows, with the address appearing as a structured value and *paris* as an object:

```
eiffel_tower:
tuple(name: "Eiffel Tower",
      address: tuple(city: paris,
                     street: "Champ de Mars"),
      description: "a famous Paris monument",
      admission_fee: 25)
```

3 Types and Classes

In O_2 the user has two ways of structuring data: types, whose instances are objects, and classes, whose instances are values. Types are recursively constructed using atomic types such as integers, floats, strings, class names, and the set, list, and tuple constructors. Instances of types are values. These types are similar to classical types in programming languages. The following expression is an O_2 type.

```
tuple (name: string,
       country: string,
       population: float,
       monuments: set(Monument))
```

This type describes cities. The **monuments** attribute has a set-structured value. Monument is a class name. A value of this type could be:

```
tuple(name: "Paris",
      country: "France",
      population: 2.6,
      monuments: set(eiffel_tower, arc_de_triomphe))
```

Recall that we use italics to denote objects. One can see from the above example that values can be arbitrarily complex. The elements of the set value of the attribute **monuments** are objects, as shown in the next subsection. In O_2 the user builds types using atomic types, such as string, float, integer, char and Boolean, and three type constructors: tuple, set, and list. There is no restriction on the use of these constructors; We have already used the set and tuple constructors; an example of use of the list constructor is given in the next subsection.

3.1 The Schema Definition Language

In O_2, the schema is a set of classes related by inheritance links (see section 5) and/or composition links. A class describes the structure *and* the behaviour of a set of objects. The structural part of a class is a type, and the behavioral part is a set of methods (see section 4). Classes are created using schema-definition commands as follows.

```
add class City
    type tuple(name: string,
               country: string,
               population: integer,
               monuments: set(Monument))


add class Monument
    type tuple(name: string,
               address: tuple(street: string,
                              city: City),
               description: string,
               closing_days: list(string),
               admission_fee: integer)
```

We denote the name of a class by capitalizing the first letter. In the example, the first class has the name City and a type which is given after the keyword **type**. Instances of this class are objects; that is, they each have a unique internal identifier and a value which is an instance of the type associated to the class. Objects are encapsulated; that is, their value is not directly accessible. They are manipulated by methods, as explained in section 4. The second class defines historical monuments. Note that classes can be mutually referencing:

City references Monument, which in turn references City. For every Monument object, the value of the `city` attribute is an object which may itself reference the Monument object. Following an approach similar to that used in Galileo (Albano, Cardelli, and Orsini 1985), the equivalence of classes is by name—as opposed to type equivalence, which is by structure (that is, the type of the values depends only on their structure. On the other hand, two classes are always distinct, and the compatibility rule is the name-equivalence rule.

3.2 Object Creation

Creation of objects is done through a system command called **new**. This **new** command takes as input the name of the class corresponding to the object to be created. The object is created with a default value depending on the type associated to the class. The default values are: the empty string, the integer 0, the float 0.0, the empty list for list types, the empty set for set types, and a tuple of default values for tuple types.

3.3 Naming and Persistence

In O_2, objects or values can be named. The following is an example of naming:

add object Eiffel_Tower: Monument

The name Eiffel_Tower will then stand for an object of class Monument. In the same way, one can name a value as follows:

add value Paris_monuments: **set**(Monument)

Paris_monuments is the name for a value of type set(Monument). In O_2, persistence is attached to names; that is, every named object or value is persistent. Such a name can be seen as a global variable which is dynamically attached to a given object or value and which makes it persistent. The attached object can be changed by assignment. For instance, we can write:

Eiffel_Tower = **new**(Monument)

This instruction assigns a newly created object to the name Eiffel_Tower. The initial value of the object is the tuple default value corresponding to the type. This object will always be accessible through the name Eiffel_Tower during the life of the system, except if the user makes another assignment.

The persistence rules are:

1. Every named object or value is persistent,

2. Every object or value which is a part of another persistent object or value is persistent.

For example, let us assume that we have made the assignment

Paris_monuments = **set**(Eiffel_Tower, *arc_de_triomphe*)

where Eiffel_Tower is a named object and *arc_de_triomphe* denotes an object of class Monument with no name. These objects are persistent; the first because it is named, and the second because it is an element of the named value. The same holds for objects or values which appear as an attribute value in the named object Eiffel_Tower.

The *extension* of a class is the set of all objects created using the **new** command applied to that class. The system provides the user with an automatic management of class extensions. This is done using a set value which collects all the objects of a class. For instance, one can write:

```
add class City with extension
        type tuple(name: string,
                   country: string,
                   population: integer,
                   monuments: set(Monument))
```

The **with extension** clause in the class definition tells the O_2 system to create a named value of type **set**(City) with name City. Moreover, every city created with the **new**(City) command will be automatically inserted in this set and will thus persist, as it is a component of a persistent set. Note that, according to our persistence rules, objects of a class without extension will not persist unless they are explicitly named or components of some other persistent object or value. Classes with no extension are a natural way of dealing with transient objects.

4 Manipulation of Objects and Values

In the object-oriented approach, objects are manipulated by *methods*. A method is a piece of code which is attached to a specific class and which can be applied to objects of this class.

4.1 Method Definition

In O_2, method definition is done in two steps. First the user declares the method by giving its signature—that is, its name, the type or class of the arguments, and the type or class of the result if there is one. Then he or she gives the code of the method.

The following is a method declaration:

```
add method increase_fee (amount: integer)
in class Monument
```

This method increases the **admission_fee** field of a Monument object. Methods can be *private* or *public*. Private methods are only visible within their class, that is, in the methods attached to that class. Public methods are visible by all classes and can be freely used. When declaring a method, the user can add the keywords **is public** in order to make it public. The default is private.

O_2 follows a multilanguage approach. This means that method programming is done in a standard programming language such as C or Basic with manipulation of O_2 objects and values. The main idea is that most of the programming is done using the programmer's favorite language. This includes iterations, control structures, and arithmetics. Access to, and manipulation of, objects and values is done using O_2 features. We give below, as an example, the code of the method *increase_fee* using the CO_2 language.

```
body increase_fee(amount: integer) in class Monument
    co2 { (*self).admission_fee += amount; }
```

The curly brackets delimit the CO_2 block of code, as in pure C. The value of an object is obtained using the "dereferencing" method "*", thus "self" is the object and "*self" is the associated value. This method is applied using a special syntax which follows the C "*" use. It illustrates the association between objects and values. As in standard programming languages, objects can be seen as pointers to values. In the example, the value "*self" is tuple structured, and access to an attribute is obtained using the dot operator. The assignment is done as in C; it increments the integer value representing the admission fee. Notice that we stick to the C syntax for manipulating O_2 values such as dereferencing or extracting a tuple field. This way of manipulating objects is syntactically very close to what is done in C++ (Stroustrup 1986). In O_2, however, this similarity is purely syntactical, as objects and values are implemented and manipulated in a special way by a persistent object manager, and the CO_2 compiler generates calls to this object manager (Vélez, Bernard, and Darnis 1989; see chapter 15).

A method is applied to an object by *message passing*, whose syntax is:

```
[receiver selector(arguments)]
```

The square brackets are used to delimit O_2 message passings, and "receiver" denotes an object to which the method with the name "selector" is applied. This eventually returns an object depending on the method code. For example, *increase_fee* is applied to a Monument object using the following message passing:

```
[Eiffel_Tower increase_fee(3)]
```

The keyword "self" in the above code will denote the object Eiffel_Tower when the method is applied.

4.2 Manipulating Values

The CO_2 language allows the construction of O_2 values using the set, list, and tuple constructors. We can, for instance, write a set value containing four integers as follows: set(1, 4, 34, -21). The following associates a value to a newly created object:

```
Eiffel_Tower = new(Monument);
*Eiffel_Tower = tuple(name: "Eiffel Tower",
                      address: tuple(city: paris,
                                     street: "Champ de Mars"),
                      description: "a famous Paris monument",
                      closing_days: list("Christmas", "Easter"),
                      admission_fee: 25);
```

This assumes the "*" method is public for the Monument class. We have seen above that we can extract a field of a tuple value using the dot operator. All the CO_2 value manipulations are done in this way, using the classical C constructs. For instance, we shall append elements to the **closing_days** list of the Eiffel_Tower object as follows:

```
*Eiffel_Tower.closing_days += list("June 6th");
```

We modify one entry of the list as follows:

```
*Eiffel_Tower.closing_days[1] = "January 1st";
```

O_2 provides the user with the usual set and list operators (union, intersection, difference, cardinality, concatenation, and so on), whose syntax follows as far as possible the C syntax.

4.3 Iterator

The iterator described here is applied on set-structured or list-structured *values*, not on objects. Indeed, objects are encapsulated, and one should not know what is the structure of the encapsulated value. Of course, the values to which the iterator is applied may be either a set (or a list) of values or a set (or a list) of objects. CO_2 provides the user with an iterator which allows for easy sets or lists manipulations.

```
for (x in S [when condition]) <statement>
```

This is an extension of the classical C iterator. It applies the given statement with the variable x bound to every element of the set (or list) value S that satisfies the optional condition. The **when** clause adds no power to the **for** iterator, but allows some optimization when the condition is directly evaluable by the object manager. For instance, we can write:

```
co2{ o2 Monument x;
     for (x in Paris_monument
     when (*x.admission_fee <= 20))
     [x increase_fee(amount)];
     }
```

The above code increases the value of the **admission_fee** attribute for all the monuments located in Paris whose admission fee is less than or equal to Fr 20. The expression "**o2** Monument x" declares an O_2 variable which is used to denote objects of class Monument. Paris_monument is a named value of type set(Monument) which is supposed to contain all the monuments of Paris. The **for** iterator is less concise but more flexible than the classical *join* operation. It is far more powerful in the context of O_2, which is a programming language and not an end-user query language.

5 Subtyping and Inheritance

Inheritance is a powerful mechanism which allows the user to define classes in an incremental way by refining already existing ones. O_2 provides the user with an inheritance mechanism based on subtyping.

5.1 Subtyping

Subtyping is a semantic relationship which connects two types. There are several ways of defining subtyping. In O_2 we defined a set-inclusion semantics for subtyping. That is, a type is a subtype of another if and only if every instance of this type is also an instance of its supertype. This allows one to say that a person is a human or that an employee is a person. The formal definition of the O_2 type system is given in Lécluse and Richard 1989. Another approach is taken in Vision (Caruso 1987): subtyping is expressed by means of a mapping from the objects of the subtype to objects of the supertype. We adopted a Cardelli-like approach (Cardelli 1984) for tuple subtyping. A tuple type is a subtype of another if it is more defined, that is, if it contains every attribute of its supertype plus some new ones and/or it refines the type of some attributes of its supertype. The following example illustrates this.

```
tuple(name: string,
      address: tuple(street: string,
                     city: City),
      description: Text,
      closing_days: list(string),
      admission_fee: integer,
      number_rooms: integer,
      rate: integer)
```

is a subtype of:

```
tuple(name: string,
      address: tuple(street: string,
                     city: City),
      description: Text,
      closing_days: list(string),
      admission_fee: integer)
```

Another characteristic of this subtyping relationship is that a set-structured type set(T) is a subtype of set(T′) if and only if T is a subtype of T′. For instance,

```
set(tuple(name: string,
          address: string))
```

is a subtype of

```
set(tuple(name: string))
```

The same relationship holds for lists.

5.2 Inheritance

Based on this subtyping relationship, O_2 offers an inheritance mechanism. We can define the Historical_hotel class as follows:

```
add class Historical_hotel inherits Monument
          type tuple (number_rooms: integer,
                      rate: integer)
```

The effect of this declaration is to define a Historical_hotel class whose associated type is a subtype of the Monument type. The user only has to give the extra attributes (the other ones are taken from the definition of the inherited class). The O_2 command interpreter checks whether the inheritance definition is legal (that is, there is no subtyping violation), and creates the subclass according to the subtyping rules. An object of the class Historical_hotel will automatically be considered an object of the class Monument. This results in the possibility of applying any method of class Monument to Historical_hotel objects. O_2 also allows for multiple inheritance, as shown below. We first define a Restaurant class.

```
add class Restaurant with extension
     type tuple (name: string,
                 address: tuple(city: City,
                                street: string),
                 menus: set(tuple(name: string,
                                  rate: float)))
add method check_rates(float): Boolean
     in class Restaurant
```

The method *check_rates* checks whether the menu rates are below a given amount. We can now define a Historical_restaurant class as follows:

```
add class Historical_restaurant with extension
     inherits Monument, Restaurant
     type tuple (redefines name: string,
```

```
                    redefines address:
                              tuple(city: City,
                                    street: string))

    add method check_rates(float): Boolean
         in class Historical_restaurant
```

Historical_restaurant inherits both from Monument and from Restaurant. The method *check_rates* checks whether the menu rates are less than twice the amount (the restaurant is historical, so it is allowed to have higher rates!). We do not detail here the conditions that method signatures must satisfy in order to be inherited through the subclasses (Lécluse, Richard, and Vélez 1988; see chapter 4).

As opposed to single inheritance, possible ambiguities may arise with multiple inheritance when an attribute or a method name is defined in two or more superclasses. There are several solutions to such ambiguities (e.g., Banerjee et al. 1987). We decided to follow an approach similar to that of Trellis/Owl (Schaffert et al. 1986). That is, the user has to explicitly redefine the attribute or method name when needed. We think that this solution is more natural than solutions where the system solves the ambiguity by ordering the superclasses. We also think it enhances the readability and maintainability of the schema. Thus the Historical_restaurant class redefines the attributes **name** and **address**, which are both present in the classes Restaurant and Monument. We do not infer the subclass relationship, which is user defined. The system just checks whether it is legal with respect to the subtyping rules.

5.3 Late Binding

An important feature of object-oriented systems, which is fully implemented in O_2, is late binding. The actual code of a method to be executed is selected not at compile time but at run time, and it depends on the type of the receiver object. The main benefit is dynamicity and the reuse of existing software; existing methods do not have to be recompiled when the code of the methods they use is changed. An example of the use of late binding is:

```
for(x in Restaurant) {
if(![x check_rate(120.50)])
  printf("restaurant %s is expensive", *x.name);
}
```

This iteration loop applies the *check_rate* method to every Restaurant object. Due to our subtyping semantics, some Restaurant objects are Historical_restaurant objects. For these, the system automatically applies the method defined in the class Historical_restaurant. This avoids the need for explicitly taking into account the different status of historical restaurants as compared to restaurants generally. Late binding is a critical operation from the performance point of view. The O_2 choice for the implementation of late binding is described in Vélez, Bernard, and Darnis 1989 (see chapter 15).

6 Interesting Features

In this section, we describe some interesting features of O_2 which improve the expressibility of the O_2 language.

6.1 Exceptional Attributes

Due to the semantics of the subtyping relationship, a tuple value can have extra attributes. If we consider the Monument class, the Eiffel_Tower object can have a value which also contains an attribute **height**. This extra attribute will not be dealt with by the methods associated to the Monument class; however, the standard operators available on tuple values will handle it. For instance, the following is correct CO_2 code:

```
{Eiffel_Tower = new(Monument);
 *Eiffel_Tower=
 tuple(name: "Eiffel Tower",
       address: tuple(street: "Champ de Mars",
                      city: Paris),
       description: "a famous Paris monument",
       closing_days: list("Christmas", "Easter"),
       height: 315);
 (*Eiffel_Tower).height = 320;
 return ((*Eiffel_Tower).height);}
```

Assuming that deencapsulation is allowed on Monument, this code first modifies the value of Eiffel_Tower and then adds a **height** attribute. Then, using the dot operator, the **height** attribute is updated; and finally its new value is returned. Note that exceptional attributes are allowed for any tuple object or value, even if not named.

6.2 Exceptional Methods

One can associate specific methods to named objects. These methods are used to characterize the exceptional behaviour of an object. For example, the Eiffel Tower is also a radio and TV broadcasting station. The attribute **power** indicates the station's broadcasting power. The *increase_power* method will be used to increase the **power** attribute of the Eiffel_Tower object. One can also override an existing method in the class of the object with an exceptional method. An example of the exceptional-method mechanism is:

```
add method increase_power (amount: float)
in object Eiffel_Tower
```

Note that the method is associated to the name rather than to a particular object, and that the actual object associated to the name Eiffel_Tower can change at run time. The late binding process will associate the exceptional method to the object currently bound to the name.

7 Type Checking

O_2 emphasizes user-defined classes and their associated types. This is a natural way to structure data. Another important motivation is type checking. The goal of O_2 is to increase the productivity of business-applications programmers. In this context, the safety of programs is critical. Thus O_2 offers a static type checker which detects illegal manipulations of O_2 objects and values when inheritance is not used. When there is full use of inheritance or of exceptional attributes, O_2 must perform some run-time type checking. Of course, since the method code of O_2 can be written in several languages which may be loosely typed (such as C), there also may be errors due to the host-language manipulations. The type-checking algorithm used in O_2 is standard. It is conceptually similar to that of Trellis/Owl (Schaffert et al. 1986), in that a variable can only be assigned values (or objects) of its declared type (or class) or of any subtype (or subclass). The user may modify the schema dynamically. In this case, a method which has not been recompiled may perform message passings which reference nonexisting methods. Of course, if the user recompiles every method which may be concerned by the schema modifications, references to nonexisting classes or methods are detected by the type checker. Other run-time errors occur with exceptional attributes. At compile time, the type checker may not know whether an attribute is exceptional or not, if it is not present in the variable declaration but is referred to in the code. Accepting such a manipulation implies that the method may fail at run time because the actual value does not possess this exceptional attribute. We accept this for the sake of expressive power. The user may choose to have safe programs by not using exceptional attributes.

8 Related Work

In this section we list the main characteristics of O_2 and see what kind of solutions others OODBSs provide. We compare O_2 to other systems on the basis of the programming language only. We are not concerned here with query facilities, the user interface, or physical management.

8.1 Other OODBs

GemStone (Maier, Otis, and Purdy 1985) is to our knowledge the first implementation of an OODBS. The philosophy of GemStone was to turn Smalltalk into a database system without significant modifications of the Smalltalk programming language. Vision (Caruso 1987) is another interesting approach; it models data in a way similar to Daplex (Shipman 1981). All information about an object is embodied in functions, which map one collection of objects onto another. However, function application follows a message-passing mechanism using a Smalltalk-like approach.

Iris (Derrett et al. 1986) also follows a functional approach; to every object is associated a set of functions which characterize its content. Orion (Banerjee et al. 1987) is another example of a functional approach; it is implemented using Lisp and has a Lisp syntax for the message passing. Vbase (Andrews and Harris 1987) follows an approach similar to that of O_2, as the corresponding language (COP) is a strict superset of the C programming language.

Although it is not a true OODBS, Trellis/Owl is another example of an object-oriented language with imperative programming. It has a conventional programming-language syntax and uses a procedure-call notation to invoke operations on objects. Trellis/Owl does not have all the database functionalities, but it provides persistence through an object repository. A common characteristic of these approaches is that they provide compile-time type checking.

The Exodus system (Carey, DeWitt, and Vandenberg 1988) is also an object-oriented system; it allows abstract definitions of data types, and it has objects and values. It has a query language named Excess. Programming is also done in the E language, which is a persistent C++.

We now list the main original features of O_2 and compare them with what is done in other OODBSs.

Objects and structured values. O_2 provides the user with both objects and structured values. We do not follow a pure object approach, as in Smalltalk or GemStone, but allow the definition of nested values built using the set, list, and tuple constructors. O_2 manipulates objects using methods, and manipulates values using operators. That is, full object-oriented features are available for objects (such as late binding and inheritance of methods), and values are manipulated as in database systems. Most OODBSs provide object constructors similar to the set and tuple constructors. The Exodus system also gives an array constructor which is similar to the O_2 list constructor.

The distinction between objects and values can also be found in Orion. In that system, however, the notion of complex value is implemented as a dependent object (Kim et al. 1987); that is, nonshared values are still objects, with a constraint enforcing their privacy. The Exodus data model (Carey, DeWitt, and Vandenberg 1988) also provides the user with this distinction. However, just as in Orion, values are second-class objects with no identity. In O_2 we enforce the distinction between objects and values in the programming language; we encapsulate objects, which can only be manipulated through methods. Exodus adopts a point of view which is less object oriented but more database oriented. In Exodus as in Orion, for the sake of query simplicity and uniformity, objects and values are manipulated in the same way.

In Iris and in Vision, one only has objects. Objects are atomic items which can be printable (like the object "3") or not. If an object is not printable, its value is characterized by a set of functions which can be either stored, thus playing the role of attributes, or computed. As opposed to O_2, where the three object constructors have exactly the same rights, due to their approach Iris and Vision manipulate complex objects that are records of functions, which can, however, be multivalued.

Multilanguage approach. O_2 follows a multi-language approach. Classes and types are created using the O_2 schema commands, but the code of methods can be implemented using several O_2 extensions. In this paper we have concentrated on CO_2; but another extension is currently under implementation, based on the Basic language. Up to now, among the existing OODBSs, O_2 is the only multilanguage system.

Type checker. O_2 has a compile-time type-checker. Systems such as GemStone that are based on a Smalltalk-like approach do not provide such a functionality, nor do systems based on Lisp, such as Orion.

On the other hand, systems based on an imperative paradigm are statically typed. For example, Trellis/Owl and Vbase, like O_2, have a strong typing. That is, every object is an instance of a type, and every variable is declared of a type. A variable can only be assigned objects of its type or of a subtype of its type. In order to have statically typed languages, types and methods are not modeled as objects and manipulated by methods; instead, they are primitive constructions manipulated by schema commands.

Persistence management. O_2 provides automatic management of persistence through named objects and values. Every named object or value is persistent, and every component of a persistent object or value is itself persistent. The name can be seen as a handle which allows the user to access an object or value after the end of a program that has defined it.

Other systems provide somewhat similar ways of managing persistence. Objects in Orion persist because they are components of persistent collections. For every user-defined type, the system generates a set-structured class that has at least one instance which groups the instances of the former class. In GemStone, the management of persistence also uses reachability information; that is, objects are persistent if they are attached to a persistence root or to another persistent object. An Exodus database is a collection of named persistent objects.

Updates. Updates are always implicit in O_2. Objects are created using the **new** command. If a class is created with extension, a named set value is created that will contain every object of the class, which will thus persist. If the class is not created with extension, the created objects will only persist if attached to other persistent objects. Deletion of objects or values is obtained by removing the links which attach them to the persistence roots (the names). Classes with extension are also provided with a *delete* method, which allows objects to be removed from the class extension when no other objects or values refer to it. GemStone and Orion have a similar update policy, as they have a similar persistence policy. In Vbase, however, every object is persistent, and temporary objects have to be deleted explicitly.

Subtyping. O_2 has a set inclusion semantics for subtyping. Objects of a subclass are objects of the superclasses. For instance, if one performs a display on the instances of Monuments, one will also see the instances of Historical_hotel. Some systems, such as Trellis/Owl and Iris, follow this approach. Iris has a set-inclusion semantics which is even more general, since an object can have several types even if these types are not related in the specialization hierarchy. We are not aware of the way ambiguities are solved in Iris. Orion has no set-inclusion semantics.

Vision has a mapping semantics: an object of a subclass has a corresponding image object in its superclass. We find this somehow unnatural. However, it provides the same kinds of functionalities, at least in the context of single inheritance, as are provided in Vision.

Solution of multiple-inheritance conflicts. In O_2 multiple-inheritance conflicts are solved by users (see section 5); Trellis/Owl proposes a similar solution. For instance, when there is an ambiguity on the inheritance of a method (an operation, in Trellis/Owl), the user must specify which one he or she wishes to inherit, or must redefine it.

In contrast, Orion automatically solves ambiguities arising from multiple inheritance. Roughly speaking, the system maintains an ordering among the superclasses which removes such ambiguities. To our knowledge, other systems, such as GemStone or Vbase, do not support multiple inheritance.

Exceptional methods and attributes. The O_2 system allows exceptional methods and attributes for objects. Exceptional methods can be associated to names. These methods are only accessible from the object currently attached to the name, and they override the methods of the class. Exceptional attributes can be added to all tuple-structured objects or values. To our knowledge, no other OODBS provides such a functionality.

8.2 Other Systems

Another interesting approach is that used in Galileo (Albano, Cardelli, and Orsini 1985). It is not really an object-oriented database management system, but it has some object-oriented features: classification, abstract types, and types hierarchies. As opposed to O_2, Galileo does not have the set constructor; it is higher order and has a function-type constructor. It has the notions of concrete and abstract types, which roughly correspond to our types and classes. Galileo presents a very interesting solution to persistence; however, it is not yet implemented to our knowledge. Another important difference from O_2 is that Galileo does not support object identity.

The Damokles database system (Dittrich, Gotthard, and Lockeman 1987) is designed for a software-engineering environment. Its designers describe Damokles as a "structurally object-oriented" database. That is, Damokles provides the user with object identity, complex objects based on the tuple constructor, and n-ary bidirectional relationships between objects. However, Damokles does not provide encapsulation, inheritance, or late binding. It is, rather, a "complex objects" system.

9 Conclusion

In this paper we have described the current features of the O_2 system. We only described the CO_2 programming language, but most of the described features are common to both CO_2 and BasicO_2, and the difference between the two languages is mainly syntactical.

The target applications for our language are (1) traditional applications, such as business and transactional (but excluding very high performance transaction-processing systems), (2) office-automation applications, and (3) spatial data management (such as geographic data management). At this stage, no specific emphasis is given to CAD/CAM, CASE, or knowledge-base applications; but we believe that, at a later stage, the system could be enhanced to serve these applications also.

Altaïr started in September 1986. We first implemented, in December 1987, a throwaway prototype (Bancilhon et al. 1988), whose data model is described in Lécluse, Richard, and Vélez 1988 (see chapter 4), in order to test and show the functionalities of the system. This gave us a lot of feedback, and we completely redesigned the system, its language, its data model (Lécluse and Richard 1989), and its architecture. The major differences between the V1 version and the throwaway prototype, from the language point of view, are (1) complex values together with objects, (2) names for objects and values, (3) the list type constructor, (4) an automatic persistence mechanism, (5) the possibility of separating classes and method definitions from the implementation, and (6) last but not least, a better merge between the O_2 syntax and the host language ones—that is, every implementation of O_2 on a given host language follows the syntax of the host language. The current prototype runs on Sun and implements all of the functionalities listed above. The BasicO_2 compiler is under implementation.

10 Acknowledgements

The authors thank F. Bancilhon and P. Kanellakis for their careful reading and comments which greatly improve the quality of this paper. The O_2 compiler was implemented by the language team of the GIP Altaïr which includes D. Excoffier, L. Haux, C. Lécluse, and P. Richard. The module which is in charge of storing and managing classes and methods was designed and implemented by S. Gamerman and C. Delcourt. The object manager has been implemented by the system team. Numerous suggestions and improvements on the language and its syntax have been proposed by the Altaïr team and in particular by F. Bancilhon.

References

Abiteboul, S., and C. Beeri. 1987. On the power of languages for manipulating complex objects. In *International workshop on theory and applications of nested relations and complex objects.*

Abiteboul, S., and P. Kanellakis. 1989. *Object identity as a query language primitive.* Internal report.

Ait-Kaci, H., and R. Nasr. 1986. LOGIN: A logic programming language with built-in inheritance. *Journal of Logic Programming.*

Albano, A., L. Cardelli, and R. Orsini. 1985. Galileo: A strongly typed, interactive conceptual language. *ACM TODS* 10(2): 230–61.

Andrews, T., and C. Harris. 1987. Combining language and database advances in an object-oriented development environment. In *Proceedings of the OOPSLA conference.*

Atkinson, M. P., and O. P. Buneman. 1987. Types and persistence in database programming languages. *ACM Computing Surveys.*

Bancilhon, F. 1988. Object-oriented database systems. In *Proceedings of the ACM PODS conference.*

Bancilhon, F., G. Barbedette, V. Benzaken, C. Delobel, S. Gamerman, C. Lécluse, P. Pfeffer, P. Richard, and F. Vélez. 1988. The design and implementation of O_2, an object-oriented database system. In *Advances in object-oriented database systems.* Springer-Verlag.

Bancilhon, F., and S. Khoshafian. 1986. A calculus for complex objects. In *Proceedings of the ACM PODS conference.*

Banerjee, J., H-T. Chou, J. Garza, W. Kim, D. Woelk, N. Ballou, and H. J. Kim. 1987. Data model issues for object-oriented applications. *ACM TOIS* 5(1): 3–26.

Bernstein, P. et al. 1988. Future directions in DBMS research. In *Workshop of the international computer science institute.*

Cardelli, L. 1984. A semantics of multiple inheritance. *Lecture Notes in Computer Science.*

Cardelli, L., and P. Wegner. 1985. On understanding types, data abstraction, and polymorphism. *ACM Computing Surveys* 17(4).

Carey, M., D. DeWitt, and S. Vandenberg. 1988. A data model and query language for Exodus. In *Proceedings of the 1988 ACM SIGMOD conference.*

Caruso, M. 1987. The VISION object-oriented database management system. In *Proceedings of the workshop on database programming languages.*

Danforth, S., S. Khoshafian, and P. Valduriez. 1987. *FAD: A database programming language.* MCC Technical Report.

Derrett, N. P., D. H. Fishman, W. Kent, P. Lyngbaek, and T. A. Ryan. 1986. An object-oriented approach to data management. In *Proceedings of the Compcon 31 IEEE computer society international conference.*

Dittrich, K., W. Gotthard, and P. Lockeman. 1987. DAMOKLES: The database system for the unibase software engineering environment. *Database Engineering* 10(1): 37–47.

Goldberg, A., and D. Robson. 1983. *Smalltalk 80: The language and its implementation.* Addison-Wesley.

Kim, W., J. Banerjee, H-T. Chou, J. F. Garza, and D. Woelk. 1987. Composite object support in an object-oriented database system. In *Proceedings of the OOPSLA conference.*

Kuper, G. M. 1985. The logical data model: A new approach to database logic. PhD thesis, Stanford University.

Lécluse, C., and P. Richard. 1988. Modeling inheritance and genericity in object-oriented databases. In *Proceedings of the ICDT conference.*

———. 1989. Modeling complex structures in object-oriented databases. In *Proceedings of the ACM PODS conference.*

Lécluse, C., P. Richard, and F. Vélez. 1988. O_2, an object-oriented data model. In *Proceedings of the ACM SIGMOD conference.*

Maier, D., A. Otis, and A. Purdy. 1985. Development of an object-oriented DBMS. *Quarterly Bulletin of IEEE on Database Engineering* 8(4).

Price, D. 1984. *Introduction to ADA.* Prentice-Hall.

Schaffert, C., T. Cooper, B. Bullis, M. Kilian, and C. Wilpolt. 1986. An introduction to Trellis/Owl. In *Proceedings of the first OOPSLA conference.*

Shipman, D. W. 1981. The functional data model and the data language DAPLEX. *ACM TODS* 6(1): 140–73.

Stroustrup, B. 1986. *The C++ programming language.* Addison-Wesley.

Vélez, F., G. Bernard, and V. Darnis. 1989. The O_2 object manager, an overview. In *Proceedings of the VLDB conference.*

CHAPTER 10

Lisp O_2: A Persistent Object-Oriented Lisp

GILLES BARBEDETTE

1 Introduction

In order to support new application domains such as CASE, office automation, or knowledge bases, a development environment has to provide both modeling power and database facilities. Modeling power requires the representation and manipulation of complex objects (such as programs, documents, or rules); database facilities require sharing and persistence between program invocations. Databases and programming languages have tried separately to cope with these types of applications.

Traditional database systems support persistence, but fail to model objects either in their structural or behavioral complexity. For instance, first-normal-form relational systems do not deal with structural complexity. Moreover, to express complex behavior, application programmers have to use a query language embedded in a programming language. They are thus faced with the well-known impedance mismatch problem (Copeland and Maier 1984): they have to learn two different languages and map continuously their different models.

In contrast, programming languages, in particular object-oriented languages (Goldberg and Robson 1983; Stroustrup 1986; Meyer 1988), offer powerful features such as encapsulation, inheritance, and exception handling that ease the design, implementation, and evolution of modular and robust applications. However, they support only a limited form of persistence through the use of files. Therefore the programmer has to flatten the highly interconnected in-core data structure onto the linear format of files. These error-prone conversions interfere with the application logic, decreasing the programmer's productivity.

Recently, efforts to integrate database and programming languages have come either from database people and produced object-oriented databases (Bancilhon et al. 1988; Banerjee et al. 1987; Andrews and Harris 1987; Maier et al. 1986) or from programming-language people and produced persistent languages (Schmidt 1977; Atkinson 1981; Albano, Cardelli, and Orsini 1985). These efforts focus on eliminating the major limitation on programmer productivity in such systems—the impedance mismatch. LispO_2 belongs in this trend. It is a Lisp-based language that supports the incremental and interactive design of applications. It provides the programmer with object orientation to cope with complex design, and persistence facilities to deal with data lifetime.

LispO_2 was developed within the Altaïr project, whose objective is to build a multilanguage object-oriented database system called O_2. This system provides a data model (Lécluse and Richard 1989a) with which the programmer can design an application schema; and it provides, for the time being, two languages, BasicO_2 and CO_2 (Lécluse and Richard 1989b; see chapter 9), which are used to implement the behavioral part of the application. LispO_2 should be distinguished from BasicO_2 and CO_2. These are intended to be used in an industrial environment, whereas LispO_2 is designed for experimenting with object orientation and persistence. Hence, although it retains the advantages of the O_2 data model, LispO_2 is autonomous. It was developed following the Lisp philosophy and using bootstrapping techniques; that is, almost all the system is implemented using the language. It thus offers the flexible architecture needed in an experimentation environment.

The remainder of this paper is organized as follows. Section 2 introduces the object-oriented features of the language. Section 3 is devoted to the integration of persistence in the language. This is followed, in section 4, by a brief outline of the implementation. Section 5 compares LispO_2 with other related approaches. I conclude by indicating future plans, in section 6.

2 Object-Oriented Features

Although several object-oriented languages (Stroustrup 1986; Goldberg and Robson 1983; Meyer 1988) and databases (Carey, DeWitt, and Vandenberg 1988; Andrews and Harris 1987; Banerjee et al. 1987; Bancilhon et al. 1988) have appeared, there is no universal consensus on the term *object-oriented* (Wegner 1987). Its meaning ranges from "prototype based" (Lieberman 1986) to "class based with inheritance" (Stroustrup 1986). LispO_2 belongs to the family of languages where the term *object-oriented* implies the conjunction of encapsulation, class, and inheritance. This section gives an informal presentation of how these notions are defined and used in the LispO_2 language. Additional features such as tailored object creation and exception handling are also described and illustrated with simple examples. The application in the examples concerns the management of a flying club whose members have a passion for antique planes.

2.1 Objects and Classes, Values and Types

To manage the complexity of applications, any modern programming language provides the programmer with both abstract and concrete representation of data. Data abstraction allows the programmer to model and organize information concerning the real world in a natural way, in terms of its functionality, without concentrating on its implantation. Concrete representation is generally used to structure the implementation of data.

LispO$_2$ is an object-oriented language and thus offers data abstraction through *objects*. Objects encapsulate a state via an operational interface. Object manipulation is achieved through *operations* and not by directly accessing the object's internal state.

LispO$_2$ also supports unencapsulated data. These are *values*. They are used both at an implementation level, to represent object states, and at a modeling level, whenever data abstraction is not useful. Thus an object can be seen as a capsule built around a value. Objects are manipulated by operations; values are manipulated by *operators*. Figure 10.1 shows how we can represent the parts of an airplane as objects. The encapsulated value of the object is an aggregate containing the name of the part (a wheel), the set of parts of which it is a component (landing gear), and its supplier (Darlington). Objects are denoted using identifiers in italics. Values are either simple, like the string "wheel", or complex, like the set **setof** *landing-gear*.

wheel = (**tupleof**
    (model-name "wheel")
    (is-part-of (**setof** *landing-gear*))
    (supplier *darlington*))

Figure 10.1. An object, *wheel*

LispO$_2$ is a class-based object-oriented language; that is, each object is generated by (is an instance of) a *class*. A class describes the structure (i.e., the state) and behavior (i.e., the operations) of its instances. Just as classes are object descriptors, *types* are value descriptors. For instance, figure 10.2 shows the type associated with the value encapsulated by the object *wheel* in figure 10.1. Classes are denoted with initial capital letters. Classes are defined using a **defclass** command as shown in figure 10.3; boldface is used for reserved words. This class definition consists of (1) the **type** clause, (2) the **operations** clause, and (3) the **has-extension** clause.

The **type** clause describes the structure abstracted by its instances. A type in LispO$_2$ is either an atomic type (such as integer, string, or float), or a complex type built from other types and classes using the tuple, set, and list constructors. Tuple types offer aggregation. Set types represent collections without duplicates.

```
(tupleof
    (model-name string)
    (is-part-of (setof Complex-part))
    (supplier Supplier))
```

Figure 10.2. Type describing the value encapsulated by *wheel*

```
(defclass Part
        ; definition of the type associated with the class
        (type (tupleof
                (name string)
                (is-part-of (setof Complex-part))
                (supplier Supplier)))
        ; definition of the operational interface
        (operations
            (virtual cost () (return integer))
            (virtual mass () (return integer)))
        ; automatic extension option
        has-extension)
```

Figure 10.3. Definition of the class Part

List types support indexable and homogeneous collections, as opposed to Lisp lists, which are head-and-tail access oriented and heterogeneous.

The **operations** clause describes the operational interface through which the user can manipulate instances of the class Part. It specifies the operations. An operation specification consists of its name and the type or class of the arguments and result, called a *signature*. The keyword **virtual** states that the operation specified cannot be implemented using only the information provided in class Part. This is further explained in section 2.2.

The **has-extension** clause provides automatic grouping of all created instances of the class into a set. It permits one to operate easily on all instances of that class. section 2.4 further details this point.

The definition of the class Part shows the benefit of providing both type and class as modeling tools. To constrain the attribute is-part-of, we use the type **setof** Complex-part instead of a class (say Setof-complex-part). Indeed, since the Part class defines an abstraction, the is-part-of attribute will be manipulated only by its operations. It is already protected, and we do not see the advantage of defining another abstraction level. In addition, the is-part-of attribute appears to be just a set of parts and not a high-level application concept like the part concept. Hence it does not need to be described by a class. In contrast, using a Setof-complex-part class would lead to an increasing complexity (and decreasing performance) in the manipulations, since we would have to define and use operations on an object instead of direct operators on a value.

In languages such as Smalltalk (Goldberg and Robson 1983) where a class is the only modeling tool, natural complex values are simulated through objects. This leads to the definition of unnecessary classes and to a kind of pollution of the abstract space.

The object/value duality is inherited from the O_2 model presented in Lécluse and Richard 1989, with a notable difference. In LispO_2 the duality relies on the fact that objects are encapsulated and values are not. In the O_2 model, values are neither encapsulated nor shared. In LispO_2, values are sharable, because Lisp is a language whose semantics is based on reference—that is, all Lisp data has an identity. Since objects and values are Lisp data, they can be shared.

2.2 Inheritance

Classes are more than just abstract data types. They are related to each other through inheritance links. These enable the modeling of semantic generalization or specialization relationships between objects in the application (e.g., an employee is a person, or a complex part is a part). A subclass inherits the structure and behavior specified by its superclasses. Moreover it can either redefine or extend them.

To have a more realistic model of airplane parts, we now define the two subclasses of Part that describe respectively complex and basic parts (see figure 10.4). The class Complex-part is said to inherit from the class Part. Hence the programmer simply specifies in the subclass the additional attributes and operations. This leads to an incremental modeling style where only differences from existing concepts are specified. Notice the structural complexity of the type associated with the class Complex-part. With complex types, we model the "complex objects" (which are in fact pure complex values) that are provided by extensions of relational systems allowing relation-valued attributes, such as Dadam et al. 1986.

In the class Basic-part, the cost and mass are stored as attributes. Hence, the *cost* and *mass* operations are just attribute-extraction operations. They are implicitly defined using the readable option (**r**), which automatically generates a read-access operation for an attribute.

The **operations** clause of the class Complex-part redefines explicitly the *mass* and *cost* operations defined as virtual in class Part. The class Part simply introduces functional properties of parts in their generality. It defines an abstract interface implemented differently in the classes Complex-part and Basic-part. This facility allows the inclusion of classes that are pure interface specifications. Such classes are useful as inheritance roots, since they represent the concept that is implemented differently in the subclasses. A similar feature can be found in the abstract classes of Smalltalk (Goldberg and Robson 1983) or the deferred facility of Eiffel (Meyer 1988).

```
(defclass Complex-part
        ; list the classes from which the class inherits
        (Part)
        (type (tupleof
                (assembly-cost integer)
                (components (setof (tupleof
                                        (quantity integer)
                                        (part Part))))))
        (operations
            (cost () (return integer))
            (mass () (return integer)))
        has-extension)

(defclass Basic-part
        (Part)
        (type (tupleof
                (cost integer r)
                (mass integer r)))
        has-extension)
```

Figure 10.4. Definitions of the classes Complex-part and Basic-part

In LispO_2 inheritance is based on subtyping and behavior refinement. If a class C' inherits from a class C, then the type of C' must be a subtype of the type of C. The following is a syntactic definition of subtyping.

- If T is an atomic type, then T' is an atomic type, and $T = T'$.
- If T is set structured, that is, of the form **setof** E (or list structured, **listof** E), then T' is set structured, that is, **setof** E' (or list structured, **listof** E'), and E' is a subtype of E.
- If T is tuple structured, that is, of the form **tupleof** $(a_1 TA_1) \ldots (a_n TA_n)$, then T' is tuple structured, that is, **tupleof** $(a_1 TA'_1) \ldots (a_m TA'_m)$ $m \geq n$, and $\forall i \in [1, \ldots, n]$ TA'_i is a subtype of TA_i.
- If T is a class, then T' is a class, and T' is a subclass of T.

For a formal description of the O_2 semantics of subtyping, the reader is referred to Lécluse and Richard 1989a.

C' may extend or redefine the operations offered by C. Redefinition occurs when C' defines an operation already defined in C. In that case, the operation of C' must have the same number of arguments as that of C. Moreover, the types of the arguments and result specified in the operation of C' must be subtypes of those specified in the operation of C.

Intuitively, these inheritance constraints ensure that a subclass introduces additional information, either by specializing or by extending the information (structural or behavioral) provided by its superclasses. Since the core of an application is the class hierarchy, inheritance based on subtyping allows the immediate detection of errors due to establishing a subclass relationship between two incomparable concepts. Moreover, it allows static type-checking of operations, as explained in section 2.6.

```
(defclass Member
    (Person)
    (operations
        (status () (return string)))) ; the status is "member"

(defclass Pilot
    (Member)
    (operations
        (status () (return string)))) ; the status is "pilot"

(defclass Mechanic
    (Member)
    (operations
        (status () (return string)))) ; the status is "mechanic"

(defclass Pilot-mechanic
    ; multiple inheritance
    (Pilot mechanic)
    (operations
        (status () (return string)))) ; the status is "pilot and mechanic"
```

Figure 10.5. Classes representing club members

LispO_2 also supports multiple inheritance, that is, a class may inherit from several direct superclasses. I illustrate this point with the example of the flying-club members given in figure 10.5 (I omit the type specifications for clarity). The members are categorized as general members, pilots, and mechanics; each category is modeled with a class. Each club member has a status, which returns the category to which he or she belongs. Let us assume that some members can both repair and pilot planes. To model this situation, we want to define a class Pilot-mechanic that inherits both from Pilot and from Mechanic. Unfortunately, such a definition leads to an inheritance conflict. The Pilot and Mechanic classes both have a *status* operation; therefore there is a name conflict in the Pilot-mechanic class. The programmer has to solve it explicitly, either by choosing which operation to inherit (the one from Pilot or the one from Mechanic) or by defining a new local operation—the solution chosen in figure 10.5.

Unlike some systems, such as Orion (Banerjee et al. 1987), to solve the conflict O_2 does not rely on the order of the superclasses given in the class definition. We believe that this solution does not offer a clear view of the inheritance paths (who inherits from whom) when the class hierarchy becomes complex. Moreover, schema manipulations such as adding an operation or a superclass change the inherited operation and thus affect unpredictably the behavior of existing programs.

Notice that, if the status operation was defined only in the Member class, adding the Pilot-mechanic class would not lead to a name conflict. Inheriting the same operation from two different paths is not a name conflict.

2.3 Operation Implementations: Methods

Operations are the specifications of the behavior provided by a class. For each operation defined in a class, there is a *method* that implements it. Methods are coded in Lisp, extended with object- and value-manipulation expressions. For instance, the method shown in figure 10.6 computes the cost of a complex part. Within methods defined in a class, the programmer can manipulate the internal representation of an instance of this class. For this, he or she needs a means to pass from an object to its associated value, that is, a means to break encapsulation: this is the *deencapsulate* operator. If x is a variable denoting an object, then "x." denotes its value.

```
(defmethod (Complex-part cost) ()
    ; initialization of the result with the assembly cost
    (let ((cost self.assembly-cost))
       ; iterate over the components of the complex part and accumulate
       ; their cost
       (foreach ((component self.components))
           (setq cost (+ cost
           ; multiply the quantity by the cost of the part
                          (* (get-field component 'quantity)
                             [(get-field component 'part) cost]))))
       ; return the total cost
       cost))
```

Figure 10.6. The *cost* method for a complex part

Besides deencapsulation, operations are the unique way to act upon objects. Applying an operation to an object consists in *sending a message* to it. Following Smalltalk terminology, the object is called the *receiver*. Message passing is expressed using brackets. In a method, the receiver of the message is automatically bound to the pseudovariable **self**.

Whereas objects are capsules and they are manipulated through operations, values are not encapsulated and they are manipulated using predefined operators. For example, the **get-field** operator allows the attribute extraction of a tuple value. Thus the expression "[(**get-field** component 'part) cost]" extracts the object stored in the attribute part and sends it the cost message. Attribute names are not denotable values of the language. This would prevent the static type checking of methods. Therefore attribute names must appear as constants. This explains the quotation mark, ', used in Lisp to indicate a constant. Since tuple-structured objects are frequently used, we offer a short notation for extracting attributes of tuple values encapsulated in objects. Hence the expression "**self**.assembly-cost" is equivalent to "(**get-field self**. 'assembly-cost)".

A notable operator on collection values (sets or lists) is the **foreach** iterator. It binds a temporary variable to each element of the collection and executes its body in this environment until a condition is satisfied or the end of the collection is reached.

We can now describe the body of the complex cost method. It iterates over the composition of the complex part, which is a set of tuple values. Each tuple value contains a component part and a quantity representing the number of times the part is involved in the composition of the complex part. Thus each iteration computes the additional cost of the component, multiplying the cost of the component by its quantity.

A complex part can be made from a basic part or from a complex one. However, in the component-cost computation "[(**get-field** component 'part) cost]", such a discrimination does not appear. This is because at run time the system calls the relevant method, which depends on whether the receiver is a basic or a complex part. This automatic method dispatching that depends on the class of the receiver is called *late binding*. It ensures the extensibility of the complex *cost* computation.

Suppose that we wish to introduce a new kind of part by defining a new subclass of Part. All we have to do is to define a *cost* operation local to the new class. The complex *cost* operation will still be correct for complex parts made from instances of this new class, *without having to be recompiled*. Thus the late binding facility ensures the reuse of methods for incoming classes.

2.4 Object Creation: Constructor

Assume that the name of a part is a key. Thus, when a new part is added, the programmer implementing the part abstraction has to check that there is not an already existing part with the same name. Those checks cannot be included in an operation, because nothing forces the *clients* of Part (i.e., the classes that reference the class Part in their methods) to call it. Moreover, it is logically bound to object creation. Therefore, we provide the programmer with the ability of tailoring the object creation in order to perform some precondition checks and some attribute initializations. This is the role of constructors. A constructor is introduced by the **maker** clause in the class definition, as shown in figure 10.7. As for operations, only a specification is given. The constructor implementation is defined separately, as shown in figure 10.8. Like **self**, **new** is a pseudo variable automatically bound to a new instance of the class.

```
(defclass Basic-part
        (Part)
        (type (tupleof
                (cost integer r)
                (mass integer r)))
        (maker (string integer integer Supplier))
        has-extension)
```

Figure 10.7. Complete Basic-part class definition

```
(defmaker Basic-part (name mass cost supplier)
   (let (conflicting-part)
      ; does the part already exist?
      (if (setq conflicting-part (part-already-exist? name))
         ; yes, it is an error, raise an exception
         (raise-exception Already-defined-part name conflicting-part)
         ; no, fill the attributes
         (setq new.name name) ...)))

(defun part-already-exist? (part-name)
   (let (found)
      ; iterate over all created parts until we find a conflict
      (foreach ((part (Part-extent)) found)
         (setq found (eqstring part-name [part name])))
      found))
```

Figure 10.8. Constructor of class Basic-part

In order to know if a conflicting part exists, there must be a container of all created parts up to now. This is the role of the class extension. A class extension records all created instances of a class. The three part classes are declared with extension. Since a basic (or complex) part is also a part, it is a member of both the Basic-part (or Complex-part) extension and of the Part extension. Inheritance between classes induces a set inclusion between their extensions. Therefore we retrieve in the Part extension all the complex and basic parts.

Hence the part-already-exist? predicate can be implemented as described in figure 10.8. Declaring the class Part with extension generates a function named Part-extent. When called, it returns the set of all parts created. Finding a conflict is just iterating over this set and checking for name equality.

Orion (Banerjee et al. 1987) also offers a class-extension mechanism. For each user-defined class C, a class Setof-C is created with two instances, representing respectively the set of the "direct" instances of C and the set of the instances of C and of its subclasses. Our approach differs from that of Orion in a number of points. In LispO_2 the extension mechanism is not automatic. The programmer has the choice whether or not to declare a class with extension. This avoids the management of unnecessary extensions. Moreover, class extensions are values, not objects. They are accessed through a function call, and thus distinguished from "normal" values and protected from accidental updates. Finally, the LispO_2 class extension gathers both the direct instances of the class and the instances of its subclasses, enforcing the natural set-inclusion semantics of inheritance as defined in the O_2 data model (Lécluse and Richard 1989b).

2.5 Coping with Faults: Exceptions

If a user of the part abstraction wants to create a base part with a name that already exists, an exception is raised by the Base-part constructor, using the **raise-exception** statement (see figure 10.8). When an operation or a constructor cannot perform its task, it warns its caller by raising an exception and terminates its execution. The caller must provide a handler for this exception. If it does not want to cope with it, it can simply raise it again. Exceptions in LispO_2 are objects that are instances of exception classes, as in Vbase (Andrews and Harris 1987). Thus raising an exception creates an instance of such a class. The state of an exception is used to pass some information from the signaler to the handler. Moreover, inheritance can be used for defining a hierarchy of exceptions. Figure 10.9 shows the definition of the Already-defined-part exception class and an example of an exception handler. Notice that the handler uses operations to access information.

2.6 Type-Checking Methods

The development environment of LispO_2 offers both an interpreter and a compiler, which perform respectively dynamic and static type checking of the object-oriented expressions (value manipulations, message passing, object creation, deencapsulation, and exception handling) occurring in methods. The interpreter supports the dynamics and debugging facilities needed in the first stages of development and traditionally associated with Lisp languages. Variables can be untyped, enabling the programmer to defer typing decisions. Therefore methods work as long as the objects bound to the variables respond to messages.

```
; exception class definition
(defexception Already-defined-part
    (type (tupleof
              (part-name string r)
              (conflicting-part Part r)))
    (maker (string Part)))

; example of a handler
(with-exception
    (setq part (make-Basic-part "seat" 123 15 supplier))
(handle
    ((ex Already-defined-part)
     (print "conflict with part " [ex conflicting-part print]))))
```

Figure 10.9. Exception class definition and exception handling

However, if during a message passing there is no pending operation in the receiver class, the execution is suspended and the programmer can either define *an operation and a method* on the fly, or give a result.

Once design decisions have been frozen, the programmer can invoke the compiler on methods. It performs static type checking of the O_2 expressions and catches the inconsistencies of the method with regard to the schema (unknown classes or operations, for instance). For this task, the type checker must know the static types associated with the variables involved in those expressions. Most of them can be inferred from the formal arguments of the method (typed in the operation signature) and the **self** and constructor applications. However, type declarations of the variables or functions used may be necessary.

The type-checking algorithm is similar to that of Trellis/Owl (Schaffert et al. 1986). Each variable (a formal argument or a local variable) can be assigned an expression whose type is a subtype of its (declared or inferred) type. The static type checking also catches the most common source of run-time errors in object-oriented languages, that is, message passing with an unknown operation. For each message-passing expression, the type checker searches for an operation in the static class of the receiver and checks that the types of the actual arguments are subtypes of those specified in the signature. In addition, the static analysis of methods checks for encapsulation. Within a method, the deencapsulate notation can be used only in an expression whose type is the class defining it or one of its superclasses.

3 Integrating Persistence Facilities in the Language

This section concentrates on issues raised by integrating persistence in the language from an application programmer point of view. Section 4.1 gives an overview of the implementation aspects. When trying to integrate persistence in a language, the designer is faced with two design goals: (1) to eliminate the impedance mismatch, and (2) to make persistence orthogonal to type.

The persistence facilities of LispO_2 must fit naturally into the underlying Lisp language model. The number of semantic and syntactic extensions needed must be as small as possible. In particular, the way that data persist between program invocations must not be too different from the way the transient data survive during a program invocation. Since in Lisp the programmer does not explicitly destroy his or her data, explicit **store** or **delete** commands have to be avoided.

Every entity of the language has the right to persist without additional programming cost. Notice that the second goal is not subsumed by the first. Some languages, such as CO_2 (Lécluse and Richard 1989b; see chapter 9) or Pascal/r (Schmidt 1977) deal with persistence by providing the programmer with types and operations syntactically and semantically well integrated with the host language. Thus they eliminate the impedance mismatch, but they do not fulfill orthogonality because data of some host types cannot persist (for example, everything that is not a relation in Pascal/R, or a C struct in CO_2). We do not restrict persistence to O_2 data (objects and values). We believe that complex applications will result in a mix of object-oriented implementation, using O_2 data, and conventional procedural implementation, using Lisp data (such as lists and vectors).

Once the objectives are set, let us see how persistence is used by the programmer. We introduce persistence as an extension of the lifetime of a Lisp data item. Due to the automatic storage management provided by Lisp systems through garbage collection, a data item is alive during a program execution if it is referenced (directly or indirectly) by a set of roots (usually the symbol table and the stack). Extending this view leads us to define some persistent roots: database variables and class extensions. Hence we introduce a persistent name space that includes all defined classes and database variables. Everything in the closure of class extensions and database variables is persistent.

For instance, to reduce the time spent to compute the mass of a complex part, we can declare a database variable whose role is to cache the mass already computed (like the memorizing facility described in Atkinson and Buneman 1987). Figure 10.10 gives the new implantation of the cost method. The first command defines a database variable called mass-memory. Its purpose is to register the parts with their computed mass and to act as a cache during the computation of masses. Defining a database variable simply introduces an entry in the persistent name space. Persistent variables are referenced in methods using the

Lisp name-space syntax. Hence the name #:db:mass-memory means the variable mass-memory defined in the database name space (i.e., the persistent name space). Persistent variables are used in the same way as ordinary variables.

```
; definition of a database variable
(defdbvar mass-memory (listof (tupleof
                                (part Complex-part)
                                (mass integer))))

(defmethod (Complex-part mass) ()
    (let (mass)
      ; see if the mass has already been computed
      (foreach ((cell #:db:mass-memory) mass)
        (if (eq (get-field cell 'part) self)
          (setq mass (get-field cell 'mass))))
      (unless mass
        ; not yet memorized
        (setq mass [self mass]) ; mass computing
        (list-insert #:db:mass-memory 0 (make-tuple (part self)
          (mass mass))))
      mass))
```

Figure 10.10. Complex *cost* method using a cache

A major database feature that we cannot easily map onto a language concept is the notion of a transaction supporting both concurrency and recovery. Therefore we just provide the programmer with the top-level command (i.e., a command that the programmer can only call at the top level of the interpreter) **with-transaction**. It begins a transaction scope, in which **abort-transaction** and **commit-transaction** have the usual semantics.

4 System Design

The implementation includes three layers: the persistent layer, which presents an interface with a system that provides database facilities; an object layer, which supports the object-oriented extension; and an application layer, which offers some predefined toolkits (for the time being, a user interface and a programming environment kernel). I outline very briefly the first two layers.

4.1 The Persistent Layer

Since we do not want to "reinvent the wheel," we need a layer that allows us to use some existing persistent facilities ranging from a Unix file system to a sophisticated object server like that of O_2 (Vélez, Bernard, and Darnis 1989; see chapter 15). Therefore we adopt the virtual-machine approach used in several language implementations (Goldberg and Robson 1983; Rees and Robson 1987) to facilitate portability. This virtual-machine defines storage structures and the reading/writing transformations from main-memory representation to those storage structures. There is one storage structure each for O_2 atomic types and constructors, for Lisp data types (list, vector, and so on), and for schema information (classes, types, operations, database variables, and methods). We use storage buckets to group logically related objects together. For pure Lisp data, those buckets are filled in a depth-first manner. In the development environment, we use the same approach for the O_2 objects and values. We plan to use this notion of storage buckets to implement clustering for an application. Every entity is tagged by its descriptor, and a particular storage bucket is devoted to the storage of classes together with their types, operations, and methods.

To handle transfer from persistent to main memory, we use a two-address space model as in Atkinson 1981. Every persistent entity has a persistent identifier, or pid. A persistence table associates pids with main-memory entities. The object-fault mechanism detects the use of a pid as a memory address and if necessary loads the object. It preserves identity and sharing.

Garbage collection in main memory deals only with data not reachable from this table (pure Lisp data or objects) and uses a stop-and-copy algorithm. Since we do not handle references coming from persistent to main memory, there may be some objects in the table which become unreachable from the persistent roots. In this case, the commit generates some garbage on disk. The benefit is that garbage collection and commit are fast because they do not perform disk access. The disk garbage is recovered in a batch way.

4.2 The Object Layer

The object layer supports the implementation of the object extension. An object is represented as a pair consisting of a class and its value. Values are tagged by their types. Tuple values are implemented using contiguous memory. Lists (or sets) are B-trees, which allow fast indexing (or fast insertion and membership checks). Each B-tree contains a header that records all classes appearing in the collection and the first object of each class in the collection. Objects of the same class are chained together. When there is an iteration containing a message-passing expression, this organization allows the late binding to be performed once for each class in the collection rather than once for each element of the collection.

The late-binding implementation uses the fact that the Schema Manager expands the operations of a class to its subclasses. Hence each class contains all the operations (inherited or locally defined) that can be applied on its instances. Therefore message passing extracts the class of the receiver object, looks for an operation in this class, and invokes its associated method.

To implement the Schema Manager we use a classical bootstrap technique in Lisp environments. Classes, types, operations, and methods are implemented as objects and thus are described by metaclasses. This allows all the schema manipulations to be implemented as operations on those objects. For instance, there is a subtype operation defined as virtual in the Type class and redefined in the Atomic-type, Set-type, List-type, Tuple-type, and Class classes. This bootstrap has allowed us to implement the system quickly and to evaluate the advantages of the language in the development of a complex application: the system itself. Moreover, the metalevel eases the extension of the language, since adding a type constructor is just adding a metaclass.

5 Related Work

Recently there has been a great deal of work aimed at integrating programming-language and database features. From the programming-language field, several attempts have been made to extend a language with persistence orthogonal to type. To implement the persistent layer, we use techniques similar to those of PS-Algol (Atkinson 1981); however, PS-Algol does not support object orientation with classes and inheritance.

Loom (Kaehler 1986) provides Smalltalk-80 with an object-oriented virtual memory and transparent object faulting. But it does not support database features such as transactions. Moreover, Smalltalk does not offers a clear semantics of (simple) inheritance, and in the standard version (Goldberg and Robson 1983), there is no static type checking. The closest work is PCLOS (Paepcke 1988), a persistent extension of the Common Lisp Object System (Demichiel and Gabriel 1987). Persistent facilities are offered through an interface that may be ported to several storage managers, including Iris's (Fishman et al. 1987). However, only the CLOS objects are allowed to persist; pure Lisp data are not. Moreover, the CLOS model is similar to Smalltalk and does not provide inheritance based on subtyping.

Object-oriented databases tend to reduce or eliminate the impedance mismatch. GemStone (Maier et al. 1986) provides database functionalities to Smalltalk including transactions, queries, and distribution. Based on Smalltalk, GemStone provides only simple inheritance and does not model complex values directly.

Orion (Banerjee et al. 1987) is a complete database system based on Lisp extended with object orientation. Name conflicts raised by multiple inheritance are solved implicitly by the system, based on the declared order of the superclasses. In $LispO_2$ we choose to notify the programmer of all name conflicts and let him or her explicitly solve them.

A last interesting point of comparison is the object/value duality provided by several systems. In $LispO_2$ this duality relies on the fact that object are encapsulated and values are not; but both can be shared. This distinguishes $LispO_2$ from the pure data model discussed in Lécluse and Richard 1989a where values are neither shared nor encapsulated. Orion (Kim et al. 1987) does not offer values but unshared objects named dependent objects, the class notion being the single modeling tool.

6 Future Work

We have implemented a first version of LispO$_2$, which includes all the features presented in this paper. The Schema Manager, the programming environment tools, and the method and application compilers are implemented using LispO$_2$. They are currently serving as benchmarks to evaluate the performance of this first implementation. The persistent layer is implemented on top of the Unix file system. Therefore it supports only a simple form of recovery and no concurrency at all. We are considering its implementation using the O$_2$ storage manager (Vélez, Bernard, and Darnis 1989; see chapter 15).

Some directions for future work are apparent from the first evaluations. Our own programming experience with LispO$_2$ encourages us to provide the programmer with a development methodology. Encapsulation and inheritance can be seen as design tools, and as such they can be misused or underused. Even without guidelines it is easy to design complex and deep class hierarchies. We are currently defining a top-down methodology, starting from an informal specification of the application and leading step by step to its implementation and test strategy. This methodology will be supported by tools in the programming environment.

Operations are the unique way to act upon objects, and we believe in encapsulation as a good development principle. However, functional decomposition of methods leads to a number of simple operations that are just data-structure manipulations. Those operations are never redefined in subclasses. Letting the programmer state explicitly which operations are redefinable offers a clear view of the points of flexibility of his or her design. Moreover, the late-binding overhead occurs only for those operations. Therefore we should obtain benefits both at the conceptual and implementation levels. Such a feature will be introduced in the next version of the language. At a physical level, we plan to integrate a clustering mechanism in the application compiler, based on the application schema and the access patterns that rely on methods.

7 Acknowledgements

We wish to thank F. Bancilhon, P. Richard, and the referees for their careful readings of this paper.

References

Albano, A., L. Cardelli, and R. Orsini. 1985. Galileo: A strongly typed, interactive conceptual language. *ACM TODS* 10(2): 230–61.

Andrews, T., and C. Harris. 1987. Combining language and database advances in an object-oriented development environment. In *Proceedings of the second OOPSLA conference.*

Atkinson, M. 1981. An Algol with a persistent heap. *Sigplan Notices* 17(7).

Atkinson, M., and P. Buneman. 1987. Types and persistence in database programming languages. *ACM Computing Surveys.*

Bancilhon, F., G. Barbedette, V. Benzaken, C. Delobel, S. Gamerman, C. Lécluse, P. Pfeffer, P. Richard, and F. Vélez. 1988. The design and implementation of O_2, an object-oriented database system. In *Advances in object-oriented database systems.* Springer-Verlag.

Banerjee, J., H-T. Chou, J. Garza, W. Kim, D. Woelk, N. Ballou, and H. J. Kim. 1987. Data model issues for object-oriented applications. *ACM TOIS* 5(1): 3–26.

Barbedette, G. 1989. LispO_2, a persistent object-oriented Lisp. In *Proceedings of the second EDBT conference.*

Carey, M., D. DeWitt, and S. Vandenberg. 1988. A data model and query language for Exodus. In *Proceedings of the ACM SIGMOD conference.*

Copeland G., and D. Maier. 1984. Making smalltalk a database system. In *Proceedings of the SIGMOD conference.*

Dadam, P. et al. 1986. A DBMS prototype to support extended NF^2 relations: An integrated view on flat tables and hierarchies. In *Proceedings of the SIGMOD conference.*

Demichiel, L. G. and R. P. Gabriel. 1987. The common lisp object system: An overview. In *Proceedings of the first ECOOP conference.*

Fishman, D., D. Beech, H. P. Cate, E. C. Chow, T. Conners, J. W. Davis, N. Denett, C. G. Hoch, W. Kent, P. Lyngbaek, B. Mahbod, M. A. Neimat, T. A. Ryan, and M. C. Shan. 1987. Iris: An object-oriented database management system. *ACM TOIS* 5(1): 46–69.

Goldberg, A., and D. Robson. 1983. *Smalltalk 80: The language and its implementation.* Addison-Wesley.

Kaehler, T. 1986. Virtual memory on a narrow machine for an object-oriented language. In *Proceedings of the OOPSLA conference.*

Kim, W., J. Banerjee, H-T. Chou, J. F. Garza, and D. Woelk, 1987. Composite object support in an object-oriented database system. In *Proceedings of the OOPSLA conference.*

Lécluse, C., and P. Richard. 1989a. Modeling complex structures in object-oriented databases. In *Proceedings of the ACM PODS conference.*

Lécluse, C., and P. Richard. 1989b. The O_2 database programming language. In *Proceedings of the VLDB conference.*

Lieberman, H. 1986. Using prototypical objects to implement shared behavior in object oriented systems. In *Proceedings of the first OOPSLA conference.*

Maier, D., J. Stein, A. Otis, and A. Purdy. 1986. Development of an object-oriented DBMS. In *Proceedings of the first OOPSLA conference.*

Meyer, B. 1988. *Object oriented software construction.* Prentice-Hall.

Paepcke, A. 1988. PCLOS: A flexible implementation of CLOS persistence. In *Proceedings of the second ECOOP conference.*

Rees, M., and D. Robson. 1987. *Practical compiling with Pascal-S.* Addison-Wesley.

Schaffert, C., T. Cooper, B. Bullis, M. Kilian, and C. Wilpolt. 1986. An introduction to Trellis/Owl. In *Proceedings of the first OOPSLA conference.*

Schmidt, J. W. 1977. Some high level language constructs for data of type relation. *ACM TODS* 2(3).

Stroustrup, B. 1986. *The C++ programming language.* Addison-Wesley.

Vélez, F., G. Bernard, and V. Darnis. 1989. The O_2 object manager: An overview. In *Proceedings of the VLDB conference.*

Wegner, P. 1987. Dimensions of an object-based language design. In *Proceedings of the second OOPSLA conference.*

Chapter 11

A Query Language for O_2

François Bancilhon
Sophie Cluet
Claude Delobel

1 Introduction

Object-oriented database systems (OODBSs) have recently received a lot of attention from the research community. Products and prototypes have been developed at a fast pace over the last few years (Banerjee et al. 1987; Bancilhon 1988; Bancilhon et al. 1988; Fishman et al. 1986; Maier et al. 1986; Atwood 1985; Caruso and Sciore 1988). However, OODBSs have to compete against relational systems, whose main strength is their query language. Therefore, one of the major problems which must be solved for OODBSs is that of the query language.

One of the main attractions of OODBSs is that they handle both data and programs in a single framework. Therefore they all come with some programming language, which is used to write the programs associated to the data. As opposed to relational query languages, these programming languages are complete; that is, they allow the user to write complete programs. However, because they are complete, they have the usual complexity of a powerful language and lack the simplicity of query languages. Thus there is still a need for a way of extracting information from the database without having to write a program. In this paper, we address the problem of designing a query language that provides this ad hoc querying facility and of integrating it in the overall system. We propose one solution for a specific object-oriented system, O_2, currently being implemented in the Altaïr group.

The paper is organized as follows: Section 2 defines what we mean by an object-oriented database system. Section 3 presents the various uses of a query language and defines the notion of a query facility. Section 4 presents and discusses the issues in designing a query language for an object-oriented database system. In section 5, we introduce the O_2 data model. Our choices concerning the design of the query language follow, in section 6. Section 7 is an informal presentation of the language. Section 8 sketches its semantic definition. We end this paper with a study of other object-oriented query languages, in section 9.

2 Object-Oriented Database System

It is not the purpose of this paper to give a definition of an object-oriented database system. The topic is subject to considerable debate, and it will probably take some time before the community agrees on a common definition. Our objective in this section is simply to set up the framework in which the query language should be discussed. We believe that an object-oriented DBMS should be (1) a DBMS, that is, it should have persistence, secondary storage management, concurrency, recovery, and an ad hoc query facility; and (2) object oriented, that is, it should have complex objects, object identity, encapsulation, types or classes, inheritance, overloading and late binding, extensibility, and computational completeness. Let us now briefly comment on each point, beginning with the object-oriented features (see chapter 1 for a more detailed discussion; see also Atkinson et al. 1989).

Complex objects are built from simple ones by applying to them object constructors. The three minimal constructors that the system should have are sets, lists, and tuples. In a model with *object identity*, an object has an existence which is independent of its value. Thus two objects can either be identical (they are the same object) or they can be equal (they have the same value). This has implications for object sharing (two distinct objects can share a common subcomponent) and for object updates (we can modify an object without changing its identity).

The idea of *encapsulation* comes from abstract data types: an object has an interface and an implementation. The interface is the specification of the set of operations (the methods) that can be performed on the object. It is the only visible part of the object. The implementation has a data part (the representation or state of the object), and a procedure part (which describes, in some programming language, the implementation of each operation).

A *type* summarizes the common structure of a set of objects with the same characteristics. It corresponds to the notion of an abstract data type. The specification of a *class* is the same as that of a type, but it is more of a run-time notion. It contains two aspects: an object factory (to generate new objects) and an object warehouse (to store all the objects of a class). Classes and types are organized into *inheritance* hierarchies. Each class (or type) can be specialized into a more specific class (or type) which inherits its methods and structure and contains some extra ones.

Methods can be redefined for more specific types. This yields *overloading*, that is, a given method name can mean different things, depending on the object to which it is applied. Overloading implies that the binding of the method name to the actual piece of code which executes it must be done at run time; this is *late binding.*

Computational completeness simply means that one can program any computable function, using the system. It is obvious from a programming-language point of view, but new from a database-system point of view. *Extensibility* means that the system comes with a set of predefined types or classes which can be extended; that is, there is a means to define new types and there is no distinction between system-defined and user-defined types.

We now turn to the database system characteristics. *Persistence* is the ability of data to survive the execution of a process, and to be eventually reusable in another process. *Disk management* includes the classical features one finds in a DBMS: index management, data clustering, and data buffering. *Concurrency* means that the system should ensure harmonious cooperation between users working simultaneously on the database. The system should therefore support the standard notion of atomicity of a sequence of operations and of controlled sharing.

Recovery means that, in case of hardware or software failure, the system should recover, that is, be brought back to some coherent point. A *query facility* consists in providing the functionality of an ad hoc query language. It does not have to be done under the form of a query language, but the service has to be provided. For instance, a graphical browser could very well be sufficient to fulfill this functionality. The service consists in allowing the user to ask reasonable queries to the database without too much difficulty. This paper discusses the issue of providing this facility with a query language.

3 Uses of the Query Language

We define an ad hoc query facility by four characteristics. It should be:

- *High level.* Reasonable queries should be easily and concisely expressed. This implies declarativity and associative access.

- *Retrieval oriented.* This language is not meant to perform computations but to extract information from a database on an ad hoc basis. Thus it is required to express a reasonable set of queries in a simple way. It trades simplicity against power. Completeness of the language as defined for relational systems is sufficient to meet this requirement.

- *Optimizable.* The system should find a good strategy to optimize user queries, using physical access paths such as indexes.

- *Application independent.* A specific user interface targeted to a given application is not an ad hoc query facility.

The second item is important; it makes the distinction between a database programming language and a query language. Recent evolutions in the database area have somehow confused the issue: a lot of work has consisted in extending the power of query languages to give computational completeness (Abiteboul and Beeri 1988; Abiteboul and Kanellakis 1989; see chapter 5). This idea is interesting, but it is not the topic of this paper. OOBDSs already have a programming language and claim to break the barrier between programming languages and data manipulation languages. The problem is to offer a simpler service with a simpler language.

Our point of view here is that a complete language (in the sense of a programming language) is too complex a tool for this ad hoc retrieval, and a special, simpler language is needed for this function. In this paper we discuss the design of this simpler language and its connection and integration in the rest of the system.

What are the objectives of such a query language? We think it can be used in three ways, which are the ways query languages such as SQL are currently used; and that it might be used in a fourth way, specific to an object-oriented query language. The languages were meant for ad hoc querying or data manipulation in an application program. They have also been used to write simple programs. In addition, an object-oriented language might be used to take shortcuts in the programming language.

3.1 For Ad Hoc Queries

All query languages are used for ad hoc querying; this is the mode privileged by relational systems. People who have simple data to extract from an information system should be given a simple means to formulate their question. Ease of expression, declarativity, and efficiency are the three main criteria that such a language should satisfy. This mode will apply to every possible system; thus it makes sense for an object-oriented database system: the user, instead of accessing the database through the programming language, will access it for simple tasks through the query language.

3.2 For Access to the Database

Relational systems were meant to be used only through their query language. SQL was also designed as a means of accessing data in a relational database from an application program (written in C, PL1 or Cobol). It is a mixed success in that use, because of the impedance mismatch (Bancilhon and Maier 1987). Normally, in an object-oriented database system there is no need for this functionality because the programming language allows for direct data manipulation: the data manipulation language and the programming language are supposed to be integrated.

3.3 For Simple Programs

Once one gives people a tool, they tend to use it for different purposes, simply because they like it or because they find it easy to use for this new purpose. Thus SQL has given rise to SQL programmers, who write entire applications in SQL directly, without resorting to any other language. Only simple applications can be written this way (due to the limited power of the language), but there are many of them. It is unclear whether, given a query language, users of object-oriented database systems will tend to use it this way; after all, they are supposed to have a good application-programming language.

3.4 For Shortcuts in the Programming Language

Assume we have a simple and easy-to-use query language to express even complex queries. This language is going to be simpler and more readable than the actual programming language of the system, and the programmer will be tempted to call it from its program to solve some data-manipulation problems. (This only applies to object-oriented systems.)

These modes of usage only make sense if we restrict ourselves to the original notion of a query language. They make absolutely no sense if we talk about extended query languages.

4 The Design of a Query Language

In this section we discuss the critical problems one must solve when designing an object-oriented query language.

1. Can the query language violate encapsulation?
2. What do we query: data, methods, or both?
3. What is the answer to a query?
4. Should the query language be integrated in the programming language?
5. What should the relationship with the type system be?

4.1 Relationship with Encapsulation

In an object-oriented system, each object has associated with it a set of methods (operations) by which one can operate on the object. The idea of encapsulation is that these methods are the *only* way to operate on objects. If the query language cannot violate encapsulation, then basically the only access to objects is through methods, and data is invisible. Conversely, if we want to see data, we must be able to violate encapsulation.

Encapsulation is a mechanism to enforce a good modularity of the code and a good programming discipline. Because the query language is only used to query the data and in an interactive mode, there is less reason to enforce encapsulation. This statement should be moderated in the case of updates (of the style "replace"). It should also be moderated in the case where the query language is embedded in the programming language. So we are back to an authorization problem: the query language should have a different behavior when it is used as an ad hoc query facility, as an embedded data manipulation language, or as a programming language.

We claim that, in the first case, it should be allowed to violate encapsulation, and that in the two other cases it should strictly respect it. Take the classical example of a stack: it is represented as an object with two operations, *pop* and *push*. When manipulating that stack in a program, we do not want the client programmers to see the stack implementation or content. However, when querying the system through a browser (assume a graphical interface), we want to see a complete picture of a stack with its entire content, rather than seeing only an icon which we can pop and push. On the other hand, if we allow the query language to violate encapsulation in the embedded or in the programming language mode, we lose all the benefit of the encapsulation approach.

We conclude that the query language should be able to violate encapsulation in the ad hoc query mode but not when used for programming purposes.

4.2 Data versus Methods

Because methods will be used by database designers to glorify data (i.e., to generate virtual attributes), it is necessary to be able to query them. For example, consider the Person object with the instance variable `birth_date`. A good way of improving this object is by introducing a "computed field" `age`, which computes the age from the birth date and the current date. This computed field is usually represented by a method of the Person object. Thus if we do not allow the user to query on methods, the user will be forced to recompute the age in the query whenever he or she needs to query on that field.

Because sometimes methods will only be used to store entire application programs, it is necessary to be able to query data directly. For example, consider the Employee object. Assume the designer has encapsulated everything and uses only two methods, *fire* and *hire*. Then there are no ways to browse through the database.

We conclude that the query language should be able to see data and apply methods to objects.

4.3 The Answer to a Query

The purpose of a query language is to extract information from a database. However, this information seldom exists as a whole; it has to be constructed. The answer to a traditional query, which filters a set according to some predicate, is a newly built set containing some or none of the old set's elements.

In the relational model, the answer to a query is a new relation. In an object-oriented system, one might think a query returns an object. But if so, to what class does it belong? Three answers are possible:

1. A query extracts only information that exists as a whole in the database.

2. The result of a query belongs to a metaclass which accepts all objects and whose methods allow displaying and printing. With this solution, we might find problems in reusing an answer without violating the encapsulation principle, since there will be no methods to do so. This is because a method implementation is dependent on the structural part of the class it is associated with. Since metaclass has no particular structure, it is impossible to define specific methods to manipulate its objects.

3. When constructing a new object, the query language creates a new class and a set of methods such that all information on its objects is accessible (a method for each attribute of a tuple structured object, an iteration method for a set structured object, etc.).

The first solution sounds rather restrictive. The third solution is definitely heavy. The conclusion is that in an object-oriented model, there is a tradeoff between the encapsulation principle and the power and efficiency of the query language.

4.4 Integration in the Programming Language

The query language could be a subset of the programming language or it could be a distinct language. In the latter case, the programming language could call the query language, and/or the query language could call the programming language.

Three situations can occur, in order of increasing interest:

1. The query language is distinct from the programming language and there is an impedance mismatch between the two languages, such as the one between SQL and C, due to the difference in style of the languages.

2. The query language is distinct, but it mixes well with the programming language and calling it from a program is fairly natural.

3. The query language is a subset of the programming language.

In the first situation we have failed in fulfilling one of the major objectives of object-oriented database systems: solving the impedance mismatch of relational systems. In the second case we have improved the situation, but the programmer still has to learn two different languages. The last case is a sure winner: there is no impedance mismatch, the user only learns one language, and he or she still has the benefit of a user-friendly query language.

4.5 Relationship with the Type or Class System

Many query languages refer to types in their query formulation, either for correctness purposes or simply to extract information. In fact, the only information needed is that concerning the structure of the data, and not the types. Programming languages need type information to increase their correctness; but in the case of ad hoc query languages we are in an interpreted mode and are not so concerned with correctness.

Concerning the form of type checking, whether we use compile-time or run-time type checking is more of a performance argument. Ad hoc queries could be type checked at run time, and canned queries could be checked at compile time.

One last important point: type information is currently used in database systems, not for correctness purposes but for performance purposes. Knowing the exact type of the data allows one to compile operations down into machine code, thus increasing performance. This is an argument for compile-time type checking. Note that no type information is needed in the query for that: the system can derive the type information from the schema. The query only references the data and the schema tells the system the type of the referenced data.

The conclusion is that no type information is needed in the query formulation; type information can be derived by the system and used for checking purposes and optimization purposes at compile time.

5 The O_2 Data Model

The O_2 data model (Lécluse, Richard, and Vélez 1988; see chapter 4) is object oriented; it features object identity, abstract typing, encapsulation, inheritance, and late binding.

Object identity. The entities of an object-oriented database are called objects. An object is a couple (identifier, value). The identifier is unique and value independent and allows reference to the object.

Abstract typing. All objects belong to a class. A class is characterized by the type of its instances and by a set of operators called methods. The object-oriented paradigm introduces the notion of abstract data types by dividing a class into two parts: the implementation, known only by its designer, and the interface, which represents the knowledge a user has of a class. The interface is a subset of the set of methods implemented by the designer. Its elements are represented by their names and signatures.

Encapsulation. An object can be manipulated (i.e., modified, accessed, deleted) only through the methods given in its class interface. Thus its behavior is strictly controlled.

Inheritance. Classes are partially ordered. A class can be refined in a subclass that will inherit its behavior.

Late binding. The actual code of a method is determined at run time.

An additional, distinctive feature of the O_2 data model is *values*. Values are characterized by their types. They may be composed of objects, and objects may be composed of values. Values do not obey the object-oriented principles:

- The structures of values, while similar to those of the objects, are visible and manipulable.
- Values have no identity.
- Values are manipulated by operators, not by methods.

Standard operators are available for tuple, set, and list values. For instance, the operator "." allows the extraction of a tuple field, iteration is possible inside a set value, and two lists can be concatenated.

Values have been introduced in the O_2 model because of the inadequacy of the object-oriented paradigm for the manipulation of structures. We particularly think of the set and list structures, to which one would often like to associate traditional set and list operators. The O_2 model, owing to its abstract and concrete types, offers a more flexible environment. The designer of a database will choose one solution or the other according to his or her needs. On one hand, the designer will obtain inheritance and encapsulation; and on the other hand, easy manipulation of the structures.

We end this section by presenting an example of an O_2 database schema. For this, we use the schema-command language of the O_2 programming interface. We represent the city-tour program of a travel agency.

```
add class Place_to_go
        type tuple(name: string,
                   address: tuple(country: string,
                                  city: string,
                                  street: string)
                   description: string,
                   phone: integer,
                   things_to_do: set(Thing_to_do))
        with extension
```

This command creates a class of objects having a tuple structure. The tuple has five fields. The **address** field is itself a tuple value. The fields **name**, **description**, and **phone** are atomic values, and the field **things_to_do** is a set of objects of the class Thing_to_do. The **with extension** clause means that there is a set value named Place_to_go which contains all the instances of that class. The following command creates the class Thing_to_do.

```
add class Thing_to_do
        type tuple (name: string,
                    description: string,
                    closing_days: string,
                    fee: integer)
        with extension
```

The next command creates the Tour class. The **schedule** field is a list of tuples. Notice that this class is created without extension.

```
add class Tour
        type tuple (name: string,
                    maximum_number: int,
                    schedule: list(tuple(what: Thing_to_do,
                                         when: Date)))
```

The last class is the Date class. This class has four methods: *day, day_in_week, month,* and *year,* returning respectively an integer, a string, a string, and an integer.

```
add class Date
        type integer
        method day: integer,
        method day_in_week: string,
        method month: string,
        method year: integer,
```

The actual code of the methods is written in the programming language of O_2.

```
add object Eiffel_Tower: Place_to_go
add object Paris_tour: Tour
```

This declares a named object of class Place_to_go with name Eiffel_Tower, and a named object Paris_tour of class Tour.

```
add value student_rate: Real
```

This declares a named value of type real, with name student_rate.

add object Today: Date

This declares a named object of type date, with name Today. The actual initialization and maintenance of these objects is not shown in this example.

6 Design Choices

The following design decisions were made for the language.

1. The query language violates encapsulation in its ad hoc mode. It does not do so in its programming or embedded mode.
2. A query returns an object or a value. Returned objects are those already existing in the database; new values can be built by a query.
3. The query language sees data and can apply methods to objects.
4. The query language is functional in nature.
5. The query language is a subset of the programming language.
6. The query language ignores types and the type hierarchy. Type checking is performed at run time in the query mode and at compile time in the programming mode.

7 The Query Language

We present the query language by means of examples on the database introduced in section 5. This presentation does not exhaust its possibilities; but it shows how to formulate simple queries on any entities of an O_2 database. Later in this section we show how to solve problems due to the complex structures we are manipulating. This is done by answering the questions:

- How does one access all levels of a structure?
- How do lists cohabit with sets inside a query?
- Is it possible to construct flat as well as nested values?

We consider the language in its ad hoc mode, which violates encapsulation. This means that objects may be considered as values, and thus that it is possible to query their structure.

7.1 Simple Queries

In the relational paradigm, sets of tuples are privileged structures. Consequently, with most relational query languages one accesses database values through set filters, called **select-from-where** in SQL or **range-retrieve-where** in QUEL. In an object-oriented model, matters are different since all structures are on a same level. Thus, although filters are still a necessity, one must be able to access the database from other angles. In the O_2 query language there are no privileged structures. One may work directly on atoms, tuples, sets, and lists.

An example of a query based on atomic values is: *What is two plus two?* It is expressed like this:

$2 + 2$

An example of a query based on tuples is, *Where is the Eiffel Tower?*

Eiffel_Tower.address

This query is one example of deencapsulation. The object Eiffel_Tower is considered here as a value. As in SQL, the "." operator allows the extraction of any tuple field. Thus, according to the O_2 model, the result of such an operation may be of any type or class.

An example of a query based on sets is, *What are the activities that cost less than ten francs?*

select x.name
from x **in** Thing_to_do
where x.fee < 10

This **select-from-where** block is a set filter. We chose an SQL-like syntax for two reasons: it is clear and easy to read, and it is very popular among applications programmers. The traditional semantics is preserved. The **from** clause indicates the filtered set, in this case the extension of the class Thing_to_do. The **where** clause conditions the elements on which the operation expressed inside the **select** clause will be executed. However, the reader should be aware of two important differences:

1. The elements manipulated inside a filter may be of any structure, whereas in the relational model they are restricted to being tuples. Consequently, we may find other operators than the field extraction in a **select** clause.

2. The elements of the resulting set need not be tuples. They can be of any type or class. In the example, they are string values.

In some cases, we might find it interesting to extract the unique element of a singleton set. This is possible through the **element** operator. For example, *What is the price of a visit to the Eiffel tower for a student?*

```
element    select  x.fee
           from    x in Eiffel_Tower.things_to_do
           where   x.name = "visit"
* student_rate
```

In this case, the filter operation results in a set containing a single value, which represents the price of a visit to the Eiffel tower. The *element* operation will return an integer that can be manipulated like any other O_2 numeric value. This is why the multiplication by the student_rate named value is permissible.

As opposed to sets, lists are ordered. This is why, knowing its position, we can access an element of a list without having to filter it. For example, *What is the first place visited on the Paris tour?*

```
Paris_tour.schedule[0].what
```

Should we be interested in more than one element or in an element whose position we ignore, we may always resort to a list-filter operation. For example, *What places do we visit with the Paris tour?*

```
select  x.what
from    x in Paris_tour.schedule
```

We chose an identical syntax for both O_2 filters so as not to needlessly complicate the language. The filtered value is the `schedule` field of the Paris_tour object, and the result is a list of objects of the Thing_to_do class.

7.2 Access to All Levels of a Structure

In the previous examples, we have seen how to work on differently structured entities. Some were named and thus directly accessible (Eiffel_Tower, Thing_to_do, student_rate, and Paris_tour) and others had to be reached after some navigation process. This was done by navigating inside the database structures. We accessed a tuple field via the "." operator, the elements of a set or a list through the two filter operators, and an element of a list with the "[ ]" operator. However, we were very reasonable since we went down several levels only through tuple attributes (for instance, x.location.address.city in the third example). This was rather simple. Things are more complex when one wants to navigate through embedded sets or lists.

We will consider an example of embedded sets; lists have an identical treatment. For example, *What things can one do in Paris for less than fr 50?*

One solution consists in building the set we want to filter, that is, the set containing the things one can do in Paris.

```
select  x.name
from    x in flatten  select  y.things_to_do
                      from    y in Place_to_go
                      where   y.address.city = "Paris"
where   x.fee < 50
```

The embedded set filter returns a set containing as many sets of things to do as there are places to go in Paris. The **flatten** operator returns a set of things to do that is the union of the previous set elements. A final filter operation gets the elements whose `fee` field has a value less than 50.

This path went through two sets; we leave the reader to imagine the complexity of such a solution should it have to go through more. Because of this complexity, the O_2 language introduces a filter that accepts logical dependencies between its variables. The query can be translated in a much nicer way:

```
select  x.name
from    y in Place_to_go
        x in y.things_to_do
where   y.address.city = "Paris" and x.fee < 50
```

This filter allows an easy navigation through sets. In the present example we are able, with a single operation, to study each thing to do at each place to go. We could go on like that through as many levels as we want.

We do not present here a formal definition of this operator. From an intuitive point of view, one can imagine the filtered set as being the subset of the Cartesian product on the variables domain whose elements respect the user-defined dependencies.

7.3 Lists and Sets inside a Query?

At this point of our study, the reader knows how to access nearly every element of an O_2 database. However, there is still one unanswered question. How does one navigate through alternated levels of sets and lists? Let us consider the following query: *What are the things to do that are not part of a tour?* We will formulate this query twice, first with two embedded filters and then with a single filter operation.

```
Thing_to_do  minus  select  x.what
                    from    x in  flatten select  y.schedule
                                          from    y in Tour
```

The named value Tour denotes a set of objects of which the `schedule` field is a list. Accordingly, the embedded filter operation returns a set of lists. The **flatten** operator has been extended to face such occurrences and flatten sets of lists (and lists of sets) into sets. Once this operation has been executed, a final set filter allows the construction of a set whose elements are things to do that are part of a tour. The last operation is a set difference with the set containing all possible things to do.

This first translation shows that, when working on a model containing lists and sets, there is an obligation to have an extended **flatten** operator. This operator returns a set, whether applied on a set of lists or on a list of sets, for an obvious semantical reason: the set structure is more general than the list structure.

We next examine the implications of the list-and-set navigation for a filter with variables dependencies.

Thing_to_do **minus** **select** x.what
from y **in** Tour
x **in** y.schedule

From an intuitive point of view, the reader should have no problem in understanding this query. It extracts all things to do from every schedule of every possible tour. One might wonder whether we used a set or a list filter. The answer is: a set filter. The lists we met in the **from** clause definition have been transformed into sets. Because the set structure is more general than the list structure, it would have been difficult to do the opposite operation.

7.4 Flat and Nested Values

We have seen how the O_2 query language gives access to all the elements of a database whatever their position in a complex structure. We are now able to extract any database entity; but query language, to be worthy of the name, has to offer more. It must give a way to construct new values (see section 4). This is needed to obtain partial information (some fields of a tuple, some elements of a set, and so on) or to create entities according to some logical criterion.

The examples that follow show how this is possible in O_2.

7.4.1 Constructing Sets and Lists

A filter constructs a new set (or list) from the elements of another. However, there is another way to construct sets (or lists) in O_2. For example, *Does a Paris tour start in the last week of March?*

define Paris_tour_start
Paris_tour.schedule[0].when ;

```
Paris_tour_start month = "March" and
Paris_tour_start day in set(25, 26, 27, 28, 29, 30, 31)
```

This is the first example of a query that resorts to a named query (Paris_tour_start) and to methods (month and day), the first that is a Boolean expression, and the first that uses the **set** constructor.

The **define** keyword introduces named queries. A named query may denote a value or an object, as is the case here with Paris_tour_start; but we will see later that it can be parameterized and denote a function. The naming of the Paris_tour_start object avoids a repetition of the path one has to follow to get it.

The **set** operator builds a set value containing its actual parameters. In this example, it was used as a programming goody. It saved us from writing six extra lines of code. Of course, there is an equivalent **list** operator.

7.4.2 Constructing Tuples

In the following query, the **tuple** operator constructs a tuple value. *What is the address and phone number of the Eiffel Tower?*

```
tuple(address: Eiffel_tower.address, phone: Eiffel_tower.phone)
```

7.4.3 Constructing Nested Structures

In O_2, to construct nested values one just has to combine the various operators. The only restrictions on those combinations are that set (or list, tuple, numerical, Boolean, or string) operators must be applied on sets (or lists, tuples, numerical values, Booleans, or strings). For example, *What is the address of the Eiffel Tower and what are the names and fees of the things that can be done there on Sundays?*

```
tuple  (address: Eiffel_tower.address,
        things_to_do: select tuple(name: x.name, fee: x.fee)
                      from x in Eiffel_tower.things_to_do
                      where not (x.closing_day = Sunday))
```

In this example, we build a tuple whose `things_to_do` attribute is a set of tuples. This set is constructed by a set filter whose **select** clause contains a tuple constructor.

7.4.4 Other Features

We end our presentation by introducing two more features: the O_2 universal quantifier, and a parameterized named query. *What are the places whose activities are all open on Sundays? What are their names and the names and fees of their activities?*

```
define names_and_fees (x)
select  tuple(name: y.name, fee: y.fee)
from    y in x ;

select  tuple(name: x.name,
              things_to_do: names_and_fees(x.things_to_do))
from    x in Place_to_go
where   for all y in x.things_to_do: y.closing_day <> "Sunday"
```

Since its use is rather trivial, we will not comment on the **for all** quantifier. As for the names_and_fees query, its purpose is to ease the formulation of the query by division into two more legible subqueries. It is interesting to note that named queries not only make for better readability but also allow query factorization.

8 Semantics of the O_2 Query Language

The query language is functional in nature. Loosely speaking, a query is an expression of the form $e(x_1, x_2, \ldots, x_n)$ where the x_is are free variables. For any database, a query defines a partial mapping which associates with each collection of n values or objects of the database, a value or an object of the database. Thus queries are parameterized, and to be evaluated they have to be assigned parameters (objects or values). Therefore only closed queries (those without any free variables) can be actually evaluated. Open queries (those with free variables) are only used to build and define other queries.

The semantics of a query $f(x_1, x_2, \ldots, x_n)$ is defined as follows. For every database, f defines a partial mapping $(\mathbf{O} \cup \mathbf{V})^n \rightarrow \mathbf{O} \cup \mathbf{V}$, where $\mathbf{O}$ is the set of persistent objects of the database and $\mathbf{V}$ the set of the possible values of the database. By "possible" we mean values whose basic components are atomic values or objects belonging to $\mathbf{O}$.

We sketch in this section the definition of the main operators. For more details, see Bancilhon, Cluet, and Delobel 1989.

We start with two queries that are the basic elements for defining the recursive process behind a functional language:

- If n is the name of a named object or value of the database, then n is a closed query. It returns the object or the value associated with this name.
- If a is an atom, then a is a closed query returning this atom.

We next enumerate the language's main operators. A formal definition is given for each of them in Bancilhon, Cluet, and Delobel 1989. We have basic queries on:

- Numerical values (+, *, / , −)
- Boolean values (*and, or, not*)

- Tuple values (the field extraction operator, denoted by a dot)
- Set values (element, inter, minus, union, flatten, count, sum, avg)
- List values (*i*th, sublist, concat, flatten, count, sum, avg)
- Objects (message passing)

We can construct values in the following manner:

- **tuple**(a_1: x_1, a_2: $x_2, \ldots, a_n$: x_n), where the a_is are distinct attribute names, is a query with free variables $x_1, x_2, \ldots, x_n$. It associates to the n objects or values $x_1, x_2, \ldots, x_n$ the tuple having its attribute a_i equal to x_i. Note that in this case the input variables can be assigned a mix of objects and values.
- **set**($x_1, x_2, \ldots, x_n$) is a query with free variables $x_1, x_2, \ldots, x_n$. It associates with all n objects $x_1, x_2, \ldots, x_n$ whose classes have a common superclass, or with all n values $x_1, x_2, \ldots, x_n$ whose types have a common supertype, the set value containing them. Note that one cannot mix objects and values in the same set.
- **list**($x_1, x_2, \ldots, x_n$) is a query with free variables $x_1, x_2, \ldots, x_n$. It associates with all n objects $x_1, x_2, \ldots, x_n$ whose classes have a common superclass, or with all n values $x_1, x_2, \ldots, x_n$ whose types have a common supertype, the list value containing them. Note that one cannot mix objects and values in the same list.

We can build predicate queries of the following forms:

- $x_1 \ \theta \ x_2$ is a query with free variables x_1 and x_2. θ stands for one of $\{=, <, >, \leq, \geq, \in\}$. The semantics is traditional. The type of the queries must be compatible with the operator.
- **for all** x **in** y: $p(x, x_1, x_2, \ldots, x_n)$ is a query with free variables $x_1, x_2, \ldots, x_n, y$. It defines a predicate taking the value *true* if all the elements of the set or list value y satisfy p($x, x_1, x_2, \ldots, x_n$).
- **exists** x **in** y: $p(x, x_1, x_2, \ldots, x_n)$ is a query with free variable $x_1, x_2, \ldots, x_n, y$. It defines a predicate taking the value *true* if one of the elements of the set or list value y satisfies p($x, x_1, x_2, \ldots, x_n$).

Since it can deal with several sets and lists in one single operation, the filter operator has a fairly complex definition. Because of space limitations, it is not defined here; once again, we refer the reader to Bancilhon, Cluet, and Delobel 1989.

Our last definition concerns named queries. Given an expression e($x_1, x_2, \ldots, x_n$) defining a query, we attach a name to that query to reuse it in other query expressions with the following statement:

define query f($x_1, x_2, \ldots, x_n$): e($x_1, x_2, \ldots, x_n$)

Then we can use f($x_1, x_2, \ldots, x_n$) in place of e($x_1, x_2, \ldots, x_n$).

9 Other Query Languages

In this survey, we examine five languages. Our interest lies in the choices that their developers made concerning the issues raised in section 4.

9.1 The Query Language for Orion

The object-oriented data model implemented in the Orion system can be considered conventional. It allows one to represent complex objects with the standard constructors: tuple and set. Similar objects can be grouped into classes. An object component may belong to a basic type or a class. A class describes the structural aspect and the behavior of the objects belonging to it. Behavior is characterized by a set of methods. The concept of class hierarchy is used to capture the refinement properties of a class into subclasses. Thus the attributes and the methods associated to a class are inherited by all the subclasses.

The query language (Banerjee, Kim, and Kim 1987) does not violate encapsulation. Only methods are queried. Access to the database is gained through the extension of the database classes.

The output of a query is always a subset of the instances of a class. There is apparently no way to produce a result which combines, with a tuple or a set constructor, instances of different classes. This is an important restriction, since this excludes the equivalence of join operations.

The syntax of a query is Smalltalk-like.

(Receiver Selector Arg1, Arg2, ...)

Receiver is the name of an object to which the message, given in the **Selector**, is sent. The **Selector** is a composition of method calls. The arguments **Arg1**, **Arg2**, ...are objects or blocks of code which result in an object.

9.2 OSQL, the Iris Query Language

Iris is a Hewlett-Packard project whose purpose is the development of an object-oriented DBMS (Fishman et al. 1986; Beech 1988). An Iris database has these features:

- Objects, which are entities that have an identity and an encapsulated value.
- Types, which are the equivalent of the Orion classes and which have an atomic, set, or tuple structure.
- A hierarchy of types, forming the base of an inheritance mechanism.
- Functions attached to types, as methods are to classes in Orion; they are the keys to object manipulation.

OSQL is not a simple query language but rather the vehicle language for the model. In that respect, Iris has been largely influenced by the relational paradigm and its standard SQL. Like SQL, OSQL serves as a data description, data manipulation, and query language. However, it cannot answer complex problems, which have to be solved by a call to external functions. Those functions have to be written in a foreign programming language. Thus we find in Iris the traditional impedance mismatch.

OSQL has an SQL-like syntax. A query is a declaration of a sequence of functions, followed by a **select-from-where** block (called an SFW block). As in SQL, an SFW block implicitly constructs a set of tuples. We do not know if this set is considered the extension of a tuple type or if the set is an object belonging to a set type. Another answer we have not found out concerns encapsulation. We do not know for sure what is queried, data or functions. To declare a function, one has to specify the type to which it belongs, its parameter type, and the type of its result. This is the only case where type information is not inferred.

9.3 The Query Language for Exodus

The Extra data model developed by the Exodus project might be considered an extension of the object-oriented paradigm. It features not only objects but also values, which are entities that do not respect the object encapsulation and identity principles. Values are typed; objects belong to classes. Extra has all the characteristics of an object-oriented model: complex structures obtained through a tuple, a set and an array constructor; classes and objects; functions attached to classes; and a multiple inheritance mechanism.

The Excess query language has a QUEL syntax and allows modification of a database as well as querying. It also provides facilities to define new functions. However, those functions cannot be associated to classes but only to types. Thus we cannot really speak of integration.

Data as well as functions can be queried. This is done without violating the encapsulation principle. Objects are queried through appropriate functions; values are queried according to their structure and appropriate functions. The output of a query is always a set value. Although we did not find out for sure, it seems that the elements of an answer are always tuple values.

9.4 Two Query Languages for O_2

Like the Extra model, O_2 has typed values and objects belonging to classes.

9.4.1 Reloop

Reloop was Altaïr's first attempt at a query language for O_2 (Delobel, Lécluse, and Richard 1988; Cluet et al. 1989; see chapter 12). It has an SQL-like syntax, respects encapsulation, and allows querying of methods and values. Although it is possible to define methods, there is no integration with the programming languages. The output of a query can be an object belonging to the database or any constructed value. The Reloop compiler has a type-inference mechanism. Reloop is semantically supported by an algebra which is defined in Cluet et al. 1989 (see chapter 12). We intend to use this algebra to optimize the filter operators of the current language.

The main drawback of Reloop is that it privileges access to set structures. This is due to the fact that a query is always an SFW block, and such a block corresponds to a set filter. This may be admissible for a relational database, whose only entities are set structured, but it cannot be admissible for an object-oriented database, one whose entities may be tuples, atoms, or sets.

9.4.2 Lifoo

Lifoo is a functional query language based on the O_2 data model. It was developed at the University of Marseille (Boucelma and Lemaître 1988). Like FQL (Buneman, Frankel, and Nikhil 1982), Lifoo defines basic functions from which new functions can be derived to query the database. The main basic functions include tuple, list, and set constructors; methods; and set operations.

Apart from the syntax, the Lifoo choices concerning the issues raised in section 4 are identical to those of Reloop.

References

Abiteboul, S., and C. Beeri. 1988. *On the power of languages for the manipulation of complex objects.* INRIA technical report no. 846.

Abiteboul, S., and P. Kanellakis. 1989. Object identity as a query language primitive. In *Proceedings of the 1989 ACM SIGMOD conference.*

Atkinson, M. et al. 1989. The object-oriented database manifesto. In *Proceedings of the international conference on deductive and object-oriented databases.*

Atwood, T. 1985. *An object-oriented DBMS for design support applications.* Ontologic Report.

Bancilhon, F. 1988. Object-oriented database systems. In *Proceedings of the ACM SIGACT-SIGMOD-SIGART conference on the principles of database systems.*

Bancilhon, F., G. Barbedette, V. Benzaken, C. Delobel, S. Gamerman, C. Lécluse, P. Pfeffer, P. Richard, and F. Vélez. 1988. The design and implementation of O_2, an object-oriented database system. In *Proceedings of the second international workshop on object-oriented database systems,* ed. K. Dittrich.

Bancilhon, F., S. Cluet, and C. Delobel. 1989. *The O_2 queries: Syntax and semantics.* GIP Altaïr Technical Report.

Bancilhon, F., and D. Maier. 1987. Multilanguage object-oriented systems: A new answer to old database problems. In *Proceedings of the second INRIA-ICOT workshop on computer science and artificial intelligence.*

Banerjee, J., H-T. Chou, J. Garza, W. Kim, D. Woelk, N. Ballou, and H. J. Kim. 1987. Data model issues for object-oriented applications. *ACM TOIS* 5(1): 3–26.

Banerjee, J., W. Kim, and K. C. Kim. 1987. *Queries in object-oriented databases.* MCC technical report no. DB 188 87.

Beech, D. 1988. A foundation for evolution from relational to object databases. In *Proceedings of the first conference on extending database technology.*

Boucelma, O., and J. Lemaître. 1988. *LIFOO, un language d'interrogation fonctionnel pour une base de donnée orienté-objet.* Université de Marseille, Technical Report.

Buneman, P., R. Frankel, and R. Nikhil. 1982. An implementation technique for database query languages. *ACM TODS* 17(2).

Carey, M., D. DeWitt, and S. Vandenberg. 1988. A data model and query language for Exodus. In *Proceedings of the ACM SIGMOD conference.*

Caruso, M., and E. Sciore. 1988. Contexts and metamessages in object-oriented database programming language design. In *Proceedings of the ACM SIGMOD conference.*

Cluet, S., C. Delobel, C. Lécluse, and P. Richard. 1989. *RELOOP, a request language on an object-oriented paradigm.* GIP Altaïr Technical Report.

Delobel, C., C. Lécluse, and P. Richard. 1988. LOOQ: A query language for object-oriented databases. In *Proceedings of the AFCET conference on knowledge and object-oriented database systems.*

Fishman, D. et al. 1986. Iris: An object-oriented database management system. *ACM TOIS* 5(1): 48–69.

Lécluse, C., P. Richard, and F. Vélez. 1988. O_2, an object-oriented data model. In *Proceedings of the ACM SIGMOD conference.*

Maier, D., J. Stein, A. Otis, and A. Purdy. 1986. *Development of an object-oriented DBMS.* Oregon Graduate Center, Report no. CS/E-86-005.

CHAPTER 12

Reloop, an Algebra-Based Query Language for O_2

SOPHIE CLUET
CLAUDE DELOBEL
CHRISTOPHE LÉCLUSE
PHILIPPE RICHARD

1 Introduction

In chapter 11 we presented the O_2 query language as it appears in the V1 prototype. We also discussed the general problem of designing a query language in an object-oriented environment. In this chapter we present an earlier experiment: the Reloop query language. Its design followed several stages (Delobel, Lécluse, and Richard 1988). The basic idea was to extend the traditional semantics of the SQL block **Select-from-where** through the introduction of object-oriented features. The Iris (Beech 1988) and Exodus (Carey, DeWitt, and Vandenberg 1988) query languages adopted similar approaches. OSQL, the Iris query language, is an SQL-like language; the Exodus query language, Excess, has a QUEL syntax.

The adaptation of SQL to the O_2 environment showed two limitations: (1) it only allows one to query collections; this is reasonable in the relational model, where relations are the only accessible database entities, but it is less defensible in a model where no particular structure is privileged; and (2) it forced us to fit every possible type of O_2 query into the SQL straitjacket.

For these reasons we dropped this first approach and adopted a functional one, which resulted in the current O_2 query language, a language better fitted to the orthogonality of the O_2 data constructors and easier to apprehend. Another solution consists in having a pure object-oriented query language, as Orion (Banerjee, Kim, and Kim 1988) has, which consists in a set of predefined methods. However, the Orion query language also has its limitations: the result of a query is always a subset of the instances of a class; and there is no apparent way to produce a result which combines, with a tuple or a set constructor, instances of different classes.

Although Reloop has been dropped, the experiment laid the basis for the optimization of the current query language. In order to semantically support the language translation into CO_2, one of the O_2 languages (Lécluse and Richard 1989; see chapter 9), we designed an algebra. We believe we can use this algebra's operators to optimize queries on collections.

The idea of having an algebra to support and to optimize the query language has been used for relational systems. The extension of that idea for object-oriented database systems has also been explored by Osborn 1988 and by Shaw and Zdonik 1989a. These algebras include the concepts of complex objects, object identity, and user-defined methods. They propose some optimization rules based on algebraic properties (Beeri and Kornatzky 1990; Shaw and Zdonik 1989b).

This paper is organized as follows. Section 2 introduces the example which we use throughout this paper. In section 3 we discuss the basic issues in the design of the language. Section 4 gives an overview of the Reloop language. Section 5 defines the semantics of the language by means of an algebra, and section 6 shows the steps that lead to its CO_2 translation. In section 7 we give some concluding remarks. Section 8 is an appendix on the construction of the algebra's macro-operators.

2 An Example

Throughout this paper we use a single example. Because of encapsulation, we separate the designer view of the database—that is, the implementation of classes—from the user's view, which contains the class interface.

2.1 The Designer's View

The designer creates a class by giving it a name, a type, and a set of methods; by describing its interface; and eventually by establishing a hierarchical relationship with other classes (the O_2 model admits multiple inheritance). We restrict the present study to names, types, and the hierarchical relationship. The example classes are Person, Female, Male, and Family:

Person = [**name**: [**first-name**: string, **last-name**: string],
age: integer,
address: [**city**: string, **zipcode**: integer]]

Female = [**name**: [**first-name**: string, **last-name**: string],
age: integer,
sex: string,
address: [**city**: string, **zipcode**: integer]]

Male = [**name**: [**first-name**: string, **last-name**: string],
age: integer,
sex: string,
address: [**city**: string, **zipcode**: integer]]

Family = [**name**: string, **mother**: Female, **father**: Male, **children**: {Person}]

Female and Male are subclasses of Person. An instance of the above schema may be:

(i_1, [**name**: [**first-name**: "John", **last-name**: "Doe"],
age: 2,
sex: "male",
address: [**city**: "Paris", **zipcode**: 75015]])

(i_2, [**name**: [**first-name**: "Joan", **last-name**: "Smith"],
age: 18,
sex: "female",
address: [**city**: "Paris", **zipcode**: 75015]])

(i_3, [**name**: [**first-name**: "Jack", **last-name**: "Doe"],
age: 19,
sex: "male",
address: [**city**: "Paris", **zipcode**: 75015]])

(i_4, [**name**: "Doe",
mother: i_2,
father: i_3,
children: {i_1}])

This database features four tuple-structured objects whose fields are:

- atomic valued (e.g., the **age** field of i_1),
- complex valued (e.g., the **name** field of i_1), or
- object valued (e.g., the **mother** field of i_4).

In the O_2 model, the constraint dictated by a tuple structure is less restrictive than in most models. All objects belonging to a tuple-structured class must be tuple valued and must possess, *at least*, all the fields present in the type definition. For instance, objects belonging to the Person class will be tuple valued and have, at least, a **name** field, an **age** field, and an **address** field. This definition allows objects of the Female class, for example, to belong to the Person class. Due to the set-inclusion semantics of inheritance in the O_2 model, objects of a subclass belong to its superclasses. The O_2 view of inheritance is that females and males are persons, therefore that Female and Male objects have Person behavior. The object whose identifier is i_2 belongs to the Female and the Person classes. The objects whose identifiers are i_1 and i_3 belong to the Male and the Person classes.

The designer may give the user access to all objects of a class, by providing a special set value which contains all the objects belonging to the class extension. This value will support only the membership and iteration operators and will have the same name as the class (Lécluse and Richard 1989; see chapter 9 for more details).

2.2 The User's View

We now consider the database from the user's point of view. As mentioned before, users are not aware of the object implementation. They receive information or cause modifications to objects via the methods made available to them by the designer. Values are a different matter. Their structure is known to the users, who use the system-defined operators to manipulate them. Figure 12.1 gives the user's view of our example database. The elements of the special value "Person" are objects of the Person class. Such an object can only be manipulated via the methods *name, address, age,* and *is-child-of.* The result of the application of *name* on one of these objects is a value whose type is [**first-name**: string, **last-name**: string]. To obtain a person's first name, one has to use the field-extraction operator on the previous result.

3 Design Issues

In the design of a query language for the O_2 system, we considered the concepts introduced by the object-oriented paradigm: object identity, typing, encapsulation, inheritance, and late binding. In fact, experience shows that only classes and encapsulation are relevant. Object identity and inheritance require that users be aware of their existence and their meaning: there is a difference between two identical objects and two "identically valued" objects. All other implications are implementation issues and are managed by the system.

A query language in the O_2 environment must also consider the manipulation of complex values. In this section we first identify difficulties due to classes and encapsulation and then discuss problems due to complex values.

Class Family:

Possible accesses to the extension via the special value "Family".

Methods:

name: Family → string

mother: Family → Female

father: Family → Male

children: Family → {Person}

Class Person:

Possible accesses to the extension via the special value "Person".

Methods:

name: Person → [`first-name`: string, `last-name`: string]

address: Person → [`city`: string, `zipcode`: string]

age: Person → integer

is-child-of: Person × Person → Boolean

Class Woman:

Possible accesses to the extension via the special value "Female".

This class inherits the Person class methods.

Other methods:

spouse: Female → Male

Class Man:

Possible accesses to the extension via the special value "Male".

This class inherits the Person class methods.

Other methods:

spouse: Male → Female

Figure 12.1. User's view of the sample database

3.1 Classes and Encapsulation

A user must have some knowledge of the schema in order to query the database. What is the user supposed to know? Since the object-oriented paradigm supports encapsulation, and since we do not want a query language to violate the principles which rule our system, we follow two rules:

- A user gets information on an object only via the methods given by its class interface; this means that he or she does not know its type and that data are invisible.

- A user accesses objects of a certain class only if there is a special value containing its extension or if a set-structured value contains some of its instances.

The first rule is related to the encapsulation principle. Encapsulation is a constraint on programming that is concerned with modularity and integrity of database applications. If we consider the query language as a tool to help in data manipulation, then we have to respect this principle to guarantee database integrity.

The second rule comes from the fact that one usually accesses entities of a database through a set. Due to encapsulation, a set object may be manipulated only through the methods associated with its class. Thus, if we wanted to access data through set objects, we would have to define an iteration method on each set-structured class. Since O_2 supports values, this is not needed.

In the relational model, a query always results in a relation. What does a query return in an object-oriented system? In most cases, the answer to a query does not correspond to an existing type or class of the database; it is an object. It has to be explicitly created using an existing class, or the user has to create a new class beforehand. We think that the creation of classes should not be performed by a query language used in ad hoc mode, since the result of a query is not going to be reused as a software component and does not need to be encapsulated. The values supported in the O_2 model are an answer to this problem. A query will either extract an existing object (in which case the class already exists in the data base) or it will extract an existing value or create a new value. Creating a new value is not a problem, since values are not encapsulated and their types are accessible.

3.2 Values

The O_2 values are very similar to complex objects of the nested relation models (Bancilhon and Khoshafian 1985; Pistor and Andersen 1986; Abiteboul and Beeri 1988; Verso 1986; Dadam et al. 1986). The only difference lies in the fact that an O_2 value may also have object components. Complex objects give rise to two kinds of problems. One must be able to access all levels of a structure, and the tools that allow the construction of unnested (flat) or nested structures must be available.

We shall see in the next section that unnesting is a rather simple problem. As for nesting, three possibilities are found in the literature. The first is to create functions whose role is to associate a collection of entities with its arguments; the second is to embed subqueries in larger queries; and the third is to use a special "nest" operator. We adopted the first two solutions for Reloop.

4 The Reloop Language

The Reloop language is SQL-like (Roth, Korth, and Batory 1988). Consequently, a Reloop query will feature the **select-from-where** block. In this section, we introduce our language through examples using the database of figure 12.1.

Our first query is a simple one: *What are the names of all minors?*

select name(p)
from p **in** Person
where age(p) < 18

The main SQL semantics has been maintained. The **select** clause defines the result (the name of some persons), the **from** clause specifies where to get the necessary information (in the special value "Person", the variable *p* representing one of its elements), and the **where** clause conditions the information (the persons must be under 18). The obvious differences one can notice are purely syntactic.

Why is "name(p)" used rather than "p name" as in SQL? In the object-oriented paradigm one has to deal with methods; methods may have multiple arguments, and we think that the functional notation is more natural to read. In fact, we have adopted this notation not only for methods but also for operators. This shields neophyte users from the semantic differences between objects and values. Moreover, whereas the first normal form of the relational paradigm allows users to manipulate tuples consisting of atomic values, in the O_2 model one deals with more complex entities and consequently one has to combine operators and methods. For instance, to get the first name of a person, we have to apply the *name* method on a Person object and then extract the `first-name` field from the result. We think that expressions like "name(p).first-name" are not easily readable; we prefer "first-name(name(p))".

Why do we introduce **in** in the **from** clause? Any expression whose result is a set value is valid in the **from** clause; we think that for complex expressions, a separator between the variable name and its domain makes reading easier.

A last comment on this query concerns the nature of its result. Most often, users request a collection of entities. That is why the result is a set value. Should the user want to select a single entity, he or she will use the Reloop operator **extract** to get the element of a set having one unique element. In the present query, the elements of the result set are values in the database. Similarly, one can retrieve database objects. Consider the query: *Find the families in which the father lives in Paris.*

select f
from f **in** Family
where city(address(father(f))) = "Paris"

An expression like "city(address(father(f)))" can be seen as a path within the object-composition hierarchy (Banerjee, Kim, and Kim 1988). We illustrate here one property of the inheritance mechanism. The method *father* delivers an object of type Male, and, as a Male is a Person, we can apply the method *address*. The result of the query is a set of objects defined in the database schema, namely, a set of families. However, users often want to construct new entities. The next examples will show how Reloop makes this possible. The following query shows the construction of tuple values: *Find the first name and age of all minors.*

```
select   [name: first-name(name(p)), age: age(p)]
from     p in Person
where    age(p) < 18
```

The answer to this query is of the following type:

```
{[name: string, age: integer]}
```

The tuple operator [ ] allows the construction of tuple values. Its arguments are field names and their domains. Domains can be defined through any Reloop expression. A field value may be a database entity, a tuple value, or a set value. We will see later how this generality solves the problem of nesting complex structures. Let us now examine the construction of a flat structure from a nested structure. Consider the query: *Find the mother of every child.*

```
select   [child: child, mother: mother(f)]
from     f in Family
         child in children(f)
```

Notice that it is valid to define a variable in the **from** clause which ranges on the result of the application of a method on another variable. As a matter of fact, any Reloop expression whose result is a set value may be used to define a variable. In this way, one can access all levels of a nested structure, whether it is in the database or is constructed. This makes unnesting easy. To unnest, one only needs to construct new tuples with elements of a nested structure. Our next example shows the construction of nested structures: Assuming that a woman may appear in different families, *find the first names of all minor children and the names of their mothers.*

```
make-method minor-children (Female: mom)
  select   first-name(name(child))
  from     f in Family
           child in children(f)
  where    age(child) < 18 and
           mother(f) = mom

  select   [mother: mom, children: minor-children(mom)]
  from     mom in Female
```

The set of minor children we want to associate with each woman is not a database entity (although each child is a database entity); it has to be constructed. This expression defines a method on the Female class whose functionality is to collect those children. This is done by examining the data for every child of every family (f **in** Family, child **in** children(f)) and by picking up the names of those children who are under 18 (age(child) < 18) and whose mothers' names are given by the method argument (mother(f) = mom). Once this method is created, one only needs to build the required tuple values with the [ ] constructor. The result type of this query is:

{[**mother**: Female, **children**: {string}]}

In this example, nesting was done on an object. However, sometimes one needs to work with values rather than with objects. In such cases we cannot use methods, since methods are only associated to objects. We plan to replace the **make_method** statement by another that will deal with values as well as objects.

We now give an alternate Reloop expression for the above query. The previous expression was inspired by languages such as COL (Abiteboul and Grumbach 1987) and OSQL (Beech 1988), the alternate by Pistor and Andersen 1986.

```
select  [mother: mom, children:  select  first-name(name(child))
                                 from    f in Family
                                         child in children(f)
                                 where   age(child) < 18 and
                                         mother(f) = mom]
from    mom in Female
```

The body of the *minor-children* method of the previous formulation is embedded in the **select** clause. The user may choose between created methods and embedded blocks.

The rules that determine the scope of a variable are similar to those in most programming languages. The variable *mom* of the nested block is the one defined in the main block, because it has not been redefined.

At this point, we summarize what we have presented of the Reloop language.

1. A **select-from-where** block creates a new set value. One can extract the element of a singleton. The elements of a constructed set may be objects or values in the database, or new tuple values constructed by the [ ] operator. The fields of a new tuple value may be objects or values extracted from the database, or any new constructed values. A **select-from-where** expression is valid in a **select** clause, and thus it is possible

to build a set of sets. Therefore the answer to a Reloop query could be anything constructed from the database entities through the tuple and set constructors.

2. The **from** clause allows access to entities contained in any set value. This is done directly if the value is named; otherwise it is done indirectly through methods, operators, or Reloop expressions on predefined variables.

3. The **where** clause of the Reloop language is very similar to that of SQL. We have three logical connectors (**and**, **or**, and **not**), and Boolean expressions built with the relational operators <, >, <=, =>, <>, **in**, and = (which stands for an object identity if applied on objects or a value equality if applied on values). Reloop also provides the universal and existential quantifiers **all** and **exist**. The difference between the **where** clause in Reloop and in SQL lies in the nature of the manipulated expressions (Reloop or SQL).

The aggregate operators of SQL (**sum**, **avg**, and so on), although not yet implemented, will be available in the final version of Reloop.

We conclude with two facilities: the **collapse** operator and the set constructor. The **collapse** operator flattens a set of sets; for example,

collapse({{1, 2}, {2, 3}}) = {1, 2, 3}

We have seen that sets could be constructed using a **select-from-where** block. The set constructor {} offers another way: it builds a set value from its arguments. If we combine **collapse** and {}, we can obtain an optimal writing of some queries. For instance, let us consider the following query: *Find all persons who have at least one child.*

```
          select  mother(f)
          from    f in Family
          where   children(f) <> {}
union
          select  father(f)
          from    f in Family
          where   children(f) <> = {}
```

This query finds all females, and then all males, with at least one child; and it merges both results. This union is possible since females and males are persons. An alternate formulation is

```
collapse (select {mother(f), father(f)}
          from   f in Family
          where  children(f) <> {})
```

Here, for each family with more than one child, a set containing the father and the mother is constructed. The result of the **select-from-where** block is a set of sets. The **collapse** operator flattens it. Notice that there is no such operator as "distinct" to eliminate duplicates. This is because we manipulate sets, and thus duplicates (and order) have no meaning.

5 Reloop Semantics through an Algebra

The main difficulty with complex objects is the nesting of complex structures. The way in which this problem is addressed differentiates the algebras of Abiteboul and Beeri 1988, Kuper and Vardi 1984, and Schek and Scholl 1986. In Reloop, the nesting problem is solved through the embedding of **select-from-where** blocks, and a restricted version of these algebras suffices.

For this section, the terminology and notation follow the O_2 data model. We introduce our algebra, and show the construction of Reloop expressions in terms of this algebra. We use the following notations:

- sig(m, c) denotes the signature $w \rightarrow t$ of the method name m in the class c.
- type associates with a Reloop expression its type expression, type(E).
- elt associates with a set type the type of the element; that is, elt$(\{t\})$ is t.
- lub is a partial function which takes as arguments two types or classes and returns their least upper bound. For instance, lub({Female}, {Male}) = {Person}.

5.1 The Algebra Operators

The algebra operators are the traditional set operators ($\cup$, $\cap$, $-$), projection (π), selection (σ), Cartesian product ($\otimes$), and an operator we call reduction (Δ), which builds a set from a set of 1-tuples by projecting each element (this operator is defined in the Kuper and Vardi 1984 algebra). We now define the basic operators by specifying their signatures and semantics.

Definition 1. The set operators **union, intersection**, and **difference** are defined on set values of the database. Since they are well known, we limit ourselves to the definition of the **union** operator:

1. $\cup$: $\{t_1\} \times \{t_2\} \rightarrow \{\text{lub}(t_1, t_2)\}$
2. $r \cup r' = \{x \mid x \in r \vee x \in r'\}$

Definition 2. The syntax of the projection operation is $\pi < a_1, \ldots, a_n > (r)$. It is defined as follows:

1. $\pi < a_1, a_2, \ldots, a_n >: \{[a_1\colon t_1, a_2\colon t_2, \ldots, a_n\colon t_n, a_{n+1}\colon t_{n+1}, \ldots, a_m\colon t_m]\} \rightarrow \{[a_1\colon t_1, a_2\colon t_2, \ldots, a_n\colon t_n]\}$

2. $\pi < a_1, a_2, \ldots, a_n > (r) = \{[a_1\colon v_1, a_2\colon v_2, \ldots, a_n\colon v_n] \mid \exists\, a_{n+1}, \ldots, a_m \in A\ [a_1\colon v_1, a_2\colon v_2, \ldots, a_n\colon v_n, a_{n+1}\colon v_{n+1}, \ldots, a_m\colon v_m] \in r\}$

The order of tuple fields is not significant.

Definition 3. The *selection* operation $\sigma < E_1\ \theta\ E_2 > (r)$ is based on a predicate expression and has as argument a set of tuple values. It filters the elements of the set which satisfy the predicate. θ is one of the traditional comparators: $\in$, $=$, $<>$, $<$, and so on. With the exception of $=$ and its opposite $<>$, these operators are defined on database values. The $=$ comparator represents object identity when applied to objects, and value equality when applied to values. E_1 and E_2 denote any computable expression whose free variable names correspond to the attribute names of the tuples belonging to the set argument. By extension, they also denote their own evaluation. The basic predicate expression $E_1\ \theta\ E_2$ may be extended through the traditional Boolean operators **and**, **or**, and **not**:

1. $\sigma < E_1\ \theta\ E_2 >: \{t\} \rightarrow \{t\}$

2. $\sigma < E_1(a_1, a_2, \ldots, a_n)\ \theta\ E_2(a_1, a_2, \ldots, a_n) > (r) = \{x \mid x \in r \wedge x = [a_1\colon v_1, a_2\colon v_2, \ldots, a_n\colon v_n, a_{n+1}\colon v_{n+1}, \ldots, a_m\colon v_m] \wedge E_1(v_1, v_2, \ldots, v_n)\ \theta\ E_2(v_1, v_2, \ldots, v_n)\}$

Definition 4. The Cartesian product, whose syntax is $\otimes < a_1, \ldots, a_n > (r_1, \ldots, r_n)$, is specified by a sequence of attribute names $a_1, \ldots, a_n$. Its arguments are sets.

1. $\otimes < a_1, \ldots, a_n >: \{t_1\} \times \{t_2\} \times \ldots \times \{t_n\} \rightarrow \{[a_1\colon t_1, a_2\colon t_2, \ldots, a_n\colon t_n]\}$

2. $\otimes < a_1, \ldots, a_n > (r_1, \ldots, r_n) = \{[a_1\colon v_1, \ldots, a_n\colon v_n] \mid \forall i \in [1, n], v_i \in r_i\}$

Definition 5. The *reduction* operation, Δ, is defined as:

1. $\Delta\colon \{[a\colon t]\} \rightarrow \{t\}$

2. $\Delta(r) = \{v \mid [a\colon v] \in r\}$

5.2 Reloop Semantics

The informal presentation of Reloop in section 3 showed that a query consists of a **select-from-where** block using expressions constructed from methods, operators (such as tuple field selection, union, and difference) and **select-from-where** blocks. In this section, we define the semantics in two steps: first the semantics of the operators and methods that form a Reloop expression, and then the semantics of a basic **select-from-where** block. For this, we exclude redundancy in our language. Consequently, we eliminate the **exist** and **all** quantifiers, which can be replaced by appropriate Boolean expressions; the {} constructor, which is equivalent to successive unions of **select-from-where** blocks; and the **collapse** operator, which can be rewritten in the following manner:

collapse(e) $\Leftrightarrow$ **select** e_2
from e_1 **in** e
e_2 **in** e_1

5.2.1 Reloop Methods and Operators

Reloop expressions use two kinds of methods. One belongs to some class interface, and its semantics is defined by its designer; the other is introduced by a **make_method** declaration, and its semantics is given by the **select-from-where** block which constitutes its body.

Reloop expressions use the following operators: **union, intersection, difference**, and tuple field selection. The Reloop set operators and the algebra set operators have similar semantics. The field-selection operation has the usual semantics:

$$\forall i \in [1, n], a_i \in \mathrm{A}, v_i \in \mathrm{V}, a_i([a_1\colon\ v_1, a_2\colon\ v_2, \ldots, a_n\colon\ v_n]) = v_i$$

5.2.2 Select-From-Where Blocks

Some **select-from-where** blocks are syntactically correct but semantically unacceptable. These are the ones using variables that were not previously defined. We provide no semantics for those. Thus we have two canonical blocks. The first constructs a set of database entities, and the second a set of tuple values.

select $E(e_1, e_2, \ldots, e_n)$
from e_1**in** E_1'
e_2**in** $E_2'(e_1)$
...
e_n **in** $E_n'(e_1, e_2, \ldots, e_{n-1})$
where condition$(e_1, e_2, \ldots, e_n)$

select $[a_1\colon\ E_1(e_1, e_2, \ldots, e_n), \ldots, a_2\colon\ E_2(e_1, e_2, \ldots, e_n),$
$a_p\colon\ E_p(e_1, e_2, \ldots, e_n)]$
from e_1 **in** E_1'
e_2 **in** $E_2'(e_1)$
...
e_n **in** $E_n'(e_1, \ldots, e_{n-1})$
where condition $(e_1, e_2, \ldots, e_n)$

The E, E_i and E_i' symbols denote any valid Reloop expression. The **where** and **select** clauses may use variables defined in the **from** clause of the block. The variable declarations in the **from** clause are ordered. For its definition, a variable may use only the variable declarations of an outer level. Cyclic declarations are not allowed. In this paper, we consider only queries which follow these rules. In fact, we can restrict our attention to expressions of the second form, since we have the following relationship:

$$\textbf{select } E \textbf{ from} \ldots \textbf{ where} \ldots = \Delta(\textbf{select } [a\colon E] \textbf{ from} \ldots \textbf{ where} \ldots)$$

This equivalence is a direct consequence of the Δ reduction operator.

Before we define the semantics of a **select-from-where** block, we have to extend the *type* function to Reloop expressions. This is done by the following inference rules:

1. $m \in M$ and $\text{sig}(m, t_1) = t_1 \times t_2 \times \ldots \times t_n \rightarrow t$ and $\forall i \in [1, n]$ $\text{type}(E_i) = t_i$ $\text{type}(m(E_1, E_2, \ldots, E_n)) = t$
2. $\text{type}(E) = [a_1\colon t_1, a_2\colon t_2, \ldots, a_n\colon t_n]$ $\forall i \in [1, n]$, $\text{type}(a_i(E)) = t_i$
3. $E = \text{select } E' \text{ from} \ldots$ $\text{type}(E) = \{\text{type}(E')\}$
4. $E = \text{select } [a_1\colon E_1, a_2\colon E_2, \ldots, a_n\colon E_n] \text{ from} \ldots$ $\text{type}(E) = \{[a_1\colon \text{type}(E_1), \ldots, a_n\colon\text{type}(E_n)]\}$

Now we are able to give the canonical **select-from-where** expression its algebraic translation.

Definition 6. A **select-from-where** expression

select $[a_1\colon E_1, a_2\colon E_2, \ldots, a_p\colon E_p]$
from e_1 **in** E_1'
...
e_n **in** E_n'
where condition

has the following algebraic translation:

$$R_1 \leftarrow \otimes\!< e_1, e_2, \ldots, e_n, a_1, a_2, \ldots, a_p >(\text{dom}(\text{elt}(\text{type}(E_1'))), \text{dom}(\text{elt}(\text{type}(E_2'))), \ldots, \text{dom}(\text{elt}(\text{type}(E_n'))), \text{dom}(\text{type}(E_1)), \text{dom}(\text{type}(E_2)) \ldots, \text{dom}(\text{type}(E_p)))$$

$$R_2 \leftarrow \sigma <\text{condition} \wedge a_1 = E_1 \wedge a_2 = E_2 \wedge \ldots \wedge a_p = E_p \wedge e_1 \in E_1' \wedge e_2 \in E_2' \wedge \ldots \wedge e_n \in E_n' > (R_1)$$

$$R_3 \leftarrow \pi\!< a_1, a_2, \ldots, a_p > (R_2)$$

The first operation builds a set that contains all tuples which can be constructed with the block variables as attributes and the output elements as attributes. Once this is done, one must select the tuples which respect the specifications given in the **select**, **from**, and **where** clauses. This is the second operation. The last step is a projection over a_i attributes.

Three important points must be noted about this translation.

1. We need the type inference that was introduced above.
2. The domain of all types must be finite. This is possible since the sets of constants and identifiers are finite.
3. This translation is not optimal.

Example. We are given the following assertions on the database:

- Person = $\{i_1, i_2, i_3\}$, where i_1, i_2, i_3 are object identifiers.
- age(i_1) = 2
  age(i_2) = 18
  age(i_3) = 19
- first-name(name(i_1)) = "John"
  first-name(name(i_2)) = "Joan"
  first-name(name(i_3)) = "Jack"
- last-name(name(i_1)) = "Doe"
  last-name(name(i_2)) = "Doe"
  last-name(name(i_3)) = "Smith"

Let us consider the query: *Find the first name and age of all adults.*

select [name: first-name(name(p)), age: age(p))]
from p **in** Person
where age(p) >= 18

The R_1 set of our algebraic construction will have the type

{[p: Person, **name**: string, **age**: integer]}

and will contain all possible tuples of the type. The selection operation will lead to the result

{[p: i_2, **name**: Joan, **age**: 18], [p: i_3, **name**: Jack, **age**: 19]}

and the projection on **name** and **age** will give

{[**name**: Joan, **age**: 18], [**name**: Jack, **age**: 19]}

6 Translation from Reloop to CO_2

The algebraic translation for the canonical **select-from-where** block does not correspond to any actual implementation. We will not translate into our host language the Cartesian products it implies. Similarly, although the restriction of our language to one canonical expression was a shorter way to define Reloop semantics, it cannot be used to define Reloop translation to CO_2, for optimization purposes. However, for reasons of clarity, we restrict this study to the canonical block.

This section introduces the CO_2 language; describes a macro-algebra; and shows how to transform Reloop expressions to CO_2 programs in terms of the macro-algebra.

6.1 The CO_2 Language

CO_2 was obtained by adding object- and value-management primitives (the O_2 part) to the C language. Database entities are manipulated through O_2 variables and by O_2 expressions in a C program. O_2 expressions are of two kinds: method calls, delimited by square brackets; and standard O_2 expressions, recognized by the keywords. Table 12.1 lists the O_2 operators used in the translation of Reloop expressions. The variable e denotes a value or an object, and the variable S a set value. The word *action* stands for any CO_2 block of code in a CO_2 **for** statement.

Table 12.1. O_2 Operators Used by the Reloop-to-CO_2 Compiler

	Syntax	Action
Operations on sets		
Add	S += set(e)	Adds e to the S set value.
Drop	S −= set(e)	Takes out e from the S set value.
Union	$S_1 + S_2$	Union of two set values.
Difference	$S_1 - S_2$	Difference of two set values.
Intersection	$S_1 * S_2$	Intersection of two set values.
Membership	S ?? e	The result is "true" if e belongs to the set value S.
Iteration		
	for (x in S) {*action*}	Applies *action* on all the elements of the S set value.

6.2 The Macro-Algebra

We need to define two macro-operators:

- $\uplus$ is a selective Cartesian product. This operator allows the creation of the iteration domain defined by the RReloop **from** clause.

- $\odot$ builds a set of tuples from a specification, and a set of tuples whose attributes allow the evaluation of the specification variables. This operator is used to construct, from an iteration domain, the result of a query featuring the tuple constructor in the **select** clause.

These two operators are constructed from the basic algebraic operators previously defined. Details of their construction are given in section 8.

Definition 7. The $\uplus$ operator is defined by:

1. $\uplus < e_1\colon E_1, e_2\colon E_2, \ldots, e_p\colon E_n > \rightarrow \{[e_1\colon \text{elt}(\text{type}(E_1)), e_2\colon \text{elt}(\text{type}(E_2)), \ldots, e_n\colon \text{elt}(\text{type}(E_n))]\}$

2. $\uplus < e_1\colon E_1, e_2\colon E_2(e_1), \ldots, e_n\colon E_n(e_1, e_2, \ldots, e_{n-1}) > = \{[e_1\colon v_1, e_2\colon v_2, \ldots, e_n\colon v_n] \mid \forall i \in [1, n]\ v_i \in E_i(e_1, e_2, \ldots, e_{i-1})\}$

The E_is denote any computable expression whose free variables are $e_1, e_2, \ldots,$ e_{i-1}. This corresponds to the restriction on the **from** clause of our canonical expression. By extension, the E_is will also denote their own evaluation.

Definition 8. The $\odot$ operator is defined by:

1. $$\odot < a_1\colon E_1(e_1, e_2, \ldots, e_n), a_2\colon E_2(e_1, e_2, \ldots, e_n), \ldots, a_p\colon E_p(e_1, e_2, \ldots, e_n) > \colon \{[e_1\colon t_1, e_2\colon t_2, \ldots, e_n\colon t_n]\} \rightarrow \{[a_1\colon \text{type}(E_1), a_2\colon \text{type}(E_2), \ldots, a_p\colon \text{type}(E_p)]\}$$

2. $$\odot < a_1\colon E_1(e_1, e_2, \ldots, e_n), a_2\colon E_2(e_1, e_2, \ldots, e_n), \ldots, a_p\colon E_p(e_1, e_2, \ldots, e_n) > (r) = \{[a_1\colon v_1, a_2\colon v_2, \ldots, a_p\colon v_p] \mid \exists [e_1\colon w_1, e_2\colon w_2, \ldots, e_n\colon w_n] \in r\ (\forall i \in [1, p],\ v_i = E_i(w_1, w_2, \ldots, w_n))$$

6.2.1 From Reloop to CO_2 via the Macro-Algebra

The σ operator and the two macro-operators we have just defined are a good framework for the interpretation of the canonical Reloop **select-from-where** block. The **from** clause specifies the iteration domain. The $\uplus$ operator allows its construction. The **where** clause restricts it to the elements which respect a certain condition. The σ operator has the same functionality. The **select** clause calls for the construction of a set of elements dependent on the iteration domain. The $\odot$ operator makes this possible. It is easy to show that

select $[a_1\colon E_1, \ldots, a_p\colon E_p]$
from e_1 **in** E_1'
e_2 **in** E_2'
...
e_n **in** E_n'

where condition

is equivalent to

$R_1 \leftarrow \uplus < e_1\colon E_1', e_2\colon E_2', \ldots, e_n\colon E_n' >$
$R_2 \leftarrow \sigma$ <condition> (R_1)
$R_3 \leftarrow \odot < a_1\colon E_1, \ldots, a_p\colon E_p > (R_2)$

We now briefly compare this new algebraic translation to the previous one. The R_2 result corresponds to a projection on the attributes $e_1, \ldots, e_p$ of the previous R_2 result. It contains the restriction of the iteration domain to the elements that satisfy the **where**-clause condition. The present final result has a structure similar to the previous one. It is constructed from the restricted iteration domain and respects the **select**-clause specifications. It corresponds to the projection on $a_1, \ldots, a_n$ of the previous R_2 result, and thus corresponds to the previous R_3 result.

Example. Let us consider the query *Find the first name and age of all adults,* whose Reloop translation is:

select [name: first-name(name(p)), age: age(p)]
from p **in** Person
where age(p) >= 18

The R_1 result of our new construction is

{[p: i_1], [p: i_2], [p: i_3]}

After the selection operation, we have

{[p: i_2], [p: i_3]}

and the final result is

{[name: Joan, age: 18], [name: Jack, age: 19]}

Once we recognize the two previous equivalences, the CO_2 translation comes easily. The corresponding CO_2 translation is

$$
\begin{array}{ll}
\left.\begin{array}{l}
\textbf{for } e_1 \textbf{ in } E_1' \\
\quad \textbf{for } \ldots \\
\qquad \textbf{for } e_n \textbf{ in } E_n'
\end{array}\right\} & \uplus < e_1 \colon E_1', \ldots > \\
\qquad\quad \left.\textbf{if } \text{condition}\right\} & \sigma \; <\text{condition}> \\
\qquad\qquad \left.\begin{array}{lcl}
e.a_1 & = & E_1; \\
\ldots & & \\
e.a_n & = & E_n; \\
\text{set} & += & \text{set}(e);
\end{array}\right\} & \odot < a_1 \colon E_1, \ldots >
\end{array}
$$

So far, we have left out declarations of variables. The tuple e variable successively denotes the result elements, and the *set* variable contains the query result.

We have implemented this technique of translation on a part of our language. This was done using the Syntax compilers compiler (Boullier and Deschamp 1988).

7 Conclusion

In this paper, we introduced the SQL-like Reloop language for the O_2 object-oriented database system. We outlined its syntax, semantics, and compilation to an imperative object-oriented language. Although more complicated than the relational SQL, we think Reloop can be easily assimilated by end users. However, Reloop does not currently support data description and update facilities. We intend to study its completeness and ponder on optimization issues.

8 Acknowledgements

The authors are greatly indebted to W. Kim for his many valuable comments and corrections on an earlier draft of this paper.

References

Abiteboul, S., and C. Beeri. 1988. *On the power of languages for the manipulation of complex objects.* INRIA technical report no. 846.

Abiteboul, S., and S. Grumbach. 1987. *COL: A logic-based language for complex objects.* INRIA technical report.

Bancilhon, F., and S. Khoshafian. 1985. A calculus for complex objects. In *Proceedings of the ACM PODS conference.*

Banerjee, J., W. Kim, and K. C. Kim. 1988. *Queries in object-oriented databases.* In *Proceedings of the international conference on data engineering.*

Beech, D. 1988. A foundation for evolution from relational to object databases. In *Proceedings of the first conference on extending database technology.*

Beeri, C., and Y. Kornatzky. 1990. Algebraic optimization of object-oriented query languages. In *Proceedings of the ICDT 90.*

Boullier, P., and P. Deschamp. 1988. *Le système Syntax, manuel d'utilisation.* INRIA rocquencourt.

Carey, M., D. DeWitt, and S. Vandenberg. 1988. A data model and query language for Exodus. In *Proceedings of the 1988 ACM SIGMOD conference.*

Cluet, S., C. Delobel, C. Lécluse, and P. Richard. 1990. Reloop, an algebra-based query language for an object-oriented database system. In *Proceedings of the first international DOOD conference.*

Dadam, P. et al. 1986. A DBMS prototype to support extended NF2 relations: An integrated view on flat tables and hierarchies. In *Proceedings of the 1986 ACM SIGMOD conference.*

Delobel, C., C. Lécluse, and P. Richard. 1988. LOOQ: A query language for object-oriented databases. In *Proceedings of the AFCET conference on knowledge and object-oriented database systems.*

Kuper, G., and M. Vardi. 1984. A new approach to database logic. In *Proceedings of the ACM PODS conference.*

Lécluse, C., and P. Richard. 1989. The O_2 database programming language. In *Proceedings of the VLDB conference.*

Osborn, S. 1988. Identity, equality and query optimization. In *Proceedings of the second international workshop on object-oriented database systems.*

Pistor, P., and F. Andersen. 1986. *Principles for designing a generalized NF2 data model with an SQL-type language interface.* Heidelberg Scientific Center, Technical Report.

Roth, M., H. Korth, and D. Batory. 1988. SQL-NF: A query language for non 1NF relational databases. In *Proceedings of the ACM SIGMOD conference.*

Shaw, G., and S. Zdonik. 1989a. An object-oriented query algebra. In *Proceedings of the DBPL conference.*

———. 1989b. Object-oriented queries: Equivalence and optimization. In *Proceedings of the DOOD conference.*

Schek, H., and M. Scholl. 1986. The relational model with relation-valued attributes. *Information Systems.*

Verso, J. 1986. *Verso: A database machine based on non-1NF relations.* Springer-Verlag.

Appendix: Construction of the Algebraic Macro-Operators

A.1 The ⊙ Operator

$\odot < a_1\colon E_1(e_1, e_2, \ldots, e_n), a_2\colon E_2(e_1, e_2, \ldots, e_n), \ldots, a_p\colon E_p(e_1, e_2, \ldots, e_n) >$ (r) is defined on "r", where typ(r) = $\{ [e_1\colon t_1, e_2\colon t_2, \ldots, e_n\colon t_n]\}$ and is equivalent to the following sequence:

$$
\begin{aligned}
R_1 &\leftarrow \otimes< a_1, \ldots, a_p, x > (\mathrm{dom}(\mathrm{type}(E_1(e_1, e_2, \ldots, e_n))),\\
&\qquad \mathrm{dom}(\mathrm{type}(E_2(e_1, e_2, \ldots, e_n))),\\
&\qquad \ldots,\\
&\qquad \mathrm{dom}(\mathrm{type}(E_p(e_1, e_2, \ldots, e_n))),\\
&\qquad \mathrm{dom}(\mathrm{type}(r)))\\
R_2 &\leftarrow \sigma < x \in r \wedge\\
&\qquad a_1 = E_1(e_1(x), e_2(x), \ldots, e_n(x)) \wedge\\
&\qquad a_2 = E_2(e_1(x), e_2(x), \ldots, e_n(x)) \wedge\\
&\qquad \ldots \wedge\\
&\qquad a_p = E_n(e_1(x), e_2(x), \ldots, e_p(x)) > (R_1)\\
R_3 &\leftarrow \pi< a_1, a_2, \ldots, a_n >(R_2)
\end{aligned}
$$

The second operation result, R_2, contains tuples whose frame is

$$[a_1\colon t_{a_1}, a_2\colon t_{a_2} \ldots, a_n\colon t_{a_n}, x\colon [e_1\colon t_1, e_2\colon t_2, \ldots, e_p\colon t_p]]$$

The x attribute value is an element of the set argument r ($x \in r$). The attributes a_i correspond to the specification $a_i = E_i(e_1, e_2, \ldots, e_n)$. We accessed the e_i values by field selection on the attributes of x:

$$(a_i = E_i(e_1(x), e_2(x) \ldots, e_n(x)))$$

A.2 The $\uplus$ Operator

$\uplus$ $(e_1\colon E_1, \ldots, e_n\colon E_n)$ is defined if $\forall i \in [1, n]$ type$(E_i) = \{t_i\}$. It is equivalent to the following sequence:

$\uplus$ $(e_1\colon E_1, \ldots, , e_n\colon E_n)$

is equivalent to

$$R_1 \leftarrow \otimes < e_1, e_2, \ldots, e_n > (\text{dom}(\text{elt}(\text{type}(E_1))), \text{dom}(\text{elt}(\text{type}(E_2))), \ldots, \text{dom}(\text{elt}(\text{type}(E_n))))$$

$$R_2 \leftarrow \sigma < e_1 \in E_1 \wedge e_2 \in E_2 \wedge \ldots \wedge e_n \in E_n > (R_1)$$

CHAPTER 13

Using Database Applications to Compare Programming Languages

SOPHIE GAMERMAN
CATHERINE LANQUETTE
FERNANDO VÉLEZ

1 Introduction

In this paper we try to establish comparison criteria for several existing approaches to the programming of database applications. We used the following methodology: (1) define a representative set of applications; (2) write the applications in the chosen languages; and (3) compare.

We are not looking at intrinsic characteristics of languages such as completeness or orthogonality as in Atkinson and Buneman 1985. Our interest is the point of view of the business-application programmer. What we want to measure is the ease of programming. We do this by comparing several languages, one or two for each style of programming. What can be compared? Real operational metrics could be the size of the code and the number of modifications implied by a schema update or by the addition of new functionality. There are also more subjective metrics, such as development time and code readability. Another element of comparison is the programming difficulties encountered with a particular language. For example, writing user interfaces with Prolog is difficult; is this due to the language or to the approach?

The applications we have chosen are a Bill of Materials application from Atkinson and Buneman 1985, and the Unix Mail. A rationale for these choices and a description of the applications can be found in section 2. These applications are only toy applications and will give us information on the adequacy of the languages only with regard to programming on a small scale. (They can, however, give hints as to the power of the languages with respect to coping with such changes as adding a new functionality to the Unix Mail. This issue will be further explored in a future paper.) The important problem of maintenance of programs is not considered here.

We have written the applications in the following languages:

1. C+SQL, which represents the current situation for application programmers using a database system. Declarative data manipulation languages such as SQL are not computationally complete (in the Turing sense), and therefore they have to be embedded in a general-purpose programming language.

2. Basic, which represents the imperative programming paradigm. Note, however, that the Basic we use is not standard, in that it allows the use of structured files with nonflat attributes. This feature is offered from its operating system environment (Pick), and it is not related in any way to the imperative programming paradigm.

3. Prolog, representing the logic-programming paradigm. We used a version of Prolog that offers a very crude form of persistency, that is, saving the current state of the programming environment and resuming it later. No connection with a database system has been attempted. This feature is not related to the logic-programming paradigm.

4. Smalltalk-80, which is the canonical representative of the object-oriented approach to programming.

5. O_2, which illustrates an integration of the object-oriented and the database-system approaches.

To make things comparable, all programs have been tested and are currently running. They are given in section 9.

This paper is organized as follows. After a description of the applications in section 2, we describe the implementation of the application in the target languages (sections 3 to 7). For each application we give some measures: the time necessary to develop the application, the size of the resulting code, and the number of tokens. The relevance of this metric, and some possible extensions, is discussed in the conclusion; we also discuss the difficulties we encountered when evaluating each language. All our measures are dependent on the programmer and her or his background. The authors have a Pascal and C background, and before this study we had some theoretical knowledge of Prolog and Smalltalk.

2 The Applications

Typical business applications often involve (1) an associative access-to-data facility, (2) a general computational capability (computations and interactive dialog with users are essential in such applications), and (3) an update facility eventually involving the checking of integrity constraints. We used two applications: a Bill of Materials application and the Unix Mail.

2.1 The Bill of Materials Application

The Bill of Materials is a toy application used in Atkinson and Buneman 1985 to compare different programming languages. It represents a fragment of a manufacturing company's parts database, in particular, the way certain parts are manufactured out of other parts: the subparts that are involved in the manufacture of a part, the cost of manufacturing a part from its subparts, and the mass increment or decrement that occurs when subparts are assembled. Four tasks to be accomplished on this database have been defined.

Task 1: Describe the database.

Task 2: Print the name, cost, and mass of every purchased part that costs more than Fr 100. Purchased parts are known as base parts.

Task 3: Print the total mass and total cost of a composite part, that is, a part made by assembling subparts.

Task 4: Record in the database a new manufacturing step, that is, how a new composite part is manufactured from subparts.

This application is interesting because it tests the capability of the languages with respect to the writing of a recursive program with computation, and the management of updates involving integrity constraints.

2.2 The Unix Mail Application

The Unix Mail (Unix 1986) provides commands to browse, display, save, delete, and respond to messages. When the user enters the command mode in order to read her or his messages, Mail displays a header summary of the messages, followed by a prompt for one of the commands listed below. Messages are listed and referred to by number. There is at any time a current message. Most commands have message numbers for arguments. If the user omits to specify a number, the current message is taken by default. The commands are:

- **delete** [message number]: Delete the specified message from the mailbox.
- **exit**: Exit from Mail without changing the mailbox.
- **headers**: Display the headers of all messages.

- **print** [message number]: Print the specified message.
- **quit**: Exit from Mail, storing the messages that have been read in the Mbox file and storing unread messages in the Mailbox. Messages that have been explicitly saved are deleted from the mailbox.
- **reply** [message number]: Send a response to the author of the message; the subject line is taken from the message.
- **save** [message number] filename: Save the specified message in the specified file.

This application implies a significant number of updates (creating and deleting messages), and the dialog with the user is important. Therefore, with this application we can test functionalities not present in the Bill of Materials application.

3 C+SQL

The applications were programmed on a Sun using the DBMS Sabrina (Sabrina 1988), developed at the Institut National de Recherche en Informatique et Automatique (INRIA). Sabrina is sold with a multilanguage interface called IML. It can be used with Pascal or C. There are four primitives:

- **call_connection** connects the program to the DBMS.
- **call_deconnection** disconnects the program from the DBMS.
- **call_sabre** executes any command of the data manipulation language or the data definition language.
- **lire_tuple** reads a tuple from a temporary relation (*lire* is French for "read").

All these primitives return a negative number when an error occurs.

3.1 Developing the Bill of Materials Application in C+SQL

We created two relations: Part and MadeFrom. Part contains information about all the parts ones can find in the company. It has four attributes: `name`, which is the key; `type`, which indicates if it is a part bought outside the company (a base part) or manufactured inside the company (a composite part); and two attributes, `price` and `mass`, which have different interpretations depending on the value of the `type` attribute. If it is a base part (`type` = 'b'), `price` is the price of the part and `mass` is its weight. If it is a part manufactured by the company (`type` = 'c'), then `price` is the cost of manufacturing the part and `mass` is the increment or decrement in mass that occurs in manufacturing the part. The relation MadeFrom contains for each composite part the name of its subparts and the needed quantity. It has three attributes: **name**, **subpart** and **qty** (quantity). There is an inclusion dependency between the **subpart** attribute of the MadeFrom relation and the **name** attribute of the Part relation.

The second task requires a simple selection query, followed by a loop to read all the relevant tuples.

The third task is implemented by a recursive function that contains a **call_sabre** primitive selecting the subparts of a given part. At each step, a temporary relation is created. In Sabrina one cannot create two temporary relations with the same name, so we had to use a global variable to distinguish the name of the next temporary relation to be created. This is only a naming problem at creation time and has nothing to do with accessing the temporary relations at a given level in a recursive call. In fact, internal identifiers of temporary relations are coded as C integers by the **call_sabre** primitive. This identifier is the input of the **lire_tuple** primitive, and so the recursion on temporary relations is handled by C.

The fourth task was very easy because Sabrina handles integrity constraints such as inclusion dependencies.

3.2 Developing the Unix Mail Application in C+SQL

We defined two relations: Message and Mailbox. The latter contains, for each user, the identifier of its messages. It has three attributes: **messId**, which is the identifier of the message; **username**, which is the name of a user who received this message; and **state**, which indicates whether the user has read the message. The relation Message contains the values of the messages, that is, the date, the sender, the title, and the text. To manage the message identifier (i.e., to insure uniqueness), we defined a **messId** relation which has one attribute, **currentId**, and only one tuple. It represents the identifier of the next message to be created.

When the program starts, the relevant messages are put in a C array, and for each message a temporary relation is created containing the names of the recipients of the message. To allow users to browse in any way through messages (using **get next**, **previous**, **first**, and **last**), we do not store messages in a temporary relation because cursors in Sabrina only allow one to scan tuples forward. Relation browsers are exactly the type of functionalities that Portal in Ingres (Stonebraker and Rowe 1986) implements.

At the end of the program we have to delete the messages that have been read, saved, or deleted. For each message the corresponding tuple in the Mailbox relation is deleted. Then we have to check if there is another recipient who has not yet read the message. If not, we have to delete the message from the Message relation.

3.3 Conclusions

We now know what *impedance mismatch* means. By using two languages with such different programming paradigms, we encountered the following difficulties:

- We had to decide where to do things, whether in C or in SQL.
- Artificial constructs such as cursors (which do not belong either to C or to SQL) had to be introduced to solve the mismatch between the two different computational models: SQL is set-at-a-time, whereas C is record-at-a-time. Furthermore, data conveyed from one system to the other are very primitive, as only atomic values can be exchanged.
- A lot of unnecessary code was introduced to handle the communication between C and Sabrina. An example is error handling: after each call to the DBMS one has to test whether any errors occurred.

As a result, the development time was rather high (eight days for both applications). The debugging phase took a long time, because it is difficult to find where bugs come from when using two languages. This was exacerbated by the fact that syntax errors in SQL queries may occur at run time in Sabrina, as the programming interface is by procedure call (i.e., no precompilation is attempted).

The problem of recursivity in the third task of the Bill of Materials application was solved by using different names for temporary relations. This would not have been possible with Oracle, because a cursor cannot be declared twice and it is not possible to have an array of cursors. Also, cursor names and relation names are restricted to being constants. Therefore, the only solution is to limit the number of recursive calls, and to declare a cursor for each step. This means that recursivity is handled by the programmer, who has to decide which cursor to use at each step.

Associative access is easy to express with a relational DBMS. Furthermore, sharing of data is possible, and therefore space can be saved. For instance, in the Unix Mail application, messages are not duplicated. All concurrency problems are dealt with within the DBMS. A further advantage is that the DBMS enforces integrity constraints, so programs are simpler to write. Other well-known advantages of relational DBMSs (data independence, disk management, and recovery) are not visible in this study, but they exist and are very useful.

4 Basic-Pick

The applications were developed on an IN-350 machine, which supports the Pick system and handles concurrency control and recovery on files (this software is called Score). The Pick system (Pick 1986) is original in its file structure. A file is a set of *items*, each item is a set of *attributes*, each attribute is a set of *values*, and each value is a set of *subvalues*. Each of these sets can be of various sizes or can be empty. Each item has an *identifier*, which is not considered an attribute. The items of a file are organized in a hash table on the identifier.

In Basic there is a **read** instruction to read an item from a file. This instruction has two parameters: the name of the file and the identifier of the item. This is not standard Basic; it is a Basic for Pick systems. To read a file sequentially one has to (1) open the file, (2) select all identifiers, and (3) read the file item by item.

4.1 Developing the Bill of Materials Application in Basic

The inventory is in the file Parts. Each item in the file contains the description of a part. The key is the name of the part. If it is a base part, the first attribute is the price and the second is the weight of the part. The third attribute is empty. If it is a composite part, the first attribute is the assembly cost, the second attribute is the mass increment or decrement that occurs when the subparts are assembled, and the third attribute contains the names and quantities of the subparts involved in the manufacture of the part. The third attribute is thus a list of values, each being a pair of subvalues: name of part and quantity. An example of the data for a base part is

wheel↑50↑10↑

where ↑ is the attribute separator. An example of the data for a composite part is

car↑200↑50↑door/4]frame/1]engine/1]...

where] is the value separator and / is the subvalue separator.

The second task is done by looking at each item and testing the existence of the third attribute and the value of the second one. For the third task, a recursive subroutine computes the price of a part, calling itself on each subpart. The fourth task manually checks the existence of the part and the subparts by reading the corresponding item in the file.

4.2 Developing the Unix Mail Application in Basic

All messages are written in a file named Mailbox. Each message is an item of this file. This solution was chosen rather than one mailbox for each user like in Unix, because with the Pick system it is not possible to access from a user directory a file of another user without explicitly creating a link on the file. That would require each user to have a link to the mailbox of every other user. It is easier to create one link from each user to a file containing all the messages. There is no problem of concurrent access to this file, because this is handled by Score.

Each user has his or her own Mbox file where messages that have been read are written at the end of the session.

The schema of the Mailbox file is:

- The first attribute is the sending date.

- The second attribute is the name of the sender.
- The third attribute is the list of recipients who have not yet read the message.
- The fourth attribute is the list of recipients who have already read the message.
- The fifth attribute is the title of the message.
- The next attributes contain the text of the message.

To insert a record in a file, the Pick file system needs an identifier. If this identifier is already used, then the old record is removed. To avoid this undesirable side effect our program allocates the identifier using a counter stored in the record numbered 0. A list of the users of the Mail system is stored on this record, to verify the possibility of sending mail to somebody. This can be done because records in a Pick file are not typed (of course, we could have stored the counter and the list of users in another file).

When a user reads mail, the Mailbox file is scanned, and the records containing messages forwarded to the user are copied into an array of records. The resulting order in the array does not necessarily correspond with the chronological order in which they were sent (this can be achieved by calling a sorting procedure).

4.3 Conclusions

Programming in Basic is not difficult for people with a background in imperative programming languages (as was our case). Only two or three days were needed to write both applications. But the resulting code is long. Furthermore, there is no independence between the physical representation and the application programs, as there is no declarative means to perform associative access.

With this specific Pick implementation of Basic, we found that persistence is not difficult because of the rich file structure of Pick. Nonflat records are convenient because they allow directly to modelize one-to-many relationships, and they avoid the join operation we would have to perform if we were restricted to flat records, as in the relational model (see the corresponding C+SQL program). A disadvantage is that when one wants to write an item on a file there is no protection against deletion of an existing item. The programmer is thus forced to keep a list of unused keys or a counter.

5 Prolog

The applications were written in Prolog II V2.2 on an SM90. In this implementation of the applications, persistence was obtained by saving the current state of the programming environment that is not using files. With this Prolog compiler it is impossible to read and write the same file while executing a program. This implies that all data must fit in memory.

5.1 Developing the Bill of Materials Application in Prolog

There are two basic relations: Base and Composite. The Base relation contains the parts bought outside, and the price and weight of each. All composite parts are in the Composite relation. The attributes of this relation are the name of the part, the cost of manufacturing the part, the mass increment or decrement that occurs when the subparts are assembled, and the list of the names and quantities of the subparts.

The second task is implemented by a single rule, very easy to write. The third task is a little more complicated, because recursion is easy but not calculation. The fourth task one was less easy because it needs a lot of if-then-else structures to verify the constraints (if the part already exists, then ..., else if the first subpart exists, then ..., else ...). Also, the *cut* and *fail* predicates are intensively used, making the program less readable.

5.2 Developing the Unix Mail Application in Prolog

All messages are kept in the Message relation, which has five attributes:

- The date
- The name of the sender
- The name of the recipient
- The title
- The content of the message, which is a Prolog list

When the program starts, the messages for the user are removed from the Message relation and inserted into the Mess relation, which has two more attributes: the number of the message, and an indication whether it was read (R), destroyed (D), or copied (C). When the user stops the program with the **quit** command, the messages that were neither read, copied, nor destroyed are inserted in the Message relation. Those which were read are written in the Mbox file.

To number messages, we need a variable to be incremented for each message removed from the Message relation. To this end, a unary predicate is defined, nb-current(y), which contains the number of the last message. When the program starts, this predicate is not in the database. The rule get-nb(x) gives the current number. If the *nb-current* predicate does not exist, it is created with parameter 1; otherwise its parameter is incremented. At the end of the program, this predicate is removed.

Concerning updates, we found lots of difficulties with the **assert** and **retract** predicates, which allow the programmer to insert and delete one clause in a Prolog program. In fact, as pointed out by Naish, Thom, and Ramamohanarao 1987 and Warren 1984, the semantics of these clauses is not defined, and thus their meaning differs from one interpreter to another.

5.3 Conclusions

For both applications the *cut* (/) and *fail* predicates are intensively used. It is not easy to understand how they work. One must understand unification to make good use of them.

It is hard to compare a line of Basic with a Prolog rule, but the Prolog program is significantly more concise and is easy to write. As in Basic-Pick, the order of the attributes is very important; there is a strong dependence between the application programs and the physical representation. If we want to change the schema of the relation (adding a new attribute, for example), all programs have to be modified.

Prolog is very well adapted for applications, such as the Bill of Materials, that have associative access to data and poor dialog with the user. The program is easily written, and the result is short. But for applications such as the Unix Mail that have a lot of updates, input-output, and if-then-else conditionals, Prolog is less suitable. We have to simulate the if-then-else by an intensive use of the predicates *cut* and *fail*. The resulting program looks like one in an imperative language. Furthermore, as we pointed out above, programming updates is not an easy task in Prolog. It seems that this problem is inherent in the logic-programming paradigm, not just in Prolog.

Persistency was not easy to deal with, but this is mainly due to the Prolog interpreter we have. There are Prolog interpreters that handle persistent data in a more general and efficient way; so this problem is not due to the logic-programming approach.

6 Smalltalk-80

The applications were programmed on a Macintosh Plus, using the two reference books Goldberg and Robson 1985 and Goldberg 1983.

6.1 Developing the Bill of Materials Application in Smalltalk-80

The database is a subclass, named DB, of the predefined class **Dictionary**. This DB class has neither an instance variable nor a class variable. It has just one instance, *Database*, which represents the whole database. The keys of the dictionary are names of parts. The values are instances of the class Description.

The class Description is a subclass of **Object**. It has three instance variables: *price*, *mass*, and *subparts*. The latter is an instance of the Subpart class. A base part has its variable *subpart* equal to nil. As full encapsulation is supported, instance variables are manipulated only through methods associated to the class. For an instance variable of name *x*, it is current practice to designate with the same name, *x*, the method that returns the value of the instance variable. The method that updates its value is commonly named "*x*: ". For each instance variable of class Description, we have the corresponding projection and update methods.

The class Subpart is a subclass of **Dictionary**. The key is a part's name and the value is a quantity. An entry named p_1 gives the quantity of parts p_1 needed to manufacture the part. This class inherits the methods of class **Dictionary** and defines no new method.

In Smalltalk there is a primitive notion of persistence; only elements of a file, are allowed to persist. To store the database on a file, we define the method *writeonfile*. The dual method *readfromfile* reads the database from a file.

Now we have to create *Database* as an instance of DB and declare it to be a global variable. In order to declare a variable to be global (that is, known to all classes and to the user's interactive system), the variable name must be inserted as a key in the predefined dictionary instance *Smalltalk*.

Smalltalk at: #Database **put: nil.**
Database <- **Dictionary new**

In Smalltalk-80, a method can return an object. The third task needs two results: the price and the mass of the part. We created a new class, named Answer. The methods associated to this class are those that project and update its instance variables *price* and *mass*. Having to define the class Answer is heavy and makes the program less understandable. The third task becomes a method, *task3*, of class DB, with the name of the part as argument. It will return an object of class Answer. Then to obtain the price and the cost of a part named *p*, one must send the message "task3: *p*" to the object *Database*. This method is not a method of class Description, because it must be sent to the name of the part, not to the part itself. So the way to do this is to attach the method to the class and not to instances. This is a well-known problem with the object-oriented approach: how to choose which method goes with which class?

6.2 Developing the Unix Mail Application in Smalltalk-80

A message will be an instance of the class Letter, which has five instance variables: *date*, *title*, *sender*, *recipients*, and *text*. The first is an instance of the predefined class **Array**. We use the predefined method **dateandTimeNow** from class **Time**. The response is an array whose first element is the current date (an instance of class **Date**) and whose second element is the current time (an instance of class **Time**). The variable *recipients* is an instance of class **Set**. The other variables will be instances of **String**.

The class Letter has one class method, *create*, which creates messages. This method has one parameter, the name of the sender. The instance methods are *date* and *date:*, *title* and *title:*, *sender* and *sender:*, *recipients* and *recipients:*, *text* and *text:*.

A mailbox is an instance of the class Mailbox, which is a subclass of **OrderedCollection**. This is to avoid writing special software to deal with order. In fact, the message protocol for class **OrderedCollection** maintains the order in which the messages arrive to a mailbox. The class Mailbox has an instance variable, *name*, which contains the name of the owner of the mailbox. The instance methods of the class Mailbox are *name*, *name:*, *header*, which displays the headers of the letters received, and *destroy: anInt*, which removes the letter numbered *anInt* from the receiver.

To find the mailbox of a user, we define the class method *selectMbox*, which uses the predefined method **allInstances** of the class **Class**. This method, when sent to a class, answers a set of all direct instances of the receiver. We send to the resulting set the message **select:** *aBlock*. This method evaluates the argument, *aBlock*, for each of the receiver's elements, and collects into a new set only those elements for which *aBlock* evaluates to *true*. The answer is this new set.

The names of the users known by the system are kept in an object of class **Set**, named *SetofUsers*.

6.3 Conclusions

This was our first experience in the object-oriented world. We can say that it was a tough one. The big difference from a classical language such as Pascal is that there is a single control structure, the message-passing mechanism. This means that conditionals, iterations, and the like are expressed in terms of messages to objects. Also, all input/output is expressed in terms of messages. As a consequence, Smalltalk-80's predefined class hierarchy is very complex, and one has to know many things about it before being able to program anything. Just to read something, compute, and then write the result is not an easy task. What made things worse was that no good documentation was available.

The advantages of using Smalltalk-80 to program our target applications are the following.

1. Once one is familiar with the predefined classes and the message-passing mechanism, it is easy to reuse the available methods. In particular, (a) programming a user-friendly interface is straightforward once one understands the behavior of the predefined class **FillInTheBlank**; and (b) dealing with the ordering of messages in a mailbox is taken into account by the predefined class **OrderedCollection**.

2. Associative access to all instances of a class is easy to achieve by using the methods **allInstances** and **perform**. Any type of expression (called a block) can be passed as arguments of these methods.

We perceived as disadvantages the following points.

1. Persistence is not easy, because the **storeOn:** method is not what we need in a database context. This drawback is not inherent in the object-oriented approach (this is one of the raisons d'être of object-oriented database systems). In fact, the **storeOn:** creates a sequence that should be interpretable as one or more expressions that will be evaluated in order to reconstruct the object. Therefore this method takes a long time if the object is large, as is usual in a database context. Furthermore, because it was not clear in the documentation how to execute an expression stored in a file (i.e., the result of **storeOn:**), we decided to decompose an object by hand by applying the method **printString:** to atomic objects.

2. It is not always easy to determine to which class a method should be associated. For example, the method *mainloop* was written as a class method associated to Mailbox; but the receiver was never used, so it could have been attached to another class. It is not clear if this is due to our lack of experience with the language or to the object-oriented approach.

3. Encapsulation hides the structure of objects by imposing methods to mediate all access to objects. Therefore one has to define methods explicitly to get and update the instance variables one wants to make visible. In the applications we studied, almost all the instance variables had to be visible, so it was cumbersome to define these projection and update methods. This drawback, which is inherent in the object-oriented approach, could be alleviated by making the system generate these methods automatically when the programmer instructs it to do so by using some kind of shorthand.

4. The absence of typing makes the programming task unreliable. One needs more time to debug typing errors. Also, the schema (the set of classes) is not easy to understand, because it has to be interpreted constantly with an external semantics.

7 The O_2 System

The applications were programmed on a Sun using O_2 and the database programming language CO_2 (Deux et al. 1990; see chapter 9).

7.1 Developing the Bill of Materials Application in O_2

Objects are created by the **new** operator. Persistence is attached to name. Every named object in the database is persistent, and every component of a persistent object is persistent. All valid parts will be kept in a named object set_of_parts of class Set_of_parts, which has a set structure:

```
add class Set_of_parts type set(Part)
  method add_new_part() is public;
```

The class Part has only one attribute, `name`. It has two subclasses: Atomic_part, which has two more attributes, `price` and `mass`; and Derived_part, which adds a new attribute, `subparts`, which is a set of pairs (part, quantity). The structure of all classes except Set_of_parts is private. The class Part has two public methods: *display_price*, which calls the private method *price* and then displays the price; and *init*, which checks whether a part with the same name already exists in the database.

We made a full use of Looks, the interface generator of O_2, which permits the easy display of objects. When an object is displayed, a click on it displays a menu of all applicable public methods.

The second task is a simple query written with the query language of O_2 (see chapter 11). For the third task, the price is computed by the *price* method of the class Part. It is displayed by the method *display_price*. When a part is displayed on the screen, the user can send it the message *display_price* just by clicking on it.

7.2 Developing the Unix Mail Application in O_2

A message is an instance of the class Message, which is a tuple with five attributes: `date`, `sender`, `to`, `subject`, and `text`. We use the predefined toolbox classes Date and Text for the attributes `date` and `text`. The class Message has the methods *delete*, to delete the message; *save*, to save it in a specified file; and *reply*, to send a response.

A mailbox is an instance of the class Mailbox and represents the mailbox for one particular user. The attributes are `name`, which represents the user name; `messages`, his or her list of messages; `controls`, the corresponding control list; and `mbox`, the user's set of saved messages. The `controls` list indicates if the message is new (N), read (R), or deleted (*). The message identifier is given by its place in the *messages* list. The object Mail_menu offers the methods *headers*, to display the headers of all messages; *display*, to print the current or the *n*th message, and *send*, to send a message to other users. When a user stops his or her mailbox program, *quit* inserts the read messages in his or her *mbox* and the unread ones in his or her *messages* list: and then the transaction is committed. The **exit** command is just an abort of the transaction.

All users are kept in the named value Usergroup, which is a set of mailboxes, and the method *select_mailbox* finds a user's mailbox. To define users we use the method *create_user*. The query language is easily used with these methods to find a specified mailbox.

O_2 manages applications with their programs, and we only had to define the application Mail_O_2, with only one main program, *init*, which is automatically executed when we start the application. The named value Usergroup maintains the persistence for all user mailboxes, and thus for all messages. We used the generic methods **display_icon** and **display_level_one** to present objects on the screen.

7.3 Conclusions

Programming in O_2 is easy for a programmer with a C background, because the language-level surgery to put the object layer on top of C is very small and therefore easy to learn. As O_2 is upward compatible with C, classical procedures such as calculations are written rather easily using C statements. For instance, starting with O_2 the programmer only has to learn the syntax for message passing and for class and method declarations. Both our applications were written and tested in less than four days. The fact that O_2 is a database system gives persistence for free. We just have to put valid parts in a named set. Also, as in Smalltalk-80, there is the clear benefit of reusing software, as exemplified by the use of the classes Text and Date.

Because of the use of the human interface generator, Looks, we got a very nice interface for the two applications using only a predefined method, **display_level_one**, which displays an object, and the function **lock**, which stops the application until the user has clicked on either the "pencil" or the "eraser" button that is displayed with the object. The fact that Looks gives the capability of triggering a method by clicking on an object avoids the need to write a large main program to display a menu and interpret the choice of the user, as in Smalltalk-80. We also used the methods of the predefined named object **Dialoger**, which permits one to display messages or to ask question to the user. As with C+SQL, we get all functionality of a DBMS, such as associative access, concurrency control, recovery, and disk management.

8 Conclusions

Table 13.1 gives the measures for C+SQL, Basic, Prolog, Smalltalk-80, and O_2 for the Bill of Materials application. Table 13.2 gives the measures for the Unix Mail Application. We give the number of lines and the number of tokens so as to use significant numbers; a Prolog rule and a Basic instruction are not directly comparable.

8.1 Development Time

Basic was the best for development time. It is easy to use, especially for people with a classical background. The development time of C+SQL is rather high. It is mostly due to the impedance mismatch, which increases the difficulty of the

Table 13.1. Measures for the Bill of Materials Application

	Time (days)	Lines	Tokens	Variables
C+SQL	2	130	400	45
Basic	1	75	300	27
Prolog	1	32	152	37
Smalltalk-80	4	86	285	29
O_2	1	76	286	11

Table 13.2. Measures for the Unix Mail Application

	Time (days)	Lines	Tokens	Variables
C+SQL	6	300	650	65
Basic	1	160	623	53
Prolog	7	142	574	141
Smalltalk-80	15	244	427	42
O_2	3	186	647	33

debugging phase. With Smalltalk-80, a lot of time was devoted to understanding the predefined classes and methods. When all this is known, the programming becomes easier; but the apprenticeship is hard. In Smalltalk, it is not always easy to do easy things; for example, there is no easy way to do a simple read or write. Similarly, it is often difficult to find where methods go. We learned that if one decides to design an object-oriented language, she or he will have to provide users with good documentation on predefined types and methods, and good tutoring.

With O_2 we didn't have so many problems. We wrote both applications in less than four days. The differences between O_2 and Smalltalk-80 are that (1) the programming language of O_2 is very close to C, (2) the set of predefined classes and methods is not very large, and (3) the human interface generator is made up of ten functions and one method, so it is very easy to learn.

8.2 Code Size

There is no significant difference in code size, except the short Bill of Materials application in Prolog. (But in the Prolog implementations of the applications, the interface is very primitive, and there is no persistence.) C+SQL is the longest, because a lot of code is developed to handle errors: after each call to Sabrina, we have to test if an error occurred. In O_2, the notion of encapsulation leads to two declarations of methods: the first to give the interface of the method, and the second to give its implementation.

8.3 Number of Variables

The number of variables measures the number of concepts and names the programmer has to introduce to develop the applications. This number is significantly higher in Prolog than in the other languages, because the programmer must name all the attributes of the relations. It is also high in C+SQL, because the programmer has to define names and variables in two languages.

8.4 Conformity to Specifications

Coming back to the specifications we gave for business applications in section 2, we now look at how the various languages met these requirements.

8.4.1 Associative Access

With C+SQL and O_2, associative access to data is handled by the DBMS. In Prolog, the unification mechanism takes care of associative access, but one has to remember the order of attributes and clauses. In the remaining three languages, one has to program a function to be applied on the elements of a set. In Basic, this is accomplished by a read on each element of a file, whereas in Smalltalk-80 we can use the method **perform**, which applies a function to each element of a set. In Smalltalk-80 the method **allInstances** gives the set of all instances of a class.

8.4.2 Computation

C+SQL, Basic, and O_2 have the computation power of imperative languages, with the same style. In Prolog, computation is done by the use of a special predicate, which has side effects that make the code less readable. In Smalltalk-80 the syntax for numerical objects is not the same as for other methods; it takes quite a long time to obtain a syntactically correct program.

8.4.3 Update Facility

It is easy to perform basic updates in all the languages except Prolog, which has no well-defined semantics for updates (Naish, Thom, and Ramamohanarao 1987). C+SQL offers built-in support for integrity constraints; the other languages do not. Furthermore, Prolog, Basic, and Smalltalk-80 are untyped, so they are not very good at protecting the user from (update) errors. A problem found with Basic is that the programmer must take care of the key value. There is no protection again the deletion of an existing item.

8.5 Other Aspects

The languages differ in three other respects: persistence, sharing, and the dialog with the user.

8.5.1 Persistence

Only the DBMSs Sabrina and O_2 deal correctly with persistence (this is what DBMSs are good for). They could be added to virtually any language. In Basic, the rich structure of the files and the read and write functions help to deal with persistent data. With Prolog and Smalltalk-80, persistence is a very painful problem.

8.5.2 Sharing

For the object-oriented systems O_2 and Smalltalk-80, sharing is handled by the system. With the other languages, the programmer has to deal with identifiers.

8.5.3 Dialog with the User

It is very easy to program an interaction in C+SQL or Basic, using the classical read and print functions. But the result is not very nice. With Smalltalk-80 it is very easy to program a user-friendly interface, once the class **View** is understood. But understanding it can take a very long time. In O_2, the dialog with the user is managed by Looks, which is very easy to learn and brings a very nice interface. In Prolog, there are only very primitive functions.

8.6 General Conclusion

The main benefits of our study are:

1. We have a better idea of the languages we examined, from the programmer's point of view.

2. We have a first notion of the kind of metrics that should be used to compare languages, also from the programmer's point of view.

To improve these metrics, it is important to evaluate such issues as the impact on the overall application when adding a new functionality and/or changing an already existing functionality. Code reusability must also be measured, especially in the object-oriented environment.

9 Acknowledgements

Thanks to C. Lepenant and J. B. Ndala who were our teachers for Pick and Basic. F. Pasquer and M. Jean-Noel spent some time with us while developing the C+SQL programs. We also want to thank F. Bancilhon and E. Simon for their careful reading of this paper.

References

Atkinson, M. P., and O. P. Buneman. 1985. Database programming language design. To appear in *Computing Survey.*

Bancilhon, F., S. Cluet, and C. Delobel. 1989. A query language for the O_2 object-oriented database system. In *Proceedings of the DBPL II conference.*

BASIC. 1986. *Manuel de référence du langage BASIC-GESTION.* IN2 (February).

Cox, B. J. 1986. *Object oriented programming, an evolutionary approach.* Addison-Wesley.

Deux, O. et al. 1990. The story of O_2. *IEEE Transactions on Knowledge and Data Engineering* 2(1).

Goldberg, A. 1983. *Smalltalk-80: The interactive programming environment.* Addison-Wesley.

Goldberg, A., and D. Robson. 1985. *Smalltalk 80: The language and its implementation.* Addison-Wesley.

Meyer, B. 1986. Eiffel: Programming for reusability and extendibility. In *Proceedings of the OOPSLA conference.*

Mylopoulos, J., P. Bernstein, and H. Wong. 1980. A language facility for designing database-intensive applications. *ACM TODS* 5(2).

Naish, L., J. Thom, and K. Ramamohanarao. 1987. Concurrent updates in Prolog. In *Proceedings of the international conference on logic programming.*

Pick. 1986. *Manuel de référence système.* IN2 (February).

PROLOG II. 1985. *PROLOG II version 2.2 manuel de référence.* PrologIA.

Sabrina. 1988. *Manuel de présentation générale de Sabrina.* Infosys S-V6-GAL2.

Schaffert, C., T. Cooper, B. Bullis, M. Kilian, and C. Wilpolt. 1986. An introduction to Trellis/Owl. In *Proceedings of the first OOPSLA conference.*

Schmidt, J. W., and M. Mall. 1980. *PASCAL/R Report.* Technical report no. 66, Fachbereich Informatik, University of Hamburg.

Shipman, D. W. 1981. The functional data model and the data language DAPLEX. *ACM TODS* 6(1): 140–73.

Stonebraker, M., and L. Rowe. 1986. The design of Postgres. In *Proceedings of the ACM SIGMOD conference on the management of data.*

Unix. 1986. *Unix reference manual.* Sun Microsystems.

Warren, D. 1984. Database updates in pure Prolog. In *Proceedings of the international conference on fifth generation computer systems.*

Appendix: The Programs

The keywords are in boldface; comments are in italic.

A.1 The C+SQL Programs

A.1.1 The Bill of Materials Application

Task 1 Creation of the two relations and declaration of the inclusion dependency between the relations MadeFrom and Part.

```
#include <stdio.h>
#include "iml.h"
main()
{ int rep = call_connection("sophie");
  if (rep ≠ 0) printf("Connection OK\n");
   else
     { printf("Connection OK\n");
       rep = call_sabre("create table Part (name char unique, price integer, mass integer,
                                    type char);");
       if (rep ≠ 0)
        { printf("Error when creating relation Part\n");
          rep = call_sabre("rollback;");
        }
        else
         { rep = call_sabre("create table MadeFrom (name char, subpart char,
                                          qty integer);");
           if (rep ≠ 0)
              { printf("Error when creating relation MadeFrom\n");
                rep = call_sabre("rollback;");
              }
             else
              { rep = call_sabre("assert includ
                                  inclusion of MadeFrom: subpart
                                  in Part: name;");
                rep = call_sabre("commit;");
              }
         }
      call_deconnection();
    }
  }
```

Task 2

```
#include <stdio.h>
#include "iml.h"
main()
{ char name[20];
  int price, mass, nrel, rep = call_connection("sophie");
  if (rep ≠ 0) printf("Connection is not possible\n");
  else
    { printf("Connection OK\n");
      nrel = call_sabre("select name, price, mass from Part where ((price < 100)
                                         and (type = 'b'));");
      if (nrel < 0) printf("Error\n");
      else if (nrel == 0) printf("No tuple\n");
      else
       {do               * Loops until the end of the relation.
         { rep = lire_tuple(nrel, name, &price, &mass);
         printf("Part = %s  Price = %d  Weight = %d\n", name, price, mass);
         }while (rep == 0);
       }
      call_deconnection();
   }
}
```

Task 3

```
#include <stdio.h>
#include "iml.h"
int global_number = 0;          * It will be the number of the next relation to be created.

int totalcost(name)             * This function returns the cost of the given part.
char *name;
{char subpart[20];
 int cost, qty, rep, nrel, totalprice;
 int number;                    * The number of the relation created in this recursive call.
 nrel = call_sabre("select into temp%d price, type from Part where name = '%s';",
                               global_number++, name);
 if (nrel < 0)
    printf("Error when selecting relation Part \n");
 else if (nrel = 0)
       { printf("Error: This part doesn't exist\n");
         return(-1);
       }
  else
     { rep = lire_tuple(nrel, &cost, type);
       if (type[0] = 'b')       * It is a base part.
          return(cost);
       else
          { number = global_number++;      * We search for the subparts of this part.
            nrel = call_sabre("select into temp%d subpart, qty from MadeFrom
                                       where name = '%s';", number, name);
            if (nrel ≤ 0)
               {printf("Error \n");return(-1);}
            else
               { totalprice = cost;
                 do              * Computes the price of each subpart.
                    { rep = lire_tuple(nrel, subpart, &qty);
                      totalprice = totalprice + (qty * totalcost(subpart));
                    } while (rep == 0);
                 return(totalprice);
               }
          }
     }
}

main()
{char  name[20];
 int rep = call_connection("sophie");
 if (rep ≠ 0) printf("Connection is not possible\n");
 else
   { printf("Connection OK \n");
     printf("Name of the part:"); gets(name);
     printf("Price: %d \n", totalcost(name));
     call_deconnection();
   }
}
```

Task 4

```
#include <stdio.h>
#include "iml.h"
int number = 0;          * It will be the number of the next relation to be created.
main()
{char name[20], answer[3], subpart[20];
 int price, mass, rep = call_connection("sophie");
 if (rep ≠ 0) printf("Connection is not possible \n");
 else
  { printf("Connection OK \n");
    printf("Name of the new part:"); gets(name);
```

```
  printf("Is it a base part? (y/n):"); gets(answer);
  if (answer[0] == 'y')      * Insertion of a base part.
    { printf("Price:"); scanf("%d", &price);
      printf("Weight:"); scanf("%d", &mass);
      rep = call_sabre("insert into Part values('%s', %d, %d, 'b');", name, price, mass);
                               * The uniqueness of the part is verified by Sabrina.
      if (rep < 0 ) printf("This part is already in the database\n");
      else printf("Insertion completed \n");
    }
  else
    { printf("Assembly cost:"); scanf("%d", &price);
        printf("Weight increment:"); scanf("%d", &mass);
        call_sabre("insert into Part values('%s', %d, %d, 'c');", name, price, mass);
        if (rep < 0) printf("This part is already in the database \n");
      else
        { printf("Name of the subpart:"); fflush(stdout);
          scanf("%s",subpart);
          while ((subpart[0] ≠ 'F') && (rep == 0))
            { printf("Quantity:"); scanf("%d",&qty);
              rep = call_sabre("insert into MadeFrom values ('%s', '%s', %d);",
                               name, subpart, qty);
              if (rep < 0 )
                { printf("This subpart doesn't exist: abort \n");
                  qty = call_sabre("rollback;");
                }
              else
                {printf("Name of the subpart:");fflush(stdout);
                 scanf("%s",subpart);
                }
            }
          if (rep == 0)
            { printf("OK \n");
              rep = call_sabre("commit;");
            }
        }
    }
  call_deconnection();
 }
}
```

A.1.2 The Unix Mail Application

Creation of the relations

```
#include <stdio.h>
#include "iml.h"
main()
{ char name[20];
  int rep = call_connection("sophie");
  if (rep ≠ 0) printf("Connection is not possible \n");
  else
    { printf("Connection OK \n");
      rep = call_sabre("create table MessId (currentId integer);");
      if (rep ≠ 0)
        { printf("Error when creating relation MessId \n");
          rep = call_sabre("rollback;");
        }
      else
        {rep = call_sabre("insert into MessId values (1);");
         rep = call_sabre("create table Message
                             (messId integer, date integer, sender char, title char,
                                    text char);");
         if (rep ≠ 0)
           { printf("Error when creating relation Message \n");
             rep = call_sabre("rollback;");
           }
```

```
        else
          { rep = call_sabre("create table Mailbox
                              (messId integer, username char, state char);");
           if (rep ≠ 0)
              { printf("Error when creating relation Mailbox \n");
               rep = call_sabre("rollback;");
              }
           else
              { printf("Creation OK\n");
               rep = call_sabre("commit;");
              }
          }
        }
      call_deconnection();
    }
}
```

The sendmail program First the number of the message to be created is read from the relation MessId. Then this relation is updated to handle the number of the next message. After that, the message can be created. For each recipient, a tuple is inserted in the Mailbox relation, then a tuple is inserted in the Message relation.

```
#include <stdio.h>
#include "iml.h"
main()
{ char query[5], username[L_cuserid], recipient[L_cuserid];
  char date[15];
  char title[20];
  char text[150];
  int number, i, car, nrel, rep = call_connection("sophie");
  if (rep ≠ 0) printf("Connection is not possible \n");
  else
    { printf("Connection OK \n");
     cuserid(username);
      * The relation MessId is read to obtain the number of the message.
     nrel = call_sabre("select * from MessId;");
     if (nrel ≤ 0)
        printf("Error when reading MessId \n");
     else
       { rep = lire_tuple(nrel, &number);
        if (rep < 0)
           {printf("Error when reading the current MessId \n");
            rep = call_sabre("rollback;");
           }
        else
          { rep = call_sabre("update MessId set currentId = %d;", (number+1));
           if (rep < 0)
              { printf("Error when updating MessId \n");
               rep = call_sabre("rollback;");
              }
           else
              { rep = call_sabre("commit;");
               printf("To: ");
               do                 * Loops to read the name of all recipients.
                { scanf("%s", recipient);
                  rep = call_sabre("insert into Mailbox values (%d, '%s', 'U');", number,
                                   recipient);
                  car = getchar();
                }while ((car ==  32) && (rep == 0));
               if (rep ≠ 0 )
                  {printf("Error \n");
```

```
                rep = call_sabre("rollback;");
                }
             else
                {printf("Title: ");
                 scanf("%s", title);
                 scanf("%s", text);
                rep = call_sabre("insert into Message values (%d, %d, '%s', '%s', '%s');",
                                  number, time(0), username, title, text);
                if (rep == 0)
                   { printf("OK \n");
                     rep = call_sabre("commit;");
                     }
                 else
                   { printf("Error \n");
                     rep = call_sabre("rollback;");
            }
          }
        }
      }
     }
   }
  call_deconnection();
 }
}
```

The mail program

```
#include <stdio.h>
#include "iml.h"
struct
{ int messId;
  char state;
  int date;
  char sender[20];
  char title[20];
  char text[150];
} tab[20];              * It will contain the messages sent to the user.
int listofuser[20];     * It will contain for each message the name of the cursor
                          which corresponds to the list of its recipients.
int number;             * Number - 1 = the number of messages received by the user.

  header()              * Print the header of each message (state, number, date , sender, title).
{ int i;
  for (i = 0; i < number; i++)
      printf("\n %c %d:  %s from %s: %s\n", tab[i].state,i, ctime(&(tab[i].date)), tab[i].sender,
                                            tab[i].title);
}

  copy(ind, NameFile)  * Saves the message number in file NameFile.
int ind;
char *NameFile;
{ FILE * fichier;
  int rep;
  char name[L_cuserid];
  if ((fichier = fopen( nameFile , "a+")) == NULL)
    printf("Error while opening file %s \n", NameFile);
  else
   { fprintf(fichier, "\nDate: %sFrom %s\n", ctime(&(tab[ind].date)), tab[ind].sender);
     fprintf(fichier, "To: ");
      do               * Loops in the temporary relation to get the names of the recipients.
      { rep = lire_tuple(listofuser[ind], name);
        fprintf(fichier, "%s ", name);
      }while (rep == 0);
    fprintf(fichier, "\nTitle: %s\n", tab[ind].title);
    fprintf(fichier, "%s\n", tab[ind].text);
```

```
    fclose(fichier);
   }
}

   display(ind)        * Displays message number "ind."
int ind;
{ int rep;
  char name[L_cuserid];
  printf( "Message %d\nDate: %sFrom %s\n", ind, ctime(&(tab[ind].date)), tab[ind].sender);
  printf( "To: ");
  do                   * Loops in the temporary relation to get the names of the recipients.
    { rep = lire_tuple(listofuser[ind], name);
      printf( "%s ", name);
    }while (rep == 0);
  printf( "\nTitle: %s\n", tab[ind].title);
  printf( "%s\n",tab[ind].text);
}

   reply(ind, user)    * Reply of "user" to message number "ind."
int ind;
char *user;
{char title[20];
 char text[150];
 int nrel, currentId, rep;
 nrel = call_sabre( "select * from MessId;" );
 if (nrel ≤ 0)
   printf( "Error when reading MessId\n" );
 else                  * We get the number of the message to be created.
   { rep = lire_tuple(nrel, &currentId);
     if (rep < 0)
       printf( "Error when reading the current MessId\n" );
     else
       { rep = call_sabre( "update MessId set CurrentId = %d;", (currentId+1));
         if (rep < 0) printf( "Error when updating MessId\n" );
         else
            { rep = call_sabre( "insert into Mailbox values (%d, '%s', 'U');",
                                        currentId, tab[ind].sender);
              if (rep < 0 )
                printf( "Error \n" );
               else
                {sprintf(title, "Re: %s", tab[ind].title);
                 printf( "Title :%s \n", title);
                 scanf( "%s", text);
                 rep = call_sabre( "insert into Message values (%d, %d, '%s', '%s', '%s');",
                                        currentId, time(0), user, title, text);
                 rep = call_sabre( "commit;" );
* The only time the database is modified is when inserting a reply and at the
  end of the session. Here we commit the transaction to unlock the relation
  MessId. Otherwise, one will be blocked when sending a mail. That means
  that if the user quits the program by "x" then everything is aborted except the
  reply and save, as in the case in the real Unix Mail.
                }
            }
       }
   }
  }
}


main()
{ char query, username[L_cuserid], read_number, nameFile[10];
  int i, nrel, nrel2, rep2, rep = call_connection( "sophie" );
  int current, last;
  if (rep ≠ 0) printf( "Connection is not possible \n" );
  else
    { printf( "Connection OK \n" );
      cuserid(username);
```

```
* We make a join between relations Message and Mailbox, and select on the user name.
nrel= call_sabre("select into mess Mailbox.messId, date, sender, title, text
                  from Mailbox,Message
                  where username = '%s' and Mailbox.messId = Message.messId
                  and state = 'U' order by date;", username);
if (nrel < 0)
  {printf("\n *** Error when joining Message and Mailbox ***\n");
   rep = call_sabre("rollback;");
  }
else if (nrel == 0)
  printf("No message \n");
else
  { number = 0;
   do        * Loops to read the messages.
    { rep = lire_tuple(nrel, &(tab[number].messId), &tab[number].date, tab[number].sender,
                       tab[number].title, tab[number].text);
     tab[number].state = 'U';
     number++;
    }while (rep == 0);
   printf("%d new messages\n", number);
   for (i = 0; i < number; i++)
    { listofuser[i] = call_sabre("select into temp%d username
                                  from Mailbox
                                  where messId = %d;", i, tab[i].messId);
     if (listofuser[i] < 0)
       printf("Error when reading the recipients list \n");
    }
   header();
   current = 0;
   last = number - 1;
   printf("?");
   query = (char) getchar();
   while ((query ≠ 'x') && (query ≠ 'q'))
    { read_number = (char) getchar();
     if (read_number == ' ')
       { read_number = (char) getchar();
        switch (read_number)
          { case 'p': current --;
                      if (current == -1) current = last;
                      break;
            case 'n': current++;
                      if (current > last) current = 0;
                      break;
            case 'l': current = last; break;
            case 'f': current = 0;
          }
       }
     if (tab[current].state == 'D')
       printf("Message deleted \n");
     else
       switch (query)
         { case 'h': header(); break;
           case 'p': display(current);
                     if (tab[current].state == 'U') tab[current].state = 'R';
                     break;
           case 's': printf("Name of the file? \n");
                     scanf("%s", NameFile);
                     copy(current, NameFile);
                     tab[current].state = 'S';
                     fflush(stdin);fflush(stdout);
                     break;
           case 'd': tab[current].state = 'D'; break;
           case 'r': reply(current, username);
         }
     printf("?"); fflush(stdout);
     query = (char) getchar();
    }
```

```
        if (query == 'x') rep = call_sabre("rollback;");
        else
          {for (i = 0; i < number; i++)
            switch (tab[i].state)
             { case 'R': copy(i, "mbox");
               case 'D':
               case 'S': rep= call_sabre("update Mailbox
                                         set state = 'R'
                                         where messId = %d and username='%s';",
                                         tab[i].messId, username);
              * The tuple in Mailbox is updated. If all recipients have read the
                message, the corresponding tuple in Message must be deleted.
                    rep = call_sabre("select * from Mailbox
                              where ((messId = %d ) and (state='U'));", tab[i].messId);
                    if (rep == 0)    * All recipients have read the message.
                     { rep=call_sabre("delete from Message where messId=%d;",
                                         tab[i].messId);
                       rep=call_sabre("delete from Mailbox where messId=%d;",
                                         tab[i].messId);
                    }
           }
        rep = call_sabre("commit;");
        }
      }
    call_deconnection();
  }
}
```

A.2 The Basic Programs

A.2.1 The Bill of Materials Application

Task 2 Each item of the file Parts is read. Attributes are read using the function **extract**, which takes as arguments the item and the number of the attribute to be extracted.

```
equ true to 1, false to 0
open "Parts" to parts else print "File error";stop      * Opens the file Parts.
select parts to lparts                                  * Gives in Lparts the list of the identifiers.
the_end=false
loop                                                    * Loops on the items.
   readnext idart from lparts else the_end=true         * Gives the next identifier in the list Lparts.
  until the_end do
  read item from parts,idart else print "File error";stop  * Reads the item.
  if (extract(item,3)=" ") and (extract(item,1)>100) then
       * If it is a base part that cost more than Fr100
     print "Part ":idart
     print "Price ":extract(item,1)                     * Gives the value of the first attribute.
     print "Weight ":extract(item,2)                    * Gives the value of the second attribute.
    end
 repeat                                                 * End of the loop.
```

Task 3 A recursive subroutine *price* computes the price of a part, calling itself on each subpart.

```
subroutine price-mass(name,price,mass,rep)       * Name = the name of the part.
                                                 * Price and mass are output.
                                                 * Rep tells if everything is OK.
equ true to 1, false to 0
equ am to char(254), vm to char(253), svm to char(252)
prompt " "
```

```
p=0
rep=true
open "Parts" to parts else print "File error";stop      * Opens the file Parts.
read item from parts, name else print "This part doesn't exist";rep=false;stop
                                              * Reads the item about the part.
list=extract(item,3)                          * Reads the third attribute.
if list=" " then p=extract(item,1) else       * If it is empty, then this is a base part.
  i=1
  loop
     ssp=extract(list,1,i)                    * Reads the ith subpart.
   until ssp=" " do
     i=i+1
     ssp.part=extract(ssp,1,1,1)              * Gets its name.
     ssp.quant=extract(ssp,1,1,2)             * The quantity.
     call price-mass(ssp.part,tamp1,tamp2,rep)  * Computes the price and the mass.
     price = price + (ssp.quant × tamp1)
     mass = mass + (ssp.quant × tamp2)
  repeat
  price = price + extract(item,1)             * Adds the assembly cost.
  mass = mass + extract(item,2)
 end
return
```

Task 4 Verification of the existence or nonexistence of a part is done by reading the record with the name of the part as key. If the read succeeds, that means that the part already exists in the database; otherwise the **read** function fails.

```
equ true to 1, false to 0
equ am to char(254), vm to char(253), svm to char(252)
prompt " "
open "Parts" to parts else print "File error";stop      * Opens the Parts file.
print "Name of the part?:":
input name
read item from parts,name then print "This part already exists in the file";stop
print "Is it a base part? (y/n):":
input response
if response="y" then                          * If it is a base part.
   print "Price of the part?:":
   input price
   print "Weight of the part?:":
   input mass
   item=price:am:mass
 end else                                     * The end of "if response = 'y'".
     print "Give the subparts list"
     list=" "
     loop                                     * Loops on the set of subparts.
        print "Name of the subpart"
        input name2
       until name2=" " do
        read item from parts, name2 else print "Part unknown";stop
                * Verification of the existence of the subpart.
        list=list:name2
        print "Quantity?:"
        input q
        list=list:svm:q:vm
       repeat                                 * End of the loop.
     print "Assembly cost?:":
     input price
     print "Weight increment or decrement:":
     input mass
     item=price:am:mass:am:list
 end
write item on parts,name                      * The new item is inserted in the Parts file.
stop
```

A.2.2 The Unix Mail Application

The sendmail program

```
equ am to char(254), vm to char(253), svm to char(252)
prompt " "
open "Mailbox" to mailbox else print "File error";stop * Opens the Mailbox file.
x=0
read tab from mailbox,0 else print "Error while reading Mailbox file";stop
number=tab<1>                              * Gets the ID of the next message.
tab<1> =tab<1>+1
list.users=tab<2>
item=timedate()
sender=oconv(x,"u50bb")                    * Gets the name of the user.
item=item:am:field(sender," ",2)
print "Recipients:":
input recip                                * Reads the list of recipients.
recip=trim(recip)                          * Deletes unnecessary blanks.
list_recip=" "
j=1
k=0                  * Loops on the set of recipients, looking at their existence.
loop
      recipient=field(recip," ",j)
    until recipient=" " do
      if index(list.users,recipient,1)=0 then
          print "User ":recipient:" is unknown"
        end else list_recip=list_recip:recipient:vm; k=k+1
      j=j+1
  repeat                                   * End of the loop.
if k=0 then print "Error: no recipient. Cancel";stop
item=item:am:list_recip:am:am
print "Subject:":
input subject
item=item:subject
loop                                       * Gets the text of the message line by line.
    text=iconv(78,"u11ed")
    print
  until text="." do item=item:am:text repeat
write item on mailbox,number
write tab on mailbox,0
```

The mail program The mail program is divided into a main program that manages the user requests by calling the right subroutine, and a set of subroutines to display a message, reply to a message, delete a message, or copy a message into a file.

```
equ true to 1, false to 0
equ am to char(254), vm to char(253), svm to char(252)
common mes(20,3)           * Variables shared by the main program and the subroutines.
common last
mat mes=0
open "Mailbox" to mailbox else print "File error";stop
user=oconv(" ","u50bb")                    * Gives the name of the user.
user=field(user," ",2)
select mailbox to lmail                    * Gives the list of IDs.
the_end=false;j=0
loop                * Loops on all the messages, keeping those addressed to the user.
    readnext ident from lmail else the_end=true
  until the_end do
    read message from mailbox,ident else print "Read error";stop
```

```
      if (index(message<3>,user,1)≠0) then
            j=j+1
            if j>20 then print "Problem—Cancel"; stop
            mes(j,1)=message
            mes(j,2)=ident
            end
  repeat
if j=0 then print "No mail for ":user;stop
the_end=false;current=1;last=j
call header                              * Displays the headers of the messages.
loop
      input quest                        * Reads the user command.
      quest=trim(quest)                  * Deletes unnecessary blanks.
      number=field(quest," ",2)
      begin case
            case number="l"; number=last
            case number="n"; number=number+1
            case number="p"; number=number-1
            case number=" "; number=current
        end case
      if (number>0) and (number≤last) and (mes(number,3)≠ "destroyed") then
            current=number
            command=field(quest," ",1)
            begin case
                  case command="p"; call print.mess(mes(number,1))
                                          mes(number,3)="read"
                  case command="d"; mes(number,3)="destroyed"
                  case command="s"; call save.mess(mess(number,1))
                                          mes(number,3)="copied"
                  case command="r"; call rep.mess(mess(number,1),user)
                  case command="h"; call header
                  case command="q"; the_end=true
                  case command="x"; stop
                  case true; print "Command unknown"
              end case
        end
  until the_end do repeat
open mbox to "Mbox" else print "Error while opening your Mbox";stop
read num from mbox,0 else print "Read error";stop
for k=1 to last
      if mes(k,3)≠0 then          * If the user has read the message.
            i=1; att3=" "         * Then his or her name must go to the fourth attribute.
            loop
                  dd=extract(mes(k,1),3,i)
               until dd=" " do
                  if dd≠user then att3=att3:dd:vm
                  i=i+1
              repeat
            mes(k,1)<3> =att3
                                  * If the third attribute is empty, that means that all
                                  * recipients have read the message, so it can be deleted.
            if mes(k,1)<3> ="" then delete mailbox,mes(k,2) else
                  mes(k,1)<4> =mes(k,1)<4>:user:vm
                  write mes(k,1) on mailbox,mes(k,2)
              end
            if mes(k,3)="read" then
                  num=num+1; write mes(k,1) on mbox,num
              end
        end
  next k
write num on mbox,0
stop


subroutine print.mess(message)       * This subroutine displays a message on the screen.
print "Date: ":message<1>
print "From: ":message<2>
```

```
list.recip=" "; i=1
loop
      recipient=extract(message,3,i)
   until recipient=" " do list.recip=list.recip:recipient:" "; i=i+1 repeat
i=1
loop
      recipient=extract(message,4,i)
   until recipient=" " do list.recip=list.recip:recipient:" "; i=i+1 repeat
print "To: ":list.recip
print "Title: ":message<5>
i=6
loop
      print message<i>
  until message<i> =" " do i=i+1 repeat
return


subroutine header            * This subroutine displays the headers of the messages.
common mes(20,3)
common last
for i=1 to last
      if mes(i,3)≠"destroyed" then
            print i:" from: ":mes(i,1)<1>:" : ":mes(i,1)<5>
        end
  next i
return


subroutine save.mess(message)   * This subroutine copies a message to a file.
print "Name of the file:":
input name
open name to file else print "Error"; return
print "Name of the item:":
input ident
write message on file,ident
return


subroutine rep.mess(message,user)    * This subroutine is used to reply to a message.
equ am to char(254), vm to char(253), svm to char(252)
open "Mailbox" to mailbox else print "File error";return * Opens the Mailbox file.
read tab from mailbox,0 else print "Error";return
number=tab<1>; tab<1> =tab<1>+1
item=timedate():am:user:am:message<2>:am:am
item=item:"Re: ":message<5>
print "From: ":user
print "To:":message<2>
print "Re:":message<5>
loop                                      * Gets the text of the message line by line.
      text=iconv(78,"u11ed");print
   until text="." do item=item:am:text repeat
write item on mailbox,number
write tab on mailbox,0
return
```

A.3 The PROLOG Programs

A.3.1 The Bill of Materials Application

```
base(windshield,50,10) →;
base(seat,100,30) →;
base(windshield wiper,10,0.5) →;
base(door,100,5) →;
base(spark plug,5,5) →;
```

```
base(wheel,50,10) →;
base(axle,150,56) →;
base(piston,30,15) →;

composite(frame,120,90,quant(wheel,4).quant(axle,1).nil) →;
composite(engine,90,30,quant(spark plug,4).quant(piston,4).nil) →;
composite(car,200,50,quant(door,4).quant(frame,1).quant(engine,1).nil) →;
```

Task 2 Evaluation of an expression is done by using the predefined rule **val**. The result of an evaluation must be an integer, a real, a string, or an identifier. **val**(t_1, t_2) computes the expression t_1 and succeeds if the result can be unified with t_2.

```
quest2 → base(x,y,z) val(inf(y,100),1)  * Makes the selection in the relation Base.
         outm("Part") outm(x)           * Prints the name, the price, and the weight of the part.
         outm("Price") outm(y)
         outm("Weight") outm(z);
```

This query is simpler than in Basic, but it is not easy to understand the **val** predicate.

Task 3 Computation of a part price. The part is either a base part or a composite part; for a composite part, the price is the assembly cost plus the price of all the subparts. The computation of the mass is similar.

```
price(part,price) → base(part,price,x);      * If it is a base part, there is nothing to calculate.
price(part,price) →
  composite(part,ass_cost,mass,l)            * If it is a composite part ...
  price-l(l,y)                               * y = price of the list l.
  val(add(ass_cost,y),price);                * Price = assembly cost + list price.
```

The price of a list is zero if the list is empty; otherwise it is the price of each subpart in the list multiplied by the required number of each subpart.

```
price-l(nil,0) →;
price-l(quant(p1,q1).l,z) → price(p1,x1) price-l(l,x2) val(add(x2,mul(x1,q1)),z);
```

Task 4 It must be verified that the part doesn't already exist. If it is a composite part, all its subparts must exist.

```
insert(part,price,weight,l) →                * Is this part in the Base relation?
  base(part,x,y)
  /
  outml("This part already exists")
  fail;

insert(part,price,weight,l) →                * Is this part in the Composite relation?
  composite(part,x,y,l')
  /
  outml("This part already exists")
  fail;

insert(part,price,weight,nil) → assert(base(part,price,weight),nil) /;
      * If it is a base part (if the list of subparts is empty), then this new fact is inserted.
```

```
insert(part,price,weight,l) →                  * If it is a composite part ...
  verif(l)                                     * The list of subparts must be valid.
  /
  assert(composite(part,price,weight,l),nil);  * Inserts the new fact.

insert(part,price,weight,l) →
  outml("one of the subparts doesn't exist")
  fail;
```

To check the validity of the subparts list, we must check that all subparts are in the database.

```
verif(nil) →;

verif(quant(p1,q1).l) → base(p1,x,y) verif(l);

verif(quant(p1,q1).l) → composite(p1,x,y,l') verif(l);
```

A.3.2 The Unix Mail Application

The following rule is triggered when the program starts.

```
to-begin →
  get_value("Your name?:",u) line
  read-mess(u)                * Reads the messages for the user.
  repeat                      * Loops on the user commands.
  outm("?")
  in-char'(c)
  command(c,u)                * Execution of the command.
  /                           * The cut is encountered only when the goal command
                                succeeds; this happens only when c = q or x.
  save-mess(u)                * The user messages are saved.
  find-rule(nb-current) suppress(1)
                              * Removes the predicate that gives the number of messsages.
  line outml("Bye bye")
  exit("message");            * Exits from Prolog.
```

The **repeat** predicate generates multiple solutions through backtracking.

```
repeat →;
repeat → repeat;
```

The following rules take care of the user commands. They all (except the exit commands **q** and **x**) fail to cause a backtrack on the **repeat** predicate of the **to-begin** rule.

```
command("q",u) → /;
command("x",u) → outml("Bye bye") quit;
command("d",u) → in-integer(t) destroy(t) / fail;
command("a",u) → in-integer(t) display(t) / fail;
command("r",u) → in-integer(t) answer(t,u) / fail;
command("e",u) → send-mess(u) / fail;
command("t",u) → header / fail;
command("c",u) → in-integer(t) copy(t) / fail;
```

The **quit** predefined predicate stops the program without modification.

The rule *read-mess* reads the messages for the user, removes them from the Message relation, gets a message number by a call to the rule get-nb(x), inserts this message with its number and an N (for new) in the Mess relation, and finally displays the header of the message: (number, date, sender, title).

In most versions of Prolog, there exists a built-in rule, **retract**, which enables a program to remove clauses from the database. This rule does not exist in version 2.2 of Prolog II, where to remove a clause $X \rightarrow Y$, one must first put the current rule pointer on the clause, using the predicate **rule**(X, Y); then remove the current rule by the predicate **suppress**(1). This sequence of operations supposes that the variables of X are completely instantiated.

```
read-mess(u) →
   message(d,e,u,t,t')
   get-nb(x)                                * Gives a number.
   rule(message(d,e,u,t,t'),nil) suppress(1) * Removes the message from the Message relation.
   assert(mess(x,"N",d,e,u,t,t'),nil)       * Inserts the message in the Mess relation.
   line out(x) outm(" ") outm(d)            * Displays the header.
   outm(" from ") outm(e) outm(":") outm(t)
   fail;
read-mess(u) →;
```

The rule get-nb(x) gives the number, x, of the current message.

```
get-nb(x) →
   nb-current(y)                  * If the predicate nb-current already exits ...
   /
   rule(nb-current(y),nil) suppress(1)   * It is removed.
   val(add(y,1),x)                * Increments the current number.
   assert'(nb-current(x),nil);    * Saves the new number.

get-nb(x) →                       * If the predicate get-nb is not already in the database ...
   val(1,x)                       * The current number is initialized.
   assert'(nb-current(x),nil);    * Inserts the new fact.
```

At the end of the program, the messages that have been read are written on the Mbox file, and the messages that have not been read are put in the Message relation. The Mess relation is destroyed.

```
save-mess(u) →                               * If the message has not been read ...
   rule(mess(x,"N",d,e,u,t,t'),nil) suppress(1)   * It is removed from the Mess relation.
   assert(message(d,e,u,t,t'),nil) fail;     * It is put in the Message relation.

save-mess(u)→                                * If the message has been read ...
   rule(mess(x,"L",d,e,u,t,t'),nil) suppress(1)   * it is removed from the Mess relation.
   output("mbox+")                           * It is written on the Mbox file.
   outm("Date:") out(d) line
   outm("From:") out(e) line
   outm("Title:") out(t) line
   display(t')
   line
   output("console") close-output fail;

save-mess(u) →                               * If the message has been copied or destroyed ...
   rule(mess(x,z,d,e,u,t,t'),nil) suppress(1);    * It is removed from the Mess relation.
save-mess(u) →;
```

The following rule displays the headers of the messages.

```
header →
   mess(x,l,d,e,u,t,t')
   line out(l) outm(" ")
   out(x) outm(" ") out(d) outm(" from ") out(e) outm(":") out(t)
   fail;
```

The following rules enable the deletion of a message numbered x.

```
destroy(x) →
   mess(x,"D",z,t,t',u,k)
   /
   outml("Message destroyed");
destroy(x) →
   rule(mess(x,y,z,t,t',u,k),nil) suppress(1)
   /
   assert(mess(x,"D",z,t,t',u,k),nil) ;
destroy(x) → outm("Message doesn't exist");
```

The rule display(x) displays the message number x. It starts by verifying that this message is not destroyed.

```
display(x) →
   mess(x,"D",z,t,t',u,k)
   /
   outml("This message has been destroyed");
display(x) →
   mess(x,"C",d,e,u,t,t')
   /
   aff(d,e,t,t');

display(x) →                          * If the message was not destroyed or copied.
   rule(mess(x,l,d,e,u,t,t'),nil) suppress(1)
   /                                  * The fact that the message was read is indicated in
   assert(mess(x,"L",d,e,u,t,t'),nil)   the second component of the tuple.
   aff(d,e,t,t');
display(x) → outml("This message doesn't exist");

aff(d,e,t,t') →
   outm("Date:") outm(d) line
   outm("From:") outm(e) line
   outm("Title:") outm(t) line
   show(t')
   line;
```

The *show* rules display a list on the screen.

```
show(nil) →;
show(a.l) → outm(a) outm(" ") show(l);
```

Sending mail:

```
send-mess(u) →
   get_value("name of the recipient?:",d)
   get_value("Title:",t)
   outm("Text:")
   in-sentence(t',t1)
   date-string(d')
   assert(message(d',u,d,t,t'),nil);
```

The following rules enable the user to answer to a message numbered x.

```
answer(x,u) →
  mess(x,"D",z,t,t',y,k)
  /
  outml("This message has been destroyed");
answer(x,u) →
  mess(x,l,d,e,u,t,text)
  /
  outm("Reply to:") out(e)          * Shows the recipient of the answer.
  line
  conc-string("Re:",t,t2)
  outm("Title:") out(t2)            * Displays the title of the answer.
  line
  outm("Text of the answer:")
  in-sentence(t',t1)                * Reads the text of the answer.
  date-string(d')
  assert(message(d',u,e,t2,t'),nil);  * Inserts the new message into the Message relation.
answer(x,u) → outml("Unknown message");
```

The rule copy(x) copies message number x onto a file. The user is asked for the name of the file.

```
copy(x) →
  mess(x,"D",z,t,t',y,k)
  /
  outml("This message has been destroyed");
copy(x) →
  rule(mess(x,l,d,e,u,t,t'),nil) suppress(1)
  /
  assert(mess(x,"C",d,e,u,t,t'),nil)
  get_value("Name of the file?:",f')
  conc-string(f',"+",f)             * This "+" is added to the write at the end of file.
  output(f)                         * The current output is the file.
  outm("Date:") out(d) line
  outm("From:") out(e) line
  outm("Title:") out(t) line
  display(t')
  line
  output("console") close-output ;  * The output is the console, and the file is closed.
copy(x) → outml("This message doesn't exist");

get_value(s,t) → outm(s) in-word(t,t1) line;
```

A.4 The Smalltalk-80 Programs

A.4.1 The Bill of Materials Application

Declaration of the class Subpart

```
Dictionary variableSubclass: #Subpart   * This class is a subclass of Dictionary.
     instanceVariableNames:' '          * There is no instance variable.
     classVariableNames:' '             * There is no class variable.

Object subclass: #Description
     instanceVariableNames:' price mass subparts'
     classVariableNames:' '
```

Methods of class Description

```
price                    * Answers the value of the price instance variable.
    ↑price

price: anInteger         * Sets the value of the instance variable price to be an Integer.
    price ← anInteger

Dictionary variableSubclass: #DB
    instanceVariableNames:' '
    classVariableNames:' '

writeonfile: aFile  * This method stores the receiver (an instance of DB) on the file aFile.
    |aName aPart aSubpart|                        * Declaration of temporary variables.
    self keysDo: [:aName | aName printOn: aFile.  * For all keys of the receiver.
            aPart ← self at: aName.
            aPart price printOn: aFile.
                    * The method printOn writes the receiver on a file.
            aPart mass printOn: aFile.
            (aPart subparts isNil)
                ifFalse:                          * If it is a composite part ...
                ['(' printOn: aFile.
                aPart subparts keysDo:            * Each subpart is written on the file.
                    [:aSubpart | aSubpart printOn: aFile.
                    aPart subparts at: aSubpart printOn: aFile
                    ]
                ')' printOn: aFile.
                ]
            ].
    aFile close
```

Task 2

```
task2
    |aName aPart|            * Temporary variables.
    self keysDo:
        [:aName |
            aPart ← self at: aName.
            ((aPart subparts isNil) & ((aPart price) > 100))
                ifTrue: [Transcript cr; show: aName]
        ]
```

Transcript (a global variable) is the name of a window in which the results are displayed using the method **show**. The semicolon is used to express a *cascade* of messages sent to the same object.

Task 3

```
Object subclass: #Answer
    instanceVariableNames:'price mass'
    classVariableNames:' '

task3: aName
    |aPart answer1 aSubpart answer2|
    aPart ← self at: aName.
            * aPart is the part for which we have to compute the price and cost.
    answer1 ← Answer new.
    (aPart subpart isNil)              * Is it a base part?
      ifTrue: [ answer1 price: (aPart price).
                answer1 mass: (aPart mass)]
      ifFalse: [ answer1 price: 0.       * If it is a composite part.
                answer1 mass: 0.
```

```
            aPart subpart keysDo:
                 [:aSubpart|          * For each subpart.
                  answer2 ← Baseatk task3: aSubpart.
                                       * task3 is computed for each subpart.
                  answer1 price: ((answer1 price)
                          + ((answer2 price) * (aPart subpart at: aSubpart))).
                  answer1 mass: ((answer1 mass)
                          + ((answer2 mass) * (aPart subpart at: aSubpart)))
                 ].
            answer1 price: (answer1 price + aPart price).
            answer1 mass: (answer1 mass + aPart mass).
            ]                          * End of the ifFalse.
↑answer1                               * The answer is returned by the method.
```

Task 4 This task implies an important dialog with the user. We will use objects of two predefined classes: **PopUpMenu** and **FillInTheBlank**. The first one will be used in the following way. A menu with labels "yes" and "no" will be displayed. Its caption is "Base part?".

```
clic ← (PopUpMenu labels: 'yes no') startUpWithCaption: 'Base part?'.
(clic=1) ifTrue: [....].
(clic=2) ifTrue: [...].
```

If the user clicks on "yes," then "clic" is made equal to 1, and the corresponding block is executed.

The **FillInTheBlank** class represent a request for information from the user. It has a method, **request:** messageString, which creates a window with two lines, centered around the cursor. The first line, in inverse video, contains the argument. The second line will contain the answer of the user. The method returns this answer.

Task 4 will be performed by the method **create** of the class DB. Its parameter will be the name of the part.

```
create: aName
    |aPart aMenu anInt setOfSub aSubp|
    (Baseatk includesKey: aName)      * Tests if the part is already in the database.
     ifTrue: [Transcript cr; show: 'This part is already in the database']
     ifFalse: [
        aPart ← Description new.
        aMenu ← (PopUpMenu labels: 'yes no') StartUpWithCaption: 'Base part?'.
        (aMenu=1)
         ifTrue:                      * If it is a base part.
            [aPart price: FillInTheBlank request: 'Price of this part?'.
            aPart mass: FillInTheBlank request: 'Weight of this part?'.
            Baseatk at: aName put: aPart]
         ifFalse:                     * If it is a composite part.
            [aPart price: FillInTheBlank request: 'Cost of manufacturing this part?'.
            aPart mass: FillInTheBlank request: 'Weight increment?'.
            setOfSub ← Subpart new.   * Creation of the subpart variable.
            aSubp ← 'continu '.
            (aSubp = 'stop')          * Loops for all component parts.
              whileFalse:
                [aSubp ← FillInTheBlank request: 'Name of the subpart?'
                (aSubp = 'stop')
                ifFalse: [
                (Baseatk includesKey: aSubp)
                                      * Verification of the existence of the part.
```

```
                    ifTrue:
                       [(setOfSub includesKeys: aSubp)
                        * Verification of the nonexistence of the part in the set of subparts.
                        ifTrue: [Transcript cr; show: 'This part is already in the set of subparts']
                        ifFalse: [anInt ← FillInTheBlank message: 'Quantity?'.
                                  setOfSub at: aSubp put: anInt ]

                        ]
                    ifFalse: [Transcript cr; show: 'Non-existent part' ]
                   ]
                   ].                    * End of the "while" loop.
              (setOfSub isEmpty)         * Tests if there are any subparts.
                ifTrue:  [Transcript cr; show: 'Set of subparts is empty—Cancel']
                ifFalse:[aPart subparts: setOfSub.
                         Baseatk at: aName put: aPart]
              ]
        ]
```

A.4.2 The Unix Mail Application

Declaration of the class Mailbox:

```
OrderedCollection variableSubclass: #Mailbox
      instanceVariableNames: 'name '
      classVariableNames: ' '

name
      ↑ name

name: aString
      name ← aString

header
      |anInt aLetter|
      anInt ← 1.
      self do: [ :aLetter |               * For each letter in the mailbox.
            Transcript cr.                * Sends a carriage return on the Transcript view.
            anInt printOn: Transcript.    * Prints the number.
            Transcript show: ' ';show: (aLetter sender);show: ' '.
            (aLetter date at: 1) printOn: Transcript.
            Transcript show: ' '.
            (aLetter date at: 2) printOn: Transcript.
            Transcript show:' ';show: (aLetter title).
            anInt ←anInt + 1]
```

For the method *destroy*, we use the predefined method **remove**. It is a method of the class **Collection**.

```
destroy: anInteger          * Removes the letter number anInteger.
      self remove: (self at: anInteger)

selectMbox: aName
      |aMailbox aSet|
      aSet ← self allInstances select :
                  [ :aMailbox | aMailbox name = aName].
      ↑ (aSet at: 1)

Object subclass: #Letter
      instanceVariableNames: 'title date sender recipient text '
      classVariableNames: ' '
```

```
create: aUser
    |aLetter aMailbox aUser2|
    aLetter ← Letter new.
    aLetter sender: aUser.
    aLetter date: (Time dateAndTimeNow).
    aUser2 ← 'continu'.
    [aUser2 =' ']              * While the name of the recipient is not an empty string.
      whileFalse:
        [aUser2 ←FillInTheBlank request: 'Name of recipient'.  * Asks for a name.
        (aUser2 =' ') and: [SetofUsers includes: aUser2]
                               * Verification of the existence of the user.
        ifTrue: [    (aLetter recipients) add: aUser2]]
    aLetter title: (FillInTheBlank request: 'Title ').
    aLetter text: (FillInTheBlank request: 'Text').
    aLetter recipients do:     * Puts the letter in the mailbox of the recipient.
        [ :aUser2 | aMailbox ← Mailbox selectMbox:aUser2.
        aMailbox addLast: aLetter]
```

The instance methods of the class Letter are the usual ones that retrieve and update instance variables. There is also *reply: aUser*, when *aUser* wants to reply to the receiver; *display*, which displays the receiver on the Transcript view; and *copy: aFile*, which copies the receiver on *aFile*.

```
reply: aUser
    |aLetter aMailbox|
    aLetter ← Letter new.
    aLetter sender: aUser.
    aLetter date: Time dateAndTimeNow.
    aLetter recipients add: (self sender).
    aLetter title: ('Re:', (self title)).
                        * The comma is the method that concatenates two strings.
    aLetter text: (FillInTheBlank request: 'Text of the reply?').
    aMailbox ← Mailbox selectMbox: (self sender).
    aMailbox addLast: aLetter

display
    Transcript cr.
    Transcript show: 'Date: '.
    (self date at: 1) printOn: Transcript.
    (self date at: 2) printOn: Transcript.
    Transcript cr; show: 'From: '; show: self sender.
    Transcript cr; show: 'To: ';
    self recipients do: [ :aUser | Transcript show:  aUser]
    Transcript cr; show: 'Title: '; show: self title.
    Transcript cr; show: self text.
    Transcript cr

copy: aFile
    |aUser|
    (self date at: 1) printOn: aFile.
    (self date at: 2) printOn: aFile.
    '.' printOn: aFile.
    self sender printOn: aFile.
    '.' printOn: aFile.
    self recipients do:
        [ :aUser | aUser printOn: aFile].
    '.' printOn: aFile.
    self title printOn: aFile.
    '.' printOn: aFile.
    self text printOn: aFile.
    '.' printOn: aFile.
```

Finally, the main program is a class method of the class Mailbox and has the name of the user as parameter.

```
mainloop: aUser
    |current clic aMailbox copied destroyed read aLetter|
    aMailbox ← Mailbox selectMbox: aUser.        * aMailbox is the mailbox of the user.
    aMailbox header.                  * Displays the headers of all letters in the mailbox.
    current ← 1.                      * The current letter is the first one.
    read ← Set new.                   * This set will contain the letters read by the user.
    copied ← Set new.                 * This set will contain the letters copied into a file.
    destroyed ← Set new.              * This set will contain the letters destroyed by the user.
    clic ← 1.
    [(clic = 8) | (clic = 9)]         * | is the disjunction.
        whileFalse:                   * Loops until the user clicks on "stop".
            [clic ← (PopUpMenu labels: 'header send reply display next remove copy quit exit')
                            startUpWithCaption: 'Help yourself'.
            clic = 1 ifTrue: [aMailbox header].
            clic = 2 ifTrue: [Letter create: aUser].
            clic = 3 ifTrue: [aLetter ← aMailbox at: current.
                            (destroyed includes: aLetter)  * Has the letter been destroyed?
                              ifTrue: [Transcript show: "Message destroyed"]
                              ifFalse: [aLetter reply: aUser]].
            clic = 4 ifTrue: [aLetter ← aMailbox at: current.
                            (destroyed includes: aLetter)
                              ifTrue: [Transcript show: "Message destroyed"]
                              ifFalse: [aLetter display.
                                        read add: aLetter]].
            clic = 5 ifTrue: [current ← current + 1.
                            (current > aMailbox size) ifTrue: [current ← 1]].
            clic = 6 ifTrue: [destroyed add: (aMailbox at: current).
                            read remove: (aMailbox at: current)].
            clic = 7 ifTrue: [aLetter ←aMailbox at: current.
                            (destroyed includes: aLetter)
                              ifTrue: [Transcript show: "Message destroyed"]
                              ifFalse: [
                                  aString ← (FillInTheBlank request: 'Name of the file ').
                                  aFile ← FileStream fileNamed: aString.
                                  aLetter copy: aFile.
                                  copied add: aLetter.
                                  read remove: aLetter]]].
                                * End of the "while" loop.
    (clic = 8)                        * If the user exits by the quit command.
      ifTrue: [ read do: [ :aLetter | aLetter copy: "mbox". aMailbox remove: aLetter].
              copied do: [ :aLetter | aMailbox remove: aLetter].
              destroyed do: [ :aLetter | aMailbox remove: aLetter]]
```

A.5 The O_2 Programs

A.5.1 The Bill of Materials Application

First we declare the classes Part, Atomic_part, and Derived_part.

```
add class Part type tuple(name: string)
    method price(): float,
    init(): Part is public,
    atomic(): Boolean is public,
    display_price() is public;

public read name in class Part;
        /* Makes the attribute name accessible from methods not of class Part. */

add class Atomic_part inherits Part
    type tuple(price: float, mass: float)
```

```
    method price(): float,
           atomic(): Boolean is public;

add class Derived_part inherits Part
    type tuple(incr_price: float,
           incr_mass: float,
           subparts: set(tuple(part: Part, qty: integer)))
    method price():float;
```

Then we declare the class Set_of_parts, and the named object set_of_parts is created and initialized.

```
add class Set_of_parts type set(Part)
    method     display() is public,
         add_new_part() is public;

public * in class Set_of_parts;        /* The structure of the class is made public. */

add name set_of_parts: Set_of_parts;
execute co2 {set_of_parts = new(Set_of_parts);}    /* Initialization of the object. */
```

Next we declare the application and programation of the *init* that starts the application.

```
add application part_manager
    program init();

body init() in application part_manager
co2 { int pid;
    prologue(0,0,500,500,"application part/subparts"); /* Opens the virtual screen. */
    /* The two following lines load specific editors. */
    set_correspondence("Choice_form", "choice");
    set_correspondence("Multichoice_form", "multichoice");
    pid = [set_of_parts display_level_one];         /* Displays the set of all parts. */
    lock(pid);
    /* Stops the application until the user clicks on the "pencil" or the "eraser". */
    epilogue();                                     /* Erases the virtual screen. */
    }
```

Task 2 Simple selection on base parts. The query is to print the name, cost, and weight of every base part that costs more than Fr 100.

```
    select part
    from part in set_of_parts
    where ([part atomic] and ([part price()] > 100))
```

The method *atomic* will return "false" if it is not a base part, and "true" if it is.

```
body atomic() : Boolean in class Part
co2 {return(false); }

body atomic() : Boolean in class Atomic_part
co2 {return(true); }
```

Task 3 Print the total cost and the total weight of a composite part. This task calls for a recursive traversal of the parts-composition hierarchy of the database. The *price* method does the job.

```
body price(): float in class Atomic_part
co2 { return(self→price); }

body price(): float in class Derived_part
co2 { float p;
      o2 tuple(part: Part, qty: integer) subpart;
      p = self→incr_price;
      for (subpart in self→subparts)
      p+=([subpart.part price] * subpart.qty);
      return(p);
      }
```

The method *display_price* displays the result.

```
body display_price() in class Part
co2 {        char * mes;
        int pid;
        mes = (char *) malloc(30);
        sprintf(mes, "The price of a %s is %d", self→name, [self price()]);
        [Dialoger  message(mes)];           /* Dialoger is a named object used to display
                                       messages or to ask questions to the user.  */
        }
```

Task 4 Record in the database a new manufacturing step.

```
body init(): Part in class Part
co2 { o2 Part part, new_part;
      o2  set(Part) set_part;
      int p;
      p = [self display_level_one];
      consult(p, &new_part);
      set_part =      select part from part in *set_of_parts
                      where (!(strcmp(new_part→name, part→name))) end;
      if (set_part ≠ set())
            { [Dialoger message("There already exists a part with that name ")];
            [element (set_part) display_level_one];
            return((o2 Part) nil);
            }
      else
            { *set_of_parts += set(new_part);
            [Dialoger message("New part created")];
            return(new_part);
            }
      }

body add_new_part() in class Set_of_parts
co2 {  o2 Part part;
      if ([Dialoger yes_no("Is it a base part?")])
            part = [new(Atomic_part) init];
      else part = [new(Derived_part) init];
      }

body display() in class Set_of_parts
co2 { o2 Part part;
      for (part in *self)
            [part display_level_one];
      }
```

A.5.2 The Unix Mail Application

Creation of the schema of the database and of the O_2 application:

```
add application Mailo2 program init();

add class Message
      type tuple(date: Date,
            sender: string,
            to: set(string),
            subject: string,
            text: Text)
      method delete() is public,
            save() is public,
            reply() is public;

public * in class Message;

add class Mailbox
      type tuple(name: string,
            messages: list(Message),
            controls: list(string),
            mbox: set(Message));

public * in class Mailbox;

add name Mail_Menu: object
      method headers() is public,
            display() is public,
            send() is public;

add name Mail_o2: object
      method select_mailbox(): integer is public,
            create_user() is public;

add name Usergroup: set(Mailbox);
add name Current_box: Mailbox;
add name Reply_box: Mailbox;
add name Current_message: integer;
add name Last_message: integer;
```

The main program is automatically executed at the beginning of the application.

```
body init() in application Mailo2
co2 { int p;
      prologue(200, 200, 700, 500, "Mail O2"); /* Establishes the client-server connection. */
      p = [Mail_O2 display_icon];
      lock(p); destroy(p);
      epilogue();                               /* Disconnection. */
};
```

Methods of the named object Mail_o2 to select and create mailboxes:

```
body select_mailbox(): integer in name Mail_o2  /* This method selects a mailbox. */
co2 {
      int p, res, i;
      o2 string name;
      o2 Mailbox a_user;
      o2 set(Mailbox) query;
      o2 list(Message) tmplist;
      o2 Message msg;
```

```
    if( Usergroup == (o2 set(Mailbox))(set()) ) {          /* Tests the Usergroup. */
        [Dialoger message("No user, create one")];
        return(0);
    }
    do { name = [Dialoger question("User name?")];         /* Selects a user. */
        query = select a_user from a_user in Usergroup
            where !strcmp(a_user→name, name) end;
    } while( query == (o2 set(Mailbox))set() );

    Current_box = element( query );
    Current_message = 1;

    if( Current_box→messages == (o2 list(Message))(list()) ) { /* Tests the mailbox. */
        [Dialoger message("No mail")];
        [Mail_menu display_icon];
    }
    else {                                                  /* Mailbox manipulation. */
        Last_message = (count(Current_box→messages));
        p = [Mail_menu display_icon];
        [Mail_menu headers];                                /* Displays headers. */
        res = lock(p);                                      /* Suspends execution. */

        if( res==CLICK_SAVE ){                              /* Saves and exits. */
            tmplist = list();
            for( msg in Current_box→messages ) {
                i = ( msg ?? Current_box→messages );
                if( !strcmp(Current_box→controls[i], "N") ) tmplist += list(msg);
                if( !strcmp(Current_box→controls[i], "R") )
                        Current_box→mbox += set(msg);
            }
            Current_box→messages = tmplist;
        }
        Current_box→controls = list();
        for( msg in Current_box→messages ) Current_box→controls += list("N");
        destroy(p);
    }
    return(1);
};

body create_user() in name Mail_o2                          /* This method creates a user. */
co2 {
    o2 Mailbox a_user;
    o2 string name;
    o2 set(Mailbox) query;

    name = [Dialoger question("User name?")];               /* Asks for a user. */
    query = select a_user from a_user in Usergroup
        where !strcmp(a_user→name, name) end;
    if( query == (o2 set(Mailbox))set() ) {                /* Creates the user. */
        a_user = new(Mailbox);
        a_user→name = name;
        a_user→messages = list();
        a_user→controls = list();
        a_user→mbox = set();
        Usergroup += set(a_user);                           /* Inserts the user. */
    }
    else [Dialoger message("User exists")];
};
```

Methods of the named object Mail_menu to manipulate a mailbox:

```
body headers() in name Mail_menu /* This method displays the headers of the messages. */
co2 {
```

```
        o2 tuple(number: integer,
                control: string,
                date: Date,
                sender: string,
                subject: string) head;
        o2 list( tuple(number: integer,
                control: string,
                date: Date,
                sender: string,
                subject: string)) Headers;
        o2 Message msg;
        int i = 0, p;

        Headers = list();
        for(msg in Current_box→messages) {
                head.number = i+1;
                head.control = Current_box→controls[i++];
                head.date = msg→date;
                head.sender = msg→sender;
                head.subject = msg→subject;
                Headers += list(head);
        }
        p = present(Headers, NO_EDIT, LEVEL_ONE, NESTED_WINDOW);
        map(p, SCREEN, MANUAL, NO_PERSIST, 0, 0);
};


body display() in name Mail_menu /* This method displays the current or the nth message. */
co2 {
        int nb;

        nb = [Dialoger question("Number of the message?")]; /* Asks for a message number. */
        if( nb < 0 || nb > Last_message || !strcmp(Current_box→controls[nb-1],"*") )
                                                        /* Tests the message number. */
                [Dialoger message("Unknown message")];
        else {
                if( nb ) Current_message = nb;
                [Current_box→messages[Current_message-1] display_all_you_can_show];
                                                        /* Displays the message. */
                if( !strcmp(Current_box→controls[Current_message-1],"N") )
                                                        /* Updates the control list. */
                        Current_box→controls[Current_message-1] = "R";
                Current_message++;
        }
};


body send() in name Mail_menu                   /* This method sends a message. */
co2 {
        int p;
        o2 Message msg;
        o2 Mailbox a_user;
        o2 set(Mailbox) query;
        o2 string recipient;

        msg = new(Message);
        msg→date = Today;
        msg→sender = Current_box→name;
        p = [msg display_all_you_can_show]; /* Asks for a message. */
        lock(p);
        for( recipient in msg→to ) {            /* Searches for the recipients. */
                query = select a_user from a_user in Usergroup
                        where !strcmp(a_user→name, recipient) end;
                if( query == (o2 set(Mailbox))set() ) [Dialoger message("Unknown user")];
                else {
                        Reply_box = element(query);
                                        /* Sends the message to the recipient's mailbox. */
```

```
                    Reply_box→messages += list(msg);
                    Reply_box→controls += list("N");
                }
        }
        destroy(p);
};
```

Methods of the class Message:

```
body delete() in class Message            /* This method deletes a message. */
co2 {
        int i;
        i = ( self ?? Current_box→messages );
        Current_box→controls[i] = "*";     /* Updates the control list. */
};

body save() in class Message              /* This method saves a message into a file. */
co2 {
        #undef NULL
        #include <stdio.h>
        FILE *fic;
        o2 string path, line;
        int i;

        path = [Dialoger question("Name of the file?")];    /* Asks for a file. */
        i = ( self ?? Current_box→messages );
        Current_box→controls[i] = "R";                      /* Updates the control list. */

        fic = fopen(path, "a");                             /* Writes the message. */
        fprintf(fic,"Date: %s, From: %s, Subject: %sOo: ", self→date, self→sender, self→subject );
        for( line in self→to ) fprintf(fic,"%s, ", line );
        for( line in self→text→text ) fprintf(fic,"30s", line );
        fflush(fic); fclose(fic);
};

body reply() in class Message     /* This method sends a response. */
co2 {
        int p, res;
        o2 Message msg;
        o2 Mailbox a_user;
        o2 set(Mailbox) query;

        msg = new(Message);
        msg→date = Today;
        msg→sender = Current_box→name;
        msg→subject = (char*)malloc( strlen(self→subject)+10 );
        sprintf( msg→subject, "Re: %s", self→subject );
        p = [msg display_all_you_can_show];
                                /* Asks for a message. */
        res = lock(p);
        if( res == CLICK_SAVE ) {
                query = select a_user from a_user in Usergroup
                                /* Searches for the recipient. */
                        where !strcmp(a_user→name, self→sender) end;
                Reply_box = element( query );
                                /* Sends the message to the recipient's mailbox. */
                Reply_box→messages += list(msg);
                Reply_box→controls += list("N");
        }
        destroy(p);
};
```

Part IV

The System

CHAPTER 14

Introduction to the System

CLAUDE DELOBEL
FERNANDO VÉLEZ

Relational database systems are implemented using well-understood technology for the efficient manipulation of large amounts of persistent, shared, and reliable data. Declarative (relational calculus) queries are automatically translated into procedural (relational algebra) queries. These are usually represented in the system as annotated algebraic trees. Their evaluation is planned by an optimizer that uses algebraic properties of the relational operators and knowledge about database sizes, access paths, indexes, and so on. Current optimizer technology is used at both query-compile time and run-time. It achieves execution plans that, even if suboptimal, are of high efficiency. The state of the art has been greatly advanced by 20 years of research in such areas as data representation, optimal transformation of queries into sequences of algebraic operations, indexing techniques, and concurrency control.

In the case of object-oriented database management systems (OODBMSs) the implementation problems are more complex and quite challenging. This is largely due to the rich and extensible nature of the new data models.

Objects are much more than flat tuples. The new data models allow (and encourage) the user to define new abstract data types, whose instances are objects. The object-oriented programming paradigm is based on the concept of inheritance hierarchies of abstract data types, combined with message passing. In this setting, query translation into "equivalent relational-like" algebraic trees is problematic. This greatly complicates optimization. In parts 2 and 3 we examined in detail how to specify an object-oriented data model, using the O_2 database programming language and query language. The critical issue, which we examine in part 4, is the efficient implementation of these new linguistic formalisms on top of an object manager.

The O_2 *object manager* represents the major part of the system and accounts for a large fraction of the project's software engineering effort. It consists of the layers of the system that deal with the representation and organization of objects into main memory and secondary memory; the transfer of data between main memory and secondary memory; the implementation of method calls; the creation and deletion of objects; the distribution in a server/workstation environment; concurrency and recovery mechanisms; indexing and some query optimization; and versions.

The design, implementation, and testing we describe here is one of a number of such recent experimental efforts. For example, similar questions about building object managers were addressed (sometimes analogously, often differently) in the Encore/ObServer (Hornick and Zdonik 1987), Exodus (Carey et al. 1990), GemStone (Maier, Otis, and Purdy 1985), Iris (Fishman et al. 1987), Orion (Kim et al. 1990), and Postgres (Stonebraker and Rowe 1986) projects. Also, implementation techniques developed for persistent programming languages, such as Smalltalk (Kaehler and Krasner 1983; Kaehler 1986), and PS-Algol (Cockshott et al. 1984), are very useful for building an object manager.

The remainder of this chapter is organized as follows. We first describe the main technical challenges, which correspond to principal components of the object manager. We then describe the successive generations of the O_2 prototype. We then put this system in perspective by describing how it addresses the technical challenges and by comparing it to other systems. We close with a roadmap of part 4.

1 The Functionality of an Object Manager

An object manager must address a variety of issues, some related to the (new) object orientation and others related to the (standard) database functionality. For example, it must provide for the direct support of many data model features, the efficient disk access of new data types, the coexistence of large- and small-sized data, and the persistence of complex objects beyond application-program executions. In addition, it is expected to provide traditional features such as facilities for data distribution and transaction management. Also, optional features of older technologies, such as version management, become more important given the potential applications of the system. Let us examine these requirements more carefully.

1.1 Direct Support for the Data Model

Direct support means that the object manager must understand the basic elements of the data model. It must (1) represent O_2 objects and values in main memory and on disk; (2) implement object identity (or provide mechanisms to simulate it; we come back to this point when we discuss efficient disk access);

(3) implement message passing to objects and, as the need arises, dynamically load methods; and (4) implement structural operations on values and objects.

Depending on the constructors used in the data model, objects may have different structures via their associated values: tuples, sets, lists, or arrays. These may be recursively composed of component objects. Furthermore, the representation of objects in main memory may be different from that on disk. For example, a disk representation could be geared to associative access, whereas a main memory representation could favor navigational operations through composite objects or put objects in a format understandable by a given programming language. In fact, the issue is: *How much knowledge about the details of the data model do the internal layers of the object manager (such as the disk management layer) need to have?* There is a tradeoff here, which we attempt to summarize in the next two paragraphs. For a more detailed discussion see the "Implementation Issues" chapter of Zdonik and Maier 1990.

When the internal layers know about the full details of the data model, there is a large potential for optimization. For example, type-specific concurrency control can be enforced if the lock manager knows which methods of a class commute with each other. However, this involves introducing data-model-related complexity at all levels of the system, and makes the entire object manager dependent on small changes in the data model's specifications. An example of this aproach is GemStone. The internal layer, Stone, understands the internal structure of objects as well as interobject references; it can therefore support garbage collection and indexes on composition paths.

When the internal layers involve a simpler data model, it is easier to reuse some components for implementing object stores for other systems or languages. However, data-model-dependent optimizations have to be implemented now in the upper layers of the system. For example, if the storage layer does not understand the notion of a tuple attribute, then indexes on collections of tuple objects cannot be implemented at this level. An example of this approach is the Encore/ObServer system. ObServer, the storage manager, handles uninterpreted, uniquely identified chunks of data. It is therefore capable of providing database support for various kinds of systems: the Encore object-oriented type system and language, or the Garden programming environment (Reiss 1987).

1.2 Efficient Access to Objects

There are three different, but interdependent, issues concerning efficient access to objects on disk. The first is related to object identity. An object identifier can be logical or physical. Logical identifiers, unlike physical identifiers, give no information about location in secondary memory. Therefore a correspondence table between logical identifiers and physical addresses is needed. Logical identifiers preserve the independence of objects with respect to location, but they decrease the access efficiency since we need an intermediate catalog to interpret and find the locations of objects. Related to object identity is the movement of data from secondary storage to main-memory storage. When objects are moved from one place to another, do they preserve their identity? The format of the object identifiers does not need to be the same in main memory and in secondary memory. Objects loaded from disk into main memory have an entry in a *resident object table.* Each entry in the table gives the address of the object in main memory. Systems like Smalltalk and PS-Algol convert disk references into main-memory addresses. The conversion is done only for objects pointing to the loaded objects. This technique is called *pointer swizzling.*

The second issue is that of clustering. Efficiency can be improved by grouping objects that are accessed simultaneously, either on the same physical page or in the same segment in secondary storage. Traditional database systems also have this *clustering* as a goal, in order to minimize the retrieval cost; however, the new data models, configuration environment and applications are quite different. Clustering can be *static* or *dynamic.* Static clustering is done at the time objects are created; dynamic clustering is done when objects are accessed. Usually the inputs of a clustering algorithm are access patterns for objects, providing information about the frequency of accesses to one object from another. The fact that objects are instances of abstract data types can be exploited; for example, the code implementing a method can be used to deduce access patterns.

The third issue is that of associative accesses. In relational systems, indexing is applied to atomic attribute values. All the techniques for optimizing queries use, up to a certain point, indexing facilities. In an object-oriented system we face new considerations: (1) objects are accessed by their identity and not by their value since the value is encapsulated; (2) objects are instances of classes, which may belong to a class hierarchy, and this hierarchy can be used to specify which classes are indexed; (3) the domain of an attribute is not necessarily atomic; it may be another class of objects, so that we can define an index not only on one attribute but also on a composition of attributes; and (4) the domain of an attribute may be a derived value computed from a method; in this case, indexing may be difficult because the result of the method can change if either the inputs of the method change or the result of the methods it invokes change.

A better integration between the query language and the host object-oriented programming language leads to these and other research questions on efficient disk access. Consequently, the scope of optimization is not limited to query optimization but becomes that of overall program optimization.

1.3 Variations in Object Size

Since objects are composed of other objects, an object may be small or large. An object is large if its size is greater than the physical page. Manipulating large objects is an essential requirement of many new applications addressed by OODBMSs.

The object manager has to provide efficient storage management facilities to handle the different types of large objects, such as large atoms (e.g., bitmaps or text), large tuples, or large sets. The existing technology of managing long fields of data (e.g., breaking up the field into small pieces and building a B-tree index for the pieces) can only offer partial solutions, and new technology must be developed.

1.4 Persistence of Objects between Program Executions

Persistence of data can be implemented in different ways: (1) by *typing*: an object has a type and we can declare that some types are persistent, so that every instance of this type is a persistent object; (2) by *reachability*: if an object is connected, through direct or indirect references, to some persistent roots, then the object is persistent; (3) by *storing*: if there is a persistent space (e.g., a file system), every object which is explicitly bound into this space is persistent; (4) by *object indication*: there can be some parameters associated with the object which indicate whether the object is persistent or not.

1.5 Database Distribution

Databases have evolved from being centralized resources to being distributed ones. For example, with the emergence of new applications such as CAD, databases tend to be used with graphical interfaces that only a dedicated single-user workstation can provide. Furthermore, this workstation has to interact with one or several servers where the permanent information is stored.

Distribution requirements can be achieved in two steps. The first is the *interconnectivity* of systems; this is currently achieved in many organizations. In an object-oriented database system the unit of processing can be considered to be the execution of a method; if we have interconnectivity, we can move this execution from one site to another to improve efficiency. The next step is *interoperability*. Two or more systems are interoperable if they can interact to perform jointly a global task. For example, a relational database system might be encapsulated as a service and be invoked from another object-oriented system.

1.6 Transaction Processing

From a database point of view, OODBMSs must provide concurrent and reliable access to objects via transaction management. The main techniques of transaction management were developed as part of the original relational database systems. In most cases, this technology abstracts a transaction as a sequence of read and write operations. One might ask whether transaction management in object-oriented systems is like transaction processing in more traditional databases; this would allow direct reuse of the available technology.

However, in OODBMSs more information is available about the operations than just read and write sets. This information can be collected by a static analysis of the methods (the only handles for objects) and can be used to increase concurrency. Moreover, for design applications classical algorithms such as two-phase locking are inadequate, because they ignore that transactions are typically very long (they might span the execution of programs). A long transaction should not lose an arbitrary amount work if a crash occurs. These facts have led to new research on design transactions. For example, one way of defining design transactions is by breaking a long transaction into a tree of *nested transactions;* another is by connecting the transaction mechanism with the versions mechanism.

1.7 Database Versions

Nontraditional applications of databases, such as CAD, OIS, and software engineering, need to track object evolution over time. Versions can record the history of the values of an object. The set of values over time of an object is called its *version set.* Individual versions in a version set may also be partially ordered according to a *derivation hierarchy,* expressing the successive derivation of an object from the user's point of view.

The interaction between version management, object identifiers, and object type has led to new research problems. (1) An object o may reference another object o'. If o' is a versionable object, which version is referenced? There are two kinds of referencing: *static* or *dynamic.* A static reference identifies one specific version. A dynamic reference is interpreted at run time to give one or several versions. This can be considered as a query against the version set. (2) When versions of the objects but not of the schema are allowed, the simplest problem of consistency is to determine which versions of two objects can form a consistent database. (3) When versions of the schema are allowed, how does one know whether two different versions of an object belong to the same class? This is one of the harder cases of the general problem of multiversion database consistency.

2 Historical View of the O_2 Approach

The O_2 object manager has been developed through two complete implementation cycles. The first involved a throw-away prototype called V0, reported in Bancilhon et al. 1988. The second produced the preindustrial prototype called V1, which is described in this book.

2.1 The V0 Object Manager

The pure object model of V0 is presented in chapter 3. No values other than atomic values were supported; nor were large atomic strings of bytes. The only bulk-data type constructor was the set constructor, and the inheritance scheme was that of simple inheritance. The persistence model was that of typing. A class was declared to be either persistent or temporary; all objects of a persistent class were persistent at creation time and could be deleted only with an explicit command.

The project started with the idea of developing server software around the Pick operating system. There was a strong nontechnical reason for this choice: Pick was the operating system of choice of the private company supporting the project. The object manager was split into a server process and a workstation process. The server process ran on an IN-8000 machine supporting the Pick file system (PFS) and the SCORE transaction manager (PFS and SCORE in combination provide a transaction-oriented storage system that handles record-structured files of varying-length attributes). The workstations were Sun machines running Unix. The connection between the workstations and the server was ensured by a serial line between a Sun server and the IN-8000. The workstation processes ran two independent modules: the schema manager, managing classes and methods; and the object manager, managing instances of classes or objects. The schema manager was implemented in an ad hoc way: information on classes and methods was loaded into C structures at application startup and saved back to a Unix file at application commit. The object manager stored objects in Pick files and used the primitives supplied by PFS and SCORE.

The V0 object manager was implemented with no concern about performance. There were no disk-management techniques (no indexing, no optimization techniques, no disk clustering, and inefficient object buffering as a result of implementing a strict LRU policy), and memory management for varying-length structures was very simple. However, the basic technique for identifying objects on disk and in memory (i.e., physical identifiers for objects and a hash-based resident-object table to retrieve them in memory) was already present in the V0 implementation.

In summary, many of the design decisions for V0 were specific to this version only, but despite the limitations of this implementation cycle a number of important goals were achieved. V0 helped in making the design of O_2 much more precise. It gave us confidence regarding the feasibility of building this new design. The various project teams gained valuable experience in order to tackle the problems of V1 and to be able to coordinate their tasks.

2.2 The V1 Object Manager

The target platform was shifted from Pick-based machines to Unix-based machines. We tried to replace PFS and SCORE with an equivalent Unix-compatible system, but the exact equivalent was not found. Our choice was to use WiSS, the Wisconsin Storage System (Chou et al. 1985)—a similar storage manager but one that has no support for rollbacks and recovery.

The functionality implemented is larger than in V0, as the final data model is more complex. Structured values were introduced, the list bulk constructor was introduced, tuples could have exceptional attributes, named objects could have exceptional behavior, and large strings of bytes were supported. The persistence model also evolved toward persistence by reachability, which in our opinion is cleaner but more difficult to implement. In fact, persistence "propagates" in a graph of objects. This is a converse of garbage collection, which has to be dealt with anyway in object managers.

The architecture also changed. The server process in V1 understands the concept of object (not only its record storage repository) and is capable of applying methods to objects. Therefore each client process in a workstation has a corresponding server-process peer in the server machine. The object buffer was put in shared memory, as were the internal structures of WiSS, including its page buffer; this entailed a painful conversion of the WiSS code to use Unix semaphores to enforce critical sections. The communication manager between the two processes became a sophisticated piece of code. In fact, embedded execution transfers may appear: if a selection operation which is to be run on the server displays one tuple per 1000 on the average (in the workstation), the two sites may act alternatively as client or server. Thus this protocol became more involved than the classical remote procedure call (RPC) mechanism.

Performance considerations are reflected in the design. First, the difference between development mode and execution mode is recognized, and the object manager is designed to support both modes. Second, the schema manager manages its data as objects, but with a special concurrency control in development mode, because schema objects are the hot spot in the system in this mode. Third, the manipulation of objects in memory was more carefully implemented and a fast dynamic linker and loader was built to accelerate message passing in development mode. Finally, both a disk clustering scheme and an indexing scheme were designed and implemented.

Let us now examine how the V1 object manager addresses the technical challenges outlined in the previous section, and compare it to some of the other implemented object managers.

3 The Capabilities of the O_2 System

3.1 Data Model and Large Objects

The O_2 object manager implements structural operations on objects, provides support for message passing, and performs associative access operations through indexes. It has a two-layer architecture in which the lower layer, the Storage Manager, is WiSS. We call the upper layer the Object Manager layer.

The O_2 data model (presented in chapter 3) distinguishes between *values*, on which we can perform any of a set of predefined primitives, and *objects,* which have identities and encapsulate values and user-defined *methods*. In the object manager, objects and values are mapped to WiSS records if they are persistent, or to records in virtual memory if they are temporary.

The design decisions for the mapping of objects and values into records in disk format are the following:

1. An object and the root of its value are stored in one record.

2. Nonatomic (i.e., constructed) values are decomposed into records on type-constructor boundaries. So for example, a tuple value containing a set-valued attribute and an integer attribute will be stored in at least two records. Atomic values are embedded in their parent record, the only exception being large strings, which are stored in one or more records.

3. List and set values are small if their corresponding record fits in one page, otherwise they are large and they consume more than one record.

4. Values have a representation that is similar to that of objects, but they behave differently: they have a *copy* semantics. For example, when returning a set-structured value attribute, the identifier of a copy of the set value is returned and, if the set is itself a set of tuple values, the copy is recursive.

The mapping of objects and values into logical units of records on disk is the most straightforward one. It has been used in various systems, including GemStone, Orion, Bubba (Copeland, Franklin, and Weikum 1990), and POMS (Cockshott et al. 1984). The main drawback of this approach is that to retrieve the whole object we have to recompose it by finding the different subcomponents. This can lead to more than one access. In O_2 this drawback is mitigated by the clustering algorithm, which attempts to store all the subcomponents in one page. Other approaches are possible. In the direction of more decomposition, object states may be subdivided at a finer granularity (an attribute or a group of attributes), as in Iris (Fishman et al. 1987) or Adaplex (Chan et al. 1982). In the direction of more composition, the Emerald system (Jul et al. 1985) goes a step further by letting component objects that have no external references to them be represented as parts of a (composite) object.

WiSS was designed, in fact, as a lower layer of a relational system, but it provides important features that make it useful as an object-oriented storage manager: (1) unique identifiers for records (see below); (2) support for data items, which can be arbitrarily long; (3) records of varying length; and (4) a record-at-a-time type of interface. In this last respect, WiSS is different from systems such as Iris and Postgres, in which the upper layers interface with the storage layer in terms of algebraic operators.

From the architectural point of view WiSS, the storage manager of O_2, provides persistent structures such as record-structured sequential files. It has a simple notion of attribute value within a record, and therefore indexes (B-tree or hash based) on a file can be defined. In this respect it is richer than the Encore/ObServer system which supports a primitive view of objects as uninterpreted blocks of data with identifiers. On the other hand, GemStone and Orion are systems built from scratch. GemStone understands the internal structure of objects and knows about object classes. As it understands interobject references, it can support garbage collection and indexes on composition paths. The Orion storage manager seems fairly close to WiSS.

3.2 Efficient Access to Objects

Object identity is implemented as a physical reference to disk space. It is equivalent to a record identifier (RID) inside WiSS. RIDs are used as identifiers for persistent objects and as physical pointers for constructed values, even though the latter are never shared. In this chapter the "identifier of a value" refers to the physical pointer of its record. To access resident records (those in a cache), we use a table hashed on RID. Our choice for physical identifiers was largely motivated by performance considerations. The alternative would be logical identifiers, which give no information about their location in secondary memory, as in GemStone (Maier, Otis, and Purdy 1985), Orion (Kim et al. 1990), and ObServer (Hornick and Zdonik 1987).

To move records on disk, the solution we adopted is to use the forward-marker technique implemented by WiSS. When accessing on disk a record which has been moved elsewhere, we perform two disk accesses: one to retrieve the forwarding RID and the other to retrieve the record. Note that if a record is further moved, there is no need to leave another marker behind, as the only reference to its current physical location is in the original marker.

When objects are loaded into main memory their identity is preserved. There is no swizzling, and objects are maintained in a resident-object hash table. The movement of an object from disk to main memory goes through different layers, since we are in a workstation/server configuration (see section 3.4).

The mapping of objects and values to files is controlled by the *placement trees* clustering technique implemented in the Object Manager layer. A placement tree expresses the way in which a composite object and its object or value components will be clustered together. Placements trees are traversed at commit time to determine the file into which the record is to be inserted. Our placement tree clustering technique is similar to the one proposed by Scholnick 1977 for the hierarchical data model. Scholnick's idea was to partition a hierarchical tree structure into subtrees and to find the best partition according to some access patterns inside the hierarchical structure. Our strategy follows the same idea, except that (1) the data model is not the same (object sharing, inheritance relationship), (2) clustering is done at commit time, and (3) clustering is invisible to the programmer, so that placement trees can be modified at any time without affecting programs. In ObServer objects are grouped into a visible segment. A segment can be composed of an object and its subobjects, in a hierarchical tree structure; and it may contain all the objects of the same type. This segment is the unit of transfer between a workstation and the server. GemStone also provides segments for clustering objects.

Indexes are provided at the Object Manager layer, using those already provided by the Storage Manager, WiSS. This is because indexes at this level take into account the specifics of the O_2 data model.

3.3 Persistence

Persistence is defined in the O_2 data model as reachability from persistent root objects or values, which are explicitly named by the programmer in the database schema definition. This is implemented by associating a reference count with each object or value. A temporary record becomes persistent by being made a component of a parent record. The corresponding RID, which is delivered only on insertion of the corresponding WiSS record, is assigned at transaction commit in order to avoid extensive message exchange between the two machines. As persistence is by reachability, there is no explicit command for deleting objects. Objects are garbage collected when they are no longer referenced.

POMS and GemStone also implement a reachability-based persistence model. By contrast, Orion, Iris, and Postgres have a persistence-by-typing model. OODBMSs based on C++ chose among two different approaches to add persistence (Atwood and Hanna 1990). The first approach is to define persistence at the level of the language, as a storage class. In this approach, followed by the ObjectStore system developed by Object Design, persistence is orthogonal to type. At creation time, the programmer indicates whether the object is persistent or temporary; if it is persistent, he or she specifies the database in which the object will be stored. The second approach is to define persistence on top of the language, through inheritance from a virtual base class. This approach is exemplified by the Eastman Kodak class-library interface. Any class that has persistent instances then includes this class in its list of superclasses, and it inherits the requisite operations. The implementor of each class must supply the actual code to implement each of these virtual operations.

3.4 Database Distribution

The object manager is constructed from both workstation and server components. Both components have (almost) the same interface. The main distinction is in the actual implementation: the workstation component is single-user (as a workstation is single-user) and memory-based; while the server version is multi-user and disk-based.

The programmer is aware of the existence of two machines, the server and the workstation; he or she may explicitly specify on which of the machines a message-passing expression is to be executed. The server component understands the concept of object; this is why we call it the *object server*. So, for example, a method scanning through a collection and selecting elements according to given criteria may run much faster on the server if the collection is large and the selectivity factor is high, because the transfer of the entire collection to the workstation is avoided.

Remote method execution has to address the cache-inconsistency problem: the state of the object cache in the workstation is potentially different from the state of the object cache in the server. As there is no easy way to know what objects a method will reference, we decided to transfer the set of updated objects from one site to the other at execution migration time.

The Orion 1 prototype (Kim et al. 1990), ObServer (Hornick and Zdonik 1987), and some prerelease versions of GemStone (Copeland and Maier 1984) employed an object-server architecture. In ObServer the server does not understand the concept of object. In Orion a different strategy is used for remote execution. First, only queries, not arbitrary methods, can be executed remotely. A query is decomposed into one-class subqueries, and each subquery is evaluated both on the station and on the server. This is to avoid having to transfer large collections from the server to the workstation at query-processing time. Next, a merging phase is required when executing each subquery, because of the cache-inconsistency problem described above.

The design choices made when partitioning database functionality between the server and workstation processes are fundamental and have to be carefully studied. To better understand the alternatives for future versions of O_2, we carried out a study of three workstation-server architectures for implementing object-oriented database systems: *object server*, *page server*, and *file server.*

3.5 Transactions and Concurrency

In the O_2 prototype the concept of transaction is the traditional one, in which serializability is the correctness criterion for a concurrent execution of transactions. The popular two-phase locking algorithm on files and pages is used.

Most OODBMSs use some form of locking. Garza and Kim 1988 describe a proposal for the Orion transaction subsystem that uses *intention* locks and introduces composite objects and classes as locking granules. In ObServer, locking is also used, but nonserializable behavior can be controlled through *notify* locks. These locks allow a group of cooperating programmers to perform a global task to synchronize their view of data: a notify lock held by a programmer can make him or her aware that other programmers are accessing the locked data. GemStone uses an optimistic concurrency-control schema.

We felt that more research was needed in order to incorporate long- and/or nested-transaction technology into the prototype. Chapter 20 is a study of what pieces of the new technology can be used in O_2 and how. It examines three aspects of this technology: (1) the constraints placed on concurrency by the object-oriented approach, (2) the possible uses of the concept of *intention locks,* first suggested by Gray 1978, and (3) the possible definition of *nested* or *multilevel transactions* in O_2 (see, e.g., Beeri, Schek, and Weikum 1988).

3.6 Database Versions

In O_2 the version-consistency problem has been investigated independently of the V1 prototype. We hope that this research will be incorporated in subsequent implementations. Instead of *object versions,* the coarser concept of *database versions* is introduced. A database version stores one consistent state of a database and is identified by a timestamp. The basic idea of the approach is to use the familiar object-oriented notions of inheritance and late binding to maintain object versions within database versions.

If we look inside a database version, we see the versions of different objects. Each database version is created by derivation from another one. Thus the set of database versions is organized as a tree, called the *derivation tree.* For example, versions 0.1, 0.2, and 0.3 would be derived from version 0, and version 0.1.1 would be derived from 0.1. The set of versions of the same object can be visualized along the derivation tree, with some nodes deleted. This is because some versions of an object may be shared by several database versions.

To avoid redundancy in storing the control information about the relationships between the object versions and the database versions, the following rule is used: if the same object version is shared by two database versions in the same derivation branch, then only the information about the ancestor is stored. One may recognize here the traditional rule of inheritance. With the concept of database versions, the dereferencing is dynamic. Suppose that object o' references object o. Then, if we are in the context of database version 0.1, o' refers to its version $o_{0.1}$ of o; if we are in the context of database version 0.2, o' refers to $o_{0.2}$, and so on. This mechanism is equivalent to the late-binding resolution process for methods.

This approach is also useful for the versioning of composite objects (see Kim, Bertino, and Garza 1989). For example, if objects are linked with other objects by the *composition* relationship and/or the *is-part-of* relationship, then, when a new version of a component object is created, its propagation to the ancestor composite objects generates cascading creations of object versions.

Finally, we would like to note that Katz and Chang 1987 have proposed mechanisms to limit the scope of change propagations and ways to disambiguate their effects. For other approaches see Agrawal and Jagadish 1989, Kim, Bertino, and Garza 1989, and Zdonik 1986.

4 A Roadmap for Part 4

The papers presented in part 4 cover most of the commonly accepted requirements for an object manager. The first three papers reflect the status of the V1 prototype as of October 1989, when it was released. The last three papers, design studies from edited conference proceedings, will be useful in future O_2 implementations.

The general architecture of the Object Manager and the main design decisions are described in chapter 15 (Vélez, Bernard, and Darnis 1989), "The O_2 Object Manager: An Overview." The O_2 object manager is the lowest layer (using WiSS) that handles persistent and temporary objects in a server/workstation environment. This paper is an edited version of a VLDB-89 publication, in which the V1 implementation was first described.

The current prototype is distributed according to a workstation/server configuration. The main choices and the protocol used for moving objects between machines and for supporting execution on various machines are described in chapter 16, "Handling Distribution in the O_2 System."

Chapter 17 "Clustering Strategies in O_2: An Overview," is a synthesis of three papers: on functionalities and specifications (Benzaken and Delobel 1990), on a cost model (Benzaken 1990), and on a benchmark (Harrus, Benzaken, and Delobel 1990) similar to that of Cattell and Skeen 1990. Chapter 17 deals with the grouping of related objects on the same disk page.

Chapter 18 (DeWitt et al. 1990), "Three Alternative Workstation-Server Architectures," presents a comparison between three basic distribution architectures: object server, page server, and file server. The object server transfers individual objects between machines (this corresponds to the actual prototype), the page server transfers disk pages, and the file server transfers pages using a remote file service mechanism such as NFS. An understanding of these alternatives is fundamental for the development of future implementations.

Chapter 19 (Cellary and Jomier 1990), "Consistency of Versions in Object-Oriented Databases," investigates the possibility of defining a database version as a consistent configuration of object versions, making critical use of the object-oriented notions of inheritance and late binding.

Chapter 20 (Cart and Ferrié 1990), "Integrating Concurrency Control," investigates the possible integration of a large spectrum of concurrency control techniques in O_2.

References

Agrawal, R., and H. V. Jagadish. 1989. On correctly configuring versioned objects. In *Proceedings of the 15th VLDB conference.*

Atwood, T., and S. Hanna. 1990. Two approaches to adding persistence to C++. In *Proceedings of the fourth workshop on persistent object systems.*

Bancilhon, F., G. Barbedette, V. Benzaken, C. Delobel, S. Gamerman, C. Lécluse, P. Pfeffer, P. Richard, and F. Vélez. 1988. The design and implementation of O_2, an object-oriented database system. In *Proceedings of the second international workshop on object-oriented database systems,* ed. K. Dittrich.

Beeri, C., H. Schek, and G. Weikum. 1988. Multi-level transactions: Theoretical art or practical need? In *Proceedings of the first international conference on extending database technology.*

Benzaken, V. 1990. An evaluation model for clustering strategies in the O_2 object-oriented database system. In *Proceedings of the third international conference on database theory.*

Benzaken, V., and C. Delobel. 1990. Enhancing performance in a persistent object store: Clustering strategies in O_2. In *Proceedings of the fourth workshop on persistent object systems.*

Carey, M. et al. 1990. The Exodus extensible DBMS project: An overview. In *Readings in object-oriented database systems.* Morgan Kaufmann.

Cart, M., and J. Ferrié. 1990. Integrating concurrency control into an object-oriented database system. In *Proceedings of the second international conference on extending database technology.*

Cattell, R., and J. Skeen. 1990. *Engineering database benchmark.* Technical Report, Sun Microsystems, Inc.

Cellary, W., and G. Jomier. 1990. Consistency of versions in object-oriented databases. In *Proceedings of the 16th VLDB.*

Chan, A. et al. 1982. Storage and access structures to support a semantic data model. In *Proceedings of the eighth VLDB conference.*

Chou, H-T., D. DeWitt, R. Katz, and A. Klug. 1985. Design and implementation of the Wisconsin storage system. *Software Practice and Experience* 15(10).

Cockshott, W. P. et al. 1984. Persistent object management systems. *Software Practice and Experience* 14(1).

Copeland, G., M. Franklin, and G. Weikum. 1990. Uniform object management. In *Proceedings of the second international conference on extending database technology.*

Copeland G., and D. Maier. 1984. Making Smalltalk a database system. In *Proceedings of the ACM SIGMOD conference.*

DeWitt, D., P. Futtersack, D. Maier, and F. Vélez. 1990. A study of three alternative workstations/server architectures for object-oriented database systems. In *Proceedings of the 16th VLDB.*

Fishman, D., D. Beech, H. P. Cate, E. C. Chow, T. Conners, J. W. Davis, N. Denett, C. G. Hoch, W. Kent, P. Lyngbaek, B. Mahbod, M. A. Neimat, T. A. Ryan, and M. C. Shan. 1987. Iris: An object-oriented database management system. *ACM TOIS* 5(1): 46–69.

Garza, J., and W. Kim. 1988. Transaction management in an object-oriented database system. In *Proceedings of the ACM SIGMOD conference.*

Gray, J. 1978. *Notes on database operating systems.* IBM research report no. RJ2188. IBM Research, San Jose.

Harrus, G., V. Benzaken, and C. Delobel. 1990. *Measuring performance of clustering strategies: The Club-0 benchmark.* Altaïr Technical Report.

Hornick M., and S. Zdonik. 1987. A shared, segmented memory for an object-oriented database. *ACM TOIS* 5(1).

Kaehler, T. 1986. Virtual memory on a narrow machine for an object-oriented language. In *Proceedings of the OOPSLA conference.*

Kaehler, T., and G. Krasner. 1983. LOOM: Large object-oriented memory for Smalltalk-80 systems. In *Smalltalk-80: Bits of history, words of advice.* Addison-Wesley.

Katz, R., and E. Chang. 1987. Managing change in a computer-aided design database. In *Proceedings of the 13th VLDB conference.*

Kim, W., E. Bertino, and J. F. Garza. 1989. Composite objects revisited. *SIGMOD Record* 18(2).

Kim, W., K. C. Kim, and A. Dale. 1987. *Indexing techniques for object-oriented databases.* MCC technical report no. DB-134-87.

Kim, W. et al. 1990. Architecture of the Orion next generation database system. *IEEE Transactions on Data and Knowledge Engineering* (March).

Jul, E., H. Levy, N. Hutchinson, and A. Black. 1985. Fine-grained mobility in the Emerald system. *ACM Transactions on Programming Languages and Systems* 7: 244–69.

Maier, D., A. Otis, and A. Purdy. 1985. Development of an object-oriented DBMS. *Quarterly Bulletin of IEEE on Database Engineering* 8(4).

Maier, D., and J. Stein. 1986. Indexing in an object-oriented DBMS. In *Proceedings of the first international workshop on object-oriented database systems.*

Reiss, S. P. 1987. Working in the Garden environment for conceptual programming. *IEEE Software* 4: 16–27.

Scholnick, M. 1977. A clustering algorithm for hierarchical structures. *ACM TODS 2(1).*

Stonebraker, M., and L. Rowe. 1986. The design of Postgres. In *Proceedings of the ACM SIGMOD conference.*

Vélez, F., G. Bernard and V. Darnis. 1989. The O_2 object manager: An overview. In *Proceedings of the 15th VLDB.*

Zdonik, S. B. 1986. Version management in an object-oriented database. *International workshop on advanced programming environments.*

Zdonik, S. B., and D. Maier (eds.). 1990. *Readings in object-oriented database systems.* Morgan Kaufmann.

CHAPTER 15

The O_2 Object Manager: An Overview

FERNANDO VÉLEZ
GUY BERNARD
VINEETA DARNIS

1 Introduction

The major objective of Altaïr is to build a new-generation development environment for data-intensive applications. The functionality of the system should include that of a DBMS, of a programming language, and of a programming environment. The target applications of the system are business applications, transactional applications (except very high performance transaction processing systems), office automation, and multimedia applications. The physical configuration we aim at consists of a server connected to a set of workstations (which may be heterogeneous). The server is the common repository for shared data. The target customers are application programmers and end users. Our main interest is in application programmers, since we consider the major problem to be the improvement of programmer productivity.

To meet these requirements, we decided to build an object-oriented database system and its programming environment. O_2 is both a database system and an object-oriented system. As a database system it provides support for accessing and updating large amounts of persistent, reliable, and shared data. As an object-oriented system it supports features such as complex objects with identity, inheritance (of classes or types), encapsulation (of an object state by the methods defined on its class), overriding (redefining methods in classes), and run-time binding of methods to objects. Our interpretations of these notions are condensed in the definition of the O_2 data model (Lécluse, Richard, and

Vélez 1988; Lécluse and Richard 1989a; see chapter 4). Section 2 presents a quick overview of the model.

O_2 has a complete programming environment. It provides tools such as editors, browsers, and debuggers. When developing an application, programmers specify a schema and write the code for methods. The schema is specified in the O_2 language. Methods are written using standard programming languages. In the current implementation of the system, methods are written in either CO_2 or $BasicO_2$, which are extensions of C and Basic respectively. The schema declarations are interpreted and handled by the Schema Manager. Methods are precompiled, then compiled by the host programming-language compiler, and they may be loaded and executed.

A first throwaway prototype was built in 1987 (Bancilhon et al. 1988). Since then we have redefined the system at all its levels: data model and language, programming environment, compilers, Schema Manager, and Object Manager. The work reported here concerns only the last module.

The Object Manager (OM) is the piece of software that handles persistent and temporary complex objects with identity. Furthermore, objects are shared, are reliable, and move from a workstation to the server and vice versa. The OM is used by all the upper modules of the system: (1) by the programming environment when the user edits objects and browses through the database, (2) by the Schema Manager, as the latter is built on top of the OM, and (3) by methods and/or applications when they are executed.

We believe that the OM synthesizes techniques proposed in the database field and in the object-oriented programming field. A similar approach is found in GemStone (Maier and Stein 1987), Orion (Kim et al. 1988), Encore (Hornick and Zdonik 1987), Vbase (Andrews and Harris 1987), and Iris (Fishman et al. 1987). However, the OM is original in the following respects. First, in the way it handles distribution: applications may run either entirely on the server or entirely on the workstation, or the programmer may migrate control from one machine to another at will when passing a message to an object. We consider this to be a powerful performance-tuning facility, not found in the systems mentioned above and well adapted to a server/workstation configuration (the first three of those systems fall in this category).

Second, the system adapts itself to a wide range of application requirements, ranging from the development of applications to the execution of data-intensive applications. We distinguish a *development mode,* in which users are programmers developing applications, from an *execution mode,* in which previously built applications are executed and the main concern is performance. The systems mentioned above do not make such a distinction; they run in a single mode.

Third, the system implements a number of facilities that make life easier for application programmers: (1) exceptional attributes for tuple objects may be attached at any time without performance degradation, (2) persistence is implemented with a simple composition-based schema in which deletions are implicit (this obviously is not new in the programming language world), and

(3) clustering issues are clearly separated from the schema information and specified by the DBA in the form of a subset of the composition graph.

The rest of this chapter is organized as follows. Section 2 discusses the functional requirements of the OM both with respect to the O_2 data model and with respect to the applications the system is intended to support. Section 3 presents the main design choices we faced when developing the OM. Section 4 presents an architectural overview of the system. Section 5 compares our system to other related work, and Section 6 concludes the paper and presents some future extensions.

2 Functional Requirements

2.1 Data Model Requirements

In what follows, we present the particularities of the model pertinent to the system design. In O_2 we distinguish between *values*, on which we can perform any of a set of predefined primitives, and *objects,* which have identity and encapsulate values and user-defined *methods*. Values can be *set-, list-,* or *tuple-structured,* or *atomic*. Each value has a *type,* which describes its structure. Objects belong to *classes*. A class has a name, a type t (specifying the common structure of the set of objects of the class), and a set of methods M. Every object of a certain class has a value of type t and has the same set of methods M.

Classes and types are partially ordered according to an inheritance relationship. Multiple inheritance is supported. Each class or type can be specialized into a more specific class or type which inherits the methods and structure of the former. The specialized class or type may add some extra methods and/or elaborate on the inherited structure. Our interpretation of tuple types follows the one proposed by Cardelli 1984, implying that inheritance has natural set-inclusion semantics: if C is a subclass of C', then the set of all possible instances of C is included in the set of all possible instances of C'. The prescriptive interpretation of tuple types implies that a tuple object or value may have "exceptional" attributes, that is, attribute values not declared in its class or type. The following O_2 code shows this:

```
class Person type tuple(name: string, age: integer);
O2 Person x;
x = tuple(name: "John", age: 27, my_opinion: "nice fellow");
```

Here, the expression "$*x$" refers to the value encapsulated in object x. Reference to values encapsulated in objects is allowed only in methods of class Person (or in other methods if the deencapsulation method, *, is exported by the creator of class Person (Lécluse and Richard 1989b; see chapter 9).

Methods are procedures that take as input objects and/or values, and return an object or a value. They are not necessarily applicative; that is, they may update existing objects or values in the database as a side effect. They are written in a programming language—in the current implementation of the system, either CO_2 or BasicO_2. The extensions we made to these languages are (1) statements to declare object classes, value types and O_2 variables, (2) message-passing expressions for objects, and (3) primitives to manipulate structured values. Methods may be redefined in more specific classes. This yields *overloading*: a given message (i.e., a given method name) may mean different things depending on the object to which it is applied. Overloading implies that the binding of the method name to the actual code which executes it must sometimes be done at run time. This is *late binding*. Static type checking is enforced on methods: in a message-passing expression, the method arguments and the result are type checked. Assigning an object or a value to an O_2 variable is type checked; so are errors arising from passing messages to values, and so on. As all possible bindings of messages to methods are type checked, we achieve static type checking even if late binding is necessary.

A *named* object or value is an object or value with a user-defined name. These objects or values are the roots of persistence. Persistence is defined in the model as follows: (1) every named object or value is persistent, (2) every component of a persistent object or value is persistent, and (3) nothing else is persistent. Therefore, persistence is *user controlled*: in order to make an object persistent, the user has to make it a component of an already persistent object. Persistence is also *orthogonal* to the type system, in that every object or value has the same right to persist. Finally, persistence is *method transparent,* in that the same method may be applied to a persistent or to a temporary object.

The set of objects of a given class is referred to as the *extension* of the class. Upon user request at class-definition time, the system offers automatic extension maintenance as follows: given a class C, it creates a named value of type set(C) with name C, and automatically inserts every newly created object of class C into it.

An O_2 *schema* consists of classes, types, named objects, and named values. A query language has been designed (Bancilhon, Cluet, and Delobel 1989; see chapter 11) which uses the distinction between objects and values and the existence, in the data manipulation language, of primitives to manipulate structured values. It can be used in an ad hoc mode or in a programming mode. The difference is that in its *ad hoc* mode it sees the value encapsulated in an object (thus violating encapsulation). The result is a query language fully embedded in the O_2 language, thus solving the impedance mismatch typical of the current integration of query languages such as SQL and general-purpose programming languages.

2.2 Application Requirements

The system should support a wide range of application requirements. Consider the three following utilization scenarios:

1. The users are programmers developing O_2 applications. The applications evolve within a programming environment which provides tools such as editors, browsers, and debuggers. They constantly define new classes and new methods, and methods are generally tested with few objects in main memory.

2. The users are end users (i.e., not necessarily programmers), and they execute applications which have been previously developed and tested. Here we have a notion of "application" which contains a set of classes and methods. In this mode, the essential concern is execution speed. Data are massive, they are shared, and they have to be reliable. The schema is static.

3. The users are programmers developing (rapid) prototypes with O_2. The data would fit in main memory in many cases and are seldom shared. Execution speed is important and the schema may be flexible.

These three scenarios imply very different and contradictory requirements. In the first scenario, which we call *development mode*, flexibility is at a premium, and therefore it is important to optimize method compilations and schema-concurrency protocols. Execution speed is less important.

In the second scenario, the *execution mode*, we need all the functionality of a database system: persistence, disk management (i.e., indexing, clustering, and smart buffering), concurrency on objects (not necessarily on the schema), and recovery. Message passing should be optimized; referencing an attribute of a tuple value should be done in "compiled mode" (i.e., the system should not interpret an attribute name); and operations on large sets and lists should be done efficiently.

In the third scenario, the *resident mode*, the system could load all persistent data in main memory to enhance execution speed. This is in contrast with what we could call *object-fault mode,* which is typical of data managers. Note that this issue is orthogonal to the preceding two: it is possible to have a mixture of resident and execution mode, as well as of resident and development mode. Furthermore, if data are private, no overhead should be incurred by any concurrency-control mechanism.

These scenarios could apply to virtually any kind of application. Another requirement, imposed essentially by office applications and spatial applications, is the efficient manipulation of multimedia data as text, images, and graphics. The main difficulty here is to manage very large structured objects.

2.3 Architectural Requirements

One of the lessons learned from the prototype reported in Bancilhon et al. 1988 was that the OM should be as *canonical* as possible, that is, that other projects should be able to use the OM as a back end in charge of persistence and transaction management for complex objects. With the current flurry of experimentation in both the database field and the programming-language field (especially in persistent programming), this has an obvious interest. To this end, the semantics of O_2 concerning classes, inheritance, and schema evolution should be taken care of at higher layers, namely, by the Schema Manager and the compilers. The parts of the OM using specific O_2 knowledge (for example, support for message passing) should be clearly isolated from the rest of the system in order to ignore them when building a stand-alone version of the system.

Another requirement is that it should be easy to downgrade the system to a single-site machine (recall that the target configuration is a server/workstation architecture).

We tried to use existing products as much as possible. We use WiSS, the Wisconsin Storage System (Chou et al. 1985), as the low-level layer of the OM to provide persistence, disk management, and concurrency control. WiSS provides the following persistent structures: record-structured sequential files, unstructured files, and long data items. All these structures are mapped into pages, the basic persistence unit. WiSS provides indexes for disk management as well as full control of the physical location of pages on disk. It runs under Unix System V but bypasses the Unix File System and does its own buffering.

3 Main Design Choices

3.1 Modes of Operation

3.1.1 Compiling Modes

The sharp differences in application requirements between development mode and execution mode drove us to build two different "compiling modes." We designed the OM in such a way that these modes affect only the compilers. They do not imply building two different versions of the OM. In any case, both modes must share the same persistent data.

Execution mode applications are the result of "deeply compiling" some classes and methods developed by a programmer, to gain speed when executing these methods. The code is optimized in the following respects.

1. Late binding is replaced by a function call whenever possible; otherwise, for those message-passing expressions that involve late binding due to overloading, an ad hoc binding primitive is generated for each case. This situation is to be contrasted with the development mode, in which it is the OM that uses late binding systematically to support all message passing.

2. Access to tuple attributes by name is replaced by physical offsets. This is not always possible, due to multiple inheritance; the position for attribute values within tuple objects may change from a class C to a class C' if the latter is a subclass of C and also of another class C''. In these cases, the compiler generates a late-binding call for attribute names.

3. No run-time method fault occurs: methods are loaded statically. In development mode, methods are loaded dynamically, because flexibility is required.

These optimizations are made possible by restricting changes to the classes used by an application. Changes dealing with the structure of a class (for example, dropping an attribute, or changing the type of an attribute or the type of the elements of a set) are disallowed. Dropping a class is also disallowed. However, the operational parts of classes and the extensibility of the system are preserved: methods can be added, dropped, or redefined, and classes may be refined into subclasses. These changes do not have an impact on existing execution-mode applications unless they are recompiled. In the current implementation, the granularity of execution-mode compilation is the entire application.

3.1.2 Transaction Modes

The OM interfaces either with a full-fledged execution mode application or with a development-mode *session*. We denote both by the term *application*. An application is composed of one or more *transactions*. For example, in a development session, the OM interacts with one of the following: the Schema Manager, when compiling a method or a schema command; the programming environment, when the programmer or the end user browses through the database and edits objects; or a method being tested during application building. It is reasonable to associate transactions to each one of these.

Our notion of transaction differs from the classical database notion of transaction (namely, an atomic and serializable sequence of database commands) in the following respects.

1. We distinguish concurrency on the schema from concurrency on objects, and allow them to be activated or deactivated independently. For example, in execution mode, one can choose to run with concurrency on objects but no concurrency on the schema. The converse makes sense when running in development mode under the Schema Manager. When concurrency is not enforced, the system inhibits access to shared data (this is an authorization issue that has been disregarded for the moment).

2. Recovery may be switched on or off. When running prototype applications, one may be willing to sacrifice safety for the sake of performance. If recovery is enforced, the programmer may set savepoints in order not to lose arbitrary amounts of work if transactions are large (for example, when designing applications in development mode).

3. A transaction may run in resident mode or in object-fault mode. This choice is specified at execution time, not at compile time: the same transaction may run in a different mode from one session to another (except if we run out of memory space; see section 4.4). A good candidate to run

in resident mode is the Schema Manager: in this case, before beginning a session, all the schema information is loaded in memory. This is a significant improvement from the first version of the system, in which this choice was built into the code. In the current version, the Schema Manager can run in object-fault mode if it wishes to.

Obviously, transactions encompass persistence of objects: at commit time, persistent objects are written to disk.

3.2 Handling Distribution

The OM has a *workstation version* and a *server version*. Both versions have almost the same interface. The main distinction is in the actual implementation: the workstation version is single-user (as a workstation is single-user) and memory based; the server version is multiuser and disk based. No application development is performed on the server (as the programming environment operates on a bitmap screen and is workstation-oriented). So the O_2 compilers and the Schema Manager exist only on the workstation.

An important problem we faced while designing the system was: given an (execution mode) application program in O_2, how do we decide which part runs on the server and which part runs on the workstation? The main goals are to make tasks run efficiently in the system configuration and to program distribution as simply as possible. We are not dealing with a distributed-query problem but with general programs, since methods are programs.

Several approaches can be taken. The simplest is to make distribution transparent to the application programmer and make everything run on a single machine. If the machine is the server, workstations are useless; and if the machine is the workstation, we may have serious performance problems if the database is large. Making distribution transparent and letting the system determine the best site is an unsolved problem up to now. Furthermore, considering the state of the art of distributed query optimization, there is little hope that this situation will change in the near future.

We decided to make the distributed architecture visible to the application programmer (but not to the end user). Issues in handling distribution and programming instructions for controlling data flow execution between the server and the workstation are described in chapter 16.

3.3 Object Access

Objects are uniquely identified and accessed by object identifiers (oids). Object identifiers could have been "logical," giving no information about their location in secondary memory, as in GemStone (Maier and Stein 1987), Orion (Kim et al. 1988), and ObServer (Hornick and Zdonik 1987). With logical identifiers a correspondence table between oids and physical addresses is needed. Moving objects in secondary memory is straightforward, but the object table might be very large, as it would contain one entry for each object in the database. Probably one disk access would be performed to retrieve the object-table entry of the object, and a second to retrieve the object. For performance reasons, we have chosen to make the object identifiers physical, that is, identifiers that reflect their location on disk. Roughly speaking, an object will be stored in a WiSS record, and the object identifier will be the record's identifier, an RID. An RID is coded in 8 bytes: a volume identifier (2 bytes), a page identifier within a volume (4 bytes), and a slot number (2 bytes) which indirectly addresses a record within a page.

A major problem with physical identifiers is moving objects on disk without changing their identifiers. If we were to change the identifier of an object *o* that we want to move on disk, we should be able to attain all objects referencing *o* to update their references; but this would imply using backward references in the composition hierarchy, and we consider these too heavy to maintain. The solution we adopted is to use forwarding markers. When accessing on disk an object which has been moved elsewhere, we perform two disk accesses: one to retrieve the forwarding RID and the other to retrieve the object. If an object is moved again, there is no need to leave another marker behind, as the only reference to its current physical location is in the original marker. WiSS already implements this mechanism as a side effect of a record update that makes the record too big for the page it resides on. We modified WiSS to give the Object Manager direct control over this mechanism.

With physical identifiers and a workstation/server configuration, a decision has to be taken upon when to assign oids to newly created objects. Objects are generally created in the workstation, and physical identifiers representing RIDs are only delivered on insertion of the corresponding WiSS record. Persistent identifiers are assigned at transaction-commit time in order to avoid extensive message exchange between the two machines. This also solves the problem of having to change the identifier of a newly created object when the system decides to cluster it afterwards (but before transaction commit) with another "owner" object (see section 3.6). Temporary oids are generated for new objects, and they are changed before commit. This also implies changing references to these objects from old (and new) objects.

3.4 Object Representation

Recall that the O_2 model distinguishes objects from values (section 2.1). In the OM, we deal only with objects and atomic values. Structured values are given an identifier and are managed as standard objects. The system supports both the primitives for manipulating values and the message-passing mechanism for objects. At the language level, objects are distinguished from values, and errors such as passing a message to a value or applying a primitive to an object will be trapped at compile time. In the OM, however, there are primitives which distinguish oids denoting objects from oids denoting values. For example, the primitive adding an oid to a set uses a different membership test depending on whether the oid denotes an object or a value: in the former case, the membership test is object identity, whereas in the latter it is value equality.

3.4.1 Tuples

On disk, a tuple is represented as a record stored in a page. When a tuple outgrows a disk page, we switch to a different representation, suitable for storing long records: the long data item (LDI) format. The oid of the tuple is unchanged: it is the RID of the original record.

In main memory, tuples are represented as a contiguous chunk containing the actual values. Only strings are stored away from the main chunk, which contains pointers to the proper locations. This way the strings may grow or shrink without requiring the entire object to change location. An exception to this rule comes from the fact that in O_2, a tuple object may have exceptional attributes (section 2.1); in such cases, the tuple object may grow in length. There is a memory-management problem for exceptional attributes: the memory management relies on the assumption that once an object is placed in main memory, its address does not change. When a tuple grows, if an in-place extension is not possible, a level of indirection for the entire tuple value is generated.

For every object, we maintain the identifier of the class to which it belongs and the identifier of the type to which its encapsulated value belongs. To interpret the names and types of exceptional attribute values, we consider that the value encapsulated in the object changes type, but the object remains in the same class.

3.4.2 Lists

Lists, which can be more accurately called *insertable arrays*, are represented as ordered trees as in Stonebraker et al. 1983 (with slight modifications to allow fast scans). An ordered tree is a tree in which each internal node contains a count of the nodes under it. It can for instance be a B-tree in which this node count is used as a key. The insertion and deletion procedures have to update node counts (this is the essential difference from standard B-tree management). More precisely, this structure creates a virtual rank field in every record, while making it possible to insert and delete an element without modifying the rank fields of all the elements that follow. This structure is efficient for storing small and large lists. The actual implementation stores the nodes of the tree as O_2 tuple objects whose fields are of predefined system types.

3.4.3 Sets

The representation for large sets of objects needs to be such that (1) membership tests are efficient, and (2) scanning the elements of the set is also efficient. WiSS provides two kinds of indexes: hash indexes and B-trees. For testing membership in a large set, hashing is better. For scanning a set, B-trees are far more efficient because, as the oids of the elements are sorted, the physical order of elements on disk coincides with the order in which they are retrieved, thereby minimizing disk-arm moves. We therefore use B-tree indexes to represent large sets.

WiSS indexes can be used for large sets of values, as far as base types (such as integer, or float) are concerned, because these types coincide with key types in WiSS. Sets of composite values are represented as sets of objects and, when testing for membership, the set is scanned to test value equality.

However, using an index for a small set would be too costly. Therefore, there is a limit under which a set is represented as a WiSS record; a convenient value for this limit is the maximum record size in WiSS. Small sets are kept ordered. This decision was motivated by the fact that large sets are kept ordered, and binary operations on sets take advantage of this uniformity: unions, intersections, and differences are programmed using merge algorithms.

3.4.4 Multimedia Objects

Two types of multimedia objects are implemented: unstructured text and bitmaps. From the user point of view, they are instances of the predefined classes Text and Bitmap. The predefined methods in these classes are *display* and *edit*. They are implemented by calls to customized functions in the programming environment. From the system point of view, texts are atomic objects of type string, and bitmaps are atomic objects of type bytes, an unstructured byte string preceded by its length. When the size of these objects exceeds the size of a WiSS page, they are stored as LDIs on disk. In the current implementation, the size of a multimedia object is limited to the size of an LDI, which is 1.6 MB. Another simplification concerns the memory management of multimedia objects: they are fetched by the programming environment primitives as a whole chunk.

3.5 Persistence

Persistence is defined in the O_2 model as reachability from persistent root objects, which are named objects or values (section 2.1). This is implemented by associating with each object a reference count. An object persists as long as this counter is greater than zero. When an object is made persistent, all its components are made persistent too; conversely, when the reference count of an object drops to zero, the reference count of all its components is decremented. Circular garbage (for example, two objects pointing to each other and not being accessible from any other object) if any, would be recovered at suitable intervals by a mark-and-sweep algorithm beginning from the persistence roots.

Space for objects in memory (and disk) is recovered at transaction commit. In fact, because an object o may be pointed to by the O_2 variables of a method (which are, by nature, temporary), even if the reference count of a o is zero, it should exist as long as it is pointed to by a variable. So unless a temporary reference count scheme is built similar to that of Kaehler 1986, objects cannot be freed from memory until commit time. We decided not to include this scheme because it adds complexity to the system, and the added benefits do not seem very large.

3.6 Clustering on Disk

Newly created, persistent objects are given a persistent identifier when they are inserted in a file at transaction commit. The mapping of objects to files depends on control data given by the database administrator describing the placement of objects: the *placement trees.* Placement trees are described extensively in chapter 17 and in Benzaken and Delobel 1990. The main idea is that if several objects are used together frequently, we should put them on disk as close to one another as possible. The main heuristic we used to postulate that two objects will be used together frequently is their relationship through composition structure. Intuitively, a placement tree expresses the way in which a composite object and its components will be clustered together. Roughly speaking, a placement tree for a class C is a subtree of the composition class hierarchy rooted at C. Several placement trees may be defined, and they may change over time. A given class may be the root of at most one placement tree, and it may or may not belong to other trees. Placement trees may consist of a single root.

To each placement tree we associate a WiSS file (this mapping is injective), and for instances of classes not belonging to any placement tree we reserve a default file. The mapping between the set of classes in the system and the set of files is therefore not unique, as a class may appear in several placement trees. For space reasons, we do not present here the set of rules governing the exact placement of objects into files.

When an object o is to be stored in the same file as an object o' because o is a component of o', we try to store o as close as possible to o'. To do so, we use the elementary clustering facility offered by WiSS. When inserting a record in a file, one has the option of specifying the identifier of another record r of the file. WiSS tries to store the new record in the same page as r on in a nearby page. By default, a (nonatomic) value v appearing as a component of an object o is placed near o. For example, if the class Department uses type setof(Person) in its structure, the system will automatically generate a branch Department $\rightarrow$ setof(Person) in the placement trees in which Department appears.

When we want to read an object identifier from disk, we must first open the file where it is stored. In the general case, we do not know the file it is stored in. This implies modifying WiSS to support automatic file opening.

3.7 Handling Concurrency at the O_2 Level

Concurrency on objects is handled by WiSS. However, the distributed architecture of the system does not make life easy. Consider a transaction executing on the workstation and updating shared objects. Before reaching the workstation, objects are read-locked. Note that it is difficult to anticipate which objects need to be write-locked, as objects are operated by methods of arbitrary complexity. As there is no concurrency control on the workstation, the problem is to ensure consistency, and to do so cheaply.

Straightforward solutions are (1) each time the transaction wants to update an object in the workstation, migrate execution to the server and perform the update there: the concurrency control mechanism of WiSS will ensure consistency; (2) update the objects locally and maintain an update log that will be executed in the server at transaction commit; (3) run the transaction in the workstation and in the server in parallel (this is less straightforward!). Solution (1) has obvious performance problems. Solution 2 seems complicated to implement, and it has contention problems as all controls are performed at commit time. Solution 3 is difficult to implement because the transaction itself may migrate its execution site from one machine to another (see section 3.2). None of these being satisfactory, we chose the following solution.

Concurrency in WiSS is handled by a two-phase locking algorithm on pages and files. WiSS has an internal **lock_page** primitive which sets locks on pages. Our solution is to move this primitive to the programming interface, and ask for write locks explicitly from the workstation before an object is updated The OM in the workstation keeps track of the pages for which a write-lock has been requested in a bitstring. In this way, useless requests are avoided. The update proceeds in the workstation asynchronously without waiting for an answer. The workstation is not informed unless the answer is "rollback," in which case the process running the transaction in the workstation is informed and the transaction is aborted. This "optimistic" approach reduces the network traffic and the work to be done by the server. At transaction commit, the workstation process asks the server process if all requested write locks have been granted (we call this *precommit*); only if this is the case are the objects transferred. This way, consistency of shared objects in the server is preserved.

Our handling of concurrency on the schema differently from that of concurrency on objects is a consequence of our application requirements (summarized in section 2.2). It is also due to the observation that in development mode, the schema is the hot spot of the system. Even executing a message-passing expression implies reading the schema information because methods belong to the schema. Therefore a custom concurrency control for the schema is being designed which takes into account semantic information about schema updates to allow for increased parallelism. It does not seem wise to put a read lock on a page each time a message passing expression is solved.

4 Overview of the System

The Object Manager (OM) is divided into four layers: (1) a layer which copes with the manipulation of O_2 objects and values and with transaction control; (2) a memory-management layer; (3) a communication layer that takes into account object transfers, execution migration, and application downloading;

and (4) on the server, a storage layer devoted to persistence, disk management, and transaction support implemented by WiSS.

The following process layout has been adopted. On the workstation, an application (i.e., an execution-mode application or the development module consisting of the programming environment, the compilers, and the Schema Manager) and the workstation version of the OM form a single process. There will be as many processes as running applications.

For each process running on a workstation, there is a *mirror* process running on the server. In addition, there may be some *terminal* application processes running on the server which do not have any corresponding "partner" on a workstation. Given the large number of such concurrent applications on the server, the OM is compiled as reentrant library modules to be shared among all applications. The lock table and the buffer managed by WiSS are shared by all processes. The object memory of the OM is also a global buffer in shared memory, as detailed below. Both versions of the OM are illustrated in figure 15.1.

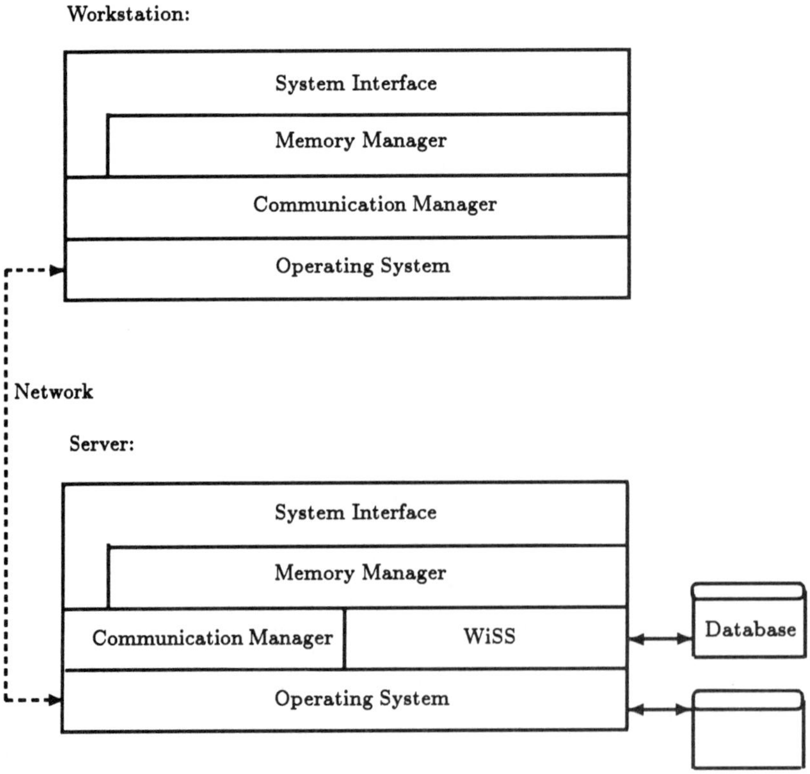

Figure 15.1. Architecture of the OM

4.1 The System Interface Module

The System Interface is the gateway to the OM. All object manipulations done by a transaction are treated by this module. It is concerned with (1) general object manipulation and manipulation of complex values, (2) support of message passing, (3) transaction control at the O_2 level, (4) implementation of indexes, and (5) physical administration support. The first four tasks are discussed below. Task 5 is the interface for the database administrator. For the time being, it concerns addition and deletion of placement trees for clustering purposes.

4.1.1 The Complex Object Manager

The object-manipulation submodule performs the following tasks:

1. Creation and deletion of structured types. (Creation of classes and methods is the responsibility of the Schema Manager and not of the Object Manager.)

2. Creation and deletion of objects. Objects are deleted only if they are not referenced by any other object.

3. Retrieval of objects by name.

4. Support for the predefined methods for objects. These are the methods of the predefined class Object, namely *value_equal, deep_equal, value_copy, deep_copy, display,* and *edit.*

5. Support for set, list, and tuple objects.

The following operators are available for sets: **union, intersection, difference, add** element, **remove** element, set **membership**, set **containment**, set **scan** for elements, and **apply methods** to all the elements of the set. For lists, we have: **concatenation, append** element, **add** at a given position, **drop first** occurrence of element, **drop element** at a given position, **get (and put) element** at a position, **get (and put) sublist** delimited by two positions, and **apply method** to all the elements of the list. For tuples, **get attribute** value and **put attribute** value.

For sets and lists, we have implemented a two-layer structure in which the upper layer takes care of logical operations (and reference counts) and the lower layer handles the data structures. Concerning sets, the upper layer has no knowledge about the differences among small and large sets. As for lists, the details of the ordered-trees implementation are managed at the lower layer exclusively.

4.1.2 The Message-Passing Manager

The message-passing submodule exists both on the workstation and on the server. In development mode, it supports late binding and also handles the application of the selected binary code to the receiver object. In execution mode, the message is replaced by a function call whenever possible, and in the few cases which remain unsolved, method-name resolution is done by the executing code in an ad hoc manner. In any case (i.e., early or late binding), the application of the method is done by the system; this has the advantage of letting the system decide dynamically on the site of application of the method (see section 6). Dynamic distribution is not yet implemented, but we have tried to leave the door open to accommodate this feature easily.

As methods and classes are implemented as objects by the Schema Manager, solving a method invocation involves retrieving a method object depending on the class of the receiver. This retrieval is done in constant time because there is no run-time lookup of the ancestors of a class. The retrieved method object gives a pointer of the entry point of the method.

4.1.3 The Transaction Manager

An O_2 transaction maps directly to a WiSS transaction. The transaction-support submodule supports the functionality described in section 3.1.2 and handles concurrency according to the strategy presented in section 3.7.

When a transaction runs in memory-resident mode, the system is given information about the persistent root objects it accesses, and fetches all objects accessible from these at transaction start. Once this is done, all interobject references are changed to memory addresses. From now on, an object identifier no longer represents a disk location but a virtual-memory address. This optimization accelerates the transaction execution considerably. Obviously, when such a transaction commits, the objects it has modified cannot be written out to disk without converting the interobject references back to persistent disk addresses.

At both sites, this submodule keeps track of the set of dirty objects (this includes newly created objects) and the set of persistent objects to be deleted from the database. When control is transferred from one site to another (at transaction commit or when migrating execution), these two sets, as well as the objects referenced to by these sets, are also transferred. In this way, transactions preserve their execution context.

4.1.4 The Index Manager

The Index Manager implements indexes that take into account the specificities of the O_2 data model—in particular, the inheritance hierarchy and the composition hierarchy. The relationship of indexes with each kind of hierarchy has been explored separately in Kim et al. 1988 and in Maier and Stein 1987. It is constructed directly above the WiSS layer supporting indexes. We currently support indexes on extensions of classes (not on arbitrary sets or lists). The selection criteria associated to an index can involve a path expression applied to members of a class, as in Maier and Stein 1987. For example, the following command creates an index on the Restaurant class which can be used to retrieve instances of restaurants given the name of the city in which they are located.

add index Rest_city_name **on class** Restaurant **path** address.city.name

In our implementation, we decompose indexes defined on paths along the composition hierarchy in a sequence of basic index components, one for each link in the path. Scans on composite indexes are compound operations on these basic indexes. Decomposing a composite index into basic ones is necessary in order to take into account updates in the intermediate links of the paths. Known advantages of this approach are that (1) if the paths of two or more indexes share a common prefix, the indexes will share the index components on the common prefix, and (2) any prefix of a path is also indexed.

Indexes also "understand" the inheritance hierarchy: the index defined above for the Restaurant class will contain entries for all restaurant objects and objects of other subclasses of the class Restaurant. Furthermore, if the city of the address of a Restaurant object is an object of a subclass of City—say, Beautiful_city—the index should still map the name of the Beautiful_city object to the restaurant. This is called *class-hierarchy indexing.* An alternative solution would be to have one index for each subclass; this is called *single-class indexing.* As inheritance in O_2 has an inclusion semantics, queries addressed to a class extension C will implicitly refer to subclasses of C as well. Kim et al. 1988 have shown that in this case, class-hierarchy indexing is better in general than single-class indexing. Fast retrieval from this index can still be performed for a query on a subclass of the indexed class. In our implementation, we structure the leaves of the index in such a way that we retrieve all objects of a subclass in a single block, without having to scan the whole leaf. This is an improvement with respect to the implementation proposed in Kim et al. 1988.

4.2 The Memory-Management Module

The Memory Manager takes care of translating object identifiers into memory addresses. This includes handling object faults for objects requested by the application and not currently in memory. It is also responsible for managing the space occupied by objects in main memory. As in Orion (Kim et al. 1988) and GemStone (Maier and Stein 1987) but unlike ObServer (Hornick and Zdonik 1987), a dual buffer-management scheme is implemented: a page buffer implemented by WiSS and an object buffer pool, the *object memory*. Objects in the page buffer are in their disk format. In the object memory, they are in their memory format.

4.2.1 On the Server

On the server, an object fault implies reading a WiSS record and transferring it between the page buffer and the server object memory. Even though an object corresponds to one WiSS record, on every object fault all the valid records on the same page as the object in question are transferred into the object memory. This read-ahead strategy is based on the fact that objects which have a strong correlation between them are clustered on the same or nearby pages, and reading an entire page (which is anyway placed in the page buffer by WiSS) will accelerate further processing.

As some degree of sharing is expected among applications, the server object memory is implemented as a data segment shared by all the concurrent processes. The shared memory management can be considered a shared-memory equivalent of the Unix *malloc/realloc/free* package. When the memory manager at the server asks for memory space, it is automatically given a chunk in the shared segment. The first process to run out of shared memory adds more memory to the common pool. Other processes automatically detect that more memory is now available and adjust their own internal data to reflect this. Figure 15.2 illustrates this mechanism.

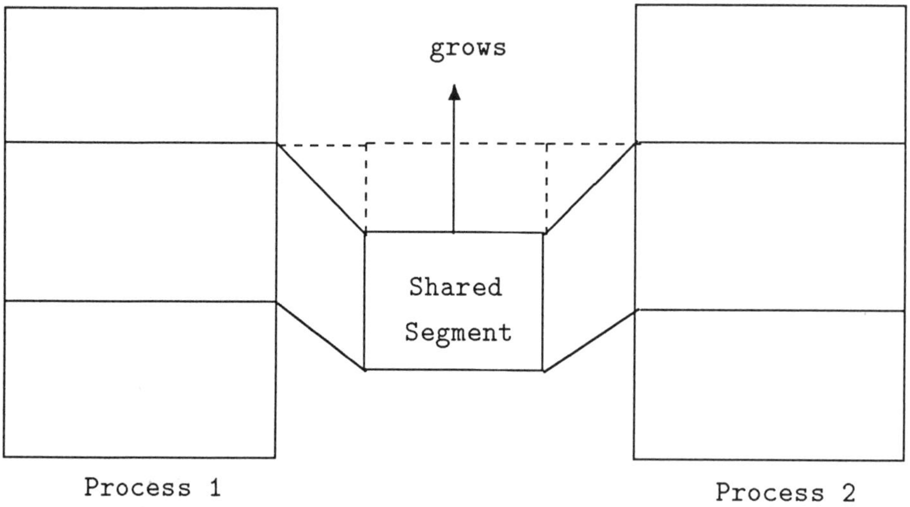

Figure 15.2. Shared memory management

4.2.2 On the Workstation

On the workstation, the object memory is private to each application. The memory allocation and deallocation tasks are left to the Unix virtual-memory mechanism. An object fault is addressed to the Communication Manager, which in turn asks the server mirror process to send the object across the network. To gain maximum reusability of code, we kept the representation format the same on disk and on the network. All objects stored in the same page as the requested object are transferred to the workstation.

4.2.3 Object Table

Both on the server and on the workstations, the memory address at which an object is stored (after reading from disk or on creation) never changes until the object migrates to another machine or is written out to disk. While an object is in memory, in order to access it given its identifier, we use an object table. This table is hashed on identifier values and contains entries for resident objects only. On the workstation each application has its own object table, whereas on the server the object table is shared among all applications.

If the table saturates, its size is doubled, all the existing entries are rehashed to the new table, the old table is freed, and execution continues. This process is limited by a threshold value which, when attained, will cause a certain number of objects to be written out to disk and free slots to be created in the table. We estimate that this situation is very infrequent, and in such cases the OM will do this object-level swapping.

4.2.4 Object Migration

When objects are migrated from one machine to another, some objects have to be handled carefully, namely, newly created objects and those which belong to a transaction running in resident mode. In both of these cases, the object identifier is a virtual-memory address which is local to the machine where it was assigned. Thus, every time a machine receives an object from the network, it checks whether the identifier has the temporary or resident flag set indicating that the receiving machine has to allocate its own memory location to hold the object. Further, as the address found in the object identifier is not valid at the receiver's site, all accesses should go through the object table, which would give the correct memory location.

4.3 The Communication Manager

4.3.1 Session Level

When an application is started on a workstation, a *mirror application process* must be started on the server in order to interact with the lower layers of the system. This mirror process is woken up also when the application process transfers execution control to the server. Thus, an activity must be always present on the server machine, to watch for application creations on workstations or on server terminals, and to start the corresponding processes. This activity is the *O_2 daemon process*, which is always running. When a connection request arrives from the server (application started from a terminal of the server), the O_2 daemon process creates terminal application process on the server and goes back in the loop, waiting for the next connection request. When a connection request arrives from a workstation (application started from a workstation), the daemon processes creates a mirror application process and loops back.

The workstation application process and the mirror application process behave differently. Whereas the workstation application process executes the code of the application as a transaction, the mirror application process is passive: it goes to sleep until receipt of an incoming message, processes it by *upcalling* the appropriate primitive, and goes back to sleep until the next message arrives or the workstation application process is ended. An application is started from a terminal of the server almost in the same way, the important point being that the terminal application process is handled by the O_2 daemon process.

The O_2 daemon process also plays an important role in case of failure detection. Abnormal process terminations are detected and managed by the following mechanism.

1. If the workstation application process terminates abnormally, the mirror application process is informed via the loss of the transport connection on which it waits for incoming messages. It can then abort the current transaction, if necessary, before exiting.

2. If the mirror application process terminates abnormally, the O_2 daemon process (the one which has created the mirror process) is notified by the operating system. The daemon then aborts the current transaction if necessary. This is possible because the O_2 daemon process registers, along with the process identifier of the mirror application process, its current transaction identifier.

4.3.2 Presentation Level

The heterogeneity between machines is handled by a presentation protocol, XDR (Sun 1986), which was chosen for its simplicity. For object moves, the size of an object when received at a site depends on the machine parameters. In order to minimize extraneous memory-to-memory copying, this size is computed from the type of the transferred object. It is used to determine the place in memory where the object data will be copied, and data transfer is done directly from network to this memory address. Another optimization consists of grouping in a single message several objects to move (for instance at commit time). This minimizes the number of network accesses.

4.3.3 Execution Migration

In the current version of the system, the execution site for a message passing is specified statically by the application programmer. Embedded execution transfers may appear. For instance, if a selection operation results in displaying one tuple per thousand, on average, the programmer may specify that the selection operation should be done on the server. The display, of course, can be done only on the workstation. In this way, the two sites may act alternatively as client or server. Our execution migration protocol is thus more than a classical, unidirectional remote-procedure-call mechanism.

5 Comparison with Related Work

In this section we attempt to compare the O_2 OM with the object managers of GemStone and Orion. It should be noted that there is a lack of agreement on higher-level object-oriented concepts for databases, so object managers actually implement different kinds of functionality.

5.1 GemStone

The GemStone system (Maier and Stein 1987), is a commercial product developed at Servio Logic. The original objective of GemStone was to make Smalltalk a database system. It is decomposed into two main layers, a lower layer called Stone and an upper layer called Gem. Roughly speaking, they correspond to the object memory and the virtual machine of the standard Smalltalk implementation. Stone has the same kind of functionalities as the O_2 OM: it provides persistence, secondary storage management, transactions, concurrency control, recovery, support for associative access, and authorization functions. Stone knows about structured objects, although the model it implements is simpler than the full GemStone model implemented by Gem (which is close to Smalltalk). The main architectural differences are that (1) Gem and Stone are structured as separate processes (a GemStone system has a single Stone process and a separate Gem process for each active user), and (2) the current mapping of processes to processors has Gem and Stone running on a server. On the workstation, an interface to GemStone (PIM) has been developed; it implements remote procedure calls to functions supplied by GemStone.

Each application initiates a session with the database, and each session consists of one or more transactions. Another similarity is the way objects are represented: on disk, objects are laid into pages, and a page may contain several objects. Objects growing larger than a page are broken into pieces and organized as a B-tree spanning several pages. Stone provides each session with a private workspace in which changes are only visible to the session. This is implemented by a shadow mechanism: each time a session modifies an object, a new copy of the object is created, and it is placed in a page that is inaccessible to other sessions. Stone uses logical identifiers for objects, so an object table organized as a B-tree is used to map an oid to a physical location in memory and on disk. The shadow copy of the object table is modified so that the object's identifier references the new copy.

Transaction management in GemStone bears little similarity to that of O_2. Aborting a transaction consists of throwing away its shadow object table, and committing consists of replacing the shared table with a shadow copy. An optimistic concurrency-control scheme is implemented. Access conflicts are checked at commit time, rather than being prevented through locking. The main disadvantage with this scheme is that a long transaction can lose arbitrary amounts of work if prevented from committing. To alleviate this problem, a pessimistic concurrency control based on locking is explored in Penney, Stein, and Maier 1987.

One of the major innovations of GemStone is its indexing mechanism to support associative access on large collections. A complete description of this mechanism can be found in Maier and Stein 1986. The main feature is that indexes can be defined on a path along the composition hierarchy, and that they index into sets rather than into classes.

5.2 Orion

Orion (Banerjee et al. 1987; Kim et al. 1988) is an object-oriented DBMS developed at MCC. It extends Common-Lisp with object-oriented programming and database capabilities. A version of Orion implements a multiuser, multitask system in which a server provides persistence and sharing of objects on behalf of several workstations. Noteworthy data-modeling concepts supported by Orion are (1) the notion of a composite object as a hierarchy of exclusive and dependent component objects, and (2) version support for objects. Orion implements associative access to objects by allowing selection conditions to be applied to a class and by allowing the user to navigate through the composition hierarchy. These is no explicit set constructor. However, the system maintains the set of all instances of a given class.

The architecture of Orion consists of the following modules: (1) a message handler, which receives all messages sent to Orion objects; (2) an object subsystem, which provides functions such as schema evolution, version control, query optimization, and multimedia information management; (3) a transaction subsystem, which provides concurrency control and recovery mechanisms; and (4) a storage subsystem, which provides access to objects on disk. The last two modules implement functionalities similar to those of the O_2 OM: the storage subsystem implements a dual buffer-management scheme (page buffer and object buffer), and it maintains a resident-object table hashed by oid. However, as oids are logical, there is another hash-based oid-to-physical-id for all objects in the database. Buffer management for objects in the object buffer is far more complex than that of O_2: fragmentation is dealt with by a garbage-collection mechanism that reclaims space occupied by objects which can still be referenced to by the application; and thus an intermediate structure, the resident object descriptor (ROD) has to be introduced between the resident-object table and the actual object. Applications point to RODs only, and these may not be swapped.

Transaction management (Garza and Kim 1988) is rather classical: concurrency control is based on a locking protocol, and recovery is based on logging. However, a composite object may be locked as a whole. To this end, the hierarchical locking protocol (Gray 1978) has been extended. A class-lattice locking protocol, which is needed to allow access to instances of a class while preventing changes to the definitions of the superclasses of the class, has also been proposed. Other important database features in Orion are indexing, authorization, and version support. Indexes may be defined on a class or on subclasses of a class, and are they used when queries are evaluated.

6 Conclusions and Future Work

In this chapter we have described the main choices involved in the design of the O_2 Object Manager, and presented its overall architecture. The OM handles shared and persistent complex objects with identity. The OM is used by all the upper modules of the O_2 system. However, a major concern throughout the design has been to build a common kernel for different object-oriented paradigms. In fact, most of the semantics of the O_2 type system has been shifted to the upper layers—the Schema Manager and the compilers. The part of the OM depending on classes and methods is essentially the message-passing mechanism. It has been isolated from the rest of the system. Outside Altaïr, the OM is currently being used as a back-end bearing persistence to a frame-based expert-system generator (Neveu and Haren 1986).

The OM combines well-known techniques from the database field and the object-oriented programming field, and has the following original aspects:

1. The programmer has full control over distribution. This is done in an easy way when passing messages to objects. The implications of this design choice on the overall architecture of the system are deep; they mainly concern memory management and transaction management.

2. The system adapts itself to a wide range of application requirements. This has led us to parameterize the modes in which a transaction may be run. An important design choice was to differentiate concurrency on the schema from concurrency on objects and to control concurrency on the schema with a different mechanism from the one that controls concurrency on objects.

3. The system makes life easier for application programmers by allowing (a) exceptional attributes for tuple objects to be attached at any time without performance degradation, (b) persistence to be implemented with a simple composition-based schema, and (c) the separation of clustering issues from the schema information.

For the next version of the system, the major thrust will be in the following directions.

- An ad hoc concurrency control for the schema, as mentioned in section 3.7, is under design and will be implemented shortly. It takes into account semantic information about schema updates to allow for increased parallelism.

- Recovery and rollbacks are not implemented in the current version of WiSS. We plan to add these shortly. To support long transactions, we also plan to provide savepoints in order not to lose arbitrary amounts of work.

- Indexes will be provided at the O_2 level (WiSS already provides B+ trees and hash-based indexes on files), that is, on large set and list objects, to support associative access on these objects. The relationship of indexes with both the inheritance hierarchy and the composition hierarchy (which has been explored separately in Kim, Kim, and Dale 1987 and in Maier and Stein 1986, respectively) will be investigated.

- Our large objects are currently limited by the size of a WiSS long data item (1.6 MB). We are looking into the possibility of modifying WiSS to be able to store large objects with virtually no size limitation.

- More work is needed toward determining when objects are badly clustered and should be moved on disk. Also, when this happens for a large number of objects, instead of making the database quiescent and changing the identifiers globally, an incremental restructuring should be used. The idea is the following. When attaining a moved object o from object o', instead of just following the forwarding marker, we also change the reference to o in o' by the forward mark, that is, its "new" identifier. The original record containing the forwarding marker will be liberated when no object refers to o by its "old" identifier (this can be handled using a reference-counter technique). This approach seems interesting, but the problem remains that moved objects may have two different oids that have to be considered equivalent.

- Versioning and authorization will be taken into account in the next version of the system. Also, more work is needed on schema evolution. The main effort is in integrating state-of-the-art techniques in the O_2 framework.

7 Acknowledgements

We thank François Bancilhon for comments on an earlier draft of this paper and for the many discussions we had during the design of the system. We also thank the following persons involved in the development of the Object Manager: Véronique Benzaken, Constance Bullier, Philippe Futtersack, Gilbert Harrus, John Ioannidis, Jean-Marie Larchevêque, and Dominique Stève. The OM also benefits from discussions with Christophe Lécluse and Philippe Richard and especially from those with Sophie Gamerman and Claude Delobel. Paris Kanellakis, Michel Scholl, and John Ioannidis read earlier drafts of this paper and suggested many improvements.

References

Andrews, T., and C. Harris. 1987. Combining language and database advances in an object-oriented development environment. In *Proceedings of the OOPSLA conference.*

Bancilhon, F., G. Barbedette, V. Benzaken, C. Delobel, S. Gamerman, C. Lécluse, P. Pfeffer, P. Richard, and F. Vélez. 1988. The design and implementation of O_2, an object-oriented database system. In *Proceedings of the second international workshop on object-oriented database systems*, ed. K. Dittrich. Springer-Verlag.

Bancilhon, F., S. Cluet, and C. Delobel. 1989. *Query languages for object-oriented database systems: Analysis and a proposal.* Altaïr Technical Report.

Banerjee, J., H-T. Chou, J. Garza, W. Kim, D. Woelk, N. Ballou, and H. J. Kim. 1987. Data model issues for object-oriented applications. *ACM TOIS* 5(1): 3–26.

Benzaken, V., and C. Delobel. 1990. Enhancing performance in a persistent object store: Clustering strategies in O_2. In *Proceedings of the fourth workshop on persistent object systems*, eds. Dearle, Shaw, and Zdonik.

Cardelli, L. 1984. A semantics of multiple inheritance. *Lecture Notes in Computer Science*, Vol. 173. Springer-Verlag.

Carey M. et al. 1986. The architecture of the Exodus extensible DBMS. In *Proceedings of the international workshop on object-oriented database systems.*

Chou, H-T., D. DeWitt, R. Katz, and A. Klug. 1985. Design and implementation of the Wisconsin storage system. *Software Practice and Experience* 15(10).

Fishman, D., D. Beech, H. P. Cate, E. C. Chow, T. Conners, J. W. Davis, N. Denett, C. G. Hoch, W. Kent, P. Lyngbaek, B. Mahbod, M. A. Neimat, T. A. Ryan, and M. C. Shan. 1987. Iris: An object-oriented database management system. *ACM TOIS* 5(1): 46–69.

Garza, J., and W. Kim. 1988. Transaction management in an object-oriented database system. In *Proceedings of the ACM SIGMOD conference.*

Gray, J. 1978. Notes on database operating systems. In *Operating systems: An advanced course.* Springer-Verlag.

Hornick M., and S. B. Zdonik 1987. A shared, segmented memory for an object-oriented database. *ACM TOIS* 5(1).

Kaehler, T. 1986. Virtual memory on a narrow machine for an object-oriented language. In *Proceedings of the OOPSLA conference.*

Kim, W., N. Ballou, H-T. Chou, J. F. Garza, D. Woelk, and J. Banerjee. 1988. Integrating an object-oriented programming system with a database system. In *Proceedings of the OOPSLA conference.*

Kim, W., K. C. Kim, and A. Dale. 1987. *Indexing techniques for object-oriented databases.* MCC technical report no. DB-134-87.

Lécluse, C., and P. Richard. 1989a. Modeling complex structures in object-oriented databases. In *Proceedings of the eighth symposium on the principles of database systems.*

Lécluse, C., and P. Richard. 1989b. *The O_2 database programming languages.* Altaïr Technical Report.

Lécluse, C., P. Richard, and F. Vélez. 1988. O_2, an object-oriented data model. In *Proceedings of the ACM SIGMOD conference.*

Maier, D., and J. Stein. 1986. Indexing in an object-oriented DBMS. In *Proceedings of the first international workshop on object-oriented database systems.*

Maier, D., and J. Stein. 1987. Development and implementation of an object-oriented DBMS. In *Research directions in object-oriented programming,* ed. B. Shriver and P. Wegner. MIT Press.

Neveu, B., and P. Haren. 1986. SMECI: An expert system for civil engineering design. In *First international conference on applications of artifial intelligence to engineering problems.*

Penney, J., J. Stein, and D. Maier 1987. Is the disk half full or half empty?: Combining optimistic and pessimistic concurrency mechanisms in a shared, persistent object base. In *Workshop on persistent object systems.*

Stonebraker, M. et al. 1983. Document processing in a relational database system. *ACM TOIS* 1(2): 143–58.

Stonebraker, M., and L. Rowe. 1987. The design of the Postgres storage system. In *Proceedings of 13th VLDB conference.*

Sun. 1986. *External data representation protocol specification.* Sun Microsystems.

CHAPTER 16

Handling Distribution in the O_2 System

GUY BERNARD
DOMINIQUE STÈVE

1 Introduction

According to the classical taxonomy of distributed systems (Tanenbaum and Van Renesse 1985), O_2 is neither a distributed operating system nor a network operating system. Rather, it is a distributed application system, where the user executes (or designs) some applications involving several machines in a transparent way, without direct access to the underlying operating system(s). Grapevine (Birrell et al. 1982; Schroeder, Birrell, and Needham 1984) is another example of a distributed application system, the target application being electronic mail. In O_2 the target applications are business, transactional, office automation, and multimedia applications.

The design of the distribution management in O_2 relies on four characteristics of the system: (1) data are structured in objects; (2) the size of the objects handled by multimedia applications may be quite large (think of a bitmap); (3) the logical topology of the system is a star, with one server machine and several workstations; and (4) these machines may be heterogeneous.

This chapter is organized as follows. The overall design of the distribution management is presented in section 2. The Object-Transfer Protocol is discussed in section 3 and the Execution-Migration Protocol in and section 4. Section 5 describes the synchronous and asynchronous workstation/server interactions. Section 6 deals with fault tolerance. Related work is reported in section 7.

2 Overall Design of the Distribution

In this section we describe the respective roles assigned to the server and the workstations, the tasks required by this dichotomy, and the main design choices.

2.1 Workstation/Server Task Assignment

There are two main approaches for designing the architecture of a system where only one site manages a data repository while the other sites have to do computation on objects (DeWitt et al. 1990; see chapter 18). In the first, the *dumb server* approach, the server deals only with pages. In the second, the *smart server* approach, the server understands the concept of an object. In O_2 we chose the smart-server approach. More work must be done on the server side (extracting and inserting objects from or into pages), but it is easy to apply methods on objects on the server, and this permits load balancing between server and workstations (see section 4). Moreover, handling heterogeneity is easier in the smart-server approach.

No concurrency control is done on the workstations, since distributed concurrency control is very difficult to implement efficiently and thus results in poor performance. If several applications running on the same workstation deal with common objects, no attempt is made to share object memory locally between these applications, and each one has its own copy under server control. Our grounds for this choice are that (1) workstations are mainly used by a single user, and the number of applications running concurrently will remain low; (2) memory space is not likely to be a scarce resource in the coming years; and (3) keeping the software as simple as possible is undoubtedly a factor in keeping response times low.

On the workstation side as well as on the server side, O_2 runs in a single process. This has important consequences, as will be seen.

2.2 Tasks Involved in Distribution

Given the choice of a smart server, the main tasks involved in distribution of the system are:

1. *Workstation startup.* Since the workstations are assumed to be diskless, the O_2 system and the database schema must be downloaded from the server machine.

2. *Object transfers.* Objects are moved from server to workstation and conversely.

3. *Execution migration.* The programmer can choose the site of execution of methods, as detailed in section 4.

4. *Interactions with the remote System Interface.* Applications running on a workstation interact with the System Interface layer of the server machine; for example, to begin, abort, or commit a transaction, and for lock requests.

5. *System monitoring.* Network or machine failures must be detected. Abnormal process terminations on both the server machine and the workstations have to be detected, too, in order to take the appropriate action. Performance monitoring and measurements of distributed executions are also useful in order to be able to tune the system.

These five tasks do not have the same requirements in terms of performance. Task 1 is not critical. First, it is performed only once when the user initializes O_2. Second, the user is not surprised by some initialization delay. Task 2 is critical. Object transfers are quite frequent for the target applications (for reading as well as for updating objects). Furthermore, object size is very variable, ranging from a tuple containing one integer field to a 1 MB bitmap.

Task 3 exists in order to enhance the overall system performance; thus it must be carefully designed. Task 4 may be invoked several times during an O_2 session, but the amount of transferred data is small; thus this task is not critical. The overhead resulting from task 5 must be as low as possible. This is not difficult to achieve since it does not imply extra message transfers in our design.

2.3 Main Design Choices

Our design choices in the implementation were made according to the criteria of simplicity, transparency, performance, and reliability. *Simplicity* (and thus portability) is achieved by choosing standard and well-proven tools. The local area network which links the workstations and the server is Ethernet; the transport protocols are TCP/IP (Postel 1981a, 1981b). No change has to be made to the host operating system. A connection-oriented transport protocol such as TCP brings reliability. Since a workstation interacts only with the server machine, connection startup time is required only once, at workstation startup. Of course, it is quite easy to modify the communication layer in order to use another general-purpose, connection-oriented protocol or "lightweight" transport protocols for local area networks, such as NETBLT (Lambert, Clark, and Zhang 1985), VMTP (Cheriton 1986), UDSTP (Lee, Chon, and Chung 1986), or Delta-t (Watson and Mamrak 1987).

Transparency results from the fact that the end user is never concerned with either the client/server task distribution or the heterogeneity of the machines. *Performance* is obtained by execution migration and by a designing an ad hoc protocol for object movement. *Reliability* is obtained by a failure-detection mechanism that prevents indefinite resource holding, which might result from an abnormal process termination.

3 Object-Transfer Protocol

Object transfer requires special attention, since the server machine is first of all an object server. The Object-Transfer Protocol was designed to allow peer machines to be heterogeneous, and to allow object sizes to vary considerably. Since the internal data representation on a workstation and on the server machine may be different, some data translation is needed in order that the correct values may be retrieved. Moreover, the size of a given object may not be the same on the two machines.

The Object-Transfer Protocol was designed with the following elements in mind.

1. The data to be transferred are typed objects.

2. Memory-to-memory copies are time-consuming. The impact of multiple copies has been pointed out as being an important factor affecting the performance of implementations of level-3 and level-4 communication protocols (Cabrera, Karels, and Mosher 1985; Mosher 1985).

3. Dynamic memory allocations are still more expensive, due to the cost of kernel calls.

4. It is much more costly to send m messages of size s each than to send a single message of size $m * s$.

3.1 Presentation Protocol

As for communication protocols, in the current prototype we use the standard presentation protocol XDR (Sun 1986). The choice of XDR was based on the following considerations:

- Although designed by Sun, XDR has been adopted in non-Sun operating systems (e.g., Unix 4.3bsd), so that implementations are available on many kinds of machines.

- XDR specifications are in the public domain.

- In SunOS and Unix 4.3bsd, the XDR interface is a set of procedures included in the C library, and is thus easily usable.

- XDR provides a means for delimiting records in a byte stream.

The layering has been designed to make it easy to switch to another presentation protocol.

In order to use XDR for O_2, two problems had to be solved.

1. Data encoded by XDR (and by most presentation protocols) are not self-describing. This means that for the correct decoding of object data, the basic structure of the data must be known by the receiver (e.g., one integer, two strings, and an object identifier).

2. With a connection-oriented transport protocol, transferred data are seen as a byte stream, and there is no *message* concept. We need this concept in O_2, since the workstation software has to know when an object transfer is completed. Moreover, a logical message may be quite large (e.g., a bitmap or a large set).

The first problem is solved in O_2 by relying on the type of the objects. The second one is solved by using the marking standard provided by XDR. The programmer may mark the logical end of a message when he or she so desires. The logical channel is implemented as a cache buffer where encoded data are stored before effective transmission on the network. The buffer is flushed either when the programmer marks an end-of-message or when the buffer is full. Buffer size is customizable and may be tuned to fit the transport-level protocol and the link-level protocol. The programmer does not have to worry about message lengths, while being sure that the number of system calls required by any actual writing is kept to a minimum. The same cache mechanism is used for receiving data.

3.2 Minimizing the Number of Messages

Whereas the cache buffer used by XDR minimizes the number of system calls for a given number of messages, another way to improve performance is to minimize the number of messages. This is achieved in O_2 in two ways. First, at transaction-commit time, the set of dirty objects is sent in a single logical message. Second, objects are mapped to files according to placement trees, as described in chapter 17 and in Benzaken and Delobel 1990. This clustering algorithm minimizes both disk access and network access: when an object fault occurs on a workstation, if the object requested is not already in object memory on the server, a page is read from disk and all the objects of the page are moved to the workstation in a single logical message. ObServer (Skarra, Zdonik, and Reiss 1986) also uses a strategy for clustering objects.

3.3 Minimizing the Number of Memory Copies

The number of memory copies may be minimized in a homogeneous environment by sending the size of the objects in front of the data. When the Communication Manager receives a set of objects, for each object of the set: (1) read its size from the network, (2) ask the Memory Manager for an address large enough to store the object, and (3) copy the incoming data from network to memory.

Unfortunately, this scheme does not work between heterogeneous computers. There are several unsatisfactory solutions, for instance:

- Provide an intermediate buffer in the Communication Manager for storing decoded data. Once receiving is completed, the local length of the object is known. This solution would imply a copy in memory. Furthermore, with buffer space statically allocated, this would set a limit to the object size, and memory space would be wasted most of the time.

- Include in each object header the maximum size the object has on all the types of machines present in the configuration. If a new type of machine is added, for which the size of some objects is larger than the previous maximum size, database objects will have to be modified. Moreover, keeping inside the objects of the database information which has nothing to do with the semantics of the objects is not a clean solution.

The solution chosen in O_2 relies on the typing of the objects. Given the class of an object, its basic structure is known (in terms of atomic types: integer, float, string, object identifier, and so on), and this permits its local size to be computed. The object header includes the type identifier of the object (which is needed anyway by other parts of the Object Manager). When an object is to be sent, its basic structure is retrieved from its type and put in the message being built. This information is also used to properly encode the object data, which are appended to the basic structure in the message. On the receiving side, the basic structure is received first; it is used to compute the local length and ask for a suitable memory address. Then data are received from the network, properly decoded and copied on the fly at the returned address. The basic structure of an object is kept in memory and is directly available if the object is to be sent later to the other site.

3.4 Serializing and Deserializing Data

O_2 objects may be quite complex; that is, some components may be pointers on memory addresses (for strings or other objects). Before emission, the object data are flattened by dereferencing the components. On the receiving side, references are rebuilt. Once again, profit is taken from object typing. Emerald also uses a serializing/deserializing mechanism (Jul et al. 1988).

4 The Execution-Transfer Protocol

The task assignment described in section 2 is, roughly speaking: "the server is responsible for data and the workstation is responsible for computation"; but the O_2 language and the O_2 system allow execution of methods on the server machine, in order to enhance performance.

Suppose that the programmer is writing a selection on a large set with a high selectivity and a simple selection criterion, and that the objects of the set do not have to be already referenced by the application. The objects of the set are thus not loaded in object memory on the workstation. Executing the selection on the workstation would imply downloading all the objects of the set on the workstation before applying the selection on them. It may be more efficient to transfer execution on the server machine, because only the selected objects will have to be moved.

We decided to make the distributed architecture visible to the application programmer (but not to the end user). The programmer will be aware of the existence of two machines (the server and the workstation) and may explicitly specify on which of the machines a message-passing expression is to be executed. For example, the programmer specifies that the message *filter,* which tests each element of the set my_set, should be run on the server:

result_object = [**on server** my_set filter];

On the other hand, methods that display an object or edit a document object must be run on the workstation, and computations on objects already loaded in object memory on the workstation should be performed on the workstation. Note that we associate location with message passing and not with methods: the same method could be run first on the server and later on the workstation, if the user so decides.

For messages without site specification, the system decides the evaluation site. The strategy we implemented is: "execute in the machine in which you are currently executing." See section 7 for expected improvements to this strategy.

At first sight, the Execution Transfer Protocol may appear to be a classical Remote Procedure Call (RPC) Protocol (Nelson 1981). However, some specificities must be pointed out.

4.1 Decoupling from Transport Protocol

RPC protocols are generally coupled with an ad hoc transport protocol. The work of Birrell and Nelson 1984, Panzieri and Shrivastava 1982, 1988, Shrivastava and Panzieri 1982, Otway and Oskiewicz 1987, and *Eden* (Lazowska et al. 1981, Black 1985; Almes et al. 1985) are examples of this approach. The same is generally true for the internal mechanisms used in distributed operating systems.

In O_2, using a reliable transport protocol permits one to avoid acknowledgement managing: if a result is available, the method was executed remotely exactly once, and the result is itself an acknowledgement.

4.2 Orphan Detection

Detecting an abnormal termination of the remote procedure is generally achieved by a probing mechanism: periodically, the caller sends a probe message to the callee to be sure that processing is still under way.

Once again, the design choices for O_2 make the task easier. Since the transport layer and the module responsible for method execution run in the same process, an abnormal termination of a method execution leads to connection closing, which is immediately detected by the process awaiting a result. We come back to this point in section 6.

4.3 Embedded Calls

Embedded calls (i.e., the remotely called procedure itself does an RPC) are generally not supported by RPC protocols. There are however some exceptions, e.g., REX (Otway and Oskiewicz 1987).

In O_2, the Execution Transfer Protocol supports embedded calls. Embedded method executions may result from a poor programming methodology (for instance when the methods have been written by different programmers, without a global view of the application); but it may also be caused by constraints on method execution (for example, a method which displays object data should be run on the workstation).

An example of embedded method executions is given in figure 16.1. The programmer specifies that the method *extract* will be applied on object List on the server machine. Method *extract* scans List and, when some predicate is true, the selected element of List is displayed on the workstation side. Finally, method *extract* returns the number of elements selected. Between execution transfers 1 and 4, the application acts as a client; that is, execution is suspended on the workstation. Between execution transfers 2 and 3, the server acts as a client. Of course, these execution transfers are transparent to the end user.

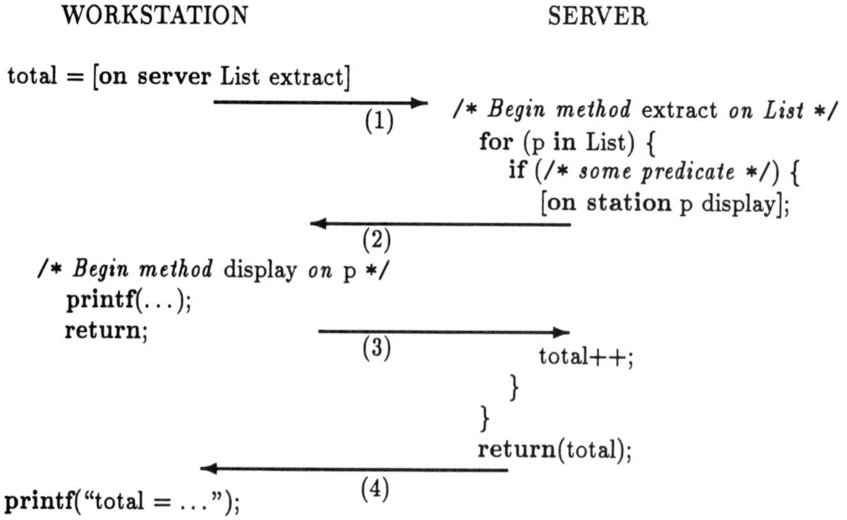

Figure 16.1. Example of embedded execution migrations

4.4 Coherence between the Two Sites

Transactions must preserve their execution context when transferring execution from one site to another. Refer to the example in figure 16.1. Suppose that before executing method *extract*, some object *o* was modified on the workstation side. This object must be transferred to the server side before execution of method *extract* begins, because this method might use object *o*. In the same way, all objects created or updated on the server side by method *extract* must be sent to the workstation before resuming execution on the workstation. Thus our Execution Transfer Protocol is much more than a simple request-response protocol.

4.5 Argument Passing

The number of arguments of the invoked method, and their basic types, are not known at precompile time; therefore an encoding/decoding scheme is provided. A first buffer, arg_buf, contains the arguments of the message passing. This buffer is used for local execution as well as for remote execution. A second buffer, desc_buf, is necessary for remote execution, because the argument values in arg_buf must be encoded/decoded when transmitted on the network. Thus the basic types of the arguments must be known by the communication module. This is achieved by desc_buf, which is filled at the same time as arg_buf with an integer (number of arguments) and, for each argument, a byte which indicates the argument type. The buffer desc_buf is sent on the network just before the (encoded) arg_buf. The desc_buf buffer is not used for local method execution.

5 Workstation/Server Interactions

The communication between an O_2 process on a workstation and the corresponding O_2 process on the server is mainly synchronous. This is the case for object faults and remote method execution, for instance. However, some interactions follow an asynchronous scheme.

5.1 Synchronous Interactions

On the server side, the O_2 process is driven by the network: it just sits in an endless loop in a dispatcher, waiting for incoming messages from the workstation. When a message arrives, the appropriate system primitive is called according to the message type and, upon return, the O_2 process comes back in the dispatcher. The loop is exited only when the O_2 process terminates on the workstation.

On the workstation side, the O_2 process is driven by the application. When a service is requested of the O_2 server process, some primitive of the System Interface or Memory Manager module is called. This primitive itself calls the appropriate primitive in the Communication Manager module (which sends a message of some type and returns without waiting for an answer). The primitive then calls a dispatcher to correctly handle the data received from the O_2 server process. The dispatcher is needed because some replies have to be received and processed without returning control to the System Interface or the Memory Manager. For instance, objects may be received by the workstation either because they were explicitly asked for, or because a remote-execution method ends on the server. Thus the dispatcher on the workstation has exactly the same behavior as the dispatcher on the server, except that the former returns after having received and processed a message of some type. The dispatcher on the workstation is called with an argument which indicates, according to the System Interface or the Memory Manager primitive that called the dispatcher, the received message type(s) which should make it return.

When the O_2 process on the server acts like a client of the O_2 process on the workstation (this is the case when an embedded remote-method call occurs), a dispatcher identical to the dispatcher on the workstation is called on the server, before returning to the main loop.

5.2 Asynchronous Interactions

Whereas most of the dialogue between the O_2 process on the workstation and the O_2 process on the server follows this synchronous scheme, there are a few cases where asynchronism is more efficient. For instance, when an application programmer modifies a method, the O_2 process on the workstation sends the method name to the O_2 process on the server and goes on without waiting for a grant. If at the same time another application programmer modifies the same method, a conflict occurs, and one of the two transactions must be aborted.

Asynchronous interactions are carried out by an out-of-band data mechanism. When an out-of-band message is received, a software interrupt is sent to the O_2 process on the workstation and appropriate processing is done immediately.

6 Fault Tolerance

Before dealing with fault tolerance, it is necessary to say a few words about the processes involved in O_2 and about the way an O_2 session is started.

6.1 Processes Involved in O_2

The processes involved in O_2, both on a workstation and on the server, are shown in figure 16.2. When an O_2 session is started on a workstation, an O_2 process must be started on the server, in order to interact with the lower layers of the system, and possibly for remote method execution. Thus an activity must be always present on the server machine, to watch for application creations on workstations (or from terminals of the server) and to start the corresponding process. This activity is the O_2 daemon process. It must be always running on the server, and it never terminates unless killed by the administrator of the system. The O_2 daemon process waits for connection requests. When a connection request arrives from a workstation, the O_2 daemon process creates an O_2 mirror process on the server and goes back into the loop, waiting for the next connection request. The O_2 daemon serves other purposes. It plays an important role in case of failure detection, and it can be used for global measurements on the O_2 system.

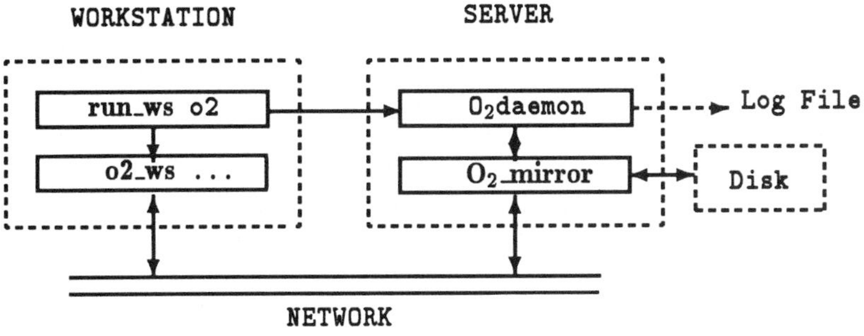

Figure 16.2. Processes in O_2

6.2 Starting O_2 from a Workstation

O_2 is started by the user on a workstation by executing the command **run_ws** with some arguments (e.g., database name, application name and interface options).

- On the workstation side, **run_ws** (1) sets up a TCP connection with the server, (2) creates a process, (3) sends on the opened connection a message containing the application name just invoked, together with the user-supplied arguments, and (4) waits for an acknowledgement from the O_2 daemon process. It then (5) derives (from the application name, the user-supplied arguments, and the environment information) the name of the executable file associated to the O_2 workstation application, and finally (6) starts it in the newly created process with (possibly) some of the user-supplied arguments. This new process is the **o2_ws** process. It inherits the TCP connection set up by the **run_ws**, and **o2_ws** begins.

- On the server side, the O_2 daemon process (1) accepts the connection, (2) creates a process, (3) recognizes that the application was started from a workstation, (4) derives (from the application name and the user-supplied arguments sent by the workstation) the name of the executable file associated to the O_2 process to start, (5) starts it in the newly created process with (possibly) some of the user-supplied arguments, and (6) sends an acknowledgement. This new process is the **o2_mirror** process. It inherits the TCP connection set up by the O_2 daemon process, and **o2_mirror** starts the dispatcher to wait for incoming messages.

6.3 Handling Abnormal Process Terminations

In this section we deal only with failure detection. Recovery is outside the scope of this paper. Failure detection in O_2 relies on the fact that all the tasks involved run in a single process. Machine or network crashes are detected by the connection loss. Abnormal process terminations, *anywhere in the O_2 modules*, result in closing the connection, which is noticed by the other site when it attempts to read or write on the network.

When a transaction begins, the O_2 mirror process sends to the O_2 daemon process the transaction identifier, together with its process identifier. When a transaction aborts or commits, a null transaction identifier is sent. This way, the O_2 daemon process knows the number and the state of the O_2 processes at any time. This information may be used for statistics (transaction durations for instance); it is also useful for failure detection and recovery.

- When an O_2 process terminates normally on a workstation, there is no currently running transaction. A message is sent by the **o2_ws** process to the **o2_mirror** process, and this latter process quietly exits.
- When an O_2 process terminates abnormally on a workstation, the connection loss is detected by the O_2 mirror process, which, if necessary, aborts the current transaction, sends a null transaction identifier to the O_2 daemon process, and exits.
- The problem is more complex when the O_2 mirror process itself terminates abnormally. The **o2_ws** process will notice the connection loss with the next read or write on the network, but it has no way to communicate with the server machine to free the locks possibly held. Here the O_2 daemon process is involved. It detects the abnormal termination of the O_2 mirror process and looks at the transaction identifier currently corresponding to that process. If the transaction identifier is non-null, then the O_2 daemon itself aborts the transaction.

On the workstation side, the calls to the communication primitives may be quite infrequent (for instance, all the objects needed for a long computation may have been downloaded from the server a long time ago). In this case, a connection loss may be detected very late. The solution we have adopted is to look periodically at the message queue, returning immediately if no message is present. This mechanism works in background, and is transparent to the user. If a connection loss is detected, a warning message is displayed for the user, who decides to continue anyway (if no modified persistent objects are to be written on disk) or to stop the session.

7 Related Work

O_2 may be compared with other workstation/server object-oriented DBMS systems.

In *GemStone* (Purdy, Schuchardt, and Maier 1987), Smalltalk objects on the workstation belong to one of two exclusive categories: proxies and deputies. Methods may be applied on proxy objects only on the server; the site for execution of methods applying to deputy objects may be chosen by the programmer. Embedded execution migrations are not possible. In O_2 the execution site is not decided by the programmer according to some object characteristics, but on the basis of message passing. Remote method execution may thus be applied on any object.

ObServer (Hornick and Zdonik 1987) provides a dumb server to workstations. The server machine does not know the concept of *object*; thus execution migration is not possible. Interactions between the workstations and the server are only asynchronous (Skarra, Zdonik, and Reiss 1986). In O_2 we combine the flexibility provided by asynchronous interactions (for schema updates) and the efficiency provided by synchronous interactions (object faults).

The O_2 prototype is currently implemented on Sun/3 machines (both for the server and the workstations). However, we are working on accommodating heterogeneity.

Using XDR systematically for object transfers appears to imply only a slight overhead. The main part of the response times for communications between workstation and server is caused by process context switching. This is the price to pay for portability on standard Unix computers: as mentioned earlier, read/write operations on the network are made through kernel calls in Unix.

Running all the O_2 software layers in a single process has several advantages. First, the *upcall* mechanism (Clark 1985) between the Communication Manager and other modules of the OM that is worked out by the dispatchers reduces to simple function calls (embedded execution migrations are made through the program stack), and this provides simplicity and efficiency. Second, fault detection may be carried out easily; no probe mechanism is needed, because connection losses are immediately detected.

Remote method execution appears to have a large impact on system performance. For a list of 1000 tuples of 300 bytes each, selecting 2 of them on the server rather than on the workstation leads to a speedup factor of 3.1 when objects are to be read from disk, and 3.5 when objects are already loaded in server memory. Embedded remote method execution leads to good results too. With the same example, if the two selected objects are displayed on the workstation (so that two successive embedded calls occur—see figure 16.1), the speedup factor is 2.2, either with or without objects loaded in server memory. Thus the end user takes advantage of a short response time while keeping the benefits of local displaying, all in a transparent way. The low granularity of the execution migration (namely the *method*) provides the programmer with great flexibility in load balancing.

Further work is needed to implement dynamic load balancing. For messages without site specification, the system currently implements message passing in the same site in which it runs. This strategy could clearly be improved by letting the system decide dynamically on the site of application of the method. The criteria might be the current workload of the server and/or the workstation, the number of objects to transfer from a site to another to preserve the execution context, and the size of the receiver object. This problem is complex, since it involves both system aspects and database aspects. An intermediate solution could be to take advantage of hints given by the application programmer (about request selectivity, for instance) and to let the system make the final choice according to its current state. This solution is now being investigated.

References

Almes, G. T., A. P. Black, E. D. Lazowska, and J. D. Noe. 1985. The Eden system: A technical review. *IEEE Transactions on Software Engineering* SE-11(1).

Bancilhon, F., G. Barbedette, V. Benzaken, C. Delobel, S. Gamerman, C. Lécluse, P. Pfeffer, P. Richard, and F. Vélez. 1988. The design and implementation of O_2, an object-oriented database system. In *Proceedings of the second international workshop on object-oriented database systems,* ed. K. Dittrich.

Benzaken, V., and C. Delobel. 1990. Enhancing performance in a persistent object store: Clustering strategies in O_2. In *Proceedings of the fourth workshop on persistent object systems*, eds. Dearle, Shaw, and Zdonik.

Birrell, A. D., R. Levin, R. M. Needham, and M. D. Schroeder. 1982. Grapevine: An exercise in distributed computing. *Communications of the ACM* 25(4).

Birrell, A. D., and B. J. Nelson. 1984. Implementing remote procedure calls. *ACM TOCS* 2(1).

Black, A. P. 1985. Supporting distributed applications: Experience with Eden. In *Proceedings of the tenth symposium on operating system principles.*

Cabrera, L. F., M. J. Karels, and D. Mosher. 1985. *The impact of buffer management on networking software performance in Berkeley UNIX 4.2BSD: A case study.* Report no. UCB/CSD 85/247, University of California, Berkeley.

Cheriton, D. R. 1986. VMTP: A transport protocol for the next generation of communication systems. In *Proceedings of the SIGCOMM '86 conference.*

Clark, D. D. 1985. The structuring of systems using upcalls. In *Proceedings of the tenth symposium on operating system principles.*

DeWitt, D., P. Futtersack, D. Maier, and F. Vélez. 1990. A study of three alternative workstations/server architectures for object-oriented database systems. In *Proceedings of the 16th VLDB conference.*

Hornick M., and S. B. Zdonik 1987. A shared, segmented memory for an object-oriented database. *ACM TOIS* 5(1).

Jul, E., H. Levy, N. Hutchinson, and A. Black. 1988. Fine-grained mobility in the Emerald system. *ACM TOCS* 6(1).

Lambert, M., D. D. Clark, and L. Zhang. 1985. *NETBLT: A bulk data transport protocol.* RFC 969, Network Information Center, SRI International.

Lazowska, E. D., H. M. Levy, G. T. Almes, M. J. Fischer, R. J. Fowler, and S. C. Vestal. 1981. The architecture of the Eden system. In *Proceedings of the eighth symposium on operating systems principles.*

Lee, D., K. Chon, and C. Chung. 1986. A reliable datagram transport protocol on local area networks. In *Proceedings of the SIGCOMM conference.*

Mosher, D. A. 1985. *A study of an Internet protocol implementation.* Report no. UCB/CSD 85/238, University of California, Berkeley.

Nelson, B. J. 1981. *Remote procedure call.* PhD thesis, Carnegie-Mellon University. Available as CMU report no. CMU-CS-81-119.

Otway, D., and E. Oskiewicz. 1987. REX: A remote execution protocol for object-oriented distributed applications. In *Proceedings of the seventh international conference on distributed computing systems.*

Panzieri, F., and S. K. Shrivastava. 1982. Reliable remote calls for distributed UNIX: An implementation study. In *Proceedings of the second symposium on reliability in distributed software and database systems.*

Panzieri, F., and S. K. Shrivastava. 1988. Rajdoot: A remote procedure call mechanism supporting orphan detection and killing. *IEEE Transactions on Software Engineering* 14(1).

Postel, J. B. 1981a. *Internet protocol: DARPA Internet program protocol specification.* RFC 791, Network Information Center, SRI International.

Postel, J. B. 1981b. *Transmission control protocol.* RFC 793, Network Information Center, SRI International.

Purdy, A., B. Schuchardt, and D. Maier. 1987. Integrating an object server with other worlds. *ACM TOIS* 5(1).

Schroeder, M. D., A. D. Birrell, and R. M. Needham. 1984. Experience with Grapevine: The growth of a distributed system. *ACM TOCS* 2(1).

Shrivastava, S. K., and F. Panzieri. 1982. The design of reliable remote procedure call mechanism. *IEEE Transactions on Computers* C-31(7).

Skarra, A., S. Zdonik, and S. Reiss. 1986. An object server for an object-oriented database system. In *Proceedings of the IEEE conference.*

Sun. 1986. *External data representation protocol specification.* Sun Microsystems.

Tanenbaum, A. S., and R. Van Renesse. 1985. Distributed operating systems. *ACM Computing Surveys* 17(4).

Vélez, F., G. Bernard and V. Darnis. 1989. The O_2 object manager: An overview. In *Proceedings of the 15th VLDB conference.*

Watson, R. W., and S. A. Mamrak. 1987. Gaining efficiency in transport services by appropriate design and implementation choices. *ACM TOCS* 5(2).

CHAPTER 17

Clustering Strategies in O_2: An Overview

VÉRONIQUE BENZAKEN
CLAUDE DELOBEL
GILBERT HARRUS

1 Introduction

In the past five years, object-oriented database systems (OODBSs) have evolved into what is likely to become the major commercial database technology of the 1990s (Bancilhon 1988; Kim 1988). Whereas the relational model provided the user only with sets of tuples as data modeling primitives, object-oriented database systems provide the database programmer with a wide variety of data modeling primitives (type constructors) including sets, lists, tuples, and references between objects (see chapter 3). In addition, one can compose these type constructors almost arbitrarily (Atkinson and Buneman 1987; Lécluse, Richard, and Vélez 1988; Lécluse and Richard 1989a; Abiteboul and Kanellakis 1989). Furthermore, OODBSs almost always provide an inheritance hierarchy for defining types.

The differences between relational database systems and OODBSs are not, however, limited to their type-definition systems. Database accesses in an OODBS are much more complex, due to the rich variety of type constructors provided. In addition to providing relational-like scans of sets or collections of objects, OODBSs foster a navigation-like access among related objects. Such interobject references would not present a performance problem if the entire database fitted in main memory; with a disk-resident database, however, following every such interobject reference may result in random disk accesses.

Without effective clustering, following a reference from one object to another may involve a disk I/O. Since a typical disk drive can only perform 30 such random accesses per second, the performance of the system may be severely limited if objects that reference one another are not clustered together. *A clustering strategy* is an attempt to reduce the I/O overhead by storing the components of a complex object in the same unit of storage.

Most of the prototypes already developed (Hornick and Zdonik 1987; Kim et al. 1987; Atwood 1985; Maier et al. 1986; Hudson and King 1989; Schek et al. 1990) attempt to perform clustering. In all such systems the segment or the page is the clustering unit, and clustering is done when the object is created. The principal goal is to store a complex record as a linearized consecutive string preserving the hierarchical structure. If the string is larger than a page, it will be mapped to a minimal number of contiguous disk pages. The approach adopted in Orion (Kim et al. 1987) defines the unit of clustering as the composite (exclusive/dependent) object. This is done at the schema level. However, we think that the user should not need to worry about physical issues; the clustering information should be transparent to the user. Furthermore, if the concept of cluster (via the notion of composite object) is part of the schema, when we want to modify the placement in secondary storage we have to perform a schema update—and data independence is not ensured.

Chang and Katz 1989 have shown that clustering exploits structural information such as composition hierarchy and inheritance properties. A simulation model has been developed which gives a comparative evaluation of different clustering strategies. The clustering algorithm studied by Chang and Katz 1989 chooses an initial placement for newly created objects which depends on the most frequently used composition links between instances.

The grouping strategies presented in the Encore system (Hornick and Zdonik 1987) seem flexible and powerful (in particular the clustering-by-value feature). In Encore, the following clustering rules may be chosen: (1) ability to store one object per segment if it is large, (2) ability to store components of a complex object together, (3) ability to group all the instances of a given class in the same segment, (4) grouping by value properties (e.g, all objects representing blue cars will be stored together). The power of these strategies relies on the fact that, in Encore, objects are shared by means of copies. However, in an environment where update operations are frequently performed, managing such copies seems likely to impair performance.

The approach adopted in the Prima project (Harder et al. 1987) uses the concept of type-molecule as a clustering mechanism for complex objects (Schoning and Sikeler 1989). This concept allows the description of flexible clustering strategies. The main drawbacks of this approach are that some objects, have to be duplicated between several complex objects, and that clustering is update dependent.

The Prima strategies rely only on the structure of objects and do not take into account the operations really performed on the database. Design decisions about clustering are under the control of the database administrator. However, to help the database administrator in taking his decision we have established a link between the access patterns of the methods of a class and the object clustering strategies for this class.

Our technique is similar to the one proposed by (Schkolnick 1977) for the hierarchical data model. The idea of Schkolnick is to partition a hierarchical tree structure into subtrees and to find the best partition according to some access patterns inside the hierarchical structure. Our strategy follows the same idea, but differs in the following respects: (1) the data model is not the same (objects can be shared, and there is an inheritance relationship); (2) clustering is done at commit time, as well as persistency; (3) clustering is transparent to the programmer, so that placement trees can be modified at any time without affecting programs.

In this chapter we propose a set of flexible clustering strategies which can evolve when the need arises. We do not try to cluster all the components of an object together; instead, we try to define grouping strategies which take into account both the structural parts of the objects (i.e., the composition hierarchy) and the operations performed on the database (i.e., the methods). To this end, we propose a cost model which evaluates the profits of a given strategy; then an algorithm is presented which builds the optimal strategy with respect to the model. Finally, we give a short summary of past and future performance-measurement activities. Most of the results presented in this chapter were published in three earlier papers, Benzaken and Delobel 1990, Benzaken 1990a, Harrus, Benzaken, and Delobel 1990.

2 The O_2 Clustering Strategies

In the O_2 system two main concepts coexist: *values* and *objects*. Values are instances of *types*, which specify their structure and are manipulated through predefined primitives. Objects have an identity (internal identifier) and encapsulate values and *methods*. Objects belong to *classes*. Each class has a name and is associated with a type as well as with a set of objects. This set of objects may be referred to, at the schema level, as the *extension* of the class. However, some classes may be declared to have no extension. Types are recursively constructed from basic types such as integer and string, using set, list, and tuple constructors. The following example illustrates class and type construction (notice that the courses on a menu are identified by numbers).

```
add class Restaurant
        type tuple(name: string
                   menu: Menu
                   chef: Chef
                   customers: set(Person))
```

add class Menu
    type tuple(**price**: integer
        courses: Course)

add class Course
    type set(integer)

add class Chef **inherits** Person
    type tuple(**specialty**: Course)

add class Person
    type tuple(**name**: string
        address: string)

Classes are partially ordered according to an inheritance hierarchy. Types and classes may be represented by a directed, labeled graph which we call the *type inheritance graph* (TIG). The TIG for the Restaurant example is given in figure 17.1. Such graphs are similar to those described by Kim, Bertino, and Garza 1989. Each node denotes a class or a type and is associated with the constructor used: tuple [ ], set { }, or list <>. When a node denotes a class it is labeled by the class name. Each edge represents either a composition link, labeled by an attribute name in the case of tuples, or an inheritance link (the dotted edges in the graph). Basic types may be represented in the TIG; but as we assumed that atomic values are always stored within the corresponding object, we limit our description to the elements which are essential for clustering purposes.

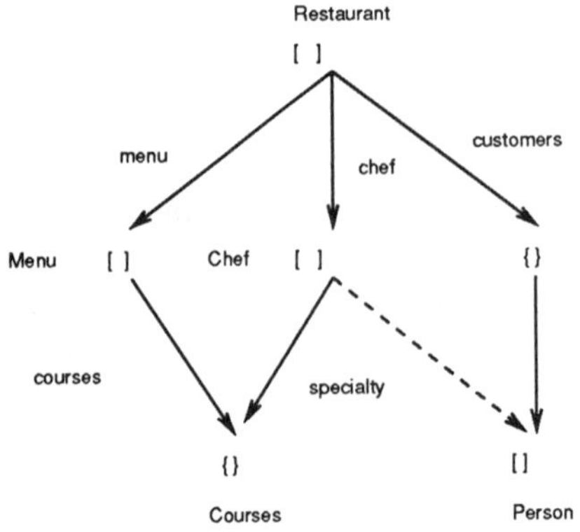

Figure 17.1. A type inheritance graph

In the O_2 system, objects are uniquely identified and are represented by a pair (i, v) where i is an object identifier and v a value. The value of an object may be composed of several other objects and/or values. Values are recursively constructed from atoms (such as integer, string, or object identifiers) using set, list, and tuple constructors. A *named* object or value is an object or value with a user-defined name.

Given a set of objects, the links between these objects may be represented by a labeled, directed graph. We call this graph a *composition object graph* (COG). The nodes denote either objects or complex values. These concepts are illustrated in the following example, which represents the database state.

(i_1, [**name**: "Taillevent"
  menu: i_3
  chef: i_4
  customers: {i_5, i_6}])
(i_2, [**name**: "La tour d'argent"
  menu: i_7
  chef: i_8
  customers: {i_6, i_9}])
(i_3, [**price**: 500
  courses: {i_{10}}])
(i_4, [**name**: "P. Dupond"
  address: "Rue des dames"
  specialty: i_{12}])
(i_5, [**name**: "F. Mitterand"
  address: "Elysee"])
(i_6, [**name**: "J. Chirac"
  address: "Hotel de ville"])
(i_7, [**price**: 600
  courses: i_{11}])
(i_8, [**name**: "P. Dupont"
  address: "Rue des abbesses"
  specialty: i_{11}])
(i_9, [**name**: "G. Bush"
  address: "The White House"])
(i_{10}, {1, 2, 3, 4, 5, 6})
(i_{11}, {1, 2, 3, 4, 5, 6, 7)}
(i_{12}, {1, 2, 3, 4})

The **customers** attribute of object i_1 is a set-structured complex value. The **menu** attribute of object i_1 is an object. The COG associated with these data is given in figure 17.2.

The COG is an abstraction which allows us to represent a complete database as well as any subset of objects of the database. The clustering strategies, which we present next, rely on the structural part of the data and on inheritance.

In the O_2 system, pure object identity is maintained. There is no sharing by copy. The clustering strategies are used when new objects are created or when

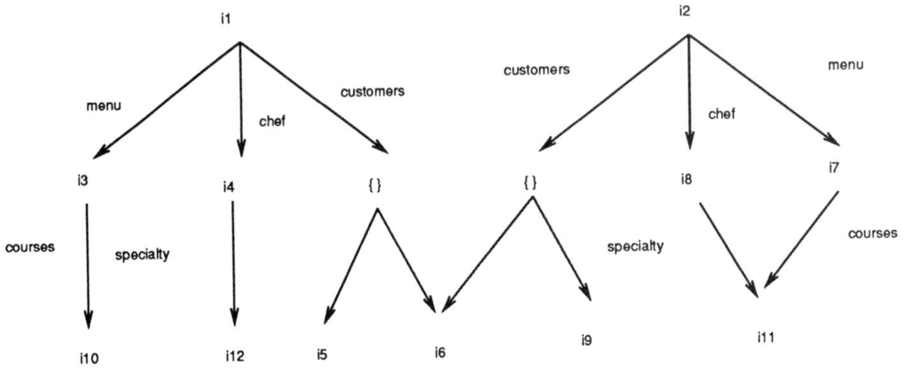

Figure 17.2. A composition object graph

links between objects are updated. At that time we have to decide whether to create a new cluster for the object or to place it in an already existing one. This is the major reason why we bind the clustering process to the concept of transaction. When an object is brought into main memory during a transaction, its location has been determined by the transaction which created it. On the other hand, newly created objects have an existence in main memory only, and it is impossible to state, before the end of the transaction, if they will be persistent. Thus we need to delay as long as possible the physical placement in secondary storage. The clustering algorithm will be invoked at the end of the transaction, that is, at commit time.

2.1 Placement Trees

Intuitively, the type structure of a class in the O_2 system may be represented as an infinite tree, in the case of recursive types (Abiteboul and Kanellakis 1989; see chapter 5). A placement tree is any finite subtree extracted from this infinite tree. A *clustering strategy* for the system classes is a set of placement trees. Given a clustering strategy, each class in the system is the root of at most one placement tree. We have chosen a finite tree for operational reasons. A placement tree for class *c* expresses the way in which components of an instance of *c* are to be clustered. Notice that the definition of a placement tree allows us to handle type recursiveness at the physical level. Figure 17.3 shows examples of clustering strategies.

In the first alternative, the placement tree for the Restaurant class states that **menu** (which is an instance of class Menu), the type **customers**, and each of the "customers" elements will be grouped with the corresponding instance of Restaurant. This means that, in a single cluster, we shall store the Menu object, its atomic components, the value `customers`, the elements of the corresponding set, and the atomic values which compose them. An instance of the class Courses may be shared by a Chef instance or a Menu instance. Therefore a Courses

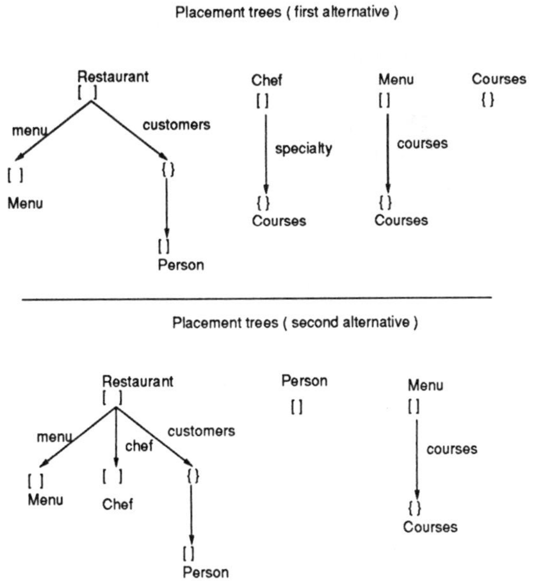

Figure 17.3. Placement trees

object may be clustered either with a Chef object or with a Menu object. Unlike in the Orion system, such a decision is taken only at run time and is not part of the database schema. In the second alternative, the placement tree for the class Person reduces to a single node. Instances of this class consist only of atoms, and we assume that atomic values are stored with the instance to which they are related. Placement trees are the inputs of the clustering algorithm. They indicate how objects may be stored; they are not part of the schema. There is no class placement tree, and no instances of placement trees.

2.1.1 Placement Trees and Complex Values

A placement tree can be used to describe how complex values may be mapped onto the physical memory. The concept of placement tree allows the database administrator (DBA) to describe, for a given class, any subtree extracted from the type graph associated with it. Such a tree may contain types (which denote complex values). Assume that a class Person is defined as follows.

```
add class Person
        type tuple(parents: tuple(father: Man
                                  mother: Woman)
                   children: set(Person))
add class Man inherits Person
add class Woman inherits Person
```

The TIG for this class is shown in figure 17.4. A placement tree for Person is shown in figure 17.5. Beside it is a subtree that groups only the values **parents** and **father**. With the subtree, in one cluster we shall have the instance of Person, the tuple complex value **parents**, and the **father** attribute of this value, which is an instance of class Man. The **mother** attribute of the tuple value will not be grouped with the instance of Person. Nevertheless, the reference to the value **mother** is stored within the Person object. If we had instead an atomic type (such as string) rather than Man, the attribute **father** would not appear in the placement subtree; the atomic value **father** would be stored with the tuple complex value **parents**.

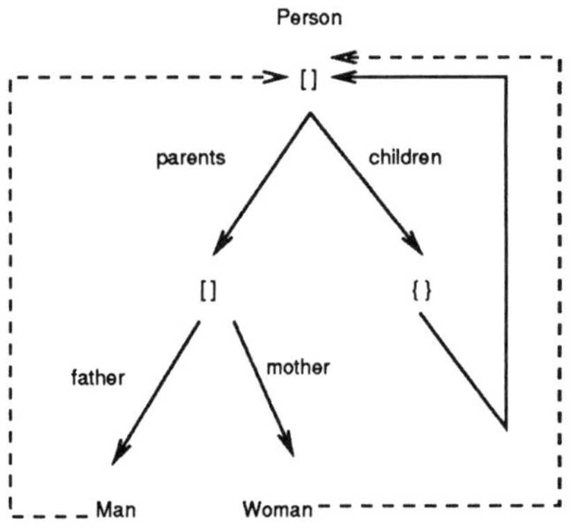

Figure 17.4. TIG for the class Person

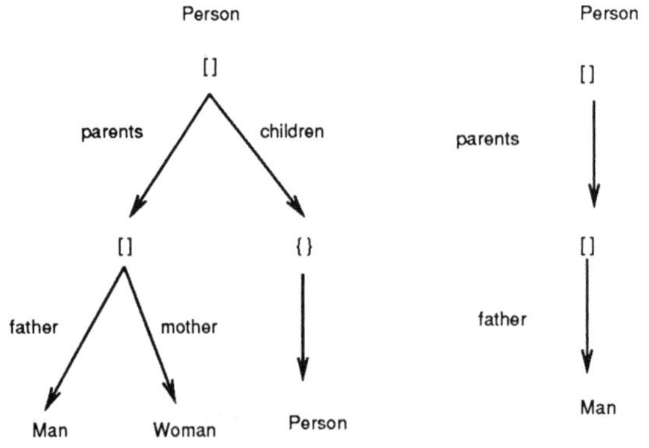

Figure 17.5. Placement tree and subtree for the class Person

2.1.2 Placement Trees and Recursiveness

Since types may be recursive, there might exist cycles in the TIG (such cycles are fully described in Kim, Bertino, and Garza 1989). Though a placement tree breaks such cycles, it allows us to manage the depth of recursivity. For the class Person of figure 17.4, we have a composition cycle with the value **children**. We may choose either of the placement trees of figure 17.6 for the class Person, where the cycle is broken at the second level. In the rightmost placement tree of figure 17.6 the value **parents** is grouped with the representations of the children of a given person.

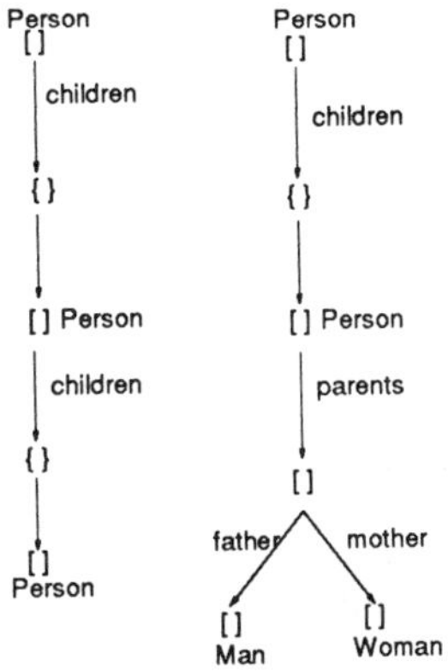

Figure 17.6. Placement trees for Person

2.1.3 Placement Trees and Inheritance

Given two classes, one being a subclass of the other, they may have completely different placement trees. If this is the case, it is because the behavior of their instances (the methods which are actually performed) is different, and so there is a real need to adopt different grouping schemes for them. However, if they have the same behavior, we want to force their placement trees to be similar. We thus introduce the concept of *consistent placement tree.* Two placement trees are consistent if the edges present in the superclass tree are either replicated or specialized in the subclass tree. The concept of consistency is closely related to the subtyping relationship, and it will affect the relationships between placement trees and file allocation. In figure 17.7 the placement tree for the class Chef is consistent with the one for Person. If the tree for Chef had only the **specialty** edge, they would no longer be consistent.

In the TIG, cycles other than composition cycles may be present. Both composition links and inheritance links compose cycles, as the class Person: Person, **parents**, **father**, Man, Person is a mixed cycle. In the placement tree in figure 17.7, however, the cycle is broken; the placement trees defined for Man and Woman are not forced to be consistent, since this is unnecessary.

The definition of placement trees is orthogonal to inheritance. When a class has no placement tree, we shall use for it the placement tree of its (first selected) direct superclass.

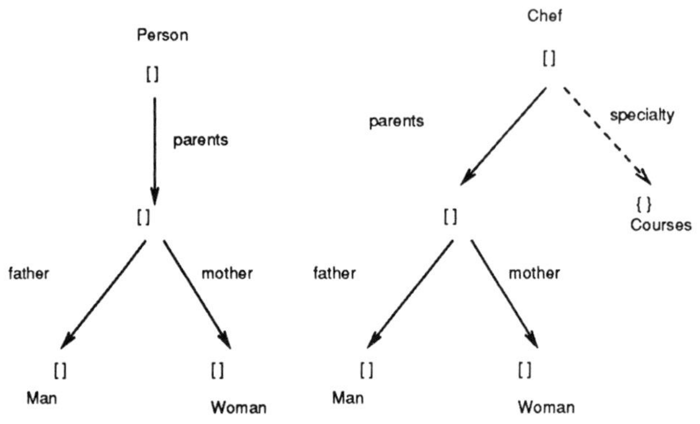

Figure 17.7. Consistent placement trees

2.1.4 Placement Trees and File Allocation

The clustering algorithm (see section 2.2) generates logical clusters. This means that some space limitations introduced by the file-system features have not been taken into account. The size of a cluster is considered unlimited, even though it depends on the characteristics of the file system. In the actual implementation of the O_2 system, we have to take into account the WiSS (Wisconsin Storage System) features (Chou et al. 1985). WiSS uses files and records; we thus have to map logical clusters to a set of records of the same file.

We shall associate a file F with each placement tree PT(c). A default file D will be reserved for those instances corresponding to classes that do not belong to any placement tree. Thus the mapping between objects of a given class and files is not unique; it depends on the following rules.

Rule 1 If the class c is the root of a placement tree and if c does not belong to any other placement trees, then all instances of c will be stored in the file, say F, associated with PT(c).

Rule 2 If c is the root of PT(c) but also belongs to many other placement trees, then instances of c might be stored either in the file associated with PT(c) or in the files associated with the other placement trees containing c.

Rule 3 If there is no placement tree for c but c belongs to other placement trees, then some instances of c will be stored in the corresponding files. However, it may be that some instances of c do not belong to any other objects. We consider, then, the poset of the superclasses of c; the following three rules apply.

Rule 3.1 If the poset has a unique least element, say c'', then instances of c will be stored in the file associated with PT(c'') if such a file exists.

Rule 3.2 If the poset has more than one least element, each being the root of a placement tree (this may happen in case of multiple inheritance), then instances of c will be stored in the file corresponding to the class selected first.

Rule 3.3 If the poset is empty, instances of c will be stored in the default file D.

Rule 4 If class c does not belong to any placement tree, the three subcases of rule 3 apply.

Table 17.1 gives the file allocation for the first set of placement trees in figure 17.3). All instances of the class Restaurant will be stored in file F_1. Instances of the class Person which are not components of a Restaurant instance will be stored in D. These rules are particularily useful in the following case. When a class c is declared to have an extension, the system automatically generates a value set (c), where each element is an object identifier. It is thus possible to retrieve all the instances of class c by scanning this set; but it would also be possible to scan the corresponding files. Such a decision is left to the optimizer, which has to choose the best strategy. For the classes which are not declared to possess an extension, it is impossible to know where their instances are stored. Thus, with the tables generated by the file-allocation rules, it is possible to scan the files in which those instances may be stored.

Table 17.1. File Allocation Table

Classes	F_1	F_2	F_3	F_4	D
Restaurant	•				
Chef		•			
Menu	•		•		
Courses		•	•	•	
Person	•				•

We associate a file with each placement tree, but this mapping is not one to one. If placement trees corresponding to subclasses of a given class are consistent, they are assigned to the same file. If one of the subclasses has a placement tree which is not consistent, it is assigned its own file.

2.2 A Clustering Algorithm

The clustering algorithm operates on a set of objects which consists of the objects newly created by the transaction (these have a temporary identifier) and those objects which have been accessed by the transaction (they have a persistent identifier). This set is described by a COG which is a subgraph of the COG that describes the whole database. This COG represents the objects which must persist at the end of the transaction. Objects are placed in logical clusters, using placement trees associated with the class of which they are instances, and according to their identifiers (disk or memory). A logical cluster is composed of a root object and a set of objects which are grouped with it. We assume that the size of a logical cluster is unlimited. The algorithm presented here is a greedy tree pattern-matching algorithm. There exist alternative algorithms based on either depth-first or breadth-first traversals of placement trees.

Algorithm 1.

Input: The COG corresponding to the transaction being executed and the list of the objects manipulated by the transaction.

1. **while** (not end of list): select an object o in the list if it is not marked.

   (a) If there is a placement tree associated with the class c of this object or with a superclass of c (if there is no PT for c), then SET = succ(o, PT(c)); that is, succ(o, PT) is the set of objects o' such that there exists a path from o to o' in PT(c), and o' is either a memory identifier or a disk identifier and is in the cluster of o (each object of the path is in succ(o, PT(c)).

   (a) If o has never been stored on disk, create a logical cluster; group each element of SET;

   (b) If o is a root object, open the old logical cluster; group all elements of SET;

   (b) mark o; mark each element of SET;

   end while

2. When the end of the list is reached, all the objects which are not marked are grouped in a default cluster.

Output: A set of logical clusters.

We give an illustration of the clustering algorithm for the classes Restaurant, Menu, and Chef. We consider the first set of placement trees shown in figure 17.3 above, and we assume that all objects are new. The set of all generated clusters is a partition of the COG nodes, and each logical cluster is a connected subgraph of the COG. From the point of view of localization, this algorithm is nondeterministic. Localization depends on the order in which objects were selected from the list. For this example, we have chosen instances of Restaurant first. Thus the algorithm generates five clusters (see figure 17.8). If we had selected Course instances first and then Menu, Chef, and Restaurant, we would have had nine clusters: three for the "courses" and two for each of "menu," "chef," and "restaurant."

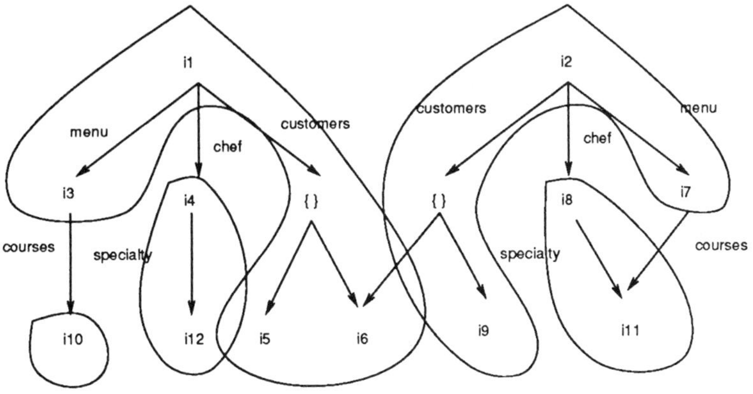

Figure 17.8. Clusters

Our objective is to minimize the I/O overhead; given a grouping strategy, it is desirable to minimize the number of clusters produced by the clustering algorithm. We assume that the exchange granularity between disk and main memory is the cluster. Under this assumption, it is possible to order the classes in such a way that we obtain as few clusters as possible. Such an order, described in Benzaken 1990b, relies upon the existence of placement trees and on the presence of the given class in other placement trees. The objects are selected according to this order. To group as many objects as possible, we select those objects which were already stored on disk and group some of their newly created components with them. Assume that object i_1 has already been placed on disk and that object i_5 has been created during this transaction; we shall cluster i_5 with i_1. Objects already existing on disk are not reclustered except in the case mentioned in Benzaken and Delobel 1990.

The clustering algorithm is actually implemented in the O_2 system. However, we need to define what constitutes good placement trees. Thus the need arises to define a cost model in order to evaluate the benefits of our clustering strategies. This model must take into account the treatments performed on the database. We present our cost model in the next section.

3 Self-adaptative Clustering Strategies

The clustering problem consists in finding a partition of the set of the objects in the database. Our approach is similar to the one adopted in Schkolnick 1977 for the hierachical model. When objects are grouped together, it is desirable that these objects be accessed together in the future. We have an operational approach; our model relies on the following information: the type graph of the system, a clustering strategy (a set of placement trees), and the set of methods associated with the classes. Given this information, we will evaluate the benefits of our clustering strategy and show how to dynamically adapt it. First, we have to define what is a good placement tree.

3.1 Definition of Good Placement Trees

We rely on the following assumptions. Given a class *c* and its associated methods (inherited or not), the following two criteria will be taken into account in order to define good placement trees.

- When a method is applied to an object (an instance of *c*) and the object has been brought into main memory in one disk access, all the object's components accessed by the method must also be brought in the same disk access. There is no object fault. This means that in a logical cluster (created according to PT(*c*)) all the objects the method needs to access are present.

- All objects that have been brought into main memory in one disk access should be used. We do not want to waste main-memory space.

These two criteria might be contradictory. Assume, for example, that a class is built from ten component classes, and that there are two methods for this class, the first one accessing two components and the second one accessing the ten components. In order to fulfill the first criterion, we would be tempted to cluster the ten components together. But if we now assume that in 90% of the cases it is the first method that is applied, then the second criterion is not fulfilled. We thus have to take into consideration the activation frequencies of methods. In the next subsection, we characterize the operations that can be performed in a method. We shall use them to derive an evaluation model for our clustering strategies. Finally, we shall use this evaluation to derive optimal strategies.

3.1.1 Syntactical Characterization of Operations

The problem we face is to get some information for a given class and its associated methods which describes the paths the methods follow in the graph that represents the type structure of this class. Given a class *c*, we shall characterize any of its methods *m* by means of expressions representing which edges in the graph describing class *c* it needs to follow.

Any O_2 method is defined by its signature and its body. The signature describes the parameters of the method, while the body is written in CO_2 source code. We are only interested in the structural part of class *c*, which method *m* needs to access. Thus we shall transform any method body into a regular expression. We call this transformation a *characterization*, and we denote it by $\mathcal{C}$. The alphabet is composed of the labels of each edge in the graph denoting class *c*. The connectors are ".", which stands for edge concatenation, and "+", which stands for conjunction. We assume that each edge in the type graph is uniquely labeled either by an attribute name (in the case of tuples) or by a unique arbitrary label (in the case of sets and lists), say $\ell_{x,y}$, where x denotes the set-structured type $x = \text{set}(y)$ or the list-structured type $x = \text{list}(y)$.

The following example illustrates such a characterization. Suppose we have for the class Restaurant the following method (written in CO_2 source code) which returns for a given Restaurant instance its Chef's specialties:

```
add method chef-specialty in class Restaurant
    body Courses
        in class Restaurant co2
{
    o2 Courses result;
    result = self → chef → specialty;
    return(result)
}
```

The characterization of chef-specialty is: $\mathcal{C}$(chef–specialty) $\equiv$ **chef.specialty**. In this example the characterization expresses the path followed by the method. It is possible to describe not only simple paths but also paths where set iterations may be described. Given such characterizations, we have an access pattern for the class.

A placement tree which is a good candidate with respect to the first criterion of section 3.1, is a tree which provides a minimal covering of the set of edges covered by the methods. We call it a *minimal covering tree* and denote it $PT^0()$.

3.2 Simplifying Assumptions

We make the following simplifying assumptions. They are not too restrictive, and they will permit us to focus on only one class at a time and its associated methods.

- We assume that there is no space problem. In other words, given a placement tree PT(c) for the class c, all the instances of c will be stored on the disk according to this placement tree. Thus all the components which should be stored in the cluster actually are stored in it.
- We suppose that when a method has to access a component o' of an object o, it must access each of the components of the path $o, o_1, \ldots, o_i, \ldots, o'$ (i.e., we do not take into consideration the index).
- When we characterize a method, we do not take into account the fact that it might have parameters. We thus assume that the set of methods associated with a class reflects the current usage pattern of the class.

3.3 Cost Function

This subsection defines the cost function of a placement tree PT(c) for class c. We use the following notation.

- $m_1, m_2, \ldots, m_l$ are the methods associated with c.

- $p_1, \ldots, p_l$ are their associated frequencies (the number of times they are called).
- $t_1, \ldots, t_n, \ldots, t_p$ are the types which compose c; c and $t_1 \ldots t_n$ are only accessed by the methods m_i associated with c.
- cost(i, j) is the cost associated with method m_i and type t_j.
  1. cost$(i, j) = \alpha$ if, for the method m_i, component $o(t_j)$ has been brought into main memory and then used. α is a profit, and thus $\alpha > 0$.
  2. cost$(i, j) = \beta$ if, for the method m_i, component $o(t_j)$ has been brought into main memory and has not been used. In this case there is waste of main memory space. β is a loss, and thus $\beta < 0$.
  3. cost$(i, j) = \gamma$ if, for the method m_i, component $o(t_j)$ has not been brought into main memory and was not needed. γ is a profit, and thus $\gamma \geq 0$.
  4. cost$(i, j) = \delta$ if, for method m_i, component $o(t_j)$ has not been brought into main memory and was needed. In this case, there is an object fault. δ is a loss, and thus $\delta < 0$.

Let PT$(c) = (V, E)$ be the placement tree associated with c. Let us consider the matrix

$$M_{l,1} = (p_1, p_2, \ldots, p_l)(\text{cost}(i, j))$$

1. If $t_j \in V$ and if m_i uses t_j, then cost$(i, j) = \alpha$.
2. If $t_j \in V$ and if m_i does not use t_j, then cost$(i, j) = \beta$.
3. If $\neg(t_j \in V)$ and if m_i does not use t_j, then cost$(i, j) = \gamma$.
4. If $\neg(t_j \in V)$ and if m_i uses t_j, then cost$(i, j) = \delta$.

The cost function F(PT(c)) associated with PT(c) is obtained by adding the coefficients of matrix $M_{l,1}$. It will reflect the object faults and the main memory overloading.

$$\text{F}(\text{PT}(c)) = \sum_{i=1}^{i=l} \sum_{j=1}^{j=n} \text{cost}(i, j) p_i$$

$$\text{F}(\text{PT}(c)) = \alpha \sum_{i=1}^{i=l} p_i Nbr\,(j; \text{cost}(i, j) = \alpha) + \beta \sum_{i=1}^{i=l} p_i Nbr\,(j; \text{cost}(i, j) = \beta) +$$

$$\gamma \sum_{i=1}^{i=l} p_i Nbr\,(j; \text{cost}(i, j) = \gamma) + \delta \sum_{i=1}^{i=l} p_i Nbr\,(j; \text{cost}(i, j) = \delta)$$

where $Nbr(j; \text{cost}(i,j) = \aleph)$ denotes the number of times $\text{cost}(i,j)$ is equal to $\aleph$. Our purpose is to find the placement tree which maximizes the cost function (i.e., which gives the greater profit). We posit:

$$\text{used} = \sum_{i=1}^{i=l} p_i Nbr\,(j\ \text{cost}(i,j) = \alpha)$$

where *used* corresponds to the number of objects used for all the methods of c.

$$\text{waste} = \sum_{i=1}^{i=l} p_i Nbr\,(j; \text{cost}(i,j) = \beta)$$

where *waste* corresponds to the number of objects uneeded and brought into main memory.

$$\text{unused} = \sum_{i=1}^{i=l} p_i Nbr\,(j; \text{cost}(i,j) = \gamma)$$

where *unused* corresponds to the number of objects which have neither been brought into main memory nor used.

$$\text{default} = \sum_{i=1}^{i=l} p_i Nbr\,(j; \text{cost}(i,j) = \delta)$$

where *default* corresponds to the number of object faults.

Assume that with this placement tree, k methods among l lead to an object fault. Let $p_{i1}, \ldots, p_{ik}$ be their associated frequencies. If k methods among l lead to an object fault, this means that the associated tree was not a minimal covering. It is interesting to know whether the minimal covering tree $\text{PT}^0(c)$, which eliminates object faults, should be better (i.e., should have a greater cost function) than a noncovering one. So we now compare the costs of $\text{PT}(c)$ and $\text{PT}^0(c)$. Objects which were unused are loaded and thus associated with the loss of waste objects. Objects which were in default are brought and are associated with the profit of used objects. Thus the cost function associated with $\text{PT}^0(c)$ is

$$\text{F}(\text{PT}^0(c)) = \alpha\,(\text{used} + \text{default}) + \beta\,(\text{ waste} + \text{unused})$$

In order to determine which of $\text{PT}(c)$ and $\text{PT}^0(c)$ is the better candidate, we compute the difference of their associated cost functions.

$$\text{F}(\text{PT}(c)) - \text{F}(\text{PT}^0(c)) = (\delta - \alpha)\text{default} + (\gamma - \beta)\text{ waste}$$

$\text{PT}^0(c)$ is the better candidate if and only if

$$(\delta - \alpha)\text{ default} + (\gamma - \beta)\text{ waste} \leq 0$$

$$\frac{\text{default}}{\text{waste}} \geq \frac{(\gamma - \beta)}{(\alpha - \delta)}$$

Both *default* and *waste* depend on the call frequencies of the methods associated with c. This inequation indicates that, if object faults correspond to methods with a low frequency, it is better to use a placement tree which is not covering and which will permit a gain of space in main memory. The coefficients α, β, γ, and δ depend on the characteristics of the system and will be fixed in time. However, if the penalization (δ) associated with object fault is the only one to vary, we obtain the curve shown in Figure 17.9.

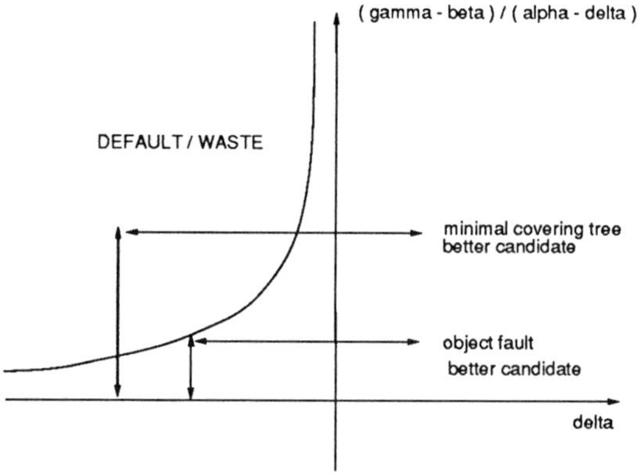

Figure 17.9. Cost function

The cost function described in this section does not take sets into account. When a method accesses a set structured type, we do not know how many elements of the set will actually be used by the method. In our first approach, we considered that either all the elements were brought in one disk access (if the placement tree allowed it) or none of them. In all cases, only one object was taken into account in the computation of the cost function. This does not correctly reflect reality. On the other hand, it might not be correct to consider that a method will always access all the components of a requested set. A refined version of the cost function which takes sets into account is described in Benzaken 1990a. Nevertheless, we are able to introduce the automatic derivation of placement trees without any lack of generality.

3.4 Automatic Derivation of Placement Trees

The objective of this section is to use the cost analysis in order to derive automatically an optimal placement tree for a class c. The naive method, which consists in building all the possible trees and computing their cost functions and then selecting the best, is not tractable. Indeed, such a construction is exponential with respect to the number of edges covered by the methods. We instead propose a linear algorithm with respect to the number of edges covered by the set of methods associated with c. This algorithm derives an optimal tree based on the following assumptions: the set of methods associated with class c is fixed, and their frequencies are also fixed. We assume that there exists PT(c).

Let $F_\tau(c)$ be the cost function associated with PT(c) at time τ. Assume that at time $\tau + d\tau$ we add the edge a. Let $\mathcal{M}_a$ be the set of methods which use edge a. We have

$$F_{\tau+d\tau}(c) = F_\tau(c) + \Delta$$

with

$$\Delta = \alpha\Delta_\alpha + \beta\Delta_\beta + \gamma\Delta_\gamma + \delta\Delta_\delta$$

$$\Delta_\alpha = -\Delta_\delta = \sum_{i \in \mathcal{M}_a} p_i$$

Methods which before adding a caused an object fault for the edge a will not cause this fault again.

$$\Delta_\beta = -\Delta_\gamma = \sum_{i \neg\in \mathcal{M}_a} p_i$$

Methods which were not using edge a now cause a main-memory overload. It is crucial to notice that the fact of adding an edge has no retroactive effect on the initial value of the cost function $F_\tau(c)$. This guarantees that there are no local maxima or minima.

3.4.1 A Derivation Algorithm

The algorithm we now present builds an optimal placement tree from the initial placement tree which reduces to a single node, by adding an edge, step by step, if this improves the cost function.

Algorithm 2.

Input: The set of edges covered by the set of methods. The frequencies associated with each edge.

> **while** (not empty set) **do**
> extract an edge a;
> compute Δ;
> **if** ($\Delta > 0$) **then** PT(c) = PT(c) + a;
> **end while**

Output: A placement tree.

This algorithm builds an optimal placement tree in linear time; the proof is given in Benzaken 1990b.

4 Performance Measurements

The cost function described in section 3 and the algorithm for deriving an optimal placement tree are obtained under the simplifying assumption that there is no space problem, that is, that a cluster fits in a physical page. Moreover, this model does not take into account the sharing of components between two or more objects. In practice, if these two conditions are not met, the actual benefits of the clustering strategies might differ from those expected. So we made a study on the effect of the size of objects on the number of disk accesses in the actual system (see section 4.1 and Benzaken and Delobel 1990).

Another argument for the studies outlined in this section is the effect of the choice of a placement tree that optimizes the traversal of a composition graph, following particular edges, on other kinds of queries. The experiments we designed in order to study this problem led us to the very first version of a clustering benchmark, CluB-0 (see section 4.2).

4.1 Early Measurements

The complete description of the measurements outlined in this section can be found in Benzaken 1990b. The main goals of these measurements were:

1. A first partial validation of the cost model: if the assumptions we made are met, the best theoretical placement tree is expected to be also the best in the actual implementation of the O_2 system.

2. A study of the effect of parameters neglected in the model, mainly the size of objects or the relationship between *logical* cluster and *physical* page.

3. A first study of the behaviour of the clustering algorithms in the actual implementation, in order to get information for a second, more precise theoretical model.

We decided to make these first experiments simple; the number of parameters had to be small enough for the results to be easily understable. Here is a sketch of the experiments and an abstract of the results and conclusions.

The class we studied is in fact a simplification of the class Restaurant described in previous sections. Its TIG is given in figure 17.10. A number of parameters can be studied:

- The placement tree: one of the eight nonempty placement trees, or no placement tree (if there is no clustering)
- The number of objects in each class
- The size of objects of each class
- The degree of sharing of objects (only objects of class c_4 can be shared)
- The calling frequencies for the methods

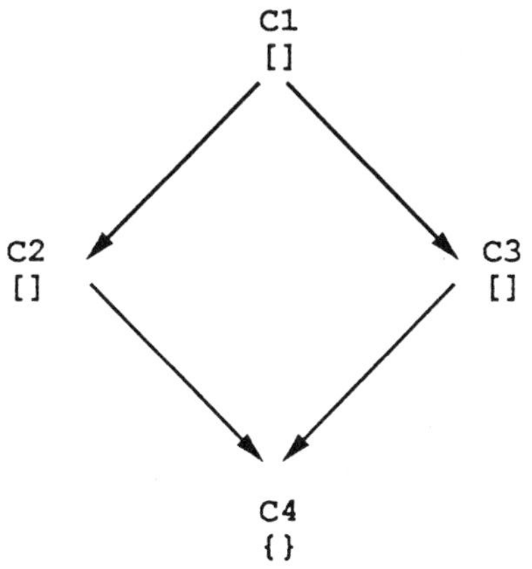

Figure 17.10. Type inheritance graph for the basic measurements

For the last parameter, we chose the worst case: equal frequencies for all methods. For various values of these parameters, the number of disk accesses made during the execution of the set of methods was recorded. The main conclusions of the study are:

1. If the assumptions are satisfied—mainly if the size of a logical cluster is less than the size of a physical page—the theoretically optimal placement tree is actually optimal. It saves from 30% to 50% on the number of disk accesses by all except one of the suboptimal trees.

2. As soon as the cluster derived from the optimal placement tree is larger than the size of a physical page, clusters smaller than this size give the best results (up to 40%).

Even on the study of this simple class, we can see that the cost model has to be modified to take into account the size of objects.

4.2 From Hypermodel to CluB-0

After these basic measurements we felt unsatisfied, as we did not catch in the results all the power of the clustering strategies in O_2. For example the ability to cluster along two or more different relationships has not been completly explored. Moreover, a placement tree can be optimal for a certain kind of query on a complex composition graph, but very bad for other kinds of query. Also, we think that comparing clustering strategies and algorithms require the definition of a common platform. We describe here what we think is a good basis for such a benchmark.

The Hypermodel Benchmark (Anderson et al. 1990), also called the Tektronix Benchmark, was a good candidate for our goals. This benchmark presents a fairly complex composition graph, with a wide range of operations. However, we did not want to reuse exactly the same composition graph, as we wanted to have total control over a small number of parameters. Moreover, a number of operations of the Hypermodel Benchmark do not directly concern clustering in O_2. For example, operations such as *rangeLookups*, that is, selections, are not part of the first version of our benchmark.

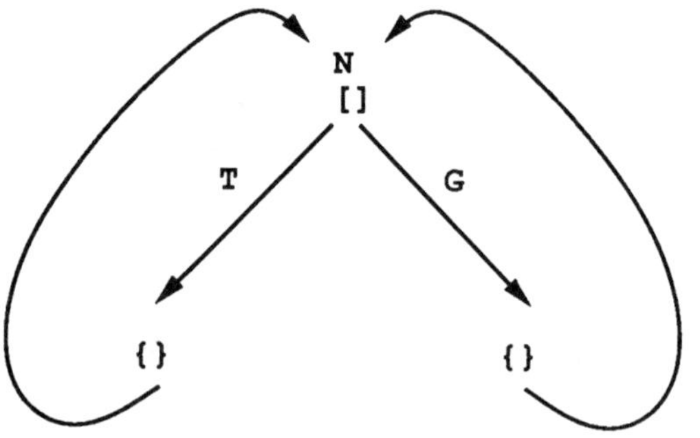

Figure 17.11. The type inheritance graph for the class N

The structure of the composition graph we choose for the CluB-0 benchmark is as follows. Only one class N is needed. The TIG for this class is shown in figure 17.11. The database consists of objects of class N, called nodes, that form a tree (relationship T) with a constant fanout f, overlapping with a graph (relationship G). Each internal node of T, say a node at depth i, is connected to exactly f distinct nodes randomly chosen from the set of nodes at depth $i+1$ (each branch in the tree has the same depth). Of course, at level 0, the two kinds of links are the same. At any other level, objects can be shared inside the graph induced by G.

Figure 17.12 shows an instance of a database. Solid lines represent the T relationship, dotted lines the G relationship. The value of f is 5 in the benchmark description, 3 in figure 17.12.

Attached to each node are some more data items, mainly a unique identifier, the list of sons for each one of the two relationships T and G, and a variable-length string. The latter allows us to make measurements on various configurations without changing physical parameters such as the page size of the internal buffers; that is, the underlying parameter is the mean number of objects per physical page.

For this study, we are interested only in queries whose performance can be modified by clustering decisions. So not all of the requests described in Anderson et al. 1990 were retained. An example of queries that will benefit from good clustering decisions is *closure traversals*, such as "Choose a node at a given level of the tree and construct the list of the subtree or subgraph that can be attained from this node" (a depth-first traversal). Some other queries are of interest; for example, scans such as "Read the unique identifier of all nodes, traversing the tree in a breadth-first manner."

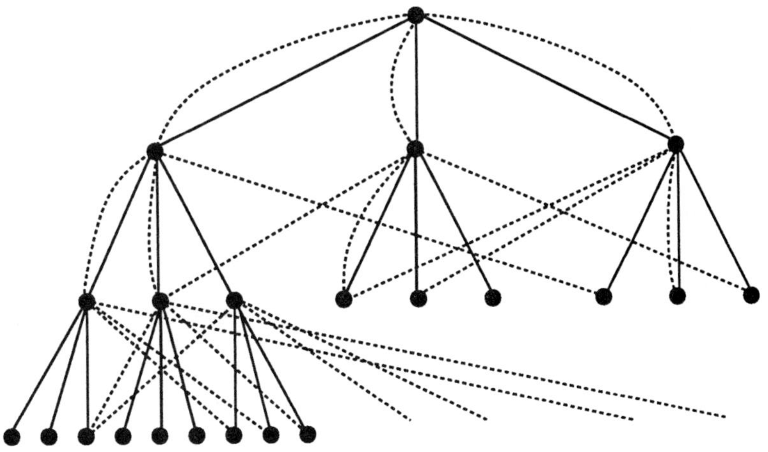

Figure 17.12. A four-level composition graph

The complete study consists in generating a number of databases obtained for various values of the parameters, such as the mean number of objects per physical page, and for various placement trees (spanning up to two levels of the hierarchies). For each of these databases, for the operations described above, the complete trace of accessed objects was used to derive some indices of performance, such as the total number of pages read during the operation, and the *switch rate*—the proportion of accesses to objects that are made in the same page as the previous access.

The main phenomena observed were:

1. For a given operation (e.g., closure traversals), the best placement tree leads to 75% fewer object faults than without any clustering. However, with the same tree and another operation, we loose 50% of the benefits we previously had with the best tree (i.e., if we had 10 disk operations we now have 15 disk I/Os). Nevertheless, clustering has a beneficial impact on the performance when it corresponds to the operations actually performed against the database.

2. Object sharing has a crucial impact on clustering performance. Such performance may be severely altered for the same tree even if few objects are shared (for the same tree, when objects are shared, we observed that the number of disk operations increases in the proportion of 30%; the probability for an object to be shared is, in this case, .26). However, the tree which is expected to be the best candidate for the corresponding operation still remains the best.

The complete benchmark and results are described in Harrus, Benzaken, and Delobel 1990.

5 Conclusion

The concept of placement trees proposed in this paper is simple and powerful enough to define clustering strategies. These strategies can evolve over time when the need arises. Our work differs from the Orion or Prima approach in the following respects: (1) we rely on the specificity of the O_2 data model, which incorporates the notions of objects and values; (2) our strategies are not part of the schema. The clustering algorithm allows us to group objects according to a given strategy. If this strategy changes, the algorithm will continue to run according to the new strategy without penalizing the global performance of the system. The algorithm is actually implemented in the O_2 system.

The measurements performed in the system allow us to select an optimal placement tree under certain assumptions. This tree leads to significantly fewer object faults. However, when the assumptions are not met, the results are quite different. Nevertheless, we are able to provide the DBA with a tool to help him or her choose adequate placement trees. In future work, we shall design another cost model which will take into account the sizes of objects.

In this paper, we do not take into account the relationships between clustering and concurrency control. As it is desirable to have a means to group objects, it would be desirable too to have the ability to ungroup objects (in the case of highly transactional objects). This point will be studied in future work.

6 Acknowledgements

We are thankful to: G.Arango for his helpful comments about the characterization of methods, P.Biriotti for the discussions we had about the cost model, and J.Ioannidis for his helpful suggestions on the derivation algorithm. We also would like to thank P.Richard, C.Lécluse, C.Bauzer-Medeiros, J.M.Larchevêque, and F.Bancilhon for helpful advice and careful reading of the paper.

References

Abiteboul, S., and P. Kanellakis. 1989. Object identity as a query language primitive. In *Proceedings of the ACM SIGMOD conference.*

Anderson, T., A. Berre, M. Mallison, H. Porter, and B. Schneider. 1990. The Hypermodel Benchmark. In *Proceedings of the EDBT conference.*

Atkinson, M. P., and O. P. Buneman. 1987. Types and persistence in database programming languages. *ACM Computing Surveys* (June).

Atwood, T. 1985. *An object-oriented DBMS for design support applications.* In *Proceedings of the IEEE COMPINT.*

Bancilhon, F. 1988. Object-oriented database systems. In *Proceedings of the ACM PODS conference.*

Benzaken, V. 1990a. An evaluation model for clustering strategies in the O_2 object-oriented database system. In *Proceedings of the third international conference on database theory.*

Benzaken, V. 1990b. *Regroupement d'objets sur disque dans un système de bases de données orienté-objet.* Phd Dissertation, Université d'Orsay.

Benzaken, V., and C. Delobel. 1990. Enhancing performance in a persistent object store: Clustering strategies in O_2. In *Proceedings of the fourth workshop on persistent object systems.*

Chang, E. E., and R. H. Katz. 1989. Exploiting inheritance and structure semantics for effective clustering and buffering in an object-oriented DBMS. In *Proceedings of the ACM SIGMOD conference.*

Chou, H-T., D. DeWitt, R. Katz, and A. Klug. 1985. Design and implementation of the Wisconsin storage system. *Software Practice and Experience* 15(10).

Harder, T., K. Meyer-Wegner, K. Mitschang, and A. Sikeler. 1987. PRIMA: A DBMS prototype supporting engineering applications. In *Proceedings of the 13th VLDB conference.*

Harrus, G., V. Benzaken, and, C. Delobel. 1990. *Measuring performance of clustering strategies: The Club-0 benchmark.* Altaïr Technical Report.

Hornick M., and S. B. Zdonik 1987. A shared, segmented memory for an object-oriented database. *ACM TOIS* 5(1).

Hudson, S., and R. King. 1989. Cactis: A self-adaptative, concurrent implementation of an object-oriented database management system. *ACM TODS* 14(3).

Khoshafian, S., M. J. Carey, and P. Franklin. 1987. *Storage management for persistent complex objects.* MCC Technical Report.

Kim, W. 1988. *A foundation for object-oriented databases.* MCC Technical Report.

Kim, W., J. Banerjee, H-T. Chou, J. F. Garza, and D. Woelk, 1987. Composite object support in an object-oriented database system. In *Proceedings of the OOPSLA conference.*

Kim, W., E. Bertino, and J. F. Garza. 1989. Composite objects revisited. In *Proceedings of the ACM SIGMOD conference.*

Lécluse, C., and P. Richard. 1989a. Modeling complex structures in object-oriented databases. In *Proceedings of the ACM PODS conference.*

Lécluse, C., and P. Richard. 1989b. The O_2 database programming language. In *Proceedings of the VLDB 15th conference.*

Lécluse, C., P. Richard, and F. Vélez. 1988. O_2, an object-oriented data model. In *Proceedings of the ACM SIGMOD conference.*

Maier, D., J. Stein, A. Otis, and A. Purdy. 1986. Development of an object-oriented DBMS. Report no. CS/E-86-005, Oregon Graduate Center.

Schek, H. J., H. B. Paul, M. H. Scholl, and G. Weikum. 1990. The DASDBS project: Objectives, experiences and future prospects. *IEEE Transactions on Knowledge and Data Engineering* 2(1).

Scheuermann, P., Y. C. Park, and E. Omiecinski. 1989. Heuristic reorganization of clustered files. In *Proceedings of the third FODO conference.*

Schkolnick, M. 1977. A clustering algorithm for hierarchical structures. *ACM TODS* 2(1).

Schoning, H., and A. Sikeler. 1989. Cluster mechanisms supporting the dynamic construction of complex objects. In *Proceedings of the third FODO conference.*

Stamos, J. 1984. Static grouping of small objects to enhance performance of a paged virtual memory. *ACM TOCS* 2(2).

Vélez, F., G. Bernard, and V. Darnis. 1989. The O_2 object manager: An overview. In *Proceedings of the 15th VLDB conference.*

Yu, C., K. Lam, M. Siu, and C. Suen. 1985. Adaptative record clustering. *ACM TODS* 10(2).

Chapter 18

Three Alternative Workstation-Server Architectures

David J. DeWitt
Philippe Futtersack
David Maier
Fernando Vélez

1 Introduction

Whereas relational database systems were the technology of the 1980s, it has recently become apparent that object-oriented database systems will be a key database technology of the 1990s. Harnessing the power of this technology will not be easy, as such systems pose many difficult engineering challenges. If one reflects on the commercialization of relational database systems, it took a full ten years to turn the first prototypes—Ingres and System R in 1976 (Stonebraker et al. 1976; Astrahan et al. 1976)—into products that customers willingly used. Given the relative complexity of object-oriented database systems, it is likely to take ten years before their technology becomes solidified.

The situation is further complicated by the emergence of the workstation-server model of computing as the standard of the 1990s in the engineering and scientific market-places—the initial target market for object-oriented database systems. In the past, the tendency has been to run database software primarily on a shared server that is accessed via a high-level query language such as SQL. A key premise of this study is that since the widespread use of 10- and 20-MIPS workstations concentrates the majority of the available CPU cycles in the workstations rather than in the server, such a distribution of functionality is no longer viable.

In addition, OODBMSs differ significantly from relational systems in the way that they manipulate data. With an OODBMS, a fair amount of an application is incorporated into the methods of the classes of which objects are instances. Moreover, while OODBMSs also provide support for associative queries over sets of objects, applications employing an OODBMS typically have a large navigational component. (For further details, see chapters 1, 5, 11, and 12; see also Atkinson et al. 1989; Abiteboul and Kanellakis 1989; Bancilhon, Cluet, and Delobel 1989; and Cluet et al. 1989). One might simply run all applications programs on a centralized server. However, such an approach is not commercially viable, as OODBMSs tend to be used for applications (e.g., CAD systems) that require the computational and graphical interface that only a dedicated workstation per user can provide. Thus a centralized solution to the problem is not acceptable. Since a distributed architecture is required, we have undertaken in this paper to examine how the functionality of an OODBMS should be distributed between a workstation and a server.

The remainder of this paper is organized as follows. Section 2 describes three alternative workstation-server architectures for an OODBMS and makes a qualitative comparison of the three. Section 3 presents our prototype implementations of these three architectures. The benchmark used to evaluate these alternative designs is given in section 4, and the results of applying this benchmark to the three prototype systems are presented in section 5. Related work is described in section 6, and our conclusions are set forth in section 7.

2 The Three Workstation-Server Architectures

There appear to be at least three markedly different approaches for architecting an OODBMS in a workstation-server environment and, within each general approach, a wide number of variations. One alternative is the *object-server* approach, so named because the unit of transfer between the server and the workstation is an object. In this architecture the server understands the concept of an object and is capable of applying methods to objects. The V1.0 prototype of O_2 (Bancilhon et al. 1988; Deux et al. 1990), the Orion 1 prototype (Kim et al. 1990), and some prerelease versions of GemStone (Copeland and Maier 1984) employ an object-server architecture.

A second alternative is the *page-server* approach. In this design, the server deals only with pages and does not understand the semantics of objects. Thus it cannot apply methods to objects. In addition to providing the storage and retrieval of database pages, the server also provides concurrency control and recovery services for the database software running on the workstations. This architecture is currently being used by the ObServer (Hornick and Zdonik 1987) and Exodus (Carey et al. 1990) prototypes.

The third design represents a further simplification of the page-server architecture. The workstations use a remote file service, such as NFS (Sun 1988), to read and write database pages directly. As with the page-server design, the server in this architecture provides concurrency control and recovery services. The current version of GemStone uses this architecture when configured for a workstation-server environment. We term this architecture the *file-server* approach.

In the following subsections we compare these three alternative architectures qualitatively, from the viewpoint of how each affects the implementation of the functionality that an OODBMS must provide. It will be obvious that there are many issues left unanswered. We have decided to concentrate our efforts on first deciding which of the three basic architectures provides the best overall performance and have ignored certain equally important issues, such as what is the best recovery strategy for any particular architecture. We will study such issues in the future.

2.1 The Object-Server Architecture

In the object-server architecture, most of the OODBMS functionality is replicated on the workstation and the server. Figure 18.1 shows one of many possible variations of this architecture. In addition, both the workstation and the server maintain caches of recently accessed objects, and methods can be applied to objects on either of them. When the workstation needs an object it first searches its local object cache for the object. If the object is not found it sends a request for the object to the server. If the object is not in the server's cache, the server retrieves the object from disk and returns it to the requesting workstation. The unit of transfer between the workstation and the server is an individual object. The server may or may not keep a copy of the desired object in its local cache, depending on the cache policy that it implements.

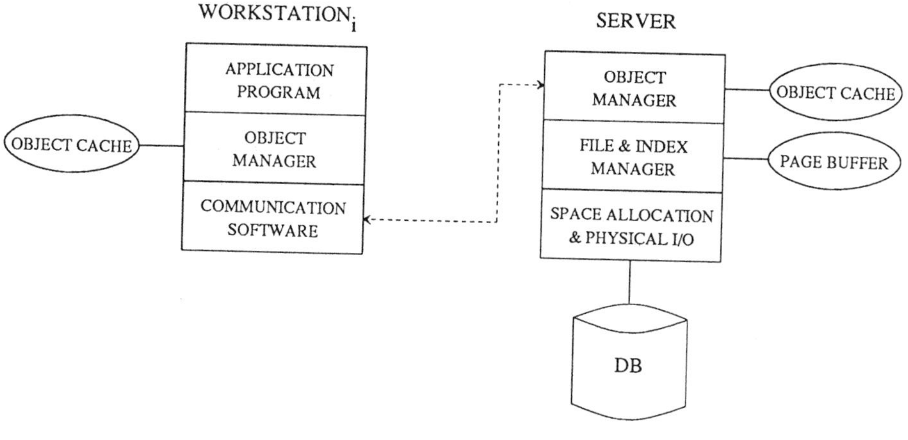

Figure 18.1. Object-server architecture

This architecture has a number of advantages. First, both the server and the workstation are able to run methods. A method that selects a small subset of a large collection can execute on the server, avoiding the movement of the entire collection to the workstation. This ability is most valuable when there is no index on the collection that can be used by the selection operation. In addition, one can balance the system workload by moving work from the workstation to the server (see chapter 16). Another advantage is that this architecture simplifies the design of the concurrency control subsystem, as the server knows exactly which objects are accessed by each application. Hence concurrency control can be almost completely centralized in the server. Furthermore, the implementation of object-level locking is straightforward. The design might also lower the cost of enforcing constraints that relate objects manipulated by an application with other objects in the database, for example, a constraint that says that the subpart graph of a mechanical assembly is acyclic. Instead of moving all the objects involved in the constraint to the workstation, the constraints may be checked at the server.

There are multiple ways of implementing recovery in such an architecture. If logging is used, the workstation can directly update objects in its own cache and then send both the modified objects and their corresponding log records to the server. A variation of this approach would be for the workstation to send the server the log records, which the server would then apply to the actual objects in the database—avoiding the overhead of copying the modified objects back to the server. In either case, updates pose a challenge to the server. When an updated object is returned to the server, the page on which the updated object resides might not be in the server's page cache. In this case, the appropriate page must be reread from disk and the update applied. Thus, each update might first incur a read operation. As we will see later, this problem never occurs with the page server design, since the unit of transfer between the workstation and server is always a full data page. In effect, the page server architectures trade off extra network traffic against reduced disk traffic. Given the relatively flat improvements in disk bandwidth compared to the forthcoming changes in local area network technology (i.e., FDDI), such a tradeoff may be the right choice.

This design suffers from some serious problems. First, in the worse case there may be one remote procedure call (RPC) per object reference, although hopefully the hit rate on the workstation's object cache will be high enough to satisfy most requests. For the server to transfer more than a single object at a time, it must be capable of figuring out which objects belong with one another, replicating the work that any clustering mechanism did when it placed objects together on a disk page.

Another major problem is that this architecture complicates the design of the server. Instead of having the server supply just the functionality that it alone can supply (e.g., sharing, concurrency control, or recovery), the server must be capable of executing arbitrary user methods. In the case of the V1.0 O_2 prototype, this meant the use of System V semaphores to coordinate access to shared memory (an expensive and slow approach) for the server's object cache and lock table.

A related problem arises when a method is applied to a group of objects that are currently distributed among the workstation's cache, the server's cache, and the disk drives which hold the database. This problem is complicated by the possibility that the same object may be in both caches as well as on the disk simultaneously. In addition, an updated version of the object may exist in the workstation's cache but not in the server's cache. Thus a method cannot execute on the server without first addressing such cache inconsistencies. O_2 V1.0 and Orion adopted different solutions to this problem. In the case of O_2 when a method (such as an associative query) is to be run on the server, the workstation flushes all the modified objects in its object cache back to the server (a fairly slow process). The Orion-1 prototype instead executes the method on both the workstation and the server (Kim et al. 1990). Since this strategy can result in duplicate copies of an object in the result, a complicated (and probably expensive) postprocessing step of duplicate elimination is required.

There are also several minor problems that occur with the object-server architecture. First, it may hinder locking at the page level as an alternative to object-level locking, since neither the workstation nor server software really deals with pages. Second, objects tend to get copied multiple times. For example, an object may have to be copied from the server's page-level buffer pool into its object cache before it can be sent to a workstation. Another copy may take place on the workstation if the object cannot be stored directly into the object cache by the networking software. Finally, since the software on a workstation simply requests an object from the server without generally being aware of the size of the object, large, multipage objects may move in their entirety, even if the application needed to access only a few bytes.

Another problem is that this design could be out of step with technology trends. Within a year or two, 10-MIPS workstations will become increasingly common, and at least 90% of the computing power will end up being concentrated in the workstations and not in the server. In such a situation it makes no sense to move work from the workstation to the server. Rather, the functionality of the server should be stripped to its bare minimum. Likewise, over the next five to ten years, FDDI will probably replace Ethernet as the standard technology for local area networks. The cost of sending a message is already almost entirely due to software overhead and not transmission time; the overhead component will definitely dominate in the future.

2.2 Page-Server Architecture

Figure 18.2 shows one possible architecture for a page server. In this architecture, the server basically consists of a large buffer pool, the I/O level of a storage system for managing pages and files, plus concurrency control and recovery servers. The upper levels of the OODBMS software run exclusively on the workstation, and the unit of transfer between the workstation and the server is a disk page. When the server receives a request for a data page, it first sets the appropriate lock on the page. Next, if the desired page is not in the server's buffer pool, the server retrieves the page from the disk and returns it to the workstation.

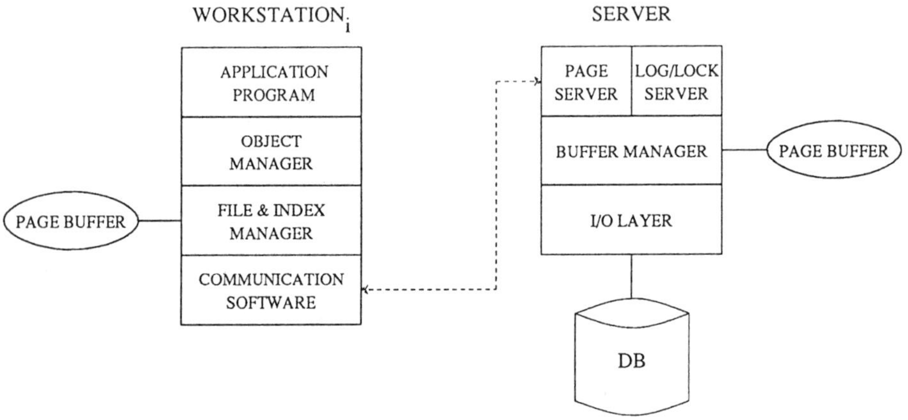

Figure 18.2. Page-server architecture

Buffering on the workstation can be done in terms of pages, of objects, or of both. The advantage of an object cache is that buffer space on the workstation is not wasted holding objects that have not actually been referenced by the application. If an object cache is used, then the cost of copying each object from the incoming data page into the local object cache will be incurred. Furthermore, if an object in the object cache is later updated, the page on which the object resides may have to be retrieved from the server again (which, in turn, may incur an I/O operation).

The primary advantage of this design is that it places most of the complexity of the OODBMS in the workstation, where the majority of the available CPU cycles are concentrated, leaving the server to perform the tasks that it alone can perform—concurrency control and recovery. Since entire pages are transferred intact between the workstation and the server, the overhead on the server is minimized. At first glance this approach may appear wasteful if only a single object on the page is needed, but in fact the cost (in terms of CPU cycles) to send 4K bytes is not much higher than the cost of sending 100 bytes. Furthermore, if the clustering mechanism has worked properly, then a significant fraction of the objects on each page will eventually end up being referenced by the client. Finally, by minimizing the load each individual workstation places on the server, one can support more workstations off a single server—delaying for as long as possible the complexities associated with supporting multiple servers.

While its simplicity makes this design very attractive, it is not without disadvantages. First, methods can be evaluated only on the workstation. Thus a sequential scan of a collection requires that all the pages in the collection be transferred to the workstation. This limitation sounds disastrous, but there are several mitigating factors. The server does the same amount of disk I/O as with the object-server design and, in the case of an indexed selection, only those pages containing relevant objects will be transferred to the workstation. Furthermore, the page server avoids all problems (e.g., having to flush the workstation's cache) that the object-server architecture encounters when executing methods on the server.

A second disadvantage is that object-level locking may be difficult to implement. Consider what happens if object-level locking is employed and two workstations update two different objects on the same data page. If classical locking protocols (Gray et al. 1976) are used, both transactions will set IX (intention lock) locks on the shared page and X (exclusive lock) locks on the individual objects. If special precautions are not taken to merge the changes to the two pages when the modified pages are written back to the server, one or the other of the updates will be lost. One possible solution is to allow only one object-level X lock on a page at a time (by making IX locks on a page incompatible). In addition, implementing non-two-phase B-tree locking protocols may be complex in this environment.

Recovery must involve both the workstation and the server with this design. With logging, the workstation must generate log records to be forwarded to the server and the server must track the dependencies between the pages and log records it receives from a workstation. However, the problem will not be as hard as recovery in a distributed database system (Lindsay et al. 1979), as long as only a single server is involved in committing the changes made by a transaction.

Finally, the performance of this design, both relative to the other architectures and in absolute terms, may be dependent on the effectiveness of the clustering mechanism. In section 5 we examine how clustering affects the performance of this design.

2.3 The File-Server Architecture

The file-server architecture is a variation of the page-server design. The workstation software uses a remote file service such as NFS (Sun 1988) to read and write database pages directly. Figure 18.3 shows such an architecture.

There are several reasons why such an architecture is attractive. First, it provides many of the advantages of the page-server architecture, such as minimizing the overhead placed on the workstation by the server. Also, since NFS runs in the operating-system kernel, by using it to read and write the database, user-level context switches can be avoided completely, improving the rate at which data can be retrieved by a remote workstation. Finally, because of its widespread use, NFS will continue to evolve and be improved. Basing a system on NFS takes advantage of these improvements.

This architecture has some serious problems in addition to those it inherits from the page-server architecture. First, NFS writes are known to be slow. Because it is a stateless protocol built on top of UDP, a write operation to a remotely mounted NFS file is flushed to disk before the request is acknowledged.

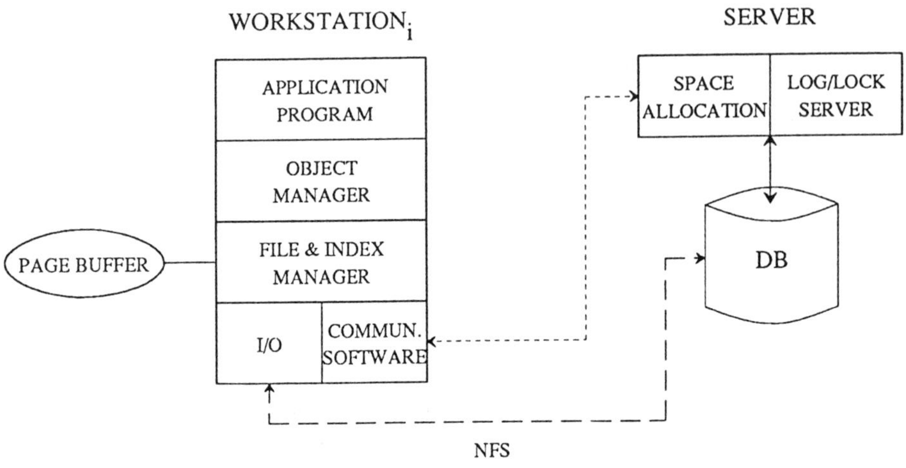

Figure 18.3. File-server architecture

(Actually, not only is the updated block flushed to disk but also the inode (a Unix file system data structure) which points to the updated block. Thus each data page write actually involves two disk I/Os. As a solution to this problem, Legato of Menlo Park, California, has recently introduced a stable RAM board for Sun servers which is used to buffer writes.)

Second, since read operations in this architecture bypass the server software completely, it is not possible to combine the request for a page with the request for a lock on a page. One can send a separate lock-request message, but such an approach negates some of the benefits of using NFS in the first place, as the cost of the lock request is likely to be very close to the cost of simply requesting the page and setting the lock as a side effect. Less costly alternatives are to use an optimistic concurrency-control scheme or to batch lock requests to reduce the overhead of setting locks. A similar problem occurs with coordinating the allocation of disk space on the server. Since sending a request to the server for an individual page is too expensive, the most reasonable solution is to have the server allocate groups of pages at a time, instead of workstations requesting a single page at a time.

3 Prototyping the Workstation-Server Architectures

This section describes our prototypes of the three alternative architectures. The basis for each of these prototypes was a stripped-down, single-user version of WiSS (Chou et al. 1985). We elected to use WiSS because it is currently being used as part of two different OODBMSs (the O_2 system from Altaïr and the ObjectStore system from Object Sciences). As shown in figure 18.4, WiSS consists of four distinct levels. Level 0 deals with the aspects of physical I/O, including allocation of disk extents (collections of physically contiguous pages) to files. Level 1 is the buffer manager which uses the read and write operations of level 0 to provide buffered I/O to the higher levels of the system. Pages in the buffer pool are managed using an LRU replacement strategy. Level 2 is the storage-structure level. This level implements sequential files, B^+-trees, and long data items. It is also responsible for mapping references to records to the appropriate references to pages buffered by level 1. Finally, level 3 implements the access methods, which provide the primitives for scanning a file via a sequential, index, or long-data item scan.

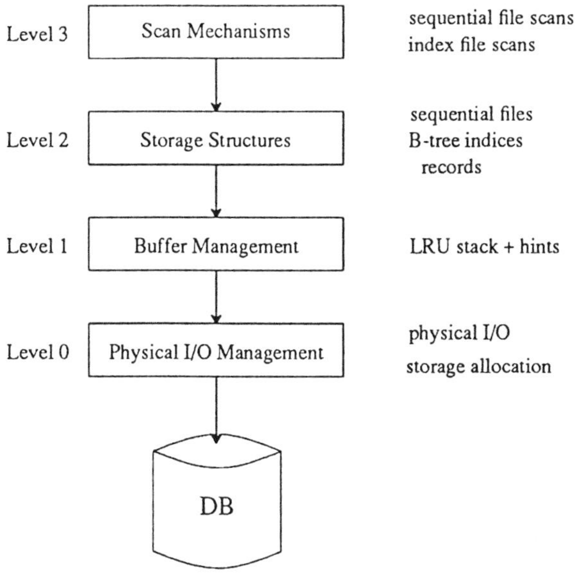

Figure 18.4. WiSS architecture

To simplify the implementation of the different prototypes, we first produced a stripped-down version of WiSS by removing support for long data items, B-trees, and all but the most primitive scans. The resulting system supports only records, files, and sequential scans without predicates. In addition to serving as the basis from which the various prototype systems were constructed, this version of WiSS also provides a lower bound against which the performance of the other systems can be compared. The ideal workstation-server version of this system would have exactly the same performance as the single-processor version.

As discussed in more detail below, the object and page servers required that we split the functionality provided by WiSS into two processes, termed the *client* and *server* processes. In the target environment, the database resides on disks attached to the machine running the server process, and the client process runs on each workstation. To provide the interprocessor communication necessary to implement such a system, we used the Sun RPC tools, including Rpcgen

(Sun 1988), which automatically generates the necessary procedure stubs given a data file that describes the message formats and the procedure names with which you wish to communicate remotely. Although this RPC package provides support for communications using both TCP and UDP, we elected to use UDP since we had no need to send streams of data larger than 8 KB.

3.1 File Server

As described in section 2, the simplest way of having a number of workstations share data is to run all the database software on the workstation and use NFS to access the database on a shared server. Since for these experiments we elected to ignore issues of concurrency control, recovery, and coordinating the allocation of disk space, prototyping this architecture simply meant running WiSS on one processor with its disk volume on a remotely mounted file system belonging to the server, as shown in figure 18.5. When level 0 of WiSS makes an I/O request to read or write a page, the NFS software takes care of executing the request on the server on behalf of the workstation.

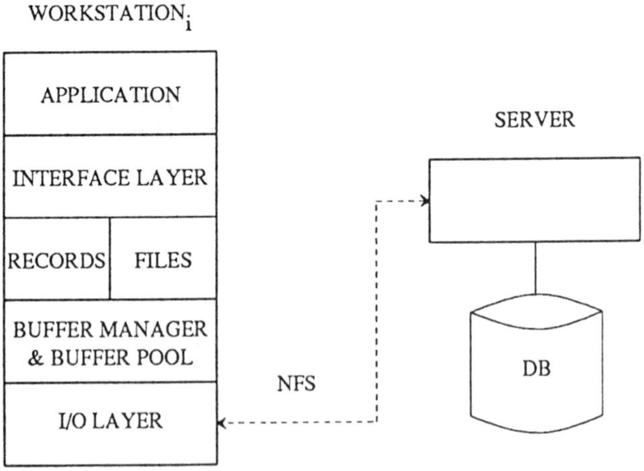

Figure 18.5. Remote file-server design

A key motivation for prototyping this design is that it provides a lower bound on how fast remote data can be accessed. Although NFS, like the version of the Sun RPC protocol that we used, is also implemented on top of UDP, data transfers occur between two kernels instead of between two user-level processes. As illustrated by the results in section 5, this difference can have a significant effect on the execution of certain kinds of queries.

3.2 Page Server

We prototyped the page-server architecture as shown in figure 18.6. The server process consists of levels 0 and 1 of WiSS plus an RPC interface to all the routines in these two levels. The workstation process consists of all the levels of WiSS except for level 0, which was replaced by a thin layer that executes requests to level 0 by sending a remote procedure call to the server process. The upper levels of WiSS were completely unaffected by these changes. Our current implementation of this design does not provide concurrency control and recovery services, but the server does support simultaneous workstation processes.

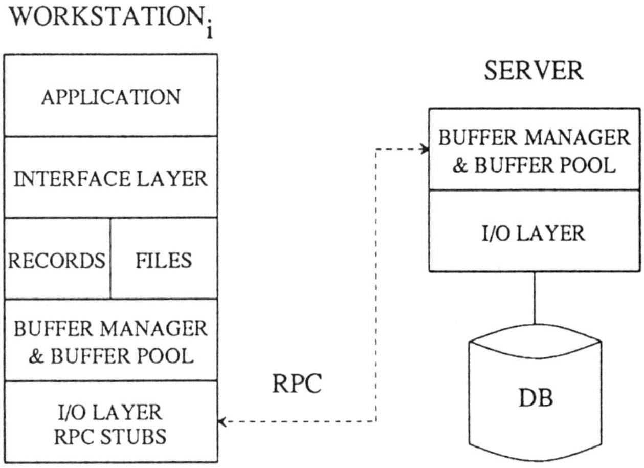

Figure 18.6. Page-server design

In a complete implementation of this design, each request for a page would also specify the lock mode desired by the workstation (e.g., S, X, or IX), avoiding the overhead of a second message to set a lock. In addition to a centralized lock table on the server, each workstation would also maintain a local cache of the locks it holds to minimize lock calls to the server.

The success of the page-server design is predicated on two factors: the extent to which related objects are clustered together on a page, and the relative cost of fetching an individual object versus a page of objects. As illustrated by table 18.1, most of the cost of obtaining a page from the server is in the overhead

Table 18.1. Cost of Fetching Objects

Size of Reply Message (bytes)	Execution Time (ms)
1	7.8
10	7.9
100	8.2
1000	9.7
4000	17.9
8000	28.4

of the RPC and communications protocols and not in transmission and copying costs. The following times were gathered between two Sun 3/80 processors (3 MIPS, 68030 CPUs) running the Sun RPC software and version 4.0.3 of the SunOS. The size of the RPC request message was 8 bytes.

3.3 Object Server

Whereas the server process in the page-server architecture only understands pages, in the object-server design it understands objects and files or collections of objects. Our object-server prototype is depicted in figure 18.7. The server process consists of all the layers of WiSS plus an RPC interface to level 3 of WiSS. The workstation process consists of the application code, a special version of level 3 of WiSS, and an object cache. This version of level 3 serves as an interface to the local object cache and to the services provided by the server process through the RPC software. Operations on files (e.g., create/destroy, open/close) are passed directly to the server. Operations on objects (really WiSS records) are handled as follows. In the case of a "read object" call, the interface layer first checks whether the object is in the local object cache. If so, the object is returned directly to the application code. When a miss on the local cache occurs, the interface layer first makes space available in the local cache (perhaps by writing a dirty object back to the server) and then requests the desired object from the server. When a new object is created, a write-through cache protocol is used because WiSS uses physical object IDs and the server is needed to place the object on a page of the appropriate file and assign an object ID. The new object

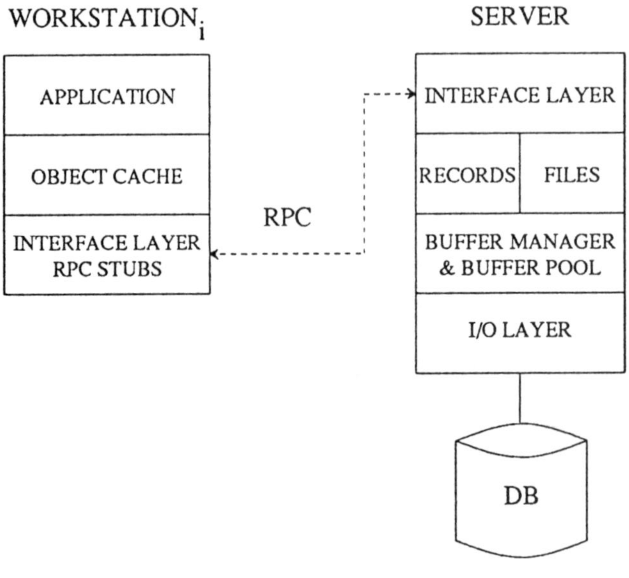

Figure 18.7. Object-server design

remains in the cache but it is marked as clean. Updates to objects residing in the cache are handled simply by marking the object dirty and flushing any remaining dirty objects to the server at commit time.

3.4 Concurrency Control and Recovery

Because we wished to complete this project in a reasonable time, it was not possible to include concurrency control or recovery services in our prototypes. We feel, however, that the results obtained are representative of the relative performance of the three architectures. With respect to concurrency control, in the object- and page-server designs, the request for a lock and the request for an object or page can be combined into a single message. If the server grants the lock, the reply message contains both the grant and the requested object or page. When this mechanism is combined with a local cache of locks already obtained, no extra messages are required to add locking to these two designs. Since lock requests cannot be combined with I/O requests in the file-server design, the results obtained for this design are undoubtedly biased in favor of it (unless optimistic concurrency control suffices).

With respect to recovery services, the performance impact of a recovery mechanism such as write-ahead logging would be identical on each design. For example, assume that log records are generated as objects are updated and that log records are grouped into page-sized chunks for transmission to the server. Since such a design is compatible will all three architectures, we contend that omitting recovery services does not significantly affect the relative performance of the three designs.

One final issue that must be addressed in complete implementations of these three architectures is how to maintain consistency among the different buffer pools. With respect to objects or pages for which locks are held until the end of transaction (the normal case), consistency is ensured by the semantics of standard locking protocols. The one case where problems might arise is with object-level locking in the page- or file-server designs. If write locks by multiple transactions are allowed on objects in the same page, then combining the changes of those transactions in the server is nontrivial. In the case of objects or pages which are locked in a non-two-phase fashion (such as is typically done for index pages to improve performance), a number of possible solutions are possible. For example, by invalidating the local copy of an object when the lock is released, consistency can be ensured at the expense of reduced performance. There are certainly better solutions, but they appear to be equally applicable to all three designs. Thus we felt that omitting cache consistency would not seriously affect our results.

4 The Altaïr Complex-Object Benchmark

To evaluate the performance of the alternative workstation-server architectures, the obvious alternatives were to use an existing benchmark or to design a specific benchmark for this evaluation. The Sun (Cattell 1988) and Hypermodel

(Anderson et al. 1990) benchmarks appeared to be the most reasonable of the existing alternatives. We opted against the Sun benchmark because it forms complex objects by choosing random objects to relate to one another. Since one measurement we wanted was the impact of the degree of clustering of the components of a complex object on the performance of the alternative designs, the Sun benchmark was not appropriate. Recently, a new version of the Sun Benchmark has been designed (Cattell and Skeen 1990) which would have been much better suited for our purposes.

Initially, the Hypermodel benchmark appeared a better match to our objectives because it provides both clustered and nonclustered groupings of objects. The problem with this benchmark is that it consists of a very large number of queries. Since we were afraid of being overwhelmed by results if we used the full Hypermodel benchmark and did not understand which subset to select, we elected to design a new benchmark that was tailored to the task of evaluating the alternative workstation-server designs. In designing this benchmark, we borrowed a number of ideas from the Hypermodel and Sun benchmarks, but attempted to limit the scope of the benchmark to a simpler database design and a smaller set of queries.

We do not consider our benchmark an OODBMS benchmark, but rather a distributed object-manager benchmark. We make the distinction because the database generator has a number of parameters controlling the physical placement of objects, such as the degree of clustering and the placement of records on pages, that are not expressible at the data-model and data-language level of an OODBMS.

4.1 Database Design

The basis for the Altaïr Complex-Object Benchmark (ACOB) is a set of 1500 complex objects. Each object is composed of seven WiSS records with the structure shown in figure 18.8. The design of this benchmark is influenced by the data model of the O_2 database system which distinguishes between values and objects. In an O_2 database, an object may have a complex structure without forcing each subcomponent to be an object. Thus it made sense for us to distinguish interobject and intraobject references and treat them differently. In particular, we put the seven records of an object on one page because we imagine them all to be part of the value of one object, and hence they would be created together when the object is created.

(4 Bytes)	(4 Bytes)	(8 Bytes)	(8 Bytes)	(88 Bytes)
WISS RECORD HEADER	KEY	LEFT CHILD	RIGHT CHILD	DUMMY STRING

Figure 18.8. Object structure

Each record is 112 bytes long. The key field is an integer whose value ranges between 1 and 1500, corresponding to the physical order of the objects in the file. The seven records that form each complex object are organized in the form of a binary tree of depth 2, as shown in figure 18.9. All interrecord (and interobject) references are in terms of physical record IDs. When an object is initially created, all seven records are placed on the same data page. Since an update to a complex object may have the unavoidable side effect of moving one or more of its component records to a different page, our benchmark provides a mechanism by which a fraction of the records within an object can be "smeared" to other pages in order to explore the effect of such updates on the performance of the different server architectures. Smearing is discussed in more detail later.

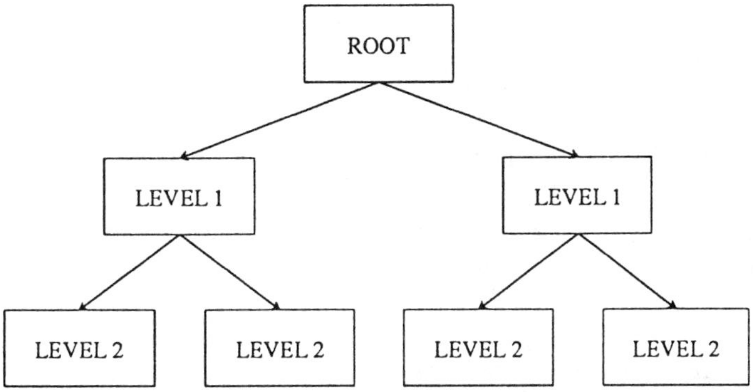

Figure 18.9. Complex-object organization

With 4-KB pages, five complex objects (consisting of seven records each) will fit on a single page. The set of 1500 objects spans 300 pages (approximately 1.2 MB). While the size of each set could be criticized as being too small to be realistic, one of the things we wanted to explore was the relative performance of the different architectures when the entire working set of the application fitted into the workstation's buffer pool. A significantly larger set size would have made such a test impossible. However, in order to minimize the effect of operating-system buffering of database pages, five identical sets of 1500 objects were used for the experiments described below, producing a total database size of about 6 MB.

The ACOB database is constructed in three phases. The first phase allocates all the records of all the objects, forming the intraobject references and filling in all the record fields. In real object-oriented databases, objects frequently reference one another in the form either of aggregation relationships (e.g., a part and its component subparts) or of M:N relationships between each other (e.g., suppliers and parts) (Anderson et al. 1990). To simulate such relationships, in the second phase we *attach* two objects to each of the four leaf records in every complex object (via the "left" and "right" fields found in each record), as shown in figure 18.10. Each triangle in figure 18.10 represents one complex of seven records, similar to the one shown in figure 18.9. These attached objects are termed "components."

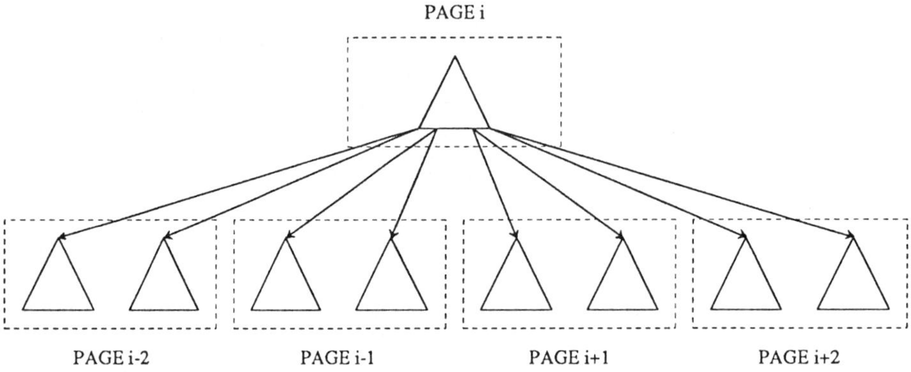

Figure 18.10. A complex object with its eight component objects

We wanted to gauge the impact of the physical clustering of complex objects on the performance of the different server designs. To this end, the second phase accepts a parameter called the *clustering factor*. Our notion of clustering is defined as follows. If object A references object B, then we say object B is *clustered* near object A if B is located within a "clustering region" around A. For example, if the size of the clustering region is five pages, B is considered to be clustered near A if B is on the same page as A or on either of the two pages physically preceding or following the page upon which A resides. Section 5 explores the effect of varying the size of the clustering region on the relative performance of the different architectures.

The clustering factor, f, can be varied from 0 to 100. It is employed as follows during the second phase of database creation. When the objects to attach to an object X are being selected, objects that are clustered near X are selected f% of the time. That is, for each attached object a random value between 0 and 99 is generated, and if this random value is less than the value of the clustering factor, one of the objects that are clustered near X is selected at random. Otherwise, a random object from the set of 1500 objects is selected.

The third (optional) phase in creating the database is to smear a fraction of the records that comprise each complex object. Smearing simulates the dispersal of records in an object over different data pages caused by database updates (either because an updated record was too long to fit on its current page or because an alternative version of a record was created and the new version does not fit on the same page with the other records of the object). If smearing is selected, one-quarter of the objects (chosen at random) are modified as follows. With a probability of 25, each of the two interior records and each of the four leaf records are "moved" to another page in the database. (The probability of being moved is computed individually on each node. However, since smearing involves swapping an internal record of one object with an internal record of another object, approximately three-eighths of the objects are actually affected by the smearing process.) As illustrated by figure 18.11, this move is accomplished by swapping the record with a corresponding record of another randomly selected object. For example, in figure 18.11, we have smeared object A by exchanging its right child with the left child of B. In a similar fashion, we have smeared a leaf node from object B by exchanging the right child of record C with the left child of record D.

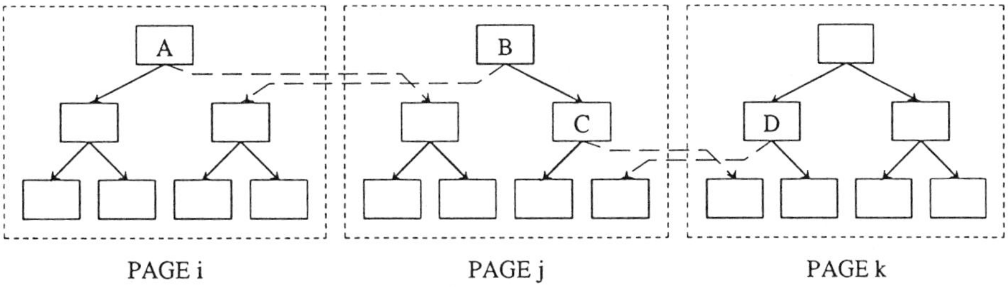

Figure 18.11. Smearing of interior and leaf records within several complex objects

4.2 Queries

4.2.1 Sequential Scan

The scan query reads all the complex objects in a set in their physical order. For each object, a breadth-first traversal algorithm is used to read the seven records that comprise the object. In our implementation of this benchmark, the record IDs of the root records are stored in a separate set. In the case of the sequential scan query, the execution times presented in section 5 include the time necessary to read the elements of this set. For the random-read and random-update queries, this set of root record IDs was read into an in-memory array as a separate processing step. The processing time for this step is not included in the execution times presented for these queries.

The scan query does not read any of the attached components of an object. Thus each record is accessed exactly once. As records are accessed, they are copied into the address space of the application program. If the records of an object have been smeared, reading an object may require access to more than one disk page.

This query has been included because it simulates reading all instances of a class. Without smearing, the query is a very good test of the instruction-path length of each design, as accesses to the database are strictly sequential, maximizing the chance that the performance of the CPU will be the limiting factor. This query, with its sequential I/O activity, was also designed to help understand the relative costs of accessing data on a disk directly attached to the processor (i.e., WiSS running on a local disk) and accessing it remotely (i.e., each of the server designs). The degree of database clustering does not have any effect on the execution time of this query.

4.2.2 Random Read

The random-read query "processes" 300 randomly selected complex objects and their components. The following sequence of operations is applied to each object selected. First the root record of the object is read. Then a partial, depth-first traversal is performed up to a tree depth of 6 (the root record is considered to be at depth 0), such that an average of 44 records from among those in the object, its 8 attached components, and the 64 root records of each of their attached components are read. This partial traversal is performed by electing to perform each stage of the depth-first traversal with a probability of 8. Thus the expected number of records read at each level is one root plus 0.8 of the children at depth 1, plus 0.8^2 of the records at depth 2, and so on up to 0.8^6 of the records at depth 6. Of the expected 44 records reads, 17 are at level 6. Our selectivity factor on this query (and also the next) is related to the structural density parameter of Chang and Katz 1989. Our selectivity of .8 appears to be in the middle of the range of structural densities actually observed in traces of access patterns from a suite of very large-scale integration tools.

This query was designed to simulate those applications in which a user checks out a collection of complex objects and selected subcomponents at the beginning of a transaction or session. As we will see in section 5, the extent to which the database is clustered has a significant effect on the execution time of this query for both the page- and file-server designs.

4.2.3 Random Update

The random-update query is basically an update version of the random-read query. Again, 300 random objects are selected for processing; but in this query the records at depth 6 that are selected for reading are also updated. On the average, for each complex object processed, 17 records are updated (out of the 44 records read). These updates are performed in place by overwriting the record with a copy of itself. Thus the structure of the database is not changed.

This query was designed to help understand some of the possible benefits of transferring individual objects between the workstation and the server. With the page- and file-server designs, complete pages, containing perhaps only a single updated record, must be transferred back to the server from the workstation. In the case of the object server, only the updated objects need to be transferred back to the server. On the other hand, the updated object must be placed back on the proper data page, but this page may no longer be in the server's page cache. In that case, the page must first be reread from the disk before the updated object can be added to it. This query is affected by the degree to which the database has been clustered and the extent to which the records in each object have been smeared.

4.3 Benchmark Organization

Using the load program plus the three queries described in the previous section, we then composed the actual benchmark that was used to evaluate the different server designs. This benchmark consisted of the following five steps, which were always executed in order. The random-number seed was set to the same value at the start of each step. As described in section 5, a wide number of versions of this benchmark were constructed by varying such parameters as the degree of clustering, whether smearing was selected or not, and the size of the workstation and server buffer pools.

1. Build five identical sets of 1500 complex objects each with the same degree of database clustering and the same choice of smearing (either on or off). The five sets are assigned names A to E, corresponding to the order in which they were constructed (thus A is the first set built and E is the last).
2. Apply the scan query on sets A through E in order. The reason for this ordering is to attempt to minimize the extent to which buffering of pages by the operating system affects the results obtained. We elected to use five sets of objects based on the relative sizes of the set of objects and the operating system buffer pool. The Sun 3/80 used as a server for our experiments had only 8 megabytes of memory. With a server that had more memory we would have either increased the number of objects in each set or expanded the number of sets employed.
3. Run the random-read query on sets A through E, in order.
4. Run the random-update query on sets A through E, in order.
5. Run the sequential-scan, random-read, and random-update queries one after another on the same set (without resetting the random-number generator between queries), first on set A, then on the other sets in order. One motivation for this final phase of the benchmark was to explore how effectively the different server designs utilized their local buffer caches.

5 Performance Evaluation

In this section we present the results of our performance evaluation of the three prototypes, using a single-site version of WiSS as a reference point. In section 5.1 we describe the hardware environment used to conduct our experiments. The results obtained while we were building the ACOB database are given in section 5.2. Section 5.3 describes our clustering and smearing experiments. Finally, in section 5.4 we explore how the size of the buffer pools on the workstation affects the architectures individually and comparatively.

5.1 Test Environment

For our experiments we used two Sun 3/80 workstation (the Sun 3/80 uses a 68030 CPU and is rated at 3 MIPS). Each workstation ran version 4.0.3 of the Sun operating system. Each machine had 8 megabytes of memory and two 100-megabyte disk drives (Quantum ProDrive 105S). The machines were run in the normal, multiuser mode, but during the tests they were not used for any other activity. The database was always constructed on the same disk drive on the server machine, to insure that any differences among the different drives did not affect the results obtained.

In configuring the different systems, we encountered a number of problems relating to buffer space allocation. The first problem was deciding how much buffer space to allocate to WiSS and the file-server prototype. Given that the default configuration for the page- and object-server designs was a 50-page (4-KB pages) buffer pool on both the workstation and the server, one option would have been to use 100-page buffer pools with both WiSS and the file-server prototype. However, this choice did not seem quite fair, because in a real environment the buffer space on the server of the page- and object-server designs would be shared among multiple workstations. In addition, 50-page buffer pools on both the workstation and the server are not as effective as a single 100-page buffer pool. Since there was no obvious right solution, we decided to use the same sized buffer pool as was used in the workstation process of the page- and object-server prototypes.

The second problem encountered was limiting the amount of buffering performed by the operating system, as the virtual memory manager of SunOS V4.0 treats both program and data pages uniformly. (Other versions of Unix typically allocate 10% of the physical memory available for buffering data pages and reserve the rest of memory for program pages.) While this feature did not affect buffering on the workstation of the page- and object-server prototypes, its impact on the file-server server prototype was to provide it with an effective buffer pool size of approximately 1500 pages! Since there is no clean way of turning this feature off, when running the file-server prototype we used a modified kernel on the workstation processor that artificially limited the size of physical memory to 292 pages (this was done by using adb to set the value of _physmem in vmunix to 0×175). The value of 292 pages was chosen so that there was enough physical memory to hold the Unix kernel, the benchmark program, a 50-page WiSS buffer pool, a 10-page NFS buffer pool, and the standard Unix utility programs.

We elected, however, not to "reduce" the size of physical memory on the processor to which the disk holding the database was attached, since each design had an equal opportunity to use this memory for buffering. More importantly, restricting the amount of memory on the server would have made the benchmark much more I/O intensive, and this change might have masked interesting differences among the architectures. The reader should, however, keep this fact in mind when interpreting the results presented throughout this paper.

5.2 Database Build Time

Table 18.2 presents the time for each of the four prototypes to build an unsmeared database with 30% and 90% clustering factors. Several observations are in order. First, each system is affected only slightly by the clustering factor. While both the file- and page-server designs are slower than WiSS, the results are not out of line, considering that both are building the database on a disk attached to a remote processor. The most startling result is that the object-server prototype is almost six times slower than the file- and page-server prototypes. As will become evident in the other tests presented below, when the object server's cache is ineffective (as with the build test), its performance is always much worse than the other designs because of the high cost of transferring objects individually. We omit the times to build a smeared database (which are somewhat higher), because the relative performance of the different systems remained the same.

Table 18.2. Time to Build an Unsmeared Database

	Time (seconds)	
	30% Clustering Factor	90% Clustering Factor
WiSS	22.0	22.6
File server	47.8	48.4
Page server	43.6	41.4
Object server	236.8	233.8

5.3 Clustering and Smearing Tests

For the next collection of tests, we fixed the workstation and server buffer pools each at 50 pages and varied the clustering factor from 10% to 90%. The WiSS and file-server buffer pools were also set at 50 pages. The clustering region was fixed at 5 pages. Figures 18.12 through 18.19 present the results that we obtained for the four benchmark queries (see section 4.2) on both unsmeared and smeared databases.

5.3.1 Scan Query

Figures 18.12 and 18.13 present the results obtained for the scan query. As expected, each design is unaffected by the clustering factor, since this query reads each object in its entirety but reads none of an object's component objects. The most startling result is the object server's extremely poor performance relative to the other designs. With an unsmeared database, the page server is approximately 11 times faster than the object server. The source of this difference is the high cost associated with fetching each of the seven records composing an object with a separate RPC operation. With the page-server design, 300 pages are fetched from the server by the workstation, one RPC call per page. With the object-server design, a total of 10,500 RPC calls are made. In order to make the object server competitive on such queries, each RPC call must fetch more than a single record. One possible solution would be for the server to return all seven records of a object in a single RPC call. This change, however, would require that the server understand the structure of an object—significantly complicating its design.

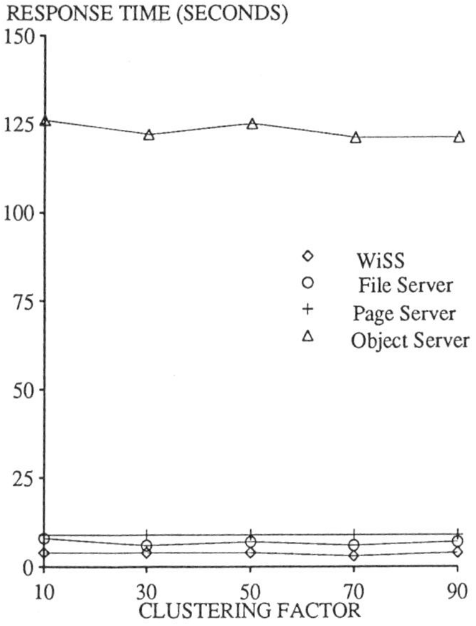

Figure 18.12. Scan query, unsmeared DB

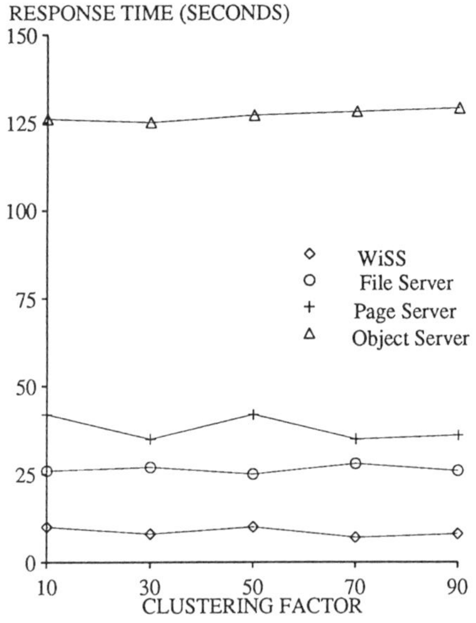

Figure 18.13. Scan query, smeared DB

When the database is smeared, the performance of the object-server design is relatively unaffected; the page- and file-server prototypes slow down significantly. Part of this slowing down is due to a fivefold increase in the number of disk I/O operations required (to approximately 1500). However, this factor accounts for only 6 seconds (the increase observed for WiSS) of the approximately 18- and 30-second increases observed for the file- and page-server architectures respectively. The remainder represents the cost of fetching an additional 1200 pages from the server. For the page-server architecture, the cost of retrieving 1200 pages via the RPC mechanism can be estimated, from the figures given in section 3.2, to be approximately 22 seconds. The 12-second difference between the two illustrates how much more efficient NFS is than a user-level RPC mechanism.

The object server is unaffected because it fetches the same number of records whether the database is smeared or not, and the increased I/O activity on the part of the server is masked by the cost of doing object-at-a-time fetches.

5.3.2 Random-Read Query

Figures 18.14 and 18.15 present the results for the random-read query. As the clustering factor is increased from 10% to 90%, the number of disk I/Os performed by each design to execute the query decreases (the buffer-pool hit rate improves by approximately 30%). This reduction improves the performance of WiSS by about 35%.

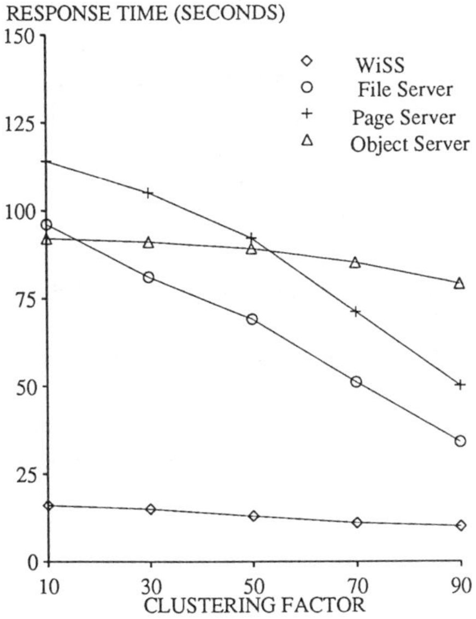

Figure 18.14. Random-read query, unsmeared DB

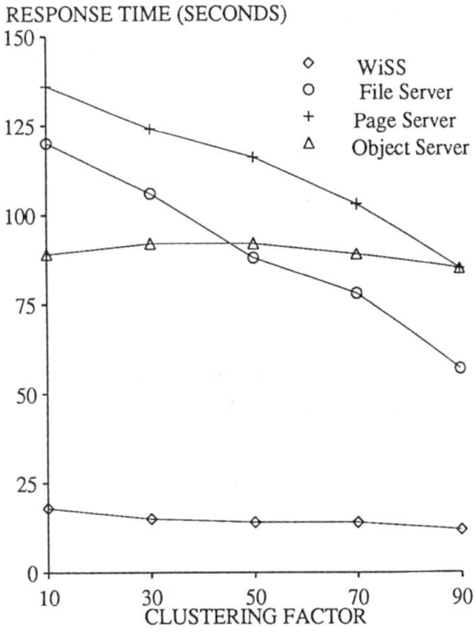

Figure 18.15. Random-read query, smeared DB

The behavior of the object- and page-server designs (both in absolute terms and relative to one another) is more complicated. First, although both systems have 50-page buffer pools in both the workstation and the server (increasing the probability that an object will be found in one of the two buffer pools), it turns out that buffer size is not the dominant factor. Instead their behavior is dominated by the costs associated with RPC access to the server. The execution of this query involves 14,623 references to WiSS records (this is independent of the clustering factor). With a 10% clustering factor, the object server has a cache hit rate of .181. When the clustering factor is increased to 90%, the cache hit rate increases to .251. The result is that 1024 fewer objects are requested from the server (10,953 instead of 11,977), producing an estimated RPC savings of only 8 seconds (the total improvement in response time is 13 seconds). The remaining 5 seconds is due primarily to the reduction in the number of disk I/Os performed by the server.

With the page-server design, as the clustering factor is increased from 10% to 90%, the buffer cache hit rate increases from .66 to .86, resulting in a saving of 3150 RPCs (from 5443 to 2293). This saving translates into an estimated RPC saving of approximately 58 seconds (consider the RPC times listed in section 3.2). The remaining 6 second improvement in response time is because the server does fewer I/Os.

The differences in performance between the page- and file-server designs is primarily due to the difference in cost between fetching a page via NFS and with an RPC call. This difference is not the result of extra copies, as we modified the output of Rpcgen to eliminate the copy normally introduced by the Rpcgen software. When the clustering factor is low (or the database is smeared as in figure 18.15), the page-server design is forced to do a large number of RPC accesses, each of which is more expensive than accessing a page via NFS.

In general, the performance of the page- and file-server designs are very sensitive to the database clustering factor. The page-server design has worse performance than the object-server design with either a smeared database or a low clustering factor, simply because each page retrieved from the server ends up fetching relatively few objects that get referenced before the page is removed from the buffer pool. On the other hand, the object server fetches only those objects it actually references. Hence its performance is relatively immune to the clustering factor or smearing. In a multiuser environment, this immunity would likely change if the bottleneck switched from the RPC mechanism to the disk arm (i.e., if each object fetched resulted in a random disk access).

5.3.3 Random-Update Query

Like the random-read query, the random-update query randomly selects 300 objects for processing; but in this case the records at depth 6 that are selected for reading during the traversal are also updated. On the average, for each complex object processed, 17 records are updated. The results are presented in figures 18.16 and 18.17.

This query illustrates the extremely poor performance of writes using NFS—the file server being more than eight times slower than WiSS at a clustering factor of 10%. As the clustering factor is increased from 10% to 90%, the response time for the file-server design improves to being only five times worse than WiSS for an unsmeared database and seven times worse for a smeared database. This improvement occurs because with a higher clustering factor the chance that a page will end up being written more than once decreases. It is important to keep in mind that these results reflect the performance of a file-server design implemented using NFS. A different remote-file service might behave quite differently.

The clustering factor and smearing again significantly affect the performance of the page-server design and, since pages flow in both directions between the workstation and the server, the impact is magnified. Furthermore, the same page may end up being written back to the server more than once.

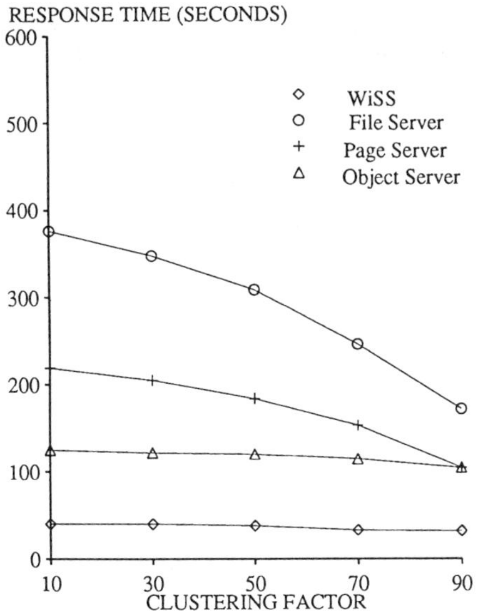

Figure 18.16. Random-update query, unsmeared DB

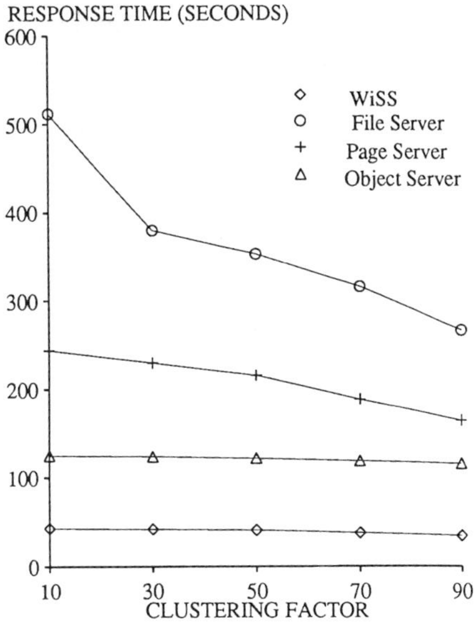

Figure 18.17. Random-update query, smeared DB

This query is the only one where the object-server design really exhibits significantly better performance than the other two designs. By fetching only those objects that are actually referenced by the application and writing back only the objects actually modified, the performance of the object-server design is relatively insensitive to clustering and smearing.

This query also illustrates that page writes with NFS are more expensive than page writes with RPC (at a clustering factor of 10%, the response time for the file server is about 20% higher than that of the page server). This difference is due to NFS being a stateless protocol: it performs the write operation before acknowledging the message. With an unsmeared database, the difference in response times decreases slightly as the clustering level is increased, because fewer pages are written more than once. (Recall that, at each clustering factor level, the same number of pages are being written by both architectures.)

5.3.4 All-Queries Tests

The final test involves running the scan, random-read, and random-update queries sequentially without flushing the workstation or server's cache between the queries. The purpose of this query is to simulate the case where a user runs an associative query against a collection in order to select a set of objects to be further manipulated and a second set of objects to be updated. The results obtained for the four different architectures are presented in figures 18.18 and 18.19.

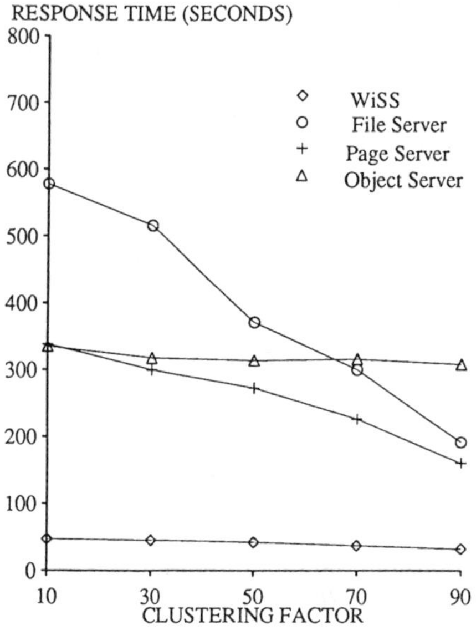

Figure 18.18. All queries, unsmeared DB

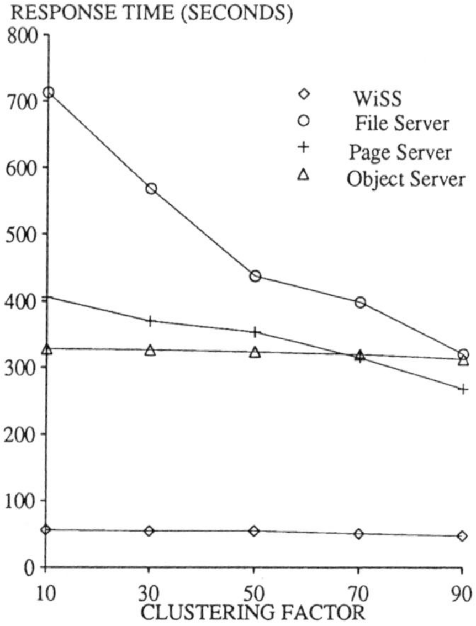

Figure 18.19. All queries, smeared DB

These graphs reveal several interesting results. First, when the database is not smeared, the page-server design outperforms the object server across almost the full range of clustering factors—primarily since the object server performs so poorly on the scan component of the experiment. Again we see that the object server's performance is relatively unaffected by changes in clustering and smearing. As expected from the results for the random-read and random-update queries by themselves, the performance of the page server improves significantly as the clustering factor is increased. Similarly, the performance of the file-server design improves as the clustering factoring is increased, because fewer NFS writes are performed. When the database is smeared, the performance of the page and file servers degrades as expected, and the object-server design provides slightly superior performance until a clustering factor of 70% is reached. Again, smearing has no significant performance impact on the object server.

5.3.5 Sensitivity to the Size of the Clustering Region

After observing the results presented above, we were curious as to the sensitivity of our results to the size of the clustering region. To test this sensitivity, we repeated the four queries using an unsmeared database and with clustering regions of one and nine pages. (Recall that our definition of *clustered* states that an object B is clustered near an object A if B lies within the clustering region surrounding A.) We used only an unsmeared database because the results in figures 18.12 through 18.19 indicate that the primary effect of smearing is to shift the file- and page-server curves by a nearly constant amount and not to change their fundamental shapes. The most interesting results we obtained are presented in figures 18.20 and 18.21.

Figure 18.20 presents the execution time of the random-read query for the page- and object-server designs for the three sizes of clustering regions. These results demonstrate that the relative performance of the different systems is indeed sensitive to the size of the clustering region. With a clustering region size of five pages, the performance of the page server is better than that of the object server only when the clustering factor is above 55%. When the clustering region is shrunk to one page, the crossover point drops to a clustering factor of about 30%, and when it is increased to nine pages the crossover point climbs to about 65%. These results reveal that the page server's performance remains very sensitive to the clustering factor, regardless of the size of the clustering region. However, they also reveal that the performance of the page server will be superior either if the degree of database clustering can be kept above 60% or if the region of clustering can be restricted to consist of only a few pages. Actually, we speculate that the absolute size of the clustering region may not matter. Rather, the key is probably the size of the clustering region relative to the size of the workstation's buffer pool.

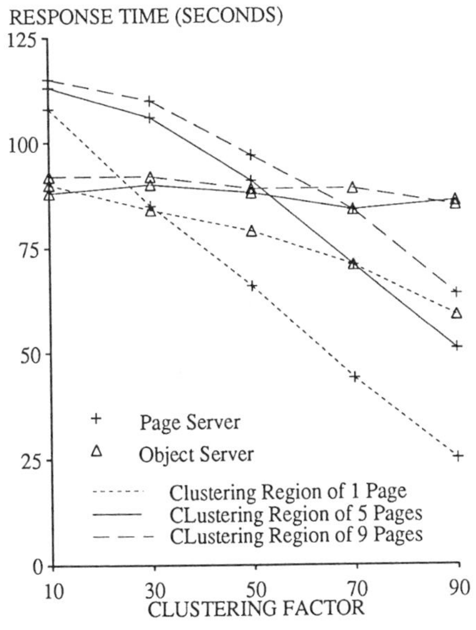

Figure 18.20. Random-read query

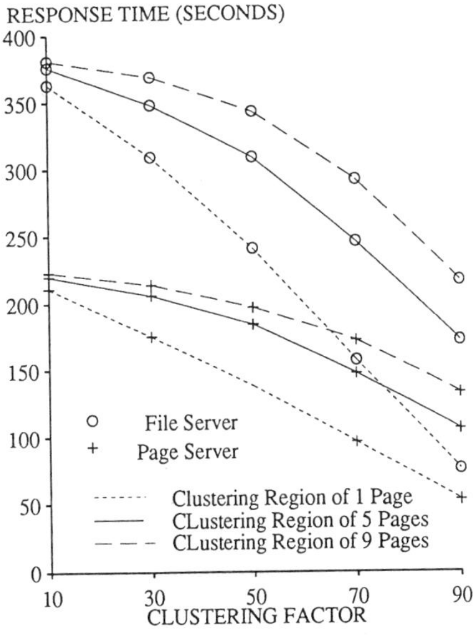

Figure 18.21. Random-update query

Figure 18.21 presents the execution time of the random-update query for the page- and file-server architectures (the object server's execution time is a fairly constant 125 seconds). Here changing the size of the clustering region simply shifts the positions of the page- and file-server architectures; it does not change their fundamental shape or spacing. Perhaps the most interesting result is that with a clustering region of one page, the page server outperforms the object server when the clustering factor is above 65%.

5.4 Impact of Workstation Buffer Space

For our final set of experiments, we selected two clustering factors (30% and 90%) and varied the size of the buffer pool on the workstation from 50 pages to 300 pages (the size of a set of 1500 objects). In the case of the file-server prototype, in addition to increasing the size of the buffer pool in 50 page increments, we also increased the "size" of the physical memory of the workstation in 50-page increments. For the page- and object-server designs, the server's buffer pool was fixed at 50-pages. The results are displayed in figures 18.22 through 18.29.

As expected, the size of the workstation buffer pool has no effect on the performance of the sequential-scan query. With the object-server design, response time actually increases. The only explanation we can offer is that this increase is an artifact of how the hash table for the object cache was organized. However, the random-read and random-update queries offer some interesting results. First, whereas the performance of the page- and file-server architectures both improve as the size of the buffer pool increases, the performance of the object server levels off once the buffer pool has been increased to 150 pages. At this point the cache size is no longer the limiting factor; the objects referenced by the query will all fit in the cache. Instead, the performance of the object server is limited by the cost of transferring objects using RPC. Since the other designs cache full pages in their buffer-pools, their performance continues to improve. One would not expect any improvement beyond a buffer-pool size of 300 pages.

For the random-read query, the relative difference between the page server and the file server diminishes as the size of the buffer pool is increased, because fewer and fewer remote accesses are necessary. Hence the performance advantage provided by using NFS decreases.

In the case of the random-update query, we observe the following. First, the file server is more sensitive than the page server to the size of the workstation buffer pool. At small buffer sizes, page-write costs are the dominating factor for the file server. However, when the whole database fits into memory, the benefits of using NFS for reads compensate for the more expensive write operations, because no pages are written more than once.

Second, the object server performs much better than the page server when the buffer size is small. At a 30% clustering factor, the buffer size has to be almost the size of the database before the page- and file-server designs outperform the object server. We conclude that more memory is not a reasonable

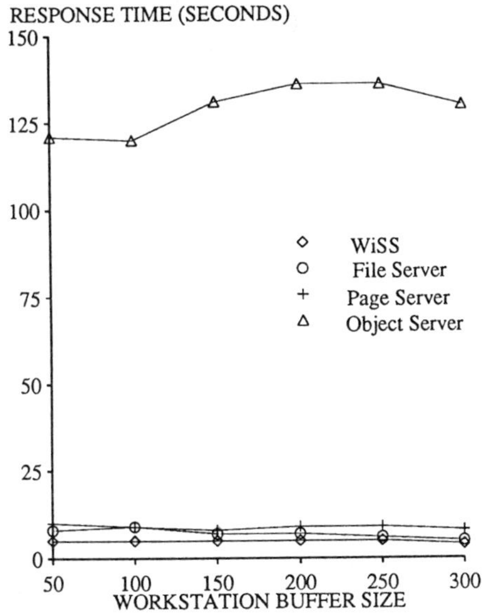

Figure 18.22. **Scan query, 30% clustering factor**

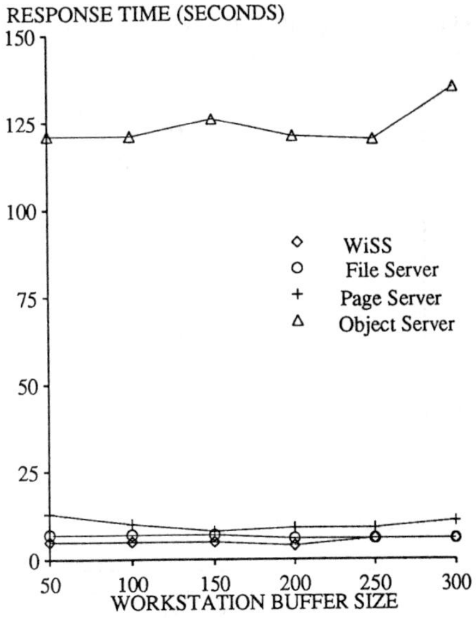

Figure 18.23. **Scan query, 90% clustering factor**

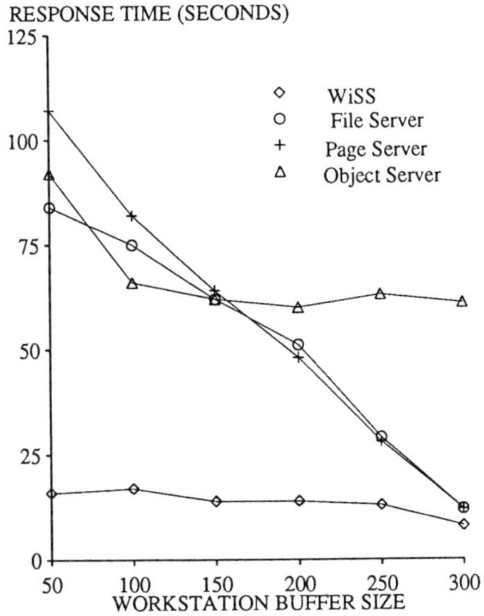

Figure 18.24. **Random-read query, 30% clustering factor**

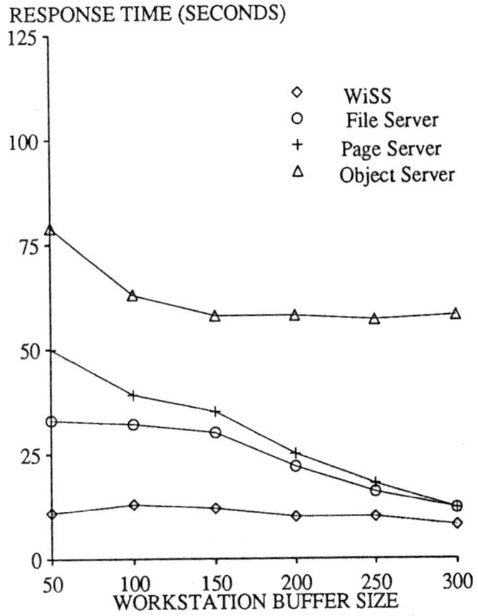

Figure 18.25. **Random-read query, 90% clustering factor**

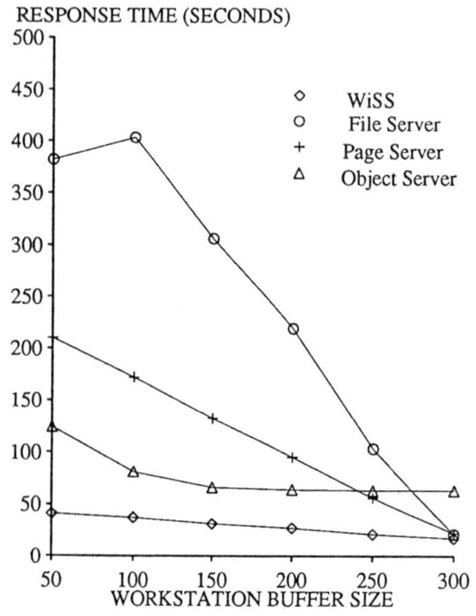

Figure 18.26. **Random-update query, 30% clustering factor**

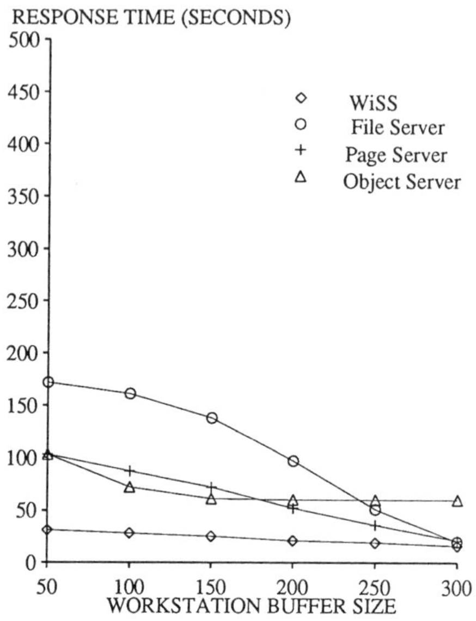

Figure 18.27. **Random-update query, 90% clustering factor**

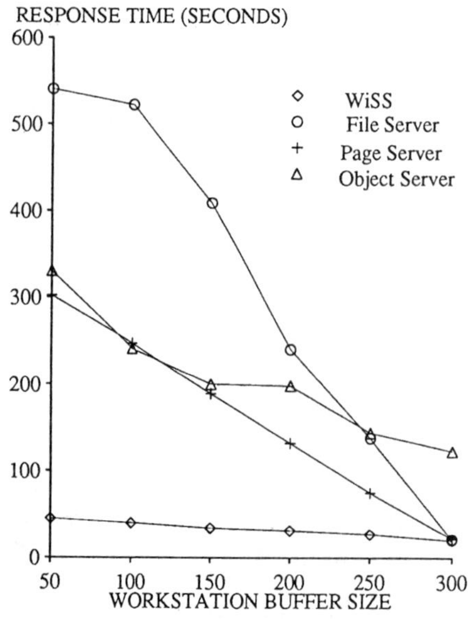

Figure 18.28. **All queries, 30% clustering factor**

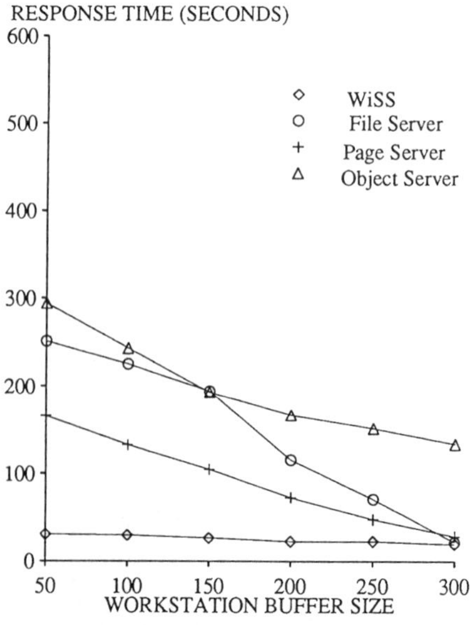

Figure 18.29. **All queries, 90% clustering factor**

substitute for effective clustering—unless the entire database will fit in main memory. With a 90% clustering factor, the performance of all three designs is very close.

For all four queries, we observe that the page server is more sensitive to the size of the workstation buffer pool than to clustering (even considering the various clustering region sizes). Except with a 300-page buffer pool, it was never the case that the pages referenced by a query would fit entirely in the buffer pool, even at a high clustering factor. Large buffer sizes do a better job at compensating for the lack of effective clustering than the opposite (i.e., effective clustering compensating small buffer sizes). For example, with the random-read query, a 200-page buffer with a 30% clustering factor performs better than a 50-page buffer with a 90% clustering factor. This behavior is even more noticeable with the random-update and all-queries tests.

6 Related Work

The previous work most similar to ours is a study by Hagmann and Ferrari 1986. They split the functionality of the university version of the Ingres system in various ways between two machines and measured CPU, disk, and network usage. Our investigation departs from theirs in several respects.

First, their work was aimed at determining the best partitioning of database function between a shared central processor and a dedicated back-end machine. Although they briefly mention workstation-server environments, the results are interpreted mainly relative to an environment with a pair of central machines. So, for example, whereas combined CPU time might be a good measure for comparing different software configurations in such an environment, it is a questionable comparison in our target environment, where workstation cycles are plentiful and server cycles are scarce.

Second, the benchmark they used was chosen to be indicative of relational data-processing loads. Our structures and operations were chosen to be representative of processing in design databases.

Finally, and most important, they did not experiment with the sensitivity of their various software configurations to physical aspects of the data or to system parameters. All of our experiments consider the effect of data placement or buffer pool sizes on the different architectures. While the direct comparisons of the performance of our prototypes must be tempered by some uncertainty as to the effect of a multiuser environment, we believe that the results on the relative sensitivity of the prototypes to data and system parameters are robust.

The AIM-P database project also investigated the workstation-server linkage (Deppisch and Obermeit 1987). Their high-level view is of two independent database systems taking advantage of a common physical format to speed transfers in a checkout model for long transactions. This differs from our view of partitioning the functionality of a single database system across two machines. In the AIM-P scheme, communication takes place at both the logical (query language) level and the physical (page) level. That work does not go into detail on architectural alternatives or provide any performance analysis. However, in spite of the differences between our model and theirs, the AIM-P techniques for concurrency control and update of auxiliary access structures might work in our context.

Our results are similar to those obtained by Stamos 1984, who simulated the behavior of different memory architectures in a nondistributed, single-user object manager, using different strategies for clustering. His conclusions are similar to some of ours, namely, that page buffering is more sensitive to clustering than is object buffering, and that object buffering shows better performance than page buffering only when buffer space is very limited relative to the size of the working set of an application. Similar architectural issues also arise in the design of distributed, object-oriented operating systems. In the Comandos system (Marques and Guedes 1989), for example, the default is for the storage system to respond with single objects when the virtual object memory has an object fault. However, logical clusters of objects can be declared, and the whole cluster is delivered when any object in it is requested.

7 Conclusions

We analyzed three different workstation-server architectures: object server, page server, and file server. The object server transfers individual objects between machines, the page server transfers disk pages, and the file server transfers pages, using a remote file service mechanism such as NFS.

We analyzed each architecture qualitatively. The main advantage of the page-server and file-server architectures is the simple design of the server, as most of the complexity of the OODBMS is placed on the workstation, an approach that coincides with the current trend toward very powerful workstations. The main drawbacks are that fine-grained concurrency is difficult to implement, that non-two-phase locking protocols on indexes must involve the workstation, and that objects cannot be manipulated in the server. An object-server architecture implies a complicated server design and suffers from the need to issue an RPC each time an object has to be read from the server. Its main advantages correspond to the page server's limitations: (1) fine-grained concurrency control can be centralized in the server; and (2) a method that selects a small subset of a large collection can execute on the server, avoiding the movement of the entire collection to the workstation. (This behavior, however, is not easy to implement.)

To compare the performance of the architectures, we built prototypes of all three, using a stripped-down version of WiSS as a starting point. To experiment with sensitivity to data placement and cache sizes, we developed our own object-manager benchmark, the Altaïr Complex-Object Benchmark.

Our main conclusions from these experiments are:

1. The object-server architecture is relatively insensitive to clustering. It is sensitive to workstation buffer sizes up to a certain point, at which point

its performance is determined by the cost of fetching objects using the RPC mechanism. For the object server to be viable, it must incorporate some mechanism for passing multiple objects or values in each message between the workstation and the server, in the same way that portals in relational systems pass groups of tuples. While it is easy to find instances where this bundling is feasible (e.g., in response to a selection over a set or a request to display the complete state of a complex object), we do not know of any general method for predicting object references, especially those that will result from invoking a method. In particular, we do not see a means to provide such a capability that could provide automatic bundling for most of the queries in either the Hypermodel (Anderson et al. 1990) or the Sun (Cattell 1988; Cattell and Skeen 1990) benchmarks, short of processing the queries on the server itself. Note that a prefetching scheme (based on transitivity or some unit of clustering) will only help with the object server if the prefetched objects are passed to the workstation in groups, rather than individually. If prefetching uses physical pages as the unit of clustering, we have the odd situation of reading a page on the server, extracting all its objects, then rebundling those same objects for transmission to the workstation.

2. The page-server architecture is very sensitive to the size of the workstation's buffer pool and to clustering when traversing or updating complex objects. While the page-server architecture is far superior on sequential-scan queries, the object-server architecture demonstrates superior performance when the database is poorly clustered or the workstation's buffer pool is very small relative to the size of the database.

3. The file server's performance is very good when reading pages of the database using NFS, but writes are slow. On the update query, and in the combination of all three queries, the file server is very sensitive to the size of the workstation buffer pool (even more so than the page server).

The above observations lead us to postulate:

1. There is no clear winner. A page-server approach seems beneficial if the clustering algorithm is effective and if the workstations have large enough buffer pools. An object-server approach will perform poorly with applications that tend to scan large data sets, but it will perform better than a page server for applications performing updates and running on workstations having small buffer pools.

2. A file-server approach based solely on NFS is ruled out, mainly because of its expensive, nonbuffered writes. Its need for separate messages for locking is also a problem.

3. A hybrid architecture may be necessary to maximize overall performance. The "naive ideal" would be to read pages through NFS and to write individual objects back to the server. The respective drawbacks would be the

aforementioned concurrency-control problem, and the fact that an object cache has to be maintained in the workstation.

Some preliminary studies of different page sizes showed very little impact on the performance of the different designs; we intend to study this issue further. In addition, we need to examine multiuser issues more carefully.

8 Acknowledgements

We would like to thank Jacob Stein for providing us with information on the current architecture used by Gemstone and Gilbert Harrus, Jon Kepecs, Rusty Sandberg, and V. Srinivasan for their help in understanding how NFS in V4.0 of SunOs operates. We would also like to thank Mike Carey, Robert Hagmann, and Mike Stonebraker for their constructive comments on an earlier draft of this paper.

References

Abiteboul, S., and P. Kanellakis. 1989. *Object identity as a query language primitive.* INRIA Techical Report.

Anderson, T., A. Berre, M. Mallison, H. Porter, and B. Schneider. 1990. The Hypermodel Benchmark. In *Proceedings of the EDBT '90 conference.*

Astrahan, M. H. et al. 1976. System R: A relational database management system. *ACM TODS* 1(2).

Atkinson, M., F. Bancilhon, D. DeWitt, K. Dittrich, D. Maier, and S. Zdonik. 1989. The object-oriented database system manifesto. In *Proceedings of the first DOOD conference.*

Bancilhon, F., G. Barbedette, V. Benzaken, C. Delobel, S. Gamerman, C. Lécluse, P. Pfeffer, P. Richard, and F. Vélez. 1988. The design and implementation of O_2, an object-oriented database system. In *Proceedings of the second international workshop on object-oriented database systems,* ed. K. Dittrich.

Bancilhon, F., S. Cluet, and C. Delobel. 1989. Query languages for object-oriented database systems. In *Proceedings of the DBPL-II workshop.*

Bretl, B. et al. 1989. The GemStone data management system. In *object-oriented concepts, databases and applications,* eds. W. Kim and F. Lochovsky. ACM Press.

Carey, M. et al. 1990. The Exodus extensible DBMS project: An overview. In *Readings in object-oriented database systems.* Morgan Kaufmann.

Cattell, R. 1988. Object-oriented DBMS performance measurement. In *Advances in object-oriented databases: Proceedings of the second international workshop on object-oriented database systems*, ed. K. Dittrich. *Lecture notes in computer science*, Vol. 334. Springer-Verlag.

Cattell, R., and J. Skeen. 1990. *Engineering database benchmark. ACM TODS* (Submitted for publication).

Chang, E. E., and R. H. Katz. 1989. Exploiting inheritance and structure semantics for effective clustering and buffering in an object-oriented DBMS. In *Proceedings of the ACM SIGMOD conference.*

Chou, H-T., D. DeWitt, R. Katz, and A. Klug. 1985. Design and implementation of the Wisconsin storage system. *Software Practice and Experience* 15(10).

Cluet, S., C. Delobel, C. L.'ecluse, and P. Richard. 1989. *RELOOP, a request language on an object-oriented paradigm.* GIP Altaïr Technical Report.

Copeland G., and D. Maier. 1984. Making Smalltalk a database system. In *Proceedings of the ACM SIGMOD international conference on the management of data.*

Deppisch, U., and V. Obermeit. 1987. Tight database cooperation in a server-workstation environment. In *Proceedings of the seventh international conference on distributed computing systems.*

Deux, O. et al. 1990. The story of O_2. *IEEE Transactions on Data and Knowledge Engineering* (March).

Gray, J. N. et al. 1976. Granularity of locks and degrees of consistency in a shared data base. In *Modeling in data base management systems,* ed. G. M. Nijssen. North-Holland.

Hagmann, R. B., and D. Ferrari. 1986. Performance analysis of several back-end database architectures. *ACM TODS* 11(1).

Hornick M. F., and S. B. Zdonik 1987. A shared, segmented memory for an object-oriented database. *ACM TOIS* 5(1).

Kim, W. et al. 1990. Architecture of the Orion next generation database system. *IEEE Transactions on Data and Knowledge Engineering* (March).

Kung, H., and J. Robinson. 1981. On optimistic methods for concurrency control. *ACM TODS* 6(2).

Lindsay, B. et al. 1979. *Notes on distributed database systems.* Technical report no. RJ2571, IBM Research Laboratory, San Jose.

Marques, J. A., and P. Guedes. 1989. Extending the operating system to support an object-oriented environment. In *Proceedings of the OOPSLA '89 conference.*

Sun 1988. *Network programming guide.* Part no. 800-1779-10, Sun Microsystems.

Stamos, J. W. 1984. Static grouping of small objects to enhance performance of a paged virtual memory. *ACM TOCS.* 2(2).

Stonebraker, M. et al. 1976. The design and implementation of Ingres. *ACM TODS* 1(3).

Vélez, F., G. Bernard, and V. Darnis. 1989. The O_2 object manager: An overview. In *Proceedings of the 15th VLDB conference.*

Zdonik, S. B., and D. Maier. 1990. *Readings in object-oriented database systems.* Morgan Kaufmann.

CHAPTER 19

Consistency of Versions in Object-Oriented Databases

WOJCIECH CELLARY
GENEVIÈVE JOMIER

1 Introduction

In recent years, development of database technology has addressed nontraditional domains, such as computer-aided design (CAD), manufacturing, management, software engineering (CASE), and office automation. Database management systems (DBMSs) devoted to these domains need to support new functions. One of the most important is *version management*, which appears necessary in new object-oriented database systems (Chou and Kim 1988; Kim, Bertino, and Garza 1989; Kim and Chou 1988, Kim et al. 1987a, 1987b, 1988; Ontologic 1987; Stonebraker and Rowe 1986; Zdonik 1986). These systems are required to manage simultaneously several versions of the same object. For instance, in computer-aided management applications, consecutive real-world states appearing one after the other have to be stored in a database. In CASE and CAD applications, a database has to store different alternatives of the same object. Such databases are called *multiversion*.

Various aspects of version management have been considered in the literature: version identification and manipulation, change notification and propagation, version primitives, functions, histories, and structures of version graphs. These aspects have been considered separately for CAD databases (Atwood 1985; Chou and Kim 1986; Fauvet 1988; Katz and Chang 1987; Katz, Chang, and Bhateja 1986; Katz and Lehman 1984; Kim and Banerjee 1985; Kim and Batory 1987; Landis 1986), information systems (Davidson and Zdonik 1986; Klahold et al. 1985), and engineering databases (Dittrich and Lorie 1985a, 1985b; Woelk and Kim 1987), taking application specificity into account. There is also considerable work concerning temporal aspects of databases using versions (Adiba 1988; Klahold, Schlageter, and Wilkes 1986; Lum et al. 1985; Stam and Snodgrass 1988). All these aspects are important; however, as soon as the database becomes large, with a great number of objects and many among them with several versions, the key problem of version management is the problem of *consistency*. Intuitively that means that the DBMS must be able to present to the user the versions of different objects that go together. If this problem is not solved efficiently, it is impossible to query and update the database consistently.

In monoversion databases the problem of consistency is stated as follows. A monoversion object is defined as a pair (object identifier, object value). A monoversion database is defined as a set of objects, and a monoversion database state as the set of values of all the objects contained in the database. A monoversion database is considered to be consistent if it accurately represents a state of the real world that it models. The real world modeled may not physically exist; for example, the designer of a design database stores a representation of a real-world state that exists only in his or her mind. Formally, database consistency is defined by consistency constraints imposed on object values. To maintain database consistency, atomic *transactions* are used, which transform one consistent state of the database into another (Gray 1978).

In multiversion databases the consistency problem is more complex. A multiversion object is defined as a pair (object identifier, set of object versions). An object version is defined as a pair (version identifier, version value). A multiversion database is defined as a set of multiversion objects. A multiversion database state is defined as the set of the values of all the object versions contained in the database.

The introduction of object versions has a fundamental consequence: generally, a multiversion database is inconsistent—that is, considered as a whole it does not reflect any state of the real world. Assume a multiversion database containing two objects: A, in two versions a_1 and a_2; and B, in one version b_1. Even if b_1 is consistent with respect to both a_1 and a_2, the multiversion database state $\{a_1, a_2, b_1\}$ is inconsistent. As a consequence, in multiversion databases the definition of a transaction as a process that transforms one consistent state of the database into another is no longer valid, because the initial state of a multiversion database is inconsistent. Thus a fundamental problem of multiversion databases is to recognize which versions of different objects are consistent together. This problem is important, because in a database composed of m objects, each one in n versions, there are up to n^m different subsets of the database containing one version of each object. Even if not all of them are consistent, and even if m and n are small, the user will quickly be lost without the help of the system.

The problem of version consistency has been pointed out in some papers referenced above, and tools to maintain *partial consistency* (Atwood 1985)—that is, consistency of parts of the database—have been proposed. They may be seen as links established between consistent versions of different objects. In

Zdonik 1986, these links are given in the form of slices; a slice is a set of object versions that have been produced by a single transaction. In Katz and Chang 1987 and in Katz, Chang, and Bhateja 1986, the links are given in the form of version histories, which maintain is–a–descendant–of and is–an–ancestor–of relationships among many versions of the same object; and configuration objects, which in CAD are parts of a design hierarchically constructed. In Ontologic 1987, consistency surfaces are proposed for tracking the state of particular versions of objects and the degree to which they are consistent with versions of other objects. In Atwood 1985, the idea of layers and contexts introduced in Pie (Bobrow and Goldstein 1980) is taken up again; a layer is a group of sets of related changes and a context is a sequence of layers. In Atwood 1985, the problem of configuring a system in software and design database domains is considered. A syntactic characterization of a correct configuration tied to a transaction model is presented. In this model each object is stamped with the signature of the transaction that created it. Then correct configurations are generated by the use of a version graph for each object and transaction dependence graphs.

The common point of all these approaches is that, by different means, they establish explicit links between consistent object versions. The storage, use, and maintenance of these links impose a heavy burden on database management. It grows rapidly with the number of objects and the number of versions of each object (Kim, Bertino, and Garza 1989). So these approaches seem to be impracticable, except in some limited or particular cases.

In this chapter a totally different solution of the consistency problem, called the *database-version approach*, is presented. Its concepts are described in section 2. In section 3 we explain how object versions are managed in the system. Section 4 is devoted to operating on objects. Section 5 deals with concurrency control. In section 6, version management of composite objects is presented and compared with other approaches. Section 7 concludes the paper.

2 The Database-Version Approach

The database-version approach is not based on the notion of partial consistency of the multiversion database. To solve the problem of multiversion database consistency, we use the same notion of consistency as is used in monoversion databases. A monoversion database stores one representation of the real-world state—strictly taken, the last one introduced by the user, which replaces the previous one. If a user of a monoversion database modifies one object, in fact he or she replaces the entire representation of one real-world state by the representation of another. Similarly, if a user of a multiversion database creates a new version of an object, in fact he or she creates a new representation of an entire real-world state. In the future, the user will need to retrieve this representation. This is possible if the multiversion database stores the set of representations of the real-world states introduced by the users. In our approach a representation of a real-world state is called *database version*. A multiversion database is defined as a set of logically independent and identified database versions (figure 19.1). Formally, a database version is defined as a pair composed of the database version identifier and the set of versions of all the objects contained in the multiversion database, one version per object. The state of a database version is defined as the set of values of all the object versions that it contains.

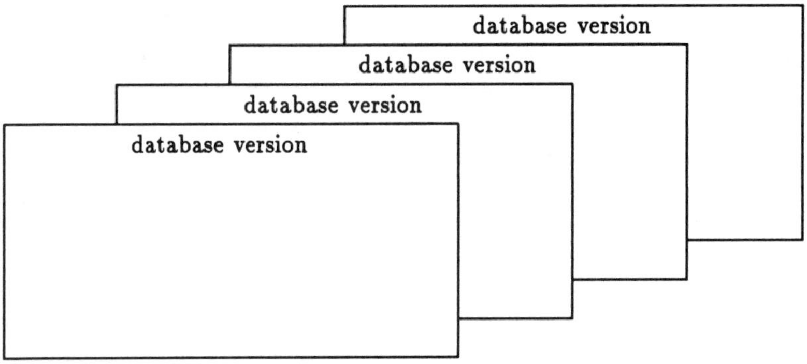

Figure 19.1. Multiversion database as a set of database versions

The concept of database versions allows the use of transactions defined as an extension of the classical definition (Gray 1978): a transaction is defined as a process that takes each member of a set of database versions from one consistent state to another consistent state. Before or after transaction execution, a database version may be empty.

In the simplest case a transaction concerns one database version. It may be nonversioning or versioning. A *nonversioning transaction* queries or updates a database version, causing its evolution independently of the evolution of the other database versions. It corresponds exactly to the notion of transaction in monoversion databases. A *versioning transaction* creates a new database version. It is addressed to a database version, the *parent* database version, and it creates a *child* database version, which is a logical copy of the parent. Thus the set of database versions is organized as a tree, called a *derivation tree*. Once created, the new database version will evolve autonomously, according to the nonversioning transactions addressed to it.

A user operates on a multiversion database in the following way. First of all he or she chooses one or more database versions. One way to do that is to specify a database version identifier used by the DBMS. However, it is more convenient to use other identifiers, which reflect the semantics of the database and which are translated into the system identifiers. For instance, in a temporal database each system identifier of a database version may be associated to a date, in a CASE application to a software configuration (Tichy 1989).

When the database version is chosen, the user may perform nonversioning transactions addressed to it, as if he or she was working on a monoversion database. The system will automatically identify object versions belonging to the database version chosen. However, the user is responsible for writing transactions properly, that is, in such a way that a transaction transforms an initial consistent state of the database version into another consistent state. By running a versioning transaction, the user may create a new (child) database version and then work on it. Finally, a user may work simultaneously on several database versions, embedding operations addressed to different database versions in a transaction. In this case, he or she may, for example, move the value of an object version from one database version to another, browse through the multiversion database, read all the different versions of an object, and so on. The only requirement is that the transaction must transform a consistent state of each database version accessed into another consistent state.

To summarize, there are two levels of operation on a multiversion database. At the upper level the user creates or deletes a specified database version. At the lower level the user reads, writes, creates, or deletes a specified object in a specified database version.

3 Object-Version Identification

Since a child database version usually differs only partially from its parent, versions of the same object contained in different database versions may have identical values. To avoid redundancy, this object version has to be physically shared by several database versions. This may be done by associating several identifiers of database versions with one object version that they share. However, the following problem arises: when a new database version is created, its identifier must be associated with one version of each object stored in the multiversion database. In a large database the association process would be inadmissibly long. To solve this problem, in the database-version approach database version identifiers are constructed in a special way. They are called *version stamps.*

As the multiversion database is organized as a tree of database versions, the version stamp of a database version is constructed in such a way that it makes it possible to identify all the version's ancestors. If a database version is the nth child of its parent, whose version stamp is p, then the child version stamp is $p.n$. The root database version is stamped 0.

The following example shows how version stamps are used to identify object versions. Consider a multiversion database composed of four database versions.

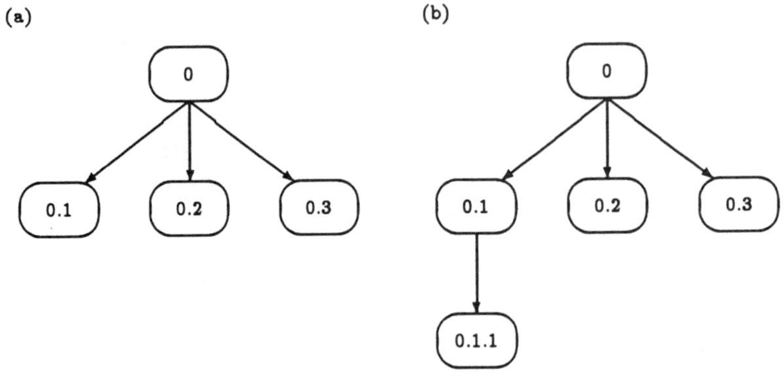

Figure 19.2. Database version derivation trees

Its derivation tree is shown in figure 19.2(a). An object A is stored in the multiversion database. From the logical point of view, one version of A appears in each database version. However, since the versions of A belonging to database versions 0.2 and 0.3 are identical, they share one physical version of A. Versions of object A are associated with the database versions by the use of version stamps as shown in table 19.1.

Table 19.1. Association of DB Version Stamps with the Versions of Object A

Versions of A	DB Version Stamps
a_0	0
a_1	0.1
a_2	0.2, 0.3

Suppose now that database version 0.1 has a child, database version 0.1.1 (figure 19.2(b)); and suppose that the version a_1 of A is shared by database versions 0.1 and 0.1.1. In this case the association of version stamps with object versions presented above does not need to be modified. It is sufficient to establish a rule saying that *If no object version is explicitly associated with a database version, then it shares the object version with its parent database version.*

Suppose that the version of A belonging to database version 0.1.1 is required. Since no version of A is stamped with 0.1.1, using the rule above, one can deduce that the desired object version is shared with the parent database version, stamped 0.1, so a_1 is found.

This mechanism works recursively for an arbitrary number of ancestors sharing an object version. It allows a versioning transaction to avoid explicit association of the version stamp of the just-created database version with a version of each object. As a result, we distinguish between an ***unshared object version***, which belongs to only one database version, and a ***shared object version***, which belongs to several database versions, associated explicitly or implicitly.

Consider now object B stored in the same multiversion database (table 19.2).

Table 19.2. Association of DB Version Stamps with the Versions of Object B

Versions of B	DB Version Stamps
b_0	0
b_1	0.2
b_2	0.1.1

From the version stamp association it follows that $\{a_0, b_0\}$, $\{a_1, b_0\}$, $\{a_2, b_1\}$, $\{a_2, b_0\}$, and $\{a_1, b_2\}$ are consistent because each pair is contained in a database version. In contrast, $\{a_1, b_1\}$ and $\{a_2, b_2\}$ are not known to be consistent.

Table 19.1 represents a multiversion object A, which is identified by its object identifier *oid_A*. A row of the table represents one object version, whose value is a_i. This value may be arbitrarily complex; in particular, it may be totally or partially composed of references to other objects, that is, of oids.

To implement our versioning strategy, we require only that (1) the identifier of an object identifies the set of its versions, because a multiversion object is the set of its versions; and (2) each object version is associated with its list of version stamps.

4 Operating on Objects

In this section we explain how the requests for object reading, updating, creating, and deleting are performed. These requests are addressed to a database version stamped s.

4.1 Reading

To perform a read request, an object version belonging to database version s must be identified and read. This procedure is presented in section 3.

4.2 Updating

To update an object in database version s, the object version that it belongs to must first be identified. Then it must be determined whether this object version is shared or not. An object version is unshared if only one version stamp is explicitly associated with it, and if all the children of this version stamp are explicitly associated with other versions of the object. Otherwise, an object version is shared.

If an object version is not shared, it can be updated without any modification of version stamps. If it is shared, then a new object version, *new*, must be created, in which changes are introduced. This version is stamped by *s*. The old object version, *old*, remains unchanged, stamped by the version stamps of all the database versions that shared it except *s*. Because of this implicit sharing, the set of stamps associated with *old* contains after the update:

1. All the stamps explicitly associated with *old* before the update, except *s* if *s* was explicitly associated with *old*, because the database version *s* could share *old* implicitly.
2. The stamps of all the children of the database version *s* which are not explicitly associated with other versions of the object. Before the update these children implicitly shared *old* with the database version *s*.

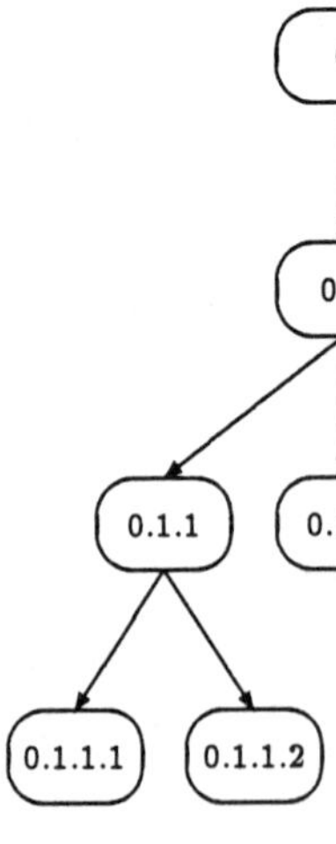

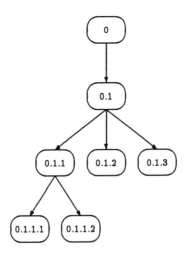

Figure 19.3. Derivation tree of database versions

The performing of an update request is illustrated by the following example. Consider the derivation tree presented in figure 19.3. An object A, stored in the database, has two versions: a_0 belonging only to the database version stamped 0; and a_1, which is shared by the remaining database versions, as shown in table 19.3(a). Table 19.3(b) shows object A after it has been updated in database version 0.1.1. Version a_1 is preserved in database versions 0.1, 0.1.1.1, and 0.1.1.2, which share it explicitly; and database versions 0.1.2 and 0.1.3, which share it implicitly. If object A is updated again in database version 0.1.1, the version stamp association remains unchanged (table 19.3(c)). Table 19.3(d) presents object A after it has been updated in database version 0.1.

Table 19.3. Version Stamp Associations after Object Updating

(a)

Versions of A	DB Version Stamps
a_0	0
a_1	0.1

(b)

Versions of A	DB Version Stamps
a_0	0
a_2	0.1.1
a_1	0.1 , 0.1.1.1 , 0.1.1.2

(c)

Versions of A	DB Version Stamps
a_0	0
a_3	0.1.1
a_1	0.1 , 0.1.1.1 , 0.1.1.2

(d)

Versions of A	DB Version Stamps
a_0	0
a_3	0.1.1
a_4	0.1
a_1	0.1.2, 0.1.3, 0.1.1.1, 0.1.1.2

Object creation and deletion is reduced to updating. Formally, all the objects that exist in the multiversion database appear in one version at each database version. Thus, to create a new object which appears only in a particular database version and not in the others, or to delete an object in a particular database version, we have to express its nonexistence in a database version. To this end a special value, *nil*, is used that means "does not exist." The *nil* version of each object is contained in the root database version stamped 0 (in the above example $a_0 = nil$).

4.3 Deletion

To delete an object in a particular database version it is sufficient to update it with the *nil* value.

4.4 Creation

To create an object in a particular database version, its *nil* version is first introduced in the root database version. Then the object is updated in the standard way.

5 Concurrency Control

Transactions are executed concurrently, and they are serialized by the concurrency controller. An access conflict happens only if two transactions accessing an object version are addressed to the same database version. No conflict happens if the transactions are addressed to different database versions, because when a shared object version is updated in one database version, it is replicated and the changes are introduced to the copy while the original remains unchanged.

Access conflicts happen between nonversioning and versioning transactions addressed to the parent database version. The reason is that the versioning transaction makes a logical copy of the parent database version to create the child. A physical copy would be useless because of object-version sharing between parent and child database versions. Since the parent database is only read by the versioning transaction, and the reading is only virtual, locking the entire database version may be avoided (Cellary and Jomier 1990).

6 Version Management of Composite Objects

In this section, the database version approach is compared with the other approaches to version management of composite objects. In these approaches, object versions refer to object versions; that is, reference resolution is static. This way of referencing deeply influences version management as presented in Kim et al. 1987a and in Kim, Bertino, and Garza 1989 and briefly described below.

Consider figure 19.4(a). A composite object A has two components, B and C. Each version of A refers to a version of B and C. Figure 19.4(b) shows the impact of the creation of a new version b_2 of B: one or more new versions of A must be created. Each new version of A associates b_2 with a version of C consistent with it; for instance, a_3 composed of b_2 and c_0, and a_4 composed of b_2 and c_2. If A is itself a component of a composite object of a higher level, E for instance, then several new versions of E must be created. The process of creation of new object versions will continue up to the root of the composite object.

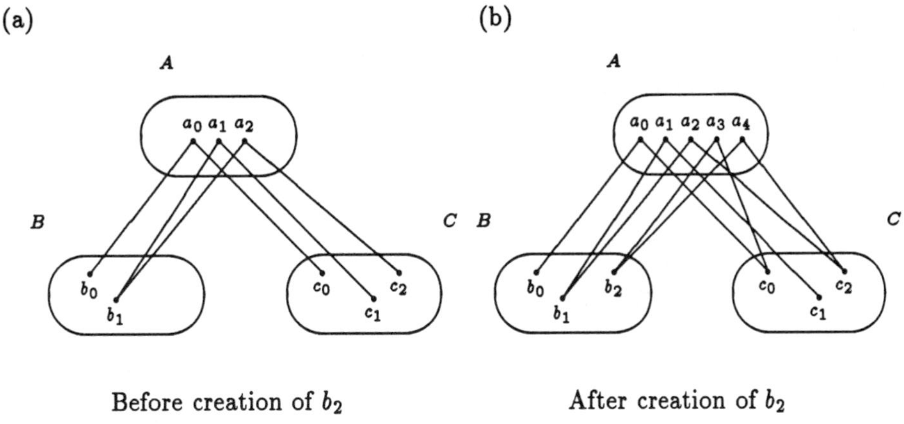

Figure 19.4. References between object versions

As noticed in Kim, Bertino, and Garza 1989 and shown in our example, the creation of object versions in composite objects may be done through the use of the is-part-of link, which permits reading a composite object bottom-up; but such links must be maintained by the system. If it does not exist, bottom-up object identification can only be done by memorizing the access path from the object root of the composition hierarchy. However, in this case, no versionable object may be shared by several composite objects (Kim et al. 1987a).

At each level of a composition hierarchy the number of object versions created grows geometrically. This reduces database system performance, since cascading creations require extra read and write operations, and extra overhead of the concurrency control if the database is multiuser.

The process of object-version creation may be performed by the user without any system support; then he or she decides at each step which object versions have to be created. Since this may be very cumbersome, another solution is *percolation* (Atwood 1985): the version manager automatically creates all the possible versions of composite objects at each level of the composition hierarchy. In this way the user avoids work, but the database is burdened by a large number of useless object versions.

The counterpart of this complex process of creation of object versions for composite objects is that many composite object versions must be deleted in the case of deletion of a version of a component object. On the other hand, in the database-version approach, version management is orthogonal to the object model, and dynamic reference resolution is used. Consider, as an example, three classes $\mathcal{A}, \mathcal{B}$, and $\mathcal{C}$, such that each object of class $\mathcal{A}$ is composed of one object of class $\mathcal{B}$ and one object of class $\mathcal{C}$. The database version derivation tree is given in figure 19.5(a). There are five objects, A, B, B', C, and C', whose versions are given in table 19.4. From table 19.4(e), object A exists in four different versions: a_0: $[b_0, c_0]$ in database version 0, a_1: $[b_1, c_1]$ in database version 0.1, a_2: $[b'_1, c_1]$ in database version 0.2, and a_3: $[b'_1, c'_2]$ in database version 0.3. Different versions of A are composed of different versions of different objects of the same class and different versions of the same object.

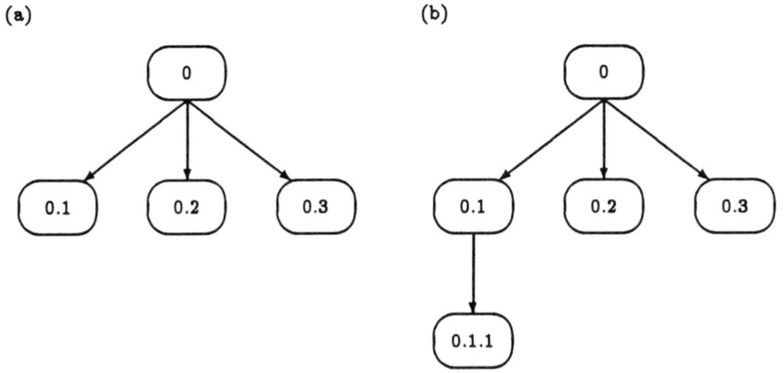

Figure 19.5. Database version derivation trees

Suppose now that a user wants to create a new version of A, composed of b_1 and a new version c_2 of C. He or she derives a new database version 0.1.1 from 0.1 (see figure 19.5(b)) and updates C in database version 0.1.1; the result is the insertion of c_2 stamped by 0.1.1 (see table 19.4(f)). All the other objects remain unchanged, and the DBMS is now able to recognize that a_1: $[b_1, c_2]$ is the version of A belonging to database version 0.1.1.

This example shows that in the database-version approach the version management does not generate cascaded creations or deletions of object versions when a component object version is created or deleted. Another consequence of the dynamic reference resolution used in the database-version approach is that the internal structure of a nonversionable object is the same as the internal structure of an object version. It is exactly the same as the internal structure of the objects in monoversion databases. Thus, in contrast to other versioning strategies, the decision whether an object is versionable does not need to be made at database creation time.

7 Conclusions

The database-version approach offers a very powerful tool for managing multiversion databases, because of version-stamp semantics. It allows one to establish object-version identification, consistency of database versions, the history of each object, the history of the database versions, and the difference between

Table 19.4. Version Stamp Association in a Composite Object

(a)

Versions of B	DB Version Stamps
b_0	0
b_1	0.1, 0.2, 0.3

(b)

Versions of B'	DB Version Stamps
b'_0	0
b'_1	0.1, 0.2
b'_2	0.3

(c)

Versions of C	DB Version Stamps
c_0	0
c_1	0.1, 0.2, 0.3

(d)

Versions of C'	DB Version Stamps
c'_0	0
c'_1	0.1, 0.2, 0.3

(e)

Versions of A	DB Version Stamps
a_0: *oid_B, oid_C*	0
a_1: *oid_B, oid_C*	0.1
a_2: *oid_B'*, *oid_C*	0.2
a_3: *oid_B'*, *oid_C'*	0.3

(f)

Versions of C	DB Version Stamps
c_0	0
c_1	0.1, 0.2, 0.3
c_2	0.1.1

database versions. This semantics must be compared with the semantics of the version identifiers used in other approaches to version management. In those approaches an object version is identified using a pair (object identifier, version identifier), where the version identifier is a local reference to the object. As a consequence, the only possibility offered besides identification is object history. The difference between the semantics of version stamps and version identifiers explains why the capabilities of versioning mechanism using version stamps includes all the capabilities of versioning systems using version identifiers.

The main advantage of the database version approach is its orthogonality to the object model, object addressing, concurrency control, access authorization, and other object-management problems. Version stamps are easy to implement and economical with respect to space. In comparison with other approaches, version-management overhead does not grow significantly with the number of object versions.

Our work on the database-version approach is in progress. We are extending it to versions of methods and schemas and are implementing it in the O_2 system.

8 Acknowledgements

The authors are grateful to François Bancilhon, Claude Delobel, David DeWitt, David Maier, Michel Raoux, and Fernando Vélez for their helpful comments and suggestions.

References

Adiba, M. 1988. Histories and versions for multimedia complex objects. *IEEE Data Engineering Bulletin* (December).

Agrawal, R., and H. V. Jagadish. 1989. On correctly configuring versioned objects. In *Proceedings of the 15th VLDB conference.*

Atwood, T. 1985. *An object-oriented DBMS for design support applications.* Ontologic Report.

Bancilhon, F., G. Barbedette, V. Benzaken, C. Delobel, S. Gamerman, C. Lécluse, P. Pfeffer, P. Richard, and F. Vélez. 1988. The design and implementation of O_2, an object-oriented database system. In *Proceedings of the second international workshop on object-oriented database systems,* ed. K. Dittrich.

Bobrow D., and I. Goldstein. 1980. *Representing design alternatives.* In *Proceedings of the conference on artificial intelligence and simulation of behavior.*

Cellary, W., E. Gelenbe, and T. Morzy. 1988. *Concurrency control in distributed database systems.* North-Holland.

Cellary, W., and G. Jomier. 1990. *Global specification of the version manager.* Altaïr Technical Report.

Chou, H-T., and W. Kim. 1986. A unifying framework for version control in a CAD environment. In *Proceedings of the 12th VLDB conference.*

Chou, H-T., and W. Kim. 1988. Versions and change notification in an object-oriented database system. In *Proceedings of the 25th ACM/IEEE design automation conference.*

Davidson, J. W., and S. B. Zdonik. 1986. A visual interface for a database with version management. In *Proceedings of the third ACM SIGOIS conference.*

Dittrich, K. R., and R. A. Lorie. 1985a. *Object-oriented database concepts for engineering applications.* IBM research report no. RJ 4691 (50029).

______. 1985b. *Version support for engineering database systems.* IBM research report no. RJ 4769 (50628).

Fauvet, M. C. 1988. *Etic: Un SGBD pour la CAO dans un environment partagé.* Thèse de l'Université de Grenoble 1, France.

Gray, J. 1978. Notes on data base operating systems. In *Operating systems: An advanced course,* eds. R. Bayer, R. M. Graham, and G. Seegmuller. Springer-Verlag.

Katz, R. H., and E. Chang. 1987. Managing change in a computer-aided design database. In *Proceedings of the 13th VLDB conference.*

Katz, R. H., E. Chang, and R. Bhateja. 1986. Version modeling concepts for computer-aided design databases. In *Proceedings of the ACM SIGMOD international conference on data management.*

Katz, R. H., and T. J. Lehman. 1984. Database support for versions and alternatives of large design files. *IEEE Transactions on Software Engineering* SE-10(2): 191–200.

Kim, W., N. Ballou, H-T. Chou, J. F. Garza, D. Woelk, and J. Banerjee. 1988. Integrating an object-oriented programming system with a database system. In *Proceedings of the OOPSLA conference.*

Kim W., and J. Banerjee. 1985. Support of abstract data types in a CAD database system. In *Proceedings of the COMPINT 85 conference.*

Kim, W., J. Banerjee, H-T. Chou, J. F. Garza, and D. Woelk. 1987a. Composite object support in an object-oriented database system. In *Proceedings of the OOPSLA conference.*

Kim W., and D. S. Batory. 1987. A model and storage technique for versions of VLSI CAD objects. In *Foundations of data organization.* Plenum Press.

Kim, W., E. Bertino, and J. F. Garza. 1989. Composite objects revisited. *SIGMOD Record* 18(2).

Kim W., and H-T. Chou. 1988. Versions of schema for object-oriented databases. In *Proceedings of the 14th VLDB conference.*

Kim, W., D. Woelk, J. F. Garza, H-T. Chou, J. Banerjee, and N. Ballou. 1987b. Enhancing the object-oriented concepts for database support. In *Proceedings of the third international conference on data engineering.*

Klahold P., G. Schlageter, R. Unland, and W. Wilkes. 1985. A transaction model supporting complex applications in integrated information systems. In *Proceedings of the ACM SIGMOD international conference on management of data*. Also in *SIGMOD Record* 14(4): 388–401.

Klahold P., G. Schlageter, and W. Wilkes. 1986. A general model for version management in databases. In *Proceedings of the 12th VLDB conference.*

Landis, G. S. 1986. Design evolution and history in an object-oriented CAD/CAM database. *IEEE CH2285-5/86/0000/0297*:297–303.

Lum V., P. Dadam, R. Erbe, J. Guenauer, P. Pistor, G. Walch, H. Werner, and J. Woodfill. 1985. Designing DBMS support for the temporal dimension. *SIGMOD Record* 14(2): 115–30.

Ontologic. 1987. *Vbase integrated object system, technical overview.* Ontologic, Inc.

Stam R., and R. Snodgrass. 1988. *A bibliography on temporal databases.* Department of Computer Science, University of North Carolina, Chapel Hill.

Stonebraker, M., and L. Rowe. 1986. *The Postgres Papers.* Memorandum no. UCB/ERL M 86/85.

Tichy, W. F. 1989. Tools for software configuration management. In *Proceedings of the 11th international conference on software engineering.*

Vélez, F., G. Bernard, and V. Darnis. 1989. The O_2 object manager: An overview. In *Proceedings of the 15th VLDB conference.*

Woelk D., and W. Kim. 1987. *Multimedia information management in an object-oriented database system.* MCC technical report no. DB-046-87.

Zdonik, S. B. 1986. Version management in an object-oriented database. In *Proceedings of the international workshop on advanced programming environments.*

CHAPTER 20

Integrating Concurrency Control

MICHÈLE CART
JEAN FERRIÉ

1 Introduction

Object-oriented database systems (Bancilhon 1988), such as Orion (Banerjee et al. 1987), Iris (Fishman et al. 1987), O_2 (Bancilhon et al. 1988), GBase, and GemStone, make it possible to deal with complex objects, both shared and persistent, that are usable through specific operations. Objects can easily be extended by creating new object classes and by reusing inherited existing methods and redefining them with overriding and late-binding properties. It is also essential that they support multiple concurrent users, but few studies have been published on concurrency control (CC) in such systems.

We describe three aspects of CC in an object-oriented DBMS. We first indicate the constraints placed on concurrency by the object-oriented approach, with respect to a classical DBMS, namely complex objects, objects (instances) grouped together into classes, multiple inheritance, specific operations (methods) on classes, and instances with richer semantics than the usual read and write operations. These constraints make it necessary to extend the principles of classical CC (Bernstein, Hadzilacos, and Goodman 1987) in order to serialize transactions.

We then propose an adaptation of the locking technique to satisfy the constraints of object-oriented CC. A particular adaptation has been implemented in the Orion system (Garza and Kim 1988), which minimizes the number of locks requested by a transaction, by using implicit locking. Nevertheless, the restricted number of lock types used in the system does not allow exploitation of all possible parallelism in an object-oriented approach. Our proposal does not have this shortcoming. We also consider the particular synchronization required when creating and deleting instances so that phantom objects can be avoided (Eswaran et al. 1976; Gray 1978).

Finally, we investigate the integration of such aspects with regard to an underlying system, providing transaction management and synchronization associated with a given granularity. We study the constraints placed on concurrency by the underlying system in the object-oriented approach, taking phantom objects into account. More specifically, the impact of both the locking granularity and the transaction model (single level or multilevel) is analyzed in detail. We show that potential concurrency is best exploited with a multilevel transaction model.

To illustrate our study of concurrency control, we use the O_2 system. The description of the O_2 system given here does not necessarily correspond to its current state of implementation, nor are the solutions we propose necessarily those that will be followed.

The paper is organized as follows. Section 2 presents transactions and O_2 objects, the physical representation of O_2 objects, and a hierarchy of abstraction levels that plays a significant part in concurrency control. Section 3 specifies constraints inherent in the object-oriented approach when dealing with classes and multiple inheritance relationships; we show how to satisfy them using a locking technique. The following sections raise the problem of integrating this method into the system used to support O_2 objects. We investigate possible solutions in accordance with the transaction model and the properties of physical objects supporting O_2 objects.

2 User Transactions and O_2 Objects

In the O_2 system a user can create objects and make them persistent and accessible to other users; he or she can also consult, modify, and delete them. A class defines an equivalence relationship between instances used through the same methods. Morever, all the instances belonging to the same class are based on the same type. Therefore, a class determines properties which specify the structure (i.e., the attributes) of instances of the class and the set of methods usable with any instance of the class. Generally classes are not independent. Using multiple inheritance, a new class may be constructed from one or several other existing classes.

The user names objects by means of an identifier called an *external name.* The methods used to manipulate objects resemble procedures and also have an external name. A user source program consists of a succession of method invocations on O_2 objects. The hierarchical construction of classes and instances in the O_2 system means that the methods consist themselves of a succession of method invocations on other objects.

At compile time, each external name of an object is translated into an *internal name*, or oid, that locates the object representation; the internal name of an instance is denoted by *iid* and that of a class by *tid.* Similarly, the external name of a method is translated into an intermediate name, denoted by *mcode*; this intermediate name is used at run time to determine, using a dynamic binding phase, the code associated with the invoked method. The same method name may in fact correspond to several possible computations, depending on the class the manipulated instance belongs to. The same holds for attributes.

When simplifying, the program resulting from compilation consists of a succession of method invocations, denoted by their mcodes, and performed on objects denoted by their oids. This program is called an O_2 transaction. For example:

begin ... $\mathtt{oid}_i\mathtt{.mcode}_k$; ... $\mathtt{oid}_j\mathtt{.mcode}_l$; ...**end**

The following classical properties (Haerder and Reuter 1983) are associated with an O_2 transaction: (1) integrity, (2) "all or none" effect (failure atomicity), (3) isolation from effects due to concurrent execution with other transactions (concurrency atomicity), and (4) persistence of a transaction's effects once committed. The transaction programmer is responsible for the integrity property, whereas the system assures the other three. In this study we limit ourselves to the implementation of property 3 without considering properties 2 and 4, which are related to fault tolerance.

The property of isolation from effects due to concurrency is achieved by transaction *serializability*. This criterion may be costly if transactions are long, thereby inducing excessive rejects or waiting. In this case, nonserializable schedules could be accepted (Garcia-Molina 1983; Sha 1985; Cart, Ferrié, and Richy 1988) using the semantics of transactions, objects, or methods.

2.1 Representation of O_2 Objects

O_2 objects are stored into WiSS records (Vélez et al. 1989; see chapter 15) located within a file. A *file*, named f, is composed of a set of *pages* of equal size. The page is the transfer unit between disk and main memory. A page p is located by the pair (f, p). Pages support *records*, of which there are two types: (1) the short record, which is smaller than (or the same size as) the page, so that several short records can be grouped within a page; and (2) the long record spread over several pages, the first page specifying the others that support the record.

Each page contains a table describing records so that the address of the rth record within the page is given by the rth table entry. Record r within page p of file f is located by the triplet (f, p, r). The hierarchical structure binding these objects (files, pages, and records) results from their hierarchical designation, as shown in figure 20.1.

O_2 objects are not duplicated; only one representation exists for any object. Broadly speaking, an O_2 object is represented in only one record and its internal name *oid* is the record name (f, p, r).

Instances of a class may be constructed either from primitive items, such as integer or string, or from instances belonging to the same class or to different

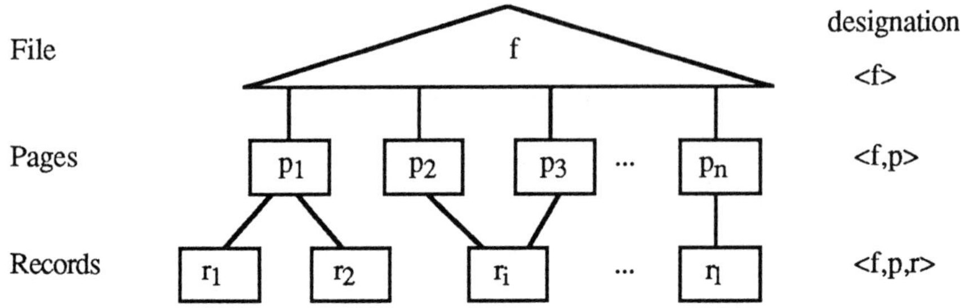

Figure 20.1. Hierarchical designation of objects

ones. The tuple or set constructors express this composition. When an instance refers to other instances, say iid_j and iid_k, its representation contains the names iid_j and iid_k of these instances but not their representations. These principles are illustrated in the following example (Bancilhon et al. 1987).

Example 1. Representation of an instance of the class Movie. Let us consider the class Movie, specified using the class Person. The structure of the instance *Casablanca* of the class Movie is shown in figure 20.2.

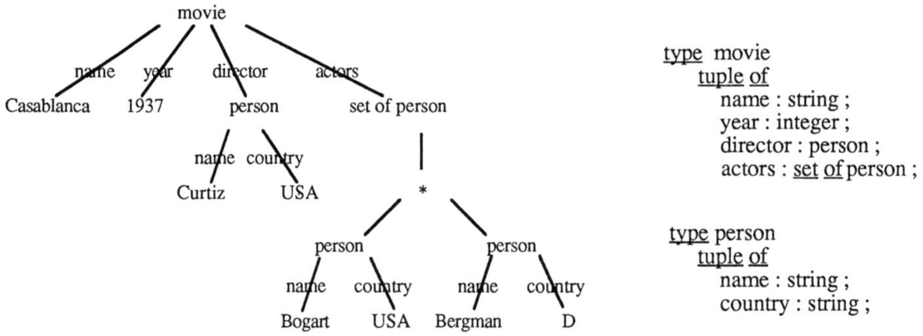

Figure 20.2. Casablanca schema

Specifically, the instance *Casablanca* is a tuple composed of:

- The instance *Curtiz* of the class Person,
- An instance of the type (for the difference between class and type, see chapter 3) set (Person), composed of the instances *Bogart* and *Bergman.*

Each instance is represented in a different record, as shown in figure 20.3.

We call the *representation* of the instance *Casablanca* the single record named by iid_i. The other records constitute representations of other instances. Similarly, the representation of the class TID contains the structure (i.e., the attributes) of instances of this class and the list of methods defined on this class and usable on its instances.

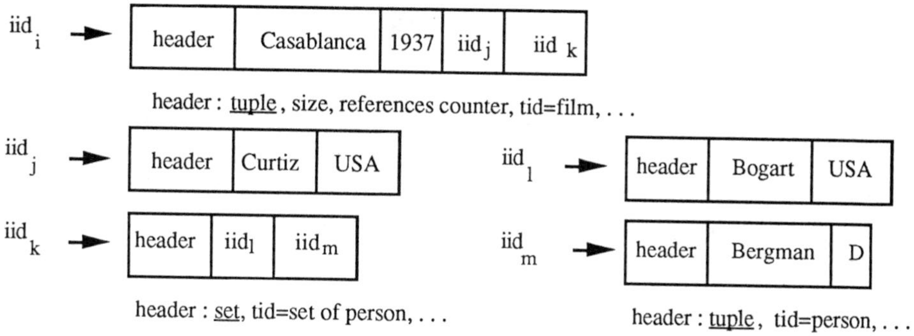

Figure 20.3. Records of the *Casablanca* object

2.2 Hierarchy of Abstraction Levels

There are two categories of objects in the system: physical and logical. Logical objects are O_2 objects usable through methods. Physical objects are pages and representations. The three types of objects (O_2 objects, representations, and pages) form a hierarchy with three levels of abstraction, such that at each level, one type of object and its operations are implemented (see figure 20.4).

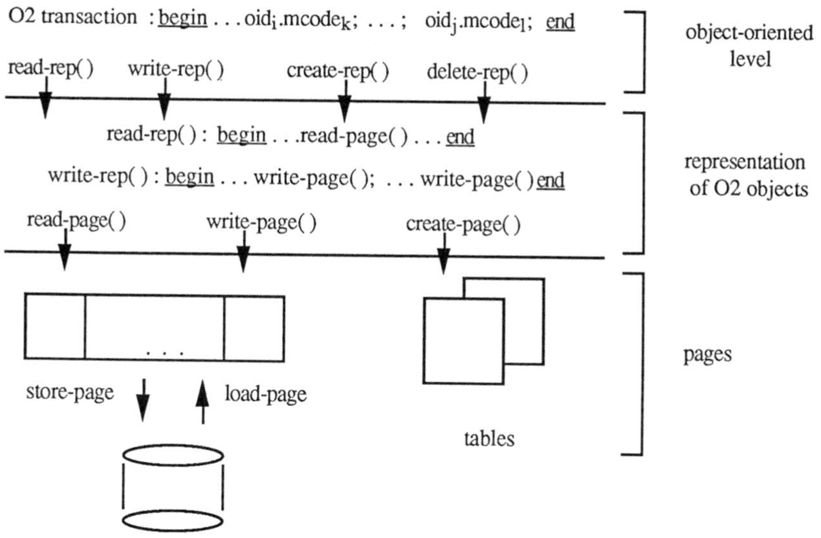

Figure 20.4. Hierarchy of abstraction levels

At the bottom level (page level) the page objects and the operations *read-page* and *write-page* are implemented. Page transfers between disk and main memory are managed at this level. At the intermediate level (representation level) representation objects usable through the operations *read-rep*, *write-rep*, *create-rep*, *delete-rep* are implemented. This implementation requires pages supplied by the bottom level.

At the top level (O_2 object level) are O_2 objects usable through methods. The invocation of a method on an O_2 object involves accessing its representation by means of the operations *read-rep* and *write-rep*. Thus any O_2 transaction request, even a simple one, involves activity of the underlying system (accesses to pages containing representations, to internal tables, etc.), which must be taken into account in concurrency control and recovery.

3 Constraints upon Concurrency

In an object-oriented system, controlling accesses to object representations is not sufficient to achieve concurrency control. Specific constraints must be taken into account, due to the fact that each object belongs to a class and due to the inheritance property between classes. Classes and instances are not independent, insofar as each instance belongs to a particular class. The clustering of instances into classes is represented by a three-level tree, called an *instance tree*. The leaves are instances and the intermediate nodes are the classes they belong to. (See figure 20.5.)

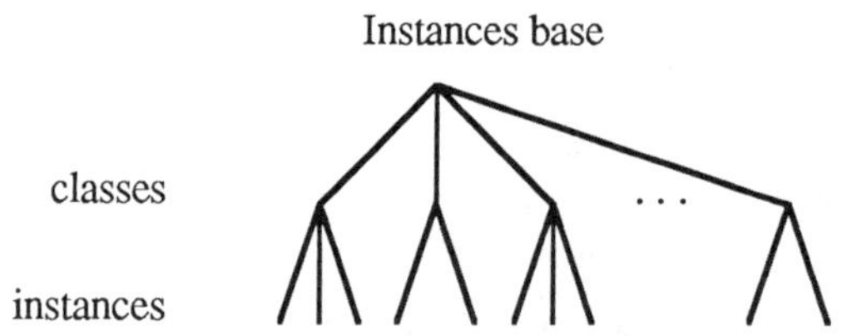

Figure 20.5. Instance tree

Similarly, classes are not independent of each other, due to the multiple inheritance relationship. The *class graph* expresses this dependency (see figure 20.6). With each class C is associated the set of its superclasses, denoted SC(C); these are classes whose properties are directly or indirectly inherited by C. Similarly, the set of subclasses of C, denoted sc(C), contains classes which, directly or not, inherit properties from C. Instances are not independent of each other, insofar as an instance i may take on as the value for an attribute any instance i'.

3.1 Classification of Methods on Classes and Instances

Classes and instances can be accessed through methods. Those performed on instances essentially consist of consultation and modification of an attribute value. Among those performed on classes are the following: consult the class definition; add or delete an attribute as well as a method in a class; change

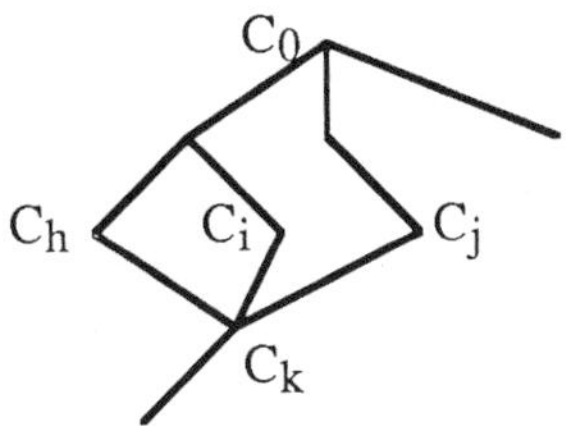

Figure 20.6. Class graph (multiple inheritance)

the domain of an attribute of a class; change the code of a method in a class; and change the inheritance relationship between classes (see chapter 7). This is possible for classes, if class definitions are implemented as objects.

Each method, depending on whether it only consults object representation or both consults and modifies it, is considered to be either a reading or a writing method. We emphasize the fact that a method m performed on an object o is classified as a reading or a writing method according to its effects on the representation of o exclusively. The effects induced on the representation of the component objects of o are not considered. They will be felt through the methods invoked by m on the components of o.

We also distinguish methods according to whether they are performed on a class or an instance. For requirements of CC, methods are classified into four categories:

- *read-c* and *write-c*, performed on classes
- *read-i* and *write-i*, performed on instances

Creation and deletion methods on classes or instances pose the problem of phantom objects, considered below.

3.2 Compatibility of Methods

We call a *real access* to an O_2 object, an access to its representation resulting from the invocation of a method on this object by a transaction. Because of dependency among objects, a real access to an object may concern other objects, though not requiring access to their representation. For those objects, we speak of *virtual access*. For instance, applying a method to an instance i induces a real access to i and a virtual one to the class of i as well as to its superclasses, since i inherits their properties.

For each real access, the induced virtual accesses are the following. Reading some class C, through *read-c(C)*, corresponds to a real read access to C and a virtual read access to its superclasses (see figure 20.7). Similarly, writing a class C, through *write-c(C)*, corresponds to a real write access to C as well as a virtual read access to all its superclasses and a write access to its subclasses (see figure 20.8).

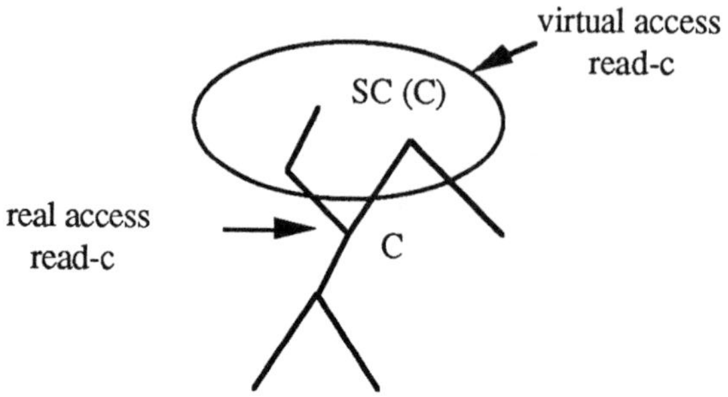

Figure 20.7. Effects induced by *read-c(C)*

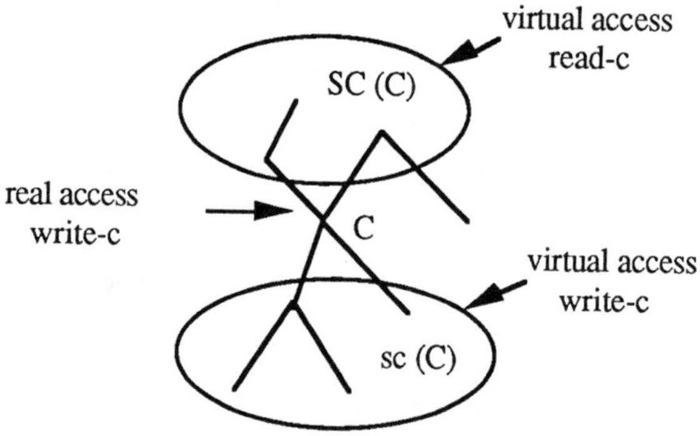

Figure 20.8. Effects induced by *write-c(C)*

Reading or writing an instance, through *read-i* and *write-i*, corresponds to a real access to the instance and a virtual access to the class and its superclasses. The virtual accesses induced by a real access are summarized below.

Real Access	**Virtual Accesses Induced**
read-c(C)	read access: $\forall C' \in \mathrm{SC}(C)$
write-c(C)	read access: $\forall C' \in \mathrm{SC}(C)$ and write access: $\forall C'' \in \mathrm{sc}(C)$
read-i(i) $i \in C$	read access: $\forall C' \in C \cup \mathrm{SC}(C)$
write-i(i) $i \in C$	read access: $\forall C' \in C \cup \mathrm{SC}(C)$

Two methods are compatible if they can be executed concurrently without having to be controlled—in other words, if the effects produced by one do not interfere with those produced by the other. Compatibility of two methods depends on whether they involve real or virtual accesses to common objects. When there are common objects, compatibility results from the semantics of *read* and *write*: only read methods are compatible. For instance, reading a class C that induces a virtual read access to its superclasses is not compatible with writing a superclass of C. Tables 20.1 and 20.2 summarize compatibilities among the methods.

Table 20.1. Compatibility of Methods on Classes and Instances

	class C		$C' \in sc(C)$		$C'' \in SC(C)$	
	read-c(C)	*write-c*(C)	*read-c*(C')	*write-c*(C')	*read-c*(C'')	*write-c*(C'')
read-c(C)	–	N	–	–	–	N
write-c(C)	N	N	N	N	–	N
read-i(i) $i \in C$	–	N	–	–	–	N
write-i(i) $i \in C$	–	N	–	–	–	N

Legend : – = compatible, N = incompatible

Table 20.2. Compatibility of Methods with Instances

	$i \in C$		$i' \in C'$ and $C' \in sc(C)$		$i'' \in C''$ and $C'' \in SC(C)$	
	read-i(i)	*write-i*(i)	*read-i*(i')	*write-i*(i')	*read-i*(i'')	*write-i*(i'')
read-i(i) $i \in C$	–	N	–	–	–	–
write-i(i) $i \in C$	N	N	–	–	–	–

3.3 Access Control of Classes and Instances

In this subsection, we describe the principles of concurrency control on O_2 objects based on locking, while disregarding the physical objects that support them. We consider two independent types of locks, C to control classes and I to control instances. Depending on whether the object has to be read or written (really or virtually), two *modes* are distinguished for each type of locks: the R mode for reading and the W mode for writing. Lock compatibility is shown in tables 20.3 and 20.4.

Table 20.3. Compatibility of Locks on Classes

	C_R	C_W
C_R	–	N
C_W	N	N

Table 20.4. Compatibility of Locks on Instances

	I_R	I_W
I_R	–	N
I_W	N	N

Integration of control into the execution schema is shown in figure 20.9. Each time a method is invoked on some object, the following actions take place. If the object is a class, locks on classes (C-type locks) are requested for the real and virtual acceses. If the object is an instance, a lock on the instance (I-type lock) is requested for the real access as well as locks on classes (C-type locks) for virtual accesses. In any case, control of a real access only takes place after virtual accesses to the classes are completed. When all the locks have been granted, the code of the method is run.

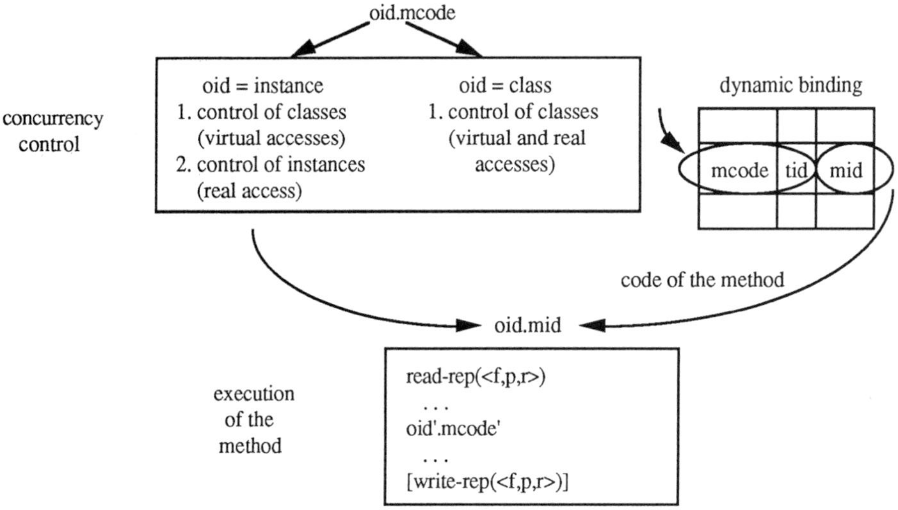

Figure 20.9. Concurrency control location when a method is invoked

From a practical point of view, the control of virtual accesses to the superclasses, with the aim of protecting them from concurrent writing, is redundant. Indeed, as a superclass C' of the class C cannot be written before the virtual accesses to its subclasses have been controlled, and as C is a subclass of C', concurrent writing of C' will not occur. For these reasons locks on superclasses do not have to be requested.

Locks granted to a transaction are held until commitment. To prevent risks of deadlock, locks on classes must be requested in the same order. This can be achieved by accessing the class graph in a predefined order (for instance, downward traversal from the root, from the left to the right).

Object-oriented CC cannot be considered without taking underlying abstraction levels into account. In sections 4, 5, and 6, we discuss physical objects supporting O_2 objects and show their impact on CC.

3.4 Creation and Deletion of Instances

A phantom is an object whose creation (or deletion) by some transaction has not been perceived by a concurrent one that follows it in the serialization order. The result is that isolation of transactions is no longer ensured. The phantom problem is more easily solved by taking into account the grouping of instances into classes. This consists in controlling any access to an instance by using the instance tree while applying the hierarchical locking protocol (Gray 1978). We briefly describe its use in an object-oriented system.

As all the locks are used to control accesses to instances, they are of the I type. There are five lock modes: R, W, IR, IW, and RIW. The compatibility of I-lock modes is shown in table 20.5. An instance can be ***explicitly*** locked only in the R or W mode to indicate whether it has to be, respectively, read or written. On the other hand a class can be locked (with an I-type lock) in any of the five modes. The ***intentional*** read mode IR (or write mode IW) on a class means that some instances of the class are or will be explicitly locked in the R (or W) mode. An R (or W) mode implies that all the instances of the class are ***implicitly*** locked in the R (or W) mode; it prevents them from being written (or read/written) by another concurrent transaction. An RIW mode on a class associates effects of both mode R and mode IW. Before an explicit lock (I_R or I_W) is placed on an instance, an intentional lock (I_{IR} or I_{IW}) must be placed on its class.

Table 20.5. Compatibility of I-lock Modes

	I_R	I_W	I_{IR}	I_{IW}	I_{RIW}
I_R	–	N	–	N	N
I_W	N	N	N	N	N
I_{IR}	–	N	–	–	–
I_{IW}	N	N	–	–	N
I_{RIW}	N	N	–	N	N

With this protocol, the phantom problem is solved merely by requiring a transaction that has to create or delete some instance, to hold an I_W lock on its class; thus creation or deletion will be done in mutual exclusion with any transaction that manipulates other instances of this class. On the other hand, minimizing the number of locks for a transaction that has to access all the instances of a class is achieved by explicitly locking (with I_R or I_W locks) the class rather than each instance separately.

I_R, I_W, I_{IR}, I_{IW}, and I_{RIW} locks on classes must not be confused with C_R and C_W locks, since they have a different meaning and are in fact completely compatible. C_R and C_W locks control access to the representation of a class; I_R, I_W, I_{IR}, I_{IW}, and I_{RIW} locks control access to instances of the class. Thus an instance write can run concurrently with a class read, which is not possible with the protocol described for Orion in Garza and Kim 1988. Indeed, in our protocol, a transaction T_1 can hold both a C_R lock on class C for virtual access and an I_W (or I_{IW}) lock on the class for real access to an instance of C, while another transaction T_2 holds a C_R lock on the same class for real access to the class.

3.5 Creation and Deletion of Classes

When creating and deleting classes, the class graph is used to avoid phantoms. For instance, the creation of a class C_k as a direct subclass of C_i and C_j is checked as a writing of these classes and is therefore controlled by a C_W lock. Any transaction that uses the class being created has to request a lock on its superclasses, and it is prevented from holding that lock as long as the transaction that created the class is not committed. Deleting a class C_k is also managed as a writing of all its superclasses.

4 Object and Operation Properties Exploited by CC

O_2 objects are built from physical objects supplied by the system, and CC implementation has to take this into account. Objects (whether logical or physical) and their operations can be characterized by properties that are exploited by CC. We specify them below.

4.1 Primitive and Constructed Objects

An object is defined by its representation and the operations that can be performed on it. For the requirements of concurrency control we separate *primitive* and *constructed* objects. Operations defined on primitive objects satisfy the following two properties:

1. An operation performed on any primitive object has no effect on the representation of other primitive objects.
2. Concurrent operations on the same primitive object are run serially; they are referred to as *indivisible* operations.

A constructed object is made from existing ones, either primitive or constructed. In the following discussion, a constructed object means an object (at some level i) made from one or several objects at lower level $(i-1)$. From this point of view, O_2 objects obtained using various constructors (such as tuple or set) are not considered to be constructed objects. The operations defined on a constructed object are built from operations defined on the component objects. The two properties verified by primitive objects are not necessarily satisfied by constructed ones. An operation on a constructed object may indeed affect another constructed one when there is a common object in their representation (such as object z in figure 20.10).

Operations on constructed objects are not necessarily indivisible, but they have to be *atomic* (i.e., as if indivisible) to ensure their isolation. In the O_2 system we regard pages as primitive objects and representations as objects built from pages.

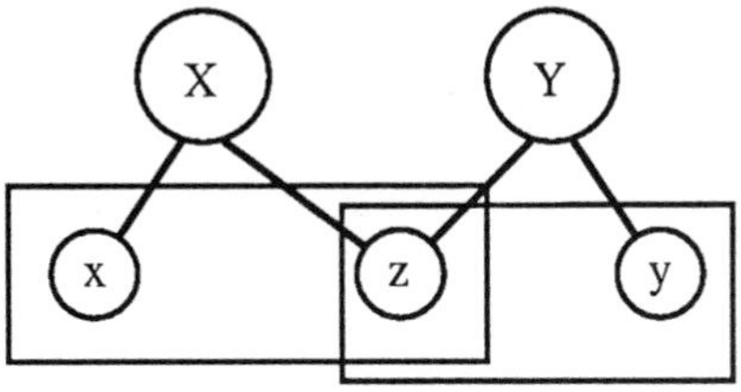

Figure 20.10. Example of constructed objects

4.2 Compatibility and Commutativity between Operations

The parallelism allowed by concurrency control depends to a large extent on the properties of compatibility and commutativity between operations defined on the objects.

Let X be a primitive or constructed object that is usable through a set of operations $\{OP_1, \ldots, OP_n\}$. The pair of operations (OP_i, OP_j) has the property of *compatibility* if, whatever the initial state of object X and the concurrent execution of these operations by two different transactions, the effects on the object X and on the transactions are the same. In other words, two compatible operations may be performed concurrently without having to be controlled. For instance, readings are compatible. When two operations are not compatible, commutativity may be used, which is a weaker property.

The ordered pair of operations (OP_i, OP_j) has the property of *commutativity* (Cart, Ferrié, and Richy 1989) if, whatever the initial state of object X, execution of operation OP_i by transaction T_1 followed by execution of operation OP_j by transaction T_2 has the same final effect on the object and the same results for the transactions as the execution in the reverse order (OP_j followed by OP_i). This definition can be more concisely formulated as follows:

$$\forall X_i \quad T_1.OP_i(X);\ T_2.OP_j(X) \sim T_2.OP_j(X);\ T_1.OP_i(X)$$

where X_i is the initial state of X and $\sim$ signifies that both executions give the same final state for object X and the same results for transactions.

It should be noted that compatible operations always commute. It is also possible to take call and return parameters into account to express conditional commutativity between operations (Schwarz and Spector 1984; Cart, Ferrié, and Richy 1988).

4.3 Independence of Objects at the Same Abstraction Level

We discuss below the significance of the independence of constructed objects when a multilevel transaction model is used. Assume that X and Y are two objects at the same abstraction level, usable through the sets of operations O_x and O_y respectively. X and Y are said to be *independent* if, whatever the initial state of X and Y and whatever the operations $OP_x \in O_x$ and $OP_y \in O_y$, the execution of OP_x by transaction T_1 followed by the execution of OP_y by transaction T_2 gives the same final states of objects X and Y and the same results for the transactions as the execution in the reverse order (OP_y followed by OP_x). The independence of objects X and Y can be more concisely expressed as follows:

$$\forall X_i, \forall Y_i \quad \forall OP_x, \forall OP_y \quad T_1.OP_x(X);\ T_2.OP_y(Y) \sim T_2.OP_y(Y);\ T_1.OP_x(X)$$

where X_i and Y_i are the initial states of X and Y, respectively.

Primitive objects are naturally independent, since an operation on a primitive object has no effect on the representation of another primitive object. As for constructed objects, if they are obtained from independent and distinct objects at lower level, they are themselves independent. If they share common objects at lower levels in their representation, they are independent on condition that all pairs of operations defined on the common objects commute. For instance, in figure 20.10 above, if x, y, and z are independent and if all pairs of operations defined on z commute, then X and Y are independent. On the other hand, the following example shows a situation where constructed objects are not independent.

Example 2. Suppose that r_1 and r_2 are two representations contained in the same page. They may be manipulated through the operations *write-rep*$(r_i, \ldots)$ and *read-rep*$(r_i, @)$. The return value @ is the address of the representation in the page (it is not the value of the representation). We assume that the length of a representation may vary, so that updating a representation may cause other representations to be moved in the page. Given these conditions, the following computations do not always give the same effects:

T_1.write-rep$(r_1, \ldots)$; T_2.read-rep$(r_2, @)$
and
T_2.read-rep$(r_2, @')$; T_1.write-rep$(r_1, \ldots)$

Indeed, when updating r_1 causes r_2 to be moved in the page, the final effect on the page remains the same but the effect on the transaction that invoked *read-rep* is different ($@ \neq @'$). The result is that r_1 and r_2 are not independent.

5 Impact of a One-level Transaction Model

A one-level transaction (Bernstein, Hadzilacos, and Goodman 1987) is modeled as a set of indivisible operations op_i on primitive objects. In the O_2 system, primitive objects are pages; pages are provided with a locking mechanism that we call physical locking, as opposed to logical locking defined on classes and instances. Given these conditions, object-oriented CC can be obtained either by using only physical locking on pages, or by combining physical and logical locking. The consequences of these two approaches are discussed in this section.

5.1 Physical Locking

When physical locking is used alone, running transactions are controlled at the page level only: when methods are invoked on O_2 objects, only induced operations on pages are taken into account by the CC. Thus the page is the only granule concerned by a lock request. In the following discussion, locks placed on pages are considered to be P-type locks. A P_R or P_W lock is used depending on the nature of operation (*read-page* or *write-page*). All locks needed to satisfy the requirements of the object-oriented approach are translated into locks on pages that contain the representations. With two-phase locking (Eswaran et al. 1976), pages (and therefore the objects they contain) remain locked until the end of the transaction. If pages simultanously contain instance and class representations, concurrency is severely decreased since it is not possible for different transactions to read the definition of a class C and to update an instance i (with $i \in C$ or $i \notin C$) concurrently if the representations belong to the same page. This consideration must be taken into account when placing objects in pages.

In any case, two transactions cannot concurrently use different instances if they are represented in the same page and the lock modes on the page are incompatible.

5.2 Physical and Logical Locking

The use of logical locks to satisfy the constraints of the object-oriented approach (see section 3) may be combined with the use of physical locks on pages. A logical lock is associated with the oid of an O_2 object and must be requested by the transaction for any virtual or real access to the object. In the case of a real access to an object, the physical lock that controls the page containing its representation must be requested once the logical lock is held.

Serializability of transactions is achieved by releasing logical locks at the end of the transaction (two-phase locking on logical locks). As for a physical lock, it may be released either at the end of the transaction (two-phase locking on physical locks), or at the end of the operation *read-page* or *write-page* on the page; in this case physical locks are called short locks. The former solution has the same drawbacks as in those mentioned in section 5.1; the latter solution avoids them. It uses a physical lock as a means of performing operations on pages in mutual exclusion so that *read-page* and *write-page* are made atomic. In fact, this technique used in the Orion system (Garza and Kim 1988) amounts to a two-level transaction model (see section 6). However, although it takes the object-oriented approach into account, it does not allow a full exploitation of it; specifically, as we will see below, it does not take advantage of method commutativity (to increase concurrency). Finally it should be noted that the use of logical locks with a one-level transaction model allows implementation of the two-phase locking hierarchical protocol to solve the phantom problem.

6 Impact of a Multilevel Transaction Model

The multilevel transaction model, which is based on nested transactions (Beeri, Schek, and Weikum 1988; Beeri, Bernstein, and Goodman 1989), takes the different abstraction levels into account. It follows directly from the hierarchical construction of operations and objects as presented in section 2.2. A transaction is modeled as a sequence of operations on objects provided at a given level of abstraction. An operation may be regarded in turn as a transaction invoking operations defined on objects at lower levels.

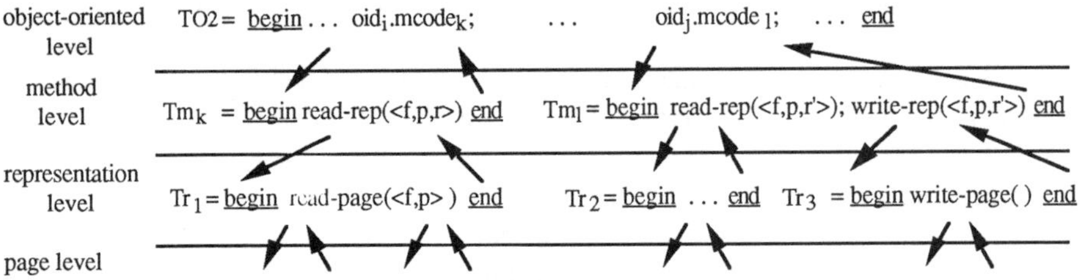

Figure 20.11. An O_2 transaction represented by nested transactions

Figure 20.11 shows the decomposition of operations in the O_2 system and the nested transactions involved in an O_2 transaction. Three levels of transaction are considered:

1. Transactions at the object-oriented level corresponding to the O_2 transactions:

   $$T_{O_2} \equiv \textbf{begin} \ldots \text{oid}_i.\text{mcode}_k; \ldots \text{oid}_j.\text{mcode}_l; \ldots \textbf{end}$$

2. Transactions at the method level; each method m is taken as a transaction T_m:

   $$T_m \equiv \textbf{begin}\ op_i(x); \ldots; op_j(y)\ \textbf{end}$$

   where x and y are representations of classes and instances named by a triplet (f, p, r), and $op_i, op_j \in \{\text{read-rep}, \text{write-rep}, \text{create-rep}, \text{delete-rep}\}$

3. Transactions at the representation level; an operation on a representation (*read-rep*, ...) corresponds to a transaction T_r:

   $$T_r \equiv \textbf{begin}\ op_k(z); \ldots; op_l(w)\ \textbf{end}$$

   where z and w are pages named by a pair (f, p) and $op_k, op_l \in \{$read-page, write-page$\}$.

The advantage of multilevel transactions over one-level transactions is that the semantics of both operations and objects can be exploited at each level of abstraction. Thus dependencies due to conflicts on primitive objects can be eliminated. The following examples illustrate this idea.

Example 3. Exploiting object independence.

Let r_1 and r_2 be representations contained in the same page p. Reading and writing a representation is expressed in terms of operations on the page, as follows:

read-rep(r) = **begin** ... read-page(p) ... **end**
and
write-rep(r) = **begin** ... write-page(p) ... **end**

The operation *read-rep* is assumed to return the value of the representation (and not the address in the page). Let us consider a concurrent execution in which transaction T_1 reads r_1 and transaction T_2 writes r_2. Accesses to the page p are made in the following order: T_1.read-page(p); T_2.write-page(p). It entails the dependency T_1.read-rep(r_1) $\rightarrow$ T_2.write-rep(r_2), due to the conflict on p. If we exploit the fact that representations r_1 and r_2 are independent, it follows that the execution T_1.read-rep(r_1); T_2.write-rep(r_2) has the same effects both on the representations r_1 and r_2 and on the transactions (the information read by T_1 is the same) as the execution in the reverse order, T_2.write-rep(r_2); T_1.read-rep(r_1). Thus the dependency $T_1 \rightarrow T_2$ can be eliminated.

Example 4. Exploiting operation commutativity.

Let A and B be two objects of the Bank-account class. They may be used through the operations (i.e., methods) *credit* and *debit*. These operations are expressed in terms of *read-rep* and *write-rep*; for instance:

credit(A) = **begin** read-rep(A); ... ; write-rep(A) ... **end**.

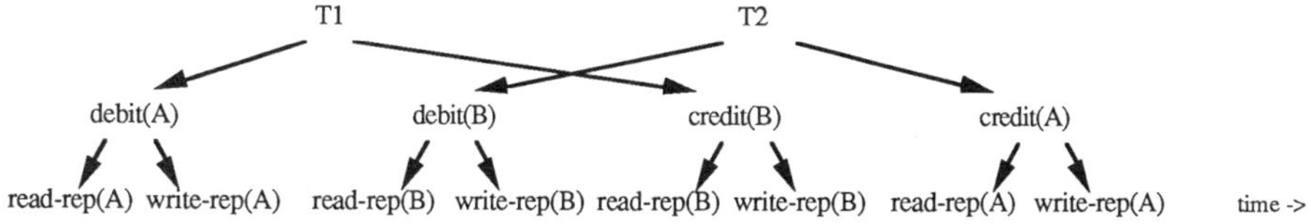

Figure 20.12. Concurrent execution of two transactions (1)

Figure 20.12 represents a concurrent execution where transactions T_1 and T_2 transfer money from one bank account to another. This execution leads to dependencies $T_1 \rightarrow T_2$ and $T_2 \rightarrow T_1$, due to conflicts on the representations of A and B, so that the transactions are not serializable. But if we consider the semantics of credit and debit, we find that the pair of operations (*debit*, *credit*) verifies the commutativity property (Cart, Ferrié, and Richy 1989). Since in this execution these operations are atomic, it is possible to apply this property so that the dependencies between T_1 and T_2 disappear and the transactions become serializable.

The multilevel transactions theory (Martin 1987; Beeri, Bernstein, and Goodman 1989) states that a concurrent execution of transactions is correct (i.e., top-level transactions are serializable) if the transactions at each level are serializable and if the serialization orders of the different levels are compatible. This result is obtained by proceeding iteratively from the lowest level. Once the serializability of transactions at a given level is achieved, transactions are then considered to be atomic operations invoked by higher-level transactions that in turn have to be serialized (using operation commutativity and object independence).

In practice, serializability is obtained at each level by the same CC methods as for one-level transactions. However, all these methods set up dependencies between transactions from conflicts due to shared objects. This leads to a limitation concerning the modeling of objects, which has not been sufficiently discussed in the literature; we examine the problem in the following subsection.

6.1 Necessity of Object Independence

Let X, Y, and Z be objects usable through operation OP and built from primitive objects x, y, z, and w used through operation *op*; we suppose that w is an object common to representations of X, Y, and Z, and that the pair of operations (*op*, *op*) does not satisfy the commutativity property. Operation OP corresponds, according to the object on which it is performed, to the following actions:

$$\begin{aligned} \mathrm{OP}(X) &= \textbf{begin } \mathrm{op}(x); \mathrm{op}(w) \textbf{ end} \\ \mathrm{OP}(Y) &= \textbf{begin } \mathrm{op}(y); \mathrm{op}(w) \textbf{ end} \\ \mathrm{OP}(Z) &= \textbf{begin } \mathrm{op}(z); \mathrm{op}(w) \textbf{ end} \end{aligned}$$

Let T_1 and T_2 be the transactions:

$$T_1 \equiv \text{begin} \ldots \mathrm{OP}(X); \ldots; \mathrm{OP}(Z) \text{ end} \quad \text{and} \quad T_2 \equiv \text{begin} \ldots \mathrm{OP}(Y); \ldots \text{end}$$

Let us consider the concurrent execution given by the tree in figure 20.13. To determine whether T_1 and T_2 are serializable, we first consider operations OP as transactions that invoke operations *op*. They are serializable (their execution is performed serially) and the dependencies due to conflicts on w are $\mathrm{OP}(X) \rightarrow \mathrm{OP}(Y) \rightarrow \mathrm{OP}(Z)$. As the operations OP are atomic, we then examine transactions T_1 and T_2, considering that operations OP are invoked in the order $\mathrm{OP}(X); \mathrm{OP}(Y); \mathrm{OP}(Z)$. Whatever CC method (in particular two-phase locking) is used, dependencies between transactions arise from conflicts on shared objects; the result is that T_1 and T_2 do not conflict and are therefore serializable (equivalence with $T_1; T_2$ or $T_2; T_1$). The problem here is that the method ignores dependencies resulting from operations on objects at lower levels. These dependencies may be ignored only if the semantics of the objects shows that they are independent. If that is not the case, transactions T_1 and T_2 are not serializable.

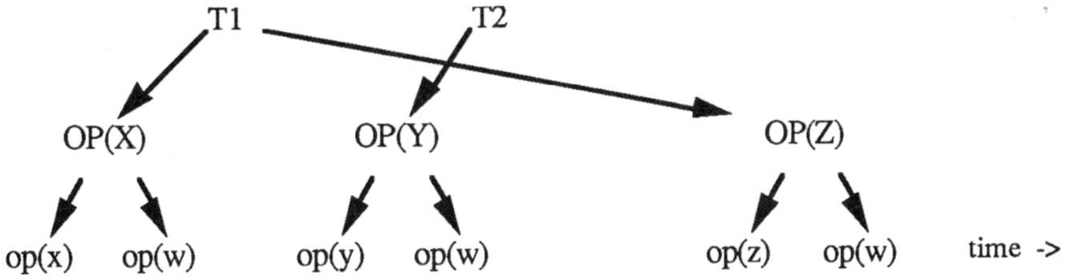

Figure 20.13. Concurrent execution of two transactions (2)

In practice, the objective is then to prove object independence (at each level), allowing use of the multilevel transaction model. Independence (see section 3.3) is ensured in the following cases:

1. When objects are constructed from distinct and independent objects at lower levels
2. When objects share some common objects in their representation and these common objects are only used by operations that commute.

6.2 Multilevel Two-phase Locking

Assuming that the objects at each level are independent, transaction serializability can be achieved at each level by the two-phase locking protocol. This implies that some types of locks have been defined at each level to control accesses to the objects of this level:

- *I*- and *C*-type locks are used to control O_2 objects
- *R*-type locks are used to control representations
- *P*-type locks are used to control pages

Figure 20.14 shows the different levels of locking. In the absence of deadlock, the two-phase locking protocol ensures that serialization orders of the different levels are compatible. It should be emphasized that a page is locked only during execution of an operation on a representation within the page. The representation of an object is locked during execution of a method; an O_2 object is locked until the end of the O_2 transaction.

In multilevel concurrency control, it is not necessary to take all abstraction levels into account. Only those that involve operations commutativity and/or object independence have to be considered. For instance, it is of no need to

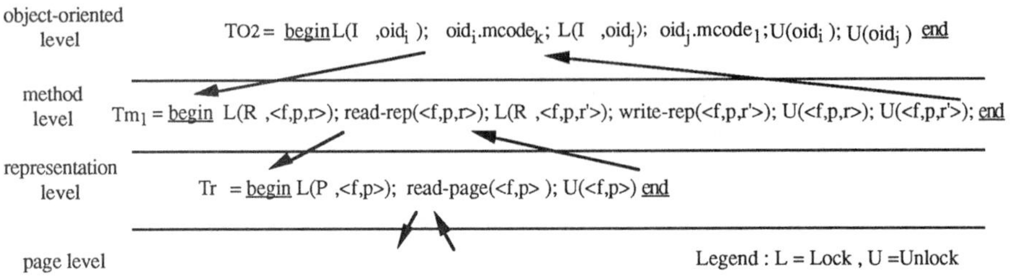

Figure 20.14. Two-phase locking protocol applied to multilevel transactions

consider the representation abstraction level if each representation fills the whole page. Similarly, there is no need to take the method level into account if method commutativity is not exploited.

6.3 Exploiting Method Commutativity

In section 3, only method compatibility (i.e., the capacity to be executed concurrently without control) is used by the CC, and lock-mode compatibility corresponds exactly to method compatibility. Thus, if m_1 and m_2 are two incompatible methods, when transaction T_1 holds a lock for performing m_1 it impedes transaction T_2 from acquiring the lock for performing m_2; T_2 has to wait until the commitment of T_1.

However, although methods m_1 and m_2 are not compatible, they may be commutative. In this case, provided that methods m_1 and m_2 are atomic, the fact that transaction T_1 holds the lock for performing m_1 no longer prevents transaction T_2 from obtaining the lock for performing m_2. The waiting by T_2 is eliminated, but method atomicity has to be ensured. It may be obtained either by a serial execution (in mutual exclusion) or by a serializable one.

The following example shows how to take advantage of method commutativity when using multilevel locking. Suppose we want to exploit the commutativity of debit and credit methods presented in example 4. New modes associated with I-type locks have to be defined and included in the compatibility table—a DEB mode for debit and a CRED mode for credit. These two lock modes are compatible, since the methods they are associated with are commutative. Thus a Bank-account object is locked until the commitment of the transaction that invoked the credit or debit method; but as the I_{DEB} and I_{CRED} locks are compatible, this provides a higher degree of parallelism.

The atomicity of debit and credit methods at run time has to be ensured by performing the sequences of operations *read-rep*( ) ...; *write-rep*( ) relative to credit and debit methods, either in mutual exclusion or in a serializable way. In this case a method is seen as a transaction, and serializability can be achieved using R-type locks on the representation. Thus incompatible but commutative methods may be performed concurrently, provided that their atomicity is ensured. This is a great advantage over mutual exclusion when methods are long.

7 Conclusion

We have shown in this paper that the structural properties of objects in an object-oriented database impose requirements on concurrency control if the dynamic creation, deletion, and update of classes are to be performed concurrently with the creation, deletion, consultation, and update of instances. These requirements can be expressed in terms of compatibility and can be implemented with a locking protocol. We have examined the problem that arises when adapting to the underlying system used to support object representations. The transaction model provided by this system and the locking granularity it imposes are determining features when a high degree of parallelism is needed. The multilevel transaction model seems best suited to fully exploiting potential parallelism, especially method commutativity. However, recovery must be adequately managed; this has not been addressed in this paper.

8 Acknowledgements

We would like to thank Michel Scholl and Fernando Vélez for providing helpful explanations of the O_2 system.

References

Bancilhon, F. 1988. Object-oriented database systems. In *Proceedings of the seventh ACM PODS conference.*

Bancilhon, F., G. Barbedette, V. Benzaken, C. Delobel, S. Gamerman, C. Lécluse, P. Pfeffer, P. Richard, and F. Vélez. 1988. The design and implementation of O_2, an object-oriented database system. In *Proceedings of the second international workshop on object-oriented database systems,* ed. K. Dittrich.

Bancilhon, F., V. Benzaken, C. Delobel, and F. Vélez. 1987. *The O_2 object manager architecture.* Altaïr technical report no. 14/87.

Banerjee, J., W. Kim, H. J. Kim, and H. F. Korth. 1987. Semantics and implementation of schema evolution in object-oriented databases. In *Proceedings of the ACM SIGMOD conference.*

Beeri, C., P. Bernstein, and N. Goodman. 1989. A model for concurrency in nested transactions systems. *Journal of the ACM* 36(2): 230–67.

Beeri, C., H. Schek, and G. Weikum. 1988. Multi-level transactions: Theoretical art or practical need? In *Proceedings of the first international conference on extending database technology.*

Bernstein, P. A., V. Hadzilacos, and N. Goodman. 1987. *Concurrency control and recovery in database systems.* Addison-Wesley.

Carey, M. J. 1983. Granularity hierarchies in concurrency control. In *Proceedings of the second ACM SIGACT-SIGMOD symposium on principles of data base systems.*

Cart, M., and J. Ferrié. 1989. Integrating concurrency control into an object-oriented database system. In *Proceedings of the second EDBT conference.*

Cart, M., J. Ferrié, and H. Richy. 1988. Le contrôle de concurrence des transactions dans les environnements orientés-objets. *Actes 4è Journées Bases de Données Avancées, Bénodet.*

______. 1989. Contrôle de l'exécution de transactions concurrentes. *Technique et Science Informatique* 8(3): 225–40.

Eswaran, K.P., J. N. Gray, A. Lorie, and I. L. Traiger. 1976. The notions of consistency and predicate locks in data base system. *Communications of the ACM* 19(11): 624–33.

Fishman, D., D. Beech, H. P. Cate, E. C. Chow, T. Conners, J. W. Davis, N. Denett, C. G. Hoch, W. Kent, P. Lyngbaek, B. Mahbod, M. A. Neimat, T. A. Ryan, and M. C. Shan. 1987. Iris: An object-oriented database management system. *ACM TOIS* 5(1): 46–69.

Garcia-Molina, H. 1983. Using semantic knowledge for transaction processing in a distributed database. *ACM TODS* 8(2): 186–213.

Garza, J., and W. Kim. 1988. Transaction management in an object-oriented database system. In *Proceedings of the ACM SIGMOD conference.*

Gray, J. 1978. Notes on data base operating systems. In *Operating systems: An advanced course.* Springer-Verlag.

Haerder, T., and A. Reuter. 1983. Principles of transaction-oriented database recovery. *ACM Computing Survey* 15(4): 287–317.

Lécluse, C., and P. Richard. 1989. Modeling complex structures in object-oriented databases. In *Proceedings of the eighth ACM PODS conference.*

Lécluse, C., P. Richard, and F. Vélez. 1988. O_2, an object-oriented data model. In *Proceedings of the ACM SIGMOD conference.*

Martin, B. E. 1987. Modeling concurrent activities with nested objects. In *Proceedings of the seventh international conference on distributed computing systems.*

Schwarz, P. M., and A. Z. Spector. 1984. Synchronizing shared abstract types. *ACM Transactions on Computer Systems* 2(3): 223–50.

Sha, L. 1985. *Modular concurrency control and failure recovery: Consistency, correctness and optimality.* Ph.D. dissertation, Department of Computer Science, Carnegie-Mellon University.

Vélez, F., G. Bernard, and V. Darnis. 1989. The O_2 object manager: An overview. In *Proceedings of the 15th international VLDB conference.*

Woelk D., and W. Kim. 1987. Multimedia information management in an object-oriented database system. In *Proceedings of the 13th international VLDB conference.*

Part V

The Programming Environment

Chapter 21

Introduction to the Programming Environment

Claude Delobel
Paris Kanellakis
Didier Plateau

Workstations with high-resolution graphics and new programming-environment techniques had a revolutionary impact on computing during the 1980s. Part 5 stresses the importance of incorporating these advances in any new database technology. Let us first comment on how this coupling of database and programming environment has evolved.

In the early 1970s the user interface to network database systems consisted simply of the data definition language and the data manipulation language. Other tools, such as a data dictionary, report generators, editing facilities, and conceptual schema design, were provided independently of the database software. With the advent of relational database systems in the late 1970s, the need to integrate all these components was already clear. Query by Example (QBE) (Zloof 1977) was one of the first efforts to integrate the interface and the query language. It is now generally recognized that relational query languages, because of their high-level primitives and elegant user interfaces, resulted in a significant increase of programmer productivity for data-processing applications. However, database support is needed during *all* phases of program development and also for many non-data-processing applications. Object-oriented databases address this need through a close coupling of the database and the programming environment.

During the 1980s, largely under the general heading of "the object-oriented approach" (Goldberg 1983; O'Brien, Halbert, and Kilian 1987; Reiss 1986; Schmucker 1986), a new major requirement emerged: that all related software components must be integrated into the database product. This synthesis of database and software tools is realizable using state-of-the-art technology. For example, technology developed for the Human-Machine Interface can be used directly in a database environment (see Cardelli 1988; Coutaz 1987).

In summary, it is highly desirable that the programmer be provided with tools and functionalities for every phase of database application development, making these programming tasks easier, quicker, and safer. This goal is a database extension of the principal goal of a complete programming environment (and incidentally of fourth-generation languages—see Goodman 1987; Martin 1985).

In part 5, we hope to demonstrate how the above goal has been, to a significant degree, attained in O_2. In the rest of this chapter we present some of the major technical challenges, a historical view of the O_2 approach, and a roadmap for part 5.

1 The Technical Challenges

The main issues that were addressed in designing the O_2 programming environment can be subdivided into two parts: the interaction between the user and the database, and the software engineering problems.

1.1 Interaction between User and Database

We draw from the extensive literature on database interfaces (e.g., Bryce and Hull 1986; Goldman et al. 1985; King and Novak 1985; MacKinlay 1986; Maier, Nordquist, and Grossman 1986; Skarra, Zdonik, and Reiss 1986; Stonebraker and Kalash 1982; Wong and Kuo 1982). Most researchers model these interfaces using a three-level approach. The three levels are related to schema, data, and queries. The *schema level* provides window views of the schema. In O_2 these views describe its components: classes, types, method names, method signatures, and the inheritance hierarchy. The *data level* provides window views of the instances in the database. It allows the basic operations on objects, such as creation, deletion, and update. Nevertheless, in an object-oriented environment these operations are only possible through methods. Consequently, the interaction between the user interface and encapsulation must be defined. The *query level* is a worksheet window where one can formulate queries and receive the results. At each level, browsing and editing are possible. A good design has to facilitate communication between these levels. Visualizations, although generally simple, involve elements of artistic design.

A particular problem is that many of the current OODB query languages are text oriented. This is, in part, a consequence of emphasizing the integration of query languages with generally accepted (text-oriented) host programming languages. Here our goal was to study which textual functions and commands could be replaced by graphical and visual actions or by keyboard and mouse events.

We summarize below some interesting specific problems addressed in designing an interface for O_2.

1. What components of the schema must be visualized, and how?
2. What data must be visualized, and how?
3. How does one display and edit large objects? What information is essential, and what can be omitted from a display? (We called this the ellipsis problem.)
4. Should the query language be integrated with the interface?
5. How should a query be formulated graphically?
6. What kinds of operations can we authorize by graphical actions? What is the relationship with the encapsulation principle?
7. Is it possible to integrate in the same window framework the three levels: schema, data, and query?
8. What are the interactions between the interface and concurrency control mechanisms?

1.2 The Software Engineering Problems

In the words of Adele Goldberg (1984, 142): "The problem of creating a friendly programming environment centers on the kind of help the system provides, and the ease with which we can cause the effect we wish to cause." The point is that *friendly* is quantified by the distance between what the user has in mind to do (e.g., program design, implementation, or testing), and how the user can do it with the system. The object-oriented approach decreases this distance by providing full use of a graphic interface, and by the everything-is-an-object philosophy, which translates into *simple communication between diverse software components.*

Various software tools are needed to support program development. These help in (a) finding and extracting information about existing functionality; (b) designing the database schema; (c) editing, testing, and debugging programs; and (d) reusing programs and compiling incrementally. Object-oriented programming greatly facilitated the various implementations and their integration in O_2.

2 Historical View of the O_2 Approach

We started in 1986 with two goals. First, we decided to develop graphic facilities to support interactive manipulation of data: form-based graphic representations together with cut-copy-paste editing facilities. Implementing these facilities required the use of an existing graphic toolkit (we felt there was no need to build another window system!). The second goal was to build the programming environment as an O_2 application, meaning that the schema is represented as O_2 objects and viewed using the graphic facilities of the system. This programming environment would mainly support schema and data browsers, class and method creation, compilation, and debugging.

In the original V0 prototype, a very limited programming environment was built: a class hierarchy browser and a full-screen editor for the manipulation of classes and methods. In the early stages of the project, the main effort was dedicated to the benchmarking of user-interface toolkits. Several commercial toolkits (the Macintosh Toolbox, MS-Windows, X Windows, HyperCard, and Aïda) were tested for their support of user-application communication in the O_2 environment.

From this experimentation, we learned that HyperCard (and its likes) provided the best functionalities. Unfortunately, it was too tightly related to a "stack of cards" data model and to the Macintosh hardware. We also concluded that general-purpose toolkits were too far from the needs of database programmers (for instance, nothing is provided to display tables), but they constituted a good basis for building the graphic facilities we envisioned. Among the toolkits commercially available at that time, we chose Aïda, a Lisp-based toolkit running on top of various window systems (X, SunView, Macintosh, MS-Windows). Portability and prototyping flexibility were the main reasons for this choice. In 1987 no standard Unix toolkit (such as Motif or OpenLook) was available. In retrospect, the choice of Aïda helped the project at the time it was made, but subsequent versions are based on a more standard and higher-performance toolkit.

For V1, a full set of graphic facilities have been implemented. Any database object can be displayed and interactively manipulated. In fact V1 fullfills both original objectives. On top of O_2 there is a programming environment that integrates browsing, editing, compiling, and debugging tools.

3 A Roadmap for Part 5

The rest of part 5 consists of five chapters. Four of these are extended and considerably modified versions of papers which have appeared in various conference proceedings.

Chapter 22 (Plateau et al. 1990) is entitled "Building User Interfaces with Looks." Looks supports the construction of user interfaces in the O_2 system. It provides facilities to display and edit objects and allows browsing of the database schema and the database objects. The system offers primitives to display objects; these primitives are generic and parameterized. When one is displaying an object, the type of the object is not specified; the parameters are the expansion depth, the style, and the placement. Since the system is dealing with complex structures, an object may be recursively composed of other objects. The expansion depth in the visualization of the object is, thus, composition dependent. There are two basic styles: a graph style and a form style. The graph style is equivalent to seeing the database objects as a semantic network, and visualizing some parts of this graph. The form style visualizes an object as a form which may recursively contain other forms. The placement parameter gives information about the position of objects on the screen. Other features are the customization of object displays and the possibility of sending a message to an object presented on the screen.

Chapter 23 (Borras et al. 1989), "OOPE, the O_2 Programming Environment," describes the programming environment for O_2. It provides functionalities for defining a database schema with classes and methods, and for editing, compiling, and testing the bodies of the methods. All these functionalities are organized into different programming tools: the *browser*, the *O_2 shell*, the *workspaces*, the *journal*, the *query manager*, and the *application manager*. The information managed by the programming environment is quite large, so the information is organized as O_2 objects stored in the database itself. Special attention is given to the debugger, which is described in greater detail in chapter 24.

Chapter 24 (Doucet and Pfeffer 1990) is entitled "Using a Database System to Implement a Debugger." The debugger is an essential part of the O_2 programming environment. It is multilanguage: it can be used with different programming languages (C and Basic). Changing from one language to another is transparent to the user. The O_2 debugger uses the O_2 data model. All the variables representing the state of a program are considered O_2 objects. The debugging is done through browsing. The debugger uses graphics rather than text to represent process states; this is done by using the functionalities of the Looks system. Chapter 24 describes the main functionalities of the debugger: interactive execution control, display of variable values, dynamic modification of variables, and providing information about the program.

Chapter 25, "Incremental Compilation in O_2," deals with the fact that database schemas can be frequently updated. We have seen in part 2 an analysis of the schema update problem; the problem examined in chapter 25 has a more pragmatic flavor. It is due to the fact that in the O_2 environment there are two basic compilation modes: a *development mode* and an *execution mode*. In the development mode, methods are dynamically linked at execution time. Furthermore, in the development mode there is a debug option that will generate code according to what the debugger needs. In the execution mode, an application is compiled into an executable code which reflects a state of the database schema. The goal of chapter 25 is to study how an incremental compiler can be used to satisfy (in a uniform framework) the requirements of the two modes.

Chapter 26 (Arango 1990), "Self-Explained Toolboxes," describes how a toolbox can be used to improve the reusability of software components. A toolbox can be seen as a part of a schema definition adapted to an application domain. The components of a toolbox are libraries of meaningful pieces of code, such as definitions of classes, procedures, functions, and programs. Chapter 26 presents an example of such a toolbox developed for business programmers.

References

Arango, G. 1990. Self-explained toolboxes: A practical approach to reusability. In *Proceedings of the 1990 TOOLS conference.*

Borras, P., A. Doucet, P. Pfeffer, and D. Tallot. 1989. OOPE, the O_2 programming environment. In *Proceedings of the sixth PRC BD3 conference.*

Bryce, D., and R. Hull. 1986. SNAP: A graphics-based schema manager. In *Proceedings of the second IEEE conference on data engineering.*

Cardelli, L. 1988. Building user interfaces by direct manipulation. In *Proceedings of the ACM SIGGRAPH workshop on user interface software.*

Coutaz, J. 1987. The construction of user interfaces and the object paradigm. In *Proceedings of the ECOOP conference.*

Doucet, A., and P. Pfeffer. 1990. Using a database system to implement a debugger. In *Proceedings of the IFIP working conference on database semantics.*

Goldberg, A. 1983. *Smalltalk-80: The interactive programming environment.* Addison-Wesley.

———. 1984. The influence of an object-oriented language on the programming environment. In *Interactive programming environment,* eds. D. Barstow, H. Shrobe, and E. Sandewal. McGraw-Hill.

Goldman, K. J., S. A. Goldman, P. C. Kanellakis, and S. B. Zdonik. 1985. ISIS: Interface for a semantic information system. In *Proceedings of the ACM SIGMOD conference.*

Goodman, D. 1987. *The complete Hypercard handbook.* Bantam Books.

King, R., and M. Novak. 1985. FaceKit: A database interface design toolkit. In *Proceedings of the VLDB conference.*

MacKinlay, J. 1986. Automating the design of graphical presentations of relational information. *ACM Transacions on Graphics* 5(2): 110–20.

Maier, D., P. Nordquist, and M. Grossman. 1986. *Displaying database objects.* Technical Report, Oregon Graduate Center.

Martin, J. 1985. *Fourth-generation languages.* Prentice-Hall.

O'Brien, P., D. Halbert, and M. Kilian. 1987. The Trellis programming environment. In *Proceedings of the OOPSLA conference.*

Plateau, D., R. Cazalens, J. C. Mamou, D. Lévêque, and B. Poyet. 1990. Building user interface with the LOOKS hyper-object system. In *Proceedings of the Eurographics workshop on object-oriented graphics.*

Reiss, S. 1986. An object-oriented framework for graphical programming. *SIGPLAN* 21(10): 49–57.

Schmucker, K. 1986. *Object-oriented programming for the Macintosh.* Hayden Book Company.

Skarra, A., S. Zdonik, and S. Reiss. 1986. An object server for an object-oriented database system. In *Proceedings of the 1986 international workshop on object-oriented database systems.*

Stonebraker, M., and J. Kalash. 1982. Timber: A sophisticated browser. In *Proceedings of the VLDB conference.*

Wong, H. K. T., and I. Kuo. 1982. GUIDE: A graphical user interface for database exploration. In *Proceedings of the VLDB conference.*

Zloof, M. M. 1977. Query-by-example: A database language. *IBM Systems Journal* 4: 325–45.

CHAPTER 22

Building User Interfaces with Looks

DIDIER PLATEAU
PATRICK BORRAS
DIDIER LÉVÊQUE
JEAN-CLAUDE MAMOU
DIDIER TALLOT

1 Introduction

End-user dialogue management represents a large part of the application code. Designing and implementing a powerful direct-manipulation graphic user interface requires time and expertise from the programmer. Such user interfaces are out of reach unless appropriate user-interface tools are provided.

In this paper, we focus on the user-interface tools needed by a programmer writing object-oriented database (OODB) applications. OODB applications cover various domains such as business, office automation, CAD, hypertext, and hypermedia systems.

OODB applications are specific for two reasons:

1. The information manipulated by the applications (and therefore the end users) is a graph connecting large composite objects. Think, for instance, of a travel agency organizing tours. The database stores information about cities, hotels, monuments, restaurants, customers, flights, and so on. Cities and hotels are represented by objects linked together: a hotel is located in a city and a city contains a set of hotels. A travel agency application needs basic tools to display, browse, and update this graph to allow the end user to perform functions such as "What about Paris?" or "Make a room reservation in the Ritz Hotel."

2. Database programmers have to compromise between application usability and software productivity. What they need are easy-to-learn, easy-to-use tools which relieve them from most of the user-interface design and implementation workload. These tools also guarantee the usability and consistency of the resulting user-interfaces

1.1 Existing User-Interface Tools

Object-oriented database programmers need a set of built-in facilities to display, browse, and manipulate interactively a graph of *hyperobjects*. Let us now discuss how far these needs are met by the existing user-interface tools.

User-interface toolkits (e.g., OSF 1989; Devin and Duquesnoy 1988; Schmucker 1986, etc.) constitute a mature technology moving toward standards. However, what they provide is a library of basic dialogue components (widgets) such as buttons and menus. They do not meet OODB applications requirements. To display a piece of data, one needs not only to compose widgets but also to implement editing operations.

User-interface editors (Cardelli 1988; Karsenty 1987; Smith 1988; Devin and Duquesnoy 1989; Hullot 1986) allow one to create widgets, to combine them interactively, and to store their description in resource files to be used by a program. This relieves the programmer from writing the corresponding code, and it provides a nice framework for tuning the user interface (color, layouts, fonts, etc.). However, user-interface editors hardly capture the dynamic aspects of widgets, such as the creation of widgets or reactions to user commands.

User-interface management systems (UIMSs), as defined in Betts et al. 1987 and Rhyne et al. 1987, address the complete construction of dialogue: not only the description of the different screen components but also how these components relate together and relate with the application and the user to capture user/application dialogue. Many UIMSs have been prototyped (e.g., Borning 1981; Sibert, Hurley, and Bleser 1986; Olsen 1986; Myers and Buxton 1986; Hermann and Hill 1988), but UIMS technology is still not mature. The UIMS research community is quite active, but few products are available and none is widely used.

Application generators are dedicated to a specific application domain. A domain is characterized by a data model that describes the information manipulated by the application. Within this framework, application generators provide facilities to control data layout, editing, and interactive behavior. Application semantics is represented by scripts. Application generators include fourth-generation languages (Martin 1985) and Hypercard-like systems (Goodman 1987).

Fourth-generation languages are parts of the programming environments of relational database systems. In relational systems, data is modeled by tables and tuples. Fourth-generation languages provide facilities for display, editing, and scripting (usually SQL queries). Information handled by Hypercard is represented by stacks and cards instead of tables and tuples (the difference is not great). Hypercard provides a nice environment to specify the graphic appearance and the interactive behavior of cards and stacks.

Application generators meet our initial requirements. The Looks system we present in this chapter belongs to this category. It is built on top of a data model and it provides facilities to display and interactively manipulate objects. However, various features make Looks significantly different from other application generators.

1.2 Looks

Looks is based on an object-oriented data model, which is much more powerful than relational or card-and-stack models. To control data layout, interactive manipulation, and dialogue construction, Looks provides various original features such as masks, links, and modes, which are described in this paper.

The rest of this chapter is organized as follows. The O_2 object-oriented data model is described in section 2. The various features of the system are described in section 3. Section 4 illustrates these features with a short programming example. As a conclusion, section 5 presents the current state of the Looks system and discusses the future of the project: evaluation, tuning and improvements, additional functions, and so on.

2 The Looks Data Model

This section gives an informal description of the data model underlying the Looks system. This data model is part of the O_2 object-oriented database system. Extensive presentation and theoretical justifications of the model can be found in Part 2.

An object is either atomic (integer, float, string, bits, Boolean, etc.) or composite. A composite object is built from atoms combined with list, set, or tuple constructors. These constructors can be arbitrarily nested. In order to illustrate our discussion on object display, we use the following example.

```
class Hotel
      type tuple(name: string,
                 address: Address,
                 facilities: list(string),
                 stars: integer,
                 rate: integer);

class Address
      type tuple(street: string,
                 city: City);
```

```
class City
      type tuple(name: string,
                 map: bitmap,
                 hotels: set(Hotel));
```

The Hotel type is a composite type built with a tuple, the attributes of which are a name (an atom of type string), an address (a reference to the Address class), a set of facilities (set of string), a number of stars (integer), and a room rate (integer). It should be noticed that the three classes defined above form a cycle: Hotel has an **address** field, Address has a **city** field, and City has a **hotels** field.

The next example shows a Hotel object.

```
ritz: tuple(name: "Ritz Hotel",
            address: ritz_address,
            facilities: list("swimming pool",
                             "bar"),
            stars: 5,
            rate: 800,000)
```

3 Main Features of Looks

This section describes the main features of Looks: generic presentations, the ability to edit presentations, masks, placements, modes, links, interactive method activation, and specific presentations.

3.1 Generic Presentations

Looks provides a generic algorithm to display objects. It can be applied to any object to build an interactive presentation. A generic presentation is an interactive component which can be edited and saved in the database. Application/end-user dialogue can be organized by means of menus that are hooked to the presentations. There is one menu per object. Menu items correspond to object methods.

Figure 22.1 shows three generic presentations of the *ritz* object defined above. Several generic presentations can be created from the same *ritz* object. The difference is the amount of information visible. To control this, a depth parameter is used. Let us illustrate how the algorithm works on the *ritz* example. Displaying an object with depth 0 creates an icon (the upper left window of figure 22.1). A menu is hooked to the icon: the menu items correspond to *ritz* methods.

Displaying with depth 1, shows the content of *ritz* (see the lower left window of figure 22.1. The display algorithm shows all *ritz* subobjects as icons; the

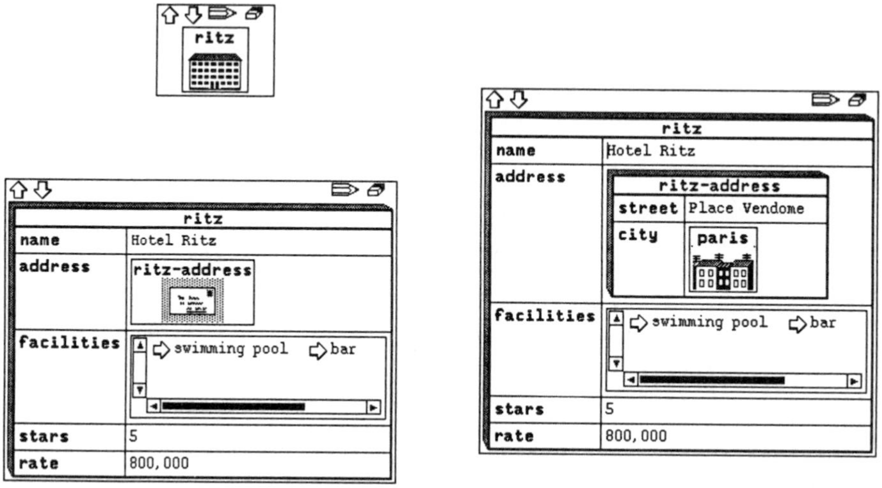

Figure 22.1. Three presentations of the *ritz* object

only subobject in this example is *ritz_address*. Menus are hooked to *ritz* and *ritz_address*.

Recursively, depth 2 presentation is obtained by applying depth 1 to *ritz* and again to *ritz_address*. Depth i is the expansion obtained by applying depth 1 to *ritz* and depth $i-1$ to *ritz_address*. For instance, the right-hand window of figure 22.1 shows depth 2 applied to *ritz*.

3.2 Editing Presentations

Generic presentations show atoms (such as integers, and strings), structures (list, set, or tuple), and objects. Each of these components can be edited.

Atoms such as integer and string are edited in a text manner; however, Booleans (viewed as two-state buttons) and bitmaps are not edited as text. Atoms can be copied and pasted within a presentation and between different presentations. Looks type-checks dynamically; for instance, one cannot type something other than a digit in an integer field.

Structures can be copied and pasted. The end user can copy a tuple and paste it on a tuple having the same type. It is also possible to cut and create elements within lists and sets. Looks performs synchronous type-checking. Any type-inconsistent manipulation is forbidden. However, if two views of the same O_2 structure do not show the same information (because one view does not show hidden attributes in a tuple, for instance), the copy/paste will be allowed by Looks if there is internal (O_2) type consistency.

Objects can be copied, pasted, and cut when they are in a list or a set. They can also be shared. Sharing is different from copying; the *copy* operation performs an object copy (a new object is created), whereas the *share* operation manipulates the object identity.

3.3 Masks

With generic presentations, the programmer's control over the amount of visible information is limited to the depth. Also, generic presentations are completely editable. Masks provide the capability to control (1) how much information is displayed and (2) which parts of this information can be edited.

Here are some masks which can be used to control the presentation of the *ritz* object.

```
O2 type mask1
read object
        read tuple(name: write string,
                   address: read object,
                   facilities: read list(read string),
                   stars: read integer,
                   rate: private integer);
```

Basically a mask is a structure similar to the corresponding object. The various components of the mask are labeled by **private**, **read**, **write** properties: **private** means hidden, **read** means visible but not editable, and **write** means visible and editable. For instance, the attribute **rate** is hidden because it is declaredOC **private** in *mask1*. The complete object and the tuple structure cannot be pasted because they are declared **read**.

To see the content of the address, the following mask can be used.

```
O2 type Mask_Hotel
        read object
            tuple(name: string,
                  address: read object
                               tuple(street: string,
                                     city: City)
                  facilities: write list(read string));
```

In this second example, the mask forces the **address** attribute to be visible. The **private**, **read**, and **write** properties are inherited through the mask structure but can be overridden. Notice also that the **rate** attribute has disappeared, which is equivalent to declaring it **private**.

3.4 Placements

Whether a generic presentation or a mask is used, once a presentation is created it has to be displayed on the screen. The placement capability provides high-level control over screen layout. Looks provides eight layout strategies: *manual, mouse, stack, top, down, right, left*, and *coordinate*.

Two strategies, *manual* and *mouse*, let end users control the layout. The layouts *stack, top, down, right, left*, and *coordinate* position a presentation P_1 relatively to another presentation P_0, provided P_0 is already on the screen. In the following discussion, we assume that a presentation P_0 is already on the screen and that the program has to map another presentation P_1.

Manual asks the end user to perform placement P_1 interactively at run time. This is done by moving a P_1 ghost on the screen.

Mouse requires that the upper left corner of P_1 match the current position of the mouse.

Stack placement consists in placing P_1 over P_0, slightly translated downward and to the right.

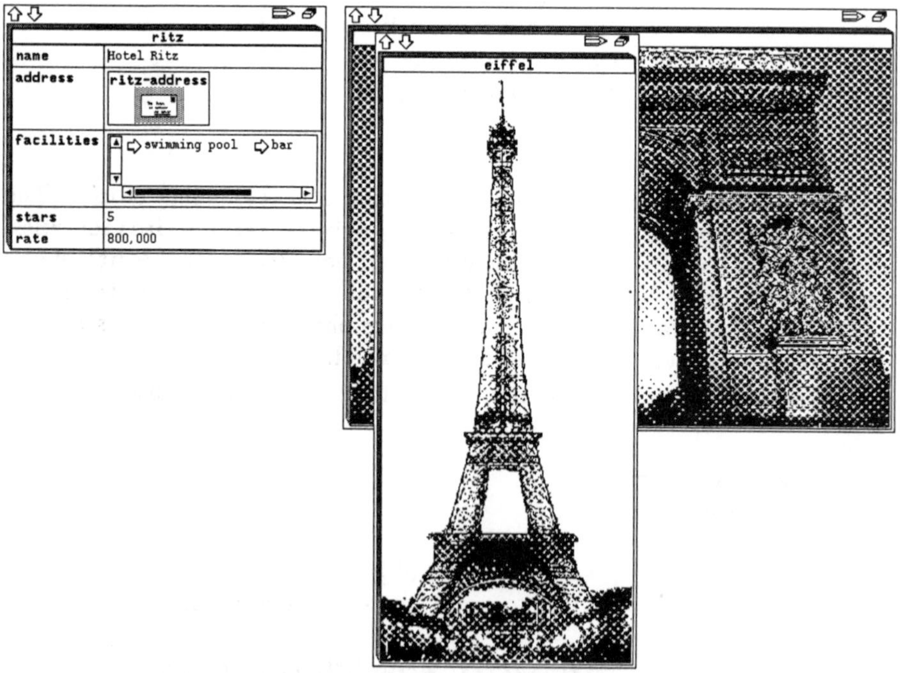

Figure 22.2. ***Right*** *and* ***stack*** *placements*

For example, in figure 22.2 the presentation of the *eiffel* object is stacked on the *arc_de_triomphe* presentation. *Top, down, right*, and *left* tile two presentations P_1 and P_0. *Down* places P_1 in the upper left corner and P_0 in the lower left corner. *Right* places P_1 in the upper left corner and P_0 in the upper right corner. *Left* places P_1 in the upper right corner and P_0 in the upper left corner. In figure 22.2 the *eiffel* presentation is to the right of the *ritz* presentation.

The *coordinate* strategy allows x and y coordinates to be explicitly defined in the program.

3.5 Modes

Modes address the problem of dialogue control. When an application is running, it is either waiting for an end-user operation (user control) or executing a method (application control). Transfer of control from the application to the user and back is a complex problem.

A method can be interrupted to get some information from the user. Later on, this method will be restarted or maybe canceled. Meanwhile, the end user is either constrained to input the required information or free to perform any other operation. Looks modes implement each of these alternatives. Assume a presentation P was created with the *mode* option. At the time P is displayed, the mode will affect the execution of the application as follows.

If mode is *wait*, the application is interrupted. Control is transferred to the end user, who is free to manipulate P as well as any other presentation. If the mode is *grab*, the application is interrupted but the end user is constrained to manipulate only P. In both cases, *wait* and *grab*, the end user restarts the method either by a *continue* or a *cancel* command. The method can then get the content of P, remove P from the screen, and give any semantics to the *continue* or *cancel* commands.

Because we are in a database environment, there is a third mode, *browse*. If P is created with the *browse* mode, displaying P will not interrupt the method. However, if later on the end user gets control, it will be possible to edit P and save it in the database without any application control.

3.6 Links

When a presentation P_0 is laid out on the screen relatively to another presentation P_1 using *top, down, right, left, stack,* or *coordinate*, a link (or a constraint) from P_0 to P_1 can be created by Looks. These links group presentations in trees, and they impact such as operations resizing, moving, removing from the screen, and saving in the database. Four kinds of link are supported: *free, geometric, content*, and *slave*. We illustrate each of them by a P_1 and P_0 example, and then generalize to a tree.

Free expresses that P_1 and P_0 are not linked. The end user is free to move, resize, erase, edit, and save P_1 and P_0 independently.

Geometric links P_0 to P_1 geometrically. Each time one of them is pushed, popped, moved, or resized, the other is pushed, popped, or moved so that the primary layout (*right, stack*, etc.) is preserved. More generally, if P_1 is part of a presentation tree, each time P_1 is moved or resized, all the tree nodes are moved in order to preserve the layout.

Content links P_0 to P_1 from the application point of view. Assume, for instance, that P_0 and P_1 were created with a *wait* mode. Each time a *continue* or a *cancel* operation is applied to P_1, the same operation is first applied automatically to P_0. More generally, when a *continue* or a *cancel* operation is performed on a presentation linked to a presentation tree, the same operation is performed, in suffix order, on the subtree issuing from the presentation.

Slave cumulates the properties of the *geometric* and *content* links.

3.7 Interactive Method Activation

Each item of an object menu corresponds to a method of the object. Looks allows the programmer to control which methods can be activated through this menu (a subset of the object methods). The item name can be different from the method name.

When an item (or a method) is selected in a menu, Looks automatically displays a presentation to collect the arguments, if there are any. Once the arguments are collected, the method is executed. At any time during argument collection, the end user can also cancel the method activation.

3.8 Specific Presentations

Generic presentations and masks allow the programmer to specify which parts of an object are visible and editable, but they do not help him or her to control the graphical aspect of the object. Furthermore, the application cannot trap user operations. For instance, one might wish to display an object as a pie chart or a bar graph. Figure 22.3 shows the same object with the generic presentation and with a specific presentation.

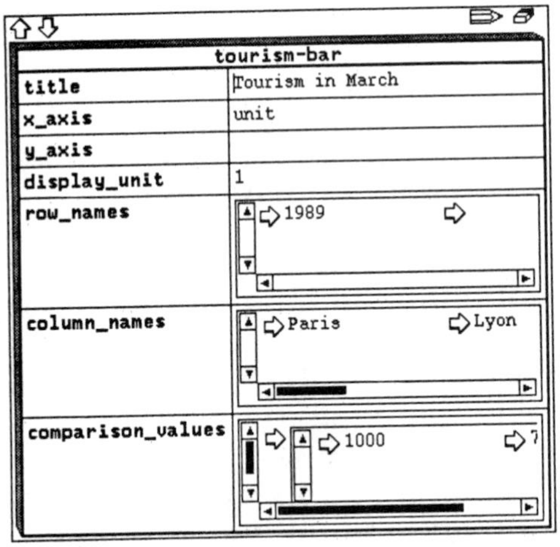

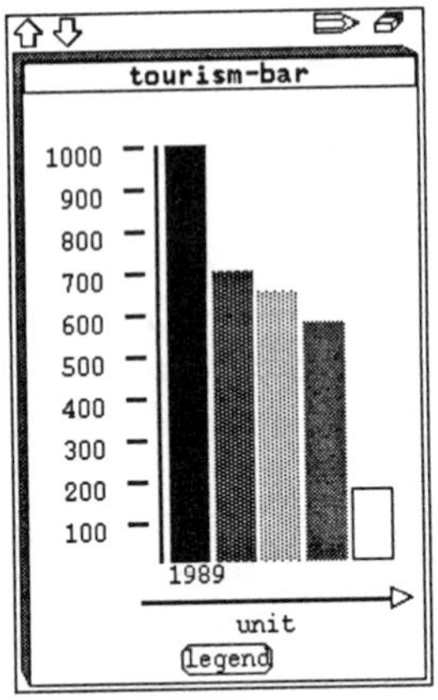

Figure 22.3. Generic and specific presentations of the same object

A specific presentation is a programming extension of Looks. When displaying an object, the application can require a specific presentation. Programming a specific presentation is similar to adding a new widget in a toolkit. The precise description of this programming process is outside the scope of this book.

4 A Programming Example

The following example illustrates the use of Looks capabilities from the programming perspective. In the example a new Hotel object is created.

hotel = **new**(Hotel);

This new Hotel object is displayed with a depth-2 generic presentation. The mode is wait; the application will be interrupted and control will be transferred to the user when the presentation is mapped on the screen.

presentation2 = **present**(hotel, generic, 2, wait);

We assume that there is a *presentation1* already on the screen; presentation2 is mapped at the right of *presentation1*. This *right* constraint will be maintained against *geometric* operations (moving *presentation1* or *presentation2*). The result will be either *continue* or *cancel*.

result = **map**(presentation2, right, presentation1, geometric);

The **map** command has interrupted the execution until the user has either canceled the creation or filled this new Hotel object with the required information. In either case, *presentation2* will be erased from the screen and removed. If the result is continue, the content of *presentation2* will be transferred to *hotel*.

if (result = continue) **consult**(presentation2, hotel);

The code should check the consistency of the data returned by the user.

unmap(presentation2); **destroy**(presentation2);

5 Conclusion

In this chapter we have described the main features of the Looks system: generic presentations, masks, placements, modes, and links. The current prototype is written in Le_Lisp (Chailloux 1986) on top of the Aïda toolkit (Devin and Duquesnoy 1988). Looks has been tested against the development of significant applications: a travel agency application (from which the examples and figures of this paper are taken) and a complete programming environment for the O_2 OODB system.

We believe the strong point of Looks is that it allows the programmer to write a reasonable user interface very quickly and without dealing directly with widgets, event queues, or other typical graphic toolkit notions. As compared to Hypercard and existing fourth-generation languages (4GLs), Looks provides additional power. The data model is richer and is extensible since one can define new classes. For each object, Looks proposes several predefined display algorithms.

Unlike most 4GLs, but like Hypercard, object presentations are graphical components which can be directly manipulated. Like most 4GLs, but unlike Hypercard, Looks is a programmer tool. The programming methodology is (1) to define the internal structures of the data manipulated by the application, and to use the generic presentations to test it; (2) to use the various tools available in Looks to refine the aspect and interactive behavior of the presentations.

We now briefly discuss the current and future improvements and evolutions. First, we are currently redesigning the external aspect and behavior of generic presentations. To do so, we are collaborating with graphic designers. Second, we plan to add an interactive presentation editor. In the current prototype, building a specific presentation (that is, changing the graphical aspect or interactive behavior of object presentations) requires programming. What we plan is an interactive tool to redraw presentations. It can be viewed as a user-interface editor specialized to deal with the problem of displaying and manipulating structures and objects. Finally, we are porting Looks on top of Motif.

References

Betts, B., D. Burlingane, G. Fisher, J. Foley, M. Green, D. Kasik, S. Kerr, D. Olsen, and J. Thomas. 1987. Goals and objectives for user interface software. *Computer Graphics* 21(2): 73.

Borning, A. 1981. The programming language aspects of thinglab, a constraint-oriented laboratory. *ACM Transactions on Programming Languages and Systems* 3(8): 353.

Cardelli, L. 1988. Building user interfaces by direct manipulation. In *Proceedings of the ACM SIGGRAPH symposium on user interface software.*

Chailloux, J. 1986. *Le-Lisp version 15.2 manuel de référence.* INRIA, Domaine de Voluceau BP 105, Rocquencourt.

Deux, O. 1989. *The story of O_2.* Altaïr Technical Report.

Devin, M., and P. Duquesnoy. 1988. *Aida version 1.2 manuel de référence.* ILOG, Gentilly.

———. 1989. *Masai version 1 manuel de référence.* ILOG Gentilly.

Goodman, D. 1987. *The complete Hypercard handbook.* Bantam Books.

Hermann, M., and R. D. Hill. 1988. *Abstration and declarativeness in user-interface development: The methodological basis of the composite object architecture.* ECIRC Technical Report.

Hullot, J. M. 1986. Sos interface. *Journées AFCET.*

Karsenty, S. 1987. *Graffiti: un outil interactif et graphique pour la construction d'interfaces homme-machine adaptables.* Ph.D. thesis, Université de Paris XI.

Lécluse, C., and P. Richard. 1989. The O_2 database programming language. In *Proceedings of the VLDB conference.*

Martin, J. 1985. *Fourth-generation languages.* Prentice-Hall.

Myers, B. A., and W. Buxton. 1986. Creating a highly-interactive and graphical user interface by demonstration. *Computer Graphics* 20(3): 249–58.

Olsen, D. R. 1986. Mike: The menu interaction kontrol environment. *ACM Transactions on Graphics* 5(4): 318.

OSF. 1989. *Motif 1.0 programmer's guide.* OSF.

Plateau, D., R. Cazalens, J. C. Mamou, and D. Tallot. 1990. Building user interfaces with the Looks hyper-object system. In *Eurographics workshop on object-oriented graphics.*

Rhyne, J., R. Ehrich, J. Bennett, T. Hewet, J. Sibert, and T. Bleser. 1987. Tools and methodology for user-interface development. *Computer Graphics* 21(2): 78.

Schmucker, K. 1986. Macapp: An application framework. *Byte* 11(8): 189–93.

Sibert, J. L., W. B. Hurley, and T. W. Bleser. 1986. An object-oriented user-interface management system. *Computer Graphics* 20(4): 259–68.

Smith, D. N. 1988. Building user interfaces interactively. In *Proceedings of the ACM SIGGRAPH symposium on user-interface software.*

CHAPTER 23

The O_2 Programming Environment

PATRICK BORRAS
ANNE DOUCET
PATRICK PFEFFER
DIDIER TALLOT

1 Introduction

A large part of the development of a database application consists of programming activity. Implementing a database application means editing and querying the schema and the data, and writing application programs. The O_2 programming environment, OOPE, is designed to facilitate this work and to reduce the development time. Therefore, it integrates the traditional database design tools with software engineering techniques and tools such as a browser, a debugger, a journal, and a test generator.

OOPE is fully object oriented. Its design was inspired by the programming environment of Smalltalk-80 (Goldberg 1983). A major concern was to provide external homogeneity. This is achieved by representing all information managed by OOPE as objects: classes, methods, programs, and applications are objects, as well as all the programming tools. The functionalities are provided by sending messages to these objects.

Another aspect of the design of OOPE is the use of graphics. Information is displayed on the screen, and user interaction is done via a graphical interface. This graphical interface is easy to understand, to use, and to remember, making OOPE a user-friendly tool. OOPE is entirely built in O_2, and all the information it handles is stored and managed using the database functionalities of O_2.

This chapter describes the design and the functionalities of OOPE. It is organized as follows. In section 2 we present the design principles of OOPE.

Section 3 explains how to program with OOPE through an example. In section 4 we compare OOPE with other programming environments. We give some perspectives on future work and improvements in section 5, and conclude with section 6.

2 Design Principles

Programming environments and software engineering environments handle a large volume of complex structured data. Most Unix programming environments use permanent or temporary files to handle this information. Furthermore, a programming environment consists of a set of different tools which communicate with each other. Such development environments require access facilities, data independence, preservation of the semantic integrity of the information, protection against failure, versioning, and support for cooperative work. Database management systems offer features in all these categories; so the use of a database system seems an obvious way to support this kind of data management. However, traditional (e.g., relational) databases have an unsuitable data model and poor performance; as explained in Didriksen, Lie, and Conradi 1986, the main reason for poor performance is the unsuitable data model. The new generation of data models, and especially the object-oriented data model, has the power to support greater modeling development. According to the definition given in Zdonik and Wegner 1985, O_2 can be considered as a database programming language because it is a language with database facilities powerful enough to describe its own environment. Therefore we have decided to build the OOPE on top of O_2 as an application.

The O_2 system stores all information as objects (Vélez, Bernard, and Darnis 1989; see chapter 15), for bootstrapping reasons. At the language level, however, classes and methods are not objects, in order to ensure static typing. The search for simplicity and uniformity led us to represent the objects used by the programmer in the same way as they are represented in the system. Classes and methods are thus represented as objects in OOPE and stored in the database. This representation is interesting for two main reasons.

First, it allows us to use the database functionalities of the O_2 system to store and manage the classes and to use O_2 methods for fast access to them. Second, the programmer can manipulate these classes and methods in the same way he or she manipulates the other database objects. This reduces the length of documentation and learning time. Following the same idea, all programming tools are represented as objects, and the data they handle is stored in the database. Thus the Journal, the Workspace, the Browser, and the O_2_Shell are objects. The O_2 Debugger is not an object in itself, but it is composed of objects. Actions are performed through methods applied to these objects.

The all-object design of the programming environment presents many advantages. First, it provides uniformity: all information is displayed and manipulated as objects, and every functionality is a method; thus the only thing the user has to know is how to manipulate objects in the system. Second, it is easily extensible: a new functionality can be added by defining a new method (or a new object with a method). Third, it provides a good integration between the various tools and functionalities provided by OOPE: information can be copied, cut, and pasted from any object to any other object. The type checking in O_2 provides verification and prevents some inappropriate manipulations.

Objects are displayed and manipulated in a uniform fashion through the Looks interface server. To standardize the behavior of the objects as much as possible, we use the generic display and editing mechanism, which allows a uniform representation of the objects and the message-passing mechanism. In order to illustrate this generic display mechanism, we define the following O_2 class.

```
class Address
      type tuple (number: integer,
                  street: string,
                  city: City,
                  zip_code: string,
                  country: Country)
```

Consider an object *o* belonging to the class Address. To display it in a generic fashion, we use the primitives **present** and **map** of Looks, as follows.

```
p = present (o, EDIT, LEVEL_ONE, NESTED_WINDOW);
map (p, SCREEN, COORDINATE, NO_PERSIST, 10, 10);
```

The primitive **present** creates a presentation for the object *o*, and **map** displays this presentation, as shown in figure 23.1 (see also chapter 22).

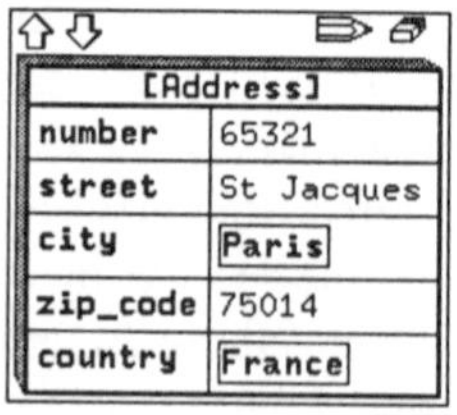

Figure 23.1. An object of the class Address

The parameters of **present** and **map** control the editability, the level of expansion, the style of display and the placement of the object.

3 Programming with OOPE

The main activities while programming an O_2 application consist of defining a schema (creating classes and method signatures) and editing, compiling, and testing the bodies of the methods. OOPE provides a set of programming tools for these activities. We first describe the available tools of OOPE, then we describe how these tools may be used to build an application.

3.1 Programming Tools

When OOPE is invoked, a window called Tools is displayed on the screen. This window contains all the programming tools represented as object icons. (see figure 23.2). A standard menu is associated with each tool. The available programming tools are the Browser, the O_2 Shell, the Workspaces, the Journal, the Query Manager, and the Applications Manager. The Debugger does not appear in the Tools window. It is automatically called when a program or a method is run in debug mode.

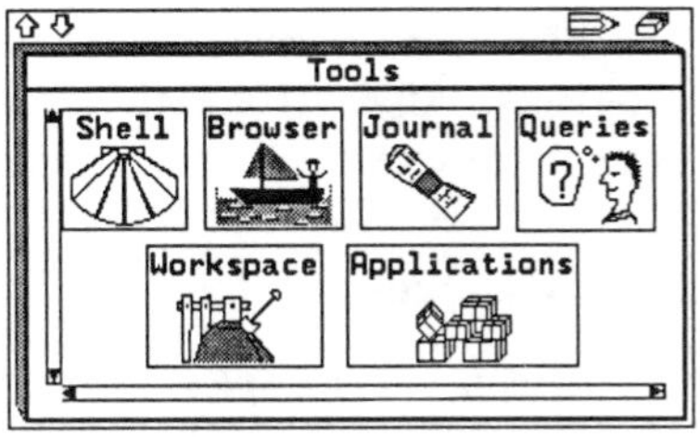

Figure 23.2. The Tools window

3.1.1 The Browser

The browser allows the user to access the objects of the database and to navigate through them. In order to display an object, the user selects the name of the object from a list. Navigation is done from a displayed object, using the browsing facility provided by Looks. In the same way, the browser can display named objects, values of named objects, and applications. The browser also allows the user to display the full class hierarchy in the form of a tree.

3.1.2 The O_2 Shell

The O_2 shell is a full-screen text editor with a direct interface to the O_2 command interpreter. It gives access to the Unix file system by allowing the reading and writing of Unix files (in order to export or import new data).

3.1.3 The Workspaces

The development of an application requires access to several classes and objects. A programmer usually needs several sessions to build a complete application, and it may take some time to retrieve all the objects and classes needed for the development of the application at the beginning of a session. The workspaces are used to store OOPE objects from one session to another, in order to save time at the beginning of a session. The workspaces are displayed in the Tools window and are immediately accessible. They can be seen as entry points to the browsing and programming activities. The programmer only has to open a workspace to retrieve his or her working data.

Being a set of objects, a workspace can contain objects of any kind: classes, methods, applications, named objects, and so on. A programmer can create as many workspaces as he or she wants, generally one for each major activity. To render a workspace persistent, it must be given a name.

3.1.4 The Journal

The journal records critical operations made on OOPE objects, their date, and an object version. Each time an object is successfully compiled, its version is stored in the journal. The objects concerned are classes, methods, programs, applications, and named objects. At any time, the programmer can retrieve a version of an object in order to restore it. Restoration is manual.

3.1.5 The Applications Manager

The Tools window contains an icon called *Applications*; this is in fact a persistent set of all applications known by the system. Using this tool, it is possible to display an existing application, to create a new one, or to run one.

3.1.6 The Query Manager

The O_2 system provides a query language (Bancilhon, Cluet, and Delobel 1989; see chapter 11) to retrieve data in the database. OOPE provides access to the query language through the query manager in the Tools window. The query manager contains a set of existing queries that can be displayed and executed. It is also possible to create and edit new queries.

3.1.7 The Debugger

Every programmer knows that bug-free programs are only achievable in Utopia; and a programming environment without a debugger is incomplete. The O_2 debugger follows the object-oriented principles of the OOPE. The debugger paradigm is the following: a program under the control of the debugger is aware of this control and will modify its internal behavior in consequence. The program itself constructs a database of O_2 objects that reflects its internal state at each step of the computation. The O_2 debugger is composed of four O_2 objects; it is fully integrated into OOPE. It behaves like any other tool and does not require the learning of a new command language.

If the programmer detects an abnormal behavior of a program, he or she may execute the program under the control of the O_2 debugger. This gives the programmer interactive control over the program's execution and over message passing, and the possibility of editing the values of variables and of executing methods and functions external to the program. The O_2 debugger supports late binding. The interested reader can find further information in Doucet and Pfeffer 1989 and 1990 (see chapter 24).

3.2 A Tour with OOPE

We propose to illustrate the use of OOPE through the example of a travel agency application. Its schema is composed of classes such as Client, City, Monument, Restaurant, and methods associated with each class.

3.2.1 Creating a New Class

Assume we wish to extend the travel agency application by creating a new class, for example, Seaside_resort as a specialization of the class City. To create a new class, we first need to display its immediate superclass. We use the browser by sending to it the ***display_class*** method (this method is an entry of the standard menu associated to the browser). Then the names of all existing classes appear on the screen in the form of a list sorted in alphabetical order (figure 23.3). Selecting the *City* item causes the display of the corresponding class.

Figure 23.3. The list of classes

A class is represented by an OOPE object with the following information: the name of the class, its type, its set of superclasses, its set of subclasses, and its set of methods (public and private). It also indicates whether the structure of the class is private or public. Additional information (such as documentation) is gathered in an **Infos** field (figure 23.4).

Now we can call up the standard menu of the class City and select the item *Add_subclass*. A template representing a new class is displayed on the screen (figure 23.5). Note that some fields have been initialized: the set of superclasses contains the class City from which the new class was built, and the type is the same as that of its superclass.

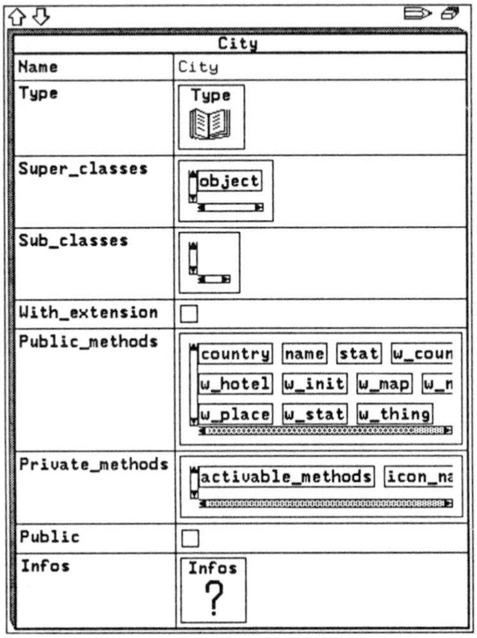

Figure 23.4. The City class

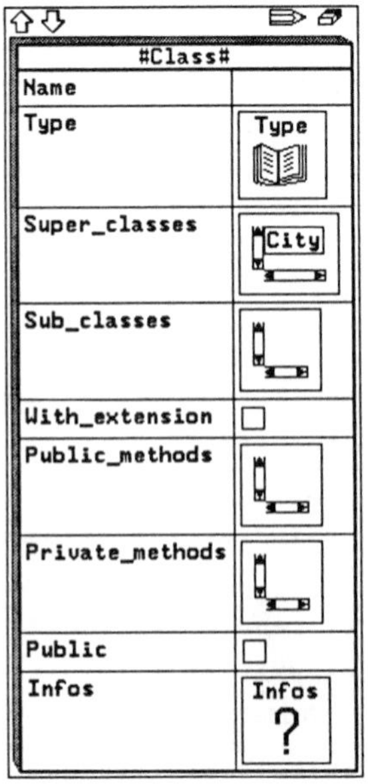

Figure 23.5. Template for a new class

The remaining fields of the template we have to fill are **Name** and **Type**. **Name** is a string; it has to be filled with the string "Seaside_resort". **Type** is a text attribute. It was initialized with the type of the class City as follows:

```
tuple(name: string,
      map: bitmap,
      hotels: set(Hotel))
```

The type of the class Seaside_resort contains all the attributes of its supertype. We add a new one, the **beaches** attribute, which gives:

```
tuple(name: string,
      map: bitmap,
      hotels: set(Hotel),
      beaches: set(tuple(name: string,
                         watching: Boolean,
                         nautic_sports: set(Sport),
                         dog_admitted: Boolean)))
```

The class is compiled by sending the *Compile* method from the standard menu of the class presentation. Then the class is created in the database schema.

3.2.2 Creating a New Method

Now assume we wish to create a method attached to the class Seaside_resort, for example, a method *beach_info* displaying the set of beaches that have lifeguards and that offer at least two water sports. To create a method, we send the message *Add_public_method* to the Seaside_resort class. (If the class is not displayed, we may use the browser to display it.) Then a template for the new method is displayed on the screen (figure 23.6).

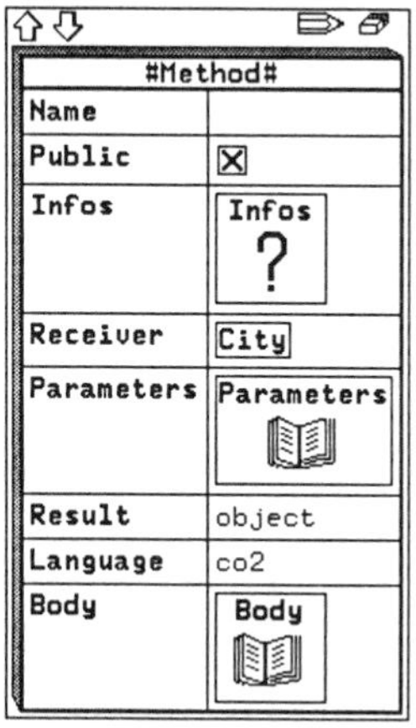

Figure 23.6. Template for a new method

A method is represented by an OOPE object with the following information: the name of the method, its parameters, the type of its result, the class to which the receiver is attached, the language in which the method is written, the body of the method, and whether the method is public or private. Additional information is grouped in an **Infos** field. Some fields have been initialized: the receiver contains the class in which the method is created, the "public" flag is set to true, the language is CO_2 (the default) and the type of the result is "object" (the default).

The fields we have to fill are **Name** and **Type**. **Name** is a string editor filled with the string "beach_info". **Body** is a text editor containing the CO_2 code of the method:

```
o2 set(tuple(name: string, water_sports: set(Sport))) result;
o2 tuple(name: string,
         watching: Boolean,
         nautic_sports: set(Sport),
         dog_admitted: Boolean) beach;
int p;

result = set();
for (beach in self->beaches)
    if ((beach.watching) || (count(beach.nautic_sports) >= 2))
      result += set(tuple(name: beach.name,
                          nautic_sports: beach.nautic_sports));

p = present (result, NO_EDIT, LEVEL_ONE, NESTED_WINDOW);
map(SCREEN, COORDINATE, NO_PERSIST, 100, 100);
```

Sending the *compile* method to the OOPE method allows the creation of the method in the database schema. If the compilation fails, an error message will be displayed in a separate window (figure 23.7).

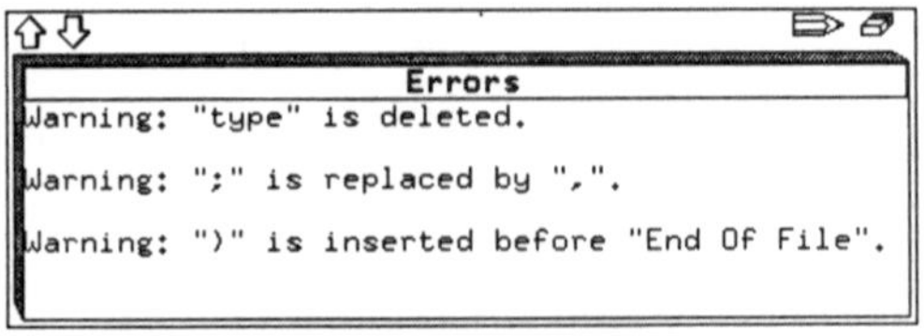

Figure 23.7. Error messages

To summarize, we have created a Seaside_resort class and a method *beach_info* belonging to that class. We may visualize the new class hierarchy using the browser (figure 23.8).

Now we would like to test the *beach_info* method. To do that, we send the message **Run_methods** to the Seaside_resort class. OOPE automatically

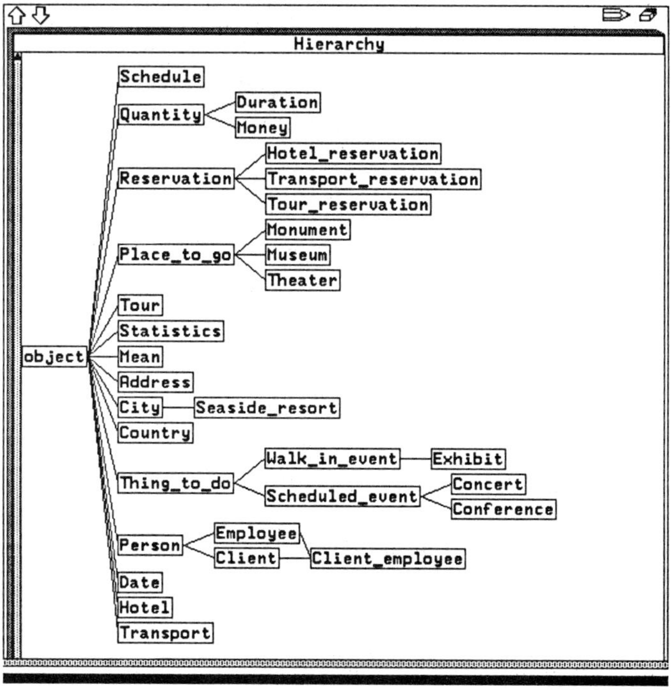

Figure 23.8. The class hierarchy

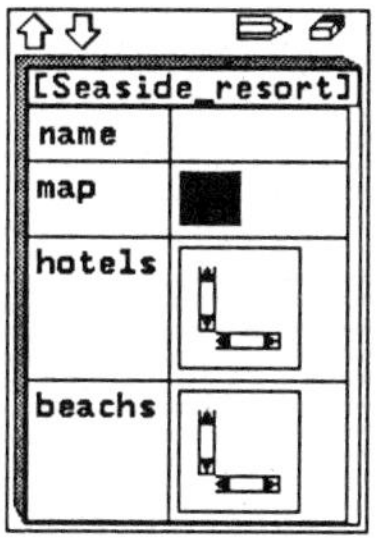

Figure 23.9. A test instance of the Seaside_resort class

creates and displays a test instance of that class (figure 23.9). The displayed instance may be edited and filled (assume we have created several Beach objects). Then we can call up the standard menu of the test instance (corresponding to all methods attached to the class Seaside_resort) and select the method we wish to execute. In our example we select the item *beach_info*, the method is executed, and the corresponding result is displayed as shown in figure 23.10.

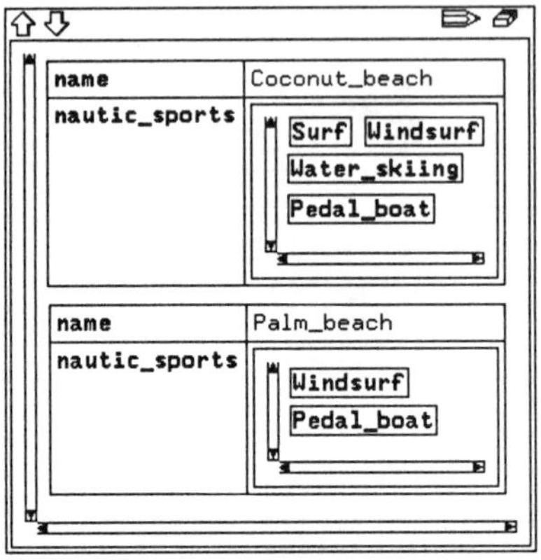

Figure 23.10. Result of the *beach_info* method

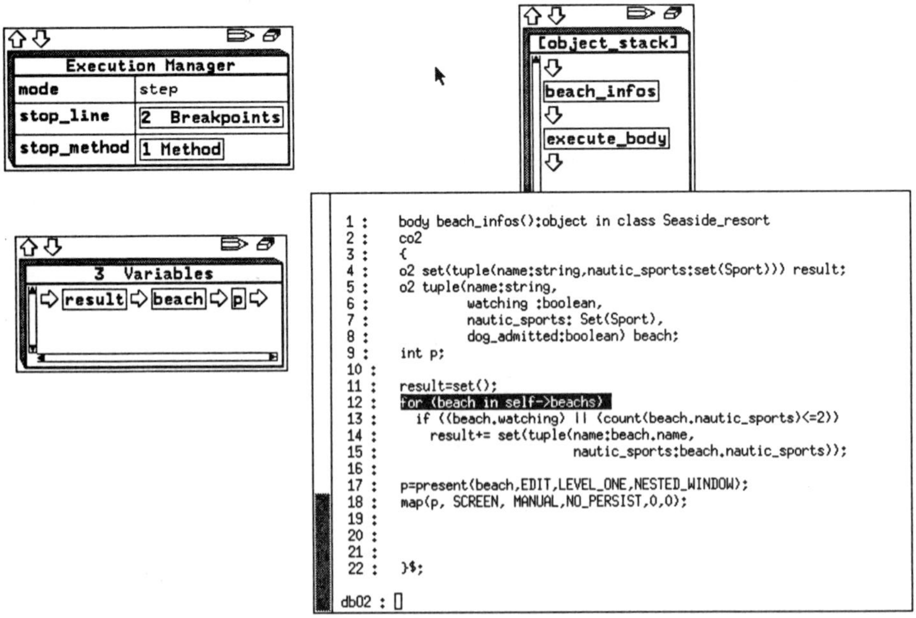

Figure 23.11. Debugger windows

Suppose the programmer has made a mistake in writing the body of the method *beach_info*, which causes an abnormal behavior. In order to localize the semantic error the programmer may run his or her program under the control of the debugger. Figure 23.11 shows a snapshot of the screen when a program is being run with the debugger. The upper left window represents the Execution Manager. This object allows the programmer to control the execution of his or her program, that is, to set and clear breakpoints on lines and methods interactively, to run the execution, and to choose an execution mode. In the window below that, the list of the variables defined in the running method are grouped as a list-structured object. By clicking on an element, the programmer can consult the value or the type structure of the corresponding variable. When the value of a variable is displayed on the screen the programmer may modify it.

The upper right window represents the object-execution Stack. It allows visualization of the sequence of messages (i.e., the execution of the program). The lower right window is a text editor. It is used to display the source code of the method. It provides a scrolling function, and line and string selection facilities. By default, the current instruction is displayed in reverse video. By executing the program instruction by instruction, the programmer will be able to discover (we hope) that he or she has typed the disjunction `||` instead of the conjunction **&&** in the **if** statement at line 13.

4 Related Work

Programming environments are essential both for programming languages and for database systems. Their functionalities are slightly different, however. Programming environments for database systems, generally called fourth-generation languages, arose later. These are ad hoc programming tools, mostly rapid ways of building carefully identified classes of small programs, such as forms systems or report generators. They are not concerned with software-engineering issues. Programming environments for traditional programming languages generally offer syntax-directed editors with many editing facilities; program verifiers; debugging tools and source-code control systems; versions managers; and configuration managers.

The main difference between these two approaches comes from the separation of data manipulation and programming languages which exists in database systems. The O_2 system provides a single language for programming and for data manipulation. Its programming environment, OOPE, merges the functionalities of the two approaches in a uniform framework. Because OODBMSs are still recent, their programming environments have received relatively little attention and are in the early stage of development. Among the existing OODBMSs Vbase (Andrews and Harris 1987), GemStone (Copeland and Maier 1984), Iris (Derrett et al. 1986), and Orion (Kim et al. 1988), only GemStone has a programming environment comparable to OOPE. It uses the one provided by Smalltalk-80 (Goldberg 1983).

Programming environments for OODBMSs such as O_2 are more related to programming environments for languages than to those for database systems; so OOPE is mostly to be compared with programming environments for object-oriented languages. Smalltalk-80 provides one of the most complete and implemented programming environments. It focuses on providing visual access to each object of the language. All information concerning an object is presented to the user via a bitmap display. Menus are used to control the accesses to objects.

Smalltalk-80's system browser (a browsing tool for classes and methods) is composed of five textual views in which items can be selected. Four of the views are fixed-list menus which contain the categories of classes of the system, the classes of a selected category, the categories of messages for a selected class, and the message selectors in the selected category. The fifth view is a text editor in which methods and classes can be defined and modified. Unlike in O_2, there is no way to display graphically the class hierarchy. Syntax-compiling errors are displayed in reverse video, and possible corrections are proposed.

Other object-oriented programming languages such as C++ (Stroustrup 1986) and Objective-C (Cox 1986) inherit from C a very efficient programming environment, mainly concerned with system building (Make, Sun 1988a) and version management (SCCS, Sun 1988b.) In general, these environments do not reflect the object-oriented features of the language. Browsing tools have a very poor performance in terms of functionalities and speed, because they are based on scanning Unix files. Debugging tools are based on DBX, which was designed for C; and most of the extensions are ad hoc solutions, except the one chosen by Sun Microsystems (Chang, Landauer, and Zhang 1989). Recently, new programming environments for C++ have been developed: ObjectWorks (ParcPlace 1989) and ET++ (Weinand, Gamma, and Marty 1989). They provide features equivalent to those of OOPE, but they do not use the possibilities of the language to manage the classes and the methods. This is mainly because C++ does not support persistence.

5 Implementation Choices and Future Improvements

The source code of OOPE is composed of 15,000 lines of CO_2 code. The current implementation of OOPE consists of 75 classes and 320 methods (we do not count the inherited methods).

OOPE represents a quite complex O_2 application. Its success in terms of functionalities and performance validates our implementation choices, as well as the use of the O_2 system as the support for a programming development tool. Our experience with the first implementation and the reactions of the O_2 developers pointed out the following problem. Using generic editors to display different information is a gain in terms of learning time, but it generates a very clicky user interface. We have decided to redefine the way the information is shown to the programmer.

New functionalities, such as the support of integrity constraints, method invariants, preconditions, and postconditions, are currently under implementation on the top of the internal layer of the O_2 debugger. We plan to introduce a test-generation tool and a versioning system for the objects, methods, and classes.

6 Conclusion

This chapter describes OOPE, the O_2 programming environment, which provides all the basic programming tools for developing small applications using an OODB: editing and compiling facilities, a browser, and a debugger. A set of goodies (the O_2 Shell, the Journal, the Workspace, and the graphical hierarchy display) improves the programmer's productivity and facilitates his or her work.

OOPE is easy to use and to understand, due to its homogeneity (all information is represented in a similar way, all functions are performed the same way), and due to its graphical interface, which allows simple manipulations of objects on the screen and avoids the need to learn a language. It is used inside the Altaïr group, and is in beta-test (with the entire prototype) in several French industries.

OOPE is entirely built in O_2. It is written in CO_2 and uses the database functionalities to manage the information it handles. OOPE combines the functionalities of programming environments for traditional languages and for database systems. It is one of the few existing programming environments for OODBMSs.

7 Acknowledgements

We thank Jean-Claude Mamou for helpful discussions during the design of OOPE and M. Atkinson, C. Delobel, C. Lécluse, and D. Plateau for their careful reading of the paper and their helpful comments.

References

Andrews, T., and C. Harris. 1987. Combining language and database advances in an object-oriented development environment. In *Proceedings of the OOPSLA conference.*

Bancilhon, F., S. Cluet, and C. Delobel. 1989. A query language for object-oriented database system. In *Proceedings of the second workshop on database programming languages.* Morgan Kaufmann.

Chang, L., D. Landauer, and Z. Zhang. 1989. Engineering C++ for multi-language programming. In *Proceedings of the first international conference on technology of object-oriented languages and systems.*

Copeland G., and D. Maier. 1984. Making Smalltalk a database system. In *Proceedings of the ACM SIGMOD conference.*

Cazalens, R., J. C. Mamou, D. Plateau, and B. Poyet. 1989. *Building user interface with the Looks hyper-object system.* Altaïr Technical Report.

Cox, B. J. 1986. *Object oriented programming: An evolutionary approach.* Addison-Wesley.

Derrett, N. P., D. H. Fishman, W. Kent, P. Lynbaek, and T. A. Ryan. 1986. An object-oriented approach to data management. In *Proceedings of the Compcon 81 IEEE conference.*

Didriksen, T., A. Lie, and R. Conradi. 1986. IDL as a data description language for a programming environment database. In *Lecture notes in computer science: Advanced programming environment.* Springer-Verlag.

Doucet, A., and P. Pfeffer. 1989. A debugger for O_2, an object-oriented language. In *Proceedings of the first international conference on technology of object-oriented languages and systems.*

______. 1990. Using a database system to implement a debugger. In *IFIP working conference on database semantics.* North-Holland.

Goldberg, A. 1983. *Smalltalk-80: The interactive programming environment.* Addison-Wesley.

Kim, W., J. Banerjee, H-T. Chou, J. F. Garza, and D. Woelk. 1988. Composite object support in an object-oriented database system. In *Proceedings of the ACM SIGMOD conference.*

ParcPlace. 1989. *Objectworks for C++.* ParcPlace System, Mountain View, Calif.

Stroustrup, B. 1986. *The C++ programming language.* Addison-Wesley.

Sun. 1988a. *Make.* Sun Microsystems.

______. 1988b. *Source code control system.* Sun Microsystems.

Vélez, F., G. Bernard, and V. Darnis. 1989. The O_2 object manager: An overview. In *Proceedings of the international VLDB conference.*

Weinand, A., E. Gamma, and R. Marty. 1989. Design and implementation of ET++, a seamless object-oriented application framework. In *Structured programming.* Springer-Verlag.

Zdonik, S. B., and P. Wegner. 1985. *A database approach to languages, libraries and environments.* Persistent programming research report no. 16, University of St. Andrews.

CHAPTER 24

Using a Database System to Implement a Debugger

ANNE DOUCET
PATRICK PFEFFER

1 Introduction

Building a debugger in a compiling environment implies the management of a symbol table. This, in turn, induces a lot of problems, such as a dramatic increase in the size of the object file, and time-consuming loading of the symbol table before the execution of the program. In most implementations, the management of this information is done by means of a file system. Thus, using a database to manage such a large amount of data seems natural. This paper describes the implementation of the O_2 debugger, which follows this idea.

The O_2 debugger is implemented in CO_2. All information managed by the symbol table is represented by O_2 objects, called *symbol databases*, which are stored in the database. This design allows the use of all the functionalities provided by the O_2 system, such as easy retrieval, querying, and versioning. It also improves performance, because it decreases considerably the time required for access to the symbol information.

This paper is organized as follows. Section 2 explains the process of compiling CO_2 code in debug mode. Section 3 presents the O_2 debugger in general and explains how information is managed. The two following sections describe how the O_2 debugger uses the database to manage its information: section 4 details the structure and the management of the symbol data base, and section 5 describes memory management during a debugging session. In section 6 we show how our design improves the performance of the debugger, in terms of time, space, and functionalities. In section 7 we compare our debugger with other debuggers having a similar design, and we conclude in section 8.

2 The Compiling Process

The debugger is tightly coupled with the compiler and the programming language. As the two languages (CO_2 and BasicO_2) provided by the O_2 system have a similar compiling process and a similar behavior in general, we discuss only CO_2.

The CO_2 compiler is a precompiler that analyses both O_2 and C expressions. The CO_2 compiler checks that all referenced classes and objects are valid and type-checks every O_2 expression. The precompiler analyses the C source code, and compilation errors never appear during the C compilation phase. The precompiler generates ANSI C code. Any C compiler can be used because it is only used to generate assembly code. In the current version of the O_2 system, we use the C compiler of the GNU Software Foundation (Stallman 1989). When a method or a program is compiled with the debug option, the generated C code is slightly different, and the CO_2 compiler creates a symbol database which is stored in the database. Figure 24.1 shows the compiling process in debug mode of a piece of CO_2 code.

3 The O_2 Debugger

3.1 Information Managed by Debuggers

We briefly present in this subsection the way that traditional debuggers support debugging in a compiling environment. During the compiling phase, a lot of information is computed to allow (among other things) type checking of variables and to define the scope of the variables. After the first stage of the compiling phase, the code generator generates assembly code, and all the previously computed information, not useful any more, is lost. When compilation is done with the debug option, this information persists and is stored in the object file. This information is in general gathered in a symbol table.

The symbol table consists of records and is inserted into the relocatable object file. Usually, each record contains three attributes: the symbol name, the symbol type, and the symbol address or value. Nesting in the symbol table is indicated by begin and end records bracketing the nested symbol. The mapping between program counter values and listing line numbers is given by the symbol-table record; this allows the debugger to convert the line numbers to program addresses and vice versa.

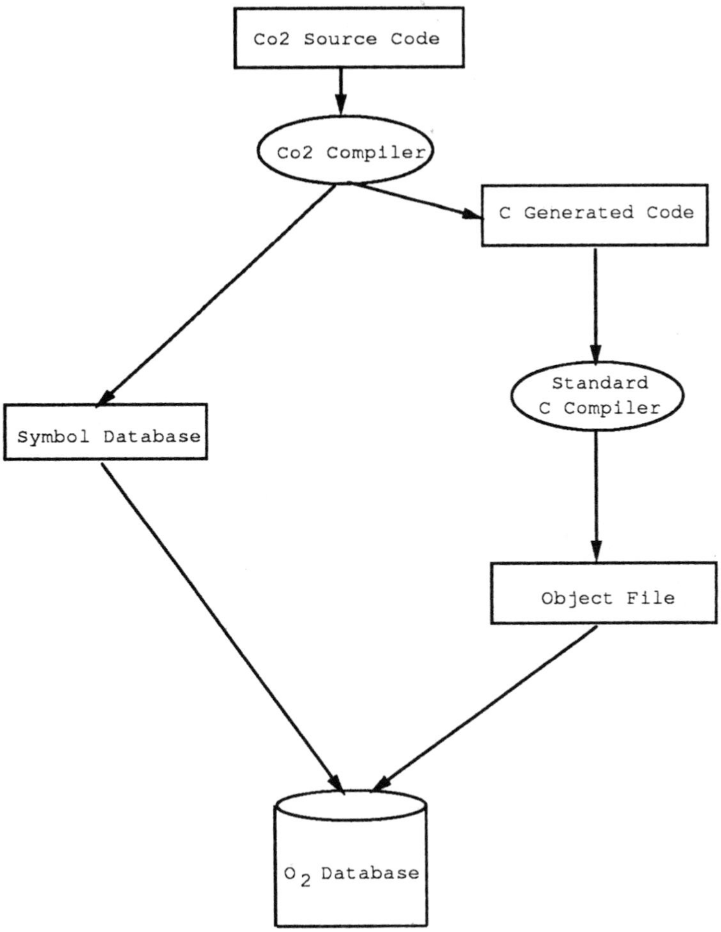

Figure 24.1. The compiling process in debug mode

The symbol tables are designed to be very compact and relatively easy for compilers to generate. The price for this compactness is poor performance access, since a linear scan or a hashing of the symbol table are the only ways to consult symbols. Recorded in the symbol table, besides the information of the records, is information on the parse tree of the program, the correspondence between nodes of the parse tree, and the executable code. In fact, the information a debugger needs is highly complex; and when organized in a flat and unnested data structure, it becomes very cryptic. We show in sections 4 and 5 the choices we made in using the O_2 object-oriented database system to store the information needed by a symbolic debugger.

3.2 The O_2 Debugger Architecture

The O_2 debugger is a symbolic debugger, written in CO_2, that supports multiple programming languages and makes intensive use of the expressive power of graphics. Its components are O_2 objects, and its functionalities are provided by methods attached to these objects. The four major objects composing the O_2 debugger are the Execution Manager, the set of symbol databases, the object-execution stack, and the Editor.

The *Execution Manager*, which allows the programmer to control the execution of a program—that is, to interactively set and clear breakpoints on lines and methods, to display the list of breakpoints, to start the execution, to choose an execution mode (line by line or step by step), and to control message passing.

The *symbol data bases* contain information about the variables declared in each method, such as their type and value and the block in which they are defined.

The *object-execution stack* is a stack of symbol databases. It is created and managed during the execution of the program. It allows visualisation of the sequence of messages and to display the information about variables and the source of a method. The elements of the object-execution stack can be examined by the programmer by opening the symbol database of the stack.

The *Editor* is used to display the source code of a method while debugging.

In this chapter we focus on the symbol database and on the object-execution stack, which make full use of the O_2 database. Further explanation on the design and the functionalities of the O_2 debugger is given in Doucet and Pfeffer 1989; in that paper we explain the debugger architecture in detail, focusing on breakpoint management and user-interface aspects.

3.3 The O_2 Debugger Paradigm

The O_2 system provides two modes for running an application: development mode and execution mode. Development mode can be used with or without debugging mode. In debugging mode, the programmer can control the program execution. A program under the control of the debugger is aware of this control and will modify its internal behavior accordingly. The program itself constructs a database that reflects its internal state at each step of the computation. This database can be consulted by the programmer, and modifications on it have side effects on the running program. For instance, if a variable is dynamically modified by the programmer during the execution of a program (at a breakpoint), the program will continue its execution with the new value instead of the old one.

Invalid data modifications are disallowed by the encapsulation. The only way to modify a variable of a running program is to use the methods defined for the corresponding class. We believe that encapsulation should, in principle, never be broken, even during a debugging session. However, debugging a program is a very special situation, where anything that could be helpful to find a bug should be allowed. Therefore the programmer is allowed to break the encapsulation in special cases.

4 The Symbol Database

4.1 Fine Granularity

Symbol tables contain all information relative to the variables and the function calls of a program, such as the type, the scope, the names of variables, and parameters. In most traditional debuggers, all this information is gathered in a single symbol table. In the O_2 system, classes and methods are represented as objects. Their creation, update, and retrieval are managed by the Class and Method Manager, which also manages the relationships between the symbols of the various methods. This representation allows a method to be taken as a symbol-table granularity. Instead of keeping only one symbol table, we decided to gather this information in a symbol database. An O_2 symbol table contains only information concerning the local variables and the parameters of a single method. Each time a method is compiled in debug mode, a new symbol table is added to the symbol database. When a variable is defined in a method, the compiler puts its class name in the symbol database. No additional work is needed at the linking stage. Uniqueness is provided by the fact that there is a single name space for classes.

This fine granularity allows efficient management of the memory space during the execution of a program, and it is also useful in the support of incremental loading.

4.2 Creation of a Symbol Database

Most of the data stored in a symbol database is computed during the first stages of the compilation, even if the debug option is off. When in debug mode, an O_2 symbol database is created, at the last stage of the compilation. Some additional information (such as the scope of variables, or the line and column number in the source code where the variables are declared) is computed and stored for debugging purposes only. Once a symbol database is created, it is stored as a regular O_2 object and thus becomes persistent.

4.3 Structure of a Symbol Database

The O_2 definition of the Symbol_ database class is given in figure 24.2. The class has the following attributes.

- `method_name`: the name of the corresponding method.
- `class_name`: the name of the class where the method has been defined.

- **blocks**: a tree of variable-scope blocks. This attribute is further explained in section 4.3.1.
- **declaration**: a list of the parameters and the local variables defined in the corresponding method.
- **block_nb**: the current block number in the tree of blocks. This information is dynamic and is therefore set at execution time.
- **line_nb**: the current line number in the source code. This information also is dynamic.
- **break_line**: a list of lines where the programmer has set breakpoints.

```
add class Symbol_database type tuple(
                    method_name: string;
                    class_name: string;
                    blocks: block_tree;
                    declaration: Table_declaration;
                    block_nb: integer;
                    line_nb: integer;
                    break_line: list(integer)
                   );
```

Figure 24.2. Definition of the class Symbol_database

Figure 24.3 and table 24.1 show a CO_2 method, *store*, with the scope of its local variables. This method is not complete; we show it to explain how the debugger deals with variable homonymy in a method. The variables *paris* and *team* are used in several blocks with different types (see table 24.1).

Table 24.1. Scope Rules for the Local Variables of Method *store*

Variable	Type or Class	Block Scope
paris	City	B1 – (B2 + B3)
	int	B2
	set(Street)	B3 – B4
	long	B4
team	set(Person)	B1 – B3
	char	B3

The next two subsections explain the attributes **blocks** and **declaration** in detail. The other attributes are self-explanatory.

```
body store() in class City;
co2
{
|   o2 City paris;
|   o2 set(Person) team;
|      ...
|
|   {
|   |  int paris;
|   |  ...
|   B2
|   |
|   }
|      ...
B1 {
|   |  o2 set(Street) paris;
|   |  char team;
|   |  ...
|   B3  {
|   |   |  long paris;
|   |   B4 ...
|   |   |
|   |   }
|   }
}
```

Figure 24.3. A method and its scope blocks

4.3.1 Dealing with the Scope of Variables

In languages such as CO_2, where nested blocks and variable homonyms are supported, a working algorithm to define the scope of a variable is very useful (particularly for dynamic binding, as explained in section 5.1.1). We present in this subsection the O_2 data structures Block_tree and Block that we use to deal with it. The same result could be obtained using a formal approach such as abstract grammars. Figure 24.4 shows the class definition of classes Block_tree and Block.

An object of class Block_tree is a list of objects of class Block. The class Block is a tuple-structured object. The attributes `block_nb`, `father`, `child1`, and `brother1` are used to define a tree organization in a one-dimensional data structure. The attributes `first_declaration` and `nb_declaration` assign a variable declaration to a set of blocks. The attributes `left_line`, `left_column`,

```
add class Block_tree type list(Block);
add class Block type tuple(
                        block_nb: integer,
                        father: integer,
                        child1: integer,
                        brother1: integer,
                        first_declaration: integer,
                        nb_declaration: integer,
                        left_line: integer,
                        left_column: integer,
                        right_line: integer,
                        right_column: integer
                        );
```

Figure 24.4. Definitions of the Block_tree and Block classes

right_line, and **right_column** define the size of the block. This information is used by the user-interface layer to display in reverse video the scope area of a variable.

4.3.2 The Table of Declarations

A list of symbols appearing as parameters and local variables is associated with each method. These symbols are gathered in the table of declarations, which is a list-structured object of class Var_info. Figure 24.5 shows the O_2 declarations of the classes Table_declaration and Var_info.

```
add class Table_declaration type list(Var_info);
add class Var_info type tuple(
                        name: string,
                        tid: co2_type,
                        block: integer,
                        line: integer,
                        column: integer,
                        ptvalue: integer
                        );
```

Figure 24.5. Definitions of the Table_declaration and Var_info classes

The attribute **tid** is a complex structured value which indicates the type structure of the variable. The **block**, **line**, and **column** attributes indicate the block number in the tree of blocks, and the line and the column number in the method where the variable is defined. The **ptvalue** attribute allows the debugger to retrieve from the process stack the value of the variable **name**. This attribute is instantiated at execution time; the O_2 debugger records in it the address of the variable **name** on the process-execution stack.

Figure 24.6 shows the symbol database for the method *scope*, the list of symbols, and the values of two blocks of the block tree.

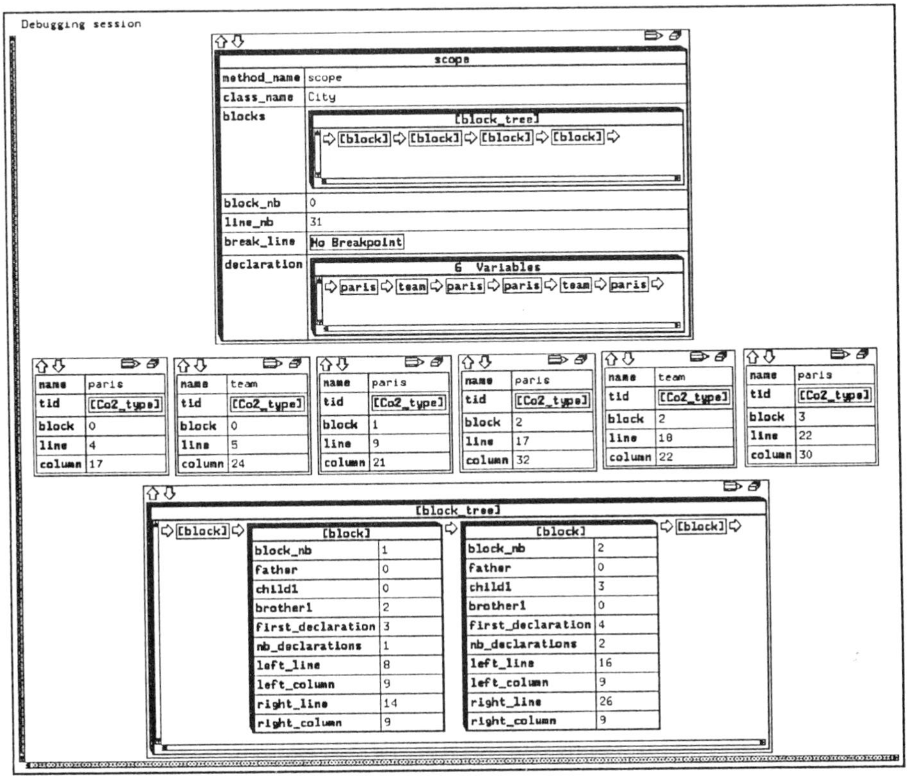

Figure 24.6. Symbol database, list of symbols, and two blocks of method *scope*

5 Database Management during the Debugger Process

In the previous sections, we have detailed the organization of the symbol database. In this section, we present two very important features of the management of the memory performed by the O_2 debugger when a process is under its control. We first explain how the dynamic binding is done, then we detail the management of the execution stack.

5.1 Dynamic Binding

5.1.1 The Lexical Scope

In CO_2 the scope-of-declaration rule is lexical, and it is not possible to define nested methods (in contrast to Pascal, where nested functions are allowed). As explained in Aho, Sethi, and Ullman 1986, there is a function named *environment* which maps a symbol name to a storage location, and a function named *state* which maps a storage location to the value held there. The *environment* function is static inside the scope of a block. On the other hand, an assignment changes the *state*. The O_2 debugger does not make any assumption about the *state*; the update of this function is supported by the standard assembly code. The storage location attached to a name is defined after the list of declarations in each block. In debug mode, the value of the function *environment* for each parameter or variable declared in the block is recorded in the attribute `ptvalue` of the corresponding symbol. In CO_2, this is done through the generation of a special C code. Table 24.2 shows an example of the C code generated to deal with dynamic binding.

Table 24.2. Code Generated to Achieve Dynamic Binding

CO_2 Code	C Generated Code
{	{
int i;	**Int** i;
o2 City paris;	**Oid** paris;
o2 tuple(name: string, age: int) p;	**Oid** p;
...	debug_set_address(1,&i);
}	debug_set_address(2,&paris);
	debug_set_address(3,&p);
	}...

The first parameter of the function *debug_set_address* indexes the current symbol name inside the declaration table. The use of this index, computed at compile time, allows a direct access to the attribute `ptvalue` and makes the *environment* function (i.e., *debug_set_address*) optimal. As we can see in this example, the O_2 debugger records for each variable the address of the *environment* function performed internally by the C compiler. This address is static throughout the lifetime of the declaration. It is sufficient to display the value of the variable associated with its type.

5.1.2 Parameter Passing

In C, parameter passing is achieved by *call-by-value*. This means that parameters are not affected after the execution of functions. In CO_2, parameters are also passed by value, except for O_2 objects, which are passed by reference. In fact, the notion of identity exists in O_2. At the CO_2 language level, as well as at the level of the O_2 system, objects are recognized by their identity. Object identifiers are named oids in our system. So, in CO_2, both *call-by-value* and *call-by-reference* parameter passing coexist.

Conventional C programmers simulate a *call-by-reference* parameter passing with the use of variable addresses. The C compiler makes a copy of each parameter, and the use of an oid is easily understandable because an oid requires 8 bytes memory and may reference an object of several kilobytes or megabytes. So the copy time (and the copy size) is crucial. In CO_2 these two modes of parameter passing are supported by the *call-by-value* mode of the C compiler.

The presence of a copy of the parameter allows the O_2 debugger to perform several modifications of variable values. For example, it allows a *call-by-reference* behavior for some C parameters. The greatest advantage of this approach is a common treatment for parameters and local variables, which are both used in a similar manner in the primitive **debug_set_address**.

5.2 Management of the Execution Stack

The O_2 debugger manages memory dynamically for debugging purposes. This management includes three major processing steps.

1. The O_2 debugger loads in central memory only the symbol database of the running methods, and when the execution is completed the symbol database is garbaged out of the memory.

2. There is no dummy copy of the symbol database or of the variables of the running methods. Only the dynamic information is copied into central memory, that is, the attributes `declaration`, `block_nb`, `line_nb`, and `break_line`. Static information such as the tree of blocks is only consulted upon special request by the programmer. Such a request will concern essentially the scope of variables. Furthermore, there is no copy of variables, as explained in section 5.1; only a link to the value is recorded.

3. All the information concerning the program state is stored in an O_2 object named the object-execution stack. This object is list structured and is managed as a stack. When a method is called, a selective copy of its symbol database is pushed into the object-execution stack. When the method execution is completed, all the previously pushed information is popped from the stack and garbaged from the central memory.

6 Evaluation of Gains

6.1 Performance Gain

The architecture we chose for the O_2 debugger, and particularly the use of the O_2 database system to store the information, provides a noticeable performance gain. As students in the relational database course, we were given the following rule about physical organization: the selection (i.e., the relational operator) should take a time proportional to the number of retrieved tuples rather than to the size of the initial relation. We consistently use this rule for the O_2 physical data organization; B-tree structures are used to store objects. The O_2 debugger only looks for the symbols it needs. The response time is thus proportional to the size of the retrieved data, and not to the size of the program.

The reading time of the symbol database is significantly reduced with the use of the O_2 debugger. Debuggers such as DBX (Adams and Muchnick 1986) and GDB (Stallman 1986) take 1 minute 45 seconds to read the symbols of the O_2 prototype on a Sun 3/60 with 12 megabytes of RAM. The O_2 debugger reads the information from the symbol database only when the programmer requires to see it, that is, when more information about a method is needed. The response time is always one order of magnitude shorter than a human interaction, for several reasons.

First, in contrast with most debuggers, in O_2 information is not gathered in a unique symbol database but distributed into many small symbol databases (one per method). A consequence of this design is that only the necessary symbols are read; the time needed to read a symbol database is thus very small.

Second, in debug mode only one primitive, **debug_set_address**, is activated to make the link between the variables and their values. The **debug_set_address** is optimal. The time taken to link a symbol with its value is equal to the time to perform a C function call, consult the symbol database, and update the attribute `pt_value`. For a method with 12 symbols (variables and parameters), the overhead is less than 2 milliseconds.

Third, detecting if a breakpoint has been set on a given line takes less time with our debugger than with traditional debuggers. The Execution Manager is also an O_2 object; among other information, it contains a list of breakpoints. A program running in debug mode consults the value of the Execution Manager, after each instruction, in order to determine its behavior. The cost of the breakpoint localization is thus proportional to the access time of an object in main memory.

6.2 Space Gain

One of the main problems encountered with debuggers is the size of the symbol database, which dramatically increases the executable file. Beander 1983 explains that an executable file for a large Bliss program can easily become six to eight times larger when the program is compiled with the debug option.

The size of a program compiled with the option *-gg* of GCC, the C GNU compiler (Stallman 1989), decreases from 5 megabytes to 1 megabyte when it is compiled without it. Furthermore, the use of a conventional Unix debugger such as DBX (Adams and Muchnick 1986), GDB (Stallman 1986), or UPS (Bovey 1987) implies activation of a fork, and thus a complete duplication of the process size. (In most cases the **vfork** Unix primitive is used. This primitive does not make a full copy of the address space of the debugger process.) Here is a further illustration. The size of our version of the GDB debugger is 2 megabytes; the size of the current O_2 prototype system is 5 megabytes. When the O_2 system is running under the control of GDB, the resulting process grows to approximately 14 megabytes. This huge need for space requires a large hardware configuration. On the other hand, the O_2 debugger demands a minimal increase in process size. The compilation with the O_2 debug option increases the amount of object code by a factor of 1.2. Furthermore, the O_2 debugger does not need either a fork or a process duplication.

6.3 Functionality Gain

The major functionality improvements of the O_2 debugger are user friendliness, support for dynamic loading, and extensibility.

6.3.1 User Friendliness

The O_2 debugger makes extensive use of all the object-oriented features of the O_2 language and system. Its integration into the programming environment (Borras et al. 1990; see chapter 23) is complete. It doesn't need any command language and is very easy to learn. As all interactions between the programmer and the program under the control of the debugger are done through the editing of objects, we can say that debugging with the O_2 debugger is like browsing through a database representing the current state of the execution.

6.3.2 Support for Dynamic Loading

The O_2 debugger supports programs loaded dynamically. This support is ensured by the granularity of the symbol database and by the dynamic management, between the central memory and the O_2 database, of the symbol databases of individual methods.

6.3.3 Extensibility

The O_2 debugger has been built as a set of classes (Symbol Database, Object-Execution Stack, and so on) and methods. It is possible to specialize classes and to define new methods. The O_2 debugger is therefore extensible, and its customization language is CO_2, BasicO_2, or both.

7 Related Work

In this section we focus on three projects similar to ours in term of static and dynamic memory management. The first project is that of the Swat debugger, which attempts to construct a multilanguage debugger. The other two projects use a database to manage the information used by a debugger.

7.1 A Similar Symbol Table Organization

The Swat Debugger (Cardell 1983) is a special-purpose tool to debug programs written in several languages. It has a symbol-table structure similar to that of our debugger. The structure of the symbol table is hierarchical, with program blocks serving as nodes in a tree. Each module (i.e., each function or procedure) may be viewed as a hierarchy and the entire program as the complete hierarchy. The linker processes the module hierarchies (or subtrees) and builds them into the complete hierarchy or symbol table. This is accomplished by simply accumulating all the symbolic information and building linkage information at the topmost level. Within each module, there may be one or more blocks. Depending on the source language, these blocks may or may not be hierarchically related.

The Swat debugger supports languages such as Fortran, C, and Pascal. These three languages have different program structures: Fortran has no block structure; C has a nested one; and Pascal has a complicated structure of nested blocks inside nested procedures. In order to deal with these different cases, in the Swat debugger each block node contains a number of links which allow the nodes to be organized into a tree. The symbolic information is ordered within the program by block; each block contains a pointer to the symbolic information gathered in a symbol node. The symbol nodes are organized as simple lists, and each symbol node has the attributes type, size, shape, storage, and address. This organization becomes complex where the language designer has improved the symbol-node structure to support user-defined types. So language-specific extensions to the symbol node were defined.

The need to support multilanguage programs led the designer of the Swat debugger to define a modular and hierarchical data structure for the symbol table. Furthermore, a special store manager was implemented for these symbol-table structures.

The main difference from the O_2 debugger is that the Swat debugger does not support the debugging of programs written in a mixture of languages. That is, the Swat environment supports programs each written in several languages but not programs or data structures in mixed languages. The multilanguage granularity for the Swat environment is therefore at the level of a module. This means that in the Swat symbol tables only the modules are labeled with the corresponding programming language, and the symbols for this module are then managed appropriately for that programming language. In O_2 all the symbols are labeled with their programming-language origin.

Another advantage of the O_2 debugger is that, unlike Swat, it is not necessary to read in the whole structure of the symbol tables before the program begins. Also, O_2 has a garbage procedure unused symbols; the SWAT debugger has no comparable procedure.

7.2 Debuggers That Use a Database

7.2.1 The Provide project

The use of a database for the postmortem debugging of programs can be found in Provide (Moher 1988). At each step of the computation, Provide stores the current state (frame) of the program in a database. Then, when the execution of the program is completed, Provide allows the programmer to use a graphical query language to browse through the different steps of the program. This is helpful in simulating simple forward and reverse execution, where series of frames are accessed by simple count-ups or count-downs, analogous to single-step execution. This atypical, but very interesting, feature is currently not supported by the O_2 debugger. We think that the possibility of postmortem debugging might be useful in database programming; but in a complete programming language such as O_2, a systematic storage of the different internal states of the program would be too expensive. (Provide is able to debug only Provide-C, a very small subset of C.) A possible solution would be to store the first state and then to store only the changes.

7.2.2 The Omega project

The Omega programming system (Powell and Linton 1983b) was an attempt to store all program information (parse tree, symbol table, version history, configuration description, etc.) in a relational database system. Debugging a program in this environment is the same as editing (Powell and Linton 1983a); the user examines and modifies data in the database. The program database contains the same type of data that a traditional compiler builds into a symbol table and a program tree. Each object class in the database is associated with a relation. For example, the following relations are mentioned by the debugger:

procedure(name, parameters, statements)
statements(class, value)
variables(name, type, value)

To support such relations, the relational database has several extensions, such as the support of lists of objects and of recursive data structures. The key idea for debugging is to incorporate program-state information within the database so that it can be manipulated with the same operations used for static information. The dynamic information, as in the O_2 debugger, is not stored in the database but is only accessible as if it were. The command language is Quel-like and is quite verbose. To express events that refer to locations in the program, a relation named Active-procedure contains at any time a tuple for each active procedure. This relation is not permanently stored in the database but computed by the debugger.

The design foundation of the Omega debugger is very similar to that of the O_2 debugger. The main difference resides in the data model of the underlying database. The modeling power of the relational database used in the Omega project does not fit well the complex data structure that a debugger needs. In fact, the attribute *value* of a tuple in the relation Variables is a pointer to the value of the variable *name*, which is not defined in the value-oriented relational data model. In the O_2 system, the variables of the program and the information of the database are of the same nature.

The design and implementation progression of the Omega debugger was the first to define an alphanumeric user interface, based on a query language. In O_2 we have used all the graphical editing facilities offered by Looks, and thus the O_2 debugger is only available through the OOPE graphical user interface.

8 Conclusion and Future Work

In this chapter we have presented the aspects of the design and implementation of the O_2 debugger related to data management. The main idea was to use as far as possible the functionalities provided by a database system to manage the information used by a debugger. The object-oriented design of our debugger was particularly adapted to this; all information is represented in the debugger by objects.

A prototype of the O_2 debugger is currently available and is being used at several sites as a beta-test version. The O_2 debugger provides a superset of the common functionalities of commercial Unix debuggers such as DBX and GDB. The functionality and performance provided by this first version validate our design choices, particularly the use of an object-oriented database to store and manage the debugging information.

We plan improvements, especially in the use of the object-oriented features of the O_2 database. The major ones are the following.

- As explained in Lécluse and Richard 1989 (see chapter 9), O_2 may be considered an object-oriented layer on top of C. This object-oriented layer may be added to other programming languages. A current version of BasicO_2 is already implemented. We have designed the O_2 debugger to support multilanguage programs; the complete implementation of the O_2 debugger in this direction remains to be completed.

- An index mechanism has been defined in the O_2 system. We will use it in order to optimize accesses to the objects used by the O_2 debugger.

- As in Provide (Moher 1988), the O_2 debugger may store in the database the value of a state of the program. A systematic storage of the state of a program is not conceivable, but the use of a version mechanism based on stamps defined in Cellary and Jomier 1990 (see chapter 19) is under consideration.

- At each step of the computation, the program state is modeled by a database; we therefore intend to use the O_2 query language to consult and control the program behavior when the O_2 system is running in its alphanumeric version.

9 Acknowledgements

We wish to thank Malcolm Atkinson, Claudia Medeiros, Claude Delobel, and François Bancilhon for their helpful comments, corrections, and suggestions on an earlier draft of the paper.

References

Adams, E., and S. S. Muchnick. 1986. Dbxtool: A window-based symbolic debugger for Sun workstations. *Software Practice and Experience* 16(7).

Aho, A. V., R. Sethi, and J. D. Ullman. 1986. *COMPILERS: Principles, techniques and tools.* Addison-Wesley Series in Computer Science.

Beander, B. 1983. VAX DEBUG: An interactive, symbolic, multilingual debugger. In *Proceedings of the symposium on high-level debugging.*

Borras, P., A. Doucet, P. Pfeffer, and D. Tallot. 1990. The O_2 programming environment. In *Proceedings of the sixth PRC BD3 conference.*

Bovey, J. D. 1987. A debugger for a graphical workstation. *Software Practice and Experience* 17(9).

Cardell, J. R. 1983. Multilingual debugging with the SWAT high-level debugger. In *Proceedings of the symposium on high-level debugging.*

Cellary, W., and G. Jomier. 1990. Object versions in databases. In *Proceedings of the 16th VLDB conference.*

Doucet, A., and P. Pfeffer. 1989. A debugger for O_2, an object-oriented language. In *Proceedings of the first international conference on technology of object-oriented languages and systems.*

Lécluse, C., and P. Richard. 1989. The O_2 database programming language. In *Proceedings of the 15th international VLDB conference.*

Moher, T. G. 1988. PROVIDE: A process visualization and debugging environment. *IEEE Transactions on Software Engineering* 14(6): 849–57.

Powell, M. L., and M. A. Linton. 1983a. A database model of debugging. In *Proceedings of the symposium on high-level debugging.*

———. 1983b. Database support for programming environments. In *Proceedings of the ACM SIGMOD international conference on databases for engineering design.*

Stallman, R. 1986. *The GNU debugger.* Technical Report, Free Software Foundation, Inc., Cambridge.

———. 1989. *The GNU CC compiler.* Technical Report, Free Software Foundation, Inc., Cambridge.

CHAPTER 25

Incremental Compilation in O_2

J. M. LARCHEVÊQUE

1 Introduction

The O_2 system (Lécluse and Richard 1989) is essentially comprised of an object manager encapsulating the database capabilities, and a programming environment which includes a compiler for the CO_2 language, a debugger, and an interpreter for schema-modification commands. The term *schema* refers to a set of definitions for persistent symbols, notably method signatures (i.e., interface types) and class definitions. The method implementations are written in the CO_2 language, an extension of C supporting bulk-data manipulation and object-oriented programming with late binding and multiple inheritance.

To address performance requirements, the CO_2 compiler must be capable of statically binding method and attribute names to addresses whenever this is consistent with late-binding semantics, and capable of optimizing late binding by using ad hoc method tables. This requirement, however, comes into conflict with the demand for incremental application development, which requires that the class hierarchy, class structures, and method signatures be free to change between the time a method is first compiled and the time it is executed. In addition, when a schema change is requested, the system must check the validity of method implementations in the context of the resulting schema before accepting the change (see chapter 7 for issues in schema updates); and this check potentially involves the code of all the methods written for the given application, which poses an acute response-time problem. On the other hand, the compiling system faces a further challenge with the necessity for advanced debugging capabilities, such as execution-stack visualization or function-call tracing. Indeed, such capabilities are inherently interpretive and likely to slow down a compiled application by a sizable factor.

A classical solution to this dilemma is to resort to multiple compilation modes and include an optimized mode in which the executable file reflects a fixed state of the schema. This solution was used in the V1 prototype of the O_2 system (Deux et al. 1990). However, in order to ensure a smooth transition from prototypes to production systems, the ideal would be to have a single mode reconciling efficient code generation with interpretive interaction. This chapter attempts to show that incremental compilation techniques have the potentiality for approximating this ideal by describing the architecture and compiler technology of a *language-based editor* (LBE) for the O_2 system.

The next section surveys the literature on LBEs, after which an overview of the O_2 LBE is given. Then the design of the semantic and syntactic components of the incremental compiler are described in some detail.

2 A Survey of Language-based Editors

The LBEs described in the literature fall rather distinctly into two categories, which may conveniently be referred to as *synthetic* and *analytic* LBEs (Degano, Mannucci, and Mojana 1988).

In a synthetic LBE, editing actions are viewed as actions on a syntax tree; typically, a program will be entered in a top-down fashion, by iteratively specifying the child nodes of the nonterminal nodes already specified (template-driven editing). Synthetic LBEs do not require incremental parsing, so research on synthetic LBEs has focused on semantic issues. In particular, the Mentor Abstract Syntax Tree editor (Donzeau-Gouge et al. 1975) has been used to investigate the automatic transformation of a semantic specification into an S-attributed scheme, which is particularly tractable in an incremental context (Hascoët 1987). Similarly, work carried out around the Cornell Program Synthesizer (Reps 1983) has provided insight into the propagation of attribute values after a subtree replacement in an AST. Furthermore, Fritzson's 1984 research has focused on sophisticated debugging and program-analysis tools in a compiled environment, the Dice system.

On the other hand, an analytic LBE allows ordinary editing of the source text. Its implementation requires incremental parsing, which so far has been the major concern of the literature devoted to analytic LBEs. Most authors achieve incrementality by extending or otherwise modifying the usual push-down automaton algorithm for bottom-up parsing. The earliest algorithm of this type is described in Ghezzi and Mandrioli 1979. The advantages of this type of approach over top-down parsing are the greater generative power of LR grammars over LL grammars, and in some cases the possibility of modifying a standard LALR parser generator to make it generate incremental parsers. Most incremental parsers store some form of parse tree to reuse the results of previous parses. Some authors have designed more space-effective structures (Celentano 1978; Yeh and Kastens 1988), but the great advantage of a parse tree is that it provides a convenient interface with a semantic analyzer.

We will assume for the sake of simplicity that the internal representation used for a source string is always a parse tree. Given a substring substitution in a string whose parse tree is available, there are two ways in which this representation can be used to speed up reparsing: either (1) the parsing automaton starts in an intermediate configuration and stops when some matching condition is satisfied, thus producing a subtree which is grafted to the unchanged part of the old parse tree; or (2) the whole input string is reparsed, but subtrees which remain valid are reused. We say that the first approach aims at *context reuse*, while the latter aims at *subtree reuse*. Most incremental parsers (Celentano 1978; Ghezzi and Mandrioli 1979; Yeh and Kastens 1988) seek context reuse, whereas the algorithm described in Jalili and Gallier 1982 seeks parse-tree reuse, and the algorithm in Ghezzi and Mandrioli 1980 is apparently unique in seeking both context reuse and subtree reuse. As shown in section 5, if semantic analysis is taken into account, subtree reuse is more significant than context reuse.

3 Main Functionalities

3.1 Programs and Applications

An application is a set of programs interacting with a database, that is, a set of objects and attached methods. A program is essentially an executable file containing an execute block and a set of methods. It is built by incrementally linking methods into its executable code, as specified by the user. Its entry point is defined by creating a CO_2 statement block (entirely analogous to a C block) and linking this block into its code. Thus an application is comprised on the one hand of a pool of objects and methods, and on the other hand of a set of autonomous executables into which some of the database methods are linked. In this paper we show how to adapt programs to schema and method changes while preserving late-binding optimizations. The problem of adapting objects to schema evolutions, however, falls outside the scope of this chapter, and so does the question of maintaining several schema versions. Furthermore, it is desirable in practice to have a schema made up of several subschemas, so as to share classes between applications without all schema changes affecting all applications; but this does not affect the present discussion in any essential way and will be ignored in this chapter.

3.2 User Interaction

The user interacts with the compiling system through editor windows and a command window.

An editor window allows ordinary editing of schema and method sources; in addition, the user may request at any moment the current text to be compiled, thus getting feedback on the effect of the last changes and the possibility of rolling back to the state corresponding to the last compile command should an error be detected. In the case of a schema source, a change may invalidate several existing methods, and the user will be offered the possibility of going ahead or of canceling the change. The compile command need not be explicitly issued; it could be bound to editing commands such as insertion of a newline, or switching from insertion to cursor motion. However, it does not seem advantageous systematically to compile up to the cursor's position, as is done in some syntactic editors (e.g., Shilling 1986), unless this procedure could be disabled when a text is being modified rather than created. (The reason for this will become clearer when the incremental parser is described.)

The command window is used to

- edit an execute block, link it to the current program, and execute it
- link a method to the current program
- request various debugging actions to be performed by inserting adequate sequences into the current program
- enter an expression, insert it into the code of a suspended method, and evaluate it
- undo the effect of some or all of the debugging commands issued during a session

If any program has been launched at least once under the LBE, it contains its own entry point and therefore can be used as an autonomous executable. The system thus presents the property of *separability* (Fritzson 1984), under which the development environment and the program developed can be run independently.

4 The Semantic Component

4.1 Code Generation

Each method and each class definition is internally represented by a decorated parse tree. Nodes in method trees have a `code` attribute containing object code interspersed with references to child nodes. Before a method is linked, the object code for this method is generated by traversing the tree from the root and in the order dictated by these references, so as to yield linear object code.

The only optimizations performed concern method calls. These are translated into ordinary function calls when a schema lookup indicates that there can be no overloading, or else they are solved using indexes assigned uniquely to sets of methods or attributes defined in related classes. Consider the following example, where c_2 is a subclass of c_1;

```
{
    c1 x;
    c2 y;
    ...
    if (cond)
        x = y;
    ...
    [x m2];
    ...
}
```

The call to the method *m* will be translated into code equivalent to

x → address_of_method_table [index_for_m2_in_c1]

This supposes that:

1. All programs of a given application have their solve tables loaded at the same address.
2. When an object is created or brought from the disk, its **address_of_method_table** attribute is set to the proper value.
3. When a method is linked into a program, the linker records its address in the relevant solve-table entries.

More sophisticated optimizations—such as static method solving through type-flow analysis, or the usual optimizations performed on a flow graph or on object code—can be performed by a daemon when the system is quiescent. Thus most optimizations are to be performed *lazily* rather than incrementally. This raises two questions: the knowledge the incremental optimizer is given about lazy optimizations; and the point of performing incremental optimizations at all, given the possibility of lazy optimizations.

As far as the first question is concerned, the simplest option is to have the incremental optimizer simply ignore the work of the lazy optimizer, which is therefore undone whenever a method is recompiled. More sophisticated schemes would attempt to preserve existing optimizations during incremental compilation. Unfortunately, our research on this subject is still too sketchy to be reported in this paper. As far as the second question is concerned, it should be noticed that, while static solving is fairly cheap if it applies only to cases which do not depend on program flow, solve-table management is not only an optimization, but an implementation of separability, that is, a device allowing an executable unit to be attached to a development environment or to function as a production program without any structural change.

4.2 Parse-time Semantic Actions

The semantic analyzer uses two distinct schemes; one for local semantic dependencies, and one for managing the dependencies between identifier uses and definitions.

The symbol definitions are the schema on the one hand, and the declarations in CO_2 methods on the other hand. The internal representations used both for the schema and the method sources consist essentially of decorated parse trees. To a subtree representing a symbol definition, we associate a list of uses, so as to be able to zero in on the places to check and modify if this definition requires to be modified. Conversely, when a terminal symbol is analyzed, it is added to a use list.

All other semantic relations are expressed utilizing a strictly S-attributed scheme, which—in the context of incremental bottom-up parsing—presents the advantages of parse-time evaluation and bottom-up update propagation. In practice, the constraints imposed by an S-attributed scheme amount to moving some computations up in the tree, which does not enlarge the scope of attribute dependencies.

In schema sources, the only symbol dependency that need be considered is the relation between a class and its superclasses. Indeed, as a method or attribute name is meaningless if the class of attachment is not known, a class node will necessarily have to be accessed to retrieve information about dependent attributes and methods (notably attribute offsets and method indexes in jump tables). So the semantic links between a set of attribute and method names and the class in which they are defined can be expressed by synthesizing all needed information in the class node.

In method implementations, the symbols used are defined either in schema sources or in declarations occurring at the beginning of CO_2 blocks. From the point of view of their scopes, these definitions form a tree, with the most deeply nested definitions associated to leaf nodes and the schema definitions associated to the root, because some schema definitions can be masked by local definitions.

5 The Syntactic Component

5.1 Conventions

The conventions adopted here are those of Aho, Sethi, and Ullman 1986. Lower-case letters occurring early in the alphabet, such as a and b, denote terminal symbols. Lower-case letters occurring late in the alphabet, such as x and y, denote strings of terminals. Early-occurring upper-case letters, such as A and B, denote nonterminals. Late-occurring upper-case letters, such as X and Y, denote symbols. Early-occurring greek letters such as α and β, denote strings of symbols. Also, first(x) denotes the first symbol of x, last(x) its last symbol, and $\$$ denotes the end of input.

The LR(1) parsing automaton uses two matrices, named respectively *action* and *goto*, which are indexed by state and symbol, as well as a parse stack where automaton states are recorded. The reading head is made to point one token past the substring already analyzed; this token is called the *lookahead* and is denoted by a. Let w be the input string. Parsing starts in state s_0, with a equal to first(w) and the parse stack initially empty. In a given state s_i, the next parse action is given by the matrix *action* as a function of s_i and the lookahead a.

Four types of actions may be indicated:

- **shift** j**:** Push state s_j on the stack. Advance the lookahead a, and go into state s_j.
- **reduce** k**:** Supposing k identifies the context-free production $A \rightarrow \alpha$, pop $\mid \alpha \mid$ items from the parse stack. Let s_j be the new stack top. The new state, which is given by goto(s_j, A), is then pushed onto the parse stack.
- **error:** Reject the input and halt.
- **accept:** Accept the input and halt.

5.2 Requirements and Assumptions for the Incremental Parser

We will assume that the grammar contains no ϵ-productions; and we will limit the task of incremental parsing to the parsing of a complete and correct program $w' = xy'z$, given the parse output of a complete and correct program $w = xyz$ differing from w' by a single substring y. Section 5.5 indicates how the algorithm can deal with erroneous programs and multiple substring substitutions.

Given the semantic component described in section 4, the following semantic actions will be triggered by the parser.

1. *Nonlocal dependencies.* When a new token is shifted, its type information is inherited from the relevant symbol definition, and the node created for this token is added to the list use for the definition. Conversely, when a definition is modified (as a result of either a schema change or a method change), new type information can be inherited in unchanged tokens and propagated upward.

2. *Attribute synthesizing.* When a nonterminal node is created (by a **reduce** action) its attribute values are synthesized. When a subtree covering y' is computed and grafted to the part of the parse tree which remains unchanged (context reuse), the attribute values at the root of the new subtree have to propagate upward to the root of the parse tree.

So, although subtree reuse is excellent for avoiding actions triggered by shifts and reductions, context reuse is useful if the propagation of attribute values after a graft is stopped as soon as the new values match the former values. The gain is particularly significant when a modification concerns a group of statements followed by many other statements, since the nesting of the concrete syntax tree will involve many superfluous reductions and attribute recomputations if no context reuse is attempted.

The algorithm will first be presented in a form guaranteeing maximal subtree reuse with no attempt at context reuse; then a scheme for maximal context reuse will be described.

As described here, the algorithm makes fairly strong assumptions on parse-table construction:

1. The *goto* matrix is canonical in the sense that it is possible to look it up in order to determine what transitions are illegal, whereas in concrete implementations undefined entries are commonly used for various purposes in order to save space.

2. The parse tables are canonical LR tables, rather than the LALR tables usually generated by compiler compilers.

3. The production descriptors give the length not only of the right-hand side but also of the left-hand side symbol of a production.

Larchevêque 1990 provides a description of a suboptimal but more pragmatic variant, currently implemented on the O_2 prototype.

5.3 Extended Example

The productions for a simple grammar are:

1. $S \rightarrow PpQ$

2. $P \rightarrow p$

3. $P \rightarrow Pp$

4. $Q \rightarrow q$

The parse table is given in table 25.1. A parse tree for the string *pppq* is given in figure 25.1. This tree is in fact a *threaded tree*, as defined in Ghezzi and Mandrioli 1979. Each node represents a stack item, in that it contains the state the automaton went into after its creation and points to the node representing the next item down the stack. In figure 25.1 each node is labeled by a (symbol, state_number) pair, and the stack threading is represented by dotted curves. In addition, we will suppose that some appropriate scheme makes it possible to map any token in the input string to the nodes dominating this token in the tree.

Table 25.1. Parse table for the example grammar

	Action			Goto		
	\$	p	q	S	P	Q
s_0		s_3		s_1	s_2	
s_1	accept					
s_2		s_4				
s_3		r_2				
s_4		r_3	s_6			s_5
s_5	r_1					
s_6	r_4					

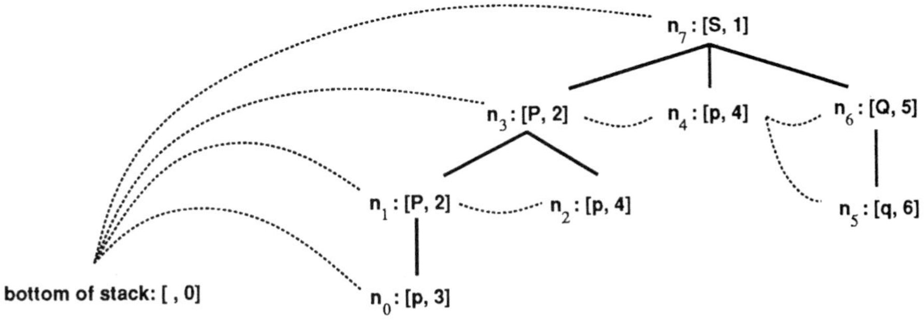

Figure 25.1. Threaded tree for the string *pppq*

To show that appropriate use of this structure allows maximal subtree reuse, let us suppose that, given the tree in figure 25.1, we want to parse the string *ppq*, obtained by deleting the third occurrence of *p*. In other words, we have

$$\begin{aligned} x &= pp \\ y &= p \\ y' &= \emptyset \\ z &= q \end{aligned}$$

We will use the variable *tos* to denote the node representing the current top of stack. We will say that a node n in a tree is *right-incident* to a terminal node t if t is the first node in the fringe of the tree rooted at n—also called the *yield* of n. Conversely, n is *left-incident* to t if t is the last node in the yield of n. A terminal node is both right-incident and left-incident to itself. In figure 25.1, for example, nodes n_0, n_1, n_3, and n_7 are right-incident to n_0, and n_5, n_6, and n_7 are left-incident to n_5.

5.3.1 Starting the Automaton

For maximal subtree reuse, we start in the state corresponding to the highest possible node left-incident to last(x). In the example, we have two nodes left-incident to n_2, namely n_3 and n_2 itself. Node n_3 is higher, but action(n_3.state, q) is **error**, so we start with tos $= n_2$ and $a = q$, which is a legal configuration.

5.3.2 Shift Action

Indeed, action(n_2.state, q) is not **error**, but **shift** 6. Two distinct situations may occur upon a shift: either the lookahead is in y', or y' has been consumed. In the former case, a node is created for a, with its **symbol** and **state** fields duly updated; and this node is pushed onto the stack, that is, assigned to *tos* and made to point to the former value of *tos*. In the latter case, a node of the parse tree that is right-incident to the lookahead node is pushed. Highest nodes are tried first for maximal subtree reuse. A nonterminal node n can be pushed if goto(tos.state, n.symbol) is defined; if so, the state returned will be the new state, and it will be recorded in n.state. In the example, y' is (trivially) consumed, and the nonterminal node n_6 satisfies the condition for being pushed (i.e., shifted), which leads us to state goto(s_4, Q), that is s_5.

5.3.3 Reduce Action

The next action to perform, action(s_5, \$), is a reduction by $S \rightarrow PpQ$. So we pop three items from the stack, and create a node for symbol S and state goto(s_0, S), which is pushed on the stack. In addition, kinship links are set up, meaning that the popped items are made children of the new node (figure 25.2).

5.3.4 Accept Action

The **accept** condition is exactly the same as in a standard LR algorithm. Figure 25.2 shows the situation when reparsing stops. At this point, some space-reclaiming procedure could be invoked to sweep all the nodes not reachable from the new root. Alternately, an incremental garbage collection of the kind described in section 5.4 could be used.

5.4 Augmenting the Parser for Optimal Context Reuse

To allow optimal context reuse, the parsing algorithm is augmented to compute the position at which the new subtree will be grafted by successive approximations during the parsing process, until the smallest possible subtree covering y' has been parsed. This computation consists in (1) marking a position in the main tree as invalid as soon as it is determined to be at or under the root of the subtree being built, and (2) recording the highest invalid position as an approximation to the root of the subtree. The node at this position will be denoted by the variable $n_{y'}$.

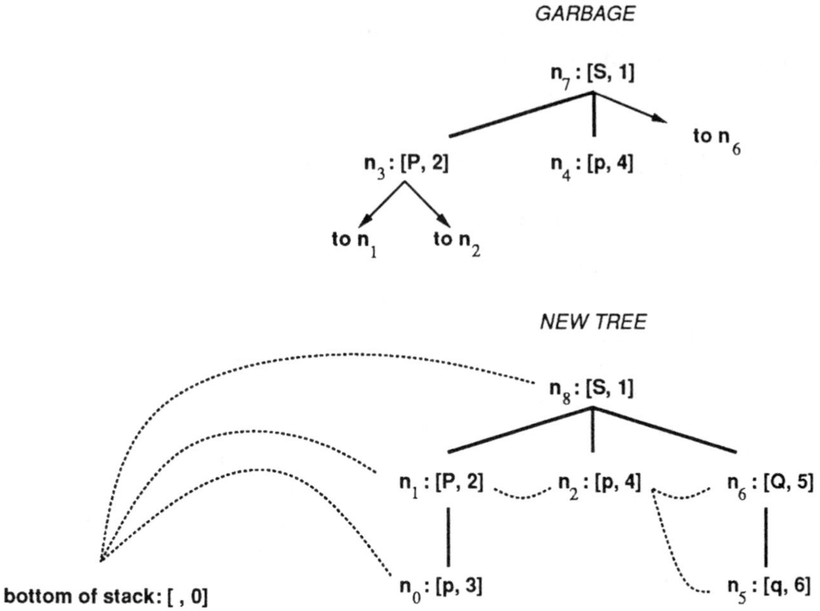

Figure 25.2. Situation as the parser is about to accept the string ppq

A node can be marked as invalid, meaning that the *position* is invalid, or as deallocatable, meaning that all the nodes under it have been marked as invalid or deallocatable, so that neither being the root of a reused subtree nor part of the context, it will not be in the parse tree for w', and can indeed be deallocated.

The following rules are applied, in which n.pred denotes the predecessor of node n in the threaded tree.

1. Initially, all the nodes representing tokens of y are successively marked as deallocatable, and $n_{y'}$ is *nil.*

2. Whenever a node dominating z is shifted, it is marked as invalid.

3. Whenever a node dominating x is on the right-hand side of a reduction, it is marked as invalid.

4. Whenever a node n is marked as deallocatable or invalid, $n_{y'}$ is set to the nearest common ancestor to n and $n_{y'}$; and all the nodes along the paths from this ancestor to n and the former value of $n_{y'}$ are marked as invalid. (The nearest common ancestor to *nil* and any node n is n; the path between *nil* and any node is empty.)

5. Whenever a node is marked as invalid or deallocatable and all its siblings are invalid or deallocatable, then its parent is marked as deallocatable and all its deallocatable siblings are swept to free storage.

6. When (1) y' has been consumed, (2) $n_{y'}$ is deallocatable, and (3) goto($n_{y'}$.pred.state, tos.symbol), $n_{y'}$ is swept to free space and replaced by *tos* (the tree rooted at *tos* is grafted).

5.5 Adding Flexibility to the Parser

5.5.1 Incomplete Programs

Suppose the reading head is past the end of w' and the action is **error**. This means more input is expected. In this case, rather than a single tree rooted at S, we are left with an intermediate state of the parse stack, that is, a list of trees whose root symbols form the beginning of a right-sentential form. This list of trees can be used in exactly the same way as a single tree for future compiles. To see that, we can represent the stack items as children of a pseudo-root ρ and (fictively) apply the marking rules of section 5.4. In the process of parsing a complete and correct w', these items will all be marked as invalid (reused under a different parent node) or deallocatable (absent from the new parse tree), so that ρ will necessarily become deallocatable and eventually disappear.

5.5.2 Erroneous Programs

When an error is detected before the input is consumed, the simplest course of action is to copy the stack to a work area so that error recovery does not interfere with the building of the tree, and leave for future compiles a tree list consisting of the parse stack before error detection and the terminal nodes starting at the point of error. As an optimization, the tree right-incident to the point of error and all largest trees covering successive adjacent strings can form a list from which nonterminal nodes have a chance to be shifted in subsequent parses.

5.5.3 Multiple Changes

Dealing with multiple changes can be useful in cases like the deletion of a pair of block boundaries. It consists in parsing $xy'_0z_0y'_1z_1 \ldots y'_nz_n$, given a parse tree for $xy_0z_0y_1z_1 \ldots y_nz_n$. The extension of the algorithm to this situation is fairly straightforward, except for the fact that a nonterminal node can be shifted only if its yield does not overlap with a y'_i.

6 Further Research

Incremental compilation seems extremely promising in all environments requiring both interactivity and efficiency. There remains, however, a significant amount of work to be carried out in understanding and using incrementality. The scheme just described suggests research topics in (1) general language implementation, and (2) database programming languages (DBPL) implementation. In the first set of topics, we could mention:

- The integration of C-like preprocessing directives to an incremental scanner, as the present implementation of the CO_2 incremental compiler relies on complete preprocessing of a method source and assumes that the lexical specification is simple enough to make it easy to map a character offset to a terminal node.

- The incremental adjustment of method indexes in response to a schema change.

- The preservation of lazy optimizations by the incremental compiler.

Concerning the implementation of DBPLs, the design of the O_2 LBE suggests further research in the following directions:

- Efficient forms of incremental program-flow analysis; in particular, type-flow analysis for solving method calls statically whenever possible, but more generally analyses allowing one to minimize the work of the run-time support of a DBPL, notably with respect to index updates, integrity constraint checking, and storage management tasks.

- The consequences of schema evolution on the management of persistent objects, notably the management of objects whose class is incompletely defined.

- The definition of persistent structures adequate to implement efficiently a cell heap such as the one used in the implementation of the CO_2 incremental compiler.

References

Aho, A., R. Sethi, and J. D. Ullman. 1986. *COMPILERS: Principles, techniques and tools.* Addison-Wesley.

Bancilhon, F. 1988. Object-oriented database systems. In *Proceedings of the seventh ACM PODS conference.*

Begwani, V. S., M. D. Schwartz, and N. M. Delisle. 1984. Incremental compilation in magpie. In *Proceedings of the SIGPLAN symposium on compiler construction, SIGPLAN Notices* 19(6): 122–31.

Boullier, P. 1984. *Contribution à la construction automatique d'analyseurs lexicographiques et syntaxiques.* PhD dissertation.

Celentano, A. 1978. Incremental LR parsers. *Acta Informatica* 10: 307–21.

Dearle, A. 1988. *On the construction of persistent programming environments.* PhD thesis, PPRR-65, Universities of Glasgow and St. Andrews.

Degano, P., S. Mannucci, and B. Mojana. 1988. Efficient incremental LR parsing for syntax-directed editors. *ACM Transactions on Programming Languages and Systems* 10(3): 345–73.

Deux, O. 1990. The story of O_2. *IEEE Transactions on Data and Knowledge Engineering* (March).

Donzeau-Gouge, V., G. Huet, G. Kahn, B. Lang, and J. J. Levy. 1975. *A structure-oriented program editor: A first step towards computer-assisted programming.* INRIA report no. R 114.

Fritzson, P. 1983. A systematic approach to advanced debugging through incremental compilation. In *Proceedings of the symposium on high-level debugging.*

______. 1984. *Towards a distributed programming environment based on incremental compilation.* Linköping studies in science and technology. Dissertation no. 109.

Ghezzi, C., and D. Mandrioli. 1979. Incremental parsing. *ACM Transactions on Programming Languages and Systems* 1:58–70.

______. 1980. Augmenting parsers to support incrementality. *Journal of the Association for Computing Machinery* 27(4): 564–79.

Hascoët, L. 1987. *Transformations automatiques de spécifications sémantiques. Applications: Un vérificateur de types incrémental.* PhD dissertation, Université de Nice.

Jalili, and Gallier. 1982. Building friendly parsers. In *Proceedings of the ninth annual ACM symposium on principles of programming languages.*

Larchevêque, J. M. 1990. Using an LALR compiler compiler to generate incremental parsers. In *Proceedings of the third international conference on compiler compilers. Lecture notes in computer science.* Springer-Verlag.

Lécluse, C., and P. Richard. 1989. The O_2 database programming language. In *Proceedings of the 15th VLDB conference.*

Reps, T. 1983. *Generating language-based environments.* PhD thesis, Cornell University. Also ACM doctoral dissertation award. MIT Press.

Shilling, J. 1986. *Incremental LL(1) parsing in language-based editors.* IBM technical report no. RC 12772.

Yeh, D., and U. Kastens. 1988. Automatic construction of incremental LR(1) parsers. *SIGPLAN Notices* 23(3).

CHAPTER 26

Self-explained Toolboxes

GUSTAVO ARANGO

1 Introduction

One approach to increasing programming productivity is the reuse of software components. Code reusability mainly involves three steps: accessing the code, understanding it, and adapting it (Prieto-Diaz and Freeman 1987). Today, there is a general agreement about the importance of reusability for sound and fast software development in the future (Arnold and Stepoway 1987; Burton et al. 1987; Embley and Woodfield 1987; Fisher 1987; Jones 1984; Kernighan 1984; Meyer 1987; Woodfield, Embley, and Scott 1987).

A common approach to reusability is to produce and maintain software libraries containing reusable components. These components are generally meaningful pieces of code, such as procedures, functions, or programs. The problem with this crude approach is not only how to design good software components, but also how to ensure that those components will be used and understood by software developers.

The object-oriented paradigm offers two important mechanisms to reduce the complexity of the problem: (1) data abstraction and information hiding, and (2) inheritance. The first allows a programmer to define a class in terms of the operations that apply to its instances. The second allows a programmer to define classes as extensions or restrictions of others. These principles should lead to an effective reuse: classes describe common and general behavior and subclasses reuse it.

Programmers often rewrite pieces of code to perform functionalities they have used before. Hence a library with these functionalities is a real help for them. A toolbox is like a library, in that it provides users with components ready to use. Furthermore, those components are easy to refine. One of our purposes is to illustrate in this paper that a toolbox in an object-oriented environment satisfies the open-closed principle: a component is open if it is still available for extension, and it is closed if it is available for use for other components (Meyer 1988).

However, the existence of object-oriented libraries is not enough to ensure the use of its components. Potential users must find these components easy to understand, and we believe that learning by example how to use a library is a promising way to an effective reuse. Consequently, we provide a mechanism to teach the use of toolbox components by generating examples.

In this chapter, we present the teaching-toolbox approach for an object-oriented environment, we give some hints for the design of such a toolbox, and we present an example of a toolbox for business programmers. The rest of this chapter is organized as follows. Section 2 presents the toolbox approach, introduces the toolbox built, and sketches some rules to help in the design of reusable components. In section 3, the explanatory mechanism is presented, using a very simple example; and then some functionalities of the toolbox are described, using more examples.

2 The Toolbox Approach

In an object-oriented environment the basic reusable component is the class. Classes are closed, because their set of operations remains unchanged and every external user has a stability guarantee. Classes are also open, because the behavior of a class can be modified by generating a specialization where implementation of a different behavior is neededOC. This section defines a toolbox and gives some hints on its design.

2.1 What Is a Toolbox?

A toolbox is a set of classes and class instances chosen for a given application domain. Object-oriented programmers may reuse the classes without changing them, or they may adapt them to satisfy a particular problem. Sometimes an instance of a class is useful to everybody; in that case, it is important to offer this particular instance to the user by making it a part of the toolbox. The best way to start toolbox development is bottom-up, from the most general utility services to the most application-specific ones. The upper-level tools should use the components of the lower-level ones.

Toolboxes are similar to Meyer's clusters (see Meyer 1989). There are some lower-level clusters, such as the basic and graphical libraries in Eiffel, which offer classes like List, Array, Tree, and Window (see Meyer 1988). The facilities provided by these clusters are also available in O_2; they may be embedded in the language as type constructors (Lécluse and Richard 1989; see chapter 9), or they may be part of the functionalities offered by the object-oriented programming environment (OOPE) or by the interface generator (Looks). Looks (Plateau et al. 1990; see chapter 22) allows the graphic display, edition, creation and message passing of objects. OOPE (Borras et al. 1990; see chapter 23) is a collection of tools that allow the browsing of the class hierarchy, the creation and compilation of classes, and the creation, compilation, debugging, and testing of methods.

Our toolbox is particularly aimed at business programmers. Some of the services and operations of the classes in the toolbox use the functionalities of the low-level layers of O_2, such as the language features for manipulation of the type constructors and the editing facilities of Looks. To choose the classes to be included in the library, we first looked into the libraries offered by some existing object-oriented programming systems, such as Smalltalk-80 (Goldberg and Robson 1983), Eiffel (Meyer 1988), C++ (Stroustrup 1986), MacApp (Schmucker 1986); and the functionalities of widely used spreadsheets such as Excel (Microsoft 1985). The main criteria for the choice of the classes in the initial library are frequency and ease of use.

2.2 Class Identification

A correct identification of the classes is crucial to the development of a stable design. There is no recipe to define what is and is not a class. A first important point is that classes should be created from objects, not from functions. Hence a first procedure is to create a list of the real objects from the application domain. Objects from the domain can be found from texts, existing applications, requirements documents for these applications, and existing libraries of functions. Objects belonging to the existing toolboxes can be deleted from the list. Afterwards, the resulting objects must be inspected to determine what services we will need them to provide.

2.2.1 The Classes of the Business-Application Toolbox

We found that business applications make heavy use of time points (dates) and money. These two objects were refined, generalized, and associated with some other objects to obtain the classes included in our library. The following paragraphs introduce the classes in the same order they were needed in the design process.

The class Date represents a point in time. This point can be described with varying precision, using seconds, minutes, hours, days, months, and years. There is also an instance of the class Date which we called *today*, representing the present date.

Dates cannot be completely designed without introducing new classes. If we are interested in information about holidays, we need the notion of a calendar; so we introduced the class Calendar to allow the use of holidays and to relate them with the dates. The need to represent the time between dates led to the inclusion of the class Duration.

Analyzing the object Money and the instances of Duration, we found that they had several commonalities. So we introduced a more general class, Quantity, from which Duration and Money will inherit. We designed the class Quantity to describe a wide variety of real-world objects; for instance, weights and distances are quantities.

Quantities are numbers tagged with a unit belonging to a unit system. For instance, 25 kilometers is a quantity having kilometers as the unit and the International Metric System (IMS) as the unit system. Two commensurable quantities can be added to produce a new one, and the operation should be correct, independently of the units used. The user need not be concerned with adjusting the units of the objects he or she is adding. The objectives of the class Quantity are to allow easy manipulation of numbers representing objects of the same unit system and to make automatic conversions between objects of different unit systems.

Quantities are often used in more complex structures, so we included the class Quantity_matrix to allow the use of matrices of quantities and to allow some comparisons among various matrices. More specifically, it is possible to perform statistical operations over a quantity matrix, and an object may be displayed as a pie chart or a bar graph. Dependency links may be established among different Quantity_matrix instances. These links are important for planning; the changes on an instance are automatically updated for all the instances related by a dependency link.

Figure 26.1 shows the class hierarchy of the toolbox.

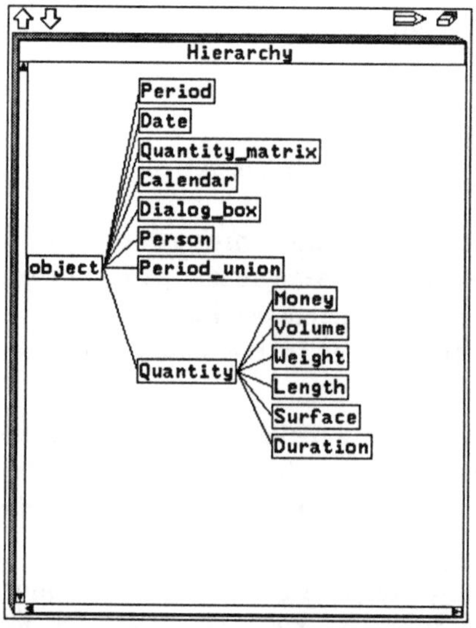

Figure 26.1. Class hierarchy of the business-application toolbox

2.3 Classification of Operations

It is useful to classify the operations that can be applied to the instances of a class, to facilitate the design of the interface of a class. There are several roughly equivalent classifications, such as (1) selectors, constructors, and analyzers (Guttag 1977), (2) functions and procedures (Meyer 1988), and (3) occur, connect, and monitor services (Coad 1989). We have made a classification by refining some of the existing ones. The goal of our detailed classification is to produce a good check list of the kind of services a programmer can define for a class.

The rest of this subsection presents the classification and some of the operations we obtained by applying it to the Date class of our toolbox.

Procedures modify the state of the object. We must be able to extract the information from a string of the form "12/3/1987,13h0'45"" and to update the object with information about the day, the month, and the year. For example, the result of applying a set_date operation to a Date instance can modify respectively its day, month, and year information.

Outputs present the object on an output device. Generally, users will reuse the methods for print and display of the class Object.

Selectors obtain information about the state of the object. We can ask the following information about a Date instance: the day, the month, the year, the hour, the minute, the second, and the day's occurrence in the year. For instance, if we apply *day_in_year* to the Date instance *20/7/1989*, we obtain 201.

Parameterized selectors are selectors that need external information to produce a result. For example:

1. To display the calendar month of a date using a particular calendar:

   show_month(calendar)

   If *default_calendar* is a Calendar instance whose only holidays are Sundays, the result of applying *show_month* with *default_calendar* to the Date instance *20/12/1989* is displayed in figure 26.2.

Figure 26.2. Calendar for December 1989

2. To find the week number using a particular calendar:

   week_in_year(calendar)

   The result of applying *week_in_year* with *default_calendar* to the date *20/5/1989* is 20.

3. To display the name of the month using a particular calendar:

   month_name(calendar)

   The result of applying *month_name* with *default_calendar* to the date *20/5/1989* is "May".

Comparisons compare equality or order. We can ask if a date is equal to or occurs before another:

compare(date)

The result of applying *compare* with *1/12/1989* to *2/12/1989* is −84600, which is the difference in seconds between the dates.

Creators produce new instances of the class. For example:

1. To obtain a future date:

   forward(duration)

   This gives the date the results from adding the duration to the date. The result of applying forward with a duration of 90 days to *23/7/1989* is 21/10/1989.

2. To obtain a date, taking holidays into account:

   forward_working_days(integer, calendar)

   The result of applying this method, taking into account five holidays not specified in *default_calendar*, to the date *20/3/1989* is 25/3/1989.

External creators produce instances of other classes. We did not find examples for the class Date. Nondate examples of external creators might be (1) the multiplication of two distances to generate an instance of the class Surface; or (2) an object migration (the destruction of an object in a given class and the creation of this object in another class), for example, to reflect a person's change in status from employed to unemployed.

Conversions pass from internal to external representations to facilitate the programming of the user interface. The result of applying *to_string* to *20/3/1989* produces the string "20/3/1989".

3 The Business-Application Toolbox

Section 3.1 explains how to learn to use a toolbox component, with a simple example. Section 3.2 gives examples of the use of the toolbox as a closed system. Section 3.3 presents two ways of using the toolbox as an open system.

3.1 The Learning Mechanism

The learning mechanism uses the service of the OOPE that makes classes and methods in O_2 first-class objects.

The main feature of OOPE is its all-object design philosophy (Borras et al. 1990; see chapter 23). A set of methods is provided to create, destroy, and modify the elements of the O_2 schema. For instance, a class is represented by an object of type tuple (see figure 23.5); the documentation information is contained in an attribute named `Infos`. The class Infos is specialized to support the explanatory characteristic of the reusable components we have built. A method is also represented by an object of type tuple (see figure 23.6); each method has an attribute `Infos`. A method *example* is defined for each class; these methods rely on a method *example* defined for the class Infos.

The activation of the method *example* generates on-line help for the class and its methods. Each method's on-line help includes (1) a display of information about the method's purpose and use; (2) generation of the code to produce a complete example of the method (this code includes object creation, initialization, and message passing and generally contains information given by the on-line-help user); and (3) the execution of the code previously generated and a display of the result (when the method is a procedure, the receiver object is displayed).

The starting point to the learning mechanism is the application of the method *example* to a class. The important problem of finding a class is not addressed here. For a mechanism to deal with this retrieval problem in large libraries of classes, see Arango, Cazalens, and Mamou 1988.

3.1.1 Results of an Example

One of the services offered by O_2 is an easy way to define dialog boxes to communicate with end users. Figure 26.3 shows the services offered by O_2 to create dialog boxes. The user has chosen a multiple-choice box. Figure 26.4 shows a text explaining the use of the method and sketching the example to be computed to inform the user about the questions he or she will be asked. Figure 26.5 displays a typical dialog box. The user's answer will enable the program to produce an appropriate example. In this case, the example is about a set of fruits—apples, oranges, and bananas—and their quantities on hand. The choice of fruit will be made using a dialog box which demands a string answer. Figure 26.6 presents the code to produce the "fruit" dialog box required by the user. Figure 26.7 shows the dialog box created by the code. The resulting dialog box is operational; a choice can be made, and its result (a list of integers) will be displayed.

3.2 Using the Toolbox

This section demonstrates the use of the toolbox through two examples.

3.2.1 Defining the Age of a Person

Assume we wish to find the age of a person represented by an instance of the Person class. The procedure *set_from_dates* of the class Duration allows the user to modify an instance to represent the elapsed time between two dates. The selector *years* of the class Duration obtains the number of years that represent the person's age. The selector *date_of_birth* of the class Person gives the person's date of birth. Let p be the Person instance and d a Duration instance; the age is computed in CO_2 as follows (message passing is delimited by square brackets):

```
o2 Duration d;
o2 Person p;

...
[d set_from_dates([p date_of_birth], Today) years];
```

Several messages can be chained; a message expression is evaluated from left to right. The declaration of variables representing instances of O_2 classes is introduced by the keyword **o2**.

3.2.2 Automatic Update of Dependent Quantity Matrix

Suppose you have a 2×2 quantity matrix called *matrix*, whose rows are (100, 200) and (500, 600). Suppose that you also have a 1×2 quantity matrix called *matrix0*, whose row (600, 800) results from adding the columns of *matrix*. To generate *matrix0* we write in CO_2:

```
matrix0 = [matrix row_add_comparison(list(0, 1))];
```

The *row_add_comparison* operation is a creator of the class Quantity_matrix. Its parameter gives a selection of the positions of the columns of *matrix* that are to be added. In this example, we are adding the first and second columns, whose positions are given by 0 and 1.

Figure 26.8 presents the standard display of *matrix* and its representation as a bar graph and the display of *matrix0* as a pie chart. These displays are generated using operations of the class Quantity_matrix. For example, the standard display of *matrix* is obtained by the following method, which is a redefinition of that provided for the class Object: [matrix display_level_one].

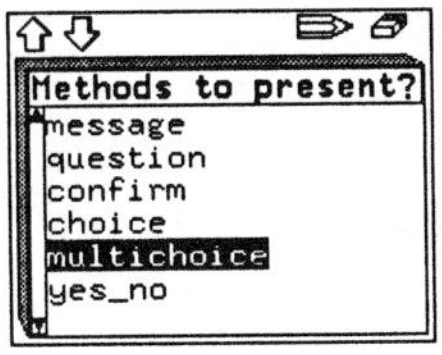

Figure 26.3. Choice of dialog boxes

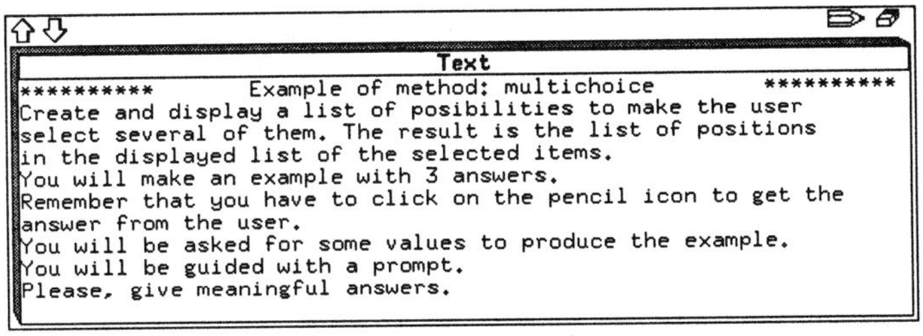

Figure 26.4. Introductory text for the method *multichoice*

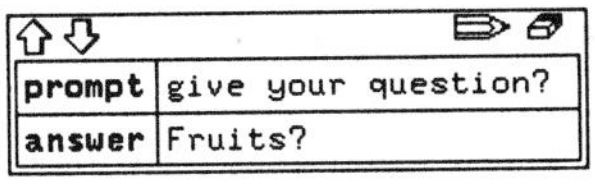

Figure 26.5. Defining the text of the question

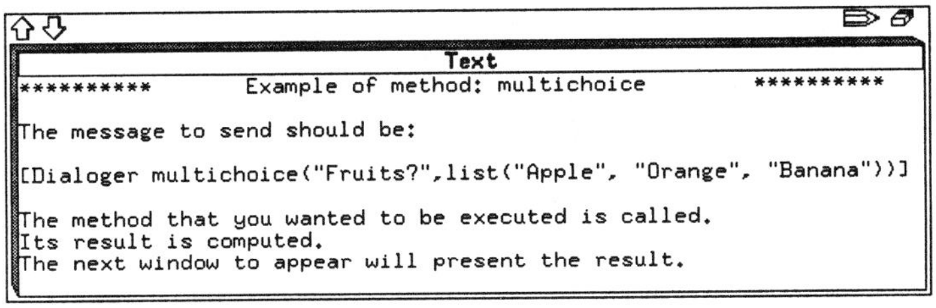

Figure 26.6. Example of code to produce a multiple-choice dialog box

Figure 26.7. Example of a multiple-choice dialog box

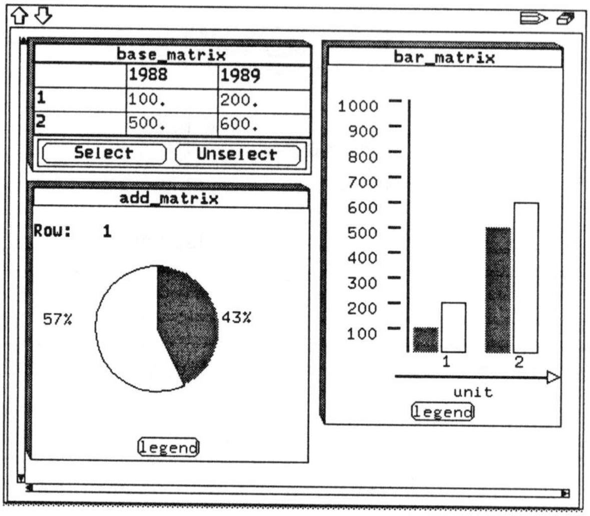

Figure 26.8. Matrix representations

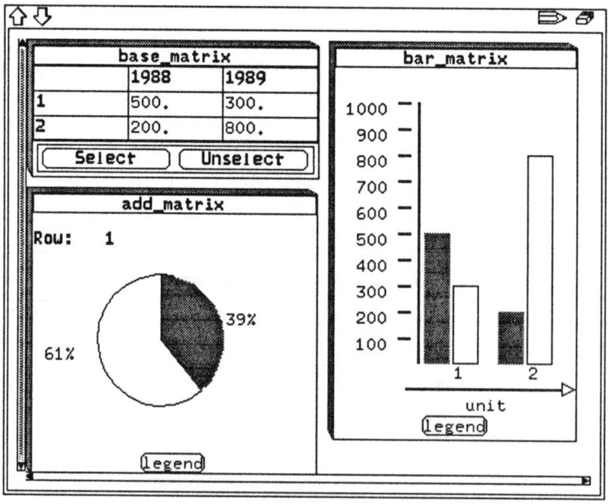

Figure 26.9. Matrix representations following an update

The *matrix* object may be edited on the screen. A click on the "pencil" icon uses the screen values to update the matrix. When an update is performed on a matrix, all the dependent matrices are automatically modified. Figure 26.9 shows the screen following an automatic update that reflects the saving of *matrix* with new row values of (500, 300) and (200, 800).

3.3 Extending the Toolbox

Users can extend the toolbox in two ways: (1) use the inheritance principle and specialize the existing classes or (2) use some predefined methods to augment the set of useful instances.

For example, we may wish to add different duration units. The predefined duration units of the toolbox are years, months, weeks, days, minutes, and seconds. The toolbox provides the possibility of defining a new unit system for computing durations; it is also possible to describe an operation that allows a user to convert a unit from the old unit system into the new one. This operation establishes a compatibility link between the old and new unit system and ensures the correct use of durations belonging to the two systems.

Suppose that Std_duration is the name of the unit system to express standard durations and My_duration is the new unit system we wish to add. The following CO_2 code allows a programmer to define the new unit system and to relate it to the old one.

```
[My_duration set_unit_system("Duration", "fortnight", "fn",
                list(tuple(name: "quarter", symbol: "qr", factor: 6.0),
                     tuple(name: "semester", symbol: "sem", factor: 12.0)))];
[My_duration declare_scale_transformation(Std_duration, list(14*24*3600.0))];
```

The arguments of the first message give the name of the new unit system, the name of the main unit, the main unit's symbol, and the list of all the other units in the unit system. The attribute **factor** gives the factor needed to transform the unit described into the main unit of the system. The second message creates the conversion function between the representation units of the old system and those of the new system; in this case, it is a simple multiplication to obtain the number of seconds in a fortnight (i.e., in two weeks).

4 Conclusions

The toolbox for the business-application programmer is operational and is part of the O_2 distribution tape. It consists of 34 classes with 450 methods, organized in a three-level hierarchy. We also provide the default calendar and the French calendar, and we have included the most widely used unit systems, such as the International Metric System.

Our approach allows us to fulfill two important goals of software reusability: the design of truly reusable components, and a way of learning the meaning and the use of reusable components. We design reusable components which are stable, easy to extend, and easy to retrieve. Stability is obtained by modeling real-world objects via classes and by choosing a class as the reusable component. This gives stability because objects change less than their operations and services. A low cost extension is obtained by using inheritance or by creating suitable instances. Easy retrieval is supported by grouping classes within a particular application domain to produce a toolbox. Well-designed toolboxes should reflect a natural way to package reusable components. Learning the contents of the toolbox is made easier by the example mechanism attached to the classes and methods in the toolbox. We plan to extend this mechanism to the toolbox instances.

The object-oriented programming languages, such as Smalltalk-80 (Goldberg and Robson 1983), often allow programmers to treat everything as an object. However, this is not the case when there is static type checking, as in Eiffel (Meyer 1988). The safety ensured at execution time in the latter case is not guaranteed where everything is treated as an object. The O_2 system and its programming environment favor the generation of toolboxes that have self-explanatory properties. OOPE provides an elegant way to bypass the restrictions produced by a static type-checking language; and the learning mechanism presented here is a good example of the functionalities that can be reached when schema elements may by handled as objects.

The next step will be to evaluate this approach to reusability, measuring the usefulness of the elements of the toolboxes and the appropriateness of the explanatory mechanism.

5 Acknowledgements

We wish to thank François Bancilhon, Christophe Lécluse, Anne Doucet, and Philippe Richard for their comments and suggestions on earlier versions of this chapter.

References

Arango, G. 1990. Self-explained toolboxes: A practical approach to reusability. In *Proceedings of the TOOLS 90 conference.*

Arango G., R. Cazalens, and J-C. Mamou. 1988. *Design of a software reusability subsystem in an object-oriented environment.* Altaïr Technical Report.

Arnold, S. P., and S. L. Stepoway. 1987. The reuse system: Cataloging and retrieval of reusable software. IEEE Computer Society International Conference (February).

Bancilhon, F., G. Barbedette, V. Benzaken, C. Delobel, S. Gamerman, C. Lécluse, P. Pfeffer, P. Richard, and F. Vélez. 1988. The design and implementation of O_2, an object-oriented database system. In *Proceedings of the second international workshop on object-oriented database systems,* ed. K. Dittrich.

Borras, P., A. Doucet, P. Pfeffer, and D. Tallot. 1990. OOPE, the O_2 programming environment. In *Proceedings of the sixth PRC BD3 conference.*

Burton, B. A., R. A. Wienk, S. A. Bailey, K. Koelher, and L. A. Mayes. 1987. The reusable software library. *IEEE Software* (July).

Coad, P. 1989. Object oriented requirement analysis. In *SAL: State of the art limited.* Documentation.

Deux, O. et al. 1989. *The story of O_2.* Altaïr Technical Report.

Embley, D. W., and S. N. Woodfield. 1987. A knowledge structure for reusing abstract data types. *ACM.*

Fisher, G. 1987. Cognitive view of reuse and redesign. *IEEE Software* (July).

Goldberg, A., and D. Robson. 1983. *Smalltalk 80: The language and its implementation.* Addison-Wesley.

Guttag, J. V. 1977. Abstract data types and the development of data structures. *CACM* 20(6).

Jones, C. T. 1984. Reusability in programming: A survey of the state of the art. *IEEE Transactions on Software Engineering* SE-10(5).

Kernighan, B. W. 1984. The UNIX system and software reusability. *IEEE Transactions on Software Engineering* SE-10(5).

Lécluse, C., P. Richard, and F. Vélez. 1988. O_2, an object-oriented data model. In *Proceedings of the ACM SIGMOD conference.*

Lécluse, C., and P. Richard. 1989. The O_2 database programming language. In *Proceedings of the VLDB conference.*

Meyer, B. 1987. Reusability: The case for object-oriented design. *IEEE Software* (March).

______. 1988. *Object-oriented software construction.* Prentice-Hall.

______. 1989. From structured programming to object-oriented design: The road to Eiffel. In *Structured programming.* Springer-Verlag.

Microsoft. 1985. *Microsoft Excel for the Apple Macintosh. User's guide.* Microsoft, Inc.

Plateau, D., R. Cazalens, D. Lévêque, J. C. Mamou, and B. Poyet. 1990. Building user interfaces with the Looks hyper-object system. *Eurographics workshop on object-oriented graphics.*

Prieto-Diaz, R., and P. Freeman. 1987. Classifying software for reusability. *IEEE Software* (July).

Schmucker, K. 1986. *Object-oriented programming for the Macintosh.* Hayden Book Company.

Stroustrup, B. 1986. *The C++ programming language.* Addison-Wesley.

Woodfield, S. N., D. W. Embley, and D. T. Scott. 1987. Can programmers reuse software? *IEEE Software* (July).

Part VI

Examples of O_2 Applications

CHAPTER 27

A Guided Tour of an O_2 Application

CONSTANCE GROSSELIN
T. MARK JAMES

1 The Altaïr Travel Agency

Let us imagine ourselves on a typical touristy street in central Paris, perhaps the rue Auber, on a sunny autumn afternoon. In front of us is the Altaïr Travel Agency, the storefront of which displays a number of inviting posters. We enter; the woman behind the counter rises to greet us.

We have here at least two instances of the class Person, whose characteristics may be described by the following O_2 schema command:

```
add class Person
    type tuple(name: string,
               first_name: string,
               birthdate: Date,
               address: tuple(number: integer,
                              street: string,
                              city: string,
                              zip_code: string,
                              country: string))
    method creation(): Person is public;
  public write name, write first_name, read birthdate in class Person;
```

The `name` and `first_name` attributes have been made visible and changeable anywhere (**write**); the `birthdate` attribute is visible anywhere (**read**), but it may be altered only by a method attached to the class Person. The attributes associated with the address are fully encapsulated; they are invisible outside of the methods of class Person. Apart from attribute access, the main operation that one would perform within the context of the class Person is the creation and initialization of an instance. This may be done anywhere (**public**).

Looking closer at the people in our agency, we recognize two subclasses: clients and employees. The subclass Client inherits all of the attributes and methods of the class Person. It also requires an extra tuple attribute representing the business conducted with a particular person, and methods to operate on that attribute. Similarly, the subclass Employee needs extra attributes and methods dealing with the employee's position in the agency.

```
add class Client
    inherits Person
    type tuple(reservations: list(Reservation))
    method total_bill(): float is public,
           balance_update(): float;
public write reservations in class Client;

add class Employee
    inherits Person
    type tuple(seniority: integer,
               title: string,
               salary: float)
    method balance_update(): float;
```

The class Reservation is defined elsewhere in this schema; its presence here is an illustration of *composition links* among classes, just as the subclass semantics is an example of *inheritance links*.

It will be useful also to define two named instances: a set value, *The_clients*, representing the totality of the agency's client base, and *agency_balance*, holding the travel agency's running account balance.

```
add name The_clients: set(Client);
add name agency_balance: float;
```

Each of the subclasses Client and Employee has an impact on the financial position of the agency; we may model this impact through methods. Clients need a method to calculate their bill, and another to record payments and update the company's overall balance. Employee salaries must be deducted from the company's balance. The last two methods mentioned are both called *balance_update*.

The method name *balance_update* exhibits the object-oriented property of *late binding*. When this method is invoked upon an object, the system determines (at execution time) the class of the object, thus deciding whether to call the *balance_update* method of class Client or that of class Employee. The CO_2

code of these two methods is quite different. For clients, we invoke the *total_bill* method to determine how much the client owes; then we use that amount to update the agency's balance.

```
body balance_update(): float in class Client co2
{ /*
    Add the bill of the client to the balance of the agency.
 */
agency_balance += [self total_bill];
return(agency_balance);
}$;
```

For employees, double the value of the **salary** attribute is subtracted from the balance. (This covers such things as sick leave, paid vacation, and social security charges.)

```
body balance_update(): float in class Employee co2
{ /*
    Twice the salary of the employee is subtracted from the balance of
    the agency.
 */
agency_balance -= self → salary * 2;
return(agency_balance);
}$;
```

Note the square-bracket notation [*object method* (*parameters*)] for the passing of a message to a receiver object. The receiver is called self in the method code.

Back in the travel agency, we notice that there is usually a second agent, but she is presently sailing the Greek isles. A poster advertising her cruise is prominently displayed behind her workstation. She belongs to a common subclass of both Employee and Client.

```
add class Client_employee
    inherits Client, Employee
    type tuple(discount: integer)
    method balance_update(): float;
```

This is an example of multiple inheritance. Instances of the class Client_employee inherit all of the characteristics of the two superclasses, including their specific tuple attributes and methods. In the case of the method balance_update, we need to specify which of the two methods of that name to inherit, or whether we wish to define a third method of that name. It is this last option that we have chosen. The system must therefore choose between three methods of the same name, depending upon the class of the receiver object.

Nothing prevents us, however, from making an explicit reference in one such method to another. For example, the method balance_update in class Employee_client makes such a reference to the method of the same name in class Employee. Thus if the agency should ever change its payroll accounting method, the change need only be administered at one point.

```
body balance_update(): float in class Client_employee co2
{ /*
      Add the discounted bill of the client-employee to the balance of the
      agency, and subtract the salary as per Employee@balance_update.
*/
agency_balance = [self Employee@balance_update] +
      ([self total_bill] * (100 - self → discount) / 100);
return(agency_balance);
}$;
```

2 Displays and Data Capture

An *application* in O_2 consists of a group of programs that serve a coherent purpose, such as the operation of a travel agency. The programs are linked by a number of variables representing common objects and values. For example, current_client is a persistent object of class Client.

```
add application altair

    variable  current_client: Client,
              place_of_stay: City,
              number_of_persons: integer,
              departure_date: Date,
              returning_date: Date

    program   init(),
              travel_information(),
              transport_reservation(),
              hotel_reservation(),
              tour_reservation(),
              bill();
```

The application altair appears on the agent's screen as a simple icon (figure 27.1). From the user's point of view, this icon is the entry point to the system. Since we are undecided as to where we would like to go for our holiday, the agent clicks on the altair icon and chooses the travel_information program. The icon and menu displays and mouse handling are governed entirely by the O_2 system, based upon nothing more than the application definition given above.

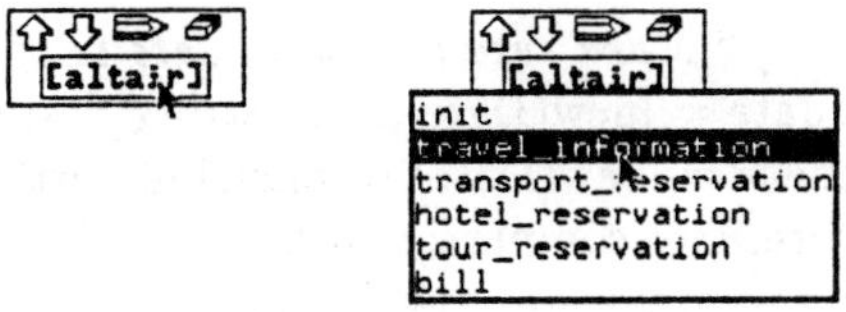

Figure 27.1. Clicking on the "altair icon" (left) brings up the application menu (right)

Now, however, some programmed CO_2 code is called into play. This is the code of the **travel_information** program.

```
body travel_information() in application altair co2
{
/*
    This program asks the user for his or her destination, the
    dates of departure and return, and the number of persons
    traveling. To help the user to choose a destination, the sys-
    tem offers some statistics about the population of tourists
    in various European countries for a selected month; and
    then in a selected country, the population of tourists in the
    cities where one can go with the travel agency.
*/
o2 tuple(name: string, first_name: string, departure: string,
        returning: string, destination: City,
        number_of_persons: integer) dest1, dest2;
int pid, pids, pidc, res, bool;

set_title("Travel Information");

bool = 0;
/* Display a data entry form. */
pid = present(dest1, EDIT, ICON, NESTED_WINDOW);
/* Display statistics icon. */
pids = present(info_statistics, NO_EDIT, ICON, NESTED_WINDOW);
/* Display the set of all cities. */
pidc = present(City, NO_EDIT, ICON, NESTED_WINDOW);

map(pids, SCREEN, COORDINATE, NO_PERSIST, 300, 0);
map(pidc, SCREEN, COORDINATE, NO_PERSIST, 300, 70);
do {
    map(pid, SCREEN, COORDINATE, NO_PERSIST, 0, 0);
    res = lock(pid);                  /* Wait for data entry. */
    if (res == CLICK_QUIT)            /* If user clicks on eraser.... */
        bool = 1;
      else                            /* If user clicks on pencil.... */
        {consult(pid, &dest2);
```

```
                    /* Make sure returning date is after departure date.*/
        departure_date = [new(Date) from_string(dest2.departure)];
        returning_date = [new(Date) from_string(dest2.returning)];
        if ([departure_date compare(returning_date)] >= 0.)
            [Dialoger message("invalid dates!")];
          else
            bool = 1;
        }
    } while (!bool);

if (res == CLICK_SAVE)
                                        /* If (and only if) user clicked on
                                        pencil, set application variables. */
    {place_of_stay = [dest2.destination copy];
    number_of_persons = dest2.number_of_persons;
    current_client → name = dest2.name;
    current_client → first_name = dest2.first_name;
    }
                                        /* Erase the three displays. */
  destroy(pid); destroy(pids); destroy(pidc);
}$;
```

The first lines of code declare two O_2 tuples and five integers, then establish the title of the screen. There follows a series of **present** and **map** instructions which govern three object and value displays (figure 27.2). The first, for the tuple variable *dest1*, will become a data entry template for the new client. The second shows an icon representing the named object *info_statistics*; if it is clicked upon, methods attached to that object will appear in a menu. The third displays the named value *City*, representing the set of all objects of class City on our database. The `lock` instruction in the `do` loop causes the program to pause while we enter the relevant data.

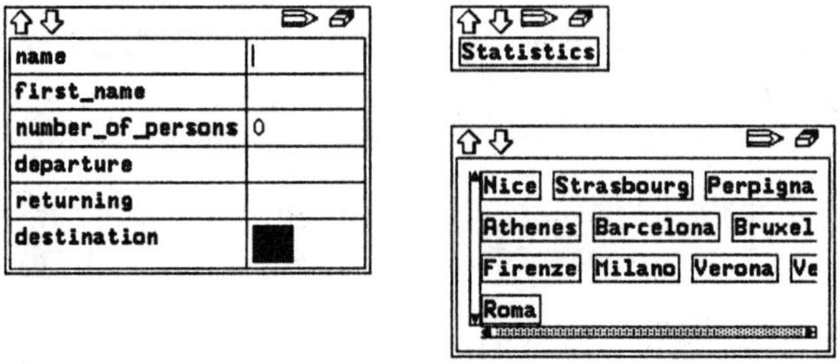

Figure 27.2. Three object and value displays

The data entry form (*dest1*) is filled out by typing into the alphanumeric fields, and by a copy-and-paste operation for the destination city object; in our case, we choose Rome. Each of the cities displayed in the set *City* is an iconic representation of an object of class City.

```
add class City
        type tuple(name: string,
                   country: Country,
                   statistics: set(Statistics),
                   map: Bitmap,
                   places_to_go: list(Place_to_go),
                   things_to_do: list(Thing_to_do),
                   hotels: list(Hotel))
        method stat(integer): integer is public;

public write name, write country, write statistics in class City;
public write hotels, write map, write places_to_go,
        write things_to_do in class City;
```

By pasting a copy of the object *Roma* into the destination field of the data mask, we make use of the concept of *object identity*; that is, both copies of the icon (as well as any other representation of or reference to the object *Roma*) designate the same persistent object, and any change made to one representation will affect all others.

When the data entry form is filled out, the agent clicks on one of the title bar icons (figure 27.3). If she clicks on the "eraser" icon (CLICK_QUIT in the program), the operation is abandoned. If she selects the "pencil" icon (CLICK_SAVE), the information from the screen is read and checked for consistency; the object variables *current_client* and *place_of_stay*, as well as the integer *number_of_persons*, are updated. In either case, the program erases the three displays from the screen (the three **destroy** instructions).

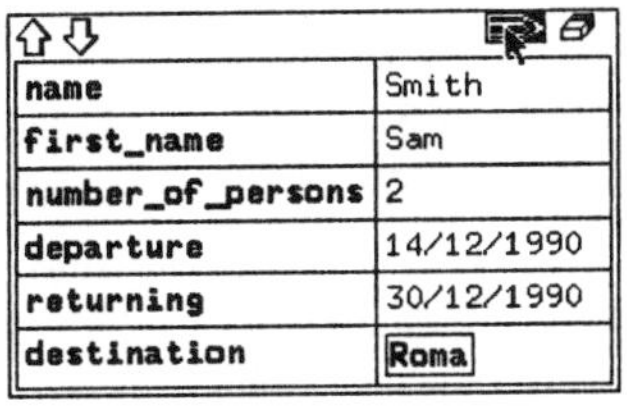
name
Smith
first_name
Sam
number_of_persons
2
departure
14/12/1990
returning
30/12/1990
destination
Roma

Figure 27.3. Clicking on the pencil icon renders persistent any changes made to the object values

3 The O_2 Query Language

We are particularly interested in Rome's ancient monuments, and so we enquire about guided tours of the monuments. The agent invokes the *tour_reservation* program from the application menu. The travel agency schema defines a class Tour with the following type:

```
add class Tour
    type tuple(capacity: integer,
               availability: integer,
               theme: string,
               city: City,
               description: list (tuple (what: Place_to_go,
                                         date: Date)),
               price: float);
```

The schema also defines a named set value, also called *Tour*, representing all of the instances of the class Tour:

```
add name Tour: set(Tour);
```

There are, of course, dozens of tours in the set *Tour*, but we are only interested in those for Rome. Now the system knows where we are going (this was recorded in the variable *place_of_stay* as soon as we decided on Rome), so it is a simple matter to find the appropriate subset of *Tour* that may interest us. This could be written in CO_2, but it is much simpler to write it using the O_2 query language.

```
o2 set(Tour) tours;
int pid1;

...
tours = select x
        from x in Tour
        where (!(strcmp (x → city → name, place_of_stay → name)))
        end;
pid1 = present (tours, NO_EDIT, ICON, NESTED_WINDOW);
...
```

In the middle of a CO_2 program, therefore, we have a snippet of query language. The variable *tours* is defined as a set of objects of class Tour (the first line), and its value is established as the set of objects that satisfy the query predicate. The predicate is itself a straightforward C string comparison, making sure that the name of the city where the tours take place is the same as that of our chosen destination. The **present** instruction which follows the query performs the same function as it did in the *travel_information* program. Figure 27.4 shows the result of the query.

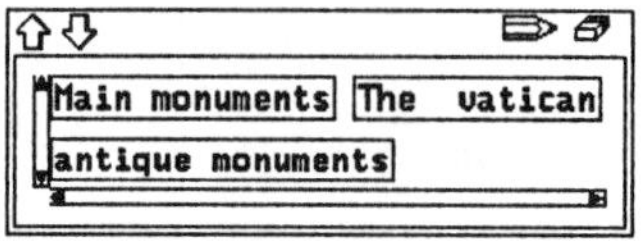

Figure 27.4. The result of the query on Rome tours

In object-oriented systems, the traditional dichotomy between programming languages and query languages does not apply. In O_2, the two share the same type structure and the same computational model; either one may operate on single records or on sets. There is thus no problem in intermixing their code in a single application.

4 Multimedia Objects

Having chosen our destination, we now wish to reserve a hotel room. The agent calls up the *hotel_reservation* program from the application menu; since the program knows our destination, it displays a map of Rome (figure 27.5) containing several sensitized spots. Some of these spots are marked with a special icon to indicate popular tourist areas; clicking on one of these brings up a photograph of that area.

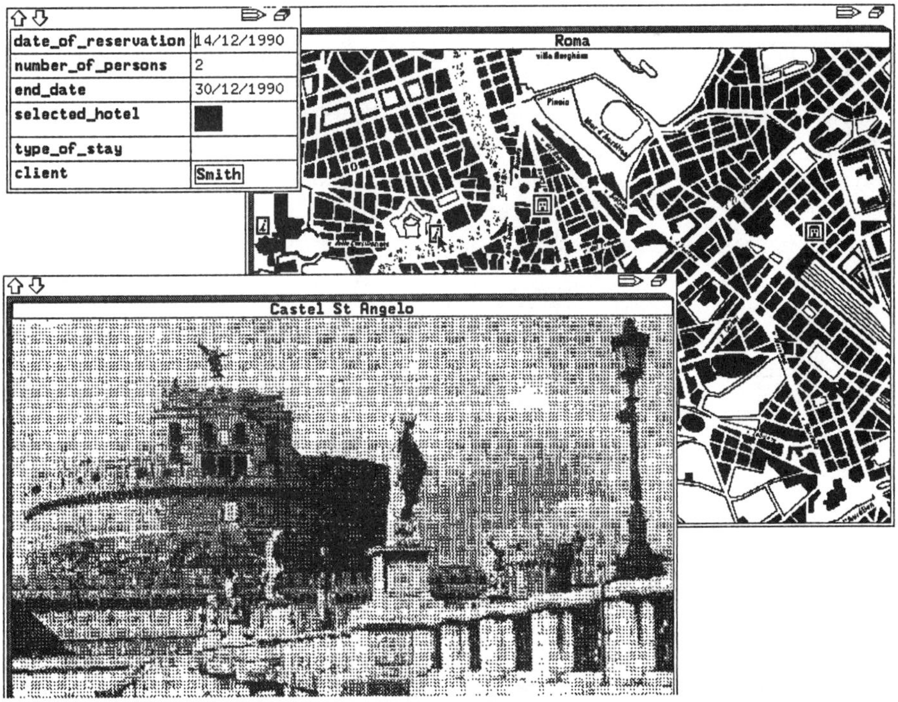

Figure 27.5. Bitmap objects with sensitized areas (note the position of the mouse cursor)

The map and photograph are displays of objects of the system-defined class Bitmap, using the same **present** and **map** instructions that we saw in section 2. These two Bitmap objects are components of objects of class City (see its definition in section 2). The map of Rome is, of course, the attribute **map** of the object place_of_stay, which in our case is identical with the object *Roma*.

pid2 = **present**(place_of_stay → map, NO_EDIT, LEVEL_ONE,
NESTED_WINDOW);
map(pid2, SCREEN, COORDINATE, NO_PERSIST, 300, 0);

The photograph of the Castel St. Angelo comes from the list of objects of class Place_to_go, whose structure includes the attribute **picture**.

add class Place_to_go
type tuple(**name**: string,
picture: Bitmap,
address: Address,
things_to_do: set(Thing_to_do));

Clicking on a bitmap display triggers the method *click* of the bitmap object concerned; this method displays the appropriate Place_to_go picture based upon the point at which the click took place. The method *click* is an *exceptional method*, in that it attaches to one single object rather than to a class as a whole.

Other spots on the map are marked with a special icon; these are hotels. Clicking on one of these causes information on that particular hotel to be displayed (figure 27.6). The display is of an object of class Hotel; as usual, it may be copied and pasted into the **selected_hotel** field of the data-capture mask. (Note in figure 27.6, the "phantom" outline of the object being copied.)

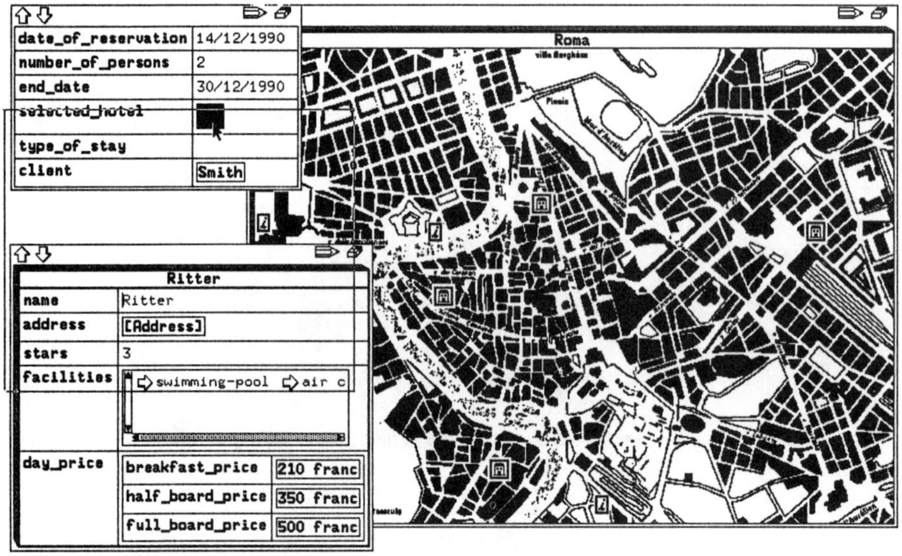

Figure 27.6. Copy and paste of an object of the class Hotel

5 The O_2 Programming Environment

Now that the trip to Rome is settled, the travel agent asks us if she can be of any further service; we ask about ski vacations in Huez. The O_2 programmer in the back room overhears this, and realizes that he has not foreseen the need for a class to represent ski resorts. Such a thing would be useful, since the agency has plenty of information on ski slopes, and the ski season is approaching. He realizes that there is no point in creating a new class from scratch; a ski resort class would logically be a subclass of the class City, and would inherit its properties. The only thing he has to do is to specify how a winter resort city differs from any other kind of tourist city.

The programmer dashes to his workstation and, in between bites of his Mars bar, invokes the Browser from his programmer's toolbox to display the definition of the class City. Under OOPE, database schema definitions are maintained as metaobjects; schema manipulations are merely methods attached to those metaobjects. Our programmer, following the procedure outlined in chapter 23, defines a new subclass of City that shares, by default, City's type specification. The programmer names the new class Winter_resort, refines its type specification by adding a new attribute slopes to the tuple (figure 27.7), and "compiles" the new class; Winter_resort is thus instantly available to the agent and her clients in the front office.

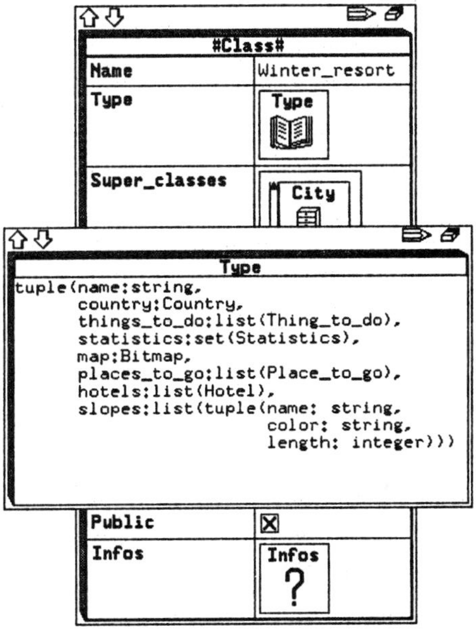

Figure 27.7. Refining the type specification for the class Winter_resort

The new attribute, slopes, of the type specification is defined as a list of tuples; each member tuple represents a ski slope at the resort in question. Each slope has a name; a level of difficulty, represented by a color; and a length in meters. Thus far, except for the possession of this new attribute, an object of class Winter_resort behaves just like an object of class City.

Peeking through the curtains, the programmer notices that we are occupied with pamphlets on ski vacations, so he decides to create a method for the class Winter_resort to display, in graphical form, information on the difficulty of a resort's ski slopes. Following the procedure outlined in chapter 23, he defines a new method, *ski_info*; into the **Body** field of the template, he enters its CO_2 code (figure 27.8). The code of the method is simple, but it does many things. After declaring variables, the central **for** loop cumulates the ski slope lengths of each color category: so many meters of green-rated slopes, so many meters of red, and so forth. The result is kept in a set value called *result*.

```
Body
/*     Compute the total length of slopes of the same color,
       and then display the result as a pie chart.
 */

o2 set(tuple (color: string, total_length: integer)) result;
o2 tuple(name: string, color: string, length: integer) piste;
o2 tuple (color: string, total_length: integer) elt;
o2 Quantity_matrix matrix;
o2 list(double) values;
o2 list(string) legends;
o2 string message;
o2 boolean found;
int p;

result = set();


for (piste in self->slopes) {
  found = false;
  for (elt in result)
    if (strcmp(elt.color, piste.color) == 0) {
      elt.total_length = elt.total_length + piste.length;
      found = true;
      break;
    }
  if (!(found))
    result += set(tuple(color: piste.color, total_length: piste.length));
}
values = list();
legends = list();
for (elt in result) {
  values += list((double)elt.total_length);
  legends += list(elt.color);
}
matrix = new(Quantity_matrix);
[matrix set_with_scalars(list(values))];
message = (o2 string) malloc(40);
sprintf(message, "Slope color distribution in %s", self->name);
[matrix create_Pie_form(message, legends)];
[matrix activate_graphics(message,"")];
```

Figure 27.8. The CO_2 code for the method *ski_info*

The second, shorter **for** loop turns this set into a pair of lists, one of floating-point numbers (*values*) holding the lengths, the other (**legends**) the corresponding colors. The lengths are then stored in a new object, *matrix*, of the system-supplied class Quantity_matrix. The advantage here is that Quantity_matrix has a number of useful methods defined; two of these are sent to the object *matrix* at the end of the code. They create (*create_Pie_form*) and display (*activate_graphics*) a pie chart showing the distribution of difficulty of the resort's slopes.

The programmer, like most of his tribe, is confident that he has made no mistakes in his code, but he is also prudent. Therefore he tests the method by dashing off a quick test program that creates a new object of class Winter_resort and invokes his method on it. Since we have been speaking of Huez, he will create the object to represent Huez and will render it persistent. The code of the test program is shown in figure 27.9. When executed, the program creates and displays a new, blank object of class Winter_resort, whose data may be entered on the screen (figure 27.10). Once this is done, the object is made persistent by including it in a persistent named set value (*City*, the set of all cities in the database). Finally, the method *ski_info* is sent to the new object; the resulting pie chart may be seen in figure 27.11.

```
Shell
execute co2
{
 o2 Winter_resort wr;
 int p;

    /*  Create an object of the Winter_resort class;
        display it on screen to fill it out. */
 wr = new(Winter_resort);
 p = present(wr, EDIT, LEVEL_ONE, NESTED_WINDOW);
 map(p, SCREEN, MANUAL, NO_PERSIST,0 , 0);
 while (lock(p) == CLICK_QUIT);
 consult(p, &wr);
 destroy(p);

    /*  Include it in a persistent set */
 City += set(wr);

    /*  Send message ski_info to new object */
 [wr ski_info];
}
```

Figure 27.9. Test program for the *ski_info* method

These changes are available instantly to the front room. As the travel agent sits down with us to plan the Huez trip and invokes the *travel_information* program once again, she is mildly surprised to see a new city in the list of available destinations: *Huez.* Curious, she clicks on this object to see what operations are associated with it, and sees the newly-created program *ski_info* (figure 27.12).

Watching from behind the curtain, the programmer smiles.

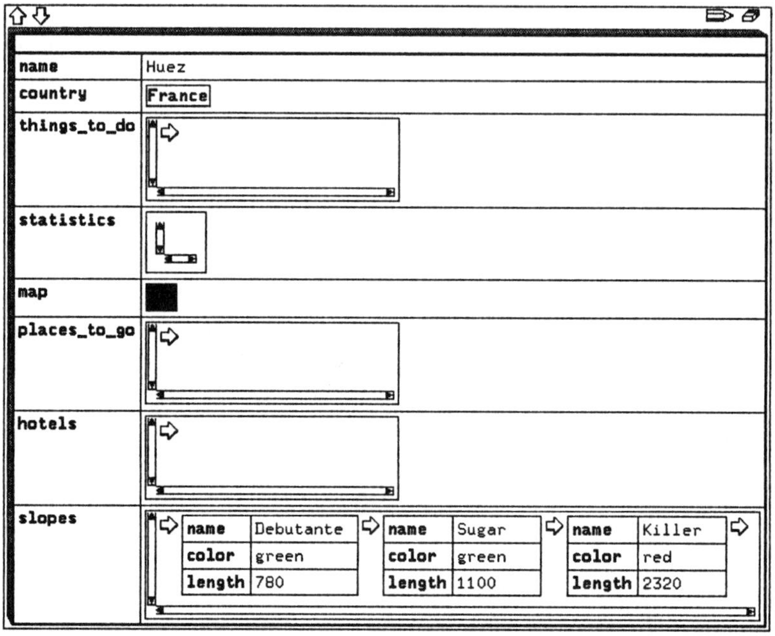

Figure 27.10. Filling out a new object of the class Winter_resort

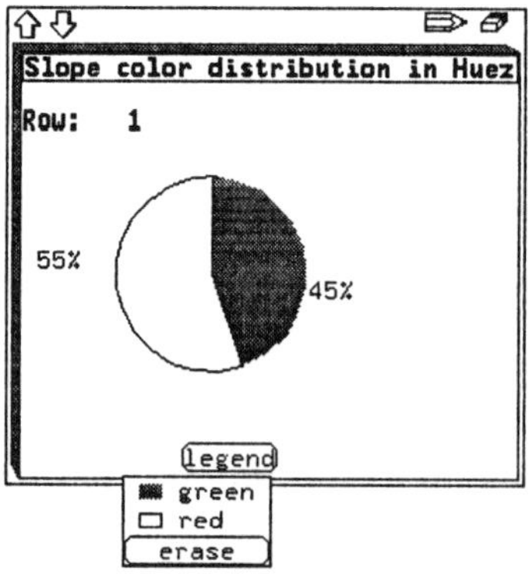

Figure 27.11. Pie chart resulting from the method *ski_info*

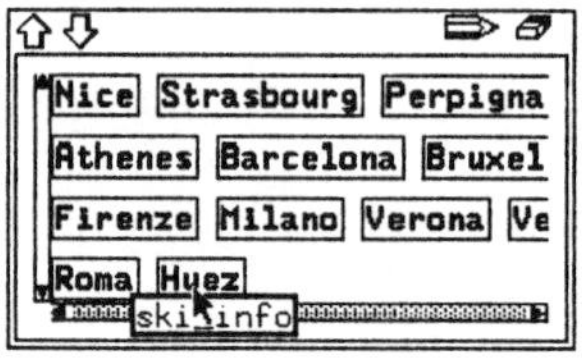

Figure 27.12. The new object *Huez* and its method

CHAPTER 28

Geographic Applications: An Experience with O_2

MICHEL SCHOLL
AGNÈS VOISARD

1 Introduction

We consider in this chapter geographic applications which require an intensive use of database systems called Geographic Information Systems (GIS). For a comprehensive study on the modeling and design of GISs, see Frank 1984 and Smith et al. 1987.

One of the characteristics of GISs is that they cover a wide range of applications dealing with objects for which neither a common definition nor a common set of functions exist. The design and implementation of a query language for geographic applications therefore becomes a complex task. Several proposals for such query languages, called spatial query languages, have recently been made in the literature (Barrera and Buchmann 1981; Frank 1982; Sack-Davis, McDonell, and Ooi 1987; Cardenas and Joseph 1988; Guting 1988; Abel 1989; Egenhofer 1989c; Ooi, Sack-Davis, and McDonell 1989). A spatial query language basically requires the capability of

1. managing, manipulating, and querying a large number of objects whose value includes geometric information as well as alphanumeric description

2. representing arbitrarily complex structures for these objects

3. applying to these objects application-dependent geometric operations

Clearly, (extended) relational systems are good candidates for fulfilling our first requirement. There exist a large number of proposals in the literature (see, for example, Sack-Davis, McDonell, and Ooi 1987; Waugh and Healey 1987;

Guting 1989; Bennis et al. 1990) based on extended relational query languages *à la* SQL. Within such languages, geometric objects are represented as tuples of flat (normalized) relations. Regular relational operations can be performed on these objects as well as application-dependent geometric operations.

The model proposed in Scholl and Voisard 1989 differs from these approaches in the following respects:

- It allows the representation of arbitrarily complex structures (in the normalized relational model, only records of atomic attributes are allowed) and the expression of more complex operations on objects such as nest and unnest (Abiteboul, Fisher, and Schek 1988). It uses the Abiteboul-Beeri complex objects algebra (Abiteboul and Beeri 1988).

- It allows one to extend general-purpose retrieval and manipulation operations with application- or user-dependent geometric operations. This is done through the use of a functional **apply** similar to the **replace** operator of Abiteboul and Beeri 1988, or the **filter** operator of FAD (Bancilhon et al. 1987), or the λ operator of Guting 1988.

However, the objective of this chapter is not to propose another spatial query language but to study the feasability of implementing relational-like spatial query languages by means of an object-oriented database system. Therefore, in this chapter we do not allow the representation of arbitrarily complex objects, and we restrict our attention to flat relations for modeling geometric objects; this is the approach followed in the literature mentioned above. Although the existing languages do not lean on a sound theoretical framework, they all, more or less, distinguish two levels: the relational or map level, and the spatial or geometric level.

The first level is the *map level.* Geographic information is represented by geographic relations called maps, whose only peculiarity is the existence of at least one geometric attribute whose abstract data type is defined at the second level. Maps are queried and manipulated through a relational-like query language which may call for functions on the geometric attributes. These functions are implemented at the second level.

The second level is the *geometric level.* There exist a given number of geometric abstract data types with the following characteristics:

- The abstract data types correspond to a given data model or representation of the geometry. Recent geometric data models (see, for example, Egenhofer 1989a; Smyth 1990) use geometric models derived from Euclidean geometry and algebraic topology.

- The internal structure of the abstract data types is hidden at the map level, that is, the user, who sees only functions (name and signature) on objects with such types.

- There exist a variety of application-dependent functions on these types. Such functions are supposed to be very general. It is not assumed that objects of geometric type are closed under these functions; and the signature of such a function may use any type (geometric or not). Because of this generality, the power of expression of such languages is not well defined, as it is with regular relational models. In consequence, the application-dependent software has a greater overhead, in particular for type verification.

Not only spatial query languages but also general-purpose extended relational systems, such as Postgres (Stonebraker and Rowe 1986) or Sabrina-Lisp, (Gardarin et al. 1989) are based on this approach. It has the advantage of providing the user with some programming facility linked to the use of high-level, general-purpose database operations. In order to study an object-oriented implementation of spatial query languages, we chose to develop a prototype of GIS on top of the O_2 system developed by Altaïr.

The remainder of this chapter reports our design choices and the current state of implementation. A definition of the map model is given in section 2, as well as a sketch of a spatial query language through examples. Section 3 describes the architecture of the prototype. Section 4 discusses the problem of implementing a spatial uery language with the database system O_2. Section 5 addresses the implementation of geometric data types; this requires the definition of an object-oriented schema.

One of the most challenging tasks of geographic applications is the design of user interfaces whose main characteristic is the visualization of (and interaction with) geometric objects. This is briefly discussed in section 6, which reports our design choices. Some conclusions on the suitability of the object-oriented approach, and more specifically of the O_2 system, for such applications are drawn in section 7. Sections 8 and 9 contain two appendices: an O_2 schema for the geometry of a map, and an extension of CO_2 for implementing relational operations.

2 Map Model and Query Language

We begin by describing some spatial query languages. It is not our purpose to give a complete definition of each language. Instead we chose a few examples to illustrate some of the most common features and operations of the languages one can find in the literature, and to express a few queries with a syntax *à la* SQL. We need first to specify what we call a *map model* and to introduce a few definitions.

We believe that looking for a model general enough to encompass a large variety of geographical applications is an enterprise bound to fail. Any map model will strongly depend on the geographic application, on the structure of the geometry visible to the user, and on the geometric functions to be applied to these objects. Of course, part of the structure is hidden to the user as well as the implementation of the functions, because of encapsulation. The more encapsulated the geometry, the cleaner the separation between application-independent database operations and application-dependent geometric operations. Encapsulation will allow modularity, that is, extensibility and customization of the geometric operations independently of the general-purpose database operations.

2.1 The Map Model

Any relation with at least one geometric attribute is called a *map*. Nongeometric attributes are called *descriptive* attributes. They are defined as usual; that is, they have a name and a definition domain (Ullman 1988). We do not require in a map the existence of descriptive attributes; a map can have geometric attributes only. These are specified by a geometric data type. Any application requires the specification of one or more types. We chose for our examples three data types: points, lines, and regions; these are described below. We show in section 5 that the object-oriented approach is extremely well adapted to the implementation of geometric types.

2.1.1 Maps

A *geographic database* is a set of maps. A map is a set of tuples. To each tuple of a map is associated a subset S of the two-dimensional plane R^2, with common alphanumeric information. The geometric attributes of the tuple represent the (possibly infinite) set S of points; the descriptive attributes represent the alphanumeric information common to all points in S. We give below an informal specification of geometric types necessary for the examples of queries to be studied.

2.1.2 Informal Specification of the Geometric Types

The geometric attribute of a map may have one of three types, depending on whether the S topology is zero-dimensional, one-dimensional, or two-dimensional.

1. A zero-dimensional geometric object of type Points is defined as a finite set of points in R^2.

2. Let an *arc* be the infinite set of points of a linear segment in R^2. Whether the *end points* of the segment belong to the arc or not is of no concern for our examples. Given a finite set of arcs A, let N be the union of end points of arcs in A. To A can be associated a graph $G = (N, E)$, where for each arc in R^2 there is a corresponding edge in E and there is no other edge in E. A is a *line* iff G is connected. A one-dimensional object of type Lines is defined as a finite set of lines.

3. A two-dimensional object of type Regions is defined as a finite set of regions; a *region* is the infinite set of points in R^2 included in and possibly on a simple polygon.

Representing geometric objects (of types Regions, Lines, and Points) as finite sets of more elementary objects (Region, Line, and Point) is motivated by the fact that the former objects are closed under operations such as intersection, union, or difference. Note that at the map level the internal structure of geometric types (set of, arc, line, region, and so on) is not visible. It is given here only for illustrative reasons. Only the following functions are visible at the map level. They can be applied to objects of types Regions, Lines, and Points.

- *included-in*, with signature Points × Regions → Boolean, has for its semantics set inclusion in R^2. Let p be of type Points and r of type Regions; included-in(p, r) is true if all points in p are in r.
- *inside*, with signature Lines × Regions → Lines, corresponds to intersection in R^2. Let l be of type Lines and r of type Regions; inside(l, r) represents all points in l which are in r.
- *inter*, with signature Lines × Regions → Boolean, tests whether a one-dimensional object crosses a two-dimensional object. Let l be of type Lines and r of type Regions; inter(l, r) is true iff the intersection of points in l with points in r is nonempty.
- *border*, with signature Regions → Lines, gives the one-dimensional boundary of a two-dimensional object.
- *Radjacent*, with signature Regions × Regions → Boolean, tests the adjacency of two-dimensional objects. *Ladjacent*, with signature Lines × Lines → Boolean, tests the adjacency of one-dimensional objects. Informally speaking, two two-dimensional objects are adjacent if their intersection is nonempty and is on their boundaries and on their boundaries only; two one-dimensional objects l_1 and l_2 are said to be adjacent if there exists one arc of l_1 colinear with one arc of l_2 (see figure 28.1).

Figure 28.1. Arcs a and b are colinear

Note that the semantics of the functions is more or less dependent on the topology of the geometric objects; this is particularly true for the three last functions. A formal specification of geometric types and in particular of the above types should use geometric modeling. Egenhofer 1989b is an attempt toward this.

2.1.3 Examples of Tuples

Here are three examples of tuples.

1. [**name**: "Fontainebleau", **vegetation**: "beech", **R**: r] represents a forest whose name is Fontainebleau and whose geometric attribute has the value r, which identifies a set of two polygons (figure 28.2). This tuple belongs to the relation Forests, whose schema is a tuple [**name**: string, **vegetation**: string, **R**: Regions].

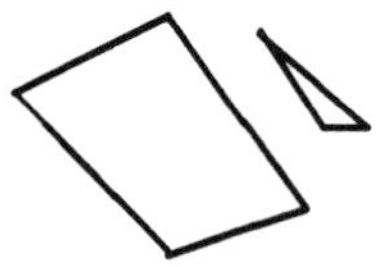

Figure 28.2. Set of two polygons represented by r

2. [**number**: "A6," **L**: l] represents highway number A6, whose one-dimensional geometry value l identifies a set that contains a single line (figure 28.3).

Figure 28.3. Set of one line represented by l

   This tuple belongs to the relation Highways, whose schema is [**number**: string, **L**: Lines].

3. [**name**: "Petit_Clamart," **P**: p] represents a highway intersection point whose name is Petit Clamart and whose geometry is a set containing a single point. This tuple belongs to the relation Crossings, whose schema is [**name**: string, **P**: Points].

Such a representation of geographic objects is simple; but it has the following limitation, due to the relational model: we forbid the use of nonatomic domains for descriptive attributes. One way of getting around this restriction is to allow complex values, as in nested relational models (Abiteboul, Fisher, and Schek 1988) or in complex-object models (Abiteboul and Beeri 1988). Object-oriented models allow an even more powerful representation of complex domains. As a simple example, the domain of a highway number is designated as "string".

Since any highway is described by an alphabetic character string followed by an integer, it would be more appropriate to define the domain of attribute **number** in the relation Highways by a type Highway_type, whose definition in terms of atomic domains is [**Alpha**: string, **num**: integer]. As another example, geometric attributes are always seen as attributes whose value is atomic. This might of course be a strong limitation.

2.2 Examples of Queries on Maps

A large number of geometric queries vary from one paper to the other in the literature. See, for example, Egenhofer 1989c, Guting 1988, and Quilio et al. 1989 for a thorough description of queries and geometric functions used at the map level. We give here only a few examples of queries on the following map schema:

Cities(**name**: string, **population**: integer, **R**: Regions)
Crossings(**name**: string, **P**: Points)
Highways(**number**: string, **L**: Lines)
Districts(**name**: string, **R**: Regions)
Forests(**name**: string, **vegetation**: string, **R**: Regions)

For each query we give the English formulation and the query itself in a language whose syntax is close to that of SQL. All queries below have a **select-from-where** form. The arguments of the **select** clause can be descriptive attributes drawn from the source maps, as well as values computed by the use of a function of the abstract geometric data type. In general, the arguments of **select** give the schema of the target relation. But the result of a query is not necessarily a map; it can be any relation whose attributes are descriptive attributes; it can also be any measure (possibly aggregate), such as length, or distance. The arguments of the **from** clause are the source maps, and the arguments of the **where** clause are a conjunct of functions whose range is Boolean. These functions are either a regular SQL predicate or a Boolean function on geometric attributes.

1. *What are the highway intersections located inside the city of Versailles?*

select Crossings.name
  from Cities, Crossings
  where Cities.name = "Versailles"
  and included-in(crossing.P, Cities.R)

2. *Display the portions of highways inside the Var district.*

select Highways.L inside Districts.R
  from Highways, Districts
  where Districts.name = "Var"
  and inter(Highways.L, Districts.R)

3. *Which are the cities adjacent to Versailles?*

```
select C1.name, C1.R
    from Cities C1, Cities C2
    where C2.name = "Versailles"
    and Radjacent(C1.R, C2.R)
```

4. *Which forests are bordered by highway A7?*

```
select Forests.name, Forests.vegetation, Forests.R
    from Forests, Highways
    where Highway.number = A7
    and Ladjacent(border(Forests.R), Highways.L)
```

In query 3, the last predicate Radjacent(C1.R, C2.R) could be expressed as: Ladjacent(border(C1.R), border(C2.R)), testing whether the two border lines have one or more colinear segments. We could also have defined a function *RLadjacent*, which would test adjacency between a two-dimensional object and a one-dimensional one. This example illustrates that the query language strongly depends on the definition of the geometric types, that is, on the spatial semantics visible at the user level. Other typical queries are given in section 5.

3 Architecture of the Prototype

A prototype of a spatial query language is being developed on top of version V1 of the O_2 system. This prototype allows querying of maps through a graphical user interface. In this section, we briefly describe the functional architecture of the prototype.

3.1 Available Functionalities

A spatial query language such as that described in section 2 is not yet available as a user interface. The querying of maps through operations, examples of which were given in section 2, corresponds to algebraic operations such as:

- Regular relational selection, projection, and join.
- Algebraic operations with geometric functions, the simplest form of which is *geometric selection*, that is, the selection of regions or lines: included in, or containing, or intersecting, etcetera, a constant window chosen on the screen. For example, *clip* selects all regions or lines that intersect a rectangle drawn by the user on the screen; *window* selects all geometric objects inside a rectangle drawn on the screen.

For a more complete definition of these algebraic operations, see Scholl and Voisard 1989.

Currently, these operations are implemented as methods run on an object (a map) through the user interface provided by Looks (Plateau et al. 1990; see chapter 22), which has been extended to deal with maps. The user first browses through the database and chooses a map he or she wishes to query. The user displays the map and chooses one or more of the following methods:

1. Display the description (alphanumeric attribute values) of objects (regions, lines, or points) containing a point selected with the mouse on the screen.

2. Project or select on descriptive attributes.

3. Clip or window.

3.2 Architecture

The implementation of these functionalities corresponds to the development in parallel of three independent modules: the interface, the map level, and the geometric level.

3.2.1 The Interface

The Looks system has been extended in Aïda (Devin and Duquesnoy 1988) to allow the display of geometric vectorized objects and a geometric interaction with the user (see section 6).

3.2.2 The Map Level

A map is represented by an object (Souf 1990). Algebraic operations are implemented by methods on map objects. This module corresponds to the programming of all CO_2 methods implementing algebraic operations on maps as well as methods for creating maps and entering actual map data. Most of this module could have been trivially implemented by using the O_2 query language (Bancilhon, Cluet, and Delobel 1989; see chapter 11). We explain in section 4 why this was not possible and why we had to program these algebraic operations in the O_2 programming language CO_2 (Lécluse and Richard 1989b; see chapter 9).

3.2.3 The Geometric Level

The geometric level corresponds to the implementation in CO_2 of the geometric data types: Regions, Lines, and Points. A tuple of a map is represented as an object. Each tuple object is composed of a subobject which represents the geometry of this object. For example, the object whose value is [`name`: "Versailles", `R`: *r*] is composed of the object with identifier *r* of class Regions. When executing a database query, a method is called whose receiver is an object representing the map. The execution of a geometric operation may be necessary; this corresponds to calling a method whose receiver is an object of class Regions. The design of the schema (classes and methods) corresponding to the internal representation of the geometry and the implementation of geometric operations is developed in section 5.

4 Implementation of the Map Level

In this section we discuss the implementation of the map level, that is, the design of methods on classes representing maps, which methods implement algebraic operations for answering database queries. We have two possibilities: either (1) these methods on map objects are implemented in the programming language of the object-oriented system, CO_2, or (2) a query language is available that is powerful enough to express the queries of the application. We examine first the second alternative, namely the use of the O_2 query language for implementing extended database queries.

4.1 Expressive Power of the O_2 Query Language

The O_2 query language is powerful enough to express database queries such as those described in section 2. For example, query 2: *Display the portions of highways inside the Var district.* This query can be expressed with as follows.

select x.L **inside**(y.R)
from x **in** Highways
y **in** Districts
where y.name = "Var" **and**
x.L **inter**(y.R)

A map, say Highways, is represented by a set value of objects representing map tuples; these objects belong to a class with structure [name: string, L: Lines]. The geometric attribute L has for its value an object of a geometric class: Lines. The geometric functions inside and inter are implemented as methods (inside and inter) of the class Lines.

The **from** arguments indicate that *x* (or *y*) is an object to be taken in a set of Highways (or Districts) objects. The **select** argument expresses that the method inside is sent to object *x.L* of class Lines, with argument object *y.R* of class Region (*x.L* is an object representing the geometry of a highway, and *y.R* is the geometry of a district). The second **where** predicate is true if the method inter, sent to *x.L* with argument *y.R*, returns "true." The result is a set that contains objects of class Lines. With the O_2 interface we can output the value of this result, but we cannot visualize it as a map.

4.2 Integration of the O_2 Query Language

In spite of its power, at the time of implementation, the O_2 query language was only available in an interactive way. This prevents the designer from using it through any graphical user interface which requires a full integration of the query language into the programming language. By full integration we mean that the query language is a subset of CO_2 and that any query (that is, any **select-from-where** block) can be utilized in a CO_2 method.

There are also features in the current definition of the O_2 query language that render the implementation of spatial query languages more difficult. In particular, the O_2 model distinguishes encapsulated objects with methods from nonencapsulated values; there is no possibility of defining user functions on these values.

For example, the result of a filter query is a value and not an object. The result of an algebraic operation (implemented by a filter instruction) usually being a map, maps should be represented by set values. This suggests that algebraic operations should be implemented by functions on set values. But this is impossible, since user-defined functions on values are not provided by CO_2. To overcome this difficulty, tuples of a map (relation) are represented by objects with a tuple structure, while the extension of the map (relation) is represented by the set of object identifiers stored in a named value.

To illustrate the use of the O_2 query language integrated with CO_2 for implementing algebraic operations let us look at standard relational projection. To represent a relational schema $R(A_1\colon D_1, \ldots, A_n\colon D_n)$ we define a class R with structure $[A_1\colon D_1, \ldots, A_n\colon D_n]$ and a named value Rext with type {R}. Thus, a relation is represented by the set Rext of tuple objects of class R. Projection $\pi_{A_i}(R)$ is implemented as follows.

V = **select**[$x.A_i$] **from** x in Rext
Text: $\{T\}$
for each v **in** V
    a = **new**(T)
    $a.A_i = v$
    Text + = $\{a\}$

The target relation is represented by a set value Text of type {T}, where T is a class with type $[A_i\colon D_i]$. The first line (O_2 query and assignment of the result to V) performs the projection. The result is a set V of tuple values. But we would like the result to be a relation whose extension is stored in Text. Then for each tuple value v of V, an object a of class T is created. The value of a is assigned to v, and a is added to Text. This implementation assumes, of course the preexistence of the class T and of the named value Text.

4.3 Implementing Generic Relational-Algebra Operations

Relational-algebra interpreters have the capability of run-time access to the relation type definitions (the schema). This is different from database programming languages which use static type checking. This problem is illustrated in Stemple et al. 1990, where the integration in the *Adabtpl* language of generic projection, selection, join, and nest is studied. It is shown that a solution exists for the first two operations, but the other two are problematic. Another approach is taken in Machiavelli (Ohori, Buneman, and Breazu-Tannen 1989). Object-oriented database programming languages have a level of polymorphism insufficient to handle query algebra capabilities, that is, to allow the implementation of generic relational operations. Consider the above example in section 4.2. One would like to implement a method ***projection*** on class R, taking as arguments the attribute names in the list $A_1, \ldots, A_n$. We encounter two problems:

- After projection, the target relation may have one of $2^n - 1$ schemas. This suggests the existence of the same number of classes for representing target relations, since it is impossible to create a new class in the body of a method in CO_2. This is the problem of dynamic class creation.
- Projecting tuple $[A_1\colon a_1, \ldots, A_n\colon a_n]$ on A_i, where the attribute name A_i is given as a parameter, is not possible with the current version of O_2; run-time access to type information is impossible. Analogous problems arise for selection, join, and other operations.

4.4 Design of a Query Language

A system designer might want to develop his of her own query language, for performance reasons. Specific applications require specific optimizations dependent on the physical organization of data; this is particularly true for geographic applications, where significant effort has been put toward the creation of efficient data structures (Samet 1989; Six and Widmayer 1988), or of efficient implementation of query languages (see, for example, Guting 1988). In order to solve the problem of dynamic class creation, it is necessary to afford the capability of writing a query language either (1) in the programming language of the database system or (2) directly on the object manager, in which case the system designer should be given a more user-friendly interface to the object manager. In section 9, we sketch a possible extension of CO_2 with a few constructs and the simulation of genericity by inheritance (Meyer 1986, 1988) in order to allow the implementation of generic relational-algebra operations. These extensions solve the problem of run-time access to type information. However, they are of limited use if dynamic class creation is not provided by the system.

4.5 Current Implementation

In order to bypass the above problems and to implement filter (**select-from-where**) queries in CO_2, an alternate approach, also suggested in Stemple et al. 1990, was chosen. It is far from elegant, and it complicates the implementation of sets of tuples (relations or maps); but it is at present the only solution for integrating generic relational-like operations in CO_2. It does not require any additional features to the type mechanism, and it does not require dynamic class creation or run-time access to type information.

The approach consists in encapsulating the attribute name with its value so that type information is manipulated by the programmer as values. All maps are implemented as objects of a single class, Map. All algebraic operations on maps are implemented by methods of this single class, and they give as output an object (a map) of that class; there is thus no need to create a new class for a target map.

Each tuple of a map is modeled as a list of tuples [attribute-name, attribute-value]. Such a schema is sketched in figure 28.4. This schema loses part of the typing power of O_2. The enforcement of constraints (such as: all tuples of a single map must have the same number of attributes and the same attribute names) is the responsibility of the programmer. Access to the attribute values and the attribute names is explicitly done by the programmer. Thanks to this subterfuge, some genericity is obtained.

```
class Map
      type tuple(name: string,
                 extension: Geotuples)
      method filter ...
      method mapOverlay ...

class Geotuples
      type set(Geotuple)

class Geotuple
      type tuple(attributes: list(Att)
                 geometry: Geos)

class Att
      type tuple(name: string)
      method compare(x: Att): Boolean

class IntAtt
      inherits Att
      type tuple(value: integer)
      method compare(x: IntAtt): Boolean

class StringAtt
      inherits Att
      type tuple(value: string)
      method compare(x: StringAtt): Boolean

class RealAtt
...
```

Figure 28.4. O_2 schema for representing maps

More precisely, all maps have a single tuple structure with two attributes: a name and an extension, which is an object of the class Geotuples. An object of class Geotuples has a set value. An element of this set represents a map tuple. It is an object of class Geotuple and has two attributes: one is a list of descriptive attributes; the other is the geometric attribute, which is an object of class Geos. There are three classes, one for each geometric type: Points, Lines, and Regions; these have a common superclass, Geos (see section 5).

Each descriptive attribute has a name and an atomic value (such as integer, string, or real). This is represented by a class hierarchy with root Att of type tuple with a single O_2 attribute whose value is the name of the descriptive attribute of the map. Methods of this class should never be executed, since a descriptive attribute is of class IntAtt, StringAtt, or some other similar class. The value of a descriptive attribute is specified in the subclass corresponding to its domain. The overloaded method *compare* of this subclass tests whether the value of the descriptive attribute is equal to the value in the argument. Other methods are provided for other comparators such as < and >.

For example, consider the map Forests(**name**, **vegetation**, **R**) and the tuple [**name**: "Fontainebleau", **vegetation**: "beech," **R**: g]. The map Forests is represented by an object of class Map with value [**name**: "Forests", **extension**: e]. e is an object of class Geotuples with value $\{f, \ldots\}$, where f represents Fontainebleau forest and is an object of class Geotuple with value [list(n, v), g]. n and v are objects of class StringAtt and g (geometry) is an object of class Geos. n has the value: [**name**: "name," **value**: "Fontainebleau"] and v has the value [**name**: "vegetation," **value**: "beech"].

5 Implementation of Geometric Functions

We do not list a complete set of classes and methods for implementing geometric operations; this set is heavily dependent on the application. Instead, we illustrate the object-oriented approach and describe the O_2 schema for implementing a few geometric functions that appear in the following queries.

5.1 Queries

1. *Which are the cities adjacent to Versailles?* (Query 3 of section 2.2)

```
select C1.name, C1.R
    from Cities C1, Cities C2
    where C2.name = "Versailles"
    and Radjacent(C1.R, C2.R)
```

2. *Which forests are bordered by highway A7?* (Query 4 of section 2.2)

```
select Forests.name, Forests.vegetation, Forests.R
    from Forests, Highways
    where Highway.number = "A7"
    and Ladjacent(border(Forests.R), Highways.L)
```

3. *Display the intersections between countries and Lake Leman.* The result indicates the French and Swiss parts of the lake. This query is on the maps Lakes(**name**: string, **R**: Regions) and Countries(**name**: string, **R**: Regions). It uses the function *Rintersection* (intersection of regions), which has the signature Regions × Regions → Regions. Rintersection(r, s) represents all points in r which are also in s.

   select Rintersection(Lakes.R, Countries.R)
   from Lakes, Countries
   where Lakes.name = "Leman"

4. *Select the parts of trails that run along (are colinear to) highways.* We use the maps Highways(**name**: string, **L**: Lines) and Trails(**name**: string, **Length**: integer, **L**: Lines), and the function *Lintersection* (intersection of lines), which has the signature Lines × Lines → Lines. Lintersection(l, m) is the maximal one-dimensional object which is in both l and m.

   select Lintersection(Highways.L, Trails.L)
   from Highways, Trails

5. *Select all bridges (i.e., intersection points of highways and rivers).* This query is on the map Highways and the map Rivers(**name**: string, **L**: Lines). We need the function *Pintersection* with signature Lines × Lines → Points. Pintersection(l, m) is not defined if l and m are adjacent (Ladjacent(l, m) is true); otherwise it is the finite set of points which are in both l and m.

   select Pintersection(Highways.L, Rivers.L)
   from Highways, Rivers

Geometric functions are implemented by methods on geometric classes, the schema of which is given in the next subsection.

5.2 Structure

Figure 28.5 displays an inheritance tree whose nodes are the geometric classes. All classes have a common root, Spatial, which represents geometric information common to all maps (e.g., referential, or scale). Section 8 gives for each class its structure and the methods necessary for implementing the above geometric functions. For the time being we are only interested in the structure of the classes. The hierarchy of geometric classes includes four subtrees with roots Geos, Arc, Arcs, and Geo.

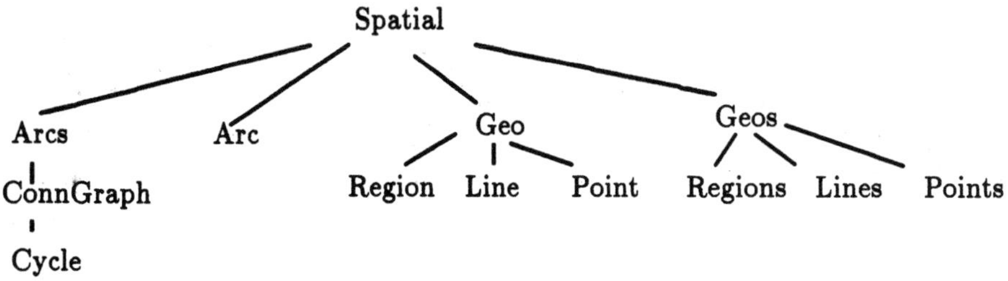

Figure 28.5. Inheritance tree for the geometric classes

The hierarchy Geos A tuple of a map has at least one geometric attribute of type Points, Lines, or Regions. Values of geometric attributes are implemented as objects of a class Geos with subclasses Regions, Lines, and Points. Objects of the class Regions (or Lines or Points) represent geometric values of type Regions (or Lines or Points). An object of class Geos (or Regions, Lines, or Points) has as its value a set of objects of class Geo (or Region, Line, or Point). An object of class Region represents a region (a simple polygon). An object of class Line represents a line (a finite set of linear segments or arcs whose associated graph is connected). An object of class Point represents a point.

For example, the tuple [`administrative-region`: "Brittany", `Roads`: l] represents the roads of Brittany (l is an object of class Lines). Each road is represented by an object of class Line. The tuple [`administrative-region`: "Brittany", `crop`: "corn", `counties`: r] represents the counties of Brittany where corn is grown (r is an object of class Regions). Each county is represented by an object of class Region.

The classes Region, Line, and Point have class Geo as a superclass. Before getting into the structure of classes of the Geo hierarchy, let us describe the classes Arc and Arcs.

The class Arc An object of class Arc represents an arc, that is, a linear segment represented by its end points (objects of class Point). The distinction between a begin point and an end point allows us to represent oriented arcs.

The hierarchy Arcs An object of class Arcs has as its value a list of objects of class Arc (it represents a list of linear segments in R^2). The class ConnGraph is a subclass of Arcs. It inherits the Arcs structure and methods and has an additional method, connect:Boolean, which checks that the set of arcs is a line (its associated graph is connected). The class Cycle is a subclass of Conn-Graph, with the additional method cyclic:Boolean, which checks that the line is a boundary of a simple polygon (in particular, that its associated connected graph is a simple cycle).

The hierarchy Geo The Geo hierarchy of classes implements atomic objects. A point (i.e., an object of class Point) is represented by its two coordinates relative to the referential. A line is represented by an object of class Line (see figure 28.6); it has a tuple structure, with one attribute whose value is an object of class ConnGraph (a line is composed of a set of connected arcs). Similarly, an object of class Region is composed of a cycle (the border of the polygon); although a region is a two-dimensional object, it is represented by its one-dimensional border. If regions with holes were to be represented, one could also add a subclass of Region called RegionWithHoles, with an additional attribute for the holes whose type is set(Cycle) (see figure 28.7). The extension of class Geo is the union of the extensions of Point, Line, and Region: an atomic object is either a point or a line or a region.

Figure 28.6. Examples of objects of class Line

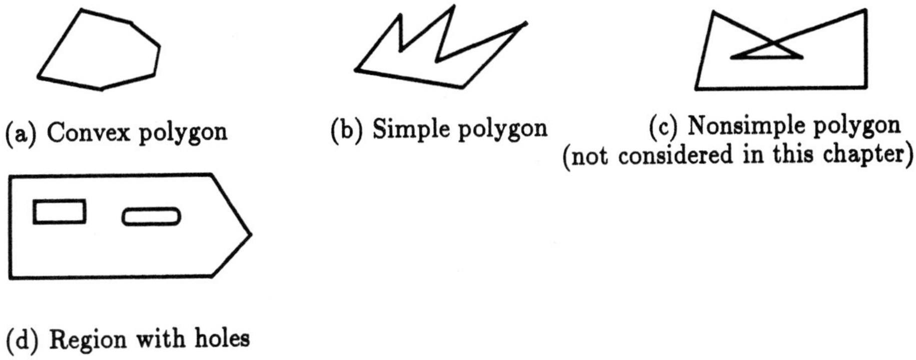

Figure 28.7. Examples of objects of class Region

Geos is modeled as a set of objects of class Geo because sets of homogeneous geometric objects are closed under operations such as intersection, union, or difference. But this modeling is somewhat arbitrary. For some applications, Geos could be structured as a set of sets of objects of class Geo. For example, assume that administrative regions are split into districts, which in turn are split into counties. In that case, one might decide to keep for the geometry of the tuple Brittany in the map France, the borders of all counties of Brittany, grouped by district, instead of either the set of district borders or the outer border of the administrative region itself. Then, depending on how much of the semantics of the geometry one wants to be visible at the map level, one has the choice between two extremes:

1. Render the structure visible at the map level; use the types Region, Line, and Point. The map level sees atomic attributes whose type is a line or a polygon. With such an approach, counties are visible in the tuple Brittany of the map France.

   ```
   [administrative-region: "Brittany",
   crop: "seaweed",
   Districts: {[District: "Morbihan",
               Counties: {[County: Groixisland,
                           Geometry: r], ...}]...}],
   ```

   where r is an object of class Region.

2. Hide the structure of geometric objects; at the map level, it is an atomic attribute (of type Regions, for example) on which some operations are performed, and its hidden structure is any complex structure whose atoms are lines or polygons. The choice of this structure would then depend not only on the application semantics but also on implementation, optimization, and performance choices.

   ```
   [administrative-region: "Brittany", geometry: r]
   ```

   where r is an object of a class with the following structure:

   ```
   [ARouterborder: Region,
   Districts: {[Districtborder: Region,
               Counties: {Countyborder: Region}]}]
   ```

Although the first approach is more appropriate, we chose the latter alternative in order to stick to the flat relational model assumed by the spatial query languages discussed in the literature. We further assumed the simplest structure for representing complex geometric objects (hierarchy Geos) in terms of atomic geometric objects (hierarchy Geo).

5.3 Methods

We present now the implementation of the geometric functions appearing in the five queries of section 5.1: Radjacent, Ladjacent, border, Rintersection, Lintersection, and Pintersection. Each function is implemented by a method of a given class (see table 28.1).

Function	Signature	Method	Class
Radjacent	Regions × Regions → Bool	adjacent	Geos
Ladjacent	Lines × Lines → Bool	adjacent	Geos
border	Regions → Lines	border	Lines
Rintersection	Regions × Regions → Regions	intersection	Geos
Lintersection	Lines × Lines → Lines	intersection	Geos
Pintersection	Lines × Lines → Points	pintersection	Lines

Table 28.1. **Implementation of Geometric Functions by Methods**

5.3.1 Adjacency

The functions Radjacent (adjacency of two-dimensional objects) and Ladjacent (adjacency of one-dimensional objects) are implemented by a single method, adjacent, defined in class Geos (see section 8). This is an advantage of object-oriented programming; at the query-language level it is not necessary to distinguish between *Radjacent* and *Ladjacent*. Whatever the type of the geometric attribute (Regions or Lines), the method *adjacent* of class Geos is executed. In its body appears the method *adj* of class Geo. This method is redefined in subclasses Region and Line. At run time, the system chooses which code is to be executed according to the class (Region or Line) of the receiver of method *adj*; this is known as overloading. Method *adj* of class Geo should never be executed.

To complete the implementation, let us look at method *adj* redefined in class Region to give an adjacency test for two polygons. Two regions are adjacent if their boundaries are colinear. The method *border* is sent to an object of class Region. It returns an object of class Cycle, to which the method *colinear* (inherited from class Arcs) is sent. This method checks whether two lists of arcs are colinear and therefore calls the method *colinear* of class Arc.

5.3.2 Intersection

To illustrate the limits of the above mechanism for implementing generic operations, we chose the operation *intersection* because it has various semantics not only according to the object type, but also within a given type. The intersection of two sets of polygons is either the empty set or a set of polygons. A naive algorithm consists of iterating on each set of polygons, using as a primitive the intersection of two elementary polygons.

The intersection of two sets of lines may have at least two interpretations. Figure 28.8 (a) shows two lines, line 1 and line 2, intersecting at a, b, cd, and ef. The intersection can be a set of points (a, b, c, d, e, and f) or a set of lines (cd and ef; see figure 28.8 (b)). In the first case it uses as a primitive the intersection of two lines, which in turn utilizes the intersection of two arcs; in the second case it uses as a primitive another operation on two lines which utilizes the colinearity of two arcs.

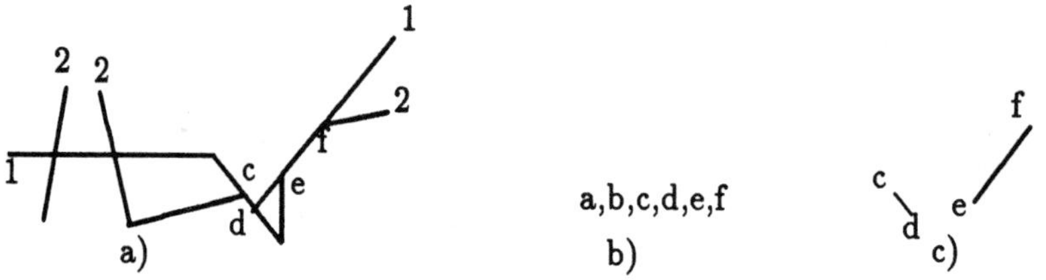

Figure 28.8. Intersection of two lines

Functions Rintersection and Lintersection are implemented by a single method, *intersection*, of class Geos. Without loss of generality, we chose to interpret intersection either as intersection of sets of regions or as an intersection of sets of lines, whose result is a set of lines (this is the second interpretation of a line intersection, as in figure 28.8 (b). We implemented a generic operation as follows: the method *intersection* of class Geos is redefined in classes Regions and Lines. Take the example of class Regions. Its body (1) enforces the method *intersection*, defined in class Geos (intersection(r)@Geos), to be applied to the object of class Regions, which is also an object of class Geos; and (2) casts the result to be of class Regions (return(Regions)). Casting and explicitly choosing which method's code should be executed in a superclass are extensions of the current version of CO_2 that will most probably be provided in a future version of CO_2. In the body of method *intersection* (class Geos) appears method *intersect* of class Geo. This method is redefined in classes Region and Line. At run time, when method *intersect* is sent to an object (of class Geo), the system chooses which code is to be executed according to the type (Region or Line) of that object (overloading). Thanks to this well-known mechanism (Meyer 1986) we obtained some genericity for intersection.

Unfortunately, when the intersection of two sets of lines is interpreted as the set of intersection points between segments of the first set of lines and segments of the second set of lines (the first interpretation of a line intersection), a new method has to be written. Its code is the same as that of the second interpretation (method *intersection* of class Geos), except that method *pintersect* of class Line is called; but this code has to be duplicated in a new method, *pintersection*, of class Lines.

In summary, this implementation of geometric functions showed the power of overloading through inheritance. With the Arcs hierarchy that inheritance allows one elegantly to check the following integrity constraints: (1) to each line is associated a connected graph, and (2) the graph associated to a simple polygon boundary is a simple cycle. We end this section with a brief discussion of the implementation of variant types in our application.

5.3.3 Variant Types

The two hierarchies with roots Geos and Geo allow us, to a certain extent, (1) to model the fact that a geometric object has one among various types, (2) to manipulate a heterogeneous set of objects (e.g., to display on a single map a mixture of regions, roads, and cities). If classes Geos, Regions, Lines, and Points are visible at the map level, then the user can decide between heterogeneous data (use of class Geos) or homogeneous data (use of classes Regions, Lines, or Points). If only class Geos is visible, the user has no way of enforcing homogeneity, since objects of class Geos represent homogeneous as well as heterogeneous data.

6 The User Interface

User interfaces play a prominent part in applications, which manipulate graphic data (such as CAD-CAM, geography, or cartography). Lately there has been increasing activity in this area. In the field of geographic applications, Egenhofer and Frank 1988 is one of the first attempts to describe the functionalities of a user interface for GISs. In this prototype, it was not our objective to design and realize a complete interface for geographic applications for two reasons: (1) there is no deep understanding yet of which functionalities are required at the interface level with respect to map display and map editing (in particular there should be an external map model independent of the database map model, although there might be some morphism from one representation to the other); and (2) the current version of Looks has been designed to display objects in nested form style which is not adequate for geographic interfaces.

We chose to implement a kernel of basic functionalities by extending Looks, with the objective of acquiring a better understanding of the minimal requirements for future versions of Looks. Of course, other applications such as CAD should be looked at. In this section we first describe the functionalities that such an interface should provide, then the current implementation. We briefly describe the interface construction with Looks, and then its extension with specific editors.

6.1 Functionalities of the Interface

Two basic features of database interfaces are (1) the display of values of objects and schemas, and (2) the capability of sending queries. When querying geographic databases, one has to enter values of parameters which are either alphanumeric or geometric. Another characteristic of geographic applications is that most of the time the geometry is not stored in raster format but in vectorized format; that is, atomic objects are of two kinds: sets of end points for representing a line, and border lines for representing two-dimensional objects.

A geographic user interface must be able to display the vectorized geometry of the objects as well as the alphanumeric description of these objects. Similarly, when one is querying, some parameters are entered with the keyboard (or with the mouse when they are identified with an icon), whereas other parameters correspond to the currently displayed geometry and are usually selected on the screen with a mouse. For example, one might ask for the names of the states adjacent to a state selected on the screen (by clicking inside the corresponding geometric polygon). We describe first the most common features related to display, then a few requirements related to geometric querying.

6.1.1 Display and Graphic Aspects

Windows First, there must exist a mapping between a map and a window of the screen where the map is to be displayed. One might want to display several maps on the screen. One might decide to display two distinct maps on a single window without actually overlaying them: one map is only a visual aid, while the other one is the current map. This implies a pile mechanism (the top map being the current map).

Scale and zoom Map scale is only one among several items of geometric data that have to be stored and that might be changed during the process of displaying, editing, or printing a map. Referential (the coordinate system) is another example of such data. The question arises whether such data are related to the map, the application, or the display process. For example, one might change the actual scale at display time just because the map to be displayed must fit into the display window. Zooming is a common feature of geographic interfaces that require a change of scale at display time.

Graphic aspects and map format There exist a variety of parameters for customizing map display. Apart from specific cartographic applications requiring very sophisticated tools, one always requires the capability of mapping a geometric object to a color, of changing its texture, of making a given object blink, and so on. Legends are another important feature for map editing. The legend might be a key for the interpretation of a map. It permits the user to grasp rapidly some characteristics of the geometric object or to group visually several objects that have the same behavior. Finally, the legend might be the value of an alphanumeric attribute that one wants to be displayed close to the corresponding geometric object. The position on the screen of the legends might be specified, as well as other graphic aspects, in a map display format; or it might be chosen interactively by the user before being stored.

6.1.2 Querying

Some common ways of geometrically selecting objects for querying are:

1. Point-selection: With the mouse, select a one- or a two-dimensional object. This implies the execution of a geometric test: Does the region (or line) contain the point?

2. Clipping: Select all objects intersecting with a given window (a simple polygon is entered by the user).

3. Windowing: Select all objects inside a given window.

The algebraic operations corresponding to these geometric selections are defined in Scholl and Voisard 1989.

6.2 Current Implementation

6.2.1 Looks

Basically, Looks (Plateau et al. 1990; see chapter 22) allows the user to interactively manipulate objects and values, either directly or through methods called by menus, and to specify the editing of objects stored in the database according to their structure and according to the existence of predefined editors. For each atomic type there is a corresponding editor (string editor, integer editor, and so on). There is also an editor corresponding to each constructor (set, list, or tuple). One displays a complex object by building complex editors, which recursively call for predefined editors.

Currently the presentation style of objects is unique. However, the capability of refining generic presentations into customized ones is under study (Mamou, J. C. 1991). Although there exists a bitmap editor, there is neither a point editor, a line editor, or a region editor. One interesting feature of Looks is its extensibility through the capability of building new specific editors. For example, knowing that a polygon is represented by a list of linear segments and that a segment is stored as a couple of end points, we may display a map with Looks by building an editor that recursively calls set editors, segment editors, and point editors.

6.2.2 Extension of Looks

Display The set of predefined editors was enriched with editors capable of displaying spatial types (points, segments, and polygons). The geometric part of a map is displayed in a window whose size is predefined. To obtain the description of a particular geometric object, the user has to click inside the region (or on the line). A point selection is executed (see above): a method is called which finds the object, and an editor containing the list of the attributes is displayed in ghost form.

Currently it is not possible to superimpose two maps in the same window, because of the bijection in Looks between an object and the window which contains it. But if the user wants to overlay two maps, he or she can explicitely call the method map overlay; a new map is created whose geometry can be displayed.

Queries There are two ways of running queries on maps.

1. Looks menus enable the end user to call CO_2 methods on a class. The methods may have only alphanumeric arguments. For example, if one asks for an overlay between two maps, the first argument of the map overlay is the object itself, and the second is an object whose name is given by the user through the argument collector of the interface. Methods may also have a geometric argument. This is the case for the methods window and clip, for which the user selects a particular area on the screen.

2. The user can use the O_2 query language. At the time of implementation, this was not possible; in the future it will be done by opening a window dedicated to queries, in which the user can edit his or her queries.

7 Conclusion

This chapter discusses the implementation of spatial query languages for geographic applications using an object-oriented database system. To demonstrate the feasibility of such an approach, a prototype is currently under implementation with version V_1 of the O_2 system developed by Altaïr.

An interface for displaying and querying spatial objects (maps) is under development. It is an extension of the O_2 interface tool Looks, which is implemented in Aïda (Devin and Duquesnoy 1988) and is connected to O_2. Simple queries to the geographic database are methods sent from the interface to a Maps class. Such a class and its methods, written in CO_2, the programming language of O_2, implement a small subset of the spatial query languages discussed in the literature. A simple spatial data model was chosen for representing geometric objects. An O_2 schema for implementing a few geometric operations has been partially implemented. A quadtree-like index (Samet 1989) is under development for accelerating access to geometric objects.

At the current stage of development, several conclusions may be drawn.

1. With the current tools available for generating interfaces, designing a customizable interface is still a difficult task for standard applications. For geographic applications which deal with spatial objects, it is even more difficult.

2. The O_2 query language offers the advantage of modeling complex structures, which is forbidden by any "extended SQL" query language. In spite of its power, however, it was not used for answering geographical queries

because it was not fully integrated with CO_2 at the time of implementation. The designer who would like, instead of using the O_2 query language, to develop in CO_2 relational operations requires a few extensions of CO_2, some of which are suggested in section 9.

3. Creating a class in the body of a CO_2 method is not allowed. This turns out to be a limitation for applications requiring a relational-like query language, that is, the integration in the programming language of generic relational operations. The O_2 query language was designed as an ad hoc query facility, that is, a short cut in the programming language to extract information from the database (Bancilhon, Cluet, and Delobel 1989; see chapter 11). It was not meant to be an SQL-like language or to permit the creation of new relations (which implies a run-time modification of the schema).

4. The object-oriented approach for developing an application turned out to be extremely efficient. Three modules were developed in parallel, independently of each other; the integration lasted only a few days.

5. The object-oriented data model of O_2 is extremely well adapted to the representation of application-dependent objects and to the implementation of extensible application-dependent functions.

6. It is not clear whether the encapsulation of application-dependent objects should be fully respected or partially violated. How much of the semantics of the geometric objects should be visible at the user level? This renders the task of designing a geographical query language more difficult and perhaps explains why there is no standard emerging for such applications.

8 Acknowledgements

The authors acknowledge the GIP Altaïr members which made available the O_2 system and any required assistance. The authors are strongly indebted to J. C. Mamou whose expertise in O_2Look and Aïda was extremely useful and who suggested with S. Cluet the map schema which was actually implemented. The clarity of the paper was significantly improved thanks to the comments of D. Plateau and particularly to the careful reading of the first draft by C. Delobel. Thanks also go to G. Ferran and R. Guting for helpful discussions. The implementation was done by A. Souf, D. Charlet, J. H. Yapi, and A. Voisard. A sample of geographic data was provided by IGN. This work also benefits from the design and implementation with R. Jeansoulin of a first prototype using the graphical software EDIX (Jeansoulin 1989). The help of F. Chauveau and P. Razac for installing O_2 at the Cedric lab was extremely appreciated.

References

Abel, D. J. 1989. SIRO-DBMS: A database toolkit for geographical informations systems. *International Journal of Geographical Information Systems* 3(2): 103–16.

Abiteboul, S., and C. Beeri. 1988. *On the power of languages for manipulating complex objects.* INRIA technical report no. 846.

Abiteboul, S., P. C. Fisher, and H. J. Schek. 1988. *Nested relations and complex objects.* LNCS 361. Springer-Verlag.

Abiteboul, S., and P. Kanellakis. 1989. Object identity as a query language primitive. In *Proceedings of the ACM SIGMOD conference on the management of data.*

Bancilhon, F., T. Briggs, S. Khoshafian, and P. Valduriez. 1987. Fad, a powerful and simple database language. In *Proceedings of the 13th VLDB conference.*

Bancilhon, F., S. Cluet, and C. Delobel. 1989. A query language for the O_2 object-oriented database system. In *Proceedings of the second workshop on database programming languages.*

Barrera, R., and A. Buchmann. 1981. Schema definition and query language for a geographical database system. In *Hot Springs, IEEE computer architecture for pattern analysis and image database management.*

Bennis, K., B. David, I. Quilio, and Y. Viémont. 1990. Géotropics: database support alternatives for geographic applications. In *Proceedings of the fourth international symposium on spatial data handling.*

Cardenas, A. F., and T. Joseph. 1988. Picquery: A high level query language for pictorial database management. *IEEE Transactions on Software Engineering* 14(5): 630–38.

Devin, M., and P. Duquesnoy. 1988. Aïda version 1.2 manuel de référence. ILOG, Gentilly.

Egenhofer, M., and A. Frank. 1988. Towards a spatial query language: User interface considerations. In *Prodeedings of the 14th VLDB conference.*

Egenhofer, M. 1989a. A formal definition of binary topological relationships. In *Proceedings of the conference on foundations on database organization and algorithms.*

Egenhofer, M. 1989b. A topological data model for spatial databases. In *Proceedings of the symposium on the design and implementation of large spatial databases.* LNCS 409. Springer-Verlag.

Egenhofer, M. 1989c. *Spatial SQL: A spatial query language.* Technical Report, Department of Surveying Engineering, University of Maine.

Frank, A. 1982. Mapquery: Data base query language for retrieval of geometric data and their graphical representation. *Computer Graphics* 16.

Frank, A. 1984. Requirements for database systems suitable to manage large spatial databases. In *Proceedings of the first international symposium on spatial data handling.*

Gardarin, G., J. P. Cheiney, G. Kiernan, D. Pastre, and H. Stora. 1989. Managing complex objects in an extensible relational DBMS. In *Proceedings of the 15th VLDB conference.*

Guting, R. H. 1988. Geo-relational algebra: A model and query language for geometric database systems. In *Proceedings of the conference on extending database technology.*

Guting, R. H. 1989. Gral: An extensible relational database system for geometric applications. In *Proceedings of the 15th VLDB conference.*

Jeansoulin, R. 1989. Le système d'information géographique orienté objet GOODIES. In *7ième congrès AFCET-RFIA.*

Lécluse, C., and P. Richard. 1989a. Modeling complex structures in object-oriented databases. In *Proceedings of the ACM PODS conference.*

Lécluse, C., and P. Richard. 1989b. The O_2 database programming language. In *Proceedings of the 15th VLDB conference.*

Mamou, J. C. 1991. Du disque à l'écran: génération d'interfaces homme-machine pour objets persistants. PhD dissertation, Université de Paris-Sud.

Meyer, B. 1986. Genericity versus inheritance. In *Proceedings of the first ACM conference on object-oriented programming systems, languages, and applications. SIGPLAN Notices* 21(11): 391–405.

Meyer, B. 1988. *Object-oriented software construction.* Prentice-Hall.

Ohori, A., P. Buneman, and V. Breazu-Tannen. 1989. Database programming in Machiavelli—a polymorphic language with static type inference. In *Proceedings of the ACM SIGMOD conference on the management of data.*

Ooi, B. C., R. Sack-Davis, and K. J. McDonell. 1989. Extending a DBMS for geographic applications. In *Proceedings of the fifth international conference on data engineering.*

Plateau, D. R. Cazalens, D. Lévêque, J. C. Mamou, and B. Poyet. 1990. Building user interface with Looks hyper-objects system. In *Proceedings of the eurographics workshop on object oriented graphics.*

Quilio, I., P. Dupuis, B. David, and J. M. Ambrosini. 1989. Report on design of architecture and interface of geotropics. ESPRIT-TR 2427-0036, Tropics Project.

Samet, H. 1989. *The design and analysis of spatial data structures.* Addison-Wesley.

Stemple, D., L. Fegaras, T. Sheard, and A. Socorro. 1990. Exceeding the limits of polymorphism in database programming languages. In *Proceedings of the conference on extending database technology.*

Sack-Davis, R., K. J. McDonell, and B. C. Ooi. 1987. GEOQL: a query language for geographic information systems. In *Proceedings of Australian and New Zealand Association for the Advancement of Science congress.*

Smith, T. R., S. Menon, J. L. Star, and J. E. Estes. 1987. Requirements and principles for the implementation and construction of large-scale geographic information systems. *International Journal of Geographical Information Systems* 1(1): 13–31.

Smyth, C. S. 1990. A reference data model for spatial and geographic applications. In *Proceedings of the fourth international symposium on spatial data handling.*

Souf, A. 1990. *Implantation d'un langage de requêtes géographiques avec le SGBD O2.* DEA Technical Report. Paris 6.

Stonebraker, M., and L. A. Rowe. 1986. The design of Postgres. In *Proceedings of the ACM SIGMOD conference.*

Scholl, M., and A. Voisard. 1989. Thematic map modeling. In *Proceedings of the symposium on the design and implementation of large spatial databases.* LNCS 409. Springer-Verlag.

Scholl, M., and A. Voisard. 1990. Object-oriented database system for geographic applications: An experience with O_2. In *International workshop on geographical databases* (ESPRIT Basic Research Series) 5(1991).

Six, H., and P. Widmayer. 1988. Spatial searching in geometric databases. In *Proceedings of the fourth international conference on data engineering.*

Ullman, J. D. 1988. *Principles of database and knowledge-base systems.* Computer Science Press.

Waugh, T. C., and R. G. Healey. 1987. The GEO-VIEW design, a relational database approach to geographical data handling. *International Journal of Geographical Information Systems* 1(2): 101–18.

Appendix I: An O_2 Schema for the Geometry of a Map

```
class Spatial
      */Information common to all geometric classes.


class Arc inherits Spatial
      tuple[begin: Point
            end: Point]
      method colinear(a: Arc): Boolean
      */Checks whether the two arcs are colinear.

      method pintersect(a: Arc): Point
      */Intersection of two linear segments.


class Arcs inherits Spatial
      list (a: Arc)
      method colinear(a: Arcs): Boolean
      */Two lists of arcs are colinear iff at least one arc
      */of one list is colinear with one arc of the other list.
      */Calls method colinear of class Arc.

      method pintersect(a: Arcs): Boolean
      */Two lists of arcs are intersecting iff at least one arc
      */of one list intersects one arc of the other list.
      */Calls method pintersect of class Arc.


class ConnGraph inherits Arcs
      method connected: Boolean
      */Checks whether the list of arcs is a connected graph.


class Cycle inherits ConnGraph
      method cyclic: Boolean
      */Checks whether the connected graph is a cycle.


class Geo inherits Spatial
      tuple[any]
      method adj(g: Geo): Boolean
            body(error)

      method intersect(g: Geo): Geos
            body(error)
```

```
class Point inherits Geo
      tuple[x: real
            y: real]


class Region inherits Geo
      tuple[ ...
            c: Cycle]
      method border: Cycle
            body(return *self.c)

      method adj(r: Region): Boolean
            body(return(self→ border→colinear(r→border)))

      method intersect(r: Region): Regions
      */Polygon intersection.


class Line inherits Geo
      tuple[ ...
            c: ConnGraph]
      method adj(l: Line): Boolean
            body(return(*self.c→colinear(*l.c)))

      method intersect(l: Line): Lines
      */The intersection of the two lines is a set of lines
      */colinear with both argument lines (see figure 28.9).
      */Calls method colinear of class ConnGraph, inherited from class Arcs.
```

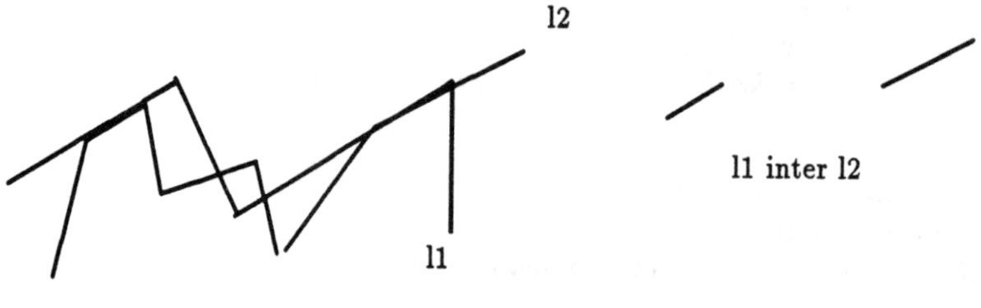

Figure 28.9. Intersection of two lines, l1 and l2

```
method pintersect(l: Line): Points
      */The pintersection of two lines is the set of intersection
      */points between arcs of each line.
      */Calls method pintersect of class ConnGraph, inherited from class Arcs.
```

```
class Geos inherits Spatial
        set(g: Geo)
        method adjacent(g: Geos): Boolean
                body(...Geo t, u ...
                    if t→adj(u) ...)

        method intersection(g: Geos): Geos
                body(
                    Geos s, v
                    Geo t, u
                    s = new(Geos)
                    for each t in *self
                        for each u in *r
                            v = new(Geos)
                            v = t→intersect(u)
                            s += v
                    return(s))


class Regions inherits Geos
        set(r: Region)
        method intersection(r: Regions): Regions
                body(return(Regions)(self → intersection(r)@Geos))


class Lines inherits Geos
        set(l: Line)
        method intersection(l: Lines): Lines
                body(return(Lines)(self → intersection(l)@Geos))

        method pintersection(l: Lines): Points
                body(
                    Points v, s
                    Line t, u
                    s = new(Points)
                    for each t in *self
                        for each u in *l
                            v = new(Points)
                            v = t → pinter(u)
                            s += v
                    return(s))


class Points inherits Geos
        set(p: Point)
```

Appendix II: Extension of CO_2 for Implementing Relational Operations

Generic operations of the relational algebra can be implemented with CO_2, given the following extensions:

1. Casting
2. Given a hierarchy of classes and a method m overloaded in each class of the hierarchy, the possibility of sending method $m@j$ from a method of subclass i, where $m@j$ refers to the code of method m of superclass j
3. A few built-in functions, to be defined below

Without loss of generality, we illustrate the mechanism on projection, using the example of selection and Cartesian product. Clearly, instead of Cartesian product, one could implement join. Similarly, one could implement an operation performing simultaneously projection and selection, join and projection, and so on. Two hierarchies are defined with roots: the classes Relation and Tuple. Relation is of type set(Tuple).Tuple has no structure defined. Any relation with schema R(A_1: $D_1, \ldots, A_n$: D_n) is an object of class R with structure set(TupleR), where TupleR is a class with structure [A_1: $D_1, \ldots, A_n$: D_n]. Class R is a subclass of class Relation. TupleR is a subclass of class Tuple.

Let us look at the implementation of projection. Two methods are needed:

1. Method Projection of class Relation, overloaded in each subclass representing a relation; the body of this method is given in figure 28.10. It defines a new object c, applies method *proj* to each tuple, and adds the resulting tuple to c.
2. Method Proj is a built-in function which, given as arguments a list of attribute names (a list of strings) and a source tuple, returns the projected tuple.

The class Relation (see figure 28.10) has subclasses RelationS with the structure set(TupleS). In each of these subclasses, the method projection is redefined as follows. The body applies to the object (self) the method projection, as defined in class Relation (projection@Relation); and it casts the result, that is, it makes the resulting set of tuples belong to subclass RelationS: return(RelationS). In each subclass TupleS the method proj is redefined similarly. The body applies proj@Tuple and makes the resulting tuple belong to class TupleS.

A projection is performed as follows:

RelationS s
r = **new**(RelationT)
r = (RelationT)s → projection(listattr)

```
class Relation
      type set(Tuple)
      method projection(listattr: list(string)): Relation
            body {
            Relation c
            Tuple t, t'
            c = new(Relation)
            for each t in *self
                  t' = t → proj(listattr)
                  c += {t'}
            return(c)}

class RelationS inherits Relation
      type set(TupleS)
      method projection(listattr: list(string)): RelationS
            body {
            return(RelationS)(self → projection(listattr)@Relation)}

class Tuple
      type any
      method proj(listattr: list(string)): Tuple
      body { built-in }

class TupleS inherits Tuple
      type tuple(A1: D1, ..., An: Dn)
      method proj(listattr: list(string)): TupleS
            body {return(TupleS)(self → proj(listattr)@Tuple)}
```

Figure 28.10. Projection

A target relation is created, that is, an object r of class RelationT; and r is assigned the result from sending the method *projection* to the source relation (object s of class RelationS) cast to class RelationT. It is assumed that class RelationT already exists.

Similarly, one can program **selection** and **product** using the following built-in methods (of class Tuple):

select(attributename: string, comparator: string, value: string): Tuple

or

select(attributename: string, comparator: string, attributename: string): Tuple

and

concat(t: Tuple): Tuple

The former sent to a tuple gives the tuple itself if it satisfies the selection criteria; the latter concatenates the tuple to which the method is sent with the tuple in argument.

Index

abstract data types, 7, 65, 83, 219, 235, 241, 327, 330, 586
access-path selection, 13
ad hoc query facility, 5, 14, 235, 236, 239, 609
alphanumeric interface, 21, 22, 41, 42
alternative architecture, 413, 418
application generators, 497, 498
associative access, 187, 236, 280, 283, 285, 287, 289, 292, 294, 329, 330, 334, 363, 364, 366
attribute
  exceptional, 28, 93, 175, 206, 210, 333, 344, 352, 365
authorization, 7, 239, 349, 363, 364, 366, 460

B-tree, 46, 55, 229, 331, 335, 352, 353, 363, 417, 419, 534
$BasicO_2$, 21, 29, 44, 188, 189, 196, 211, 216, 344, 346, 524, 535, 538
benchmark, 192, 193, 231, 340, 404–407, 412, 423–425, 427, 429–431, 441–443, 492
  Sun, 424
  Tektronix, 52, 405
  Wisconsin, 54
Bill of Materials Application, 278, 280, 281, 283, 284, 286, 287, 290, 292, 293, 297, 304, 308, 313, 318
breakpoints, 41, 519, 526, 528, 534
browser, 14, 39, 40, 236, 239, 282, 344, 347, 492, 493, 508, 509, 511, 513, 515, 516, 520, 521, 581
buffer manager, 50, 419
business-application, 207, 278, 557, 558, 561, 565

class
  extension, 25, 26, 52, 147, 155, 160, 163, 168, 170, 173, 179–181, 200, 210, 224, 225, 227, 259, 359
  hierarchy, 28, 39, 40, 51, 64, 65, 67–73, 129, 132, 133, 137, 150, 151, 168, 221, 222, 252, 289, 330, 354, 492, 511, 516, 517, 520, 541, 557, 558, 598
  name, 24, 30, 65, 67–69, 100, 104–106, 118, 119, 122, 123, 131–133, 140, 147, 150, 197, 198, 388, 527
clustering, 43, 45, 46, 51, 179, 229, 231, 330, 333, 334, 336, 340, 345, 347, 354, 357, 365, 373, 385–390, 397, 398, 404–408, 414, 416, 417, 424, 426, 428, 429, 431, 435–438, 442, 443, 468
  algorithm, 51, 330, 335, 373, 386, 390, 391, 394–397, 404, 408, 443
  factor, 426, 431, 434–441
clustering manager, 44, 51
CO_2, 21, 29–31, 37, 41, 44, 53, 64, 70, 105, 188, 189, 196, 201, 202, 206, 209, 211, 216, 227, 257, 271, 272, 274, 290, 344,

346, 398, 399, 516, 520, 521, 523, 524, 526, 528, 529, 532, 533, 535, 541, 543, 546, 553, 562, 565, 572, 575, 578, 582, 587, 593–596, 604, 608, 609, 616
code
  generation, 191, 192, 542, 544
  generator, 524
  optimizations, 47, 104, 329, 349, 543–545, 553, 596
code reusability, 10, 143, 295, 555
communication manager, 44, 49, 50, 334, 360, 361, 373, 377, 381
compiler, 15, 43, 44, 47, 61, 172, 188, 189, 191, 192, 201, 211, 212, 225, 226, 231, 254, 271, 274, 286, 344, 348, 350, 356, 365, 493, 524, 525, 527, 532, 533, 535, 537, 541, 542, 548, 553
complex object manager, 44, 45, 357
composite object, 51, 64, 173, 174, 329, 336, 338, 339, 354, 364, 386, 449, 456, 457, 459, 496, 498
composition
  hierarchy, 51, 52, 262, 320, 351, 358, 359, 364, 366, 386, 387, 457
  links, 24, 147, 198, 386, 393, 572
  object graph, 389, 390
computational completeness, 5, 12, 235–237
computer-aided design (CAD), 4, 447
computer-aided software engineering (CASE), 4
concurrency, 5, 13, 18, 43, 47, 48, 228, 231, 235, 236, 283, 292, 331, 338, 340, 347–349, 354, 355, 358, 363, 365, 442, 444, 456, 463–465, 468, 477
concurrency control, 43, 48, 283, 292, 327, 329, 334, 340, 348, 355, 363–365, 370, 408, 412–416, 420, 421, 423, 442, 449, 456, 457, 460, 463, 464, 468, 471, 472, 474, 475, 481, 483, 491
  optimistic, 48, 338, 355, 363, 418, 423
configuration, 43, 55, 179, 182, 330, 336, 340, 343, 344, 348, 350, 351, 374, 406, 430, 441, 449, 451, 519, 535, 537, 543, 550
consistency, 33–35, 43, 44, 48, 74, 82, 85, 128–130, 136–143, 148, 149, 151, 155, 159, 163, 168, 170, 172, 174, 176, 179, 332, 337, 338, 340, 355, 393, 423, 448, 449, 458, 497, 500, 505, 577
  behavioral, 146, 148, 149, 151, 159, 160, 173, 174
  structural, 146, 148–151, 154, 156, 159, 172–174
copy elimination, 103, 116, 117, 123
covariance, 130, 131, 135, 136, 139, 142

data buffering, 13, 236
data clustering, 13, 236
data complexity, 118
data description language (DDL), 64, 73
data manipulation language (DML), 7, 14, 31, 61, 64, 65, 185, 186, 237, 239, 279, 281, 346, 489
database administration utilities, 15
database build time, 431
database distribution, 331, 337
database instance, 70, 95, 154, 172
database programming language (DBPL), 21, 22, 29, 31, 61, 74,

186–188, 190, 192, 193, 196, 237, 290, 327, 509, 552, 596
database schema, 9, 22, 72, 73, 149, 150, 242, 263, 337, 370, 391, 491–493, 515, 516, 581
database transformation (db-transformation), 99, 103
database versions, 74, 332, 338, 339, 450–454, 456, 458, 459
debugger, 40–42, 344, 347, 493, 508, 509, 511–513, 518, 520, 521, 523–528, 531–538, 541
deep equality, 83
design transaction, 16, 332
development mode, 33, 41–43, 48, 52, 54, 55, 172, 180
dio-transformation, 116, 117, 123
disk manager, 21, 22, 41–43
distribution, 15, 33, 49, 230, 328, 331, 340, 344, 350, 358, 365, 369–371, 411, 565, 583
dynamic binding, 465, 529, 531, 532
dynamic loading, 535

editors, 40, 344, 347, 497, 519, 520, 542, 544, 605, 607
encapsulation, 5, 7, 8, 13, 17, 31, 63, 71, 77, 93, 98, 155, 160, 187, 206, 211, 215, 216, 222, 225, 226, 231, 235, 238–242, 244, 245, 252, 253, 257, 259–261, 288, 290, 293, 343, 345, 346, 490, 491, 526, 527, 587, 588, 609
execution manager, 40, 41, 518, 526, 534
execution mode, 33, 41–43, 47, 48, 54, 55, 172

file allocation, 393–395
file-server, 413, 417, 418, 420, 423, 428, 430–432, 434, 436, 438, 442, 443
fourth-generation language, 7, 490, 497, 506, 519

geographic database, 588, 605, 608
geographic information systems, 585
geometric types, 588, 589, 592

Identity Query Language (IQL), 99, 107
incremental compilation, 493, 542, 545, 552
incremental parser, 542–544, 547
index management, 13, 236
index manager, 44, 51, 358
inheritance
  constraint, 10
  inclusion, 10
  method, 63, 65, 71, 132, 133
  multiple, 15, 28, 47, 71, 72, 94, 95, 135, 136, 147, 148, 151, 154, 160, 162, 173, 174, 204, 205, 210, 221, 230, 253, 257, 345, 348, 395, 463, 464, 468, 469, 573
  specialization, 11
  substitution, 10
  type, 65, 104, 119, 120, 388, 405, 406
insertable arrays, 46, 352
integrity constraints, 15, 175, 280, 282, 283, 294, 520, 604
interactive consistency checker, 151
iterator, 31, 32, 202, 203, 223

journal, 493, 508, 509, 511, 512, 521

language-based editor, 542
language processor, 21, 22, 41, 42
large objects, 330, 334, 366, 491
large sets, 55, 64, 330, 347, 352, 353, 357
late binding, 5, 11, 12, 33, 47, 54, 65, 71, 74, 78, 128, 129, 133, 171, 172, 205–208, 211, 223, 229, 235, 236, 241, 242, 259, 339, 340, 346, 348, 357, 358, 513, 541, 572

library, 43, 191, 337, 356, 372, 497, 555–557
Lifoo, 190, 254
LispO_2, 188–190, 192, 216, 217, 219–221, 225, 227, 230, 231
lists, 5, 13, 27, 32, 36, 41, 46, 51, 65, 66, 202, 204, 218, 223, 227, 229, 235, 242, 244–249, 251, 271, 329, 347, 352, 357, 358, 385, 398, 500, 536, 537, 582, 603
lock, 37, 44, 48, 292, 329, 338, 355, 356, 364, 371, 380, 414, 415, 417, 418, 421, 423, 442, 443, 456, 463, 464, 471–474, 476–478, 480, 481, 483, 576
  modes, 473, 477, 482
  type of, 471
locking
  logical, 476, 477
  physical, 476, 477
Looks, 21, 22, 35–37, 40–42, 291, 292, 295, 492, 493, 498–500, 502–506, 510, 511, 538, 556, 557, 593, 605, 607, 608

masks, 499, 501, 504, 505
menu, 36, 204, 205, 291, 292, 315, 387, 389–391, 396, 497, 499, 500, 504, 511, 513, 515, 517, 520, 574–576, 578, 579, 607, 608
message passing, 29, 30, 41, 43, 44, 47, 179, 201, 207, 208, 222, 225, 226, 229, 251, 292, 327, 329, 334, 347, 348, 355, 357, 362, 375, 377, 381, 513, 556, 561, 562
messages, 34, 41, 54, 225, 280–286, 289, 291, 292, 311, 312, 314, 346, 362, 364, 365, 372, 375, 377, 379, 381, 423, 443, 508, 516, 519, 520, 526, 562
method
  commutativity, 482
  exceptional, 29, 175, 206, 207, 210, 580
  private, 26, 39, 201, 291
  public, 26, 31, 147, 161, 201, 291
method schema, 74, 128–136, 138–143
  monadic, 74, 130, 135–140, 156
  recursion-free, 130, 131, 135–137, 156
method schema, 74
mode
  debugging, 526
  development, 33, 334, 344, 347–349, 355, 357, 493, 526
  execution, 334, 344, 347–350, 358, 493, 519, 526
  resident, 48, 347, 349, 350, 358, 361
multimedia objects, 47, 353, 579

naming, 25, 62, 95, 100, 111, 135, 199, 249, 282
nested relational models, 590

o-value, 100, 101, 105–107, 109, 114, 115, 119–123
o-value assignment, 105, 106, 121
O_2 data model, 185, 192, 216, 225, 235, 241, 242, 254, 266, 334, 336, 337, 408, 493
O_2 database programming language, 188, 192, 327
O_2 query language, 190, 245, 248, 256
O_2 shell, 511
object
  assignment, 6, 133, 134
  class, 28, 170, 335, 346, 463, 537
  complex, 5, 6, 17, 28, 43, 45, 51, 63, 78, 79, 112, 113, 118, 179, 187, 196, 209, 211, 215, 219, 235, 252, 257, 261, 266, 328, 343, 344, 347, 357, 365, 424–426, 428, 429, 434, 443, 463, 586, 590, 607

copy, 6, 501
creation, 30, 52, 53, 199, 216, 223, 225, 455, 561
equality, 6
fetching, 421, 443
identifier, 7, 45, 46, 50, 63, 65–67, 69, 70, 73, 79, 99, 175, 179, 197, 270, 329, 330, 332, 350, 351, 354, 358, 359, 361, 372, 374, 388, 389, 395, 448, 453, 459, 533, 595
identity, 5–7, 14, 23, 46, 74, 77, 78, 83, 98, 99, 196, 211, 235, 241, 257, 259, 265, 267, 328, 329, 336, 352, 389, 501, 577
lists, 246, 529, 537, 580, 600
manager, 21, 22, 31, 41–45, 172, 179, 196, 201, 202, 212, 327–330, 332–334, 336, 337, 339, 344, 351, 355, 357, 363, 365, 366, 374, 442, 541, 596
migration, 361, 560
object-fault, 48, 229, 347, 349, 350
object-server, 338, 412, 413, 415, 417, 422, 430–432, 434–438, 442, 443
object-transfer protocol, 369, 372
representation, 45, 351, 468, 469, 483
sets, 8, 9, 24, 38, 40, 51, 64, 77, 80–82, 84, 86, 87, 89–91, 93, 95, 128, 133, 134, 180, 198, 235, 243, 248, 263, 345, 346, 353, 373, 387, 389, 395, 396, 412, 429, 435, 436, 448, 512, 543, 578, 600, 601, 605
table, 50, 330, 333, 350, 361, 363, 364
tuples, 5, 11, 13, 32, 65, 68, 102, 160, 327, 329, 330, 497, 534, 586, 594, 595
versions, 338–340, 448–452, 456–458, 460
object-oriented database system (OODB), 3–5, 12, 14, 15, 18, 21, 55, 63, 65, 75, 78, 95, 98, 99, 104, 128, 129, 146, 149, 172–175, 187, 190, 193, 195, 196, 216, 234, 235, 237, 238, 240, 257, 274, 290, 331, 338, 343, 385, 411, 447, 463, 498, 525, 586, 608
office information systems (OIS), 4
oid assignment, 69, 70, 73, 105, 106, 115, 119–122
OOPE, 21, 22, 31, 37–42, 44, 493, 508–513, 516, 519–521, 538, 556, 561, 566, 581
operation
closure traversals, 406, 407
read, 381, 414, 418
read-page, 467, 477–479
sequential scan, 416, 419, 427
update, 172, 173, 386
write, 381
write-page, 467, 477–479
overloading, 11, 61, 65, 71, 74, 128–130, 133, 151, 235, 236, 346, 348, 400, 544, 603, 604
overriding, 5, 11, 28, 78, 343, 463

page-server, 412, 415, 416, 420–423, 431–434, 436, 437, 442, 443
parameter passing, 532, 533
parse tree, 106, 525, 537, 542–544, 546–548, 550–552
parsers, 542, 543
percolation, 457
performance, 4, 13, 17, 22, 33, 47–49, 52, 54, 55, 77, 186, 205, 211, 219, 231, 241, 333, 334, 336, 343, 344, 349–351, 355, 365, 370–374, 381, 385–387, 404, 406–408, 413, 417, 419, 423–427, 429, 431–438, 441–444, 457, 492, 509, 520, 523–525, 534, 538, 541, 596, 602

persistence, 5, 13, 18, 25, 26, 43, 49, 50, 62, 72, 73, 147, 179, 199, 200, 208–211, 215, 216, 227, 229, 230, 235, 236, 285, 288, 290, 292–295, 328, 331–333, 337, 344, 347, 348, 350, 353, 356, 363–365, 465, 520
phantom objects, 464, 469
placement trees, 51, 336, 354, 357, 373, 387, 390–398, 402, 404, 407, 408
presentation protocol, 49, 362
presentations, 34, 35, 491, 499–506, 607
programming environment, 21, 22, 37, 43, 55, 195, 228, 231, 279, 286, 329, 343, 344, 347, 349, 350, 353, 356, 489–493, 497, 505, 508, 509, 512, 519–521, 535, 541, 556, 566, 581
programming paradigm, 16, 99, 129, 279, 283, 287, 327
programming tools, 39, 493, 508, 509, 511, 519, 521

query
  interpreter, 21, 22, 41–43
  language, 3, 4, 7, 14, 22, 23, 29, 31, 32, 78, 99, 100, 103, 105, 115, 119, 121, 185–188, 190, 193, 203, 208, 215, 235–241, 244, 245, 248, 250, 252–254, 256, 257, 259–261, 291, 327, 330, 346, 411, 441, 489–491, 512, 537–539, 577–579, 585–587, 592–596, 602, 608, 609
  optimization, 13, 14, 328, 330, 350, 364

receiver class, 39, 70, 150, 226
recovery, 5, 14, 18, 43, 48, 228, 231, 235, 236, 283, 292, 328, 333, 347, 349, 363–365, 380, 412–417, 420, 421, 423, 468, 483, 552
relation name, 100, 101, 105, 106, 115, 116, 118, 119, 283
relational database system, 3, 4, 14, 17, 186, 327, 331, 385, 411, 489, 497, 537
Reloop, 190, 193, 253, 254, 256, 257, 261–267, 269, 271–274
remote procedure call, 34, 49, 334, 363, 375, 414, 421
representation system, 16
reusability, 10, 63, 143, 295, 360, 493, 555, 565, 566
roadmap, 62, 74, 187, 192, 328, 339, 490, 492
rule-based formalism, 100, 103

schema evolution, 15, 33, 128, 129, 146, 172, 348, 364, 366, 543, 553
schema manager, 21, 22, 41, 43, 44, 47, 48, 54, 172, 179, 229–231, 333, 334, 344, 348–350, 356–358, 365
secondary storage management, 5, 13, 235, 363
serializability, 14, 16, 338, 465, 477, 480–482
server version, 42, 43, 337, 350, 419
shallow equality, 6, 83
single-class indexing, 52, 359
subtyping, 26–28, 65, 67, 68, 70, 78, 79, 87–89, 91, 94, 95, 147, 150, 173, 196, 203–206, 210, 220, 221, 230, 393
swizzling, 330, 336
symbol databases, 523, 526, 534
symbol table, 41, 227, 523–525, 527, 536, 537
syntax tree, 542, 548
system interface, 357, 371, 377, 378

toolbox, 291, 492, 493, 555–559, 561, 562, 565, 566, 581

toolkits, 228, 492, 497
transaction
  manager, 44, 47, 48, 333, 358
  multilevel, 338, 464, 475, 478–483
transport protocol, 49, 371, 373, 375
tuples, 5, 11, 13, 55, 102, 120, 185, 186, 235, 243, 245, 249, 253, 254, 262, 263, 266, 267, 270, 272, 276, 282, 333, 352, 357, 381, 385, 388, 398, 443, 576, 581, 588, 590, 596, 597, 616
type
  checking, 9, 12, 15, 70, 71, 80, 111, 155, 186, 189, 207, 208, 223, 225, 226, 230, 241, 244, 346, 510, 524, 566, 596
  hierarchy, 68, 244
  inference, 15
  system, 9, 17, 62, 78, 84, 91–95, 99, 102, 119, 185, 203, 238, 329, 346, 365, 535

uniformity, 9, 17, 43, 47, 208, 353, 509
Unix Mail Application, 280, 282–284, 286, 288, 291, 292, 299, 306, 310, 316, 321
updates, 6, 7, 33, 40, 48, 52, 74, 78, 99, 103, 142, 146, 148, 149, 152–154, 156, 159, 162, 163, 166, 168, 170, 172, 174–176, 179–182, 209, 225, 235, 239, 280, 281, 287, 288, 294, 359, 414, 417, 423, 425, 426, 428, 443, 450, 458, 553
  class, 153, 162, 163, 173
  method, 152, 154
  schema, 48, 74, 75, 146, 148, 149, 152, 153, 156, 171, 172, 174, 176, 180, 182, 278, 355, 365, 381, 386, 493, 541
  type, 152, 159
user interface, 34, 179, 207, 228, 236, 278, 489, 490, 492, 496, 497, 506, 520, 538, 560, 587, 592, 593, 595, 605, 606
  geographic, 606

V0 prototype, 62, 188, 492
V1 prototype, 62, 189, 190, 192, 193, 256, 338, 339, 542
value
  complex, 23, 43, 51, 62–64, 173, 179, 196, 208, 211, 219, 230, 259, 357, 389, 391, 392, 590
  manipulation, 29, 30, 202, 225
  pure, 100, 104, 122, 123
version
  consistency, 448
  database-version, 451, 457, 458, 460
  derivation hierarchy, 332
  derivation tree, 339, 450, 452, 454, 457, 458
  management, 328, 332, 447–449, 456–459, 520
version V1, 21, 592
view definition, 15

window views, 490
Wisconsin Storage System (WiSS), 43, 333, 348, 394
workspace, 40, 363, 493, 509, 511, 512, 521
workstation version, 42, 43, 350, 356
workstation-server architecture, 338, 340, 412, 423, 442